SOURCEBOOK ON FEMINIST JURISPRUDENCE

Cavendish
Publishing
Limited

London • Sydney

SOURCEBOOK
ON FEMINIST
JURISPRUDENCE

Hilaire Barnett, BA, LLM
Lecturer in Law
Queen Mary & Westfield College

Cavendish
Publishing
Limited

London • Sydney

First published in Great Britain 1997 by Cavendish Publishing Limited,
The Glass House, Wharton Street, London WC1X 9PX
Telephone: 0171-278 8000   Facsimile: 0171-278 8080

British Library Cataloguing-in-Publication Data.

Barnett, Hilaire A
Sourcebook on feminist jurisprudence
1. Feminist jurisprudence
I. Title
340.1'1'082

ISBN 1 85941 113 4

Printed and bound in Great Britain

[W]omen have sat indoors all these millions of years, so that by this time the very walls are permeated by their creative force, which has, indeed, so overcharged the capacity of bricks and mortar that it must needs harness itself to pens and brushes and business and politics. But this creative power differs greatly from the creative power of men. And one must conclude that it would be a thousand pities if it were hindered or wasted, for it was won by centuries of the most drastic discipline, and there is nothing to take its place. It would be a thousand pities if women wrote like men, or lived like men, or looked like men, for if two sexes are quite inadequate, considering the vastness and variety of the world, how could we manage with one only?[1]

Virginia Woolf, 1929

1   *A Room of One's Own* (1929) (Penguin, 1993), p 79.

PREFACE

The literature on feminist jurisprudence is now both extensive and impressive. Whilst the modern feminist quest for equality may be traced to the writings of Mary Wollestonecraft in the 18th century, and that of John Stuart and Harriet Mill in the 19th century, the scholarship on women and law is of more recent origins. However, with the revitalised interest of the 1960s through to the current time, feminist jurisprudence has come of age. No longer is it possible to view feminist legal scholarship as a 'minority' interest. Whether the interest lies in identifying and campaigning for the removal of the remaining legal disabilities of women, or in theorising about the manner in which law reflects and reinforces gender-based inequalities, or in infusing traditional legal scholarship and teaching with a feminist perspective, feminism has become a mainstream discipline.

In this book I have attempted to reflect the richness and variety of feminist scholarship. The book is divided into four parts and 12 chapters. In Part I, factual data on the position of women throughout the world is provided through the United Nations, 1990 and 1995 Reports. The manner in which women have been treated, in differing parts of the world, in the past and present, as a result of cultural norms is considered in Chapter 2. In Chapter 3, the scope and evolution of feminist jurisprudence is considered. Chapter 4 is devoted to three articles outlining the methods used by feminist scholars in order to advance their work. Part II is devoted to central concepts in feminist jurisprudence: those of patriarchy and gender. In Part III the role of women in political and legal theory through the ages is considered. Positivism, liberalism, Marxism and social contract theory have provided fertile areas for feminist inquiry. Also considered are the feminist debates in contemporary jurisprudence. In Part IV the key issues facing feminist jurisprudence are discussed. Violence against women, the treatment of women in the legal system, pornography, women and medicine and the status of women under international law are considered in this Part.

Inevitably, given the wide-ranging nature and volume of feminist legal scholarship, and the limits of space, the compilation of this collection has proved to be a selective exercise. I have endeavoured to present some of the now-seminal work on feminist legal thought and some of the challenging and more recent literature. It has also been my objective to give adequate attention and space to the ever-increasing Australian and British scholarship on feminist jurisprudence.

Production of this collection has been delayed by some nine months because of the difficulties caused by copyright permission requests. Requests ignored has been a principal problem, as have permissions being granted on prohibitive terms and conditions. It has been my principal aim to produce a book which will serve as a working tool for students; not to provide an expensive reference work which would find its way only into specialist library collections. As a result, the cost of copyright permissions inevitably and regrettably had to play a role in the inclusion or exclusion of many works. I am most grateful to all the authors who have helped me to get permission through personally contacting their recalcitrant publishers. Without their personal help, this collection would be the poorer.

My thanks are due to many friends and colleagues who have actively encouraged the development of this book. If through either inclusion or exclusion of some material I have failed to match their expectations I hope to be forgiven. My thanks also go to Jo Reddy, Kate Nicol and Cathy West of Cavendish Publishing.

Hilaire Barnett
Queen Mary and Westfield College
University of London
March 1997

ACKNOWLEDGMENTS

Grateful acknowledgment is made for the following:

Albury, R, 'Law Reform and Human Reproduction: Implications for Women', in Simms, M (ed), *Australian Women and the Political System* (Longman, Melbourne, 1984)

Aristotle, *The Republic*, translated by T Sinclair, revised by Trevor J Saunders (Penguin Classics, 1962)

Atkins, S and Hoggett, B, *Women and the Law* (Blackwells Publishers, 1984)

Barnett, H, *Province of Jurisprudence* (Legal Studies, 1995)

Bartlett, K, 'Feminist Legal Methods', 1990 *Harvard Law Review* 100

Bender, L, 'From Gender Difference to Feminist Solidarity: Using Carol Gilligan' (1990) *Vermont Law Review*

Bottomley, A, *Feminism, the Desire for Theory and the Use of Law* reproduced by permission of the author

Brownmiller, S, *Against Our Will: Men, Women and Rape* (Simon & Schuster, 1975)

Butler, M, 'Early Liberal Roots of Feminism: John Locke and the Attack on Patriarchy' in *Feminist Interpretations and Political Theory*, Lyndon Shanley, M and Pateman, C (eds) (Polity, 1991)

Byrnes, A, 'Women, Feminism – Some Current Issues' (1992) *Australian Yearbook of International Law* 12

Cain, P, 'A Feminist Jurisprudence – Grounding the Theories' *Berkeley Women's Law Review* Vol 4:2 pp 191–214 c 19 by *Berkeley Women's Law Review*, reprinted by permission

Charlesworth, H, Chinkin, C and Wright, S, 'Feminist Approaches to International Law'. Extracts reproduced with permission from 85 *AJIL* 613 (1991) © The American Society of International Law.

Collins, H, *Marxism and the Law* (Oxford University Press, 1982) reprinted by permission of Oxford University Press

Connors, J, *Mainstreaming Gender Within the International Framework*, reproduced by permission of the author

Connors, J, *Violence Against Women (Background paper for UN 4th Conference on Women – Beijing 1995)*, reproduced by permission of the author

Cornell, D, 'Sexual Difference, the Feminine, and Equivalency: A Critique of MacKinnon's Towards a Feminist Theory of the State', reprinted by permission of The Yale Law Journal Company and Fred B Rothman and Company from *The Yale Law Journal* Vol 100 pages 2247–2275

Daly, M, *Gyn/Ecology* (The Women's Press, 1991)

Daly, M, *Beyond God the Father* (The Women's Press, 1973)

de Beauvoir, S, *The Second Sex* (Everyman's Library, 1993)

Delmar, R 'Looking again at Engel's "Origins of the Family"' in *The Rights and Wrongs of Women*, Mitchell, J and Oakley, A (eds) (Penguin, 1976)

Duncan, S, 'The Mirror Tells its Tale' in *Feminist Perspectives on the Foundational Subjects of Law*, Bottomley, A (ed) (Cavendish Publishing Limited, 1996)

Edwards, S, *Battered Women Syndrome* (New Law Journal, 1993)

Estrich, S, 'Rape', reprinted by permission of The Yale Law Journal Company and Fred B Rothman and Company from *The Yale Law Journal* Vol 95 pp 1087–1184

Finley, L, 'Breaking Women's Silence in Law: The Dilemma of the Gendered Nature of Legal Reasoning' Vol 64, Issue 5, *The Notre Dame Law Review* (1989) 886–910 Reprinted with permission. © by *Notre Dame Law Review*, University of Notre Dame.

Grosz, E, *What is Feminist Theory in Feminist Law Challenges: Law and Social Theory*, Pateman and Grosz (eds) (Allen & Unwin, Sydney, 1986)

Hardy, T, *The Mayor of Casterbridge* (Macmillan General Books, 1975)

Harris, 'A Race and Essentialism in Feminist Legal Theory' (1990) *Stanford Law Review* 42

Hester, M, *Lewd Women and Wicked Witches* (Routledge, 1992)

Irigary, L, *Thinking the Difference* (The Athlone Press Ltd, 1994)

Jackson, E, 'The Problem with Pornography' (1995) *Feminist Legal Studies* (Deborah Charles Publications)

Kingdom, E, *Consent, Coercion and Consortium ... in What's Wrong with Rights?* (Edinburgh University Press, 1991)

Lacey, N, 'Feminism and the Tenets of Conventional Legal Theory' (1996) (*Humboldt Forum Rechts* 11 http:\\www.rewi.hu-Berlin.de\HFR\11-1996) reproduced by permission of the author

Lacey, N, *Theories of Justice and the Welfare State* (Social and Legal Studies, 1992)

Langton, R, 'Whose Rights? Ronald Dworkin, Women & Pornography' 19(4) *Philosophy & Public Affairs* (Princeton University Press, 1990)

Littleton, C, 'In Search of Feminist Jurisprudence' (1987) *Harvard Women's Law Journal*

MacKinnon, C, *The Problem of Marxism and Feminism in Towards a Feminist Theory of the State* (Harvard University Press, 1989)

MacKinnon, C, 'Francis Biddle's Sister: Pornography, Civil Rights and Speech and Difference and Dominance: On Sex Discrimination in Feminism' in *Feminism Unmodified* (Harvard University Press, 1987)

MacKinnon, CA, *Only Words* (HarperCollins Publishers Ltd, 1995)

Matsuda, M, 'Liberal Jurisprudence and abstracted Visions of Human Nature: A Feminist Critique of Rawls' Theory of Justice' (1986) *New Mexico Law Review*

McColgan, A, 'In Defence of Battered Women Who Kill' (1992) *Oxford Journal of Legal Studies*

McLean, S, 'Female Victims in the Criminal Law' from *The Legal Relevance of Gender*, McLean and Burrows (eds) (Macmillan, 1988)

Menkel-Meadow, C, 'Portia in a Different Voice' *Berkeley Womens Law Review* Volume 1 pp 39–63 © 1985 by *Berkeley Women's Law Review*, reprinted by permission

Mill, JS, 'Subjection of Women' in *On Liberty and Other Writings* by JS Mill, 1869, (Cambridge University Press, 1989)

Mitchell, J, *The Ideology of the Family in Women's Estate* (Penguin Books, 1971)

Mossman, MF, 'Feminism and Legal Method' (1987) *Wisconsin Women's Law Journal*

Naffine, N, 'Possession Erotic Love in the Law of Rape' (1996) *Modern Law Review* 57, 18–23 (Blackwell Publishers)

Naffine, N, *Law and the Sexes* (Allen & Unwin, Sydney, 1990)

O'Donovan, K, *Sexual Divisions in Law* (Weidenfeld, 1985)

O'Donovan, K, *The Medicalisation of Infanticide* (Criminal Law Journal)

Okin, SM, *Philosopher Queens and Private Wives in Women in Western Political Thought* (Princeton University Press, 1979)

Olsen, F, 'Feminism and Critical Theory: an American Perspective' in (1990) *Journal of Sociology of Law* (Harcourt Brace & Company Ltd)

Pagels, E, 'What Became of God the Mother?' in *The Signs Reader* (University of Chicago Press, 1978)

Pateman, C, *The Disorder of Women* (Blackwell Publishers, 1989)

Pateman, C, *The Sexual Contract* (Blackwell Publishers, 1988)

Plato, 'Symposium' (trans, Joyce, M) in *Plato: The Collected Dialogues*, Hamilton, E and Cairns, H (eds) (Princeton University Press, 1963) © 1963 by Princeton University Press. Reprinted by permission of Princeton University Press

Plato, *The Republic* (trans, Lee, D) (Penguin Classics, 1955, 2nd edn, 1974)

Rhode, D, 'The "Woman's Point of View"' (1988) *Journal of Legal Education* 38

Rhode, D, 'Feminist Critical Theories' 42 *Stanford Law Review* 617 (1990) © 1990 by the Board of Trustees of the Leland Stanford Junior University

Rifkin, J, 'Towards a Theory of Law and Patriarchy' (1980) *Harvard Women's Law Journal* 3 © 1980 by the Presidents and Fellows of Harvard College

Sachs, A and Hoff Wilson, G, *Sexism and the Law* (Blackwell Publishers, 1978)

Scales, AC, 'The Emergence of a Feminist Jurisprudence: An Essay', reprinted by permission of The Yale Law Journal Company and Fred B Rothman and Company from *The Yale Law Journal* Vol 95 pp 1373–1403

Sheldon, S, 'Who is the Mother to make the Judgement?' (1993) *Feminist Legal Studies* (Deborah Charles Publications)

Smart, C, *Feminism and the Power of Law* (Routledge, 1989)

The World's Women 1995 – Trends and Statistics (United Nations Publications Board)

Stubbs, M, 'Feminism and Legal Positivism' (1986) *Australian Journal of Law and Society*

Thornton, M, 'Feminist Jurisprudence: Illusion or Reality?' (1986) 3 *Australian Journal of Law and Society* 5

Thornberry, C, 'What Price the Missus Now?' (1970) *The Guardian*, 29 December

Van Bueren, G, 'International Protection of Family Members' Rights' (1995) *Human Rights Quarterly* 732 (John Hopkins University Press)

Walby, S, *Theorising Patriarchy* (Blackwells Publishers, 1990)

West, R, 'Deconstructing the CLS-FEM Split' (1986) *Wisconsin Women's Law Journal* 2

Williams, J, 'Deconstructing Gender' (1989) *Michigan Law Review*

Wolgast, E, 'Pornography and the Tyranny of the Majority' in *The Grammar of Justice* (Cornell University Press, 1987). Reprinted form Elizabeth H Wolgast: The Grammar of Justice © 1987 by Cornell University. Used by permission of the publishers, Cornell University Press

Woolf, V, *A Room of One's Own,* extract reproduced by permission of The Society of Authors as the literary representative of the estate of Virginia Woolf

Wright, S, 'Patriarchal Feminism' (1993) *Feminist Legal Studies* (Deborah Charles Publications)

Grateful acknowledgment is made to Butterworths for permission to reproduce extracts from *All ER Law Reports*; to the Incorporated Council of Law Reporting for England and Wales for permission to reproduce extracts from the *Law Reports* and *Weekly Law Reports*; and to Harvard College for extracts from *Harvard Law Review.*

The extract reprinted on page 443 from *Pornography – Men Possessing Women* by Andrea Dworkin, published in Great Britain by The Women's Press Ltd, 1981, 34 Great Sutton Street, London EC1V 0DX is used by permission of The Women's Press Ltd. Parliamentary and Crown copyright is reproduced with the permission of the Controller of HMSO.

Every effort has been made to trace all the copyright holders but if any have been inadvertently overlooked the publishers will be pleased to make the necessary arrangement at the first opportunity.

CONTENTS

Contents

PART I

INTRODUCTION

CHAPTER 1

FACTUAL DATA ON THE WORLD'S WOMEN

The United Nation's Report, *The World's Women, 1970–90*,[1] provides a wealth of statistical and other data relating to women's position in the world. This global survey reveals how inherent is the inferior position of women throughout the world:

THE WORLD'S WOMEN, 1970–90

Regional Trends: 1970–90

Over the past 20 years there have been important changes in what women do – out of choice or necessity, depending on the hardships and opportunities they face.

In Latin America and the Caribbean, women in urban areas made some significant gains according to indicators of health, childbearing, education and economic, social and political participation, but there was little change in rural areas, and the serious macroeconomic deterioration of many Latin American countries in the 1980s undercut even the urban gains as the decade progressed.

In sub-Saharan Africa, there was some improvement for women in health and education, but indicators in these fields are still far from even minimally acceptable levels in most countries. Fertility remains very high, and there are signs that serious economic decline – coupled with rapid population growth – is undermining even the modest gains in health and education. Women's economic and social participation and contribution is high in sub-Saharan Africa. But given the large differences between men and women in most economic, social and political indicators at the start of the 1970s, the limited progress in narrowing those differences since then and the general economic decline, the situation for women in Africa remains grave.

In northern Africa and western Asia, women made gains in health and education. Fertility declined slightly but remains very high – 5.5 children in northern Africa and 5.3 in western Asia. Women in these regions continue to lag far behind in their economic participation and in social participation and decision-making.

In southern Asia, women's health and education improved somewhat. But as in Africa, indicators are still far from minimally acceptable levels – and are still very far from men's. Nor has economic growth, when it has occurred, helped women – apparently because of their low social, political and economic participation in both urban and rural areas.

In much of eastern and southeastern Asia, women's levels of living improved steadily in the 1970s and 1980s. Many of the inequalities between men and women – in health, education and employment – were reduced in both urban and rural areas and fertility also declined considerably. Even so, considerable political and economic inequalities persist in much of the region – because women are confined to the lowest paid and lowest status jobs and sectors and because they are excluded from decision-making.

---

1   United Nations (1991).

Throughout the developed regions, the health of women is generally good and their fertility is low. But in other fields, indicators of the status of women show mixed results. Women's economic participation is high in eastern Europe and the USSR, northern Europe and northern America – lower in Australia, Japan, New Zealand and southern and western Europe. Everywhere occupational segregation and discrimination in wages and training work very much in favour of men In political participation and decision-making, women are relatively well represented only in northern Europe and (at least until recently) eastern Europe and the USSR.

Gaps in policy, investment and pay

Resounding throughout the statistics in this book is one consistent message. Major gaps in policy, investment and earnings prevent women from performing to their full potential in social, economic and political life.

Policy gaps

Integration of women in mainstream development policies. The main policy gap is that governments seldom integrate the concerns and interests of women into mainstream policies. Development policies typically emphasise export oriented growth centred on cash crops, primary commodities and manufactures – largely controlled by men. Those policies typically neglect the informal sector and subsistence agriculture – the usual preserve of women. Even when women are included in mainstream development strategies, it is often in marginal women-in-development activities.

Much of this gap is embodied in laws that deny women equality with men in their rights to own land, borrow money and enter contracts. Even where women now have *de jure* equality, the failures to carry out the law deny equality *de facto*. Consider Uganda, which has a new constitution guaranteeing full equality for women. One women's leader there had this assessment: 'We continue to be second-rate citizens – no, third-rate, since our sons come before us. Even donkeys and tractors sometimes get better treatment'.[2]

Counting women's work. A second policy gap is that governments do not consider much of women's work to be economically productive and thus do not count it. If women's unpaid work in subsistence agriculture and housework and family care were fully counted in labour force statistics, their share of the labour force would be equal to or greater than men's. And if their unpaid housework and family care were counted as productive outputs in national accounts, measures of global output would increase 25% to 30%.

Even when governments do consider women's work to be economically productive, they overlook or undervalue it. Until recently, labour force statistics counted production narrowly, excluding such activities as grinding grain and selling home-grown food at the market. The International Labour Organisation widened the definition in 1982 but the application of the new standard is far from universal, and in most countries and regions only a small part of women's production is measured. Without good information about what women really do – and how much they produce – governments have little incentive to respond with economic policies that include women.

---

2   Miria Matembe, 'Speaking Out for Women in Abuja' (1989) *Africa Recovery*, vol 3, No 3, United Nations publication.

Investment gaps

Education. There are also big gaps between what women could produce and the investments they command. Households – and governments – almost always invest less in women and girls than in mean and boys. One measure of this is enrolment in school: roughly 60% of rural Indian boys and girls enter primary school, but after five years, only 15% of the girls are still enrolled, compared with 35% of the boys.

The losses from investing less in girls' education are considerable. Studies in Malaysia show that the net return to education at all levels of wages and productivity is consistently 20% higher for girls and young women than for boys and young men. And that does not include the second-round benefits of reduced fertility, improved nutrition and better family care.

One consequence of women's low educational achievement is that it puts them at a disadvantage to their husbands when making major life decisions about the work they do, the number of children they have and the way they invest family income.

Health services. Another investment gap is in health services. Women need, and too seldom receive, maternal health care and family planning services. And families often give lower priority to the health care of girls than boys. Where health services are being cut back, as they so often are under economic austerity programmes, the health needs of women are typically neglected.

Productivity. These gaps in investing in women's development persist in the investments that governments might make to increase their economic productivity. Governments give little or no support to activities in which women predominate – notably, the informal sector and subsistence agriculture. Indeed, government policies typically steer women into less productive endeavours. The infrastructure that might underpin their work is extremely inadequate. And the credit available to them from formal lending institutions is negligible. Often illiterate, usually lacking collateral and almost always discriminated against, women must rely on their husbands or on high-priced moneylenders if they want to invest in more productive ventures.

Pay gaps

Lower pay. There also are big gaps between what women produce and what they are paid. Occupational segregation and discrimination relegate women to low-paying, low-status jobs. And even when women do the same work as men, they typically receive less pay – 30 to 40% less on average worldwide. Nor are their prospects for advancement the same as men's, with deeply rooted prejudices blocking them from the top.

No pay. Another pay gap is that much of women's work is not paid and not recognised as economically productive. The work is considered to be of no economic importance is not counted, which brings the discussion back to policy gaps.

Trends in childbearing and family life

Giving women the means to regulate their childbearing enhances their ability to shape their own lives. Modern family planning methods make it far easier for women today to limit their fertility and, as important, to pick the timing and spacing of their births. Almost everywhere, the access to and the use of family planning are increasing, but not as rapidly as they might.

Fertility rates are declining in many developing countries but remain at quite high levels in most countries in Africa, in the southern Asia region and in countries of western Asia. Influencing the falling rates are broader use of effective family planning methods, changing attitudes about desired family size and reductions in infant mortality. With the spread of modern contraception, women are better able to limit their fertility. But safe contraception must be available and accepted by both women and men, and in some societies men often do not allow women to practise family planning.

The childbearing gap between developed and developing regions remains wide. In Asia and Africa, a woman typically has her first child at about age 19 or even earlier, her last at 37, for a childbearing span of 18 years. In some countries – such as Bangladesh, Mauritania, Nigeria, the Sudan and Yemen – girls often start having children at age 15. Compare this with developed regions, where a woman typically has her first child at 23 and her last at 30, for a span of only seven years. Women in developed regions have fewer children over a shorter span of years and thus need to devote a smaller part of their lives to childbearing and parenting.

Family planning and health service have helped women in many ways – improving their overall health status and that of their children and increasing their opportunities to take an expanded role in society.

Childbearing exposes women to a particular array of health risks. But the broader availability of family planning and maternal health services has reduced some of the risks of pregnancy and childbirth – delaying the first birth, allowing longer spacing between births, and reducing pregnancies among women who have had four or more births and thus face the greatest risk of haemorrhaging after giving birth. Complications from childbearing nevertheless remain a major (avoidable) cause of death for women in many developing countries – especially where family planning services are poor or hard to reach, where malnutrition is endemic among pregnant women and where births are not attended by trained personnel.

Healthier mothers are more likely to have full-term pregnancies and strong children. With more resources, they are better able to nurture their children. Better educated mothers are more likely to educate their children. The positive outcome: healthier, better educated families.

Poor women generally miss out on this positive cycle. Because they have little or no education, they have little knowledge of health practices and limited economic opportunities. They have no collateral for borrowing to invest in more productive activities. Simply trying to ensure that the family survives takes all their time. The unhappy outcome: sick, poorly educated families – and continuing poverty.

Poor teenage girls, the most vulnerable of mothers, face even greater obstacles. Cultural pressures, scant schooling and inadequate information about and access to family planning make them most likely to have unhealthy or unwanted pregnancies. In developed and developing countries alike, mothers aged 15–19 are twice as likely to die in childbirth as mothers in their early twenties, and those under 15 are five times as likely. They are less likely to obtain enough education or training to ensure a good future for themselves and their children.

Trends in marriages and households

In developed and developing regions alike, women now spend less time married and fewer years bearing and rearing children. Couples are marrying later and separating or divorcing more, in part because of their increased mobility and migration.

Throughout much of the world – the exceptions are in Asia and the Pacific – households are getting smaller and have fewer children. There are fewer multigenerational households, more single-parent families and more people living alone. Smaller households suggest the gradual decline of the extended family household, most evident in western developed countries, but also beginning to be apparent in developing countries. Also evident is a decline in the strength of kinship and in the important of family responsibility combined with greater reliance on alternative support systems and greater variations in living arrangements,

Because more women are living (or forced to live) alone or as heads of households with dependents, their responsibility for their family's survival and their own has been increasing since 1970. Motherhood is more often unsupported by marriage and the elderly are more often unsupported by their children – trends that increase the burden on women. And even for women living with men, the man's income is often so inadequate that the woman must take on the double burden of household management and outside work to make ends meet.

Women face another burden that is invisible to the outside world: domestic violence. It is unmeasured but almost certainly very extensive. Domestic violence is masked by secretiveness and poor evidence, and there are social and legal barriers to its active prevention. Men's attacks on women in their homes are thought to be the least reported crimes – in part because such violence is seen as a social ill, not a crime. Women's economic independence – and the corresponding ability to leave an abusive man – are essential for preventing violence and for fostering self-esteem. And as the awareness of women's rights becomes more universal and enforceable, more women will be opposing domestic violence.

Economic life

Economic growth in many of the developed regions has provided new opportunities for women in economic participation, production and income – despite persistent occupational and wage discrimination and the continuing exclusion of women's unpaid housework from economic measurement.

Some countries in Asia and a few in other developing regions were also able to sustain strong economic growth rates, again providing new opportunities for women despite even more pervasive social and economic obstacles to their economic advancement. But in most countries in the developing regions, as well as in eastern Europe and the USSR, the economic outlook was far worse in 1990 than in 1970. And worldwide the population living in the poorest countries increased dramatically. This mixed economic growth has created new obstacles to women's economic participation and their progress towards equality with men – seriously undercutting previous advances. And whether in circumstances of economic growth or decline, women have been called on to bear the greater burdens, and receive the fewest benefits.

Women are the first to be dismissed from the salaried labour force by economic downturns and the contractions under stabilisation and adjustment programmes. With essentials less affordable because of rising inflation and falling subsidies, women have little choice but to work harder and longer. And when the demand for workers rises, as in Brazil in the late 1980s, the men find jobs at their old wages while the women must take jobs at even lower pay than before.

Women's working world

Women's working world continues to differ from men's in the type of work, the pay, the status and the pattern of entering and leaving the work force. The biggest difference is that women continue to bear the burden of managing the household and caring for the family and that men continue to control the resources for production and the income from it. In agriculture, for example, women continue to be left labour-intensive tasks that consume the most time.

Women everywhere contribute to economic production. As officially measured, 46% of the world's women aged 15 and over – 828 million – are economically active. At least another 10 to 20% of the world's women are economically productive but not counted as part of the labour force because of inadequate measurement.

Women are left to provide child care, to provide food and health care, to prepare and process crops, to market goods, to tend gardens and livestock and to weave cloth, carpets and baskets. Much of this work does not benefit from investment, making it very inefficient and forcing women to work very hard for meagre results. In the worst cases, technological investments end up exploiting women – improving their productivity but barring them from any access or control over the profits.

The pattern, then, is that women work as much or more than men. Although women spend less time in activities officially counted as economically productive and make much less money, they spend far more in home production. If a woman spends more time in the labour force, she still bears the main responsibility for home and family care, and sleep and leisure are sacrificed.

Men's participation in the labour force has fallen everywhere. Women's, by contrast, has fallen significantly only in sub-Saharan Africa, where economic crises have been most widespread. Women's share in the total labour force is increasing in most regions. in many parts of the developed regions, there have been increases in women's economic activity rates over the past two decades. Women's highest shares in wage and salaried employment are in eastern Europe and the Soviet Union, something that could change as new economic policies create widespread unemployment there.

In Africa, most public and wage employees are men, leaving women either in subsistence agriculture or to create whatever opportunities they can in the informal sector.

In Asia and the Pacific, the picture is mixed. Women's economic activity rates (in official statistics) are very low (under 20%) in southern and western Asia, but fairly high (35 to 40%) in eastern and southeastern Asia. Women's wage and salary employment rose considerably (from 44 to 57% of the total, excluding southern Asia), reflecting significant expansion of economic opportunities for women.

In Latin America, women's economic participation grew fastest but remained at low levels (31% in urban areas, 14% in rural). The increase reflects greater economic necessities arising from the ongoing economic crises of the 1980s.

Occupational segregation and wage discrimination

Everywhere in the world the workplace is segregated by sex. Women tend to be in clerical, sales and domestic services and men in manufacturing and transport. Women work in teaching, care-giving and subsistence agriculture and men in management, administration and politics. Looking at job categories in more detail reveals even sharper segregation. For example, in teaching, women predominate in elementary or first level education while men predominate in higher education.

Women hold a mere 10 to 20% of managerial and administrative jobs worldwide and less than 20% of the manufacturing jobs. In Singapore barely 1% of working women are in managerial work, compared with nearly 10% for a much larger number of working men. Even when women work in male dominated occupations, they are relegated to the lower echelons. Among all the organisations of the United Nations system, for example, women hold only 3% of the top management jobs and 8% of senior management positions, but 42% of the entry-level civil service slots, suggesting that women are not usually promoted or hired directly into higher levels. Of the top 1,000 corporations in the United States, only two are headed by a women, a mere two-tenths of 1%.[3]

In every country having data, women's non-agriculture wage rates are substantially lower than men's. In some countries, the gap is around 50% and in only a very few is it less than 30%. The average gap is between 30% and 40% and there is no sign that it is substantially narrowing.

Even where women have moved into occupations dominated by men, their income remains lower. Take Canada, where women have made solid inroads into administration, management, engineering, physical sciences, university teaching and law and medicine. Between 1971 and 1981 they accounted for nearly a third of the growth in these professions. Women in these professions earned about 15% more than women in other professional categories but they still lagged 15 to 20% behind their male counterparts.

The informal sector

One wedge of opportunity for women is the informal sector, including self-employment. Crucial to the survival strategies of many women, the informal sector also opens important long-term opportunities where salaried employment is closed to women, declining or inadequate. Women work in the informal sector because of necessity and convenience. It requires less skill and education. It has fewer biases in favour of men. And it is easier to reconcile with cultural norms that keep women near the home, for there is less conflict between working hours and household tasks. But informal employment is far less secure an employer than the formal workplace and productivity is often low.

Incomes may be lower in the informal sector for several reasons. One is the absence or high cost of credit. Another is lack of government support. A third is exploitation by larger firms controlling raw materials or markets. And although women's participation in the informal sector is increasing, the returns are declining. Studies show that there is greater difference in the earnings of men and women in the informal sector than in the formal. Women in the informal sector are vulnerable to even slight deteriorations in an economy. Especially in highly indebted countries, informal sector returns have fallen even more than formal sector returns, as more people are pushed into the informal sector. Despite the meagre earnings, the informal sector has been women's only recourse for surviving the economic crises in Africa and Latin America during the 1980s.

---

3   Chief Executives of the Business Week 1000: A Directory (19 October, 1989) Business Week.

Public life and leadership

Women are poorly represented in the ranks of power, policy and decision-making. Women make up less than 5% of the world's heads of State, heads of major corporations and top positions in international organisations. Women are not just behind in political and managerial equity, they are a long way behind. This is in spite of the fact that women are found in large numbers in low-level positions of public administrations, political parties, trade unions and businesses.

The picture barely improves at other decision-making levels. Fifty United Nations' Member States have no woman in any of their top echelons of government. Although women have made some incursions in the past 20 years in parliaments and at middle management levels, their representation in these areas still averages less than 10% and less than 20% respectively. Their parliamentary representation would have to increase by 35 to 50 percentage points to reach parity with men. The eastern European and USSR parliaments are exceptions. Women have made up about a fourth of the parliamentary bodies there and played an important role. But recent elections show a significant drop in women's representation in these countries, just as parliaments – as a result of political changes – have become more important.

Women continue to be denied equal access to high-status and high-paying positions but there has been some progress since the United Nations Decade for Women began in 1976. Many countries have set up special offices to review complaints of discriminatory practice in political parties, parliaments, unions and professional organisations. Israel, Venezuela and several European countries have quotas to guarantee women more equal participation in the leadership of political parties. Trade unions in Canada, Norway and the United Kingdom have reserved a designated percentage of political seats for women. Women are also defining their own paths in politics. Increasing numbers are entering political life through nongovernmental organisations, women's movements and associations of professional women. And women are increasingly active in the politics of their communities and locales.

Community and grass roots participation have long been an extension of women's traditional place in the community and responsibility for the health and well-being of their families. The past 20 years have seen a burgeoning of groups headed by or heavily made up of women. Discriminatory practices, increasing poverty, violence against women, environmental threats, military build-ups, family and economic imperatives and the negative consequences of economic adjustment and stabilisation programmes have all increased women's needs to band together to change conditions or policies. Women in both the developed and the developing regions have discovered that they can translate their efforts to protect themselves into effective political action.

Demands for equal status

International efforts to establish the rights of women culminated in 1979 with the General Assembly's adoption of the Convention on the Elimination of All Forms of Discrimination Against Women. The Convention confronts stereotypes, customs and norms that give rise to the many legal, political and economic constraints on women. The legal status of women receives the broadest attention – for basic rights of political participation, civil rights and reproductive rights. One hundred and two countries have ratified the Convention, legally binding themselves to incorporate the Convention's demands in their policies.

In 1985 the Nairobi Forward-looking Strategies for the Advancement of Women were approved by 157 countries gathered to assess the achievements and failures of the United Nations Decade for Women. The Strategies demand that governments:

- Play key roles in ensuring that both men and women enjoy equal rights in such areas as education, training and employment.
- Act to remove negative stereotypes and perceptions of women.
- Disseminate information to women about their rights and entitlements.
- Collect timely and accurate statistics on women and monitor their situation.
- Encourage the sharing and support of domestic responsibilities.

Even with progress in legislation, women – especially poor women – are still a long way from receiving social recognition for what they do. *De facto* discrimination on the grounds of sex is insidious but widespread. For example, the Bangladesh Constitution guarantees the equal rights of men and women and sanctions affirmative action programmes in favour of women but as the data reveals the status of women in Bangladesh is among the lowest in the world. It is encouraging, then, that policy makers there have stepped up efforts to implement programmes for women, particularly in health and education.

Many societies deny women independence from family and male control, particularly where girls are married at a very young age to much older men. According to estimates from the World Fertility Survey, almost half the women in Africa, 40% in Asia and 30% in Latin America are married by the age of 18. Men are on average four to eight years older. And a woman's social status is often linked entirely to her reproductive role. Failure to bear children – or even to bear sons – is cause of ostracism, divorce and even brutality in areas of Africa and southern Asia.

The Nairobi Strategies restate demands in the 1957 and 1962 international conventions for equal status of women and men in marriage and in the dissolution of marriage. In addition to such reforms in marriage laws and practices, efforts to improve women's economic status and autonomy – to reflect their economic responsibilities and contributions – can bring them closer to an equal footing with men in and out of the household.[4]

OVERVIEW OF THE WORLD'S WOMEN IN 1995[5]

Issues of gender equality are moving to the top of the global agenda but better understanding of women's and men's contributions to society is essential to speed the shift from agenda to policy to practice. Too often, women and men live in different worlds, worlds that differ in access to education and work opportunities, and in health, personal security and leisure time. *The World's Women, 1995*, provides information and analyses to highlight the economic, political and social differences that still separate women's and men's lives and how these differences are changing.

How different are these worlds? Anecdote and misperception abound, in large part because good information has been lacking. As a result, policy has been ill-informed, strategy unfounded and practice unquestioned. Fortunately, this is

4   *The Worlds Women, 1970–90* (HMSO, 1991), pp 1–6.
5   *United Nations Report* (HMSO, 1995).

beginning to change. It is changing because advocates of women's interests have done much in the past 20 years to sharpen people's awareness of the importance of gender concerns. It is changing because this growing awareness has, by raising new questions and rephrasing old, greatly increased the demand for better statistics to inform and focus the debate. And it is changing because women's contributions – and women's rights – have moved to the centre of social and economic change.

The International Conference on Population and Development, held in Cairo in 1994, was a breakthrough. It established a new consensus on two fundamental points:

–   Empowering women and improving their status are essential to realising the full potential of economic, political and social development.

–   Empowering women is an important end in itself. And as women acquire the same status, opportunities and social, economic and legal rights as men, as they acquire the right to reproductive health and the right to protection against gender based violence, human well-being will be enhanced.

The International Conference on Population and Development drew together the many strands of thought and action initiated by two decades of women's conferences. It was also the culmination of an active effort by women's groups to lobby international forums for women's issues. At the United Nations Conference on Environment and Development in Rio de Janeiro in 1992, nongovernmental organisations pushed for understanding the link between women's issues and sustainable development. At the World Conference on Human Rights in Vienna in 1993, women's rights were finally accepted as issues of international human rights.

At the Population Conference and later at the World Summit for Social Development, held in Copenhagen in 1995, the terms of discourse shifted. Not only were women on the agenda – women helped set the agenda. The empowerment of women was not merely the subject of special sessions about women's issues. It was accepted as a crucial element in any strategy seeking to solve social, economic and environmental problems. And building on the advances made in the recognition of women's human rights at the World Conference in Vienna, women's human rights became a focus of the debate in Cairo. The rights approach, advanced by women's groups, was added to the core objectives of development policy and the movement for women's equality.

To promote action on the new consensus, this second edition of *The World's Women* builds on the first, presenting statistical summaries of health, schooling, family life, work and public life. Each has to be seen in proper context, however. Yes, there have been important changes in the past 25 years and women have generally made steady progress, but it is impossible to make sweeping global statements. Women's labour force participation rates are up in much of the world, but down in countries wracked by war and economic decline. Girls' education is improving, but there are hundreds of millions of illiterate women and girls who do not complete primary schooling, especially in Africa and southern Asia.

It is also important to look at a range of indicators. Women's political participation may be high in the Nordic countries, but in employment Nordic women still face considerable job segregation and wage discrimination. Women's higher education may be widespread in western Asia, but in many of those countries there are few or no women in important political positions and work opportunities are largely limited to unpaid family labour.

The World's Women presents few global figures, focusing instead on country data and regional averages. There are myriad differences among countries in every field and *The World's Women* tries to find a meaningful balance between detailed country statements and broad generalisation. Generalisations are primarily drawn at the regional and subregional levels where there is a high degree of uniformity among countries. For all the topics covered, *The World's Women* has tapped as many statistical sources as possible, with detailed references as a basis for further study. Specialised studies are used when they encompass several countries, preferably in more than one region, so as to avoid presenting conclusions relevant in only one country.

Indicators relevant to specific age groups are crucial to understanding women's situation. The Programme of Action of the International Conference on Population and Development identified equality for the girl-child as a necessary first step in ensuring that women realise their full potential and become equal partners with men. This edition of *The World's Women* responds to this concern by highlighting the experience of the girl-child. Evidence of prenatal sex selection and differences in mortality, health, school enrolment and even work indicates that girls and boys are not treated equally.

The experience of the elderly is more difficult to describe from the few available data. Although elderly people constitute a valuable component of societies' human resources, data on the elderly are insufficient for regional generalisations. Considering that the numbers of elderly are growing rapidly in all regions, this gap needs to be addressed.

Education for empowerment

In the Programme of Action of the International Conference on Population and Development, education is considered one of the most important means to empower women with the knowledge, skills and self-confidence necessary to participate fully in development processes. Educated women marry later, want fewer children, are more likely to use effective methods of contraception and have greater means to improve their economic livelihood.

Through widespread promotion of universal primary education, literacy rates for women have increased over the past few decades – to at least 75% in most countries of Latin America and the Caribbean and eastern and southeastern Asia. But high rates of illiteracy among women still prevail in much of Africa and in parts of Asia. And when illiteracy is high it almost always is accompanied by large differences in rates between women and men.

At intermediate levels of education, girls have made progress in their enrolment in school through the second level. The primary-secondary enrolment ratio is now about equal for girls and boys in the developed regions and Latin America and the Caribbean and is approaching near equality in eastern, southeastern and western Asia. But progress in many countries was reversed in the 1980s, particularly among those experiencing problems of war, economic adjustment and declining international assistance – as in Africa, Latin America and the Caribbean, and eastern Europe.

In higher education enrolments, women equal or exceed men in many regions. They outnumber men in the developed regions outside western Europe, in Latin America and the Caribbean and western Asia. Women are not as well represented in other regions, and in sub-Saharan Africa and southern Asia they are far behind – 30 and 38 women per 100 men.

The Framework for Action to implement the World Declaration on Education for All states that it is urgent to improve access to education for girls and women and to remove every obstacle that hampers their active participation. Priority actions include eliminating the social and cultural barriers that discourage – or even exclude – girls and women from the benefits of regular education programmes.

Seeking influence

Despite progress in women's higher education, major obstacles still arise when women strive to translate their high-level education into social and economic advancement. In the world of business, for example, women rarely account for more than 1% or 2% of top executive positions. In the more general category of administration and management including middle levels, women's share rose in every region but one between 1980 and 1990. Women's participation jumped from 16% to 33% in developed regions outside Europe. In Latin America, it rose from 18% to 25%.

In the health and teaching professions – two of the largest occupational fields requiring advanced training – women are well represented in many countries but usually at the bottom levels of the status and wage hierarchy. Similarly, among the staff of an international group of agriculture research institutes, women's participation at the nonscientific and trainee levels is moderate, but there are few women at management and senior scientific levels.

The information people receive through newspapers, radio and television shapes their opinions about the world. And the more decision-making positions women hold in the media, the more they can influence output; breaking stereotypes that hurt women, attracting greater attention to issues of equality in the home and in public life, and providing young women with new images, ideas and ideals. Women now make up more than half of the communications students in a large number of countries and are increasingly visible as presenters, announcers and reporters, but they remain poorly represented in the more influential media occupations such as programme managers and senior editors.

In the top levels of government, women's participation remains the exception. At the end of 1994 only ten women were heads of state or government; of these ten countries only Norway had as many as one third women ministers or subministers. Some progress has been made in the appointment of women to ministerial or subministerial positions but these positions are usually tenuous for them. Most countries with women in top ministerial positions do not have comparable representation at the subministerial level. And in other countries, where significant numbers of women have reached the subministerial levels, very few have reached the top. Progress for women in parliaments has also been mixed and varies widely among regions. It is strongest in northern Europe, where it appears to be rising steadily.

Missing from this summary is women's remarkable advance in less traditional paths to power and influence. The importance of the United Nations Decade for Women and international women's conferences should not be underestimated, for these forums enabled women to develop the skills required for exercising power and influence, to mobilise resources and articulate issues and to practise organising, lobbying and legislating. Excluded from most political offices, many women have found a voice in nongovernmental organisations (NGOs) at the grass roots, national and international levels. NGOs have taken issues previously ignored – such as violence against women and rights to reproductive health – and brought them into the mainstream policy debate.

Since the women's conference in Nairobi in 1985, many grass roots groups have been working to create new awareness of women's rights, including their rights within the family, and to help women achieve those rights. They have set agendas and carved out a space for women's issues. And as seen in recent United Nations conferences, NGOs as a group can wield influence broad enough to be active partners with governments in deciding national policies and programmes.

Reproductive health – reproductive freedom

With greater access to education, employment and contraception, many women are choosing to marry later and have fewer children. Those who wait to marry and begin childbearing have better access to education and greater opportunities to improve their lives. Women's increased access to education, to employment and to contraception, coupled with declining rates of infant mortality, have contributed to the worldwide decline in fertility.

The number of children women bear in developed regions is now below replacement levels at 1.9 per woman. In Latin America and in most parts of Asia it has also dropped significantly. But in Africa women still have an average of six children and in many sub-Saharan African countries women have as many or more children now than they did 20 years ago.

Adolescent fertility has declined in many developing and developed countries over the past 20 years. In Central America and sub-Saharan Africa, however, rates are five to seven times higher than in developed regions. Inadequate nutrition, anaemia and early pregnancies threaten the health and life of young girls and adolescents.

Too many women lack access to reproductive health services. In developing countries maternal mortality is a leading cause of death for women of reproductive age. The World Health Organisation (WHO) estimates that more than half a million women die each year in childbirth and millions more develop pregnancy-related health complications. The deteriorating economic and health conditions in sub-Saharan Africa led to an increase in maternal mortality during the 1980s, where it remains the highest in the world. An African woman's lifetime risk of dying from pregnancy related causes is one in 23, while a North American woman's is one in 4,000. Maternal mortality also increased in some countries of eastern Europe.

Pregnancy and childbirth have become safer for women in most of Asia and in parts of Latin America. In developed countries attended delivery is almost universal, but in developing countries only 55% of births take place with a trained attendant and only 37% in hospitals or clinics. Today new importance is being placed on women's reproductive health and safe motherhood as advocates work to redefine reproductive health as an issue of human rights.

The Programme of Action of the International Conference on Population and Development set forth a new framework to guide government actions in population, development and reproductive health and to measure and evaluate programmes designed to realise these objectives. Instead of the traditional approach centred on family planning and population policy objectives, governments are encouraged to develop client-centred management information systems in population and development and particularly reproductive health. including family planning and sexual health programmes.

Fewer marriages – smaller households

Rapid population changes, combined with many other social and economic chances, are being accompanied by considerable changes in women's household and family status. Most people still marry but they marry later in life, especially women. In developing regions, consensual unions and other nonformal unions remain prevalent, especially in rural areas. As a result of these changes, many women – many more women than men – spend a significant part of their life without a partner, with important consequences for their economic welfare and their children's.

In developed regions, marriage has become both less frequent and less stable, and cohabitation is on the rise. Marriages preceded by a period of cohabitation have clearly increased in many countries of northern Europe. And where divorce once led quickly to remarriage, many postpone marriage or never remarry.

Since men have higher rates of remarriage, marry at an older age, and have a shorter life expectancy, most older men are married, while many older women are widows. Among women 60 and older, widowhood is significant everywhere – from 40% in the developed regions and Latin America to 50% in Africa and Asia. Moreover, in Asia and Africa, widowhood also affects many women at younger ages.

Between 1970 and 1990 household size decreased significantly in the developed regions, in Latin America and the Caribbean and in eastern and southeastern Asia. Households are the smallest in developed regions, having declined to an average of 2.8 persons per household in 1990. In eastern Asia the average household size has declined to 3.7, in southeastern Asia to 4.9. In Latin American countries the average fell to 4.7 persons per household, and in the Caribbean to 4.1. In northern African countries household size increased on average from 5.4 to 5.7.

In developed countries the decline in the average household size reflects an increase in the number of one-person households, especially among unmarried adults and the elderly. In developing regions the size of the household is more affected by the number of children although a shift from extended households to nuclear households also has some effect. Household size remains high in countries where fertility has not yet fallen significantly – for instance, in some of the African and western Asian countries.

Work – paid and unpaid

Women's access to paid work is crucial to their self-reliance and the economic well-being of dependent family members. But access to such work is unequal between women and men. Women work in different occupations than men, almost always with lower status and pay.

In developing countries many women work as unpaid family labourers in subsistence agriculture and household enterprises. Many women also work in the informal sector, where their remuneration is unstable, and their access to funds to improve their productivity is limited at best. And whatever other work women do, they also have the major responsibility for most household work, including the care of children and other family members.

The work women do contributes substantially to the well-being of families, communities and nations. But work in the household – even when it is economic – is inadequately measured, and this subverts policies for the credit, income and security of women and their families.

Over the past two decades, women's reported economic activity rates increased in all regions except sub-Saharan Africa and eastern Asia, and all of these increases are large except in eastern Europe, central Asia and Oceania. In fact, women's labour force participation increased more in the 1980s than in the 1970s in many regions. In contrast, men's economic activity rates have declined everywhere except central Asia.

The decline in women's reported labour force participation in sub-Saharan Africa stands out as an exception – dropping from a high of 57% in 1970 to 54% in 1980 to 53% in 1990.

In 1990 the average labour force participation rate among women aged 15 and over ranged from a high of 56 to 58% in eastern and central Asia and eastern Europe to a low in northern Africa of 21%. The participation rates of men vary within a more limited range of 72 to 83%. Because so many women in developing countries work in agriculture and informal household enterprises, where their contributions are underreported, their recorded rates of economic activity should be higher in many cases. The estimated increase in southern Asia – from 25% of women economically active in 1970 to 44% in 1990 – may be due largely to changes in the statistical methods used rather than to significant changes in work patterns.

Although work in subsistence production is crucial to survival, it goes largely under-reported in population and agricultural surveys and censuses. Most of the food eaten in agricultural households in developing countries is produced within the family holding, much of it by women. Some data show the extent of women's unreported work in agriculture. In Bangladesh, India and Pakistan, government surveys using methods to improve the measurement of subsistence work, report that more than half of rural women engage in such activities as tending poultry or cattle, planting rice, drying seeds, collecting water and preparing dung cakes for fuel. Direct observation of women's activities suggests that almost all women in rural areas contribute economically in one way or another.

The informal sector – working on own-account and in small family enterprises – also provides women with important opportunities in areas where salaried employment is closed or inadequate. In five of the six African countries studied by the Statistical Division of the United Nations Secretariat, more than one third of women economically active outside agriculture work in the informal sector, and in seven countries of Latin America 15 to 20%. In nine countries in Asia the numbers vary – from less than 10% of economically active women in western Asia to 41% in the Republic of Korea and 65% in Indonesia.

Although fewer women than men participate in the labour force, in some countries – including Honduras, Jamaica and Zambia – more women than men make up the informal sector labour force. In several other countries, women make up 40% or more of the informal sector.

In addition to the invisibility of many of women's economic activities, women remain responsible for most housework, which also goes unmeasured by the System of National Accounts. But time-use data for many developed countries show almost everywhere that women work at least as many hours each week as men, and in a large number of countries they work at least two hours more than men. Further, the daily time a man spends on work tends to be the same throughout working life. But a woman's working time fluctuates widely and at times is extremely heavy – the result of combining paid work, household and childcare responsibilities.

Two-thirds to three-quarters of household work in developed regions is performed by women. In most countries studied, women spend 30 hours or more on housework each week while men spend around ten hours. Among household tasks, the division of labour remains clear and definite in most countries. Few men do the laundry, clean the house, make the beds, iron the clothes. And most women do little household repair and maintenance. Even when employed outside the home, women do most of the housework.

Efforts to generate better statistics

The first world conference on women in Mexico in 1975 recognised the importance of improving statistics on women. Until the early 1980s women's advocates and women's offices were the main forces behind this work. Big efforts had not yet been launched in statistical offices – either nationally or internationally.

The collaboration of the Statistical Division of the United Nations' Secretariat with the International Research and Training Institute for the Advancement of Women (INSTRAW) – beginning in 1982 – on a training programme to promote dialogue and understanding between policy makers and statisticians, laid the groundwork for a comprehensive programme of work.

By the time of the world conference in Nairobi in 1985 some progress was evident. The Statistical Division compiled 39 key statistical indicators on the situation of women for 172 countries, and important efforts at the national level included the preparation of *Women and Men in Sweden*, first published in 1984 and with sales of 100,000.

Since Nairobi numerous developments have strengthened and given new momentum to this work. The general approach in development strategy has moved from women in development to gender and development. The focus has shifted from women in isolation to women in relation to men – to the roles each has, the relationships between them and the different impacts of policies and programmes.

In statistics the focus has likewise moved from attention to women's statistics to gender statistics. There now is a recognition, for example, that biases in statistics apply not only to women but also to men – in their roles as husbands and fathers and in their roles in the household. That recognition reaches beyond the disaggregation of data by sex to assessing statistical systems in terms of gender. It asks:

–   Do the topics investigated on statistics and the concepts and definitions used in data collection reflect the diversities of women's and men's lives?

–   Will the methods used in collecting data take into account stereotypes and cultural factors that might produce bias?

–   Are the ways data are compiled and presented well suited to the needs of policy makers, planners and others who need such data?

The first *World's Women: Trends and Statistics*, issued in 1991, presented the most comprehensive and authoritative compilation of global indicators on the status of women ever available. The book's data have informed debates at international conferences and national policy meetings and provided a resource to the press and others. Its publication greatly contributed to the understanding of data users and created, for the first time, a substantial global audience for statistical gender-based information. This audience has demanded, in turn, more and better data. The book also stimulated more work on the compilation of statistics and led to *The World's Women, 1995*, being prepared as an official conference document for the Fourth World Conference on Women in Beijing in 1995.

As gender issues receive greater priority in the work programmes of international organisations. support to the Statistical Division of the United Nations Secretariat and to national efforts to improve this work have gathered strength at UNFPA, UNICEF, UNDP, WFP, UNIFEM and INSTRAW, among others. ILO, FAO, WHO, UNESCO and UNHCR are also rethinking statistical recommendations and guidelines in their work to better understand women's activities and situations, and products of this change are evident in *The World's Women, 1995*.

The World's Women, 1995, shows considerable development in the statistics available on women and men and in ways of presenting them effectively. But it also points to important needs for new work to be addressed in the Platform for Action of the Fourth World Conference on Women. Some problems identified by the first world conference – such as the measurement of women's economic contribution and the definition of the concepts of household and household head – are still unresolved. But significant improvements have been made in many areas. Data users know much more today than 20 years ago about how women's and men's situations differ in social, political and economic life. And consumers of data are also asking many more questions that are increasing the demand for more refined statistics. Still other areas not commonly addressed in the regular production of official statistics have only begun to be explored: the male role in the family, women in poverty and women's human rights, including violence against women.

Important in today's more in-depth approach are:

– Identification of the data needed to understand the disparities in the situation, contributions and problems of women and men.
– Evaluation of existing concepts and methods against today's changed realities.
– Development of new concepts and methods to yield unbiased data.
– The preparation of statistics in formats easily accessible to a wide array of users.

None of this is easy or without cost. Every step requires considerable effort and expertise. All require integrated approaches that pull together today's often fragmented, specialised efforts and take a fresh look at methods and priorities in, say, education, employment, criminal justice, business, credit and training. All require a broader, more integrated treatment of social and economic data. And all require special efforts to improve international comparability. But required above all – for true national, regional and global assessments of the social, political and economic lives of women and men – is agreement on what the key issues are and support for how to address them.

The objective is always to produce timely statistics on women and men that can inform policy, refine strategy and influence practice. After two decades of efforts, improved gender statistics are doing much to inform policy debate and implementation. But to provide truly effective monitoring at all levels requires continuity and reinforcing the dialogue between statisticians and the consumers of statistics – policy makers, researchers, advocates and the media.[6]

---

6   *The World's Women, 1995*, pp xvii–xxiv (United Nations Report, HMSO).

CHAPTER 2

WOMEN AND CULTURE

In this chapter, the historical and traditional position of women in society is considered, not from a specifically legal standpoint, but rather from a broad political, sociological and philosophical perspective. Whatever importance is given to law as a phenomenon, the dependence of law upon the social base must be appreciated. Law does not exist in a vacuum – it is intimately connected with society. While it may be difficult at times to trace the evolution of society from one dictated purely by nature to a society with distinctive cultural mores and distinctive laws resting on those mores, the influence of both nature and culture on law is undeniable.[1] This is particularly true in relation to the position and role of women in society. The biological fact of being female, and all the associated implications and consequences of this, translated itself early into cultural mores which distinguished between men and women. Men – having superior physical strength – took control of the public sphere of life: the control of law and government. Having asserted dominance in the public sphere, women became relegated to the private domain of home and family. By examining some of the empirical data concerning the treatment of women at differing times, it becomes possible to see the common strands of thought in relation to women, albeit being expressed in differing ways, in differing societies.

In the first extract, *Toward a Theory of Law and Patriarchy*[2] Janet Rifkin explains the role of law in masking social and political questions such as women's subordination in patriarchal culture. Cultural taboos – such as the universal prohibition against incest – gave rise to legal rules which then in turn reinforced the cultural force of the prohibition. Allied to this is the role ascribed to women as the property of their men: property to be exchanged between men under cultural norms which harden into legal rules. Law becomes the symbol of masculine authority and patriarchal society.

Mary Daly develops this theme in her book *Gyn/Ecology*.[3] Analysing the practices of Chinese footbinding, Hindu suttee and African female circumcision from a feminist perspective, Mary Daly reveals the true meaning of the practices: the control of women under the authority of men.

The extract from Marianne Hester's *Lewd Women and Wicked Witches*[4] considers the 16th and 17th century practice in England and continental Europe of persecution and trial of women accused of witchcraft. Statute law was used to legitimise the practice and to bolster the belief in the power and evil of witchcraft. In Marianne Hester's analysis the single unifying thread which runs through the story of witch persecution is that the victims were invariably women who were not under the control of a man: spinsters or widows.

---

1   See below for analysis of the development from cultural mores to law.

2   (1980) 3 *Harvard Women's Law Journal* 83.

3   The Women's Press, 1991.

4   Routledge and Kegan Paul, 1992.

An extract from Thomas Hardy's *The Mayor of Casterbridge*[5] is included to illustrate another form of patriarchal practice: that of wife-sale. Wife-sale represented a semi-formal method by which the husband's property in the wife would be transferred from one man to another. As will be seen, wife-sale was not a flight of literary imagination, but firmly rooted in fact.

Religion has played an authoritative and contributory role to the perception of women as different from, and subordinate to, men. Whatever the accuracy of the frequently made claim that Western society is increasingly 'secular', the legacy of religious beliefs and texts continues to permeate, however directly or indirectly, Western society. In this section, the interpretations offered by feminist scholars Elaine Pagels and Mary Daly reveal that women have, from the earliest times of Christianity, been interpreted out of religious text and, worse, portrayed as unequal, undeserving of equality.

The chapter concludes with three extracts from socio-legal theorists who, in differing ways, trace the evolution from culture to law. In the first extract from Emile Durkheim's *The Division of Labour in Society*[6] the author explains that while it is morality which brings about, and explains, cohesion in society, it is law which symbolises that solidarity. Morality is unmeasurable: law is measurable — a visible index of solidarity. Thus law is the sum of the cultural norms in society.

The extract from Eugen Ehrlich's *Fundamental Principles of the Sociology of Law*[7] also explains the cultural basis of law. Law does not, as Ehrlich explains, have an existence independent of society but rests on society itself. A true understanding of law can only be gleaned by an examination of the 'living law' in society: those cultural norms which have arisen out of social life.

Writing at the turn of the century in the United States of America, William Graham Sumner portrayed the emergence of law as a natural evolution from nature to culture to law. This early historical/anthropological approach, for all its simplicity, presents powerful evidence of the durability of the culturally-ingrained ethos which law continues to display in its patriarchal, exclusionary, attitudes.

William Graham Sumner's work is perhaps the most explicit in terms of explaining the evolution from nature through culture to law. In Sumner's analysis, in early society, man reacts in an unthinking manner to the circumstances of life. With experience, human conduct becomes less purely reactive and becomes regularised by a perception of the utility of acting in a certain manner. Here are the 'folkways' of society. Gradually, these folkways will become hardened into the mores of society – the cultural values of that society which form the foundation for laws which will emerge only gradually and only once the mores of the society are sufficiently defined to represent a firm basis for the introduction of formal rules of law. Judicial decisions, and statutes, will come into being only at a relatively late stage of evolution of society, and must be grounded in the mores of society.

---

5   1886 (Macmillan Press, 1975).
6   1893.
7   1936.

TOWARD A THEORY OF LAW AND PATRIARCHY[8]
Janet Rifkin[9]

The power of law is that by framing the issues as questions of law, claims of right, precedents and problems of constitutional interpretation, the effect is to divert potential public consciousness from an awareness of the deeper roots of the expressed dissatisfaction and anger. The ideology of law serves to mask the real social and political questions underlying these problems of law. At the same time, the paradigm of law which historically has been and continues to be the symbol of male authority is not only unchallenged but reinforced as a legitimate mechanism for resolving social conflict. In the end, patriarchy as a form of power and social order will not be eliminated unless the male power paradigm of law is challenged and transformed. In order to challenge the male paradigm of law, the origin of law as a form of male authority and power must be discovered and examined more thoroughly ...[10]

Nature, Culture and Women

The efforts to find and explain the origins of patriarchy have led some scholars to examine mythology, fables and kinship bonds. Kate Millett, for example, in *Sexual Politics*, claims that 'myth and kinship ties are the most lasting vestiges of that vast historical shift whereby patriarchy replaced whatever order preceded it and instituted that long government of male over female'.[11] In this context, she turns to Aeschylus's *Oresteia* trilogy and its final play *The Eurmenides*,[12] in which he presents a confrontation between paternal authority and maternal order. In the first two plays, we saw Clytemnestra, rebelling against the masculine authority of husband and king, kill Agamemnon upon his return from Troy, and her son Orestes revenge his father's death by killing her. In so doing Orestes provokes the rage of the Furies who accuse him of matricide. In the third play they put him on trial, assured that justice will be done. They are not prepared, however, for the emergence of the new form of patriarchal justice articulated by Athena, who says:

> No mother gave me birth. Therefore, the father's claim
> And male supremacy in all things, save to give
> Myself in marriage, wins my whole heart's loyalty.
> Therefore a woman's death, who killed her husband, is,
> I judge, outweighed in grievousness by his ...[13]

Through Athena's deciding vote, Orestes is acquitted and his patrimony is reinforced. The Furies lament helplessly:

> The old is trampled by the new!
> Curse on you younger gods who override
> The ancient laws...![14]

---

8 (1980) 3 *Harvard Womens' Law Journal* 83. (Footnotes edited.)

9 At the time of writing, Assistant Professor, University of Massachusetts.

10 *Ibid*, p 87.

11 *Sexual Politics* (1970), p 110.

12 The play is also known as *The Furies*.

13 Aeschylus, *The Eumenides* (172AD) 11, 73–42. P Vellacott, trans (1956), in K Millett *Sexual Politics*, p 114.

14 *Ibid*, pp 173, 11, 776–78.

In this fable, law emerges as a symbol of patriarchal authority. However, the complex and fundamental connections between law and patriarchy in a more general historical context have not been adequately developed and these connections are essential to an understanding of political and social power.

In *The Elementary Structure of Kinship*[15]Levi-Strauss, in analysing the meaning of the universality of incest taboos, also analyses the role of women in pre-state societies. He suggests that the concept of women as the property of men that is based in the universal notion of the exchange of women emerges as a fundamental tenet of culture. The origins of the social order then are grounded on the conception of women as the property of men; the patriarchal social order is the basis of culture itself.

Levi-Strauss begins by asking where nature ends and culture begins. He suggests that the 'absence of rules seems to provide the surest criterion for distinguishing a natural from a cultural process'.[16] He finds that the incest taboo is a phenomenon which has the 'distinctive characteristics both of nature and of its theoretical contradiction, culture. The prohibition of incest has the universality of bent and instinct and the coercive character of law and institution'.[17] The rule against incest gives rise to rules of marriage, which although varying somewhat from group to group, are universally based on the taboo against incest. The rules of marriage also universally are based on the idea of exchange, and in particular the exchange of women. The exchange of women is a universal mode of culture, although not everywhere equally developed. Levi-Strauss asserts further that the incest taboo 'is at once on the threshold of culture, in culture, and in one sense ... culture itself'.[18] Since, as he shows, the exchange of women is integrally connected to the incest taboo, it can also be said that the exchange of women, as objects of male property, is also on the threshold of culture, in culture and is culture itself.

Levi-Strauss states that the role of exchange:

> ... in primitive society is essential because it embraces material objects, social values and women. But while in the case of merchandise this role has progressively diminished in importance in favour of other means of acquisition as far as women are concerned, reciprocity has maintained its fundamental function ... because women are the most precious possession [and] a natural stimulant.[19]

He asserts the universality of the exchange of women by stating:

> The inclusion of women in the number of reciprocal presentations from group to group and from tribe to tribe is such a general custom that a whole volume would not be sufficient to enumerate the instances of it.[20]

The notion of women as male property is at the heart of the cultural-social order. Matrimonial exchange is only a particular case of those forms of multiple exchanges embracing material goods, rights and persons:

---

15 C Levi-Strauss *The Elementary Structure of Kinship* (2nd edn), J Bell and J von Starmer, trans (1969).

16 *Ibid*, p 8.

17 *Ibid*, p 10.

18 *Ibid*, p 12.

19 *Ibid*, p 62.

20 *Ibid*, p 63.

> The total relationship of exchange which constitutes marriage is not established between a man and a women ... but between two groups of men, and the woman figures only as one of the objects in the exchange, not as one of the partners between whom the exchange takes place.[21]

Even where matrilinear descent is established, the woman is never more than the symbol of her lineage. And Levi-Strauss disposes of the myth of the 'reign of women' which he says is 'remembered only in mythology [as] an age ... when men had not resolved the antimony which is always likely to appear between their roles as takers of wives and givers of sisters, making them both the authors and victims of their exchanges'.[22]

The origin of culture as reflected in kinship systems is universally based on the idea that women are the property of men to be exchanged between individuals or groups of males. Levi-Strauss sees a 'masculinity of political authority' when political power takes precedence over other forms of organisation. Early political philosophy, as reflected by the writings of Aristotle, did not challenge this universal social fact. Aristotle, who developed a philosophy of politics and power, also saw political authority as masculine and saw women as non-participants in the political world.[23]

Aristotle radically bifurcates public (political) from private (apolitical) realms. Fully realised moral goodness and reason are attainable only through participation in public life, and this involvement is reserved to free, adult males. Women share in goodness and rationality in the limited sense appropriate to their confinement in a lesser association, the household. Indeed, it can be said with no exaggeration that women in Aristotle's schema are idiots in the Greek sense of the word, that is, persons who do not participate in the polis.[24]

The political analysis of Aristotle upholds a male-dominant power paradigm which 'serves to perpetuate an arbitrary bifurcation between that which is politics and that which is not. ... Implicit within the paradigm is a concept of persons which admits into the privileges of full personhood ... only those individuals who hold dual statuses as both public and private persons [ie men]'.[25] The male-dominant paradigm of political power is also the paradigm of law. The historical image of maleness – objective, rational and public – is the dominant image of law.

Law, in mythology, culture and philosophy, is the ultimate symbol of masculine authority and patriarchal society. The form of law is different in varying social groups, ranging from kinship bonds, custom, and the tribal rules in pre-State societies, to written codes in modern society. The point, however, is that law in State and non-State contexts is based on male authority and patriarchal social order.[26]

---

21 *Ibid*, p 115.

22 *Ibid*, p 118.

23 R McKeon (ed), *Politics*, (1941) pp 1127–30, 1194–97, 12, 13, 1252a–1253a, 1259b–1260b. On Aristotle see further below.

24 *Ibid*, p 455.

25 *Ibid*, p 472.

26 *Toward a Theory of Law and Patriarchy*, pp 88–92. See also Luce Irigary, *Thinking the Difference*; K Montin, trans (The Athlone Press, 1994).

Empirical Evidence of Patriarchy

There exists much historical evidence revealing the extent to which women have traditionally been controlled and oppressed by men, in differing societies at differing times. Theologian Mary Daly has examined some of the brutal practices, for example, the Chinese practice of binding the feet of young girls to emphasise their femininity, the Hindu practice of widow-sacrifice, and African female circumcision. As Marianne Hester reveals, the persecution of 'witches' in Continental Europe and in England represented a means by which women who were not under the control of a father or husband – and therefore represented a threat to a patriarchal order – were tried and put to death. Also considered through the literary eyes of Thomas Hardy is 'wife-sale' which facilitated the semiformal transfer of ownership of a wife to another man. Each of these illustrations convey powerful cultural messages which emphasise the cultural subservience in which women were traditionally held.[27]

Chinese female footbinding

GYN/ECOLOGY[28]
Mary Daly

The Chinese ritual of footbinding was a 1000-year-long horror show in which women were grotesquely crippled from very early childhood. As Andrea Dworkin so vividly demonstrates, the hideous three-inch-long 'lotus hooks' – which in reality were odiferous, useless stumps – were the means by which the Chinese patriarchs saw to it that their girls and women would never 'run around'. All of the components of the Sado-Ritual Syndrome are illustrated in this atrocity.

1. First, there was the familiar fixation on 'purity'. In contrast to their counterparts in such countries as India, Chinese males did not have to confine their wives and daughters in purdah in order to protect their 'purity', but saw to it instead that their prisoners were hopelessly crippled. The foot purification (mutilation) ensured that women would be brainwashed as well, since their immobility made them entirely dependent upon males for knowledge of the world outside their houses. Moreover, since torture and mutilation of a small girl was carried out by her mother and other close female relatives, the lesson of 'never trust a women' was branded upon her soul, and emotional dependency upon the seemingly less involved males was guaranteed. She was not supposed to know that men were the real masterminds of her suffering. Thus her mind was purely possessed, and it became axiomatic that the possessor of tiny feet was a paradigm of feminine goodness.

2. The second element of the syndrome – erasure of male responsibility – is evident in footbinding. From the Chinese male's point of view, there was no question of his blame or moral accountability. After all, women 'did it to themselves'. One man, cited by Howard S Levy, described his sister's ordeal as a child, when she was forced to 'walk' with bound feet:

---

27 In Chapter 12 the role of the agencies of international law in eliminating remaining cruel practices against women is examined.

28 Mary Daly, *Gyn/Ecology* (The Women's Press, 1991).

Auntie dragged her nobbling along, to keep the foot circulating. Sister wept throughout but mother and auntie didn't pity her in the slightest, saying that if one loved one's daughter, one could not love her feet.[29]

There is a kind of ignorant arrogance in this man's assertion that the older women (the token nurturers) felt not pity. According to his own account, they performed this ritual mutilation out of fear that otherwise the girl would not be marriageable. This was a realistic fear, since for 1000-year-period Chinese males – millions of them – required this maiming of female feet into 'lotus hooks' for their own sadistic, fetishistic, erotic pleasure.[30]

3. Chinese gynocidal foot-maiming 'caught on' rapidly and spread widely. The brutal rite (a family affair, 'enjoyed' by all the members) which scholars say commenced in the period between the T'ang and Sung dynasties, spread like a cancer throughout China and into Korea. By the 12th century it was widely accepted as correct fashion among the upper classes. The mothers who belonged to families claiming aristocratic lineage felt forced to bind the feet of their daughters as a sign of upper-class distinction. Not to mutilate their daughters was unthinkable to them, for it meant that men would find them unattractive and would refuse to marry them. Themselves physically and mentally mutilated, the mothers paradigmatically acted out the role prescribed for them as mutilators of their own kind. As muted 'members' of patriarchal society, their imaginations too were forced into hierarchical patterns. A mother who 'loved' her daughter would have upwardly imitative ambitions for her, and the only possible expression of this would be insuring that she would be made attractive to a suitable husband. Since one requirement for this high status was the possession of 'golden lotuses', this sado-ritual spread downward, even to women of the lowest classes in some areas.[31]

Daly castigates male interpretations of footbinding, and continues:

4 ... the use of female token torturers affects not only the primary victims of the original rituals, the maimed mothers and daughters, who are turned against each other. In addition to this primary level of dividing and conquering women, there are others. Women of 'other' cultures are deceived by sado-scholarship which 'proves' that women like to main each other, documenting the 'fact' that 'women did it'. This false knowledge fosters female self-loathing and distrust of other women. This deception affects not only the few women who read 'primary' sources but also those exposed to derivative resources, such as grade-school textbooks, popular magazines, like *National Geographic*, and 'educational' television programmes.

5. The fifth element in the Sado-Ritual Syndrome – ritual orderliness – is illustrated in the 1000 year long female massacre, Chinese footbinding, which was archetypically obsessive and repetitive. This ritual involved extreme fixation upon minute details in the manufacture and care of 'tiny feet'. There were rules for the size of the bandages, the intervals between applications of tighter and tighter bandages, the roles of various members of the family in this act of dismemberment, the length of the correct 'foot', the manner in which the boot-bound women should sit and stand the washing of the re-formed feet (to be done

29 Howard S Levy, *Chinese Footbinding: The History of a Curious Erotic Custom* (New York, Walton Rawls, 1966).

30 Mary Daly, *op cit*, pp 135–37.

31 *Ibid*, p 139.

privately because of smell and ugliness hidden by ointments and fancy shoes). There were also rites of fashion connected with the refashioned feet. 'Beautiful' tiny shoes were designed for various occasions and ceremonies, and the women wore fashionable leggings to hide their monstrously misshapen ankles.

Hindu suttee

Suttee is the practice whereby a widow is compelled to put herself to death on the flames of her husband's funeral pyre. Officially banned in 1829, widowhood remains an unattractive state: remarriage for widows was traditionally forbidden the opportunities available for self-support almost non-existent. Much of the problem of widowhood is associated with the traditional practice of female children being married – often as young as seven or nine years of age – to men of middle age, guaranteeing his earlier demise than hers. Theologian Mary Daly[32] considers the practice of suttee:

GYN/ECOLOGY

Hindu Suttee

The Hindu rite of suttee spared widows from the temptations of impurity by forcing them to 'immolate themselves', ie to be burned alive, on the funeral pyres of their husbands. This ritual sacrifice must be understood within its social context. Since their religion forbade remarriage and at the same time taught that the husband's death was the fault of the widow (because of her sins in a previous incarnation if not in this one) everyone was free to despise and mistreat her for the rest of her life. Since it was a common practice for men of 50, 60, or 70 years of age to marry childbrides, the quantitative surplus of such unmarriageable widows boggles the imagination. Lest we allow our minds to be carried away with astronomic numerical calculations, we should realise that this ritual was largely confined to the upper caste, although there was a tendency to spread downward. We should also realise that in some cases – particularly if the widow was an extremely young child before her husband's unfortunate (for her) death – there was the option of turning to a life of prostitution, which would entail premature death from venereal disease. This, however, would be her only possible escape from persecution by in-laws, sons, and other relatives. As a prostitute, of course, she would be held responsible for the spread of more moral and physical impurity.

If the general situation of widowhood in India was not a sufficient inducement for the woman of higher caste to throw herself gratefully and ceremoniously into the fire, she was often pushed and poked in with long stakes after having been bathed, ritually attired, and drugged out of her mind.[33] In case these facts should interfere with our clear misunderstanding of the situation, Webster's invites us to recover women's history with the following definition of suttee, '*the act of custom of a Hindu woman willingly cremating herself or being cremated on the funeral pyre of her husband as an indication of her devotion to him*' (Mary Daly's emphasis). It is thought-provoking to consider the reality behind the term devotion, for indeed a

---

32 *Gyn/Ecology* (The Women's Press, 1991).

33 See P Thomas *Indian Women through the Ages* (New York, Asia Publishing Company, 1964), p 263. This author describes the situation in Muslim India of widows who tried to escape cremation, writing that 'to prevent her escape, she was usually surrounded by men armed with sticks who goaded her on to her destination by physical force'.

wife must have shown signs of extraordinarily slavish devotion during her husband's lifetime, since her very life depended upon her husband's state of health. A 13-year-old wife might well be concerned over the health of her 60-year-old husband.

Joseph Campbell discusses suttee as the Hindu form of the widely practised 'custom' of sending the family or part of it 'into the other world along with the chief member'.[34] The time honoured practice of 'human sacrifice', sometimes taking the form of live burial, was common also in other cultures, for example in ancient Egypt. Campbell notes that Professor George Reisner excavated an immense necropolis in Nubia, an Egyptian province, and found, without exception, 'a pattern of burial with human sacrifice – specifically, female sacrifice: of the wife and, in the more opulent tombs, the entire harem, together with the attendants'.[35] After citing Reisner's description of female skeletons, which indicated that the victims had died hideous deaths from suffocation, Campbell writes:

> In spite of these signs of suffering and even panic in the actual moment of the pain of suffocation, we should certainly not think of the mental state and experience of these individuals after any model of our own more or less imaginable reaction to such a fate. For these sacrifices were not properly, in fact, individuals at all; that is to say, they were not particular beings, distinguished from a class or group by virtue of any sense or realisation of a persona, individual destiny or responsibility.[36]

I have not italicised any of the words in this citation because it seemed necessary to stress every word. It is impossible to make any adequate comment.

At first, suttee was restricted to the wives of princes and warriors, but as the scholar, Benjamin Walker, deceptively puts it, '*in course of time the widows of weavers, masons, barbers and others of lower caste adopted the practice*'[37] (Mary Daly's emphasis). The use of the active voice here suggests that the widows actively sought out, enforced, and accepted this 'practice'. Apparently without any sense of inconsistency the same author supplies evidence that relatives forced widows on the pyre. He describes a case reported in 1796, in which a widow escaped from the pyre during the night in the rain. A search was made and she was dragged from her hiding place. Walker concludes the story of this woman who 'adopted the practice' as follows:

> She pleaded to be spared but her own son insisted that she throw herself on the pile as he would lose caste and suffer everlasting humiliation. When she still refused, the sons with the help of some others present bound her hands and feet and hurled her into the blaze.[38]

The same author gives information about the numerical escalation of suttee:

> Among the Rajputs and other warrior nations or northern India, the observance of suttee took on staggering proportions, since wives and concubines *immolated themselves* by the hundred. It became customary not only for wives but for mistresses, sisters, mothers, sisters-in-law and other

34 J Campbell, *The Masks of God: Oriental Mythology* (New York, Viking Press, 1962), p 62.

35 *Ibid*, p 60.

36 *Ibid*, p 65.

37 B Walker, *The Hindu World: An Encyclopedic Survey of Hinduism* (New York, Praeger, 1968), Vol II, p 461.

38 *Ibid*, p 464.

near female relatives and retainers *to burn themselves* along with their deceased master. With Rajputs it evolved into the terrible right of *jauhar* which took place in times of war or great peril *in order to save the honour of the womenfolk of the clan*. (Mary Daly's emphasis.)[39]

Again the victims, through grammatical sleight of hand, are made to appear as the agents of their own destruction. The rite of jauhar consisted in heaping all the females of the clan into the fire when there was danger of defeat by the enemy. Thousands of Hindu women were murdered this way during the Muslim invasion of India.[40] Their masters could not bear that they should be raped, tortured, and killed by foreign males adhering to 'different' religious beliefs, rather than by themselves.

The term custom – a casual and neutral term – is often used by scholars to describe these barbarous rituals of female slaughter. Clearly, however, they were religious rites. Some scholars assert that an unscrupulous priesthood provided the religious legitimisation for the practice by rigging the text of the *Rig Veda*. Priests justified the ritual atrocity by their interpretations of the law of Karma.[41] Furthermore, the typical mind-diverting orderliness of murderous religious ritual was manifested not only in the ceremonial bathing and dressing of the widows, but included other details of timing and placement. If the widow was menstruating, she was considered impure, and thus a week had to pass after the cessation of her period before she could commit suttee. Since impurity also resulted from pregnancy, suttee had to be delayed two months after the birth of the child.[42] For the event itself, the widow was often required to sit with the corpse's head in her lap or on her breast.[43] The orderliness is that of ritual: repetitive, compulsive, delusional.

This horror show was made possible by the legitimating role of religious rite, which allows the individual to distinguish between the real self, who may be fearful or scrupulous, and the self as role-performer. This schizoid perception on the part of those participating in the ritual carries over to the scholars who, though temporally or spatially distanced from the rite, identify with it rather than with the victims. Joseph Campbell placidly writes of the tortured and sacrificed woman:

> Sati, the feminine participle of sat, then, is the female who really is something in as much as she is truly and properly a player of the female part: she is not only good and true in the ethical sense but true and real ontologically. In her faithful death, she is at one with her own true being.[44]

Thus the ontological and moral problems surrounding female massacre are blandly dismissed. Campbell is simply discussing a social context in which, for a woman, to be killed is 'good and true', and to cease to exist is to be. His androcratically attached detachment from women's agony is manifested in paragraph after paragraph. After describing the live burial of a young widow

39 *Ibid*, pp 462–63.

40 P Thomas, *op cit*, p 223.

41 P Thomas, *op cit*, p 297.

42 VL Bullough, *The Subordinate Sex: A History of Attitudes Toward Women* (Penguin Books, 1974), p 241.

43 E Thompson, Suttee: *A Historical and Philosophical Enquiry into the Hindu Rite of Widow Burning* (Allen and Unwin, 1928), p 40.

44 *The Masks of God*, p 66.

which took place in 1813, this devotee of the rites of detached scholarship describes the event as 'an *illuminating*, though *somewhat* appalling, glimpse into the deep, silent pool of the Oriental, archaic soul' (Mary Daly's emphasis). What eludes this scholar is the fact that the 'archaic soul' was a woman destroyed by patriarchal religion (in which he is a true believer) which demands female sacrifice.

The bland rituals of patriarchal scholarship perpetuate the legitimisation of female sacrifice. The social reality, unacknowledged by such myth-masters, is that of minds and bodies mutilated by degradation. The real social context included the common practice of marrying off small girls to old men, since brahmans have what has been called a 'strange preference for children of very tender years'. Katherine Mayo, in an excellent work entitled with appropriate irony *Mother India* shows an understanding of the situation which more famous scholars entirely lack. Her work is, in the precise sense of the word, exceptional. She writes:

> That so hideous a fate as widowhood should befall a woman can be but for one cause – the enormity of her sins in a former incarnation. From the moment of her husband's decease till the last hour of her own life, she must expiate those sins in shame and suffering and self-immolation, chained in every thought to the service of his soul. Be she a child of three, who knows nothing of the marriage that bound her, or be she a wife in fact, having lived with her husband, her case is the same. By his death she is revealed as a creature of innate guilt and evil portent, herself convinced when she is old enough to think at all, of the justice of her fate.[45, 46, 47]

African female circumcision

The practice of female circumcision – predominantly on the African continent – reveals the extent to which cultural demands, determined by men, can dictate cruelty and violence in the name of 'purity'. The practice is widespread, and is a continuing phenomenon even among women who have emigrated to the West. So deep are the false symbols generated by circumcision that women – mothers and relatives – participate in the practice, even once settled in Western democracies. Mary Daly writes as follows:

African Genital Mutilation: the Unspeakable Atrocities[48]

> There are some manifestations of the Sado-Ritual Syndrome that are unspeakable – incapable of being expressed in words because inexpressibly horrible. Such are the ritual genital mutilations – excision and infibulation – still inflicted upon women throughout Africa today, and practised in many parts of the world in the past. These ritualised atrocities are unspeakable also in a second sense; that is, there are strong taboos against saying/writing the truth about them, against naming them. These taboos are operative both within the segments of phallocracy in which such rituals are practised and in other parts of the

---

45 Katherine Mayo, *Mother India* (New York: Blue Ribbon Books, 1927), esp pp 81–89; 51–62.

46 Mary Daly, *op cit*, pp 115–19.

47 For a recent account of the failure of Indian law to protect women against harassment and death, see Christopher Thomas, 'Indian Law Fails to Protect Women' (1996) *Times*, 10 January 1996.

48 *Gyn/Ecology* (The Women's Press, 1991), Chapter 5.

Fatherland, whose leaders co-operate in a conspiracy of silence. 'Hags'[49] see that the demonic rituals in the so-called underdeveloped regions of the planet are deeply connected with atrocities perpetrated against women in 'advanced' societies. To allow ourselves to see the connections is to begin to understand that androcracy is the 'State of Atrocity', where atrocities are normal, ritualised, repeated. It is the 'City of Atrophy' in which the archetypal trophies are massacred women.

Those who have endured the unspeakable atrocities of genital mutilation have in most cases been effectively silenced. Indeed this profound silencing of the mind's imaginative and critical powers is one basic function of the sado-ritual, which teaches women never to forget to murder their own divinity. Those who physically survive these atrocities 'live' their entire lifetimes, from early childhood or from puberty, preoccupied by pain. Those women who inhabit other parts of the planet cannot really wish to imagine the condition of their mutilated sisters, for the burden of knowing is heavy. It is heavy not merely because of differences in conditions, but especially because of similarities which, as I will show later in this passage, increase with the march of progress of phallotechnology.

The maze of lies and silences surrounding the genital mutilation still forced upon millions of young girls in many African countries continues to be effective. Yet is becoming the subject of increasingly widespread attention. Fran P Hosken presents the following important definitions of the practices usually lumped under the vague and misleading expression 'female circumcision':

1. Sunna Circumcision: removal of the prepuce and/or tip of the clitoris.

2. Excision or Clitoridectomy: excision of the entire clitoris with the labia minora or some or most of the external genitalia.

3. Excision and Infibulation (Pharaonic Circumcision): This means excision of the entire clitoris, labia minora and parts of the labia majora. The two sides of the vulva are then fastened together in some way either by thorns ... or sewing with catgut. Alternatively the vulva are scraped raw and the child's limbs are tied together for several weeks until the wound heals (or she dies). The purpose is to close the vaginal orifice. Only a small opening is left (usually be inserting a slither of wood) so the urine or later the menstrual blood can be passed.[50]

It should not be imagined that the horror of the life of an infibulated child/woman ends with this operation. Her legs are tied together, immobilising her for weeks, during which time excrement remains within the bandage. Sometimes accidents occur during the operation: the bladder may be pierced or the rectum cut open. Sometimes in a spasm of agony the child bites off her tongue. Infections are, needless to say, common. Scholars such as Lantier claim that death is not a very common immediate effect of the operation, but often there are complications which leave the women debilitated for the rest of their lives.[51] No statistics are available on this point. What is certain is that the infibulated girl is mutilated and that she can look forward to a life of repeated encounters with 'the little knife' – the instrument of her perpetual torture. For

---

49 A term used by Daly throughout her work to denote, in a self-mocking manner, the work of feminists.

50 See Hosken, WIN News (1976) 2, p 30.

51 Jacques Lantier, *La Cité Magique et Magie en Afrique Noire* (Paris: Librairie Artheme Fayard, 1972), p 279.

women who are infibulated have to be cut open – either by the husband or by another woman – to permit intercourse. They have to be cut open further for delivery of a child. Often they are sewn up again after delivery, depending upon the decision of the husband. The cutting (defibulation) and re-sewing goes on throughout a women's living death of reproductive 'life'. Immediate medical results of excision and infibulation include 'haemorrhage, infections, shock, retention of urine, damage to adjacent tissues, dermoid cysts, abscesses, keloid scarring, coital difficulties, and infertility caused by chronic pelvic infections. In addition, we should consider the psychological maiming caused by this torture.

Yet this is an 'unmentionable' manifestation of the atrocity which is phallocracy. The World Health Organisation has refused for many years to concern itself with the problem. When it was asked in 1958 to study this problem it took the position that such operations were based on 'social and cultural backgrounds' and were outside its competence. This basic attitude has not changed. In fact there has been a conspiracy of silence:

International agencies, the UN and UN agencies, especially WHO and UNICEF (both devoted to health care) development agencies (such as the US Agency for International Development) non-governmental organisations working in Africa, missionaries and church groups concerned with health care, also women's organisations including World Association of Girl Guides and Girl Scouts, YWCA, and the Associated Country Women of the World, and others working in Africa, all know what is going on. Or they have people in Africa who know. This quite aside from the health departments and hospitals in African countries and the MDs, especially gynaecologists, who get the most desperate cases. The doctors know all. But they don't speak.

It is important to ask why such a variety of organisations and professions have other priorities. Why do 'educated' persons babble about the importance of 'tribal coherence' and 'tradition' while closing their eyes to the physical reality of mutilation? We might well ask why 'female circumcision' was reinforced in Kenya after 'liberation' and described by President Kenyatta, in his book *Facing Mount Kenya*, as an important 'custom' for the benefit 'of the people'. Hosken maintains that in the socialist countries in Africa clitoridectomy and infibulation are practised on a vast scale without comment from the governments or health departments. Again, one must ask why. Why do anthropologists ignore or minimise this horror? Why is it that the Catholic church has not taken a clear position against this genital mutilation (which is practised upon some of its own members in Africa)? Why do some African leaders educated in the West continue to insist upon the maiming of their own daughters?

These questions are profoundly interconnected. The appearance of disparateness among these groups and of their responses (or non-responses) masks their essential sameness. Even the above-named organisations whose membership is largely female and androcratic since they are willing to participate in the conspiracy of silence. Socialists, Catholics, liberal reformers, population planners, politicos of all persuasions – all have purposes which have nothing to do with women's specific well-being unless this happens to fit into the 'wider' aims.

The components of the Sado-Ritual Syndrome are present in African excision and infibulation. The obsession with purity if evident. The clitoris is 'impure' because it does not serve male purposes. It has no necessary function in reproduction. As Benoite Groult points out, hatred of the clitoris is almost universal, for this organ is strictly female, for women's pleasure.[52] Thus it is by nature 'impure', and the

---

52 *Ainsi Soit-Elle* (Paris: Bernard Grasset, 1975), p 96.

logical conclusion, acted out by the tribes that practice excision and infibulation, is purification of women by its removal. Furthermore, it is believed that excision encourages fidelity, that is, moral 'purity', for there is a 'decrease in sensitivity from the operation'. The term 'decrease' here is a euphemism for loss. These women have been de-sensitised, 'purified' of the capacity for sexual pleasure. The ideology among some African tribes which explains and justified this brutal robbing from women of their clitoris – the purely female organ – displays the total irony of the concept of purity. There is a widespread belief among the Bambaras and the Dogons from Mali that all persons are hermaphroditic and that this condition is cured by circumcision and excision. Since they believe the boy is female by virtue of his foreskin and the girl is male by her clitoris, the sexes are purified (that is, officially distinguished) by the rites of puberty. Thus the removal of the purely female clitoris is seen as making a woman purely female. In fact, its purpose is to make her purely feminine, a purely abject object.

Infibulation goes even further, displaying yet other dimensions of the androcratic obsession with purity. For the 'sewn women' are not only deprived of the organ of pleasure. Their masters have them genitally 'sewn up' in order to preserve and redesign them strictly for their own pleasure and reproductive purposes. These women are 100% pure because 100% were enslaved. Their perpetual pain (or the imminent threat of this) is an important condition for their perpetual purity, for pain preoccupies minds, emotions, imagination, sensations, prohibiting presence of the self.

The second component of the syndrome, erasure of male responsibility, is present by virtue of male absence at the execution of the mutilation. In most cases, it is not males who perform the brutal operations, although male nurses and surgeons now do it in some modern hospitals. Moreover, there are comforting myths, ideologies, and clichés which assure political leaders and other males that they are blame-free. Together with the hermaphroditic myth, described above, there is the justification that 'this is the way of teaching women to endure pain'. There is also the belief among the Bambaras that a man who sleeps with a non-excised women risks death from her 'sting' (clitoris). The Mossis believe that the clitoris kills children at birth and that it can be a source of impotence among men. A basic belief that justifies all, erasing all responsibility, is of course that these rites keep women faithful. What is erased is the fact that these 'faithful' wives have been physically reconstructed for male purposes. They have been deprived of their own sexuality and 'tightened up' for their masters' pleasure – tightened though devices like wounding and sewing and through the tension of excruciating pain. Erasure of all this on the global level occurs when leaders of 'advanced' countries and of international organisations overlook these horrors in the name of 'avoiding cultural judgment'. They are free of responsibility and blame, for the 'custom' must be respected as part of a 'different tradition'. By so naming the tradition as 'different' they hide the cross-cultural hatred of women.

The massive spread of female genital mutilation throughout African has been noted by responsible Searchers. Accurate statistics are impossible to obtain, since the operation is usually performed in secret. Nevertheless the ritual, which is of ancient origin, is known to be widespread from Algeria in the north to the Central African Republic in the south, and from Senegal and Mauritania in the West to Somalia in the east.[53]

---

53 *Gyn/Ecology* at pp 154–61.

The use of women as token torturers is horribly illustrated in this ritual. At the International Tribunal on Crimes Against Women the testimony of a woman from Guinea was brought by a group of French women. The witness described seeing 'the savage mutilation called excision that is inflicted on the women of my country between the ages of ten and 12'.[54]

The fact that 'women did it – and still do it – to women' must be seen in this context: the idea that such procedures, or any part of them, could be women-originated is only thinkable in the mind-set of phallocracy, for it is, in fact, unthinkable. The use of women to do the dirty work can make it appear thinkable only to those who do not wish to see. Yet this use of women does effectively blunt the power of sisterhood, having first blocked the power of the self.

Most horrifying is the fact that mothers insist that this mutilation be done to their own daughters. Frequently it is the mother who performs the brutal operation. Among the Somalis, for example, the mother does the excising, slicing and final infibulation according to the time-honoured rules. She does this is such a way as to leave the tiniest opening possible. Her 'honour' depends upon making this as small as possible, because the smaller this artificial aperture is, the higher the value of the girl.[55]

It should not be thought that barbaric practices in relation to women occurred and in some instances continue to occur only in non-European countries. Much evidence exists of the practice of seeking out, placing on trial and subsequently killing women who were suspected of 'witchcraft'. As Marianne Hester explains, in the following extract, there existed common characteristics between the women put on trial: most commonly the characteristic being that the women in question were not under adequate male control and thus represented a threat to the patriarchal ordering of society.

Witchcraft

LEWD WOMEN AND WICKED WITCHES[56]
Marianne Hester[57]
European Female Witch Trials

The central feature of male supremacy as it exists today is the eroticised inequality between men and women. Taking the early modern witch-hunts as the focus, I will examine how this understanding of inequality between men and women may also be relevant to analysis of historical phenomena.[58]

The witch-hunt period was a time of major social change where existing social structures, beliefs and relationships were undergoing transformations including, potentially, also men's and women's roles. At that particular time a number of

---

54 *Ibid*, p 163.

55 *Ibid*, p 165. Note: the refusal or failure of the mother to 'circumcise' her daughter may lead to her divorce.

56 Marianne Hester, *Lewd Women and Wicked Witches: A Study of the Dynamics of Male Domination* (Routledge and Kegan Paul, 1992). (Footnotes edited.)

57 At the time of writing, Lecturer in Social Studies and Adult Education at the University of Exeter.

58 Marianne Hester, *op cit*, p 107.

economic, political, legal, ideological and religious factors combined, which allowed and also prompted persecution for witchcraft. I shall argue here that the witch-hunts were an attempt at maintaining and restoring male supremacy within this context.

During the 16th and 17th centuries, primarily in Continental Europe and Scotland, but also in England and Scandinavia, thousands of people were condemned to imprisonment and death accused of the crime of 'witchcraft'. To make obvious the intensity of persecution at this time, the period has been called the 'witch-craze'. The term 'craze' is in some ways problematic because it implies that the witch-hunts were carried out by crazed individuals in the exhibition of momentary madness. Nonetheless, the early modern period does stand out as unique within the history of witchcraft, and it is important therefore, to differentiate this period where extensive witch-hunting took place.

Significantly, the witch-hunts were mainly directed against women. In England more than 90% of those formally accused of witchcraft were women, and the few men who were also formally accused tended to be married to an accused witch or to appear jointly with a woman.

Using a revolutionary feminist approach it may be shown that the witch-hunts provided one means of controlling women socially within a male supremacist society, using violence or the threat of violence, and relying on a particular construct of female sexuality. This specific instance of the social control of women, using the accusation of witchcraft, was a product of the sociohistorical context at the time. As a result only certain women – usually older, lower-class, poor, and often single or widowed – were directly affected. To understand why the social control of women took this form at this time we need to examine events leading up to, and taking place during, the witch-hunt period, which in England was largely between the mid-16th and the mid-17th centuries, and we also need to examine reasons for the eventual decline of the persecutions.[59]

Legislation

While a witchcraft state of little significance existed during the reign of Henry VIII, the first important witchcraft law was placed on the statute books in 1563, soon after Elizabeth I became Queen. It has been suggested that this piece of legislation came about because it was feared that witchcraft would be used as a means to dethrone the Queen. Mary Queen of Scots was said to be involved in such an anti-Elizabeth plot.[60] The 1563 law saw witchcraft as a serious offence involving the following penalties:

1   Bewitching an individual to death warranted the death penalty (hanging).

2   Other use of witchcraft or sorcery to injure people or animals warranted one year's imprisonment for a first offence and the death penalty for a subsequent offence.

Most of those who were brought to trial for witchcraft were either acquitted or imprisoned, and those sentenced to death were hanged. In Europe and Scotland the death penalty was carried out by burning, and it is often thought that the same applied to England. But that was not the case. In England 'burning to death' was only the penalty for treason or petty treason. Treason was defined as threat to, or murder of, the monarch by his/her subjects, and petty treason was murder of the master or mistress by his/her servants, and murder of a husband

---

59   *Ibid*, pp 107–08.

60   See W Notestein, *The History of Witchcraft in England from 1558 to 1728* (1911) (New York, Thomas Y Crowell, 1968), pp 18–19.

by his wife. Thus in England a woman would be burnt to death if she was deemed to have used witchcraft to kill her husband, employer, or monarch.

James I had a new witchcraft law which was placed on the statute books in 1604 and harsher than the previous. That law remained in force until 1736 when the witchcraft legislation in England was repealed. James I's law extended the use of the death penalty to instances where evil spirits had been used to cause harm, and thereby placed much greater onus on the accused having 'spirits' or 'familiars'. This change came about because of the wish, by the judiciary, for stricter standards regarding proof of witchcraft: what they now wanted was sworn evidence that the witch kept a familiar or bore the devil's mark on her person; most decisive of all, they hoped for her free confession that she had entered into a pact with Satan.[61] To us this might seem rather odd 'proof', but for many Jacobean judges familiars were an actuality, as was the devil. Like the Elizabethan law, James I's law also had imprisonment as the penalty for other use of witchcraft, extending this to the death penalty for a second offence.

The particular nature of the crime of witchcraft is very important. This varies between England and different European and Scandinavian countries, for instance, in Europe the direct linkage with Satanism is important. Unlike crimes such as theft or robbery, witchcraft was not merely a crime or sin related to an individual person – although that is often how it appeared in the English trials – it was a crime directly against God, because the perpetrator sided specifically with the devil. Perhaps by inference, it was also a crime against mankind because of the way men were seen as being closer to God than women, reflected within the church as well as political hierarchies.[62]

Numbers

Use of witchcraft to cause harm was one of the major crimes throughout the Elizabethan and Jacobean periods. In Essex during Elizabeth I's reign it was the third most common crime after theft and burglary; and during James I's reign it came fifth after theft and burglary, homicide/infanticide and highway robbery.[63]

The number of executions for witchcraft, primarily of women, which took place throughout the witch-hunt period in England have been estimated by Ewen at 'less than 1000' between 1542 and 1736 – that is, between the passing of the first witchcraft statute and the repealing of the last.[64]

The vast majority of witchcraft cases coming before the courts occurred in England during the reign of Elizabeth I, that is between 1563 and 1603. The numbers do, of course, refer to recorded figures, including those accusations of witchcraft not ending up in court, were probably much larger. It might seem surprising that Elizabeth allowed many fellow women to be imprisoned or murdered for the crime of witchcraft during her reign, and somewhat ironic that the only rule by a female monarch during the witch-craze period saw the greatest number of cases. However, Elizabeth I's rule is not characterised by positive legislation or other support for women. She has been described as an 'honorary male' who 'having established herself as an exceptional women, did nothing to upset or interfere with male notions of how the world was or should be organised'.[65] As with Margaret Thatcher and other exceptional women today,

61   K Thomas *Religion and the Decline of Magic* (Weidenfeld & Nicolson, 1971).

62   *Ibid*, pp 126–27.

63   Marianne Hester, *op cit*, pp 126–28.

64   LC Ewen, *Witch Hunting and Witch Trials* (1929) (Frederick Miller, 1971).

65   A Heisch, 'Queen Elizabeth I and the Persistence of Patriarchy' (1980) 4 *Feminist Review*.

Elizabeth I was able to act as a monarch contrary to the view of women at the time, because she continued to express her support for the prevalent gender ideology. She was able to remain unmarried, for instance, by becoming the one respectable alternative allowed: a virgin queen, married to England in the way nuns were married to God.

During James I's reign, from 1603 to 1620, the recorded figures for witchcraft accusations were much lower than those in the Elizabethan period. The underlying trend was of a decrease from then until the repeal of the witchcraft legislation in 1736, although accusations of witchcraft seem to have continued at a local level until the 20th century, and indeed also precede the witch-hunt period.

It is perhaps surprising that the number of prosecutions should have continued to decrease during James I's reign, because of his instrumental role in fuelling the Scottish witch-hunts during the 1590s. As King of Scotland, James wrote *The Daemonology* (1597) stressing that witches did indeed exist, that they were a threat to the social order, and that they should preferably be eradicated. He had come to these conclusions after witchcraft had supposedly been used to harm his bride-to-be, Anne of Denmark, and himself. James, however, had always maintained some scepticism regarding witches' supposed powers, believed that fraud or delusion was often involved in 'bewitching', and was consequently involved in facilitating the decrease in prosecutions towards the end of his reign.[66]

Gender Relations and the Economy

There is some general agreement amongst historians and social scientists that the 16th and 17th centuries were part of the period that saw the transition from feudalism to capitalism, characterised by petty commodity production. This largely pre-industrial period exhibited various capitalist and industrial, as well as feudal features of production. Within the context of this book, it is important to ask what the links were between male-female relations and the capitalist economic development taking place at the time.[67]

Having examined the respective economic roles of men and women, Marianne Hester concludes that:

Overall, then, women were finding it difficult throughout the period to make a living and their income was generally lower than men's. If single they might find work as servants, if married, they were dependent on their husbands. But if widowed they could be in either a threatening or vulnerable position, sometimes able to carry out a trade or craft left them by their husbands, but if unable to do this more likely to be dependent on others for financial support. Alternatively, widows might end up owning land, and proportionately women lower down the social scale inherited larger amounts of land than their aristocratic sisters. Generally, however, women at the lower end of the social scale, widowed and with children seem to have been some of the most vulnerable individuals in the community. Since women in the peasantry tended to marry late, precisely because of problems of financial security, older women were also likely to have young children.

By looking at the material concerning socio-economic changes in the 16th and 17th centuries, it begins to become apparent that those accused of witchcraft also

---

66   Marianne Hester, *op cit*, pp 128–29.
67   *Ibid*, p 137.

tend to be those who were among the most vulnerable in the economy, that is, labouring women, widowed and possibly older, and poor. Or otherwise those in competition with men for work in lucrative areas, that is, women carrying out a craft or trade, and most specifically, widows, who were more able to do so.[68]

In England, prior to divorce becoming available as a judicial (as opposed to parliamentary) process in 1857 – and then on discriminatory and limited grounds – the remedies for marital breakdown were predominantly informal. Simple separation through the disappearance of (usually) the husband, was an effective means of severing relationships. While the ecclesiastical courts adopted a punitive view of separation and subsequent informal unions, and would punish those who were detected, the risk taken represented the only practical means of family realignment. Evidence exists, however, of a more formal practice of 'disposing' of an unwanted wife – that of wife-sale – whereby, with or without the connivance of the wife, the husband would publicly 'transfer ownership' of the wife to another man.

Wifesale

THE MAYOR OF CASTERBRIDGE[69]

Thomas Hardy

'For my part I don't see why men who have got wives and don't want 'em, shouldn't get rid of 'em as these gipsy fellows do their old horses,' said the man in the tent. 'Why shouldn't they put 'em up and sell 'em by auction to men who are in need of such articles? Hey? Why, begad, I'd sell mine this minute if anybody would buy her.'

'There's them that would do that,' some of the guests replied, looking at the woman, who was by no means ill-favoured.

'True,' said a smoking gentleman, whose coat had the fine polish about the collar, elbows, seams, and shoulder-blades that long-continued friction with grimy surfaces will produce, and which is usually more desired on furniture than on clothes. From his appearance he had possibly been in former times groom or coachman to some neighbouring county family. 'I've had my breedings in as good circles, I may say, as any man,' he added, 'and I know true cultivation, or nobody do; and I can declare she's got it – in the bone, mind ye, I say – as much as any female in the fair – though it may want a little bringing out.' Then, crossing his legs, he resumed his pipe with a nicely adjusted gaze at a point in the air.

The fuddled young husband stared for a few seconds at this unexpected praise of his wife, half in doubt of the wisdom of his own attitude towards the possessor of such qualities. But he speedily lapsed into his former conviction, and said harshly – 'Well, then, now is your chance; I am open to an offer for this gem of creation.'

She turned to her husband and murmured. 'Michael, you have talked this nonsense in public places before. A joke is a joke, but you may make it once too often, mind!'

'I know I've said it before; I meant it. All I want is a buyer.'

---

68   *Ibid*, pp 143–44.
69   (1886) Macmillan (1975) pp 32–36.

At that moment a swallow, one among the last of the season, which had by chance found its way through an opening into the upper part of the tent, flew to and fro in quick curves above their heads, causing all eyes to follow it absently. In watching the bird till it made its escape the assembled company neglected to respond to the workman's offer, and the subject dropped. But a quarter of an hour later the man, who had gone on lacing his furmity more and more heavily, though he was either so strong-minded or such an intrepid torper that he still appeared fairly sober, recurred to the old strain, as in a musical fantasy the instrument fetches up the original theme. 'Here – I am waiting to know about this offer of mine. The woman is no good to me. Who'll have her?'

The company had by this time decidedly degenerated, and the renewed inquiry was received with a laugh of appreciation. The woman whispered; she was imploring and anxious: 'Come, come, it is getting dark, and this nonsense won't do. If you don't come along, I shall go without you. Come!' She waited and waited; yet he did not move. In ten minutes the man broke in upon the desultory conversation of the furmity drinkers with, 'I asked this question, and nobody answered to it. Will any Jack Rag or Tom Straw among ye buy my goods?' The woman's manner changed, and her face assumed the grim shape and colour of which mention has been made.

'Mike, Mike' said she, 'this is getting serious. O! – too serious!'

'Will anybody buy her?' said the man.

'I wish somebody would,' said she firmly. 'Her present owner is not at all to her liking.'

'Nor you to mine,' said he. 'So we are agreed about that. Gentlemen, you hear? It's an agreement to part. She shall take the girl if she wants to, and go her ways. I'll take my tools, and go my ways. 'Tis simple as scripture history. Now then, stand up, Susan, and show yourself.'

'Don't, my chiel,' whispered a buxom staylace dealer in voluminous petticoats, who sat near the woman; 'yer good man don't know what he's saying.'

The woman, however, did stand up. 'Now, whose auctioneer?' cried the hay-trusser.

'I be,' promptly answered a short man, with a nose resembling a copper knob, a damp voice, and eyes like buttonholes. 'Who'll make an offer for this lady?'

The woman looked on the ground as if she maintained her position by a supreme effort of will.

'Five shillings,' said some one, at which there was a laugh.

'No insults,' said the husband. 'Who'll say a guinea?'

Nobody answered; and the female dealer in staylaces interposed. 'Behave yerself moral, good man, for Heaven's love! Ah, what a cruelty is the poor soul married to! Bed and board is dear at some figures, 'pon my 'vation 'tis! '

'Set it higher, auctioneer,' said the trusser.

'Two guineas!' said the auctioneer; and no one replied.

'If they don't take her for that, in ten seconds they'll have to give more,' said the husband. 'Very well. Now, auctioneer, add another.'

'Three guineas – going for three guineas,' said the rheumy man.

'No bid?' said the husband. 'Good Lord, why she's cost me fifty times the money, if a penny. Go on!'

'Four guineas!' cried the auctioneer.

'I'll tell ye what – I won't sell her for less than five,' said the husband, bringing down his fist so that the basins danced. 'I'll sell her for five guineas to any man that will pay me the money, and treat her well; and he shall have her for ever, and never hear aught o' me. But she shan't go for less. Now then – five guineas – and she's yours. Susan, you agree?'

She bowed her head with absolute indifference.

'Five guineas,' said the auctioneer, 'or she'll be withdrawn. Do anybody give it? The last time. Yes or no?'

'Yes,' said a loud voice from the doorway. All eyes were turned.

Standing in the triangular opening which formed the door of the tent was a sailor, who, unobserved by the rest, had arrived there within the last two or three minutes. A dead silence followed his affirmation.

'You say you do?' asked the husband, staring at him.

'I say so,' replied the sailor.

'Saying is one thing, and paying is another. Where's the money?'

The sailor hesitated a moment, looked anew at the woman, came in, unfolded five crisp pieces of paper, and threw them down upon the table-cloth. They were Bank-of-England notes for five pounds. Upon the face of this he chinked down the shillings severally – one, two, three, four, five.

The sight of real money in full amount, in answer to a challenge for the same till then deemed slightly hypothetical, had a great effect upon the spectators. Their eyes became riveted upon the faces of the chief actors, and then upon the notes as they lay, weighted by the shillings, on the table.

Up to this moment it could not positively have been asserted that the man, in spite of his tantalising declaration, was really in earnest. The spectators had indeed taken the proceedings throughout as a piece of mirthful irony carried to extremes; and had assumed that, being out of work, he was, as a consequence, out of temper with the world, and society, and his nearest kin. But with the demand and response of real cash the jovial frivolity of the scene departed. A lurid colour seemed to fill the tent, and change the, aspect of all therein. The mirth-wrinkles left the listeners' faces, and they waited with parting lips.

'Now,' said the woman, breaking the silence, so that her low dry voice sounded quite loud, 'before you go further, Michael, listen to me. If you touch that money, I and this girl go with the man. Mind, it is a joke no longer.'

'A joke? Of course it is not a joke!' shouted her husband, his resentment rising at her suggestion. 'I take the money: the sailor takes you. That's plain enough. It has been done elsewhere – and why not here?'

''Tis quite on the understanding that the young woman is willing,' said the sailor blandly. 'I wouldn't hurt her feelings for the world.'

'Faith, nor I,' said her husband. 'But she is willing, provided she can have the child. She said so only the other day when I talked o't!'

'That you swear?' said the sailor to her.

'I do,' said she, after glancing at her husband's face and seeing no repentance there. 'Very well, she shall have the child, and the bargain's complete,' said the trusser. He took the sailor's notes and deliberately folded them, and put them with the shillings in a high remote pocket, with an air of finality.

The sailor looked at the woman and smiled. 'Come along!' he said kindly. 'The little one too – the more the merrier!' She paused for an instant, with a close glance at him. Then dropping her eyes again, and saying nothing, she took up the child and followed him as he made towards the door. On reaching it, she turned, and pulling off her wedding-ring, flung it across the booth in the hay-trusser's face.

'Mike,' she said, 'I've lived with thee a couple of years, and had nothing but tempers. Now I'm no more to 'ee; I'll try my luck elsewhere. Twill be better for me and Elizabeth-lane, both. So good-bye!'

Seizing she sailor's arm with her right hand, and mounting the little girl on her left, she went out of the tent sobbing bitterly.

A stolid look of concern filled the husband's face, as if, after all, he had not quite anticipated this ending; and some of the guests laughed.

'Is she gone?' he said.

'Faith, ay; she's gone clane enough,' said some rusties near the door.

He rose and walked to the entrance with the careful tread of one conscious of his alcoholic load. Some others followed, and they stood, looking into the twilight. The difference between the peacefulness of inferior nature and the wilful hostilities of mankind was very apparent at this place. In contrast with the harshness of the act just ended within the tent was the sight of several horses crossing their necks and rubbing each other lovingly as they waited in patience to be harnessed for the homeward journey. Outside the fair, in the valleys and woods, all was quiet. The sun had recently set, and the west heaven was hung with rosy cloud, which seemed permanent, yet slowly changed. To watch it was like looking at some grand feat of stagery from a darkened auditorium. In presence of this scene after the other there was a natural instinct to abjure man as the blot on an otherwise kindly universe; till it was remembered that all terrestrial conditions were intermittent, and that mankind might some night be innocently sleeping when these quiet objects were raging loud.

'Where do the sailor live?' asked a spectator, when they had vainly gazed around.

'God knows that,' replied the man who had seen high life. 'He's without doubt a stranger here.'

'He came in about five minutes ago,' said the furmity woman, joining the rest with her hands on her hips. 'And then 'a stepped back, and then 'a looked in again. I'm not a penny the better for him.'

'Serves the husband well be-right,' said the staylace vendor. 'A comely respectable body like her – what can a man want more? I glory in the woman's spirit. I'd ha' done it myself – od send if I wouldn't, if a husband had behaved so to me! I'd go, and 'a might call, and call, till his keacorn was raw; but I'd never come back – no, not, till the great trumpet, would I!'

'Well, the woman will be better off,' said another of a more deliberative turn. 'For seafaring natures be very good shelter for shorn lambs, and the man do seem to have plenty of money, which is what she's not been used to lately, by all showings.'

'Mark me – I'll not go after her!' said the trusser, returning doggedly to his seat. 'Let her go! If she's up to such vagaries she must suffer for 'em. She'd no business to take the maid – 'tis my maid; and if it were the doing again she shouldn't have her!'

Perhaps from some little sense of having countenanced an indefensible proceeding, perhaps because it was late, the customers thinned away from the tent shortly, after this episode. The man stretched his elbows forward on the table, leant his face upon his arms, and soon began to snore. The furmity seller decided to close for the night, and after seeing the rum-bottles, milk, corn, raisins, etc, that remained on hand, loaded into the cart, came to where the man reclined. She shook him, but – could not wake him. As the tent was not to be struck that night, the fair continuing for two or three days, she decided to let the sleeper, who was obviously no tramp, stay where he was, and his basket with him. Extinguishing the last candle, and lowering the flap of the tent she left it and drove away.

Thomas Hardy's portrayal of wife-sale is well documented in legal texts.[70] Prior to 1857, divorce in England could be obtained only by way of an Act of Parliament: an expensive undertaking beyond the grasp of the wealthy elite.[71] For the majority in society, the breakdown of the marital relationship resulted either in continued unhappiness or in simple desertion. Where a husband abondoned his wife and informally established a new family relationship elsewhere, he was at risk of detection and prosecution before the ecclesiastical courts. A second risk was that the wife would run up debts for which he would remain responsible. On the other side of the coin, the wife remained vulnerable to her husband seizing 'her' property which legally belonged to him. In order, therefore, to minimise, if not eliminate such difficulties, wife-sale became an option. Wife-sale represented a non-legal, but nevertheless, semi-formal public transference of the husband's right of property in his wife to another man: the women being conceptually regarded by both law and society, as a mere chattel. Unlike Hardy's illustration of the phenomenon where the wife was sold apparently 'spontaneously', many wife-sales took on a certain ritualism and formality. The wife, in order to emphasise the property aspect of her transfer, would commonly be physically taken to the local cattle-market with a leather halter around her neck. There she would be placed for sale to the highest bidder. Frequently there would have been a prior arrangement as to this property transfer. It may have been that the wife had already found another partner, and that all was required for the sake of the publicity (and thereby dubious legitimacy) of the transaction was a public spectacle in which money changed hands for her person, whereby the 'former' husband was absolved on any further liability to maintain her. Frequently the deal would be sealed with a celebratory drink at the local hostelry. Where such practices came to the attention of the courts, they were denounced as unlawful as being contrary to 'public decency and good manners'.

The statistical significance of wife-sale, according to Lawrence Stone, has been exaggerated. In its 'peak years' of 1780 to 1850, there were fewer than three hundred (recorded) cases in England. Nonetheless, wife-sale carries with it immense symbolism as to status of women and the manner in which women were viewed as chattels of their husbands.

70　See, for example, C Kenny, 'Wife Selling in England' (1920) 45 *Law Quarterly Review*, 496; Lawrence Stone, *The Road to Divorce* (Oxford University Press, 1992), p 141.

71　Between 1700 and 1857, a mere 322 divorces were secured through Act of Parliament.

Women in religous texts

WHAT BECAME OF GOD THE MOTHER? CONFLICTING IMAGES OF GOD IN EARLY CHRISTIANITY[72]
Elaine H Pagels

Unlike many of his contemporaries among the deities of the ancient Near East, the God of Israel shares his power with no female divinity, nor is he the divine husband or lover of any. He scarcely can be characterised in any but masculine epithets: King, Lord, Master, Judge, and Father. Indeed, the absence of feminine symbolism of God marks Judaism, Christianity, and Islam in striking contrast to the word's other religious traditions, whether in Egypt, Babylonia, Greece, and Rome or Africa, Polynesia, India, and North America. Jewish, Christian, and Islamic theologians, however, are quick to point out that God is not to be considered in sexual terms at all. Yet the actual language they use daily in worship and prayer conveys a different message and gives the distinct impression that God is thought of in exclusively masculine terms. And while it is true that Catholics revere Mary as the mother of Jesus, she cannot be identified as divine in her own right: if she is 'mother of God', she is not 'God the Mother' on an equal footing with 'God the Father'.

Christianity, of course, added the Trinitarian terms to the Jewish description of God. And yet of the three divine 'Persons', two – the Father and Son – are described in masculine terms, and the third – the Spirit – suggests the sexlessness of the Greek neuter term 'pneuma'. This is not merely a subjective impression. Whoever investigates the early development of Christianity – the field called 'patristics', that is, study of 'the fathers of the church' – may not be surprised by the passage that concludes the recently discovered, secret Gospel of Thomas: 'Simon Peter said to them [the disciples]: Let Mary be excluded from among us, for she is a women, and not worthy of Life. Jesus said: Behold I will take Mary, and make her a male, so that she may become living spirit, resembling you males. For I tell you truly, that every female who makes herself male will enter the Kingdom of Heaven.'[73] Strange as it sounds, this only states explicitly what religious rhetoric often assumes: that the men form the legitimate body of the community, while women will be allowed to participate only insofar as their own identity is denied and assimilated to that of the men.

Further exploration of the texts which include this Gospel – written on papyrus, hidden in large clay jars nearly 1,600 years ago – has identified them as Jewish and Christian Gnostic works which were attacked and condemned as 'heretical' as early as AD 100–150. What distinguishes these 'heterodox' texts from those that are called 'orthodox' is at least partially clear: they abound in feminine symbolism that is applied, in particular, to God. Although one might expect, then, that they would recall the archaic pagan traditions of the Mother Goddess, their language is to the contrary specifically Christian, unmistakably related to a Jewish heritage. This we can see that certain Gnostic Christians diverged ever more radically from the Jewish tradition than the early Christians who described God as the 'three Persons' or the 'Trinity'. For instead of a monistic and

72 Elizabeth Abel and Emily K Abel (eds) *The Signs Reader: Women, Gender and Scholarship* (Chicago, University of Chicago Press, 1978).

73 A Guillaumount, H Ch Puech, G Quispel, W Till, Yassah Abd-al-Masih (eds), *The Gospel According to Thomas* (hereafter cited as 'ET') (London: Collins, 1959) logion 113–14.

masculine God, certain of these texts describe God as a dyadic being, who consists of both masculine and feminine elements. One such group of texts, for example, claims to have received a secret tradition from Jesus through James, and significantly, through Mary Magdalene.[74] Members of this group offer prayer to both the divine Father and Mother: 'Through Thee, Father, and through Thee, Mother, the two immortal names, Parents of the divine being, and thou, dweller in heaven, mankind of the mighty name ...'[75] Other texts indicate that their authors had pondered the nature of the being to whom a single, masculine God proposed, 'Let us make mankind in our image, after our likeness' (Genesis 1:26). Since the Genesis account goes on to say that mankind was created 'male and female' (1:27) some concluded, apparently, that the God in whose image we are created likewise must be both masculine and feminine – both Father and Mother.

The characterisation of the divine Mother in these sources is not simple since the texts themselves are extraordinarily diverse. Nevertheless, three primary characterisations merge. First a certain poet and teacher, Valentinus, begins with the premise that God is essentially indescribable. And yet he suggests that the divine can be imagined as a Dyad consisting of two elements: one he calls the Ineffable, the Source, the Primal Father; the other, the Silence, the Mother of all things.[76] Although we might question Valentinus's reasoning that Silence is the appropriate complement of what is Ineffable, his equation of the former with the feminine and the latter with the masculine may be traced to the grammatical gender of the Greek words. Followers of Valentinus invoke this feminine power, whom they also call 'Grace' (in Greek, the feminine tern 'charis') in their own private celebration of the Christian Eucharist: they call her 'divine, eternal Grace, She who is before all things'.[77] At other times they pray to her for protection as the Mother thou enthroned with God, eternal, mystical Silence'.[78] Marcus, a disciple of Valentinus, contends that 'when Moses began his account of creation, he mentioned the Mother of all things at the every beginning, when he said, 'In the beginning God created the heavens and the earth', for the word 'beginning' (in Greek, the feminine arche) refers to the divine Mother, the source of the cosmic elements. When they describe God in this way different gnostic writers have different interpretations. Some maintain that the divine is to be considered masculo-feminine – the 'great male-female power'. Others insist that the terms are meant only as metaphors – for, in reality, the divine is neither masculine nor feminine. A third group suggests that one can describe the Source of all things in either masculine or feminine terms, depending on which aspect one intends to stress.[79] Proponents of these diverse views agree, however, that the divine is to be understood as consisting of a harmonious, dynamic relationship of opposites – a concept that may be akin to the eastern view of ying and yang but remains anti-thetical to orthodox Judaism and Christianity.[80]

---

74 L Dunker, F Schneidewin (eds), *Hippolytus, Refutationis Omnium Haeresium* (hereafter cited as 'Ref') (Gottingen, 1859) 5.7.

75 Ref 5.6.

76 WW Harvey (ed), *Iranaeus, Adversus Haereses* (hereafter cited as 'AH') (Cambridge, 1857) 1.11.1.

77 *Ibid*, 1.13.2.

78 *Ibid*, 1.13.6.

79 *Ibid*, 1.115–21.1.3; Ref 6.29.

80 Pages 97–99.

The author continues to examine the texts, and finds – in differing sources – the characterisation of the divine Mother as either the Holy Spirit or as Wisdom. However, these texts – treating the male and female as of equal divine importance – met with rejection. Elaine Pagels continues:

> All the texts cited above – secret 'gospels', revelation, mystical teachings – are among those rejected from the select list of 26 that comprise the 'New Testament' collection. As these and other writings were sorted and judged by various Christian communities, every one of these texts which gnostic groups revered and shared was rejected from the canonical collection as 'heterodox' by those who called themselves 'orthodox' (literally straight-thinking) Christians. By the time this process was concluded, probably as late as the year AD 200, virtually all the feminine imagery for God (along with any suggestion of an androgynous human creation) had disappeared from orthodox Christian tradition.
>
> What is the reason for this wholesale rejection? To look for the actual, historical reasons why these gnostic writings were suppressed is an extremely difficult proposition, for it raises the much larger question of how (ie by what means and what criteria) certain ideas, including those expressed in the texts cited above, came to be classified as heretical and others as orthodox by the beginning of the Third century.[81]

As these texts suggest, then, women were considered equal to men, they were revered as prophets, and they acted as teachers, travelling evangelists, healers, priests, and even bishops. In some of these groups they played leading roles and were excluded from them in the orthodox churches, at least by AD 150–200. Is it possible, then, that the recognition of the feminine elements in God and the recognition of mankind as a male and female entity bore within it the explosive social possibility of women acting on an equal basis with men in positions of authority and leadership? If this were true it might lead to the conclusion that these gnostic groups, together with their conception of God and human nature, were suppressed only because of their positive attitude toward women. But such a conclusion would be a mistake – a hasty and simplistic reading of the evidence. In the first place, orthodox Christian doctrine is far from wholly negative in its attitude towards women. Second, many other elements of the gnostic sources diverge in fundamental ways from what came to be accepted as orthodox Christian teaching. To examine this process in detail would require a much more extensive discussion than is possible here. Nevertheless the evidence does indicate that two very different patterns of sexual attitudes emerged in orthodox and gnostic circles. In simplest form gnostic theologians correlate their description of God in both masculine and feminine terms with a complementary description of human nature. Most often they refer to the creation account of Genesis 1, which suggest an equal (or even androgynous) creation of mankind. This conception carries the principle of equality between men and women into the practical social and political structures of gnostic communities. The orthodox pattern is strikingly different: it describes God in exclusively masculine terms, and often uses Genesis 2 to describe how Eve was created from Adam and for his fulfilment. Like the gnostic view, the orthodox also translates into sociological practice: by the late 2nd century, orthodox Christians came to accept the domination of men over women as the proper, God-given order – not only for the human race, but also for the Christian churches. This correlation between

---

81 At p 103.

theology, anthropology, and sociology is not lost on the apostle Paul. In his letter to the disorderly Corinthian community, he reminds them of a divinely ordained chain of authority: as God has authority over Christ, so the man has authority over the women, argues Paul citing Genesis 2: 'The man is the image and glory of God, but the woman is the glory of man. For man is not from women, but woman from man; and besides, the man was not created for the women's sake, but the woman for the sake of the man.'[82] Here the three elements of the orthodox pattern are welded into one simple argument: the description of God corresponds to a description of human nature which authorises the social pattern of male domination.[83]

Mary Daly has analysed the relationship between religion and the subordinate status of women in society. In the passages which follow, Daly examines the traditional – male – interpretation of the story of Adam and Eve.

BEYOND GOD THE FATHER: TOWARD A PHILOSOPHY OF WOMEN'S LIBERATION[84]

Mary Daly

The story of the Fall of Adam and Eve is not given serious weight in the modern consciousness, it would seem.[85]

The fact is, however, that the myth has projected a malignant image of the male-female relationship and of the 'nature' of women that is still deeply embedded in the modern psyche. In the Christian tradition it continues to colour the functioning of the theological imagination. Berdyaev found it possible to write the amazing comment that 'there is something base and sinister in the female element'.[86] What is equally amazing (verified by this author's experience) is that theological students, confronted with such a passage, frequently are unable to see anything remarkable or significant about it. The myth has in fact affected doctrines and laws that concern women's status in society and it has contributed to the mind-set of those who continue to grind out biased, male-centred ethical theories – a point to be developed in a later chapter. The myth undergirds destructive patterns in the fabric of our culture. Literature and the mass media repeat the 'temptress Eve' motif in deadly earnest, as do the rationalisations for social customs and civil laws, such as abortion legislation, which incorporate punitive attitudes toward women's sexual function.[87]

In view of the fact that the destructive image of women that was reflected in and perpetuated by the myth of the Fall retains its hold over the modern psyche – even though in a disguised and residual manner – it is not adequate for theologians simply to intellectualise and generalise the alleged content of the myth as an expression of a universal state of alienation. Indeed this approach is intellectually bankrupt and demonic. It amounts merely to abandoning the use of

---

82   1 Cor 11: 7–9.

83   Pages 105–6.

84   The Women's Press, 1973.

85   *Beyond God the Father*, p 44.

86   N Berdyaev, *The Beginning and the End*, RM French trans (Gloucester, Mass: YMCA Press, 1952).

87   For striking examples of this punitive attitude as implied in abortion legislation, see L Lader *Abortion II: Making the Revolution* (Boston: Beacon Press, 1973).

explicitly sexist theological imagery while failing to acknowledge its still persistent impact upon society. Such silence about the destructiveness of the myth's specific content is oppressive because it conveys the message – indeed becomes the message – that sexual oppression is a non-problem. It is not good enough to talk about evil abstractly while lending implicit support to traditional images that legitimate specific social evils.

The Myth Revisited

The story of the Fall was an attempt to cope with the confusion experienced by human beings trying to make sense out of the tragedy and absurdity of the human condition. Unfortunately, as an exclusively male effort in a male-dominated society, it succeeded primarily in reflecting the defective social arrangements of the time. The myth was both symptom and instrument of further contagion. Its great achievement was to reinforce the problem, of sexual oppression in society, so that women's inferior place in the universe became doubly justified. Not only did she have her origin in the man; she was also the cause of his downfall and all his miseries. Humourless treatises on the subject of Eve's peculiar birth and woeful sinfulness written by the indefatigable fans of Adam down through the millennia are their own best parodies. Yet a hoax of cosmic proportions took a few thousand years to be seen through. Having at last noticed the incongruity, theologians have dismissed it from their attention. Few have even barely begun to glimpse the significance of the tragedy of sexual injustice that was inadvertently 'revealed' by the story of the Fall.

The fact that the myth cultivated a backward-looking consciousness and, taken as an overall perspective on the world, constituted an obstacle to progress, was noted by Teilhard de Chardin as early as 1933 (in an essay entitled *Christologie et Evolution*). The story conveys to the popular imagination the idea that the best has already been; paradise seems to be located in the past. The specific nature of the backward-looking vision which Teilhard failed to acknowledge is fixation upon a one-sided and distorted image of half the human species – and also of the other half (Adam is pictured as a servile and arrogant dunce) – which prevents the becoming of psychically whole human beings.

Other critics of the tradition such as Hesnar, looking at it from a psychoanalytic point of view, have pointed out that it encourages an all-pervasive guilt feeling that condemns life and its instinctive joys. The refusal of life is experienced as frustration, which becomes self-accusation and aggression against the self. Logically, this would appear to lead to self-annihilation, but what usually happens is that it is at least partially transformed into aggression against others. In this way, the self-hatred encouraged by Christianity becomes a perversion of the basic desire and need to communicate with others and so fosters hatred, oppression and even war.[88] The specific form of aggression which such critics fail to take adequately into account is that which makes women into objects. They do not really deal with the fact that the projection of 'the Other' – easily adaptable to national, racial, and class differences – has basically and primordially been directed against women.

To summarise: theologians and scholars generally have failed to confront the fact that in the myth of the Fall the medium is the message. Reflection upon its specific content and cultural resides of this content leads to the conviction that, partially through this instrument, the Judeo-Christian tradition has been aiding

88   Dr A Hesnard, *Morale sans Péche* (Paris: Presses Universitaires de France, 1954).

and abetting the sicknesses of society. In a real sense the projection of guilt upon women is patriarchy's Fall, the primordial lie together with its offspring – the theology of 'original sin' – the myth reveals the 'Fall' of religion into the role of patriarchy's prostitute. This is not to say, of course, that religion was ever in a true paradise, dispensing pure revelation, free of idolatry and of servitude to unjust social arrangements. The point is simply that by its built-in bias and its blind reinforcement of prejudice the myth does express the 'original sin' of patriarchal religion. The message that it unintentionally conveys – the full implications of which we are only now beginning to grasp – is that in patriarchy, with the aid of religion, women have been the primordial scapegoats.[89]

Naming

Mary Daly next proceeds to examine the Fall in relation to the 'naming' – or more accurately, 'false naming' of women. Naming is the process whereby masculine, patriarchal labels are attached to concepts – such as God – whereby women are excluded from linguistic definition. What is needed, Daly argues, is a 're-naming' of concepts which is inclusive, rather than exclusive of women.

The Fall and False Naming

The myth of the Fall can be seen as a prototypic case of false naming. Elizabeth Cady Stanton was indeed accurate in pointing out the key role of the myth of feminine evil as a foundation for the entire structure of phallic Christian ideology.[90] As I have indicated, the myth takes on cosmic proportions since the male's viewpoint is metamorphosed into God's viewpoint. It amounts to a cosmic false naming. It misnames the mystery of evil, casting it into the distorted mould of the myth of feminine evil. In this way images and conceptualisations about evil are thrown out of focus and its deepest dimensions are not really confronted. Implied in this colossal misnaming of evil is the misnaming of women, of men, of God. Consequent upon this dislocation of the mystery of evil has been a dislocation of the Christian 'solution'.

Out of the surfacing woman-consciousness is coming the realisation that the basic counteraction to patriarchy's false naming of evil has to come primarily from women. By dislodging ourselves from the role of 'the Other', that is, by saying inwardly and outwardly our own names, women are dislodging the mystery of evil from this false context and thus clearing the way for seeing and naming it more adequately.

Effects of the Myth

As one author puts it: 'the fall of man should rightly be called the fall of woman because once more the second sex is blamed for all the trouble in the world.'[91] The attitude of negativity on the part of the male is directed against women. This, clearly, was the prevailing psychological climate which engendered the myth and sustained its credibility. However, there is more to the problem than this. The myth has provided legitimisation not only for the direction of the self-hatred of the male outward against women, but also for the direction of self-hatred

---

89 *Beyond God the Father*, pp 45–47.

90 Letter to the Editor, 'The Critic' (1896) cited in Aileen S Kraditor (ed), *Up From the Pedestal*, (Chicago: Quadrangle Books, 1968), p 119.

91 HR Hays, *The Dangerous Sex: The Myth of Feminine Evil* (New York: GP Putnam's Sons, 1964), p 88.

inward on the part of women. As long as the myth of feminine evil is allowed to dominate human consciousness and social arrangements, it provides the setting for women's victimisation, by both men and women.

It is now quite commonly known that it is characteristic of any oppressed group that its members suffer from a divided consciousness. Freire has described this phenomenon:

> The oppressed suffer from the duality which has established itself in their innermost being. They discover that without freedom they cannot live authentically. Yet, although they desire authentic existence, they fear it. They are at one and the same time themselves and the oppressor whose consciousness they have internalised.[92]

As contradictory, divided beings, the oppressed do not fully grasp the paralysing fact that the oppressor, having invaded the victims' psyches, now exists within themselves. They are caught in a web of self-defeating behaviour.

This problem, which has been perceived as the dilemma of all oppressed groups, is most tragically the case with women – divided beings par excellence. Having been divided against the self, women want to speak, but remain silent. The desire for action is by and large reduced to acting vicariously through men. Instead of living out the dynamics of the authentic self, women generally are submerged in roles believed to be pleasing to males. When a rebel tries to raise up her own identity, that is, to create her own image, she exposes herself to threatened existence in sexist society. This is partly because both women and men identify with the goals of the super-ordinate group and therefore see the rebellious female as 'the enemy'. It may also be said that, in attacking her, women are also attacking the male in the sense that she is a surrogate victim, a more vulnerable object for repressed resentment. It seems that sexist society generates a chronic inability to realise the location of the problem, to ferret out the cause of the destruction.

Patriarchal religion adds to the problem by intensifying the process through which women internalise the consciousness of the oppressor. The male's judgment having been metamorphosed into God's judgment, it becomes the religious duty of women to accept the burden of guilt, seeing the self with male chauvinist eyes. What is more, the process does not stop with religion's demanding that women internalise such images. It happens that those conditioned to see themselves as 'bad' or 'sick' in a real sense become such. Women who are conditioned to live out the abject role assigned to the female sex actually appear to 'deserve' the contempt heaped upon 'the second sex'.[93]

THE TRANSITION FROM CULTURE TO LAW AND LEGAL THEORY

Legal theory derives from social and political theory: social and political theory form the foundation on which legal theory rests. Early theoretical attempts to see law as a reflection of the cultural mores of society were offered by Emile Durkheim, Eugen Ehrlich and William Graham Sumner. The central tenets of each theorist's thought will be briefly examined here. The writers – in differing ways – each view law as a reflection of culture and no more. The value of such approaches – from a feminist perspective – lies in illustrating the close links

---

92 Freire, *Pedagogy of the Oppressed*, p 32.
93 *Beyond God the Father*, pp 47–49.

between law and cultural – patriarchal – values, and the manner in which law is grounded in society. Once this is appreciated, the sheer magnitude of the feminist endeavour becomes starkly clear: the endeavour is one which requires the realignment of deeply held patriarchal attitudes and arrangements which have become translated into law as a natural outcome of the evolution of society from nature to culture to law. The central tenets of these theorists will be considered before considering the implications of such theories from a feminist perspective.

THE DIVISION OF LABOUR IN SOCIETY[94]

Emile Durkheim[95]

The French sociologist Emile Durkheim was principally concerned with an examination of the manner in which societies are bound together, and the evolution of society from its early form in which shared values predominate to more complex society where there will be demonstrated a diffusion of values. In seeking to explain societal bonding and change, Durkheim employs two principal concepts: organic and mechanical solidarity. Because cultural values, or the morality of society, cannot be empirically quantified, Durkheim utilises law as a visible symbol of society's solidarity: law is thus a reflection of the 'consciousness' of society. In 'simple' societies, exemplified by an absence of division of labour, Durkheim believes, the law will be predominantly repressive, for law is used to uphold and reinforce the collective conscience of society. Penal law serves this purpose: where deviant behaviour is experienced the law and legal process will step in to reaffirm society's values through punishing the offender. As society diversifies and becomes more complex and the division of labour becomes more marked, the need for predominantly penal, repressive law diminishes. The law in a complex society will be increasingly concerned with restitutive law – that is to say laws which do not express the 'collective vengeance' of society, but laws which are designed to realign relationships in order to provide restitution for wrongs suffered. Durkheim's empirical work has been subjected to much academic criticism. It has been demonstrated, for example, that 'simple' societies have a significant degree of division of labour which Durkheim denies;[96] and that societies do not evolve from 'organic solidarity' to 'mechanical solidarity' in the manner in which Durkheim suggests.[97] Nevertheless, Durkheim's thought continues to exert a powerful influence on sociological jurisprudence, and the core of his thought illustrates vividly the linkage between culture and law. In *The Division of Labour in Society* Durkheim writes that:

> We have not merely to investigate whether in [complex] societies, there exists a social solidarity arising from the division of labour. This is a self-evident truth, since in them the division of labour is highly developed, and it engenders

---

94 1893. See generally, Alpert, *Emile Durkheim and His Sociology* (1961); S Lukes and A Scull, *Durkheim and the Law* (1983); RBM Cotterrell (1991) 25 *Law and Society Review* 923.

95 1858–1917.

96 See Stanislaw Malinowski, *Crime and Custom in Savage Society* (1926).

97 See, *inter alia*, RD Schwarz and JC Miller (1964) 70 *American Journal of Sociology* 159.

solidarity. But above all we must determine the degree to which the solidarity it produces contributes generally to the integration of society. Only then shall we learn to what extent it is necessary, whether it is an essential factor in society cohesion, or whether, on the contrary, it is only an ancillary and secondary condition for it. To answer this question we must therefore compare this social bond to others, in order to measure what share in the total effect must be attributed to it. To do this it is indispensable to begin by classifying the different species of social solidarity. ...

However, social solidarity is a wholly moral phenomenon which by itself does not lend itself to exact observation and especially not to measurement. To arrive at this classification, as well as this comparison, we must therefore substitute for this internal datum, which escapes us, an external one which symbolises it, and then study the former through the latter.

That visible symbol is the law. Indeed, where social solidarity exists, in spite of its non-material nature, it does not remain in a state of pure potentiality, but shows its presence through perceptible effects. Where it is strong it attracts men strongly to each other, ensures frequent contacts between them, and redoubles the opportunities available to them to enter into mutual relationships. Stating the position precisely, at the point we have now reached it is not easy to say whether it is social solidarity which produces these phenomena or, on the contrary, whether it is the result of them. It is also a moot point whether men draw closer to one another because of its dynamic effects, or whether it is dynamic because men have come closer together. However, for the present we need not concern ourselves with elucidating this question. It is enough to state that these two orders of facts are linked, varying with each other simultaneously and moving in the same direction. The more closely knit the members of a society, the more they maintain various relationships with one another or with the group collectively. For if they met together rarely, they would not be mutually dependent, except sporadically and somewhat weakly. Moreover, the sum of these relationships is necessarily proportioned to the sum of legal rules which determine them. In fact, social life, wherever it becomes lasting, inevitably tends to assume a definite form and become organised. Law is nothing more than the most stable and precise element in this very organisation. Life in general within society cannot enlarge in scope without legal activity similarly increasing in a corresponding fashion. Thus we may be sure to find reflected in the law all the essential varieties of social solidarity.[98]

As for Emile Durkheim, for Eugen Ehrlich the law is grounded in society. Ehrlich is less concerned with the 'positive law' – the law of the State – than with the 'living law' – those rules which arise out of society and which in fact regulate social relations. This living law represents the real law for differing groups in society, for which the positive law of the State may have little practical relevance. If, therefore, the sociologist is to understand the forces which control the life of differing groups, he or she must seek the empirical evidence of the living law: merely to expound a positivistic theory of State law is, from this perspective, a sterile activity. Ehrlich developed his theory through studying nine differing 'tribes' living in Bukowina, a remote area of the Austro-Hungarian empire. The central thrust of Ehrlich's work is revealed in the following passage.

98   At pp 24–25.

FUNDAMENTAL PRINCIPLES OF THE SOCIOLOGY OF LAW[99]

Eugen Ehrlich[100]

The legal proposition is not only the result, it is also a lever, of social development; it is an instrumentality in the hands of society whereby society shapes things within its sphere of influence according to its will. Through the legal proposition man acquires a power, limited though it be, over the facts of the law; in the legal proposition a willed legal order is brought face to face with the legal order which has arisen self-actively in society.[101]

The sociology of law then must begin with the ascertainment of the living law. Its attention will be directed primarily to the concrete, not the abstract. It is only the concrete that can be observed. What the anatomist places under the microscope is not human tissue in the abstract but a specific tissue of a specific human being; the physiologist likewise does not study the functions of the liver of mammals in the abstract, but those of a specific liver of a specific mammal. Only when he has completed the observation of the concrete does he ask whether it is universally valid, and this fact, too, he endeavours to establish by means of a series of concrete observations, for which he has to find specific methods. The same may be said of the investigator of law. He must first concern himself with concrete usages, relations of domination, legal relations, contracts, articles of association, dispositions by last will and testament. It is not true, therefore, that the investigation of the living law is concerned only with 'customary law' or with 'business usage'. If one does any thinking at all when one uses these words – which is not always the case – one will realise that they do not refer to the concrete, but to that which has been universalised. But only the concrete usages, the relations of domination, the legal relations, the contracts, the articles of association, the dispositions by last will and testament, yield the rules according to which men regulate their conduct.[102]

But the scientific significance of the living law is not confined to its influence upon the norms for decision which the courts apply or upon the content of statutes. The knowledge of the living law has an independent value, and this consists in the fact that it constitutes the foundation of the legal order of human society.[103]

FOLKWAYS[104]

William Graham Sumner

Definition and mode of origin of the folkways. If we put together all that we have learned from anthropology and ethnography about primitive men and primitive society, we perceive that the first task of life is to live. Men begin with acts, not with thoughts. Every moment brings necessities which must be satisfied at once. Need was the first experience, and it was followed at once by a blundering effort to satisfy it. It is generally taken for granted that men inherited some guiding

---

99 Trans WL Moll (1936). See Littlefield (1967) 19 *Maine Law Review* 1; and D Nelken 'Law in Action or Living Law?' (1984) 4 *Legal Studies* 157.

100 1862–1922.

101 At p 203.

102 At pp 501–02.

103 *Ibid*.

104 1906.

instincts from their beast ancestry, and it may be true, although it has never been proved. If there were such inheritances, they controlled and aided the first efforts to satisfy needs. Analogy makes it easy to assume that the ways of beasts had produced channels of habit and predisposition along which dexterities and other psychophysical activities would run easily. Experiments with newborn animals show that in the absence of any experience of the relation of means to ends, efforts to satisfy needs are clumsy and blundering. The method is that of trial and failure, which produces repeated pain, loss, and disappointments. Nevertheless, it is a method of rude experiment and selection. The earliest efforts of men were of this kind. Need was the impelling force. Pleasure and pain, on the one side and the other, were the rude constraints which defined the line on which efforts must proceed. The ability to distinguish between pleasure and pain is the only psychical power which is to be assumed. Thus ways of doing things were selected, which were expedient. They answered the purpose better than other ways, or with less toil and pain. Along the course on which efforts were compelled to go, habit, routine, and skill were developed. The struggle to maintain existence was carried on, not individually, but in groups. Each profited by the other's experience; hence there was concurrence towards that which proved to be most expedient. All at last adopted the same way for the same purpose; hence the ways turned into customs and became mass phenomena. Instincts were developed in connection with them. In this way folkways arise. The young learn them by tradition, imitation, and authority. The folkways, at a time, provide for all the needs of life then and there. They are uniform, universal in the group, imperative, and invariable. As time goes on, the folkways become more and more arbitrary, positive, and imperative. If asked why they act in a certain way in certain cases, primitive people always answer that it is because they and their ancestors always have done so. A sanction also arises from ghost fear. The ghosts of ancestors would be angry in the living should change the ancient folkways.

The folkways are a societal force. The operation by which folkways are produced consists in the frequent repetition of petty acts, often by great numbers acting in concert or, at least, acting in the same way when face to faced with the same need. The immediate motive is interest. It produces habit in the individual and custom in the group. It is, therefore, in the highest degree original and primitive. By habit and custom it exerts a strain on every individual within its range; therefore it rises to a societal force to which great classes of societal phenomena are due. Its earliest stages, its course, and laws may be studied; also its influence on individuals and their reaction on it. It is our present purpose so to study it. We have to recognise it as one of the chief forces by which a society is made to be what it is. Out of the unconscious experiment which every repetition of the ways includes, there issues pleasure or pain, and then, so far as the men are capable of reflection, convictions that the ways are conducive to societal welfare. These two experiences are not the same. The most uncivilised men, both in the food quest and in other ways, do things which are painful, but which have been found to be expedient. Perhaps these cases teach the sense of social welfare better than those which are pleasurable and favourable to welfare. The former cases call for some intelligent reflection on experience. When this conviction as to the relation to welfare is added to the folkways they are converted into mores, and, by virtue of the philosophical and ethical element added to them they win utility and importance and become the source of the science and art of living.[105]

---

105 *Folkways*, pp 2–3.

Sumner goes on to explain that together with the development of folkways among the group, there develops a hostile, antagonistic view of member of 'other groups' who do not share the same folkways and mores.

> 'Enthnocentrism' is the technical name for this view of things in which one's own group is the centre of everything, and all others are scaled and rated with reference to it. Folkways correspond to it to cover both the inner and the outer relation. Each group nourishes its own pride and vanity, boasts itself superior, exalts its own divinities, and looks with contempt on outsiders. Each group thinks its own folkways the only right ones, and if it observes that other groups have other folkways, these excite its scorn.[106]

As society and societal organisation develops, the folkways become the 'right' way of acting: whatever has proved to be the preferred manner of acting in a given situation will assume a moral force in the society.

> *The folkways are 'right'. Rights. Morals.* The folkways are the 'right' ways to satisfy all interest, because they are traditional, and exist in fact. They extend over the whole of life. There is a right way to catch game, to win a wife, to make one's self appear, to cure disease, to honour ghosts, to treat comrades or strangers, to behave when a child in born, on the warpath, in council, and so on in all cases which can arise. The ways are defined on the negative side, that is, by taboos. The 'right' way is the way which the ancestors used and which has been handed down. The tradition is its own warrant. It is not held subject to verification by experience. The notion of right is in the folkways. It is not outside of them, of independent origin, and brought to them to test them. In the folkways, whatever is, is right. This is because they are tradition, and therefore contain in themselves the authority of the ancestral ghosts. When we come to the folkways we are at the end of our analysis. The notion of right and ought is the same in regard to all folkways, but the degree of it varies with the importance of the interest at stake. The obligation of conformable and co-operative action is far greater under ghost fear and war than in other matters, and the social sanctions are severer, because group interests are supposed to be at stake. Some usages contain only a slight element of right and ought. It may well be believed that notions of right and duty, and of social welfare, were first developed in connection with ghost fear and other worldliness, and therefore that, in that field also, folkways were first raised to mores. 'Rights' are the rules of mutual give and take in the competition of life which are imposed on comrades in the in-group, in order that the peace may prevail there which is essential to the group strength. Therefore rights can never be 'natural' or 'God-given', or absolute in any sense. The morality of a group at a time is the sum of the taboos and prescriptions in the folkways by which right conduct is defined. Therefore morals can never be intuitive. They are historical, institutional, and empirical.

World philosophy, life policy, right, rights, and morality are all products of the folkways. They are reflections on, and generalisations from, the experience of pleasure and pain which is won in efforts to carry on the struggle for existence under actual life conditions. The generalisations are very crude and vague in their germinal forms. They are all embodied in folklore, and all our philosophy and science have been developed out of them.[107]

---

106 *Folkways*, p 13.
107 *Folkways*, pp 28–29.

As society progresses from 'folkways' to 'mores', the need for institutions and laws arises. It is imperative that law rest firmly on the mores in society:

> *Laws.* Acts of legislation come out of the mores. In low civilisation all societal regulations are customs and taboos, the origin of which is unknown. Positive laws are impossible until the stage of verification, reflection and criticism is reached. Until that point is reached there is only customary law, or common law. The customary law may be codified and systematised with respect to some philosophical principles, and yet remain customary. The codes of Manu and Justinian are examples. Enactment is not possible until reverence for ancestors has been so much weakened that it is no longer thought wrong to interfere with traditional customs by positive enactment. Even them there is reluctance to make enactments, and there is a stage of transition during which traditional customs are extended by interpretation to cover new cases and to prevent evils. Legislation, however, has to seek standing ground on the existing mores, and it soon becomes apparent that legislation, to be strong, must be consistent with the mores.[108]

> *How laws and institutions differ from mores.* When folkways have become institutions or laws they have changed their character and are to be distinguished from the mores. The element of sentiment and faith inheres in the mores. Laws and institutions have a rational and practical character, and are more mechanical and utilitarian. The great difference is that institutions and laws have a positive character, while mores are unformulated and undefined. There is a philosophy implicit in the folkways; when it is made explicit it becomes technical philosophy. Objectively regarded, the mores are the customs which actually conduce to welfare under existing life conditions. Acts under the laws and institutions are conscious and voluntary; under the folkways they are always unconscious and involuntary, so that they have the character of natural necessity. Educated reflection and scepticism can disturb this spontaneous relation. The laws, being positive prescriptions, superseded the mores so far as they are adopted. It follows that the mores come into operation where laws and tribunals fail. The mores cover the great field of common life where there are no laws or police regulations. They cover an immense and undefined domain, and they break the way in new domains, not yet controlled at all. The mores, therefore, build up new laws and police regulations in time.[109]

What can be gleaned from such theories from a feminist perspective? Over and above the centrally important fact that law arises out of society, and is thus culturally dependant, we may gain further insights. In Durkheim's work, for example, we find in the insistence on concentrating on law as a visible index of social solidarity existing in differing societies characterised by the extent of the division of labour, that women, unless they are equally economically active as men, fail to be considered at all. Given the time in which Durkheim was writing, 1936, there was be no society exhibiting organic solidarity, it was the solidarity of the economic or professional group, in which such conditions prevailed. Moreover, throughout his work, Durkheim is addressing the public sphere of life as the central determinant of the type of solidarity which exists in society at any one time. Accordingly there is no consideration whatsoever of the private domain in which most women laboured and lived. And, even if

108 *Folkways*, p 55.
109 *Folkways*, pp 56–57.

Durkheim were writing at a time in which there existed economic parity in the public domain between men and women, his theory would still not be able to explain the role of law in relation to the private domain in which women continue to labour in addition to their 'public' economic labour.

If the focus shifts to Eugen Ehrlich's work, we find different considerations. Ehrlich was concerned with the private domain: the manner in which the family regulated itself, the relationships between parents and children. However, despite this focus Ehrlich's work cannot accommodate the feminist perspective, for it takes the 'natural', patriarchal, ordering of society as a correct and necessary foundation for the enactment of State law. Ehrlich has been much criticised for failing to consider the role of State law in inculcating changing beliefs – its educative role[110] – but he may also be criticised for failing to direct attention to the justice of existing societal relations on which law should be based. Ehrlich's insistence that justice arises out of society – out of the living law – appears persuasive until viewed through feminist eyes. Through feminist eyes, Ehrlich's 'justice' looks very much like women's oppression and exclusion from that concept of justice. The same criticism must lie in relation to Sumner's thesis. What is natural – inequality and patriarchy – is viewed as a correct basis for legal ordering. That this cannot produce a society concerned for the needs and aspirations of women as equal citizens is all too obvious.

---

110 See, for example, R Mnookin and L Kornhauser (1979) *Yale Law Journal* 950 and H Jacob (1992) 26 *Law and Society Review* 565.

CHAPTER 3

THE EVOLUTION AND SCOPE OF
FEMINIST JURISPRUDENCE

The position of the world's women has traditionally, historically and culturally been one of being consigned to the position of the 'second' – and inferior – sex. In this book the explanations for the discriminations and inequalities endured by women in the past and present are explored through the eyes of feminist scholars. It is the aim of feminist scholars both to explore the manner in which such discriminations may be identified and eliminated, to explore and seek to eliminate the inequalities which are created by, or supported by, law. Further than this, feminist legal scholarship is engaged in the task of theorising the origins and causes of the gendered nature of society and law. By what means did men assume 'superiority' in society? By what means is this assumed 'superiority' reflected in law and legal institutions? By what means can feminists in general, and feminist legal scholars in particular, not only throw light on the inequalities under which women exist, but also move forward to eradicate the inequalities and quicken the movement towards the full and equal participation in society?

There is no simple, or single, answer to the question 'what is feminist jurisprudence or legal theory?' There exists, however, a unifying strand of thought throughout the literature – that is, that law reflects the interests of men in society, largely although not totally, remaindering the position of women in society to that of second class citizens. Feminist jurisprudence – in its many guises – seeks to unmask the traditional and too often ignored inequalities in society which are supported by law, and to suggest – in differing ways – the manner in which such continuing inequalities may be redressed. Inequalities based on gender in many aspects of the substantive law have long been evident to feminist scholars. Whether it is the criminal law, family law, employment law or property law, discrimination based on gender has represented a real and problematic feature of law. As will be discussed later, the extent to which law creates and sustains inequalities in society is a complex matter. It must be recognised at the outset that it cannot be assumed that there is any true agreement between jurists concerning the role of law in society – or indeed agreement over the very meaning of the word 'law'. The academic debate concerning such large and intractable questions which form the core of traditional jurisprudence is reflected in feminist jurisprudence.

Feminist Legal Theory as an academic discipline took earliest root most firmly in the United States of America, in Canada and in Australia. Nowadays, some 50% of undergraduate law courses in Australia and Canada feature of feminist legal theory component, either as a discrete subject or as a core part of the Legal Theory or Jurisprudence curriculum.[1] The United Kingdom was slower to respond, and in 1991 Carol Smart was to argue that '[F]eminist jurisprudence has not been taken seriously' in traditional jurisprudence

---

1   See Hilaire Barnett, 'The Province of Jurisprudence Determined – Again!' 1995, 15 *Legal Studies*, p 88.

courses.[2] By 1995, however, feminist legal theory had taken firm root within the context of jurisprudential thought and study in United Kingdom universities.

There now exists a wide and diverse corpus of literature on feminist legal theory. While interest in the position of women in society has been evident since the time of Plato[3] and Aristotle,[4] the concern for the legal position of women may be traced to the late 18th century with the writing of Mary Wollstonencraft.[5] In England in the 19th century with the expansion of the electoral franchise, the traditional disenfranchisement of women formed a focus of attention for English writers such as John Stuart Mill and Harriet Mill.[6] The 'modern' feminist movement may be traced to 1949 with the classic work of Simone de Beauvoir.[7] In was not to be until the late 1960s and early 1970s, however, that sustained and systematic pressure grew for an improvement in the status of women in Western society. The focus of feminist writers such as Germaine Greer,[8] Betty Freidan,[9] Kate Millet,[10] Juliet Mitchell,[11] Eva Figes[12] and others was not directed specifically to the question of law and its relationship to the position of women in society, but rather represented a broad sociological and philosophical attack on the inequalities visited upon women in society.

Out of this broad ranging movement grew feminist jurisprudence. Feminist jurisprudence focuses on the manner in which law reflects and reinforces the position of women in society. As will be seen, feminist legal theorists take many differing approaches to the issue of equality of women. There exists, however, a common theme in feminist writings, namely the view that the law – variously and traditionally portrayed by Western 'liberal' jurists as a body of rules serving to regulate all members of society – is neither class- nor gender-neutral. Feminist jurisprudence seeks to explode the 'liberal' (male) mythology of law. By concentrating, in differing ways, upon the manner in which law supports and reinforces the inequalities and disabilities under which women labour in society, law is seen as anything but gender-neutral. Law becomes, from this particular perspective, a force in society created by men, practised by men, applied by men – for the (not necessarily conscious) purpose of maintaining traditional patriarchal dominance. Viewed from the feminist perspective, law,

---

2   Carol Smart, 'Feminist Jurisprudence' in P Fitzpatrick (ed), *Dangerous Supplements* (Pluto Press, 1991).

3   c 427–347 BC.

4   384–22 BC.

5   Mary Wollstonencraft, *A Vindication of the Rights of Women* (1792).

6   John Stuart Mill, *The Subjection of Women* (1869) and JS and Harriet Mill, 'The Enfranchisement of Women' (1851) in *The Westminster Review*.

7   *The Second Sex* (1949).

8   *The Female Eunuch* (1971).

9   *The Feminine Mystique* (1963).

10   *Sexual Politics* (1970).

11   *Woman's Estate* (Penguin Books, 1971) and *The Rights and Wrongs of Women*, J Mitchell and A Oakley (eds) (Penguin Books, 1976).

12   *Patriarchal Attitudes* (1970).

far from reflecting a gender-neutral liberally inspired body of rules reflecting societal values, becomes a force of oppression of women who comprise some 50% of the population.

WHAT IS FEMINIST JURISPRUDENCE?

On the tenth anniversary of the introduction of the *Harvard Women's Law Journal*, Christine Littleton took the opportunity to overview the development of feminist jurisprudence in the Journal's first decade:

IN SEARCH OF A FEMINIST JURISPRUDENCE[13]

Christine A Littleton

'Feminist jurisprudence' has certainly come of age. At the January 1987 annual meeting of the Association of American Law Schools, participants were offered a day long 'Mini-Workshop in Emerging Traditions in Legal Education and Legal Scholarship', including feminist jurisprudence. Like other contemporary movements, it can be viewed both as a critique within legal education and scholarship and as a direct challenge to their very structure.

First, feminist jurisprudence criticises the law's omission of and bias against women's concerns, offering its insights as a supplement and corrective. Simple inclusion is not, however, the primary goal of feminist jurisprudence.[14] Rather, feminist legal theorists routinely speak of challenging, subverting or transforming legal relations at their core. If feminist jurisprudence is not simply addition of missing pieces within legal education and scholarship, what is it?

We might begin with Catharine MacKinnon's suggested definition: 'Feminist jurisprudence is an examination of the relationship between law and society from the point of view of all women'.[15] This definition, while succinct and comprehensive, must be unpacked. Feminists have discovered the endless variety of women's experience[16] and the different ways in which law affects our experience.

Heather Wishik has proposed a framework of inquiry for feminist jurisprudence:

(1)   What women's experiences are addressed by an area of law?

(2)   What assumptions or descriptions of experience does the law make?

(3)   What is the area of distortion or denial so created?

(4)   What reforms have been proposed, and how will they affect women both practically and ideologically?

(6)   In an ideal world, how would women's situation look?

(7)   How do we get there from here?[17]

---

13   Christine A Littleton,' In Search of a Feminist Jurisprudence' (1987) 10 *Harvard Women's Law Journal*, p 1.

14   See H Wishik, 'To Question Everything: The Inquiries of Feminist Jurisprudence' (1986) 1 *Berkeley Women's Law Journal* 64 (describing 'compensatory scholarship' as a necessary but insufficient development in legal scholarship about 'women and law').

15   CA MacKinnon, Panel Discussion, 'Developing Feminist Jurisprudence' at the 14th National Conference on Women and Law, Washington DC 1983, quoted in H Wishik, *op cit*, p 64.

16   See H Eisenstein and A Jardine, *The Future of Difference* (1980).

17   H Wishik, *op cit*, pp 72–75.

If these are, as they seem to me, the right (although not the only) questions to ask, then feminist jurisprudence necessarily involves more than 'examination' – it also demands active struggle for change.

'Jurisprudence', as traditionally practised (ie as practised by men), considers overarching questions usually ignored or assumed by scholars in narrow doctrinal fields. It includes studies of the 'nature' of law and legal reasoning, sources of legal obligation and legitimacy of legal systems, and the relationship between law and the social structure. On this definition, Janet Rifkin's article 'Toward a Theory of Law and Patriarchy'[18] clearly qualifies. 'Law plays a primary and significant role in social order, states Rifkin, and 'is powerful as both a symbol and a vehicle for male authority'.[19] By my reckoning, Rifkin's is easily the most cited piece the Harvard Women's Law Journal has ever published. Her work challenges traditional understandings of the way law functions within (and in relation to) social institutions, but its focus is on the traditional questions of jurisprudence.

Feminist jurisprudence has also embraced forms of scholarship not usually seen as 'jurisprudential'. Women's law journals regularly include sociological studies,[20] articles advocating legal reform, and tactical advice. These categories are not new to law reviews, but are treated somewhat differently. Women's law journals tend not to devalue law reform pieces simply because the are 'reformist' or 'advocacy'. Similarly, they do not treat sociological data and theory as 'not really law', nor do they eschew practitioner oriented pieces. What role in the 'development of a feminist jurisprudence' is played by such pieces?

Sociological data is central to feminist methodology, grounded as it is in the discovering, sharing, and analysis of women's concrete experience. While the practice of sociology has been 'male'[21] in ways that are similar to the practice of law, feminists cannot afford to ignore the fragments of women's experience that can be gleaned from it. To the extent that women's law journals enable feminist lawyers and legal scholars to gain access to such data, they offer some of the building blocks of feminist legal theory.

Questions about the value of legal reform have been raised within every social movement that radically challenges existing hierarchies.[22] As a critique of the entire structure of law, feminist jurisprudence must likewise ask whether 'cleaning up' particular legal doctrines can do anything other than legitimate the patriarchal order.[23] Yet feminist 'law reform' writing is valuable for two interrelated reasons.

First, as feminists, we cannot disregard the suffering of individual women or groups of women. Our experience of being told to place our legitimate demands

18   Janet Rifkin, 'Toward a Theory of Law and Patriarchy' (1980) 3 *Harvard Women's Law Journal* (on which see Chapter 2).

19   *Ibid*, p 84.

20   See eg Kater, 'Reflections on Women and the Legal Profession: A Sociological Perspective' (1978) 1 *Harvard Women's Law Journal* 1; C Menkel-Meadow 'Portia in a Different Voice: Speculations on a Women's Lawyering Process' (1986) 1 *Berkeley Women's Law Journal* 39. (On which see Chapter 6.)

21   See S Walby, *Patriarchy at Work* (1986) pp 7–16 (criticising 'near total focus on men' in sociological theory pertaining to work).

22   See eg Bell, 'Forward: the Civil Rights Chronicle's (1985) 99 *Harvard Law Review* 1.

23   See eg Polan, 'Toward a Theory of Law and Patriarchy' in *The Politics of Law*, D Kairys (ed), 1982, p 294.

on the back burner until 'more important' problems were solved should make us especially sensitive to the dangers of ignoring immediate human pain in the service of theoretical revolution. While legal reform, based on division among women will perpetuate the very structures we resist, reform that opens paths to additional struggles must be part of feminist jurisprudence. Any broadening of equality guarantees, any new legislation designed to ease women's double burden of work and family, any plausible attempt to make the legal system live up to the lip service it pays our concerns, should be embraced as long as it will not make the next demand on behalf of women less likely to succeed.

Second, even when legal reform efforts fail, they may still serve the feminist legal enterprise. If such efforts are clearly grounded in the purported availability of fundamental rights for all, their very failure demonstrates the hypocrisy of the legal system. Feminist law reform advocacy offer the legal system two choices: live up to your promises, or be exposed as a naked system of power and domination. While we should not expect the imminent demise of an exposed system, neither should we lose an opportunity to point out that the emperor is inadequately clothed.

Finally, when feminist jurisprudence criticises both the forms and the categories on which current legal concepts are based, why include in feminist legal periodicals suggestions to practitioners on the use of existing doctrine? This question is clearly posed in the disagreement between a major strand in critical legal studies (CLS) scholarship and many feminists on the usefulness of rights discourse. CLS critiques rights analysis by suggesting that people might believe that a grant of abstract rights equals the concrete ability to exercise such rights, that energies better used in community action and political struggle are diverted into endless rounds of litigation, and that reliance on lawyers replaces self-reliance and leadership development. Feminists point out the CLS scholarship has failed to account for women's concrete experience of empowerment through making rights based claims. While acknowledging that abstract rights, in and of themselves, do not alter the relationship between oppressed and oppressor, feminists have begun to explore the 'dialectic' between legal formulations of rights and concrete claims made upon the system. The distinction is between uncritical use of legal loopholes for short term advantage and self-conscious strategising that takes account of our larger enterprise.

The underlying pragmatism of feminist jurisprudence develops from the requirements of good feminist methodology and theory. Feminists cannot ignore the concrete experience of women; it is the foundation of both feminist theory and practice. And theory that does not work in practice is bad theory. Thus, in its attempt to achieve the elusive goal of 'praxis', feminist jurisprudence plays both ends, but to find a middle, but to expand the repertoire of resistance.

Conclusion

Definitions of feminist jurisprudence can be either inclusive or exclusive. I have self-consciously aimed at the former. While lacking the elusive certainty of clear boundaries, inclusive definitions are far more suitable to this, and I hope every, stage of the feminist enterprise. Rather than seeking merely to distinguish ourselves from others, in the time-honoured manner of traditional male legal discourse, feminists must explore the paradox of commonality in diversity that is our experience as women. Part of the strength of the feminist jurisprudence which the Harvard Women's Law Journal has helped to foster has been the embracing of just this paradox.

What is Feminist Theory?[24]

Elizabeth Grosz

[If we continue to speak this sameness, if we speak to each other as men have spoken for centuries, as they have taught us to speak, we will fail each other. Again ... words will pass through our bodies, above our heads, disappear, make us disappear.[25]]

In the 60s, feminists began to question various images, representations, ideas and presumptions, traditional theorem developed about women and the feminine. To begin with, feminists directed their theoretical attention to patriarchal discourses, those which were either openly hostile to and aggressive about women and the feminine, or those which had nothing at all to say about women. Feminists seemed largely preoccupied with the inclusion of women in those spheres from which they had been excluded, that is, with creating representations which would enable women to be regarded as men's equals. Instead of being ignored by and excluded from theory, women were to be included as possible objects of investigation. Issues of direct relevance to women's lives – the family, sexuality, the 'private' or domestic sphere, interpersonal relations – were to be included, in some instances for the first time, as a relevant and worthy object of intellectual concern. Generally, feminists continued to rely on the methods, techniques, concepts and frameworks of traditional patriarchal theories, especially in leftist or radical form, using them to develop accounts of women's oppression. Some of the relevant names circulating in feminist discourses at the time included Marx, Reich, Marcuse, McLuhan, Laing, Cooper, Sartre, Fanon, Masters and Johnson. Women used these texts in their attempts to include women as the equals of men in the sphere of theoretical analysis, developing out of various theories of (class or race) oppression by modifying and adjusting their details in order to account for women's specific oppression.

Among the relevant features or characteristics describing this phase in the development of feminist theory could be the following:

1.   Women and the feminine become worthwhile objects of theory and research. Having been neglected, or denied value in patriarchal terms, women become focal points of empirical and theoretical investigation.

2.   Women and the feminine, as excluded or neglected objects in traditional theoretical terms, are now conceptualised as men's equals – as the same as men in relevant socio-economic and intellectual terms.

3.   While elements or components of patriarchal discourses may be criticised, questions about their more basic framework and assumptions, whether ontological, epistemological or political, remain unasked.

4.   While remaining critical toward the attitude of patriarchal discourses to the position of women, feminist theory is largely concerned with 'women's issues', those which directly affect women's lives, leaving other, 'broader' or more 'public' issues uncriticised.

5.   Patriarchal discourses were subjected to an either/or decision: either they were considered thoroughly infiltrated with patriarchal values and thus need to be rejected; or they are capable of 'rectification' so that women can now be

---

24   Elizabeth Grosz, 'What is Feminist Theory?' in Carole Pateman and Elizabeth Grosz (eds), *Feminist Challenges: Law and Social Theory* (Allen and Unwin, 1986), pp 190–205.

25   Luce Irigary, 'When Our Two Lips Speak Together', *Signs*, 6, 1, pp 69–79.

included. Patriarchal discourses, in other words, were either rejected outright or were more or less wholeheartedly accepted (with 'minor adjustments').

However, within a short period it became clear that the aim of including women as men's equals within patriarchal theory contained a number of problems not anticipated at the outset. Perhaps most strikingly, it became increasingly clear that it was not possible simply to include women in those theories where they had previously been excluded, for this exclusion forms a fundamental structuring principle and key presumption of patriarchal discourses. Many patriarchal discourses were incapable of being broadened or extended to include women without major upheavals and transformations. There was no space within the confines of these discourses to accommodate women's inclusion and equal participation. Moreover, even if women were incorporated into patriarchal discourses, at best they could only be regarded as variations of a basic humanity. The project of women's equal inclusion meant that only women's sameness to men, only women's humanity and not their womanliness could be discussed. Further, while women could now be included as the objects of theoretical speculation, their positions as the subjects or producers of knowledge was not raised. In other words, in adopting the role of the (male) subjects of knowledge, women began to assume the role of surrogate men.

As subjects of knowledge, women were faced with a dilemma. They could either remain detached from the 'objects' of their theoretical investigations (where these objects are women or femininity), in which case women may be considered to retain their 'objectivity' and, neutrality'; or women could maintain a closeness to and identification with their 'objects'. In the first case, such women, while gaining the approval of their male colleagues and possibly some position of respect within academic communities, must nevertheless disavow their own positions as women. In the second case, by their self-inclusion within the category of objects investigated, many women lose the detachment needed to be considered 'scientific' or 'objective', resulting, perhaps, in ridicule or some form of academic secondariness. Yet such women, through the risks they thus take in questioning the most general assumptions and givens of intellectual inquiry, retain some possibility of maintaining identities as women. In the long run this may have led to questioning the use and value of the distinction between subject and object, transforming the very grounds of current debate.

In abandoning such attempts to include women where theory excluded them, many feminists came to realise that the project of women's inclusion as men's equals could not succeed This was because it was not simply the range and scope of objects that required transformation: more profoundly, and threateningly, the very questions posed and the methods used to answer them, basic assumptions about methodology, criteria of validity and merit, all needed to be seriously questioned. The political, ontological and epistemological commitments underlying patriarchal discourses, as well as their theoretical contents required re-evaluation from feminist perspectives, as it became increasingly clear that women could only be included in patriarchal texts as deviant or duplicate men: the *a priori* assumptions of sameness or interchangeability, sexual neutrality or indifference, the complete neglect of women's specificities and differences, could not be accommodated in traditional theoretical terms. The whole social, political, scientific and metaphysical underpinning of patriarchal theoretical systems needed to be shaken up.

While problematic and ultimately impossible, the aspiration towards an equality between men and women was nevertheless politically and historically necessary. Without such attempts, women could not question the naturalness or seeming inevitability of women's second class status as citizens, subjects, sexual beings etc. This aim of equality served as a political, and perhaps as an experiential, prerequisite to the more far-reaching struggles directed towards female autonomy – that is, to women's right to political, social, economic and intellectual self-determination. This seems probably the most striking shift in feminist politics since its revival in the 60s.

This basic shift from a politics of equality to a politics of autonomy may have created an uneasy tension within feminist circles, for these two commitments are not necessarily compatible. Autonomy implies the right to see oneself in whatever terms one chooses – which may imply an integration or alliance with other groups and individuals or may not. Equality, on the other hand, implies a measurement according to a given standard. Equality is the equivalence of two (or more) terms, one of which takes the role of norm or model in unquestionable ways. Autonomy, by contrast, implies the right to accept or reject such norms or standards according to their appropriateness to one's self-definition. Struggles for equality imply an acceptance of given standards and a conformity to their expectations and requirements. Struggles for autonomy, on the other hand, imply the right to reject such standards and create new ones.

Feminists concerned with questions surrounding women's autonomy and self-determination are, ironically, no less concerned with the work of male or masculinist theory than their equality oriented counterparts, although the male proper names have changed significantly over the 20 year period of feminism's existence as a self-consciously political intervention into theory. The names of Freud, Lacan, Nietzsche, Derrida, Deleuze, Althusser, Foucault in France, and Richard Rorty, Anthony Wilden, Frederic Jameson, Stephen Heath, Terry Eagleton, Paul de Man etc, in England and North America constitute just some of the 'names' with which contemporary feminist theory has engaged. But what has dramatically changed is the feminist attitude towards and use of patriarchal discourses. Instead of these discourses and their methods and assumptions providing uncriticised tools and frameworks by which women could be analysed as objects, now these discourses become the objects of critical feminist scrutiny. Such discourses and methods are now tactically used without necessarily retaining general commitment to their frameworks and presumptions. Feminists do not seem so eager to slot women into pre-existing patriarchal categories and theoretical spaces; instead, it is women's lives, and experiences, that provide criteria by which patriarchal texts can be judged. Basic, unspoken assumptions of patriarchal theories, the ways in which they develop and gain precedence, their use of criteria and methods of inclusion and exclusion are all beginning to be analysed from feminist perspectives. Women asserted themselves not as objects but as subjects of knowledge with particular perspectives and points of view often systematically different from men's. Such perspectives or viewpoints are not simply 'subjective' in the sense of individual, personal or idiosyncratic positions – 'subjectivity' being seen as an interference with the 'objective' procedures of knowledge in just the same way that men's theoretical productions are a function of their lived positions in the world. The production of discourse is, for the first time, being examined as a process of sexual division and exclusion.

Feminists of autonomy can be contrasted with feminists committed to struggles of equality on at least the following points:

1.   Women become both the subjects as well as the objects of knowledge; but, in occupying the position of subject, feminists do not continue to produce knowledge as if they were men, as if knowledge were sexually indifferent.

Women's femininity is asserted as a theoretical undertaking, with a number of consequences, among them:

2. In assuming the positions of knower or subject, the methods, procedures, presumptions and techniques of theory are all put into question.

3. Feminists develop perspectives not just on or about women and women's issues' but about any object at all – including other theories, systems of representation etc.

4. Feminists don't simply assert the either/or alternative, based on 'expelling unsound' or patriarchal elements or wholesale adoption of theoretical viewpoints. Instead, while attempting to 'work through' patriarchal texts, understanding how they work and how they exert their dominances, feminists attempt to use what they can of these theories – often against themselves! No longer simply condemning or accepting certain discourses, now they are analysed, examined and questioned – actively engaged with and challenged in their operations.

5. Feminist theory challenge both the content and the frameworks of discourses, disciplines and institutions, attempting to present alternatives or develop them where they did not yet exist.

These interventions and interrogations may have produced one of the most subversive challenges to patriarchal theory that this century, or epoch, has seen: 'It is a major historical event which holds the promise of enabling a more complete challenge to domination than has yet been possible before'.[26] In the diverse disciplines constituting the social sciences and humanities, in which most feminist, theorists received their training, many matured from a position akin to apprenticeship (where women learned the skills of prevailing (masculine) forms of scholarship and research) to a position of relative self-determination (where women are able to use the techniques and skills they have acquired against the very disciplines in which they were trained). These disciplines, and the specific texts and practices associated with them, have become the objects of feminist analysis and criticism. Theory, rather than 'Woman' is now the terrain of contestation between feminists and non- or anti-feminists.

Feminist struggles for autonomy, self-determination and a viable place which women can occupy as women in the theoretical and socio-political universe have developed into a two pronged or dual faceted form. On the one hand, feminist theory has radically questioned and attempted to undermine the presumptions, methods and frameworks of phallocentric or patriarchal discourses and disciplines. On the other hand, feminist theory has simultaneously attempted to explore and develop alternatives to these phallocentric systems, bringing into being new, hitherto unarticulated, feminine perspectives on the world. In other words, today feminist theory is involved in both an anti-sexist project, which involves challenging and deconstructing phallocentric discourses; and in a positive project of constructing and developing alternative models, methods, procedures, discourses etc.

The anti-sexist project clearly implies a thorough knowledge of and familiarity with prevailing theoretical paradigms and their histories. Such an endeavour means working with, understanding and reflecting on those theoretical systems which comprise women's history and their contemporary situation, and

---

26 G Finn and A Miles (eds), *Feminism in Canada: From Pressure to Politics* (Montreal: Black Rose Books, 1982).

participating in women's oppression. Yet anti-sexism is largely negative and reactive, aiming to challenge what currently exists, what is presently dominant and responsible for women's phallocentric position in theoretical representation. Such a critical, reactive project is necessary if feminist theory is to avoid the intellectual perils of abstraction, idealisation or irrelevance. It risks projecting an ideal or utopian future for women which is unanchored in or unrelated to what exists here and now. It risks a series of commitments it may wish, on reflection, to reject. It risks repeating problems of the past without recognising them as problems or learning from them. The critical, anti-sexist project is directed against the methods, assumptions and procedures by which patriarchal discourses reduce women to a necessary dependence on men as well as against more insidious, structural expressions of misogyny, which, rather than making sexist pronouncements about women instead present perspectives on the world from a masculine point of view as if such a position were sexually neutral.

If, however, feminist theory remains simply reactive, merely a critique, paradoxically it affirms the very paradigms it seeks to contest. It remains on the very grounds it wishes to question and transform. To criticise prevailing theoretical systems without posing viable alternatives is to affirm such theoretical systems as necessary. Although feminist theory must retain a familiarity with these systems, it must also establish a theoretical distance from too close an adherence to them. If feminist theory does not extend beyond the terms of anti-sexism, it remains bound up with a politics of sameness or equality even while criticising it. The limited but strategically necessary aim of destabilising and dismantling patriarchal discourses is only the first stage or prerequisite for a more encompassing and threatening challenge to patriarchal domination – the struggle for autonomy, implying struggles for the right to different paradigms, theoretical tools, and possibly even a reconceptualisation of the entire system of knowledge and acceptable theoretical methods.

Coupled with the anti-sexist project, feminists are thus involved in the positive task of experimenting with and creating alternatives to patriarchal theoretical norms. Feminist theory can no longer be content with adapting patriarchal theories so that they are capable of analysing woman – which in itself is a phallocentric endeavour, for it reduces women to theories and categories appropriate for and developed from masculine points of view. The positive components question and displace the very foundations upon which traditional theories are based.

It cannot be specified in advance what an autonomous feminist theory would involve, for this contradicts the very idea of autonomy, the right to choose and define the world for oneself. In their diversity and multiplicity, women claim the right to define their own aims and goals. Although it cannot be specified using one or many models, feminist theory can nevertheless be outlined negatively, for it seems clear that there are a number of theoretical assumptions it would not wish to reproduce. It cannot be regarded, for example, as the reverse or opposite of patriarchal texts, transforming their objects but not their underlying assumptions. On the contrary, it attempts to move beyond them, their frameworks and their limits.

In other words, feminist theory cannot be accurately regarded as a competing or rival account, diverging from patriarchal texts over what counts as true. It is not a true discourse, nor a mere objective or scientific account. It could be appropriately seen, rather, as a strategy, a local, specific, concrete, intervention with definite political, even if provisional, aims and goals. In the 1980s, feminist theory no longer seems to seek the status of unchangeable, trans-historical and trans-geographic truth in its hypotheses and propositions. Rather, it seeks effective forms of intervention into systems of power in order to subvert them and replace them with others more preferable. Strategy implies a recognition of the current situation, in both its general, structural features (macrolithic power alignments), and its specific, detailed, regionalised forms (microlithic power investments). It needs to know the spaces and strategies of its adversaries in order to undermine their positions within an overall system. it must thus be aware of the kinds of counterstrategy or tactics used by phallocentric discourses to deploy in order to seek the points of vulnerability. All forms of strategy, in short, involve recognising what is in order to move on to what should be. Strategy always involves short term aims, seen as necessary for the achievement of longer term ideals, which themselves are capable of being modified and transformed during the processes of struggle. As a form of strategy, feminist theory needs to use whatever means are available to it, whether these are 'patriarchal' or not. Phallocentric insights, concepts and theoretical tools are evaluated in terms of their usefulness, their functioning in particular contexts, rather than in terms of an ideal but impossible purity. As strategy, it is necessarily implicated in the systems it wishes to challenge. Aspirations to a theoretical purity, a position 'untainted' by patriarchal impingements, that is, forms of theoretical separatism where patriarchal terms and practices are rejected, seem naive. They are unable to struggle with, or thus move beyond the patriarchal terms that return to haunt them. In order to challenge and move beyond patriarchal models, feminists must be able to use whatever means are at hand, including those of the very systems it challenges.

As a series of strategic interventions into patriarchal texts, feminist theory does not simply aim to reveal what is 'wrong' with, or false about, patriarchal theories – to replacing one 'truth' with another. It aims to render patriarchal systems, methods and presumptions unable to function, unable to retain their dominance and power. It aims to make clear how such a dominance has been possible; and to make it no longer viable. Since feminist theory lacks the means to directly confront a sophisticated patriarchal theoretical regime in creating alternatives, feminists have had to resort to forms of intellectual guerrilla warfare, striking out at the points of patriarchy's greatest weakness, its blindspots.[27] The grounds and terrain upon which patriarchy develops its arguments reveals their partial and partisan instead of universal or representative position. Patriarchal intellectual systems are unlikely to allow such attempts at political subversion to proceed uncontested. In fact, it is clear that traditional discourses and the positions they support have developed a series of counter-strategies and tactical response to the incursions of feminism, and indeed, women, into its fields of operation. These range from more or less personal or petty tactics to more serious, far ranging threats – from personal ridicule, ignorance, stereotyping, to forms of counterattack including wilful misrepresentation, being refused access to professional status and/or a livelihood or having one's work co-opted or neutralised. Such counterattacks are by no means mutually exclusive and are exercised with greater or lesser strength according to the degree of threat feminist theories and objections pose. Without at least some awareness of the range and ferocity of these counterattacks, feminism may be unable to effect the wide ranging subversions it seeks. It need not be committed to patriarchal discourses and their values, yet without understanding them in detail, feminists will be unable to move beyond them.

---

27 See Luce Irigaray, *Speculum of the Other Woman* (Cornell University Press, 1985).

In summary, feminist theory involves, first, a recognition of the overt and covert forms of misogyny in which discourses participate. This means developing the skills of recognising what makes these discourses patriarchal – including their explicit pronouncements about men and women, and their respective values, as well as the capacity to see how such theories divide up the world according to masculine interests. Second, it involves an ability to recognise patriarchal discourses in terms of their absences, gaps, lacunae, around the question of women and the feminine, understanding how these silences function to structure and make patriarchal discourses possible. Third, feminist theory must be capable of articulating the role that these silences and masculinist representations play in the suppression of femininity, and of affirming the possibility of other, alternative, perspectives, making patriarchal texts unable to assert their hegemony; and fourth, it must develop viable methods for superseding phallocentric systems of representation even if this means relying on patriarchal methods, using them as a starting point for new directions in theoretical research. By its very existence, such forms of feminist theory demonstrate that patriarchal discourses are not neutral, universal or unquestionable models, but are the effects of the specific (political) positions occupied by men ...

... [F]eminist theory can be provisionally located at the interface of the negative, anti-sexist project and a more positive, speculative, project. It is the refusal of a number of central values, concepts and operations necessary for the functioning of patriarchal theory, and an affirmation of the alternatives to these given forms of discourse. Among the central concepts and values questioned by feminist theory is a core of assumptions shared by most, if not all of the social sciences. In particular, it has seriously questioned patriarchal adherences to the following theoretical commitments:

1.   Commitment to a singular or universal concept of truth and methods for verifying (or falsifying) truth. Few theories aspiring to the status of scientific objectivity and truth, conventionally understood, accept their own historicity and the effects that context, environment and particular circumstances have on the production and evaluation of theory. In particular, such theoretical aspirations cannot acknowledge the costs (the silences, exclusions and invalidations) on which they are founded: in seeking the status of truth, they seek a position beyond history and outside power.

2.   Its commitments to objectivity, observer neutrality and the context – independence as unquestioned theoretical values. These are closely related to the overevaluation of science and truth as models for knowledge. Objectivity is considered as a form of interchangeability or substitutability of observers or experimenters, as a check against individual bias. This ideal of interchangeability is based on the assumption of a similarity of viewpoint and position between observers – who must be 'appropriately trained'. This assumption is necessarily blind to the different structural positions men and women occupy, their different degrees of access to suitable training, and their (possibly) different relations to their disciplines. The neutrality and universality of many patriarchal discourses presumed in the social sciences is thus sex-blind – unable to acknowledge the different social positions of men and women in presuming a neutral, interchangeable subject.

3.   The commitment to a universal subject of knowledge, a subject presumed to have certain qualities and features: the ability to separate itself from feelings, emotions, passions, personal interests and motives, socio-economic and political factors, the past, one's aspirations for the future etc. This subject of knowledge is capable of achieving a distance from the object known, thus

being able to reflect on it. It is, however, a subject incapable of accepting its own limits, its materiality and historicity, its immersion in socio-economic and political values. The subject is conceived as disembodied, rational sexually indifferent subject – a mind unlocated in space, time or constitutive interrelations with others; a status normally only attributed to angels![28]

4. The commitment to a fixed, static truth, an immutable, given reality, a guaranteed knowledge of Being and access to Reason. Such an ahistorical view cannot account for the variability and historical nature of what counts as true except in terms of a greater and greater access to and knowledge of the truth, that is, except in terms of historical views being false views. It refuses to endorse the possibility of a 'politics of truth', of the political investments in truth. Truth, as a correspondence or veridical reflection of reality, is a perspectiveless knowledge, a knowledge without a point of view – or, what amounts to the same thing, a truth claiming a universal perspective.

5. The commitment to the intertranslatability of concepts, terms, truths, propositions and discourses. As embodied in a prepositional form, knowledge 'is not regarded as dependent on its particular modes of formulation', but on the underlying thoughts it is presumed to express. Language is considered a vehicle for the communication of pre-existent thoughts or ideas. It is seen merely as a medium, a dispensable tool for the transmission of thought, rather than being seen as thought's necessary condition. In denying the materiality of language, prevailing discourses can avoid recognising their dependence on and debt to tropes, figures of speech, images, metaphors etc. evoking the feminine, women or maternity. Patriarchal discourses ignore the complicity of discursive systems with oppressive social structures, and the dependence of discourses on particular positions established by particular modes of language.

There are, of course, many positive features that can be briefly sketched out in general ways which do not pre-empt women's various attempts at self-determination. Included among them are:

1. Intellectual commitments, not to truth, objectivity and neutrality, but to theoretical positions openly acknowledged as observer and context-specific. Rather than deny its spatio-temporal conditions and limits, feminist theory accepts and affirms them, for they are its *raison d'etre*. Following Nietzsche, it seems prepared to avow its own perspectivism, its specific position of enunciation, its being written from a particular point of view, with specific aims and goals.

2. In acknowledging its conditions of production, feminist theory seems prepared to question the value of the criteria of objectivity and scientificity so rigidly and imperialistically accepted by intellectual orthodoxies. This is not, however, an admission of any 'subjective bias'. The very distinction between objective (knowledge) and subjective (opinion) is put into question. Feminists seem prepared to accept that the knower always occupies a position, spatially, temporally, sexually and politically. This is a corollary of its perspectivism. It is neither subjective nor objective, neither absolute nor relative. These alternatives, for one thing, cannot explain the productive investments of power in the production of knowledges. This does not, however, mean that feminist theory used no criteria of evaluation or self-

---

28 *cf* Luce Irigaray, *L'Ethique de la Différence Sexuelle* (Paris: Minuit).

reflection. Rather, its norms of judgment are developed from inter-subjective, shared effects and functions; and in terms of a discourse's intertexual functions, its capacity to either undermine or affirm various dominant systems and structures.

3. Instead of presuming a space or gulf between the rational, knowing subject and the object known, feminist theory acknowledges the contiguity between them. Prevailing views of the rational subject posit a subject artificially and arbitrarily separated from its context. This creates a distance required for its separation from the emotions, passions, bodily interferences, relations with others and the socio-political world. Feminist theory seems openly prepared to accept the constitutive interrelations of the subject, its social position and its mediated relation to the object. For feminists (in so far as they uphold such a notion) the rational subject is not free of personal, social and political interests, but is necessarily implicated in them. Theories are seen as sexualised, as occupying a position in relation to the qualities and values associated with the two sexes, or the attributes of masculinity, and femininity. But to claim a sexualisation of discourses and knowledges is not to equate the discourse's position with that of its author or producer; there is no (direct) correspondence between feminine or feminist texts and female authors, or between phallocentric texts and male authors. The sexual 'position of the text' can only be discerned contextually and in terms of the position which the speaking subject, (the implicit or explicit 'I' of the text), speaks from; the kind of subject (implicitly) presumed as the subject spoken to (or audience), and the kind of subject spoken about (or object). As well as the range of various subjects posited in any or all texts, the text's position also depends on the kind of relations asserted between these different subjects. In the case of feminist theory, the subject, object and audience are not dichotomously divided into mutually exclusive and mutually exhaustive categories (subject/object, knower-master/ignorant-disciple, teacher/pupil, self/other etc) but may be defined more in terms of continuities and/or differences. The speaking subject, the subject spoken to and the subject spoken about may be equated; but in any case, there is a constitutive interrelatedness presumed between all three terms. This means, for example and to take a concrete case, that men do not speak with greater objectivity about women's oppression, as some male academics recently asserted with great sincerity. Men too are necessarily implicated in and part of women's oppression. It is of course clear that their relations to such oppression must be very different from women's. In short, particular interests are served by every theoretical position and in any textual or discursive system. The politics or 'power' of the text cannot, however, be automatically read off from what the text overtly says, but, more frequently from how it says it, what is invoked, and what is thus effected. Feminist theory has the merit over prevailing discursive systems of being able not only to accept but to actively affirm its own political position(s) and aspirations, to accept that, far from being objective in the sense of 'disinterested' and 'unmotivated', it is highly motivated by the goals and strategies involved in creating an autonomy for women. Such motivation or purposiveness, however, does not invalidate feminist theory, but is its acknowledged function, its rationale.

4. Because it refuses to accept the pre-given values of truth, objectivity, universality, neutrality and an abstract reason, feminist theory – along with some contemporary male theorists is not committed to or motivated by these values. It sees itself in terms of a critical and constructive strategy. It is neither abstraction, blueprint nor handbook for action, nor a distanced form

72

of reflection. These views for one thing, imply a theory outside or beyond practice. In questioning the dichotomous conceptualisation of the relation between theory and practice, feminist theory considers itself both a 'theoretical practice' – a practice at the level of theory itself, a practice bound up with yet critical of the institutional frameworks within which the production of theoretical discourses usually occurs, a practice involving writing, reading, teaching, learning, assessment and numerous other rituals and procedures; as well, it is a 'practical theory' – a theory openly seen as a part of practice, a tool or tactic playing a major part in the subversive, often dangerous assault on one particular site of the functioning of patriarchal power relations – the sphere of knowledge, which provides patriarchy with rationalisations and justifications for its ever expanding control. Feminist theory is an interweaving of strands that are simultaneously theoretical and practical. It is a site where dominant discourses, subjugated discourses, voices hitherto silenced or excluded, forms of coercion and control as well as concerted forms of resistance are able to be worked through in relation to each other. It is a threshold for the intervention of theories within concrete practices, and the restructuring of theory by the imperatives of experience and practice, a kind of hinge or doorway between the two domains. In aiming at a destruction of misogynistic theory and its fundamental assumptions and at establishing a positive influence on day-to-day and structural interactions between the sexes, it is neither a prelude to practice, nor a reflection on practice because it is already a form of practice within a specific region of patriarchy's operations.

5. Feminist theory, similarly, cannot be conceived in terms of the categories of rationality or irrationality. Since at least the 17th century, if not long before, reason has been understood in dichotomous terms, being characterised oppositionally and gaining its internal coherence only by the exclusion of its 'others' – the passions, the body, the emotions, nature, faith, materiality, dreaming, experience, perception, madness or many other terms. In questioning this binary mode of categorisation, feminists demonstrated that reason is a concept associated with the norms and values of masculinity, and its opposites, or 'others', with femininity. Feminist theory today is not simply interested in reversing the values of rational/irrational or in affirming what has been hierarchically subordinated, but more significantly, in questioning the very structure of binary categories. In short, feminist theory seeks to transform and extend the concept of reason so that instead of excluding concepts like experience, the body, history, etc, these are included within it or acknowledged as necessary for reason to function. In taking women's experiences and lives as a starting point for the development of theory, feminism attempts to develop alternatives to the rigid, hierarchical and exclusive concept of reason. It seeks a rationality not divided from experience, from oppression, from particularity or specificity; a reason, on the contrary, that includes them is a rationality not beyond or above experience but based upon it.

6. In challenging phallocentrism, feminist theory must also challenge the evasion of history and materiality so marked in theoretical traditions in the West. In conceiving of itself as a rational, private, individual activity and struggle towards truth and knowledge, a pure, intellectual activity, it must also deny its status as a historical and political product. Predominant theoretical traditions refuse to accept their dependence on the materiality of writing, on practices involved in training, producing, publishing and promoting certain methods, viewpoints and representatives, on struggles for

authority and domination. In opposition to these prevailing theoretical ideals, feminist theory openly acknowledges its own materiality as the materiality of language (language being seen as a weapon of political struggle, domination and resistance), of desire (desire as the will to achieve certain arrangements of potentially satisfying 'objects' – the desire for an identity, a sexuality and a recognised place in culture being the most clear-cut and uncontentious among feminists) and of power (power not just as a force visible in the acts, events and processes within political and public life, but also as a series of tactical alignments between institutions, knowledges, practices involved with the control and supervision of individuals and groups); in more particular terms, the alignments of male socioeconomic domination with the forms of learning, training, knowledge, and theory.

7. In rejecting leading models of intellectual inquiry (among them, the requirements of formal logic, the structuring of concepts according to binary oppositional structures, the use of grammar and syntax for creating singular, clear, unambiguous, precise modes of articulation and many other assumed textual values), and its acceptance of the idea of its materiality as theory, feminist theory is involved in continuing explorations of and experimentation with new forms of writing, new methods of analysis, new positions of enunciation, new kinds of discourse.

No one method, form of writing, speaking position, mode of argument can act as representative, model or ideal for feminist theory. Instead of attempting to establish a new theoretical norm, feminist theory seeks a new discursive space, a space where women can write, read and think as women. This space will encourage a proliferation of voices, instead of a hierarchical structuring of them, a plurality of perspectives and interests instead of the monopoly of the one – new kinds of questions and different kinds of answer. No one form would be privileged as the truth, the correct interpretation, the right method; rather, knowledges, methods, interpretations can be judged and used according to their appropriateness to a given context, a specific strategy and particular effects.

Feminist theory is capable of locating itself historically, materially, enunciatively and politically in relation to patriarchal structures. During its development over the last 25 years it has emerged as a capacity to look at women in new, hitherto unexplored ways by refusing to reduce and explain women's specificity to terms that are inherently masculine; it has developed the ability to look at any object from the point of view of perspectives and interests of women, of understanding and going beyond phallocentrism in developing different kinds of theory and practice. This description may sound like an idealised or utopian version of what a self-conscious and politically committed, active and informed theoretical practice should involve. Perhaps. It is not yet clear how far along this utopian path feminist discourses have come. But as the essays published here testify, feminist theory is in the process of developing along these diverse trajectories. It is in the process of reassessing the theoretical heritage it needs to supersede in order to claim a future for itself. This future may initiate a new theoretical epoch, one capable of accepting the full implications of acknowledging sexual difference. Theory in the future would be seen as sexual, textual, political and historical production. Although this may threaten those who adhere to the values of phallocentrism, it may open up hitherto unimagined sites, sources and tools for theoretical exploration. An autonomous femininity may introduce, for the first time in our recorded history, the possibility of dialogue with an 'alien voice', the voice of woman.

FEMINIST JURISPRUDENCE: ILLUSION OR REALITY?[29]
Margaret Thornton

... A feminist perspective corrodes the very essence of liberal legalism with its assumptions of universalism, equality and neutrality. Not only does it highlight the falsity of these assumptions, but a feminist analysis brings out the inner core of meaning of an act for women, it rejects the high level of abstraction. Indeed, the experiential dimension may be all important.[30]

A feminist approach to law must also challenge the hegemonic, sex-based structures of capitalist formation. The fragility of recent feminist gains must alert us to be ever watchful, for it is a function of legalism to constrain and hedge in the political gains of women in order to protect and maintain the *status quo*.

Feminism, therefore, seeks to create a new vision of the world from the perspective of women: it is not content to accept the male standard as an objective and universal truth which purports to encompass all. The iconoclasm of feminist critiques of the substance and form of law are necessary steps towards comprehending the role of the law in effecting the perversion of the feminine in its portrayal as a homogeneous and inferior standard. Feminist scholarship, then, aims to be 'perspective transforming'.[31]

However, is this new feminist perspective, acquired as a result of the unmasking of the mystique of law, sufficient to constitute a feminist jurisprudence? Jurisprudence is defined as 'the science or philosophy of law' and, as Judith Shkear has pointed out, analytical jurisprudence is 'solely a science of definitions':

> The major part of any work entitled 'jurisprudence' consists of demonstrations of the 'real meaning of such terms as right, duty, tort, crime, and contract'.[32]

The focus of jurisprudence, as it is presently understood, tends to be directed towards the exposition of the law as it is within narrow, positivistic parameters. There is little understanding of the study of law as an interdisciplinary, contextual and critical exercise, for it is accepted that the law in itself is a complete entity which is capable of producing 'right' answers.

The language of liberal jurisprudence reflects a society of free and equal individuals who act as independent, self-defining agents. As has been pointed out throughout this paper, the seeds of invidiousness which attach to women as inferiors and as inhabitants of the private sphere have denied us access to this society of equals. Law has underpinned and legitimised this exclusion, and liberal jurisprudence ignores the way that the ideology of law operates to isolate law from the social context in which it exists. Since this ideology serves a functional purpose, jurisprudence is likely to be just as unresponsive to feminism as it has been to challenge by other social and intellectual movements such as Marxism, Legal Realism and the contemporary Critical Legal Studies movement, all of which have been assiduous in their task of deconstructing the specific doctrines of liberal legalism. So elusive is the theoretical task of inquiry, let alone

---

29 Margaret Thornton, 'Feminist Jurisprudence: Illusion or Reality' (1986) 3 *Australian Journal of Law and Society* 5.

30 KA Lahey, *Until Women Themselves Have Told All there is to Tell* (1986).

31 M Strathern, 'Dislodging a World View: Challenge and Counter-Challenge in the Relationship between Feminism and Antropology' (1985) 1 *Australian Feminist Studies* 1.

32 J Shklar, *Legalism* (Harvard University Press, 1964).

the task of transformation, that Stewart depicts the efforts of (nonfeminist) sociologists of law as producing no more than a looking glass effect:

> But through the looking glass the sociologist can glimpse the carcasses of the attempts that since the Renaissance have repeatedly been made, then one after another abandoned, to enrich jurisprudence itself with a specific study of society.[33]

Though a feminist jurisprudential telos may be recondite, there is a danger that, if feminists are too assiduous in compressing feminist scholarship into a traditional jurisprudential framework in the short term, it may lose its critical edge. Scales' article 'Towards a Feminist Jurisprudence' would seem to be an example of this somewhat overly cautious approach.[34] Scales does not set out to postulate a theory of law, as she herself acknowledges, but to demonstrate 'the necessity of making a feminist evaluation of our jurisprudence and of taking a jurisprudential view of feminism'. While she recognises the fallacy inherent in the liberal vision, that is, the maleness of the norm of equality, her analysis focuses on the sex-unique problems arising from pregnancy and breast feeding, as revealed in a number of American Supreme Court cases. Dismissing both the liberal view and the assimilationist view which seeks to minimise sexual difference, Scales proposes her own 'incorporationist' approach which would recognise women's uniqueness in respect of female sex specificity.

It would seem, however, that a focus on reproductive differences alone is too limited to constitute a 'feminist jurisprudence' because it does no more than reaffirm women's association with nature and nurture, although it is recognised that it could have the potential to expose the law to the politics of reproduction, a fundamental area of human endeavour hitherto invisible. The conflation of women and reproduction is nevertheless overly restrictive, because it suggests a nonexistent homogeneity amongst women. Indeed, the Scales' model does not appear to be visibly different from conventional liberal jurisprudence which is able to accommodate sex-based differential treatment in cases where to do otherwise might be conceptualised as irrational, an asseveration which is ultimately damaging to the rule of law.

A transformative vision requires not just that women be 'let in' to existing male society with a perspective on 'women's issues', but that the entire gamut of human jurisprudence be reappraised to take cognisance of the feminine. The focus on reproductive differences alone has the effect of perennially confining women to the margin and otherwise accepting the continued irrelevance of women to public sphere concerns. The meretricious claim to universalism of the prevailing androcentrism would consequently remain unchallenged.

Feminist legal scholarship, in common with the feminist project generally, has the twin aims of challenging the existing norms and of devising a new agenda for theory:

> In other words, today's feminist theory is involved in both an anti-sexist project, which involves challenging and deconstructing phallocentric discourses; and in a positive project of constructing and developing alternative models, methods, procedures, discourses, etc.[35]

---

33 I Stewart, 'Sociology in Jurisprudence: The Problem of Law as Object of Knowledge', in B Fryer (ed), *Law, State and Society* (Croom Helm, 1981).

34 AC Scales, 'Towards a Feminist Jurisprudence' (1981) 56 *Indiana LJ* 375 (extracted in Chapter 4).

35 Elizabeth Grosz, *op cit* (extracted above).

Given the fact, however, that women have been entirely excluded from a legal tradition which spans several millennia, it is ingenuous to imagine that a fully fledged feminist jurisprudence is likely to spring forth from the feminist movement instantaneously. Such naivety also fails to acknowledge that the impenetrability of the carapace of autonomy which envelopes the law and immunises it against challenge is such that a transformed gynocentric jurisprudence must necessarily remain elusive – at least for the time being.

EVOLUTION AND FLUX IN FEMINIST JURISPRUDENCE

The feminist legal movement at first centred on the specific detailed areas of legal discrimination against women. For example, writers such as Albie Sachs and Joan Hoff Wilson provided an early comparative analysis of the legal position of women in the United Kingdom and in the United States of America.[36] Susan Atkins and Brenda Hoggett concentrated upon the idea of legal equality – or inequality – in employment law, in relation to the role of women within the traditional family and the position of women under the Welfare State and in relation to citizenship.[37] Katherine O'Donovan analysed the liberal dichotomy of society into 'public' and 'private' spheres and examined the problem of the legal position of women in relation to the family,[38] and subsequently, in conjunction with Erika Szyszczac analysed the notion of legal equality in employment law and practice.[39] Carol Smart has also analysed the legal position of women under English family law.[40] By concentrating on specific areas of the law, the writers of this phase of legal feminism unmasked the myth of law's gender neutrality and simultaneously pressed the case for legal equality. The task is not yet finished. In *Law and the Sexes*, Ngaire Naffine explains the concerns of this 'first phase feminism'.

LAW AND THE SEXES[41]
Ngaire Naffine[42]

The largest body of feminist work on law is about the pursuit of formal equality for women: from the acquisition of citizenship to the introduction of anti-discrimination legislation. It describes a male monopoly in the public sphere which a male controlled law has supported systematically. Its goal has been the removal of legal constraints on women to compete freely with men in the marketplace.

---

36 Albie Sachs and Joan Hoff Wilson, *Sexism and The Law: A Study of Male Beliefs and Judicial Bias* (Martin Robertson, 1978).

37 Susan Atkins and Brenda Hoggett, *Women and The Law* (Blackwell, 1984).

38 Katherine O'Donovan, *Sexual Divisions in Law* (Weidenfeld and Nicolson, 1985).

39 Erika Szyszczac, *Equality and Sex Discrimination Law* (Blackwell, 1988).

40 Carol Smart, *The Ties That Bind* (Routledge & Kegan Paul, 1984).

41 Ngaire Naffine, *Law and the Sexes* (Allen and Unwin, 1990).

42 At the time of writing, Research Fellow, University of Adelaide and Visiting Scholar, Australian National University.

This first phase of writing contends that legal men have used their position of dominance to keep the public sphere a male preserve.[43] In the courts and in the parliaments, men have actively sought to exclude women from positions of influence. the aim of feminists is thus to have women placed fully on the legal agenda, to have full rights extended to women.

A distinguishing feature of the first phase is its tendency to accept, and approve, law's own account of itself when it is not dealing with women. Law is seen therefore to be essentially a rational and fair institution concerned with the arbitration of conflicting rights between citizens. The problem with law is that it has not yet developed full and effective public rights for women. It was once overtly discriminatory. Today it indirectly denies women rights by constituting a subordinate, domestic role for them in the private sphere.

In the first-phase analysis, the present character and outlook of law is largely left intact. They prevailing idea is accepted that law should be (and can be) impartial and reasoned. The objection is to the failure of law to adhere to its own professed standards when it invokes discriminatory laws and practices. That is, the objection is to bad law.[44]

Ngaire Naffine evaluates the work of first phase feminism as follows:

Notwithstanding subsequent developments in feminist legal thinking which (as we will see) have greatly extended the challenge of the first-phase theorists, it would be wrong to see this early work as fatally flawed by the limitations of its vision, as too short-sighted in its focus on the male personnel of law. The contribution of the first phase to women's struggle for legal change has been considerable. Not only does it represent the first feminist excavation into the male foundations of law, the first archaeological dig, but its challenge to male dominance of legal institutions and to discriminatory legislation has been instrumental in reshaping and reforming much of the law for women. Indeed one writer [Susan Moller Okin] goes so far as to say that it represents 'the single most important feminist legal strategy ... the theoretical underpinning of the entire women's rights movement in law'. By demonstrating how laws which constrain only one of the sexes, and seem to work for the benefit of the other, fail to meet the law's own self-professed standards (of fairness, rationality and impartiality), it has indicted law on its own terms and supplied the intellectual framework for women's demands for equal treatment. Its sustained attack on legal sexism have also come close to winning for women formal equality within the substantive law.[45, 46]

The feminist legal movement has developed further from the specific task of unmasking the reality of law as gendered and unequal, although much remains to be achieved in that regard. In 'second phase feminism' the idea that law is gender-neutral, essentially good but in need of realignment to accommodate women's claims to equality under law, is rejected. Feminism has moved on to look at 'law' in the abstract, and considering its essential characteristics. The concern here is less with individual substantive rules of law and their justice or

---

43   On the public/private dichotomy see Chapter 5

44   Ngaire Naffine, *op cit*, pp 3–4.

45   *Ibid*, p 6.

46   See also K O'Donovan, 'Fem-Legal and Socio-Legal: An Incompatible Relationship', in P Thomas (ed), *Reviewing Socio-Legal Studies* (Dartmouth, 1996).

otherwise in relation to women, but rather with law in its entirety. Ngaire Naffine explains:

LAW AND THE SEXES[47]
Ngaire Naffine

The second-phase feminists are more swingeing in their critique of law's claim to impartiality and justice for all. These are merely high-minded principles which legal men have employed as protective cover. They obscure law's actual partiality: its preference for men and their view of the world. The truth is that men have fashioned a legal system in their own image. They have developed a harsh, uncaring, combative, adversarial style of justice which essentially reflects their own way of doing things and therefore quite naturally advantages the male litigant. Law treats people as unfeeling automatons, as selfish individuals who care only for their own rights and who feel constantly under threat from other equally self-absorbed holders of rights. This is a male view of society, they say, which ignores and devalues the priorities of women – those of human interdependence, human compassion and human need.

Second-phase feminists also take issue with law's conception of its own objectivity. This is a highly suspect notion, they say, not just because it has been used as a smoke screen to conceal male bias but because it invokes a particular approach to a social world with which many feminists take issue. Law's objectivity, they say, seeks to invoke a detached, dispassionate approach to social conflict. In the rhetoric of law, impartiality is secured by the maintenance of a healthy distance between the 'fact-finder' and the subjects of the dispute. This is the means by which judges maintain their closely guarded neutrality and hence their objectivity. To second-phase feminists, detachment may not be the best approach to resolving disputes: involvement and close proximity to the subject may be better ... .[48]

The proposition that law is imbued with the culture of men moves beyond the claim that law is made by men and therefore tends to entrench their position of dominance. The indictment is more far-reaching. Law, it is said, is conceived through the male eye; it represents the male perspective. It starts from the male experience and fails to recognise the female view ... .

There is little point in seeking to improve women's position within this masculine legal framework: it has no room for women. What is needed is social revolution, not reform.[49]

From the radicalism of this second phase, feminist scholars have moved into the inquiry concerning the relevance of law to a patriarchal society. Postmodernism, characterised by its rejection of all-encompassing ground theory and the admission of doubt, uncertainty and fragmentation has exerted a heavy influence on recent feminist jurisprudential thought. Ngaire Naffine explains:

Third-phase feminist theory concedes that law is both male-dominated and full of biases, one of which pertains to the sex of the litigant. However, it resists the

---

47 Ngaire Naffine, *op cit*.

48 *Ibid*, p 7.

49 *Ibid*, pp 7–8.

notion that law represents male interests in anything like a coordinated or uniform fashion. The reason is that law is not the coherent, logical, internally consistent and rational body of doctrine it professes to be. Part of the feminist challenge here is to the very concepts law has employed to represent itself as a fair and impartial institution. Law, they say, is not to be regarded – as it has traditionally – as a neutral and dispassionate institution which accordingly resolves disputes and organises social relations justly. The various epithets conventionally used to describe law, such as 'rational', 'autonomous' and principled', are in fact male legal ideals. They describe a set of qualities to which men might aspire but they are not, and could not be, the truth of law because nothing is life is every organised in this way. Vital dimensions of human existence, dimensions conventionally associated with women, are missing from law's depiction of itself. The reality of law is that it is 'as irrational, subjective, concrete and contextualised as it is rational, objective, abstract and principled'.[50]

Another concern of the third-phase feminists is to show that while law presents itself as autonomous and value-neutral, the truth is that law reflects the priorities of the dominant patriarchal social order, priorities which are themselves not always coherent or consistent but which generally constitute women as the subordinate sex. Also central to third-phase feminism is an explicit rejection of grand theory and a commitment to the study of particular instances of law's oppression of women.

Theorising about law and society has thus taken centre stage. Building upon the empirical data without which no such movement would have been possible, feminist jurists nowadays are seeking to synthesise the work, to place it within theoretical context and to explore feminist jurisprudence both as a discrete discipline, and as an alternative to traditional jurisprudence. Parallels may here be drawn with the evolution of sociological jurisprudence. Traditional jurisprudence has seen a similar evolution. From an analysis of laws and legal systems, and the systematisation of legal thought through legal positivism, attention turned to the exploration of the role of law in society and the interconnectedness and interdependence of law and society. The sociology of law movement explored law as a phenomenon employing the techniques of sociological empirical research. Contemporaneously, jurists were theorising about their own discipline – seeking to understand the role of law, the significance or otherwise of law as an instrument, the potential for law as a means of social change, and sociological jurisprudence occupies a central place in late 20th century thinking about law from a theoretical perspective.

Carol Smart has also critically assessed the need for – and desirability of – considering the position of women from a broader conceptual standpoint.[51] Smart cautions also against an overemphasis on law as a mechanism through which an advance in the position of women in society will be achieved – arguing that we should take care not to overestimate the power of law. It is a natural, but not necessarily desirable, assumption on the part of lawyers that law alone can produce social change. Smart argues that law 'has an overinflated view of itself', and by concentrating on law alone, feminist legal theorists may

50 F Olsen, 'The Family and the Market: A Study of Ideology and Legal Reform' [1984] 96 *Harvard Law Review*, p 156.
51 Carol Smart, *Feminism and the Power of Law* (Routledge and Kegal Paul, 1989).

fall into a self-limiting trap which obviates the need to view the position of women in far broader terms than law alone. Notwithstanding that caveat, the power of law to affect and determine social relations between individuals in society must be acknowledged. Whilst law is culturally dependent, and will reflect traditionally – socially/culturally – and politically determined social relationships, law possesses unique transformatory power – at least in the superficial regulation of relations in society, if not the power to alter consciousness within society.

FEMINISM AND THE POWER OF LAW[52]
Carol Smart[53]

Law's Power

The aspect of power I have focused on has been in terms of law as a discourse which is able to refute and disregard alternative discourses and to claim a special place in the definition of events. My concern has been with law as a system of knowledge rather than simply as a system of rules – although these two things are clearly related if one accepts that knowledge creates the potential to exercise power (ie through rules). In the first chapter I took issue with Foucault's formulation of the place of law (or the system of juridical rights) as a mode of regulation which is likely to diminish as disciplinary mechanisms (ie psychiatry) develop. He posits two modes of 'contrivances' of power, the 'old' form which is juridical power and the 'new' forms of discipline, surveillance, and regulational. He suggests that the old form will be gradually colonised by the new. However, whilst I accept that there are examples of this colonisation, I have also suggested that the process may work both ways and that the power of law may be enhanced by harnessing disciplinary modes to traditional legal methods by extending law into new terrains created by new techniques. The main example I provided of this was the way in which reproductive technologies have created the potential for new biological and social relationships and how this has created a new field in which law can apply its traditional tenets. I have suggested that rather than abandoning the field to the doctors and social workers or psychiatrists, law has striven to define the parameters of new relationships and that the creation of 'new' arenas has led to an extension of law into more and more intimate areas of personal life. Hence whilst medicine has the power to disorganise the patriarchal family, law has striven to ensure that it does not. The freezing of human embryos, for example, has not preoccupied the psychiatrists and social workers nearly so much as the lawyers who wish to define ownership and inheritance rights and to impose a legitimate family structure on the human tissue.

I am therefore less certain that law's traditional power is diminishing; rather there is a symbiotic relationship between the two modes (of discipline and of rights) and it cannot be presumed that law's part in this will diminish. This raises a dilemma, however, for it law's power is extending it seems to call for greater attention from feminism, not less.

De-centring Law

There have always been two components to feminism's engagement with law. One has been to resist legal changes which appear detrimental to women, the

---

52 *Ibid.*
53 At the time of writing, Lecturer in Sociology, University of Warwick.

other has been to use law to promote women's interests. The latter increases legislative provisions and empowers law, the former withstands damaging changes but only maintains the status quo. In terms of practical politics these strategies have often been reactive and ad hoc and they do not appear to reflect any coherent feminist analysis of law.

It is therefore important to develop a clearer vision of law. In Chapter Four I have argued against the idea of a theory of law and the development of a totalising theory such as that to be found in early Marxist analysis of law or some feminist analyses. The problem which then arises is whether, without such a general theory, it is ever possible to develop anything other than ad hoc tactics. Yet this is really a false problem. General theories never provide clear tactics, they are always open to interpretation precisely because the general theory operates at a level of considerable abstraction. So it is just as valuable to consider in detail how law operates in different fields and to analyse it its specificity rather than generality. In consequence the vision of law I have outlined is not one that is unified but refracted. That is to say that law does not have one single appearance, it is different according to whether one refers to statute law, judge-made law, administrative law, the enforcement of law, and so on. It is also refracted in that it is frequently contradictory even at the level of statute. Hence legislation to preserve foetal life coexists with legislation which provides therapeutic abortions. Different legislation may have, therefore, quite differing goals; it cannot be said to have a unified aim. The law is also refracted in the sense that it has different applications according to who attempts to use it. For example, migrant families using the 'right to family life' against repressive governments which prevent such families from living together indicates the progressive potential of law. For individual men to use the 'right to family life' against individual women in order to defeat women's autonomy is quite a different matter. Finally law may have quite different effects depending on who is the subject of the law. Hence abortion laws may have different meanings for black or native women on whom abortions are pressed, than for white women who feel they can exercise 'choice'. So if law does not stand in one place, have one direction, or have one consequence, it follows that we cannot develop one strategy or one policy in relation to it.

It also follows that we cannot predict the outcome of any individual law reform. Indeed the main dilemma for any feminist engagements with law is the certain knowledge that, once enacted, legislation is in the hands of individuals and agencies far removed from the values of the women's movement. So does this lead to the conclusion that law should be left unchallenged? This is not the position to which I believe my analysis inevitably leads. My conclusion is that feminism needs to engage with law for purposes other than law reform and with a clear insight into the problems of legitimating a mode of social regulation which is deeply antithetical to the myriad concerns and interest of women.

Precisely because law is powerful and is, arguably, able to continue to extend its influence, it cannot go unchallenged. However, it is law's power to define and disqualify which should become the focus of feminist strategy rather than law reform as such. It is in its ability to redefine the truth of events that feminism offers political gains. Hence feminism can (re)define harmless flirtation into sexual harassment, misplaced paternal affection into child sexual abuse, enthusiastic seduction into rape, foetal rights into enforced reproduction, and so on. Moreover the legal forum provides an excellent place to engage this process of redefinition. At the point at which law asserts its definition, feminism can assert its alternative. Law cannot be ignored precisely because of its power to define, but feminism's strategy should be focused on this power rather than on constructing legal policies which only legitimate the legal forum and the form of law. This strategy does not preclude other forms of direct action or policy formation. For example, it is important to sustain an emphasis on nonlegal strategies and local struggles. However, it is important to resist the temptation that law offers, namely the promise of a solution. It is equally important to challenge the power of law and to insist on the legitimacy of feminist knowledge and feminism's ability to redefine the wrongs of women which law too often confines to insignificance.[54]

Carol Smart thus reveals an ambivalence towards the law, in part recognising law's power, in part arguing against too great a reliance on law and legal strategies. The dangers of overreliance on law as a mechanism for social change have been identified and analysed by sociological jurists: there are well documented limits to the power of law.[55] However, what must also be given adequate recognition is the successes which have been achieved through the analysis of discrimination under the law and the pressure for change in the law which has been effected by feminist scholars. The work undertaken in what Ngaire Naffine describes as 'first wave feminism' cannot be underestimated in its importance for securing greater equality for women. The legal disabilities of women in relation to property ownership and control; the position of women in the family; the position of women in employment have all been significantly advanced by the pressure for legal reform. Discrimination still exists – particularly in the field of employment[56] – but great advances have been made, and the role of feminist legal scholars must be recognised and applauded. Law may be a blunt instrument in securing changing social attitudes relating to deeply entrenched prejudicial attitudes, whether they be racist or sexist. Law, however, sets the standard for appropriate attitudes; provides the mechanisms for the redress of grievances where actual behaviour and the required legal standard of behaviour part company. To 'de-centre' law, or to apparently reduce in importance the role of law, is to ignore too great a part of feminist scholarship. The pioneering work of 'first phase' feminist lawyers who explored the discrimination within law and contributed to the movement towards equality should not be underestimated in its importance. That most formal legal inequality between the sexes has been removed in, for example, employment law and family law, is a direct consequence of the feminist endeavour. Moreover, de-emphasising the importance of law is to ignore the very real need for legal rights and remedies in the face of discrimination. The maxim 'no remedy without a right' must be borne in mind. Whilst this is true for society in general, it is particularly significant for those citizens who have traditionally been regarded as second class members of society – women and minority groups. Law must remain as a focal weapon in the support of rights, and as a tool for developing further the realisation of real equality between the sexes. For these reasons, the 'de-centreing' of law – a central tenet of the Critical Legal

---

54 *Ibid*, pp 162–65.
55 See for example, A Allott, *The Limits of Law* (Butterworths, 1980); RBM Cotterrell *The Sociology of Law: An Introduction* (Butterworths, 1984).
56 For example in the restrictive attitude towards women in the armed forces.

Studies movement[57] – which is suggested by Carol Smart and by critical legal theorist has not been universally welcomed by feminist scholars.[58]

A powerful argument against the 'de-centreing of law' has been made, for example, by the black feminist scholar Patricia Williams. In *The Alchemy of Race and Rights*,[59] Patricia Williams portrays her experience as a black female American, contrasting it with the experience of her white male colleague. Whereas her colleague – in the matter of renting a property – felt little need for the formalities of contract, Patricia Williams regarded legal formalities as an essential process through which she could achieve her objective: for her 'rights' and the language of rights is a fundamentally important and empowering concept. Without legal rights, she argues, black Americans – and particularly black female Americans – are unable to achieve equal treatment. From this perspective, law is and must remain centre stage.

In the article which follows, Anne Bottomley critically analyses the position which Carol Smart adopts in relation to feminism and legal theory[60] and considers the difficulties inherent in the relationship between feminist legal scholarship and traditional legal theory.

FEMINISM, THE DESIRE FOR THEORY AND THE USE OF LAW[61]

Anne Bottomley[62]

> '... the field of law poses quite specific problems for feminist theory which may not be found in other fields...'[63]

What am I? A woman. A feminist. A lawyer working in the academy. In my everyday work I teach – in the areas of property law and equity and trusts. In all aspects of my work I am aware of myself as both woman and feminist. Indeed I entered my area of work specifically because of my gender and my commitment to feminism. How then does my feminism inform my work? How far does my work inform my feminism? I find these questions very difficult and realise, even as I pose them, that generally it is so much easier to presume at least one fixed referent than to have to recognise that I am not at all sure what I mean by 'my feminism', let alone the (many) ways in which it informs (or is informed by) my work.

For us, as academics, the projects of utilising our work for feminism and bringing our feminism into the academy leads us straight into a demand 'for theory'. Indeed recent feminist work has increasingly addressed the problem of what specifically *feminist* theory might be, rather than simply the utilisation of existing theoretical paradigms. I was very interested in a piece published in *Feminist Legal Studies* by an Australian feminist, Shelley Wright, in which she very honestly

---

57 See Chapter 8
58 See further, Chapter 8
59 Harvard University Press, 1991.
60 In Carol Smart, 'The Women of Legal Discourse' (1992) *Social and Legal Studies*, p 29
61 Seminar paper, European University Institute, Florence, 1993.
62 School of Law, University of Kent.
63 Carol Smart, 'The Women of Legal Discourse' (1992) *Social and Legal Studies*, p 29.

worried through the problem of how far 'feminist' theoretical work had been predicated within dominant theoretical discourses:

> It is not surprising that modern secular feminism should have followed the paths that modern secular masculine revolutions have taken. We have no other models. We are our fathers' daughters, undutiful or otherwise.[64]

Her concern to consider the possibility of an authentically feminist theory has become a familiar problem to us. For the moment I just want to approach the issue through the problem of the practice of theory itself. I want to draw out what I think are two quite different imperatives which often become confused in our work. The first is the development of theory within the imperative of the academy. It is a demand for inclusion; it is derived from our identity as academics, which is *then* fed by our identities as women and as feminists. The second imperative is the use of our work as a resource for feminism – for productive change. For making futures possible for ourselves as women; a world of different gender relations. Some of us are sometimes lucky enough to be able to move with these imperatives in one direction, in which the latter is privileged and the former simply benefits. But too often for most of us it is the former which compels our work into an engagement with theory; even though we would prefer not to recognise this. This is the way in which we will achieve recognition within the academy, in which we might be given a space in which we can even afford to present ourselves as feminist. Indeed in recent years, in England at least, it has become a means of advancement for women academics, as well as a palliative in some faculties for men searching for new theoretical paradigms as they bear witness to the failures of the old master narratives. My point is not to criticise and demand political purity, but rather that we must try and be more honest in recognising the imperatives which impact on our work. Therefore I want to pose questions of our practice of theory; not to challenge it but to context it.

Carol Smart's article, 'The Women of Legal Discourse',[65] begins by not only recognising that 'feminist socio-legal theory has been developing in exciting and ... controversial ways over the last twenty years ...' but also asserts that 'the field of law poses quite specific intellectual and political problems for feminist theory'. A major concern at the beginning of her paper is not only with a resistance to theory within legal work, but also the imperative to engage with law. She outlines the positions which she sees as resistant to theory, including:

> ... a form of resistance to all theory ... based ... on the argument that, because law is a practice which has actual material consequences for women, what is needed in response is counter-practice not theory. This constituency demand 'practical' engagement and continually renders (mere?) theoretical practice inadequate .... These ... elements present a major obstacle to proponents of feminist legal theory as they (we) are met with the frustrations of being ignored or seen as outmoded in and by law and are simultaneously moved to renounce theory by the oral imperative of doing something in or through law.'

I could now move very easily into a critique of this presentation; using it as a point of differentiation to allow me to present my own ideas. All too easily the sub-text becomes 'why she is wrong and why I am right'. It is particularly

---

64 Shelley Wright, 'Patriarchal Feminism and the Law of the Father' (1933) *Feminist Legal Studies*, p 134. (Extracted at in Chapter 5.)

65 *Op cit.*

difficult for me in trying to avoid this strategy, because the central thesis of this paper is to argue for a reassessment of the way in which we engage in, and utilise, the practise of theory. Therefore what I am about to argue is most easily presented in a mode of critique; but before I address my concerns with Carol Smart's position, I want to signal two important countervailing tendencies which are (I believe) present in feminist work but so taken for granted that we often lose sight of them.

The first is simply that I have more in common with, for instance the work of Carol Smart, that I do with the work of non-feminists. We share a common aspiration and commitment, our feminism. Therefore the terms in which I address her work, or the work of other feminists' theories, must start with a recognition of this.

Secondly between feminists we are engaged in a continual dialogue of possibilities – essentially possibilities for futures; we tell each other stories and weave our fantasies about these possible futures. We carry into these stories our own particular narratives, our histories of time and place, our biographies of the articulate (our intellectual traditions and training) and the inarticulate (our fears and desires), and as one tells one story, another presents a counterpoint, perhaps because of a different intellectual tradition or simply a different perspective. It is a series of presentations in which we have to resist the idea that the final presentation is the final truth but recognise that both our desire, and our work-situation as academics, push us towards an assumption of a narrative in which can effect closure. The wise part of us knows that this is not the case, but that does not matter, it does not detract from the enterprise. What matters more is that we might lose sight of realising that our desire both compels us towards closure and makes it impossible at the very same time. Indeed such is also the motor for academic work – that all theories can only be hypothesis, to be continually tested, worried through and beyond. But I want to add a crucial aspect in regard to feminist work in the academy – and I will pose it simply as a rhetorical question. Do any of us really believe, or want to believe, that our feminism is finally to be tested here? If I turn this question a little it reveals a deep paradox in our work, a paradox which allows the position I have taken above: it is that on the one hand we demand and require inclusion into the academy, and at the very same time we refuse to finally be contained in the academy. If I turn this figure a little again, what we see is that for feminists it is a question of what theory can do for us, what it makes possible for us, rather than looking to theory for a validation of our senses of self or our aspirations for change. It can be part of our feminism but cannot incorporate our feminism; indeed our feminism operates as excess, always propelling us forward. But I have to be careful here, twice now I have used a lineal figure – I have talked of beyond and forward. In fact I want to suggest that this figure is far too simplistic an account of our activities – I want to image rather a continual movement between points which are themselves not fixed. For instance a movement between different theoretical positions, or between 'theory' and 'practice', between claims to 'subjectivity' and denial of the authenticity of 'subjectivity', etc: it is a movement which I want to keep open, recognising paradox, difference, tension etc., not wanting to avoid them, but rather seeing them in relation – a way in which we continue to have stories to tell to each other. What holds us together as listeners I have already suggested, but what might separate us to the point where we can no longer share this process, is not recognising the patterns of dissonance which necessarily play through our work. By this I mean the differences in our intellectual traditions and the tendency in much work undertaken in the academy to privilege the practices of the academy, including most importantly the desire to define and delineate, to articulate and to capture that which is actually beyond. Beyond because it is both excess and because it is part of other practices. Therefore we have to both continually try and capture which we mean by 'feminism' or 'justice', for instance, and at the very same time know that we cannot, except in immediate (material) circumstances, through which we then play both our biographies and our fantasies of possibilities. For this reason I very carefully earlier in my paper said simply 'feminism': as with 'justice' it is a figure too powerful and too necessarily open, to do anything more, or less, than be immediate and, conversely, keep on the horizons of our desire.

I am aware that my position requires one crucial leap of faith and one very fundamental flaw. The leap of faith is that we can keep and share the aspiration of feminism and afford to recognise its aspect as desire, as beyond theory, beyond articulation. But I do have two points which may help. The first is simple – we are actually doing that all the time; it is simply that we also continually present our desire as something we are just on the edge of achieving. (Few of us are brave enough to lay claim to having achieved it.) Secondly, that it is in fact freeing to recognise that there will always be an excess, and to concentrate on telling stores through which we can explore our desire – stories of the immediate or stories of the archetype, whether in myth or the reproduction of grand theory. All circle around the absent centre: as along as they continue to enable us that is all that matters. So then my flaw – how do we know they are enabling? Cannot I afford to say that we must test that both by our direct experiences, which includes the judgment of our intellect but not only that, as well as the seeming strength of our fantasies of possible futures? Whilst I must recognise the dangers of my position; is the only option open to me to retreat to an orthodoxy which has already failed me? Or can I not take the risk and try and build a new epistemology in which the present orthodoxy is only one element of the possible strategies available to me? Again I could argue that that is what we all do all the time anyway (and perhaps it is crucial to continue to do this without attempting to articulate the practice in the way I am doing!); but within the terms of the methodology I am attempting to articulate, I am convinced that at this juncture it is important to reassess the practice of theory, particularly for those of us who stand in the eye of the paradox – being both feminists and academics.

So now you have my attempt to articulate my methodology – a mixture of pragmatism, strategy and desire! My question is always – what does this enable? What futures does this make possible?

How then does this affect my reading of Carol Smart? Firstly I think that is important to recognise the influences of her discipline of origin – she is a sociologist. Therefore the methodologies she employs tend to derive from this background. I suggest that this includes a tendency to utilise categories and models through which to describe and evaluate material. Therefore models of 'law' are employed and different models counterpoised etc. Further there is a tendency to differentiate between 'practice' and 'theory'; in which 'practice' should be informed by 'theory' but of itself is simply data for theoretical work. At this level of reading I have many problems with the construction of her methodology. In particular her characterisation of the constituencies resistant to theory seems unhelpful. However if we recognise them as simply 'resistances' rather than forces which are anti-theoretical, then I return to my point about countervailing tendencies. Much as she is warning against no-theory, they [the resistances] are warning against theory at the expense of engagement with law. The importance is the tension between them; not a choice of one or other but a warning to each other. For Smart herself this (fruitful) problematic is clearly signalled in her work:

> We must remain critical ... without abandoning law as a site of struggle ...Moreover, more work needs to be done in tracing how women have resisted and negotiated constructions of gender ...[66]

However there are tendencies in her approach which could become antithetical to mine. Firstly I am concerned that the process of model building, and the very models built, can become taken too seriously. It is rather as if they begin to have a life of their own, rather than that they are simply attempts to make sense of a confused world. This tendency is, for me, well illustrated in a piece by Drucilla Cornell when she utilises in one paper, Derrida, Lacan and Levinas through an overarching model taken from Luhmann:

> ... we need Luhmann to adequately understand how the gender hierarchy functions as a system so as to be structurally coupled with other systems.[67]

However she does go on to say:

> In the light of the current situation, we need to understand why hope is still possible. If systems theory and the philosophy of the limit are in alliance with feminism, then it can only be an alliance, because theory does not change the world, although it can help us see how and why it can be changed. It is still up to feminists to dream of a different world ... beyond the gender hierarchy and try to make it a reality.[68]

In truth when I read her paper it seemed to me that this paragraph is not said in strength but rather with a kind of hopelessness – having spent so much time constructing her theory she then has to finally allow that it does not deliver what she in some part of herself knows she needs. She does not, to me, seem comfortable with the excess. I may be being unfair but that is the way I hear it. One of the problems may well be that she is attempting to address again two audiences and two imperatives – her male colleagues and her display of her ability to deploy theory, and her female/feminist colleagues who have a different expectation of the possibilities of the deployment of the masters. In the same way Carol Smart has to pull herself back from the imperative of her models and recognise, in her papers not so much aspirations for change, but rather the need to address an immediacy, a pragmatic demand for response and resistance to the situation we find ourselves in now. Both these papers are addressed to theory but both have to recognise that the feminism of their authors finally escapes being caught within their theoretical frames. That does not mean that their theories are wrong or that they are even unuseful – it simply requires of us a recognition that beyond and behind our incursions into theory lies our feminism.

However, two aspects of the current presence of feminists in theoretical work do need to be addressed. They interrelate but are best presented separately. the first is the possibility of a specifically feminist theory; the second is the deployment of this possibility to offer new life to theory itself. In other words what is sometimes being presented, and received, in the academy, is an image of current theoretical practices as partial, and therefore doomed, because they do not incorporate the feminine and the possibility of, by bringing the feminine into the practice of theory, a new 'reality' of completeness and wholeness. Feminism, by signalling absence and demanding recognition of this absence, seems to set an agenda for a

---

66 Carol Smart, 'The Women of Legal Discourse' (1992) *Social and Legal Studies*, p 40.

67 Drucilla Cornell, 'The Philosophy of the Limit: Systems Theory and Feminist Legal Reform', in Cornell et al (ed), *Deconstruction and the Possibility of Justice* (Routledge, 1992), p 89.

68 *Ibid.*

demand for presence. When we figure the feminine as lack, we move towards an imperative of incorporation; of the addition of the missing element. Of recovery of the lost, the externalised: that which is not spoken demands a voice.

In work on law this operates to not only build a new model of law as gendered, but also to begin to try and image a model of law in which gender is both recognised and incorporated.

To reach this position requires two moves. Firstly it requires what is essentially descriptive work on law in which the emphasis is on law as a gendered system. Therefore it also tends towards a model of law which exemplifies this position. The second is that it requires a positing of the feminine subject as both external and a 'thing' capable of and requiring presence in law. The promise of this, the desire, is that by the recognition of, and incorporation of this subject, the law would be so radically transformed as to become no longer partial but rather complete.

It is a good story. It is one which allows us to not only to critique partialities but also to offer possibilities not only to ourselves but to other lost souls. The story is compelling; it feed from stories of loss, of separation and a desire to be reunited. A recent paper by Peter Goodrich displays its potential. He begins by quoting Lace Irigaray:

> In order to make the ethics of sexual difference possible, it is necessary to retrace the ties of feminine genealogies ... at the levels of law, religion, language, truth, wisdom ... to introduce into the history of reason an interpretation of the forgetting of feminine genealogies and thereby reestablish their economy ... .[69]

In an earlier draft of this paper he summarised the project:

> ... In contemporary terms the question is not simply that of recovering feminine genealogies, it is also that of comprehending the extent of the legal repression of the feminine, not simply in terms of legal doctrine but equally in terms of legal method and the conceptions of justice ...

However, his work in tracing the figure of the feminine in the history of the common law reveals a number of important elements. Firstly the ambiguity and plasticity of the figure of Woman. Both revered and feared the figure takes on all that is that which is most desired, all that which is beyond as well and that which connotes those things which cannot be spoken or incorporated and therefore must be avoided. Secondly, whilst it is clear that this is a narrative constructed by and for men, women are also a presence, however marginal their voices, they are there: a series of complaints which speak both actual circumstance, their own needs and their desires. They both figure as excess and themselves construct excess. In both these patterns what is displayed in the very fragility of the attempt to construct a legal discourse; it is powerful in that it connotes both a series of practices and a narrative of law and yet in both aspects it is continually fragile.

From this I take two major points for my thesis. The first is that we have to avoid a temptation to over-construct a model of law as gendered which takes law too seriously as a simple, powerful, discursive practice. We must distinguish between the non-discursive elements of law and the attempts to create a coherence to modern law as rational. We have to distinguish between what

---

69 Peter Goodrich, 'Gynaetopia: Feminine Genealogies in Common Law' (1993) *Journal of Law and Society*, p 276.

academics write about law and the actuality of legal practice. I am well aware that the dominant ethos in so many ways does radically disadvantage us as women; but I also think that the politics of difference allows us, and indeed compels us, to recognise the inconsistencies, contradictions etc within legal practice and the attempts made to present a picture of uniformity, consistency and logic. The figure of Woman is constantly within both the practice and discourse of law; so is the feminine, on the edge, at the margins but part of the process, even in the attempt to project and utilise the figure as 'other'. Recognising the figure is to recognise that the power of law rests on a very fragile base; as attempt to constantly affirm and reaffirm the enlightenment project of the rational individual – the subject brought into relation through law. It constantly fails to meet these aspirations; in this sense the figure of the feminine, a constant movement of absence/presence, is a recognition of this; even when seemingly projected as external to law.

For good historical and contemporary reasons we want to reject this role. We want to cease to be cast in the image of desire and become participants in the discourse – to make a dialogue. But then we move to our second problematic: to do this we need to present our case by asserting for ourselves a subjectivity and demanding the recognition of this in law. In other words we posit ourselves as both external and having an authentic presence which demands recognition. In England this aspect of the development of feminist theory has often been labelled as 'positivist' and is seen as running counter to the postmodernist tendencies of much contemporary theoretical work on law. I think that there is definitely a danger that it can be both presented and received in this way. My concern is that in doing so it not only posits a feminine subject, based on an analogy to the masculine subject, but it also feeds into grand narratives which present 'law' as a unified and coherent discourse within its own terms and to which we simply need to addend our own. My point is that we should rather use our insights to recognise that law does not deliver within its terms of presentation; that the unified male subject is only very tenuously held together and is a central aspect of law's fragility.

I would pose the same question as Rosi Braiddoti:

> ... are today's feminist closet humanists wanting to rescue the shaken edifice of reason, resting on some realist theory of truth? Or are they radical epistemologists, having given up the idea of gaining access to a real fixed truth? In other words, what is the image of theoretical reason at work in feminist thought?[70]

Her concern to find new ways of thinking in which she characterises 'the feminist as a critical thinker, unveiling and criticising the modalities of power and domination in all theoretical discourse including her own'[71] seems to me so important to remember and so easy to lose sight of. She answers my problem of why I find it so difficult to articulate what I want to say by focusing on where my needs come from and recognising my desire:

> ... Feminist theory expresses women's ontological desire, women's structural need to express themselves as female subjects ... as corporeal and consequently sexed beings .... the disposition of the subject towards thinking

---

70 Rosi Braidotti, 'On the Female Feminist Subject', in Gisela Bock and Susan James (eds), *Beyond Equality and Difference* (Routledge, 1992), p 181.

71 *Ibid*, p 181.

... is a pre-discursive element, which is in excess of, and nevertheless indispensable to, the act of thinking as such ...[72]

The recognition of this desire becomes then situated in an understanding both of the contexting of the desire and the possibilities of really activating patterns of truly radical change. For her, premised very much within the work of Gilles Deleuze:

It is less a question of founding the subject than of elucidating the categories by which the female feminist subject can be adequately represented.[73]

What she emphasises is the 'multi-layered structure of the subject'. It is this which I really want to carry forward. If the politics of difference impel us to adopt a strategy towards law which is based on naming law as gendered and a claim for recognition then of the specificity of our own genders needs and aspiration; we should recognise it as a strategy. The strategy should lead us towards a clearer recognition of law itself as plural; if we can open up and expand that plurality by such a strategy so much the better. The strategy is pragmatic; for it to be enabling it must address both our desire and the multiplicity of different futures. The danger is that it might simply feed back into a reengagement with the modernist project; a project which reinforces an attempt to present and represent law as a coherency. Much much more coherent now because of our own incorporation.

We no longer want to be the objects of desire but we must not lose our own desire. We must demand recognition but not hold ourselves simply to a demand for recognition and an engagement within patterns which have already failed us. Truly radical work now demands that we tell each other good stories but not become entrapped within them. As Peter Goodrich says:

There is no reason, either in history or in doctrine, why different laws cannot govern different genres, separate statuses or the plural identities of legal persons.[74]

We must not lose sight of the 'plural identities of legal persons'; and of the plural possibilities within law. To keep hold of this we must develop immediate strategies as well as keep in sight the horizons of our desire. That our feminism goes beyond our ability to articulate, that it cannot be finally represented either in theory or in law is our strength. It makes possible future rather than simply grafts us on to existing histories.

---

72 *Ibid*, p 182.

73 *Ibid*, p 190.

74 Peter Goodrich, *op cit*.

CHAPTER 4

FEMINIST LEGAL METHODS

In the quest for equality feminist scholars have adopted a number of methods. Among these, consciousness-raising has played a significant role, not only for feminist legal scholars but for all feminists. From a feminist perspective, society as traditionally ordered, particularly Western 'liberal' societies, establishes a mask – a facade – of gender-neutrality and equality. The tenets of liberalism – representative democratic government under the rule of law – creates the impression that all citizens have equal rights and equal value in society. Once, however, the veneer of liberalism is scratched, it becomes apparent that behind liberalism there lies a vast reservoir of discrimination and inequality. Such discrimination and inequality is not reserved for women: all minority groups in society have suffered the historical and contemporary experience of discrimination. So successful has liberalism been in portraying society as a community of equal genderless, raceless, classless, ageless and equally-able-bodied persons, that a conscious and systematic effort is required in order to unmask the reality of inequality and oppression. As Catharine MacKinnon explains:

> Liberal legalism is thus a medium for making male dominance both invisible and legitimate by adopting the male point of view in law at the same time as it enforces that view on society.[1]

Moreover, society and law have traditionally been so ordered that the role of women has been confined to the 'private sphere' of life,[2] and excluded from full participation in civic life. Fostering and maintaining the mythology of the 'natural' role of women as the carers and nurturers in society, disguises the unequal opportunities for women in the 'public sphere', whether that be political participation or employment opportunities. Female consciousness-raising is educative, seeking to reveal and unmask the falsehoods hidden behind the shroud of political theory.

Feminist legal methods also entail the detailed analysis of specific laws, their application and enforcement. Much of the discrimination previously suffered by women in the field of employment law and family law, to take but two examples, has been reversed by the painstaking scholarship involving detailed analysis of specific legal rules. In England, the law – being the product of predominantly male legislators and male judges, has proven a stubborn subject: it was not until 1990, for example, that husband's immunity from prosecution for rape was removed. Furthermore, as will be seen in Chapter 9, the criminal justice system is deeply resistant to evolution and reform in relation to women who – having suffered years of violent persecution at the hands of their male partners – finally break under the strain and kill their violent partners.

---

1   CA MacKinnon, *Toward Feminist Jurisprudence,* in *Toward a Feminist Theory of the State* (Harvard University Press, 1989), p 237.

2   On the public/private dichotomy see Chapter 5.

Feminist scholars are also engaged in the process of deconstructing literary, social and legal texts in order to reveal the manner in which women have traditionally been excluded. The supposedly 'gender-neutral', rational, objective language of law masks this exclusion. What feminist legal scholars strive for is full inclusion in law and legal language. The effect of 'gender-neutral' legal language goes beyond a failure to include women. Also implicit in the mask of law is the silencing of women and women's concerns and women's rights. Women must seek to be heard; to be given a voice; to be recognised as equal citizens under the law.

Feminist method is also concerned with the task of theorising about law and inequality. What role does law play? To what extent is the law 'gendered'? What role should – and could – law play? Is law the most appropriate vehicle through which to effect fundamental change in societal attitudes? Whilst there may be little consensus on such questions, the questions are increasingly being asked.

In the three articles which follow, Katherine Bartlett, Ann Scales and Mary Jane Mossman address the importance of and range of methods employed by feminist legal scholars.[3]

FEMINIST LEGAL METHODS[4]
Katharine Bartlett[5]

Introduction

'Doing' and 'Knowing' in Law

In what sense can legal methods be 'feminist'? Are there specific methods that feminist lawyers share? If so, what are these methods, why are they used, and what significance do they have to feminist practice? Put another way, what do feminists mean when they say they are 'doing law,' and what do they mean when, having done law, they claim to be 'right'?

Feminists have developed extensive critiques of law and proposals for legal reform. Feminists have had much less to say, however about what the 'doing' of law should entail and what truth status to give to the legal claims that follow. These methodological issues matter because methods shape one's view of the possibilities for legal practice and reform. Method 'organises' the apprehension of truth; it determines what counts as evidence and defines what is taken as verification.[6] Feminists cannot ignore method, because if they seek to challenge existing structures of power with the same methods that have defined what counts within those structures, they may instead 'recreate the illegitimate power structures [that they are] trying to identify and undermine'.[7]

Method matters also because without an understanding of feminist methods, feminist claims in the law will not be perceived as legitimate or 'correct'. I

---

3 See also Chapter 6 for analysis of the potential for Carol Gilligan's theory of differing male and female moral reasoning for legal interpretation and application.

4 Katharine Bartlett, 'Feminist Legal Methods' (1990) 100 *Harvard Law Review*, 829. (Footnotes edited.)

5 At the time of writing, Professor of Law, Duke University School of Law.

6 CA MacKinnon, 'An Agenda for Theory' (1982), 7 *Signs* 515, p 527

7 P Singer, 'Should Lawyers Care About Philosophy?' (1989) *Duke Law Journal* 1752.

suspect that many who dismiss feminism as trivial or inconsequential misunderstand it. Feminists have tended to focus on defending their various substantive positions or political agendas, even among themselves. Greater attention to issues of method may help to anchor these defences, to explain why feminist agendas often appear so radical (or not radical enough), and even to establish some common ground among feminists.

As feminists articulate their methods, they can become more aware of the nature of what they do, and thus do it better. Thinking about method is empowering. When I require myself to explain what I do, I am likely to discover how to improve what I earlier may have taken for granted. In the process, I am likely to become more committed to what it is that I have improved. This likelihood, at least, is a central premise of this article and its primary motivation.

I begin this article by addressing the meaning of the label 'feminist', and the difficulties and the necessity of using that label. I then set forth in Part II a set of legal methods that I claim are feminist.

All of these methods reflect the status of women as 'outsiders', who need ways of challenging and undermining dominant legal conventions and of developing alternative conventions which take better account of women's experiences and needs. The methods analysed in this article include (1) identifying and challenging those elements of existing legal doctrine that leave out or disadvantage women and members of other excluded groups (asking the 'woman question'); (2) reasoning from an ideal in which legal resolutions are pragmatic responses to concrete dilemmas rather than static choices between opposing, often mismatched perspectives (feminist practical reasoning); and (3) seeking insights and enhanced perspectives through collaborative or interactive engagements with others based upon personal experience and narrative (consciousness-raising).

As I develop these methods, I consider a number of methodological issues that feminists have not fully confronted and that are crucial to the potential growth of feminist legal theory and practice. I examine, for example, the relationship between feminist methods and substantive legal rules. Feminist methods emerged from feminist politics and find their justification, at least in part, in their ability to advance substantive feminist goals. Thus, one might argue that the methods I describe are not really methods at all, but rather substantive, partisan rules in the not-very-well-disguised shape of method. I argue, however, that the defence of any particular set of methods must rest not on whether it is nonsubstantive – an impossibility – but whether its relationship to substantive law is defensible. I defend the substantive elements of feminist methods and argue that these methods provide an appropriate constraint upon the application of substantive rules.

Throughout my analysis of feminist legal methods, I also critically examine the place of feminist methods within the general context of legal method. I reject the sharp dichotomy between abstract, deductive ('male') reasoning, and concrete, contextualised ('female') reasoning because it misdescribes both conventional understandings of legal method and feminist methods themselves. The differences between the two methodologies, I argue, relate less to differences in principles of logic than to differences in emphasis and in underlying ideals about rules. Traditional legal methods place a high premium on the predictability, certainty, and fixity of rules. In contrast, feminist legal methods, which have emerged from the critique that existing rules overrepresent existing power structures, value rule-flexibility, and the ability to identify missing points of view.

'Feminist' As a Descriptive Label

Although this article necessarily represents a particular version of feminism, I refer to positions as feminist in a broad sense that encompasses a self-consciously critical stance toward the existing order with respect to the various ways it affects different women 'as women'. Being feminist is a political choice about one's positions on a variety of contestable social issues. As Linda Gordon writes, 'feminism ... is not a 'natural' excretion of [woman's] experience but a controversial political interpretation and struggle, by no means universal to women'.[8] Further, being feminist means owning up to the part one plays in a sexist society; it means taking responsibility – for the existence and for the transformation of 'our gendered identity, our politics, and our choices'.[9]

Use of the label 'feminist' has substantial problems. First, it can create an expectation of feminist originality or invention that feminists do not intend and cannot fulfil. This expectation itself demonstrates a preoccupation with individual achievement and ownership at odds with the feminist emphasis on collective, relational discovery. Feminists acknowledge that some important aspects of their methods and theory have roots in other legal traditions. Although permeated by bias, these traditions nonetheless have elements that should be taken seriously. Still, labelling methods or practices or attitudes as feminist identifies them as a chosen part of a larger, critical agenda originating in the experiences of gender subordination. Although not every proponent of feminist practice and reform is unique, these components together address a set of concerns not reached by existing traditions.

Second, use of the label 'feminist' has contributed to a tendency within feminism to assume a definition of 'woman' or a 'women's experiences' that is fixed, exclusionary, homogenising and appositional, a tendency that feminists have criticised in others. The tendency to treat woman as a single analytic category has a number of dangers. For one thing, it obscures – even denies – differences among women and among feminists, especially in race, class, and sexual orientation, that ought to be taken into account. If feminism addresses only oppressive practices that operate against white, privileged women, it may readjust the allocation of privilege, but fail either to reconstruct the social and legal significance of gender or to prove that its insights have the power to illuminate other categories of exclusion. Assuming a unified concept of 'woman' also adopts a view of the subject that has been rendered highly problematic. Poststructural feminists have claimed that woman has no core identity but rather comprises multiple, overlapping social structures and discourses. Using woman as a category of analysis implies a rejection of these claims, for it suggests that members of the category share a set of common, essential, ahistorical characteristics that constitute a coherent identity.

Perhaps the most difficult problem of all with use of the terms 'feminist' and 'woman' is its tendency to reinstate what most feminists seek to abolish: the isolation and stigmatisation of women. All efforts to take account of difference face this central dilemma. Although ignoring difference means continued inequality and oppression based upon difference, using difference as a category of analysis can reinforce stereotyped thinking and thus the marginalised status of

---

8   Linda Gordon, 'What's New in Women's History', in T de Lauretis (ed), *Feminist Studies/Critical Studies* (1986) 20, 30.

9   Alcoff, 'Cultural Feminism Versus Post-Structuralism: The Identity Crisis in Feminist Theory' (1988) 13 *Signs* 405, p 432.

those within it. Thus, in maintaining the category of woman or its corresponding political label 'feminist' to define those who are degraded on account of their sex, feminists themselves strengthen the identification of a group that thereby becomes more easily degraded.

Despite these difficulties, these labels remain useful. Although feminists have been guilty of ethnocentrism and all too often fail to recognise that women's lives are heterogeneous, that women who have had similar experiences may disagree about political agendas, and that women's gender is only one of many sources of identity, gender remains a category that can help to analyse and improve our world. To sustain feminism, feminists must use presently understandable categories, even while maintaining a critical posture toward their use. In this article, I retain feminist as a label, and woman as an analytical category, while trying to be sensitive to the misleading or dangerous tendencies of this practice. I try to acknowledge the extent to which feminist methods and theory derive from, or are related to, familiar traditions. I also try to avoid – to the extent one can – the ever present risks of ethnocentrism and of unitary and overgeneralisations. Where I fail, I hope I will be corrected, and that no failures, or corrections, will ever be deemed final.

Feminist Doing in Law

When feminists 'do law', they do what other lawyers do: they examine the facts of a legal issue or dispute, they identify the essential features of those facts, they determine what legal principles should guide the resolution of the dispute, and they apply those principles to the facts. This process unfolds not in a linear, sequential, or strictly logical manner, but rather in a pragmatic, interactive manner. Facts determine which rules are appropriate, and rules determine which facts are relevant. In doing law, feminists like other lawyers use a full range of methods of legal reasoning – deduction, induction, analogy, and use of hypotheticals, policy, and other general principles.

In addition to these conventional methods of doing law, however, feminists use other methods. These methods, though not all unique to feminists, attempt to reveal features of a legal issue which more traditional methods tend to overlook or suppress. One method, asking the woman question, is designed to expose how the substance of law may silently and without justification submerge the perspectives of women and other excluded groups. Another method, feminist practical reasoning, expands traditional notions of legal relevance to make legal decision-making more sensitive to the features of a case not already reflected in legal doctrine. A third method, consciousness raising, offers a means of testing the validity of accepted legal principles through the lens of the personal experience of those directly affected by those principles. In this part, I describe and explore the implications of each of these feminist methods.

Asking the Woman Question

A question becomes a method when it is regularly asked. Feminists across many disciplines regularly ask a question – a set of questions, really – known as 'the woman question'[10] which is designed to identify the gender implications of rules and practices which might otherwise appear to be neutral or objective. In this section, I describe the method of asking the woman question in law as a primary method of feminist critique, and discuss the relationship between this method

10 See eg C Gould, 'The Woman Question: Philosophy of Liberation and the Liberation of Philosophy', in C Gould and M Wartofsky (eds), *Women and Philosophy* (1976), p 5; Hawkesworth, 'Feminist Rhetoric' (1986) 16 *Political Theory*, 444, pp 452–56.

and the substance of feminist goals and practice. I also show how this method reaches beyond questions of gender to exclusions based upon other characteristics as well.

The Method

The woman question asks about the gender implications of a social practice or rule: have women been left out of consideration? If so, in what way; how might that omission be corrected? What difference would it make to do so? In law, asking the woman question means examining how the law fails to take into account the experiences and values that seem more typical of women than of men, for whatever reason, or how existing legal standards and concepts might disadvantage women. The question assumes that some features of the law may be not only non-neutral in a general sense, but also 'male' in a specific sense. The purpose of the woman question is to expose those features and how they operate, and to suggest how they might be corrected.

Women have long been asking the woman question in law. Legal impediments associated with being a woman were, early on, so blatant that the question was not so much whether women were left out, but whether the omission was justified by women's different roles and characteristics. American women such as Elizabeth Cady Stanton and Abigail Adams may seem today all too modest and tentative in their demands for improvements in women's legal status.[11] Yet while social stereotypes and limited expectations for women may have blinded women activists in the eighteenth and nineteenth centuries, their demands for the vote, for the right of married women to make contracts and own property, for other marriage reforms, and for birth control challenged legal rules and social practices that, to others in their day, constituted the God-given plan for the human race ... .[12]

Feminists today ask the woman question in many areas of law. They ask the woman question in rape cases when they ask why the defence of consent focuses on the perspective of the defendant and what he 'reasonably' thought the woman wanted, rather than the perspective of the woman and the intentions she 'reasonably' thought she conveyed to the defendant.[13] Women ask the woman question when they ask why they are not entitled to be prison guards on the same terms as men;[14] why the conflict between work and family responsibilities in women's lives is seen as a private matter for women to resolve within the family rather than a public matter involving restructuring of the workplace;[15] or why the right to 'make and enforce contracts' protected by section 1981 forbids discrimination in the formation of a contract but not discrimination in its interpretation.[16] Asking the woman question reveals the ways in which political choice and institutional arrangement contribute to women's subordination. Without the woman question, differences associated with women are taken for

---

11   See D Riley, *Am I That Name?: Feminism and the Category of 'Women' in History* (1988).

12   Katherine Bartlett, *op cit*, pp 831–38.

13   See S Estrich, *Real Rape* (1987), pp 92–104.

14   See W Williams, 'Women's Rights', 7 *L Rep* 175.

15   See Dowd, 'Work and the Family' (1989) 24 *Harv CR-CL Law Review* 79; F Olsen, 'The Family and the Market' (1983) 96 *Harvard Law Review* 1497; N Taub, 'From Parental Leaves to Nurturing Leaves' (1985) 13 *NYU Rev L & Social Change* 381; J Williams, 'Deconstructing Gender' (1987) *Michigan L Rev* 797; W Williams, *Equality's Riddle*.

16   *Cf*, 'The Supreme Court, 1988 Term – Leading Cases' (1989) 103 *Harvard Law Review*, 137, p 330.

granted and, unexamined, may serve as a justification for laws that disadvantage women. The woman question reveals how the position of women reflects the organisation of society rather than the inherent characteristics of women. As many feminists have pointed out, difference is located in relationships and social institutions – the workplace, the family, clubs, sports, childrearing patterns, and so on – not in women themselves. In exposing the hidden effects of laws that do not explicitly discriminate on the basis of sex, the woman question helps to demonstrate how social structures embody norms that implicitly render women different and thereby subordinate.

Once adopted as a method, asking the woman question is a method of critique as integral to legal analysis as determining the precedential value of a case, stating the facts, or applying law to facts. 'Doing law' as a feminist means looking beneath the surface of law to identify the gender implications of rules and the assumptions underlying them and insisting upon applications of rules that do not perpetuate women's subordination. It means recognising that the woman question always has potential relevance and that 'tight' legal analysis never assumes gender neutrality.

The Woman Question: Method or Politics

Is asking the woman question really a method at all, or is it a mask for something else, such as legal substance, or politics? The American legal system has assumed that method and substance have different functions, and that method cannot serve its purpose unless it remains separate from, and independent of, substantive 'bias'. Rules of legal method, like rules of legal procedure, are supposed to insulate substantive rules from arbitrary application. Substantive rules define the rights and obligations of individuals and legal entities (what the law is); rules of method and procedure define the steps taken in order to ascertain and apply that substance (how to invoke the law and to make it work). Separating rules of method and procedure from substantive rules, under this view, helps to ensure the regular, predictable application of those substantive rules. Thus, conventional and reliable ways of working with substantive rules permit one to specify in advance the consequences of particular activities. Method and process should not themselves have substantive content, the conventional wisdom insists, because method and process are supposed to protect us from substance which comes, 'arbitrarily', from outside the rule. Within this conventional view, it might be charged that the method of asking the woman question fails to respect the necessary separation between method and substance. Indeed, asking the woman question seems to be a 'loaded', overtly political activity, which reaches far beyond the 'neutral' tasks of ascertaining law and facts and applying one to the other.

Of course, not only feminist legal methods but all legal methods shape substance; the difference is that feminists have been called on it. Methods shape substance, first, in the leeway they allow for reaching different substantive results. Deciding which facts are relevant, or which legal precedents apply, or how the applicable precedents should be applied, for example, leaves a decision-maker with a wide range of acceptable substantive results from which to choose. The greater the indeterminacy, the more the decision-maker's substantive preferences, without meaningful methodological constraints, may determine a particular outcome. Not surprisingly, these preferences may follow certain patterns reflecting the dominant cultural norms.

Methods shape substance also through the hidden biases they contain. A strong view of precedent in legal method, for example, protects the *status quo* over the interests of those seeking recognition of new rights. The method of distinguishing law from considerations of policy, likewise, reinforces existing power structures and masks exclusions or perspectives ignored by that law. The endless academic debates over originalism, interpretivism, and other theories of constitutional interpretation demonstrate further that methodological principles convey substantive views of law and make a difference to legal results.

Feminist Practical Reasoning

Some feminists have claimed that women approach the reasoning process differently than men do.[17] In particular, they say that women are more sensitive to situation and context, that they resist universal principles and generalisations, especially those that do not fit their own experiences, and that they believe that 'the practicalities of everyday life' should not be neglected for the sake of abstract justice. Whether these claims can be empirically sustained, this reasoning process has taken on normative significance for feminists, many of whom have argued that individualised fact-finding is often superior to the application of bright line rules,[18] and that reasoning from context allows a greater respect for differences[19] and for the perspectives of the powerless. In this section, I explore these themes through a discussion of a feminist version of practical reasoning.

The Method

As a form of legal reasoning, practical reasoning has many meanings invoked in many contexts for many different purposes. I present a version of practical reasoning in this section that I call 'feminist practical reasoning'. This version combines some aspects of a classic Aristotelian model of practical deliberation with a feminist focus on identifying and taking into account the perspectives of the excluded. Although this form of reasoning may not always provide clear decision methods for resolving every legal dispute, it builds upon the 'practical' in its focus on the specific, real life dilemmas posed by human conflict – dilemmas that more abstract forms of legal reasoning often tend to gloss over. In focusing on the 'real' rather than the abstract, practical reasoning has some kinship to legal realism and critical legal studies, but there are important differences which I will explore in this section.

Practical Reasoning

According to Amelia Rorty, the Aristotelian model of practical reasoning holistically considers ends, means, and actions in order to 'recognise and actualise whatever is best in the most complex, various, and ambiguous situations'.[20] Practical reasoning recognises few, if any, givens. What must be done, and why and how it should be done, are all open questions, considered on the basis of the intricacies of each specific factual context. Not only the resolution of the problem, but even what counts as a problem emerges from the specifics of the situation itself, rather than from some fore-ordained definition or prescription.

Practical reasoning approaches problems not as dichotomised conflicts, but as dilemmas with multiple perspectives, contradictions, and inconsistencies. These

---

17 See C Gilligan, *In a Different Voice* (1982); M Belenky, B Clinchy, N Goldberger and J Taruile, *Women's Ways of Knowing* (1986).

18 K Bartlett, 'Re-Expressing Parenthood' (1988) 98 *Yale Law Journal*, 293, 321–26; Sherry (1986) 72 *Va LR* 543, pp 604–13.

19 See Minow and Spelman, 'Passion for Justice' (1988) 10 *Cardozo I Rev* 37, 53; A Scales (1986) 95 *Yale LJ* p 1388 (extracted below).

20 Amelia Rorty, *Mind in Action* (1988), p 272.

dilemmas, ideally, do not call for the choice of one principle over another, but rather 'imaginative integrations and reconciliations',[21] which require attention to particular contexts. Practical reasoning sees particular details not as annoying inconsistencies or irrelevant nuisances which impede the smooth logical application of fixed rules. Nor does it see particular facts as the objects of legal analysis, the inert material to which to apply the living law. Instead, new facts present opportunities for improved understandings and 'integrations'. Situations are unique, not anticipated in their detail, not generalisable in advance. Themselves generative, new situations give rise to 'practical' perceptions and inform decision-makers about the desired ends of law.

The issue of minors' access to abortion exemplifies the generative, educative potential of specific facts. The abstract principle of family autonomy seems logically to justify a state law requiring minors to obtain their parents' consent before obtaining an abortion. Minors are immature and parents are the individuals generally best situated to help them make a decision as difficult as whether to have an abortion. The actual accounts of the wrenching circumstances under which a minor might seek to avoid notifying her parent of her decision to seek an abortion, however, demonstrate the practical difficulties of the matter. These actual accounts reveal that many minors face severe physical and emotional abuse as a result of their parents' knowledge of their pregnancy. Parents force many minors to carry to term a child that the minor cannot possibly raise responsibly; and only the most determined minor will be able to relinquish her child for adoption, in the face of parental rejection and manipulation. Actual circumstances, in other words, yield insights into the difficult problems of state and family decision-making that the abstract concept of parental autonomy alone does not reveal.

Practical reasoning in the law does not, and could not, reject rules. Along the specificity-generality continuum of rules, it tends to favour less specific rules or 'standards', because of the greater leeway for individualised analysis that standards allow. But practical reasoning in the context of law necessarily works from rules. Rules represent accumulated past wisdom, which must be reconciled with the contingencies and practicalities presented by fresh facts. Rules provide signposts for the appropriate purposes and ends to achieve through law. Rules check the inclination to be arbitrary and 'give constancy and stability in situations in which bias and passion might distort judgment ... Rules are necessities because we are not always good judges'.[22]

Ideally, however, rules leave room for the new insights and perspectives generated by new contexts. As noted above, the practical reasoner believes that the specific circumstances of a new case may dictate novel readings and applications of rules, readings and applications that not only were not, but could not or should not have been determined in advance. In this respect, practical reasoning differs from the view of law characteristic of the legal realists, who saw rules as open-ended by necessity, not by choice. The legal realists highly valued predictability and determinacy, but assumed that facts were too various and unpredictable for lawmakers to frame determinate rules. The practical reasoner, on the other hand, finds undesirable as well as impractical the reduction of contingencies to rules by which all disputes can be decided in advance.

---

21 *Ibid*, p 274.
22 See M Nussbaum, *The Fragility of Goodness: Luck and Ethics in Greek Tragedy and Philosophy* (1986).

Another important feature of practical reasoning is justification. The legal realist view is that rules allow a certain range of manipulation; judges may select on the basis of unstated, external considerations those interpretations that best serve those considerations. Thus, the 'real reason' for a decision – the social goals the decision-maker chooses to advance – and the reasons offered in a legal decision may differ. Practical reasoning, on the other hand, demands more than some reasonable basis for a particular legal decision. Decision-makers must offer their actual reasons – the same reasons that form its effective intentional description. This requirement reflects the inseparability of the determinations of means and ends; reasoning is itself part of the 'end,' and the end cannot be reasonable apart from the reasoning that underlies it. It reflects, further, the commitment of practical reasoning to the decision-maker's acceptance of responsibility for decisions made. Rules do not absolve the decision-maker from responsibility for decisions. There are choices to be made and the agent who makes them must admit to those choices and defend them.

Feminist practical reasoning

Feminist practical reasoning builds upon the traditional mode of practical reasoning by bringing to it the critical concerns and values reflected in other feminist methods, including the woman question. The classical exposition of practical reasoning takes for granted the legitimacy of the community whose norms it expresses, and for that reason tends to be fundamentally conservative. Feminist practical reasoning challenges the legitimacy of the norms of those who claim to speak, through rules, for the community. No form of legal reasoning can be free, of course, from the past or from community norms, because law is always situated in a context of practices and values. Feminist practical reasoning differs from other forms of legal reasoning, however, in the strength of its commitment to the notion that there is not one, but many overlapping communities to which one might look for 'reason'. Feminists consider the concept of community problematic[23] because they have demonstrated that law has tended to reflect existing structures of power. Carrying over their concern for inclusionism from the method of asking the woman question, feminists insist that no one community is legitimately privileged to speak for all others. Thus, feminist methods reject the monolithic community often assumed in male accounts of practical reasoning, and seek to identify perspectives not represented in the dominant culture from which reason should proceed.

Feminist practical reasoning, however, is not the polar opposite of a 'male' deductive model of legal reasoning. The deductive model assumes that for any set of facts, fixed, pre-existing legal rules compel a single, correct result. Many commentators have noted that virtually no one, male or female, now defends the strictly deductive approach to legal reasoning. Contextualised reasoning is also not, as some commentators suggest,[24] the polar opposite of a 'male' model of abstract thinking. All major forms of legal reasoning encompass processes of both contextualisation and abstraction. Even the most conventional legal methods require that one look carefully at the factual context of a case in order to identify similarities and differences between that case and others. The identification of a legal problem, selection of precedent, and application of that

---

23 See Abrams, 'Law's Republicanism' (1988) 97 *Yale LJ* 1591, pp 1606–07; Sullivan, 'Rainbow Republicanism' (1988) 97 *Yale LJ* 1713, p 1721.

24 See eg, M Matsuda, 'Liberal Jurisprudence and Abstracted Visions of Human Nature: A Feminist Critique of Rawls Theory of Justice' (1986) 16 *New Mexico LR* 613 (extracted in Chapter 8); Ann Scales, *supra*.

precedent, all require an understanding of the details of a case and how they relate to one another. When the details change, the rule and its application are likely to change as well.

By the same token, feminist methods require the process of abstraction, that is, the separation of the significant from the insignificant.[25] Concrete facts have significance only if they represent some generalisable aspect of the case. Generalisations identify what matters and draw connections to other cases. I abstract whenever I fail to identify every fact about a situation, which, of course, I do always. For feminists, practical reasoning and asking the woman question may make more facts relevant or 'essential' to the resolution of a legal case than would more nonfeminist legal analysis. For example, feminist practical reasoning deems relevant facts related to the woman question – facts about whose interests particular rules or legal resolutions reflect and whose interests require more deliberate attention. Feminists do not and cannot reject, however, the process of abstraction. Thus, though I might determine in a marital rape case that it is relevant that the wife did not want sexual intercourse on the day in question, it will probably not be relevant that the defendant gave a box of candy to his mother on St Valentine's Day or that he plays bridge well. No matter how detailed the level of particularity, practical reasoning like all other forms of legal analysis requires selecting and giving meaning to certain particularities. Feminist practical reasoning assumes that no a priori reasons prevent one from being persuaded that a fact that seems insignificant is significant, but it does not require that every fact be relevant. Likewise, although generalisations that render detail irrelevant require examination, they are not *a priori* unacceptable.

Similarly, the feminist method of practical reasoning is not the polar opposite of 'male' rationality. The process of finding commonalities, differences, and connections in practical reasoning is a rational process. To be sure, feminist practical reasoning gives rationality new meanings. Feminist rationality acknowledges greater diversity in human experiences and the value of taking into account competing or inconsistent claims. It openly reveals its positional partiality by stating explicitly which moral and political choices underlie that partiality, and recognises its own implications for the distribution and exercise of power. Feminist rationality also strives to integrate emotive and intellectual elements and to open up the possibilities of new situations rather than limit them with prescribed categories of analysis. Within these revised meanings, however, feminist method is and must be understandable. It strives to make more sense of human experience, not less, and is to be judged upon its capacity to do so ... .

Consciousness-raising

Another feminist method for expanding perceptions is consciousness-raising. Consciousness-raising is an interactive and collaborative process of articulating one's experiences and making meaning of them with others who also articulate their experiences. As Leslie Bender writes, 'Feminist consciousness-raising creates knowledge by exploring common experiences and patterns that emerge from shared tellings of life events. What were experienced as personal hurts individually suffered reveal themselves as a collective experience of oppression'.[26]

---

25 *Cf*, K Llewellyn, *The Bramble Bush* (1960), p 48.

26 L Bender, 'A Lawyer's Primer on Feminist Theory and Tort' (1988) 38 *L Legal Educ* 3, 9; see also Z Eisenstein, *Feminism and Sexual Equality*, 1984, pp 150–57; T De Lauretis, *Alice Doesn't: Feminism, Semiotics, Cinema* (1984), p 185; J Mitchell, *Woman's Estate* (1971), p 61.

Consciousness-raising is a method of trial and error. When revealing an experience to others, a participant in consciousness-raising does not know whether others will recognise it. The process values risk taking and vulnerability over caution and detachment. Honesty is valued above consistency, teamwork over self-sufficiency, and personal narrative over abstract analysis. The goal is individual and collective empowerment, not personal attack or conquest.

Elizabeth Schneider emphasises the centrality of consciousness-raising to the dialectical relationship of theory and practice. 'Consciousness-raising groups start with personal and concrete experience, integrate this experience into theory, and then, in effect, reshape theory based upon experience and experience based upon theory. Theory expresses and grows out of experience but it also relates back to that experience for further refinement, validation, or modification'.[27] The interplay between experience and theory 'reveals the social dimension of individual experience and the individual dimension of social experience' and hence the political nature of personal experience.

Consciousness-raising operates as feminist method not only in small personal growth groups, but also on a more public, institutional level, through bearing witness to evidences of patriarchy as they occur, through unremitting dialogues with and challenges to the patriarchs, and through the popular media, the arts, politics, lobbying, and even litigation. Women use consciousness-raising when they publicly share their experiences as victims of marital rape, pornography, sexual harassment on the job, street hassling and other forms of oppression and exclusion, in order to help change public perceptions about the meaning to women of events widely thought to be harmless or flattering.

Consciousness-raising has consequences, further, for laws and institutional decision-making more generally. Several feminists have translated the insights of feminist consciousness-raising into their normative accounts of legal process and legal decision-making. Carrie Menkel-Meadow, for example, has speculated that as the number of women lawyers increases, women's more interactive approaches to decision-making will improve legal process.[28] Similarly, Judith Resnik has argued that feminist judging will involve more collaborative decision-making among judges.[29] Such changes would have important implications for the possibilities for lawyering and judging as matters of collective engagement rather than the individual exercise of judgment and power.

The primary significance of consciousness-raising, however, is meta-method. Consciousness-raising provides a substructure for other feminist methods – including the woman question and feminist practical reasoning – by enabling feminists to draw insights and perceptions from their own experiences and those of other women and to use these insights to challenge dominant versions of social reality.

Consciousness-raising has done more than help feminists develop and affirm counter-hegemonic perceptions of their experiences. As consciousness-raising has matured as method, disagreements among feminists about the meaning of certain experiences have proliferated. Feminists disagree, for example, about whether women can voluntarily choose heterosexuality, or motherhood; or about whether feminists have more to gain or lose from restrictions against

27 (1986) 61 *NYU Law Rev* 589 pp 602–04.
28 See Menkel-Meadow (1985) 1 *Berkeley Women's LJ* 39, pp 55–58. (Extracted in Chapter 6.)
29 See Resnik, 'On the Bias: Feminist Reconsiderations of the Aspriations for our Judges' (1988) 61 *S Cal L Rev* 1877, pp 1942–43.

pornography, surrogate motherhood, or about whether women should be subject to a military draft. If they disagree about each other's roles in an oppressive society: some feminists accuse others of complicity in the oppression of women.[30]

Feminists disagree even about the method of consciousness-raising; some women worry that it sometimes operates to pressure women into translating their experiences into positions that are politically, rather than experientially, correct.[31]

These disagreements raise questions beyond those of which specific methods are appropriate to feminist practice. Like the woman question and practical reasoning, consciousness-raising challenges the concept of knowledge. It presupposes that what I thought I knew may not, in fact, be 'right'. How, then, will we know when we have got it 'right'? Or, backing up one step, what does it mean to be right? And what attitude should I have about that which I claim to know?[32]

THE EMERGENCE OF FEMINIST JURISPRUDENCE[33]
Ann Scales[34]

Feminist Method Revisited

The term feminist jurisprudence disturbs people. That is not surprising, given patriarchy's convenient habit of labelling as unreliable any approach that admits to be interested, and particularly given the historic *a priori* invalidation of women's experience. That long standing invalidation also causes women, including feminist women, to be reluctant to make any claims beyond the formal reach of liberalism. Further, we are taught to ascribe the legal system's successes to the principle of detachment. In the understandable rush to render feminism acceptable in traditional terms, it is sometimes suggested that we ought to advertise our insight as a revival of the Legal Realism of the 1930s. We are surely indebted to the Realists for their convincing demonstration that the law could not be described, as the positivists had hoped, as a scientific enterprise, devoid of moral or political content. The Realists' description of the influence of morality, economics, and politics upon law is the first step in developing an antidote for legal solipsism. In the end, however, the Realists did not revolutionise the law but merely expanded the concept of legal process. The Realists did not press their critique deeply enough; they did not bring home its implications. In the face of their failure, the system has clung even more desperately to objectivity and neutrality. 'The effect of the Realists was much like the role that Carlyle pronounced for Matthew Arnold: 'He led them into the wilderness and left them there'.[35]

Feminism now faces the charge levelled at Realism, that it destroys the citadel of objectivity and leaves nothing to legitimate the law. Our response to this state of

---

30 See CA MacKinnon, *An Agenda for Theory* (1982) *op cit*, pp 198–205 (accusing women who defend First Amendment values against restrictions on pornography of collaboration).

31 See Colker (1988) 68 *BUL Rev* 217 pp 253–54 (noting that consciousness-raising may influence women to adopt 'inauthentic' expressions of themselves).

32 *Feminist Legal Methods*, pp 838–67.

33 (1986) 95 *Yale LJ* 1373.

34 Professor of Law, University of New Mexico.

35 R Stevens, *Law School: Legal Education in America from the 1950s to the 1980s* (1983), p 156.

affairs begins with an insight not exclusive to feminist thought: The law must finally enter the 20th century. The business of living and progressing within our disciplines requires that we give up on 'objective' verification at various critical moments, such as when we rely upon gravity,[36] or upon the existence of others',[37] or upon the principle of verification itself. Feminism insists upon epistemological and psychological sophistication in law: jurisprudence will forever be stuck in a postrealist battle of subjectivities, with all the discomfort that has represented, until we confront the distinction between knowing subject and known object.

Feminist method is exemplary of that confrontation. The physics of relativity and quantum mechanics demonstrate that nature is on our side: nature itself has begun to evince a less hierarchical structure, a multidirectional flow of authority which corroborates our description of perception. We warmly embrace the uncertainty inherent in that perceptual model, recognising the humanity, and indeed, the security, in it. And because we do not separate the observer from the observed, 'feminism is the first theory to emerge from those whose interest it affirms'.[38] Feminist method proceeds through consciousness-raising. The results of consciousness-raising cannot be verified by traditional methods, nor need they be. We are therefore operating from within an epistemological framework which denies our power to know. This is an inherently transformative process: It validates the experience of women, the major content of which has been invalidation.

> Feminism criticises this male totality without an account of our capacity to do so or to imagine or realise a more whole truth. Feminism affirms women's point of view by revealing, criticising, and explaining its impossibility. This is not a dialectical paradox. It is a methodological expression of women's situation ... Women's situation offers no outside to stand on or gaze at, no inside to escape to, too much urgency to wait, no place else to go, and nothing to use but the twisted tools that have been shoved down our throats. If feminism is revolutionary, this is why.[39]

Consciousness-raising is a vivid expression of self-creation and responsibility. To Wittgenstein's insight that perceptions have meaning only in the context of experience, feminism would add that perceptions have meaning only in the context of an experience that matters. Consciousness-raising means that dramatic eyewitness testimony is being given; it means, more importantly, that women now have the confidence to declare it as such. We have an alternative to relegating our perception to the realm of our own subjective discomfort. Heretofore, the tried and true scientific strategy of treating nonconforming evidence as mistaken worked in the legal system. But when that evidence keeps turning up, when the experience of women becomes recalcitrant, it will be time to treat that evidence as true.

The foundations of the law will not thereby crumble. Though feminism rejects the notion that for a legal system to work, there have to be 'objective' rules, we admit that legality has (or should have) certain qualities. There must be something reliable somewhere, there must be indications of fairness in the system, but neither depends on objectivity. Rather, we need to discard the habit

36 See T Kuhn, *The Structure of Scientific Revolutions* (2nd ed, 1970), p 108.
37 See L Wittgenstein, *Philosophical Investigations*, G Anscombe, trans (3rd edn, 1968).
38 CA MacKinnon, *An Agenda for Theory* (1982) *op cit*.
39 CA MacKinnon, *Toward Feminist Jurisprudence* (1989), *op cit*, pp 637, 639.

of equating our most noble aspirations with objectivity and neutrality. We need at least to redefine those terms, and probably to use others, to meet our very serious responsibilities.

My admission that feminism is result-oriented does not import the renunciation of all standards. In a system defined by constitutional norms such as equality, we need standards to help us make connections among norms, and to help us see 'family resemblances'[40] among instances of domination. Standards, however, are not means without ends: They never have and never can be more than working hypotheses. Just as it would be shocking to find a case that said, 'The petitioner wins though she satisfied no criteria,' so it must ultimately be wrong to keep finding cases that say, 'Petitioner loses though the criteria are indefensible'. In legal situations, a case is either conformed to a standard or the standard is modified with justification. That justification should not be that 'we like the petitioner's facts better'; rather, it is that 'on facts such as these, the standard doesn't hold up'.

The feminist approach takes justification seriously; it is a more honest and efficient way to achieve legitimacy. The feminist legal standard for equality is altogether principled in requiring commitment to finding the moral crux of matters before the court. The feminist approach will tax us. We will be exhausted by bringing feminist method to bear. Yet we must force lawmakers and interpreters to hear that which they have been well trained to ignore. We will have to divest ourselves of our learned reticence, debrief ourselves every day. We will have to trust ourselves to be able to describe life to each other – in our courts, in our legislatures, in our emergence together.

FEMINISM AND LEGAL METHOD: THE DIFFERENCE IT MAKES[41]

Mary Jane Mossman

> The fact that our understanding of *homo sapiens* has incorporated the perspective of only half of the human race makes it clear that women's studies is not an additional knowledge merely to be tacked on to the curriculum. It is, instead, a body of knowledge that is perspective transforming and should therefore transform the existing curriculum from within and revise received notions of what constitutes an 'objective' or 'normative' perspective.[42]

These words appeared in *A Feminist Perspective in the Academy: The Difference it Makes*, a book of essays about the impact of feminist ideas on a number of academic disciplines, including literature, drama, economics, sociology, history, political science, anthropology, psychology, and religious studies. The authors of these essays suggested that a feminist perspective has only just begun to 'affect the shape of what is known and knowable in their respective disciplines'.[43] The authors also asserted that a feminist perspective 'challenges deeply held, often sacred beliefs, beliefs that are rooted in emotions and expressed in primitive imagery'. As well, it 'challenges vested interests, and uproots perspectives which

---

40 Wittgenstein, *op cit*, p 32.
41 (1987) *Wisconsin Women's Law Journal* (Footnotes edited).
42 Langland and Gove (1981), p 3.
43 *Ibid*, p 2.

are familiar, and, because familiar, comfortable'. In short, 'feminist ideas are a challenge to the *status quo*'.[44]

Given these perceptions about the transforming impact of feminism on the world of ideas in general, it is curious that this collection did not include an essay about the impact of feminist ideas on law. Moreover, what seems at first glance a mere oversight becomes on closer inspection a question of great significance: to what extent can feminist theory impact, if at all, on the structure of legal inquiry? In the law's process of determining facts, choosing and applying principles, and reaching reasoned decisions, is there any scope for feminism's fundamental challenge to our 'ways of knowing?'

This question needs to be addressed in the context of the definition of feminism adopted by the editors of *A Feminist Perspective in the Academy*:

> All feminists ... would agree that women are not automatically or necessarily inferior to men, that role models for females and males in the current Western societies are inadequate, that equal rights for women are necessary, that it is unclear what by nature either men or women are, that it is a matter for empirical investigation to ascertain what differences follow from the obvious physiological ones, that in these empirical investigations the hypotheses one employs are themselves open to question, revision, or replacement.[45]

The first part of this definition, especially its assertion that 'equal rights for women are necessary' assumes the existence of inequality and the need for societal change; in this respect, it represents a clear challenge to the *status quo*.

Yet, it is the latter part of the definition which represents an even more fundamental challenge: feminism's quest for an understanding of the nature of men and women demands a reassessment of the structure of our inquiry and the ways in which we ask our questions. Not only are the answers subject to scrutiny, but also the ways in which we search for them. In challenging the validity of 'facts,' the possibility of 'neutrality' and the equity of 'conclusions' which result from such analysis, a feminist perspective directs attention to our 'ways of knowing' about men and women as well as to our efforts to seek greater equality for women. Such a quest, moreover, may require new methods of inquiry; as Jill McCalla Vickers has suggested, women may 'learn little of themselves useful for achieving change by employing the intellectual tools of their oppressors'.[46]

Can a feminist agenda be accommodated within the legal system? Traditionally, legal method has operated within a highly structured framework which offers little opportunity for fundamental questioning about the process of defining issues, selecting relevant principles, and excluding irrelevant ideas. In this context, decision-making takes place according to a form which usually 'sees' present questions according to patterns established in the past, and in a context in which ongoing consistency in ideas may be valued more often than their future vitality.

In beginning to explore this relation between feminism and legal method, I decided to try to identify the features of legal method in practice, and to do so in the context of 'women's rights' cases where the claims being asserted might be

---

44 *Ibid*, pp 2–3.
45 Barnes, as quoted in Langland and Gove, p 3.
46 Macalla and Vickers, in Miles and Finn (1982), p 32.

expected to reflect feminist ideas and objectives. In this case study of two early 20th century cases, the approaches used by judges in deciding claims concerning new roles for women in society are very well illustrated. With the benefit of our historical perspective, moreover, it is clear that the structure of the legal inquiry significantly affected both these decisions. This conclusion, moreover, provides the basis for beginning to assess the potential impact of feminism's 'transforming perspective' in present day challenges to achieve sex equality.

The Idea of Difference

Just a few years before the 19th century drew to a close, Clara Brett Martin was admitted to the practice of law in Ontario, the first woman to become a lawyer in the British Commonwealth. Her petition for admission was initially denied by the Law Society on the basis that there were no precedents for the admission of women as lawyers. However, in 1892 a legislative amendment was passed permitting women to be admitted as solicitors; three years later, another legislative amendment similarly permitted women to be admitted as barristers. Clara Brett Martin herself was finally admitted in February 1897 as a barrister and solicitor.

Because of the admission arrangements in Ontario, it was the Law Society of Upper Canada, rather than a superior court, which reviewed the issue of Clara Brett Martin's entitlement to admission as a lawyer. By contrast, there was a court challenge in the Province of New Brunswick when Mabel Penury French sought admission as a lawyer there in 1905.[47] When her application was presented to the court, the judges decided unanimously that there were no precedents for the admission of women, and denied the application. In the next year, however, after the enactment of a legislative amendment, French was admitted as a lawyer in New Brunswick.[48] The same pattern of judicial denial of the application followed by legislative amendment) occurred again some years later when she applied for admission by transfer in British Columbia, and in a number of the other Canadian provinces when women applied for admission as lawyers.

In contrast to the cases where women sought to enter the legal profession and were denied admission by the courts, the celebrated Privy Council decision in the *Persons* Case[49] determined that Canadian women were eligible to participate in public life. In the *Persons* case, five women challenged the meaning of the word 'persons' in s 24 of the British North America Act. Section 24 provided that the Governor General 'shall ... summon qualified Persons to the Senate,' and there was no express requirement that Senators be male persons. Yet, even though the language of the section was gender-neutral, no woman in Canada had ever been summoned to become a member of the Senate.

The Supreme Court of Canada considered a reference as to the meaning of the word 'persons' in the British North America Act in 1928, and concluded that women were not eligible to become Senators. On appeal to the Privy Council the next year, the decision was reversed. Ironically, it was in the Privy Council, and not in the indigenous courts of Canada, that the claim of 'equal rights for women' to participate in public life was successful. The decisions in these cases offer an interesting historical picture of legal process in the cultural milieu of the

---

47   *In re French* (1905) 37 NBR 359.

48   6 Ed VII c 5 (1906).

49   *Reference re: Meaning of the Word 'Persons' in s 24 of the British North America Act* (1928) SCR 276; *Edwards v AG for Canada* [1930] 1 AC 124.

early 20th century. In the cases about the admission of women to the legal profession, judges accepted the idea that there was a difference between men and women, a difference which 'explained' and 'justified' the exclusion of women from the legal profession. Yet, the Privy Council's decision in the *Persons* case completely discounted any such difference in relation to the participation of women in public life.

The issue is why there were these differing approaches: was it the nature of the claims, the courts in which they were presented, or the dates of the decisions? More significantly, what can we learn from the reasoning in these cases about the nature of legal method, especially in the context of challenges to 'deeply held beliefs, vested interests, and the *status quo*'? In other words, what do these cases suggest about the potential impact of feminism on legal method? *French's* case in New Brunswick provides a good illustration of judicial decision-making on the issue of women in law. Her case was presented to the court for direction as to the admissibility of women by the president of the Barristers' Society of New Brunswick (as *amicus curiae*), and the court decided that women were not eligible for admission. Indeed, Mr Justice Tuck emphatically declared that he had no sympathy for women who wanted to compete with men; as he said: 'Better let them attend to their own legitimate business'.[50] Mr Justice Tuck did not expand on his views as to the nature of women's 'legitimate business'. However, it seems likely that he would have agreed with the views expressed by Mr Justice Barker in the case. Relying on the decision of the United States Supreme Court in *Bradwell v. Illinois* in 1873,[51] Mr Justice Barker adopted as his own the 'separate spheres' doctrine enunciated there: ... 'the civil law, as well as nature herself, has always recognised a wide difference in the respective spheres and destinies of man and woman. Man is, or should be, woman's protector and defender. The natural and proper timidity and delicacy which belongs to the female sex evidently unfits it for many of the occupations of civil life. The constitution of the family organisation, which is founded in the divine ordinance as well as in the nature of things, indicates the domestic sphere as that which properly belongs to the domain and functions of womanhood'.[52]

The language of the *Bradwell* decision expressed very clearly an unqualified acceptance of the idea of difference between men and women, a difference which was social as well as biological. From the perspective of legal method, however, it is significant that no evidence was offered for his assertions about the 'timidity and delicacy' of women in general; no authorities were cited for the existence of 'divine law'; and no studies were referred to in support of the conclusion that the domestic sphere belonged 'properly' to women (and vice versa). The court merely cited the existence of divine and natural law in general terms.

The legal reasoning used by Mr Justice Barker does not seem consistent at all with the recognised principles of legal method: the reliance on relevant and persuasive evidence to determine facts, the use of legal precedents to provide a framework for analysis, and a rational conclusion supported by both evidence and legal principles. Yet, if Barker, J's ideas are not the product of legal method, what is their source?

The answer, of course, is that the ideas he expressed were those prevailing in the cultural and professional milieu in which he lived. The ideas of mainstream

---

50 At pp 361–62.
51 83 US (16 Wall) 130.
52 *In re French* (1905) 37 NBR 359, p 365.

religion, for example, emphasised the differences between men and women. Moreover, even where women and men were regarded as equal in the eyes of God (in the ideas of reformers such as Calvin, for example), women were still expected to be subordinate to men, their subordination reflecting 'the divinely created social order' in which God 'ordained' the subjugation of wives to their husbands.

The idea of a divinely created 'social office' in the religious tradition, which required women and, men to perform quite different social roles, was reinforced by secular ideas in philosophy in which the role of the family prescribed defined roles for women. Even John Stuart Mill, who was well known for his progressive views about the rights of women, considered that equal rights to education, political life, and the professions could be granted only to single women without the responsibilities of family. Moreover, even if Mr Justice Barker had turned to scientific thought at the turn of the century, he would have found these views confirmed. Because scientific inquiry took place within an already existing framework of knowledge, it was almost inevitable that scientists would find the answers to questions they asked rather than to others which they did not ask, and confirmation of differences rather than similarities between women and men.

The ideas described from religion, philosophy, and science were those current in the mainstream of intellectual life at the turn of the century. There were, of course, other ideas also current at that time: ideas of religious equality among the Shakers, and also with liberals such as the Grimke sisters; ideas about sex equality, however flawed, in the work of philosophers like Mill and scientific ideas about the influence of environment on traits of men and women. Yet such ideas were less well accepted than those in the mainstream, those so warmly embraced in the court by Barker, J.

What is significant here is the court's uncritical acceptance of ideas from the mainstream of intellectual life, as if they were factual rather than conceptual. Moreover, in accepting these ideas and making them an essential part of his decision, Barker, J. provided an explicit and very significant reinforcement of the idea of gender-based difference. In this way, the particular decision denying French's claim to practice law had an impact well beyond the instant case. Thereafter, in the law, as well as in other intellectual traditions, there was a recognised and 'legitimate' difference between women and men.

Two other points must also be mentioned. It is significant to an assessment of legal method that the ideas about the role of women, first expressed in the *Bradwell* case in 1873, were adopted without question over thirty years later in *French's* case in 1905. That the court apparently did not question the appropriateness of applying a precedent from an earlier generation, and from a foreign jurisdiction, seems remarkable. The possibility of distinguishing the earlier decision is clear; and the court's acceptance, without question, of the *Bradwell* decision as both relevant and apparently binding is initially perplexing. As well, the *Bradwell* decision relied in part on the inability of married women to enter into contracts because of their common law disability, still in existence in 1873. Barker J might have been expected to comment on the fact that married women's property legislation, both in Canada and in the United States, had erased most of these disabilities by 1905, thereby providing a further reason for distinguishing rather than following *Bradwell*. As such analysis demonstrates, the *Bradwell* precedent was not self-applying; there was a choice to be made by the court in *French*. The more difficult problem, therefore, is to explain the reasons for the judicial choice. Even more fundamentally, the ideas accepted in *Bradwell* and restated in *French* were quite inconsistent, and probably known to be so by the judges, with the reality of women's work outside the home at the turn of the century. In Canada, as well as in Great Britain, very few of the women whom the judges knew, whether they were litigants, or cleaners of the courtroom, or servants in the home, actually corresponded in any way to the judicial representation. At the time when the judges were speaking, more than a million unmarried women alone were employed in industry, while a further three quarters of a million were in domestic service. For the great majority of Victorian women, as for the great majority of Victorian men, life was characterised by drudgery and poverty rather than by refinement and decorum.[53]

Despite this reality, Mr Justice Barker reiterated without criticism or qualification the authoritative statement from *Bradwell* that 'the paramount destiny and mission of women' was that of wife and mother – because 'this is the law of the Creator'.[54] The conflict which is apparent to us between the judicial description of all women, and the known conditions in which at least some of them lived at that time, suggests a further element of legal method: abstraction from the real lives of women. Indeed, what seems evident is a willingness to use the ideas of (male) theologians, philosophers, and scientists as the basis of 'reality,' in preference to the facts of life in the real lives of actual women.

The judicial approach evident in *French* changed significantly, however, by the time of the *Persons* case. There is little mention of the idea of gender-based difference in the analysis of either the Supreme Court of Canada or the Privy Council in that case. In the Supreme Court of Canada, Mr Justice Mignault referred to the petitioners' claim only as a 'grave constitutional change',[55] and Mr Justice Anglin restated the 'apologia' from *Chorlton v Lings*[56] that:

> ... in this country in modern times, chiefly out of respect to women, and a sense of decorum, and not from their want of intellect, or their being for any other such reason unfit to take part in the government of the country, they have been excused from taking any share in this department of public affairs.[57]

However, nothing in the judgments of the Supreme Court of Canada reflects the rhetoric and ideas expressed by Mr Justice Barker in Mabel French's case. And, by contrast, Lord Sankey commenced his opinion in the Privy Council by stating:

> The exclusion of women from all public offices is a relic of days more barbarous than ours, but it must be remembered that the necessity of the times often forced on man customs which in later years were not necessary.[58]

His words represented a clear signal that, although the treatment of women in the past may have been understandable in the context of those times, the world had changed.

In the *Persons* case, that is all there is about the difference between men and women. The contrast between the reliance on gender-based difference as incontrovertible fact in *French* at the turn of the century, and the virtual absence

---

53 A Sachs and J Hoff Wilson, *Sexism and the Law* (1978), p 54.
54 At p 366.
55 At p 303.
56 (1868) LR 4 CP 374.
57 At p 283.
58 At p 128.

of such ideas in the *Persons* case in the late 1920s, seems highly significant. It seems, indeed, to offer an explanation for the differing outcomes in the two cases: when difference was emphasised in *French*, women were excluded from membership in the legal profession, while when it was discounted in the *Persons* case, women were included with men in opportunities to participate in public life.

This analytical approach, based as it is on the methodology actually observed in these two judicial decisions, suggests that the dictates of legal method were not strictly followed in the decision-making process. In addition to this approach, however, it is necessary to assess the legal method actually described by the judges in the cases. The contrast between what they said they were doing, and what they actually did, also offers some important insights into legal method. To this contrast we now turn.

The Principles of Legal Method

The stated reasons in these cases were consistent with well established principles of legal method. The principles can be analysed in terms of three aspects: (1) the characterisation of the issues; (2) the choice of legal precedents to decide the validity of the women's claims; and (3) the process of statutory interpretation, especially in determining the effect of statutes to alter common law principles. Both the principles themselves and their application to these specific claims are important for an understanding of the potential impact of feminism on legal method.

Characterising the Issue

In both *French* and the *Persons* case, the judges consistently characterised the issues as narrowly as possible, eschewing their 'political' or 'social' significance, and explaining that the court was interested only in the law. For example, in the *Persons* case in the Canadian Supreme Court, Chief Justice Anglin stated pointedly:

> In considering this matter we are, of course, in no wise concerned with the desirability or the undesirability of the presence of women in the Senate, nor with any political aspect of the question submitted. Our whole duty is to construe, to the best of our ability, the relevant provisions of the BNA Act, 1867, and upon that construction to base our answer.[59]

Even the Privy Council which came to a distinctly different conclusion framed the scope of its inquiry as narrowly as possible. Clearly evident in these judicial statements is a felt need to distance the court from the 'political' or moral issue, and a desire to be guided only by neutral principles of interpretation in relation to abstract legal concepts. The judges' confidence in the principles of legal method as a means of deciding the issue, even confined so narrowly, is also evident. While their comments suggest an awareness of broader issues, there is a clear assertion of the court's limited role in resolving such disputes.

Equally clearly, the women claimants never intended to bring to the court a 'neutral' legal issue for determination; they petitioned the court to achieve their goals, goals which were unabashedly political. In the face of such claims, however, the court maintained a view of its process as one of neutral interpretation. More significantly, the court's power to define the 'real issues' carried with it an inherent absence of responsibility on the part of the (male) judges for any negative outcome. It was the law, rather than the (male) person

---

59   At pp 281–82.

interpreting it, which was responsible for the decision. The result of such a characterisation process, therefore, is to reinforce the law's detachment and neutrality rather than its involvement and responsibility; and to extend these characteristics beyond law itself to judges and lawyers. Yet, how can we accommodate this characterisation of detachment and neutrality with the opinions expressed, especially in *French*, about the role of women? The ideas about gender-based difference expressed forcefully by Mr Justice Barker in that case appear very close to an expression about the 'desirability' of women as lawyers and not merely a dispassionate and neutral application of legal precedents. Thus, at least in *French*, there is inconsistency between the legal method declared by the judges to be appropriate, and the legal method actually adopted in making their decisions. In this context, the expressed idea of detachment and neutrality both masks and legitimates judicial views about women's 'proper' sphere,

Using Precedents in the Common Law Tradition

The existence of women's common law disability was regularly cited in both these cases as the reason for denying their claims to be admitted to the legal profession and to take part in public life. The judges used numerous precedents for their conclusion. For example, Chief Justice Anglin cited as a 'fact or circumstance of importance ... that by the common law of England (as also, speaking generally, by the civil and the canon law ...) women were under a legal incapacity to hold public office ... .[60] At the end of the 19th century, of course, there were a number of respects in which women (especially married women) suffered disabilities at common law: married women were denied the right to hold interests in property until the married women's property statutes, and all women were denied the right to vote until the 20th century. As well, however, courts regularly asserted that, because of women's common law disabilities, there were no precedents for admitting women to the legal profession or to full participation in public life.

It has been suggested that the absence of such a common law precedent can be traced to Lord Coke who (apparently without the benefit of precedent) 'had stated that women could not be attorneys' 300 years previously.[61] What is clear, at least, is that the absence of precedents declaring women eligible to take part in public life and enter the legal profession created a significant handicap for those presenting arguments in favour of the women's claims. From a broader perspective, this difficulty epitomises the negative effects of the doctrine of precedent on newly emerging claims to legal rights. If a precedent is required to uphold a claim, it is only existing claims which will receive legal recognition; the doctrine of precedent thus becomes a powerful tool for maintaining the *status quo* and for rationalising the denial of new claims. Seen in this light, the law itself is an essential means of protecting the *status quo*, notwithstanding the challenge of feminist ideas.

Yet, if this conclusion is correct, how can we explain the Privy Council decision, a decision in which the same conceptual framework of law was viewed very differently. After canvassing the precedents, Lord Sankey stated:

> The fact that no woman had served or has claimed to serve such an office is not of great weight when it is remembered that custom would have prevented the claim being made or the point being contested. Customs are

---

60   At p 283.
61   A Sachs and J Hoff Wilson, *op cit*, p 32.

apt to develop into traditions which are stronger than law and remain unchallenged long after the reason for them has disappeared. The appeal to history therefore in this particular matter is not conclusive.[62]

Obviously, the Privy Council was less concerned with the absence of precedent in their decision-making than the judges in *French*. Is this approach simply an early example of a court of highest jurisdiction deciding not to be bound by precedent in appropriate cases, or is there some other explanation?

One suggestion is that the decision of the Privy Council in 1929 simply reflected the spirit of the times in relation to the role of women. Much had indeed changed since Clara Brett Martin and Mabel Penury French had sought admission to the legal profession at the turn of the century. As was noted earlier, there had been legislation enabling married women to enter into contracts and to hold interests in property even before the end of the 19th century. In the early part of the 20th century, moreover, women had participated successfully in World War One, and they had attained suffrage in many jurisdictions after the War and the benefit of the Sexual Disqualification Removal Act in England in 1919. It may, therefore, be quite accurate to conclude that the explanation is not one of 'legal logic'; instead, it is evident that 'what had changed was not ... the modes of reasoning appropriate to lawyers, but the conception of women and women's position in public life held by the judges.'[63]

At the same time, if this explanation is accepted, it is difficult to account for the differences in perspective of the judges of the Supreme Court of Canada in 1928 from those in the Privy Council in 1929. It is true that Lord Sankey sat in the English Cabinet alongside Margaret Bondfield, the first woman to hold Cabinet office in Britain; and it is, therefore, possible that he had become accustomed to the idea of women holding public office as a result of this 'precedent'. This conclusion, of course, depends on the assumption that no similar role models existed in Canada. Yet such a conclusion denies the importance of the roles of the five women challengers in the *Persons* case: Henrietta Muir Edwards was the Alberta Vice-President of the National Council of Women for Canada, Nellie McClung and Louise McKinney had been members of the Legislative Assembly in Alberta, while Irene Parlby was then a member of the same Legislative Assembly and of its Executive Council; and Emily Murphy was the first woman police magistrate in Alberta. It is therefore difficult, if not impossible, not to accept these Canadian women as 'precedents' equal to Margaret Bondfield. What, then, is the explanation for these differing perspectives and the different outcomes which resulted in the two courts? In terms of the legal method described by the judges, of course, there is no answer to this question. Neither the judgments in the Supreme Court of Canada nor Lord Sankey's opinion in the Privy Council expressly consider the reality of women's experience at that time at all, and they specifically do not consider the reality of experience for the actual women claimants in the *Persons* case. Thus, even if the judges' perspectives on women's place were different in the two courts, there is virtually nothing in their judgments expressly reflecting them. For this reason, it is impossible to demonstrate that Lord Sankey's differing perspective was the reason for the different outcome in the Privy Council. At the same time, it is hard to find any other convincing explanation.

---

62   At p 134.

63   A Sachs and J Hoff Wilson, *op cit*, p 42.

What does, of course, seem clear is the existence of judicial choice in the application of precedents. In the process of choosing earlier cases and deciding that they are binding precedents, judges make choices about which aspects of earlier cases are 'relevant' and 'similar,' choices which are not neutral but normative. In suggesting that the earlier decisions (relied on by the Supreme Court of Canada as binding precedents) were not determinative, Lord Sankey was declaring that the earlier decisions should not be regarded as exactly the same as the situation before the court in the *Persons* case. In this way, Lord Sankey's decision demonstrates the availability of choice in the selection of facts, in the categorisation of principles and in the determination of relevance. At the same time, his opinion completely obscures the process and standards which guided the choice he actually made. To the myth of 'neutrality,' therefore, Lord Sankey added the 'mystery' of choice.

Interpreting Statutes and Parliament's Intent

The interpretation of the law relating to women's claims was complicated by the need for judges to construe statutes as well as take account of common law principles. in some earlier cases, for example, women had challenged their exclusion from rights in statutes where the statutory language referred to 'men'. Such claims were based on the 1850 legislation[64] in England which provided that 'words importing the masculine gender should be deemed and taken to include females, unless the contrary was clearly expressed'. In *Chorlton v Lings*, a case involving the right to be registered to vote under legislation which gave such a right to any 'man,' the court dismissed the women's claim on the basis that it could not have been the wish of Parliament to make so drastic a change; had Parliament wished to enable women to vote, it would not have used the word 'man' in setting out the qualifications for voting in the statute.

Even in the statutes which used gender-neutral language, however, there were problems of statutory interpretation in relation to these cases. The legislation reviewed in the *Persons* case, as well as that at issue in the admission of both Martin and French, used the word 'person' in describing the qualifications for being appointed to the Senate and called to the bar respectively. In the *Persons* case in the Supreme Court of Canada, Chief Justice Anglin expressed his surprise that such a monumental change in the position of women could be conferred by Parliament's use of such insignificant means; as he stated rhetorically: 'Such an extraordinary privilege is not conferred furtively'.[65] Not surprisingly, he concluded that the women's claim must be dismissed because there was no evident express intent on the part of Parliament to effect the change advocated by them; the use of the word 'person' was not, by itself, sufficient.

A similar result occurred in French's challenge in the New Brunswick court. The legislation governing the admission of lawyers used the word 'person'; indeed, the legislation in New Brunswick had used gender-neutral language for many years. Unfortunately, this latter fact reinforced the judges' conclusion that the statute could not have been intended to include women, since they had never been lawyers.[66] Mr Justice Barker had doubt at all as to the appropriate resolution of this problem of statutory interpretation, concluding that any

---

64 Lord Brougham's Act 1850 (Imp) c 21.

65 At p 285.

66 At pp 370–71.

suggestion that the word 'person' encompassed females was a 'radical change' indeed.[67]

Thus, Canadian judges uniformly interpreted the word 'person' in a way which seemed most consistent with their time and experiences. For them, it was radical indeed to think of a woman in public office or in the legal profession, and their interpretation of the statutory language reflected their own understanding of what Parliament might have intended, had Parliament considered the matter explicitly. Presumably, the judges also felt confidence that members of Parliament, (male) people much like the judges themselves, would have agreed with their interpretation.

Once again, however, the opinion of the Privy Council is different. After reviewing at some length the legislative provisions of the BNA Act, Lord Sankey stated conclusively:

> The word 'person' ... may include members of both sexes, and to those who ask why the word should include females, the obvious answer is why should it not. In these circumstances the burden is upon those who deny that the word includes women to make out their case.[68]

Lord Sankey cited no precedent to support this presumption in favour of the most extensive meaning of the statutory language, even though it expressly contradicted the principles of statutory interpretation adopted by all the judges in the decision of the Supreme Court of Canada. In the end, just as the Privy Council decision was puzzling in relation to the effect of legal precedents about women's common law disabilities, it is also difficult to reconcile Lord Sankey's conclusions about the interpretation of the statute to the principles and precedents accepted in the Supreme Court of Canada. Clearly, the Privy Council departed from the Supreme Court's approach to legal method in reaching its conclusion to admit the women's claim. What remains unclear are Lord Sankey's reasons for doing so.

Feminism and Legal Method

In such a context, what conclusion is appropriate about feminism's potential for perspective transforming in the context of legal method? The analysis of these cases illustrates clearly the structure of inquiry identified as legal method. First of all, legal method defines its own boundaries: questions which are inside the defined boundaries can be addressed, but those outside the boundaries are not 'legal' issues, however important they may be for 'politics' or 'morals,' etc. Thus, the question of women becoming lawyers or Senators was simply a matter of interpreting the law; it did not require any consideration of utility or benefit to the women themselves or to society in general. The purpose and the result of the boundary defining exercise is to confer 'neutrality' on the law and on its decision-makers; in so doing, moreover, the process also relieves both the law and its decision-makers of accountability for (unjust) decisions – ('our whole duty is [only] to construe ... the provisions of the [constitution]').

More serious is the potential for judicial attitudes to be expressed, and to be used in decision-making (either explicitly or implicitly), when there is no 'objective' evidence to support them; because of the myth of neutrality which surrounds the process, such attitudes may acquire legitimacy in a way which strengthens and reinforces ideas in 'politics' and 'morals' which were supposed to be outside the

---

67 At p 371.
68 At p 138.

law's boundary. After the decision in *French*, for example, women were different as a matter of law, and not just in the minds of people like Mr Justice Barker. Thus, the power to name the boundaries of the inquiry (and to change them, if necessary) makes legal method especially impervious to challenges from 'the outside'.

Second, legal method defines 'relevance' and accordingly excludes some ideas while admitting others. Some facts, such as inherent gender-based traits, were regarded as relevant in *French*, for example, while in both cases the actual conditions in which women lived their lives were not relevant at all. What was clearly relevant in both cases were earlier decisions about similar circumstances from which the judges could abstract principles of general application. That all of the earlier cases had been decided by men, who were interpreting legislation drafted when women had no voting rights, was completely irrelevant to the decision-making in the cases analysed; even though the cases represented direct challenges to the continuation of gender-exclusive roles and the circumstances of the historical context may seem quite significant to women now. The irony of solemn judicial reliance on precedent in the context of significant efforts by women to change the course of legal history underlines the significant role of legal method in preserving the *status quo*.

Finally, the case analysis demonstrates the opportunity for choice in legal method: choice as to which precedents are relevant and which approach to statutory interpretation is preferred; and choice as to whether the ideas of the mainstream or those of the margins are appropriate. The existence of choice in legal method offered some possibility of positive outcomes in the women's rights cases, at the same time as legal method's definition of boundaries and concept of relevance ensured that positive outcomes would seldom occur. Lord Sankey's opinion in the Privy Council is an example of choice in legal method, however, which is as remarkable for its common sense as it is for its distinctiveness in legal method. Yet because Lord Sankey obscured the reasons for his choice, he also preserved the power and mystery of legal method even as he endowed women with the right to be summoned to the Senate. Thus, the opportunity for choice of outcome, positive as it appears, will not automatically lead to legal results which successfully challenge 'vested interests' or the '*status quo*', especially in relation to the law itself.

The conclusion that legal method is structured in such a way which makes it impervious to a feminist perspective is a sobering one. Within the women's movement, it has concrete consequences for the design of strategies for achieving legal equality: it suggests, for example, the general futility of court action for achieving significant change in women's rights, even though such action may be useful to monitor interpretation by courts or to focus attention on legal problems. For a feminist who is also a lawyer, however, the effort of 'double-think' may be both taxing and ultimately frustrating; the needs of clients require her to become highly proficient at legal method at the same time as her feminist commitment drives her to challenge the validity of its underlying rationale.

This dilemma also exists for feminist scholars. Feminist legal scholars are expected to think and write using the approaches of legal method: defining the issues, analysing relevant precedents, and recommending conclusions according to defined and accepted standards of legal method. A feminist scholar who chooses instead to ask different questions or to conceptualise the problem in different ways risks a reputation for incompetence in her legal method as well as lack of recognition for her scholarly (feminist) accomplishment. Too often, it seems almost impossible to be both a good lawyer and a good feminist scholar.

This dilemma is similarly acute for feminist law teachers and students. With the advent of large numbers of women law students and increased numbers of women on law faculties, many have concluded that there is now a feminist perspective in the law school. Such a conclusion ignores the power of legal method to resist structural change. For example, discussions about whether feminist law teachers should create separate courses with feminist approaches and content, or whether we should use such approaches and content in 'malestream' courses, or whether we should do both at once, etc, clearly confirm the 'reality' of the existing categories of legal knowledge, and reinforce the idea of the feminist perspective as 'Other'. While the separate course approach marginalises the feminist perspective, the process of 'tacking on' feminist approaches to malestream courses only serves to emphasise what is really important in contrast to what has been 'tacked on'. Even efforts to give equal time to the feminist perspective and to reveal the essential maleness of the 'neutral' approach may underline that what is male is what really has significance. On this basis, adding women's experience to the law school curriculum cannot transform our perspective of law unless it also transforms legal method.

Taking this conclusion seriously, as I think we must, leads to some significant conclusions for women who are feminists and who are lawyers, law teachers and law students. It is simply not enough just to introduce women's experience into the curriculum or to examine the feminist approach to legal issues, although both of these activities are important. Yet, especially because there is so much resistance in legal method itself to ideas which challenge the *status quo*, there is no solution for the feminist who is a law teacher except to confront the reality that gender and power are inextricably linked in the legal method we use in our work, our discourse, and our study. Honestly confronting the barriers of our conceptual framework may at least permit us to begin to ask more searching and important questions ... .

PART II

CENTRAL CONCEPTS IN FEMINIST JURISPRUDENCE

CHAPTER 5

PATRIARCHY: PUBLIC AND PRIVATE

Before considering the many and varied means by which sexual discrimination and inequality is rooted in the law, it is necessary to consider a central concept of feminist jurisprudence: that of patriarchy. For feminist scholars, the concept of patriarchy – of male power, control and dominance – represents a powerful reminder of female exclusion and powerlessness. Patriarchy has been defined as:

(1) a form of social organisation in which a male is head of the family and descent, kinship, and title are traced through the male line; and

(2) any society governed by such a system.[1]

As anthropologist Bradislow Malinowski has detailed, patriarchal societies are the norm throughout the world. A few matriarchal societies nevertheless remain, and there is evidence to suggest that matriarchal societies were widespread in times long past.[2] Friedrich Engels analysed the reasons for the transition from matriarchal society to patriarchal society, arguing that the transition is effected at the point in time in which individuals acquire private property. On this view, patriarchy is explained as a matter of economic management and succession through the male line.[3] However, even where matriarchal societies continue to exist, it is clear from Malinowski's research, that the question of property management – and thus power – remains in male hands, for property management is vested not in the female head of the family, but rather in her male kin.

Patriarchy manifests itself in every forum – within the family, in religion, in employment, and in political life. Patriarchal attitudes in part explain the phenomenon of violence against women, both within the family unit and between strangers. In the transition from culture to law,[4] the concept of patriarchy illuminates much that is otherwise unclear about the 'maleness' of the law and the legal process.[5]

The male assumption of the natural right of control and power in all fora is the subject of feminist analysis and in this chapter that analysis is considered.

In *Theorizing Patriarchy*,[6] Sylvia Walby analyses the structure of contemporary patriarchy: in modes of production; in relations in paid work; in relations within the State; in male violence; in sexual relations and in relations in cultural institutions.

---

1   *Collins English Dictionary* (1991, 3rd edn).

2   B Malinowski, *Sex and Repression in Savage Society* (1927) (Routledge and Kegan Paul, 1927).

3   F Engels, *The Origins of the Family, Private Property and the State* (1884) (Lawrence and Wishart, 1940).

4   See Chapter 2.

5   See, in particular, Chapter 10 on the legal system's response to victims of rape and domestic violence.

6   Blackwell, 1990.

In *Pornography: Men Possessing Women*,[7] radical feminist author Andrea Dworkin analyses patriarchy as consisting of 'a metaphysical assertion of self' and concept which 'expresses intrinsic authority'.[8] Subsumed within this assertion of authority is the denial of women's power; the right to physical strength; the power – through that physical strength – to subordinate by forms of fear – 'symbols of terror'[9] – individual women and women as a class. Men also assume, Dworkin writes, the power of 'naming', that is to say, the power to define thought, experience and language, to the exclusion of women. Fifth, Dworkin identifies the power of ownership. Men, traditionally and contemporarily, hold the power to own women, to deny them the right to own property in their own name, deny them the right to refuse intercourse in marriage (a position which held true in the United Kingdom until 1991). Finally, Dworkin identifies the power to control women through financial control, through dominating positions of power and influence in society, and through relegating women to less remunerative positions. Finally, the seventh tenet of male power is, for Dworkin, the power of sex. Women from this point of view are defined as sexual objects in the stereotypical definition given to female sexuality by male power. In Dworkin's words, 'sexual power illuminates his very nature'.[10] Andrea Dworkin's powerfully angry words – however intuitively appealing to the reader – offer little succour to those for whom some reconciliation between the sexes – on the basis of true equality – is both desirable and necessary. By way of contrast, Shelley Wright, in the passage which follows, whilst tracing the origins of patriarchy, and the transition from religious to secular patriarchy, offers an insight into the means by which progress towards full and equal citizenship might be achieved.

Patriarchy is neither a vacuous concept, nor does it exist in a vacuum. As the extracts which follow reveal, patriarchy is sited in both the 'public' and 'private' spheres of life. In the second part of this chapter, the dichotomy between the 'public' and 'private' realms of life are considered.

THEORISING PATRIARCHY[11]

Sylvia Walby[12]

Patriarchy needs to be conceptualised at different levels of abstraction. At the most abstract level it exists as a system of social relations. In contemporary Britain this is present in articulation with capitalism and with racism. However, I do not wish to imply that it is homologous in internal structure with capitalism. At a less abstract level patriarchy is composed of six structures: the patriarchal mode of production, patriarchal relations in paid work, patriarchal relations in the state, male violence, patriarchal relations in sexuality, and patriarchal

---

7   Andrea Dworkin, *Pornography: Men Possessing Women* (The Women's Press, 1981).

8   *Ibid*, p 13.

9   *Ibid*, p 15.

10   *Ibid*, p 24.

11   Sylvia Walby, *Theorising Patriarchy* (Blackwell, 1990).

12   At the time of writing, Lecturer in Sociology, the London School of Economics and Political Science.

relations in cultural institutions. More concretely, in relation to each of the structures, it is possible to identify sets of patriarchal practices which are less deeply sedimented. Structures are emergent properties of practices. Any specific empirical instance will embody the effects, not only of patriarchal structures, but also of capitalism and racism.

The six structures have causal effects upon each other, both reinforcing and blocking, but are relatively autonomous. The specification of several rather than simply one base is necessary in order to avoid reductionism and essentialism. The presence of only one base, for instance, reproduction for Firestone[13] and rape for Brownmiller,[14] is the reason for their difficulty with historical change and cultural variation. It is not necessary to go to the other extreme of denying significant social structures to overcome the charge of essentialism, as some of the postmodernist poststructuralists have done. The six identified are real, deep structures and necessary to capture the variation of gender relations in Westernised societies.

Patriarchal production relations in the household are my first structure. It is through these that women's household labour is expropriated by their husbands or cohabitees. The woman may receive her maintenance in exchange for her labour, especially when she is not also engaged in waged labour. Housewives are the producing class, while husbands are the expropriating class.

The second patriarchal structure within the economic level is that of patriarchal relations within paid work. A complex of forms of patriarchal closure within waged labour exclude women from the better forms of work and segregate them into the worse jobs which are deemed to be less skilled.

The State is patriarchal as well as being capitalist and racist. While being a site of struggle and not a monolithic entity, the State has a systematic bias towards patriarchal interests in its policies and action.

Male violence constitutes a further structure, despite its apparently individualistic and diverse form. It is behaviour routinely experienced by women from men, with standard effects upon the actions of most women. Male violence against women is systematically condoned and legitimated by the State's refusal to intervene against it except in exceptional instances, though the practices of rape, wife beating, sexual harassment etc, are too decentralised in their practice to be part of the State itself.

Patriarchal relations in sexuality constitute a fifth structure. Compulsory heterosexuality and the sexual double standard are two of the key forms of this structure.

Patriarchal cultural institutions completes the array of structures. These are significant for the generation of a variety of gender-differentiated forms of subjectivity. This structure is composed of a set of institutions which create the representation of women within a patriarchal gaze in a variety of arenas, such as religions, education and the media.[15]

Walby identifies two principal arenas in which patriarchy is expressed – the public and the private:

---

13 Shulamith Firestone, *The Dialectic of Sex: The Case for Feminist Revolution* (New York: Morrow, 1970).

14 Susan Brownmiller, *Against Our Will: Men, Women and Rape* (Harmondsworth: Penguin, 1976).

15 Sylvia Walby, *op cit*, pp 20–21.

I am distinguishing two main forms of patriarchy, private and public. Private patriarchy is based upon household production as the main site of women's oppression. Public patriarchy is based principally in public sites such as employment and the State. The household does not cease to be a patriarchal structure in the public form, but it is not longer the chief site. In private patriarchy the expropriation of women's labour takes place primarily by individual patriarchs within the household, while in the public form it is a more collective appropriation. In private patriarchy the principle patriarchal strategy is exclusionary; in the public it is segregationist and subordinating.

The change from private to public patriarchy involves a change both in the relations between the structures and within the structures. In the private form household production is the dominant structure; in the public form it is replaced by employment and the State. In each form all the remaining patriarchal structures are present – there is simply a change in which are dominant. There is also a change in the institutional forms of patriarchy, with the replacement of a primarily individual form of appropriation of women by a collective one. This takes place within each of the six patriarchal structures.[16]

Table I.1[17]

PRIVATE AND PUBLIC PATRIARCHY

Form of patriarchy	Private	Public
Dominant structure	Household production	Employment/State
Wider patriarchal structures	Employment State Sexuality Violence Culture	Household production Sexuality Violence Culture
Period	C19th	C20th
Mode of expropriation	Individual	Collective
Patriarchal strategy	Exclusionary	Segregationist

16 *Ibid*, pp 23–24.
17 *Ibid*, p 24.

PATRIARCHAL FEMINISM AND THE LAW OF THE FATHER[18]
Shelley Wright[19]

The Genealogy of Patriarchy

If words themselves are important then the word 'patriarchy' must be of central significance to Western feminists. We might continue our work towards a redefinition of femininity and feminism with an etymology or genealogy of this particular word, in order to discover its role in the subjugation of women and the discipline of the body, as well as the possibilities for resistance, and the creation of new alliances. If 'patriarchy' is a Master-narrative devised by men masquerading as human beings, then it must have a history, a context, a cartography of knowledge which can be traced. It is not monolithic and can be changed, escaped from or destroyed.

The derivations of this word, and its structures through centuries of Western European culture, carry within them its roots in Judeo-Christian thought. The 'Word', either spoken or written, was the vehicle by which both Judaism and Christianity were propagated throughout the Mediterranean and Europe. Judaism, Christianity, and later Islam, are religions of 'The Book' and the social structures with which they are associated are cultures that have always placed a high value on language, especially literary language. The 'text' has always been of enormous significance in European and middle Eastern cultures.

> In the beginning was the Word, and the Word was with God, and the Word was God ... And the Word was made flesh, and dwelt among us, (and we beheld his glory, the glory as of the only begotten of the Father), full of grace and truth.[20]

Within the terms of the Biblical text, particularly after the translation of the Jewish canon into Greek 250 years before Christ, we can see the development of some interesting themes. 'Patriarchy' refers to a rulership which is emphatically tied to procreation – the male reproductive role. It is rule by a man in a very specific, misconstrued and exaggerated gender role – the role of the Father. It is a rulership which openly relegates the female reproductive role to the inconsequential and which allows women little other than a reproductive role to play, as freedom to do anything else might diminish male control over security of descent. The only significant role that women play is to safeguard the purity and potency of this line where male guardianship breaks down or is ineffective. Blood, semen, genealogy and power, are inextricably tied together in a narrative of ideological distortion of enormous influence.[21]

Taking the story further into the New Testament, while continuing to look back for a larger picture of Judeo-Christian sources, patriarchy can be seen as not only a description of tribal structures or religious ideology, nor only as a means of describing an institutionalised governmental system. It is also the primal myth of creation, death, redemption and resurrection which has remained with us in everything we have done, said or thought for thousands of years. We live in a

---

18 Shelley Wright, 'Patriarchal Feminism and the Law of the Father' (1993) 1 *Feminist Legal Studies* 115.

19 At the time of writing, Lecturer in Law, University of Sydney.

20 *The Gospel According to St John* I, 1–14, King James Version, first published in England in 1611.

21 See Northrop Frye, *The Great Code: The Bible and Literature* (Penguin, 1990).

secular society, but this Judeo-Christian founding myth of perception, of knowledge and power, is the pattern on which much of our own 'truth' is based.

The genealogy of patriarchy continues within the structures of Western history, first by the Roman and Orthodox Churches, and then in the burgeoning of the nation state in which 'patriarchy' becomes associated with the Father/King, the paternal head of *'le patrie'*, the nation state. Patriarchal religious structures were challenged during the Reformation, and patriarchal political structures during the European revolutions of the 17th and 18th centuries. A detailed history of the increasing subordination of women during and after these revolutionary challenges to patriarchy is described in detail elsewhere.[22] What is important is, that at a time when men were demanding political and economic freedom from the patriarchal rule of the Father/King, or the monarchy itself was being 'domesticated', as in England under Queen Victoria,[23] women were being ever more sharply subjected to the patriarch's rule within the private sphere of the home. This 'privatisation' of patriarchy had been evident since at least the Protestant Reformation of the 16th century and ran parallel with the growth of bourgeois capitalism and the idea of liberalism in political structures. Jean-Jacques Rousseau and Adam Smith, Martin Luther and Samuel Johnson, Edmund Burke and Robespierre could all agree on one thing – the inferiority and subservience of women.[24] The old patriarchy was killed, only to be replaced by a new patriarchy masquerading as the liberal democratic 'fraternity' of men so aptly described by Carole Pateman as the 'fraternal contract'.[25]

Crucial to the perpetuation of this structure since the 19th century has been the discipline of the body, particularly the female body. The discipline of the female body in order to control and finally eradicate women as subjects-for-themselves (or as sisters) is a fundamental component of patriarchy. In the Judeo-Christian model, in which we find the genealogy of women's oppression in Western cultures, control and discipline of the body and the consequent continuing visibility of 'Woman' as a mirror for the male ego has been endemic. As Irigaray, among others, has written, women are physical containers which have their value as exchange within patriarchal economic and symbolic structures.[26] Within unmitigated patriarchy, ie that which existed prior to the fraternal contract of the late 18th century, women were literally exchanged as property or symbols of property. Since that time, women have continued to be characterised not as subjects or authors of our own lives, but as objects, containers of the male desire to retain patriarchal power within the fraternal contract. As the physical exchange of women declined in the West (at least for white middle-class women) the incorporation of femininity within women's minds and bodies as the objects of male desire increased. One means of constructing this has been, and still is, romantic love as the basis of heterosexual relations, rather than simple exchange. Because men are never simply the inhabitants of particular masculine bodies, but are always Man moving towards Mastery, Woman has remained the measure of exchange by which this universalising Mankind, this patriarchal linkage of power and masculinity, is given value. This is the Law of the Father which we

22 See Anderson and Zinsser, *A History of Their Own*, Pt II.
23 1837–1902.
24 See E Kennedy and S Mendus (eds) *Women in Western Political Philosophy: Kant to Nietzsche* (Wheatsheaf, 1987).
25 See C Pateman, *The Disorder of Women* (Polity Press, 1989).
26 Luce Irigary, 'The Power of Discourse and the Subordination of the Feminine', in M Whitford (ed), *The Irigaray Reader* (Blackwell, 1991).

have internalised as his daughters, which our brothers have internalised as his sons – and heirs.

Patriarchal Feminism

It is almost impossible to envision a non-patriarchal social structure – the one we have has been with us for so long and is so pervasive. Feminism, as it developed out of the revolutionary changes in Europe of the 18th and 19th centuries, is based on an assumption that is rarely questioned. The assumption is that freedom or personal autonomy is an intrinsic need for human beings, including women, which has been forcibly denied us. The autonomous development of the individual is described, at least rhetorically, as an inherent right of everyone. Early feminists demanded that this rhetoric could not logically be denied to women, at least not to white middle class women of Western Europe. The Law of the Father became expressed as the 'rule of law', inscribed within legal structures as available to ensure freedom and equality for everyone. Women, and others, captured for themselves the power of this rhetoric to demand that the freedom which was denied to so many, not just women, be made a reality.

The fraternal contract and the rule of law,[27] the modern masks behind which patriarchy and the Law of the Father maintain their power, are the tools by which liberatory claims have been made and to some extent have been won. It is not illogical that women and others have made gains even within patriarchy, including both political suffrage and partial control over reproduction. One of the earliest examples of an undutiful daughter, that is one who demanded the fulfilment of the promise of the fraternal contract on behalf of herself and other women, is Mary Wollstonecraft.[28] She was speaking out of the experience of that first major revolution against the Father/King, the French Revolution, which succeeded only in replacing him with modern democratic patriarchy, the fraternal contract.

What is this 'autonomy', this 'freedom', this 'equality' for which we make our rebellious demands? What is the 'slavery' to which so many have been subjugated and from which the fraternal contract and the rule of law are meant to deliver us? Both slavery and freedom, as we understand them, are defined within patriarchy itself. Slavery cannot exist unless the alternative of freedom exists to define its limits. The lack of personal autonomy presupposes the existence of that which is lacking. The core of patriarchal feminism is that women cannot be slaves within patriarchal structures unless it is possible for us to be free as defined by patriarchy itself. It cannot be said that women have been denied something unless there is something there to be denied. If the need or desire or capacity for personal freedom is not an intrinsic human quality, then it can only exist as a social construct. In our case, this means that our demands for liberation and equality have been determined by the constraints of patriarchy as it now exists, ie the liberal, democratic, fraternal contract. The particular type of slavery which women suffer under this particular form of 'patriarchy' is not necessarily the same as that which women, or others, suffer under different social constructions, patriarchal or otherwise. Freedom is equally culturally defined.

Western patriarchal institutions rest on an either/or dichotomy of gender. This dichotomy, would appear to form the basis for a generalised concept of difference which places one side of the divide in a position of dominance over the other. The reliance on difference and hierarchy informs attempts at change or

---

27   On women in political theory, see Chapter 8.

28   Mary Wollstonecraft, *Vindication of the Rights of Woman* (1792) (Penguin, 1985).

restructuring. Freedom and slavery are also perceived in terms of difference and hierarchy. Feminists have demanded that freedom, within patriarchal terms, be extended to themselves and to others. Most feminisms that we are familiar with in the West are therefore what I would term 'patriarchal feminisms'. This is not to deny the importance of empowerment which such feminist efforts have gained for some women. But recognising feminism's deep connection to the ideology it is attempting to subvert, might help us to recognise some of the inconsistencies and blindnesses for which we are often accused.

A basic reading of what is meant by 'patriarchy' in the Western Judeo–Christian tradition that we live in, has been traced back no further than the written evidence of the Old Testament. The word itself is a Graeco/Christian translation of a Hebrew word. 'Patriarchy' as icon is based on sacred scripture. An examination of this scripture seems to indicate that there is a basic either/or distinction being made, and that the core distinction is male/female. More importantly this core concept seems to be intimately connected with procreation, reproduction, birth, life, genealogy, inheritance, racial purity and religious or political hegemony. The ethic which emerges is one based on aggressive masculinity, concentrating on the male gender role in conception and birth. The power structure is not just male oriented, but Father oriented. This power structure legitimates a whole host of what have been identified as 'problems' – the subjugation of women being a major, but not the only, one. The structure does not appear to adequately coincide with material economic bases of either an agricultural or an urban society, hence the failure of Marxist feminist analyses to adequately explain the persistence of patriarchy and its collaboration with capitalism.[29] Patriarchy as a means of social ordering has survived and adapted itself up to the present time. It is a paradigm so immune to overthrow that it has resisted even the most obvious evidence that its basic assumptions about sex and procreation are biological nonsense and that its effects are manifestly unjust.

Undutiful Daughters

The latest revival of feminism is at last having a noticeable effect on previously impervious patriarchal structures. Women are gaining access to education, jobs, financial independence and life options that we have never had before. But even the optimism engendered by real gains has to be tempered by one major drawback. The feminism which has gained the most attention, and which is what most people mean by 'feminism', is Eurocentric patriarchal feminism. It is feminism which draws its own ideology out of libertarian, or Marxist, or other visions of liberation, which are themselves permeated with Judeo–Christian ideology or its secular descendants' structures. Why else do we talk about 'liberal' feminism, or 'Marxist' feminism or even 'poststructuralist' or 'deconstructionist' feminism? Our discourse is taken from the predominant patriarchal ideology, the Master-narrative, or its masculinist alternatives. This is not surprising. Our subjugation is determined by patriarchy and its alternatives are also found within this ideology. Where else can we hope to find it? We ourselves are shaped by the structures within which we have been brought up, within which we live. Our very selves are culturally bound. If, within patriarchy, we perceive ourselves as enslaved, then it is to patriarchal definitions of freedom, such as they are, that we turn for sources of resistance. It is not surprising that modern secular feminism should have followed the paths that modern secular masculine revolutions have taken. We have no other models. We are our fathers' daughters, undutiful or otherwise.

---

29 On Marxist theory, see Chapter 8.

Parricide

The political and economic revolutions of the last 200 years put on the agenda, for the first time in European and Judeo–Christian history, the massive project of destroying the patriarchal King/Father. The revolutions only partially succeeded, driving the patriarch underground into the home where he has exercised far greater tyranny over women and children; or upstairs into the civil service and the State where he has been idealised and ideologised into a kind of 'folk king' or an abstracted patriarch called 'the people': or exported to the Third World in the guise of 'development'. The imagery of the warrior, the irresponsible male maturing into the despotic father, with women as nurturing chattels, remains virtually unchanged.

What may be of some hope is that the destruction of the patriarchal King/God, although incomplete, may still be in progress. Once men put this on the agenda they could, and can, no longer prevent women from demanding that the project be completed. It is all women, not younger or subservient men, who have borne the greatest burden within this structure and it is we who have the most to gain from its destruction (not just 'deconstruction'). Once men had provided the revolutionary models for destroying the father, feminism, as part of patriarchal ideology in its new secularised still masculine form, could no longer be contained. Every masculine form of revolution or resistance, none of which have succeeded in finally escaping patriarchy, has given birth to a feminist vision which has been more radical, and therefore more threatening. Masculinist revolutions have always drawn back from incorporating the feminist vision of real destruction of the patriarch, partly out of fear, but also partly out of a deep nostalgia for the initiation – the rebirth into Fatherhood and power. But it is important to remember that patriarchy, although still alive and strong, has been under siege by all revolutions and resistances, both masculine and feminine, for the last 200 years.

Liberalism merely domesticated the tyrant, took it upon itself to civilise and privatise the patriarch and bring him under control. The fraternal contract was an attempt to liberate sons so that all men might have the opportunity of becoming the Father. There was never any real commitment to destroying patriarchy. Socialism never achieved more than to create another patriarch in working class clothes, or to dress the working man in business suits and domesticate him as the liberal masters had done. The old man dies hard. Feminists who insisted, and continue to insist, that only parricide will do, simply frighten and infuriate men who can see themselves in far greater solidarity with their fathers and grandfathers than with their mothers and sisters, who have always terrified or mystified them. Sex, the old fractured knowledge of good and evil, keeps coming back to haunt us. Subjectivities of male/female, dominance and submission are not good places to find visions of egalitarianism or liberation. However, patriarchal feminism incorporates the radical challenges to patriarchy partially commenced in the 18th century. The great hope is that men, as well as women, have begun to see that the patriarch has to die.

This cannot be seen as an unmitigated source of optimism. If feminism itself is shaped by the masculinist agenda for change, then the alternative to patriarchy (whatever that might be) which is likely to succeed is unlikely to meet feminist demands for women. 'Equality' is not in fact what we want, even on a deep level, when the substance of 'equality' is masculinist, not feminist. Nor would we want a 'liberty' that is defined in terms solely of the antithesis to patriarchal slavery. In this sense radical feminists are perfectly correct in viewing liberal or even Marxist feminisms with extreme suspicion. It may be that one day we will have a world in which women and men share equally in the balance of power – but if it is a corporatist materialist world of environmental and human extinction, not in the sense of nuclear holocaust, but through the instrumentality of McDonald's and General Motors, where nothing is free because what's left of anything spontaneous or beautiful is in a museum, what have we really gained?

Listening to Different Voices

> Let them come and see men and women and children who know how to live, whose joy of life has not yet been killed by those who claimed to teach other nations how to live.[30]

It becomes crucial to listen to other visions, other voices. Patriarchal feminism is not the only possibility. We are beginning to understand that our sisters, and possibly also their brothers, in non-patriarchal cultures may have something to teach us. Non-patriarchal cultures are not necessarily non-masculinist. Masculine domination does not have to take form within a patriarchal model. Indigenous cultures, for example, though often masculinist in the sense that men make most of the important decisions, are not necessarily patriarchal in structure; where they are it is often borrowed from Eurocentric notions of patriarchy.[31] There may even be cultures which are not patriarchal or masculinist at all – they only look as if they are because our male sociologists and anthropologists and historians keep seeing them within their own terms of reference – patriarchy. Similarly there are other forms of patriarchy itself, such as in Confucian East Asia, which are not the same as our own Judeo-Christian variety.[32] Islamic patriarchy has followed its own genealogy, for many centuries. Women and men of other traditions, not only feminists, may be able to offer alternative visions outside of Eurocentric patriarchy that can help us redraft our own agendas, so long as we recognise that these are their visions and not ours.[33]

We also need to listen to the voices of those women and men who are refashioning the 'discipline of the body', either through the exploration of sexuality, particularly homosexuality, or through practising new ethics of eating, dressing or inhabiting space. The physically or mentally disabled may be able to teach us something about the limitations of bodily space and the capacity for change within our own limits. We must see eating disorders for what the name itself implies. They are patterns of eating in rebellion against order, against the discipline of the body. But the disorder is self-destructive rather than liberatory. It is a narcissistic disorder which prevents the creation of solidarity outside the

---

30 Chinua Achebe, *No Longer at Ease*, quoted in Vandada Siva, *Staying Alive: Women, Ecology and Development* (Zed Books, 1989), xiv.

31 See, for example, the description of Central Australian Aboriginal culture through the eyes of a white feminist anthropologist in Diane Bell, *Daughters of the Dreaming* (Melbourne: McPhee Gribble, 1983).

32 See Hatch Afshar, 'Women, Marriage and the State in Iran' in Hatch Afshar, *Women, State and Ideology: Studies from Africa and Asia* (London: MacMillan Press, 1987); Margot Badrian and Miriam Cooke (eds), *Opening the Gates: A Century of Arab Feminist Writing* (Bloomington: Indiana University Press, 1990) and Deniz Kandiyoti, *Women, Islam and the State* (Philadelphia: Temple University Press, 1991).

33 There is a growing literature of crucial importance within so-called 'Third World feminism' that is slowly reaching a wider audience in the West. See the most recent collection of essays in Mohanty, Russo and Torres, *Third World Women and the Politics of Feminism* (Indiana University Press, 1991). Note the variety of meanings which Law can have; it does not need to be attached to a patriarchal concept of sovereignty. See 'Having Children: Women's Reproductive Choices' in Graycar and Morgan, *The Hidden Gender of Law* (Sydney: Federation Press, 1990).

object self. It is damaging not only for the women suffering these 'illnesses', but these disorders also have a political context. They are evidence of the failure of patriarchal feminism itself, and the failure of Western patriarchal women, to reach beyond the fraternal contract to others for whom hunger is not a representation of narcissism, but the worst of all oppressions.

Refashioning our understanding of the discipline of the body also means reshaping the debates over abortion, reproductive technology, pornography, prostitution and sexual violence. The 'sexual revolution' of the 1960s gave birth to 'second wave' feminism at the same time, and partly as a result of, reproductive freedom for women. But the law of reproductive control did not disappear, it shifted into our bodies and minds, and the bodies and minds of men. Violence against women (and men and children), whether it be physical aggression through war, killing, battery, incest and rape; or whether it be representational aggression through pornography and the display of extreme violence; or whether it be economic aggression through labour exploitation, prostitution and entrenched poverty, is only the most obvious and outward manifestation of this control – all of it mediated through legal structures. The shift in control of reproduction from the overtly male to the apparently female seems only to have exacerbated the outward manifestation of violence, just as the fraternal contract failed to complete the project of parricide, so the partial surrender of control over reproduction to women (a kind of enfranchisement of the female body) has failed to destroy the Law of the Father. The continuing presence of patriarchy is seen in the increasing discipline of the body reflecting the still pervasive male fear of female desire/rejection – so it is still women who must be made afraid of male desire and male rejection. The controversies which birth control, abortion and reproductive technologies continue to generate is evidence of how important this aspect of patriarchy is. The development of legal control over women as containers of life is not new, it is merely being spoken of in a refashioned language, the language not of a patriarchal God and the Law of the Father, but of technology and the rule of law.

Beyond Good and Evil

Is it the case that all resistances, all alternatives, all feminisms, must be determined by patriarchy and the Law of the Father? Perhaps what we are trying to end is not just patriarchy, not just masculinism, not just male/female or even female/male, but either/or itself. Not by synthesising the old dichotomies; not by androgyny; not through anger and denial; not through separation; but through love.

Love as the basis of an ethic beyond patriarchy seems both naive and overly optimistic. I would suggest that it is neither. The meaning of love itself needs to be redefined. It is not contained in the words 'care' or 'responsibility', although it must include those things. It is not taken from current visions of patriarchal relationships – although it may be possible that once the Father is dead, loving fatherhood by men in parental roles may be easier. We cannot rely on mother/daughter relationships either – although again maternal love has something of symbiosis and unlimited giving about it that we find nowhere else. But these are relationships that do not allow us to go beyond dependency. Nor can it be a love taken from models of sexuality, romance or 'being in love' because all these are permeated with inequalities largely derived from patriarchal ideologies of heterosexuality – although again, this kind of love has something of 'letting go', of surrender about it which we may also need to learn, without the consequence of dominance/submission.

Sisterhood could be one form that allows women to be independent and together at the same time and that might take us beyond good and evil, beyond patriarchal feminism and its associated rivalries, betrayals and acrimonious debates. 'Sisterhood' was raised as a banner of identification and change in the late 1960s when feminism began its latest siege of patriarchal structures and has since become a cliché and an object of ridicule. It seems to have been abandoned, partly because of the failure of 'undutiful' daughters to recognise our own allegiance with the Father – to get past our own identity as white, heterosexual, middle-class, liberal or Marxist feminists. Because we remain daughters, however rebellious, we have trouble identifying as sisters women who are not of our ' family' – our cultural or psychological or ideological heritage. Black women, indigenous women, women of colour, lesbians, women of the Third World, even conservative women rightly condemn feminists for our racism, competitive narrowness, our rigidity, our apparent dogmatism.

If sisterhood is to become a reality, it must be a sisterhood which has escaped from the Father – a sisterhood based on the absolute destruction of the Father. But this idea of sisterhood must not revert to nostalgia and sentimentality in the return to the Mother. Our mothers are also our sisters; we are grown women not children. By using 'sisterhood' as a feminist strategy, we might be able to escape our own identification with the voice of the Father and the inheritance of patriarchy. By eliminating the quest for Father's approval we may get rid of much of our competitiveness, our anger and betrayal. What anger we feel towards each other might be anger that is real, and not disguised jealousy or hidden denial. Our differences would not tear us apart, but might form the means to teach us how to be loyal to each other. Although the words of the first patricidal revolution were masculinist, they contain a real truth that we in the West have largely forgotten. Liberty and equality cannot be seen outside of solidarity.

This call for parricide and for sisterhood is not a call for violence against individual men, nor is it merely Utopian. It is a practical agenda, a matter of day to day choices. Within my own work it means listening to the voices of black or lesbian women which I have hitherto ignored, rather than looking to the Master-narratives of history, philosophy and law, whether written by men or by their female brothers. It means making daily choices. Will this action help or hurt a sister? Will speaking in this forum further the feeling of solidarity between women and women or, sometimes, between women and men, within this context at this time? Do I know what messages I am receiving, or giving? Am I acknowledging what I have, or for which I am responsible? Who are my allies? And what is my own allegiance worth? What of myself am I prepared to share with others? These are hard questions, hard choices that I am only just beginning to learn.

Nor does the call for parricide and sisterhood prevent, or resolve, the divisions that exist among us. The need to search for feminist, or feminine, voices will remain. Sisterhood should not presuppose sameness, merger, the disappearance of the individual in all her uniqueness. It should not, cannot, silence anger. Our anger and the anger of our sisters, and brothers, is real and justified. We need to hear and acknowledge it, not withdraw into defensiveness, denial and blame. I have seen – and experienced – too much scapegoating. Diversity within solidarity does not eliminate conflict, it contains it within the wider alterity of love. Sustained commitment to the process of liberation is essentials

This brings us to the possibility of alliances with men. In order for this to happen, men must learn something about brotherhood that is not tribal, not simply a preparation for the initiation into the Father. Men must learn the lessons they failed to grasp 200 years ago. In order to destroy the Father it is not enough to behead a king or declare independence from an Old World monarchy. Patriarchy, in its Western Judeo–Christian formulation, as it has been exported and as it is continuing to be exported, will not die until men kill the Father in themselves. The Warrior, the Hero, the Pastoral Shepherd, the Leader, the Boss, the Professor, the Master, the Corporate Director, the Great Artist or Author – all have to die to be replaced by a brother, a partner in solidarity, who is made of a masculinity that is not in training for hegemony.[34]

THE PUBLIC/PRIVATE DICHOTOMY

Central to orthodox Western liberalism and the idea of maximisation of individual liberty is regulation of the public sphere of life – to the extent consistent with protecting individual liberty – and the privacy of private life. The implications for feminist theorists of this sharp divide is profound. Women's role and women's work traditionally relates so closely to the 'private sphere' of life – the home and the family – that it becomes ignored by liberalism: women are in large measure simply irrelevant to liberalism. Thus, for many women – irrespective of class, race or age – there very existence is defined out of political theory: they are simply disentitled to participation in the public sphere. In this section the writings of John Stuart Mill, Carole Patemen and Katherine O'Donovan reveal the problems which liberalism, with its insistence on a private (unregulated) sphere of life, causes for feminism and the difficulties which feminism causes for liberalism and its defenders.

John Stuart Mill

John Stuart Mill may be regarded as one of the most important feminist writers of the 19th century. Mill campaigned for the enfranchisement of women, for their entry into the professions and public offices. As importantly, he analysed the social position of women *vis-à-vis* their husbands. The following passages from *The Subjection of Women* (1869) reveal the far-sightedness of Mill's thinking.

THE SUBJECTION OF WOMEN[35]
John Stuart Mill

The object of this essay is to explain as clearly as I am able, the grounds of an opinion which I have held from the very earliest period when I had formed any opinions at all on social or political matters, and which, instead of being weakened or modified, has been constantly growing stronger by the progress of reflection and the experiences of life: That the principle which regulates the existing social relations between the two sexes – the legal subordination of one sex to the other – is wrong in itself, and now one of the chief hindrances to human improvement; and that it ought to be replaced by a principle of perfect equality, admitting no power or privilege on the one side, nor disability on the other.[36]

---

34 Shelley Wright, *op cit*, pp 128–40.
35 John Stuart Mill, *The Subjection of Women* (1869) (Cambridge University Press, 1989).
36 *Ibid*, p 119.

The generality of a practice is in some cases a strong presumption that it is, or at all events once was, conducive to laudable ends. This is the case, when the practice was first adopted, or afterwards kept up, as a means to such ends, and was grounded on experience of the mode in which they could be most effectually attained. If the authority of men over women, when first established, had been the result of a conscientious comparison between different modes of constituting the government of society; if, after trying various other modes of social organisation – the government of women over men, equality between the two, and such mixed and divided modes of government as might be invented – it had been decided, on the testimony of experience, that the mode in which women are wholly under the rule of men, having no share at all in public concerns, and each in private being under the legal obligation of obedience to the man with whom she has associated her destiny, was the arrangement most conducive to the happiness and well being of both; its general adoption might then be fairly thought to be some evidence that, at the time when it was adopted, it was the best: though even then the considerations which recommended it may, like so many other primeval social facts of the greatest importance, have subsequently, in the course of ages, ceased to exist. But the state of the case is in every respect the reverse of this. In the first place, the opinion in favour of the present system, which entirely subordinates the weaker sex to the stronger, rests upon theory only; for there never has been trial made of any other: so that experience, in the sense in which it is vulgarly opposed to theory, cannot be pretended to have pronounced any verdict. And in the second place, the adoption of this system of inequality never was the result of deliberation, or forethought, or any social ideas, or any notion whatever of what conduced to the benefit of humanity or the good order of society. It arose simply from the fact that from the very earliest twilight of human society, every woman (owing to the value attached to her by men, combined with her inferiority in muscular strength) was found in a state of bondage to some man. Laws and systems of polity always begin by recognising the relations they find already existing between individuals. They convert what was a mere physical fact into a legal right, give it the sanction of society, and principally aim at the substitution of public and organised means of asserting and protecting these rights, instead of the irregular and lawless conflict of physical strength. Those who had already been compelled to obedience became in this manner legally bound to it. Slavery, from being a mere affair of force between the master and the slave, became regularised and a matter of compact among the masters, who, binding themselves to one another for common protection, guaranteed by their collective strength the private possessions of each, including his slaves, as well as the whole of the female. Any many ages elapsed, some of the ages of high cultivation, before any thinker was bold enough to question the rightfulness, and the absolute social necessity, either of the one slavery or of the other. By degrees such thinkers did arise: and (the general progress of society assisting) the slavery of the male sex has, in all countries of Christian Europe at least (although, in one of them, only within the last few years) been at length abolished, and that of the female sex has been gradually changed into a milder form of dependence. But this dependence, as it exists at present, is not an original institution, taking a fresh start from considerations of justice and social expediency – it is the primitive state of slavery lasting on, through successive mitigations and modifications occasioned by the same causes which have softened the general manners, and brought all human relations more under the control of justice and the influence of humanity. It has not lost the taint of its brutal origin. No presumption in its favour, therefore, can be drawn from the fact of its existence. The only such presumption which it could be supposed to have, must be grounded on its having lasted till now, when so many other things which came down from the same odious source have been done away with. And this, indeed, is what makes it strange to ordinary ears, to hear it asserted that the inequality of rights between men and women has no other source than the law of the strongest.[37]

Less than forty years ago, Englishmen might still by law hold human beings in bondage as saleable property: within the present century they might kidnap them and carry them off, and work them literally to death. This absolutely extreme case of the law of force, condemned by those who can tolerate almost every other form of arbitrary power, and which, of all others, presents features the most revolting to the feelings of all who look at it from an impartial position, was the law of civilised and Christian England within the memory of persons now living: and in one half of Anglo-Saxon America three or four years ago, not only did slavery exist, but the slave trade, and the breeding of slaves expressly for it, was a general practice between slave states.[38] So true is it that unnatural generally means only uncustomary, and that everything which is usual appears natural. The subjection of women to men being a universal custom, any departure from it quite naturally appears unnatural.[39]

On one of the inevitable outcomes of patriarchal power, Mill writes:

It is a political law of nature that those who are under any power of ancient origin, never begin by complaining of the power itself, but only of its oppressive exercise. There is never any want of women who complain of ill usage by their husbands. There would be infinitely more, if complaint were not the greatest of all provocatives to a repetition and increase of the ill usage. It is this which frustrates all attempts to maintain the power but protect the woman against its abuses. In no other case (except that of a child) is the person who has been proved judicially to have suffered an injury replaced under the physical power of the culprit who inflicted it. Accordingly wives, even in the most extreme and protracted cases of bodily ill-usage, hardly ever dare avail themselves of the laws made for their protection: and if, in a moment of irrepressible indignation, or by the interference of neighbours, they are induced to do so, their whole effort afterwards is to disclose as little as they can, and to beg off their tyrant from his merited chastisement.

All causes, social and natural, combine to make it unlikely that women should be collectively rebellious to the power of men. They are so far in a position different from all other subject classes, that their masters require something more from them than actual service. Men do not want solely the obedience of women, they want their sentiments. All men, except the most brutish, desire to have, in the women most nearly connected with them, not a forced slave but a willing one, not a slave merely, but a favourite. They have therefore put everything in practice to enslave their minds. The masters of all other slaves rely, for maintaining obedience, on fear; either fear of themselves, or religious fears. The masters of women wanted more than simple obedience, and they turned the whole force of education to effect their purpose. All women are brought up from the very earliest years in the belief that their ideal of character is the very opposite to that of men; not self-will, and government by self-control, but

---

37 *Ibid*, pp 122–24.

38 *Ibid*, p 127.

39 *Ibid*, p 130.

submission, and yielding to the control of others. All the moralities tell them that it is the duty of women, and all the current sentimentalities that it is their nature, to live for others: to make complete abnegation of themselves, and to have no life but in their affections. And by their affections are meant the only ones they are allowed to have – those to the men with whom they are connected, or to the children who constitute an additional and indefeasible tie between them and a man. When we put together three things – first, the natural attraction between opposite sexes; secondly, the wife's entire dependence on the husband, every privilege or pleasure she has being either his gift, or depending entirely on his will; and lastly, that the principal object of human pursuit, consideration, and all objects of social ambition, can in general be sought or obtained by her only through him, it would be a miracle if the object of being attractive to men had not become the polar star of feminine education and formation of character. And, this great means of influence over the minds of women having been acquired, an instinct of selfishness made men avail themselves of it to the utmost as a means of holding women in subjection, by representing to them meekness, submissiveness, and resignation of all individual will into the hands of a man, as an essential part of sexual attractiveness. Can it be doubted that any of the other yokes which mankind have succeeded in breaking, would have subsisted till now if the same means had existed, and had been as sedulously used, to bow down their minds to it? If it had been made the object of the life of every young plebeian to find personal favour in the eyes of some patrician, of every young serf with some seigneur; if domestication with him, and a share of his personal affections, had been held out as the prize which they all should look out for, the most gifted and aspiring being able to reckon on the most desirable prizes; and if, when this prize had been obtained, they had been shut out by a wall of brass from all interests not centreing on him, all feelings and desires but those which he shared or inculcated; would not serfs and seigneurs, plebeians and patricians, have been as broadly distinguished at this day as men and women are? and would not all but a thinker here and there, have believed the distinction to be a fundamental and unalterable fact in human nature?

The preceding considerations are amply sufficient to show that custom, however universal it may be, affords in this case no presumption, and ought not to create any prejudice, in favour of the arrangements which place women in social and political subjection to men. But I may go farther, and maintain that in the course of history, and the tendencies of progressive human society, afford not only no presumption in favour of this system of inequality of rights, but a strong one against it; and that, so far as the whole course of human improvement up to this time, the whole stream of modern tendencies, warrants any interference on the subject, it is, that this relic of the past is discordant with the future, and must necessarily disappear.[40]

The general opinion of men is supposed to be, that the natural vocation of a woman is that of a wife and mother. I say, is supposed to be, because, judging from acts – from the whole of the present constitution of society – one might infer that their opinion was the direct contrary. They might be supposed to think that the alleged natural vocation of women was of all things the most repugnant to their nature; insomuch that if they are free to do anything else – if any other means of living, or occupation of their time and faculties, is open, which has any

40   *Ibid*, pp 132–34.

chance of appearing desirable to them – there will not be enough of them who will be willing to accept the condition said to be natural to them. If this is the real opinion of men in general, it would be well that it should be spoken out. I should like to hear somebody openly enunciating the doctrine (it is already implied in much that is written on the subject) – 'It is necessary to society that women should marry and produce children. They will not do so unless they are compelled. Therefore it is necessary to compel them.' The merits of the case would then be clearly defined. It would be exactly that of the slaveholders of South Carolina and Louisiana. 'It is necessary that cotton and sugar should be grown. White men cannot produce them. Negroes will not, for any wages which we choose to give. Ergo they must be compelled.' An illustration still closer to the point is that of impressment. Sailors must absolutely be had to defend the country. It often happens that they will no voluntarily enlist. Therefore there must be the power of forcing them. How often has this logic been used! and, but for one flaw it in, without doubt it would have been successful up to this day. But it is open to the retort – First pay the sailors the honest value of their labour. When you have made it as well worth their while to service you, as to work for other employers, you will have no more difficulty than others have in obtaining their services. To this there is no logical answer except 'I will not', and as people are now not only ashamed, but are not desirous, to rob the labourer of his hire, impressment is not longer advocated. Those who attempt to force women into marriage by closing all other doors against them, lay themselves open to a similar retort. If they mean what they say, their opinion must evidently be, that men do not render the married condition so desirable to women, as to induce them to accept it for its own recommendations. It is not a sign of one's thinking the boon one offers very attractive, when one allows only Hobson's choice, 'that or none'. And here, I believe, is the clue to the feelings of those men, who have a real antipathy to the equal freedom of women. I believe they are afraid, not lest women should be unwilling to marry, for I do not think that any one in reality has that apprehension; but lest they should insist that marriage should be on equal conditions; lest all women of spirit and capacity should prefer doing almost anything else, not in their own eyes degrading, rather than marry, when marrying is giving themselves a master, and a master too of all their earthly possessions.[41]

Mill devotes Chapter 2 of *The Subjection of Women* to the issue of marriage.

Marriage being the destination appointed by society for women, the prospect they are brought up to, and the object of which it is intended should be sought by all of them, except those who are too little attractive to be chosen by any man as his companion; one might have supposed that everything would have been done to make this condition as eligible to them as possible, that they might have no cause to regret being denied the option of any other. Society, however, both in this, and, at first, in all other cases, has preferred to attain its object by foul rather than fair mains: but this is the only case in which it has substantially persisted in them even to the present day. Originally, women were taken by force, or regularly sold by their father to the husband. Until a late period in European history, the father had the power to dispose of his daughter in marriage at his own will and pleasure, without any regard to hers. The Church, indeed, was so far faithful to a better morality as to require a formal 'yes' from the woman at the marriage ceremony; but there was nothing to shew that the consent was other than compulsory; and it was practically impossible for the girl to refuse

---

41   *Ibid*, pp 144–45.

compliance if the father persevered, except perhaps when she might obtain the protection of religion by a determined resolution to take monastic vows. After marriage, the man had anciently (but this was anterior to Christianity) the power of life and death over his wife. She could invoke no law against him; he was her sole tribunal and law. For a long time he could repudiate her, but she had no corresponding power in regard to him. By the old laws of England, the husband was called the lord of the wife; he was literally regarded as her sovereign, inasmuch that the murder of a man by his wife was called treason (petty as distinguished from high treason), and was more cruelly avenged than was usually the case with high treason, for the penalty was burning to death. Because these various enormities have fallen into disuse (for most of them were never formally abolished, or not until they had long ceased to be practised) men suppose that all is now as it should be in regard to the marriage contract; and we are continually told that civilisation and Christianity have restored to the woman her just rights. Meanwhile the wife is the actual bond servant of her husband: no less so, as far as legal obligation goes, than slaves commonly so called. She vows a lifelong obedience to him at the altar, and is held to it all through her life by law. Casuists may say that the obligation of obedience stops short of participation in crime, but it certainly extends to everything else. She can do no act whatever but by his permission, at least tacit. She can acquire no property but for him; the instant it becomes hers, even by inheritance, it becomes *ipso facto* his. In this respect the wife's position under the common law of England is worse than that of slaves in the laws of many countries ...[42]

In the immense majority of cases[43] there is no settlement: and the absorption of all rights, all property, as well as all freedom of action, is complete. The two are called 'one person in law', for the purpose of inferring that whatever is hers is his, but the parallel inference is never drawn that whatever is his is hers; the maxim is not applied against the man, except to make him responsible to third parties for her acts, as a master is for the acts of his slaves or of his cattle. I am far from pretending that wives are in general no better treated than slaves; but no slave is a slave to the same lengths, and in so full a sense of the word, as a wife is. Hardly any slave, except one immediately attached to the master's person, is a slave at all hours and all minutes; in general he has, like a soldier, his fixed task, and when it is done, or when he is off duty, he disposes, within certain limits, of his own time, and has a family life into which the master rarely intrudes. 'Uncle Tom' under his first master has his own life in his 'cabin', almost as much as any man whose work takes him away from home, is able to have in his own family. But it cannot be so with the wife. Above all, a female slave has (in Christian countries) an admitted right, and is considered under a moral obligation, to refuse to her master the last familiarity. Not so the wife: however brutal a tyrant she may unfortunately be chained to – though she may know that he hates her, though it may be his daily pleasure to torture her, and though she may feel it impossible not to loathe him – he can claim from her and enforce the lowest degradation of a human being, that of being made the instrument of an animal function contrary to her own inclinations.[44]

---

42   *Ibid*, pp 146–47.

43   The nobility could enter a settlement whereby the wife's property was protected from the husband's usage, although it could not – save by the terms of the settlement – by used by the wife.

44   *Ibid*, pp 146–48.

Marriage is the only actual bondage known to our law. There remain no legal slaves, except the mistress of every house.[45]

The 'subjection of women' described by John Stuart Mill, reinforced by law, has proven slow to pass. It was, for example, to be as late as 1970 before the United Kingdom Parliament accepted that laws which effectively retained the concept of 'woman as property' were no longer reflective of the demand for equality. Cedric Thornberry considers the reforms in the article which follows:

WHAT PRICE THE MISSUS NOW?[46]

Cedric Thornberry[47]

From New Year's Day, actions for damages for adultery, breach of promise to marry, enticement, harbouring and seduction of a child or spouse are abolished.[48] Thus, towards the end of the 20th century, one of the legal bastions of the Englishmen's right to treat his family as his property is removed.

Opinion polls in recent years have shown that the right is still regarded by most of the population as sacred. However unpalatable to the liberals' ideal of England, the brutal fact is that we are a nation of Andy Capps and his Missuses. Way back in 1912 the Royal Commission on Divorce noted that the idea of getting money for your wife was peculiar among civilised peoples to the Anglo-Saxons, and that foreigners could not understand how English law could sustain it. And when the Law Commission gingerly advised the abolition of these legal enormities two years ago its members were well aware that they were going against the popular will.

It is not, for once, the fault of the lawyers that these things have survived. Most judges (though there are Andy Capps on the Bench as well) have for years seemed baffled by the retention of these actions. Deserted husbands have had to be dissuaded by their lawyers from claiming damages 'because it will alienate the Court'. Though the legislature casually re-enacted the right to damages in 1965 it has been clear for many years that the majority of MPs were unhappy about it – as they showed earlier this year when the whips were taken off and they were given a free vote. We have the law which we not only deserve but desire.

Women slaves

Women's Liberation asserts that woman is still the most colonialised people on earth. Slavery, as such, was effectively abolished in England 250 years ago. Yet the legal history and modern rationale of the damages claim is founded on the idea of bondage. The action began while a woman was in all ways regarded as the husband's property. Everything she had went to him on marriage. Her earnings were his. She was viewed as a child and 'subject to physical punishment at his hands (provided it was moderate in extent)'.

The logic of this was that a wife, however eager, was unable to consent to going to bed with her lover. So the law made an irrebuttable presumption that intercourse was forcible. In 1620 one man was sued by an irate husband for 'for that he took his wife away for five years, *simul cum* her gown and petticoat, and

---

45   *Ibid*, p 196.

46   *The Guardian*, 29 December 1970.

47   At the time of writing, Lecturer in Law, London School of Economics and Political Science.

48   Law Reform (Miscellaneous Provisions) Act 1970.

lived with her in a suspicious manner'. The law was that because husband and wife were one, and that one was the husband, intercourse with the wife was assault and battery (and probably rape) on him.

Though they later became more sophisticated the law's assumptions did not greatly change with the centuries, even after the married woman became, in the late 19th century, as more or less responsible legal person. Tracing the history of the English family through the damages cases is truly a melancholy tale of man's inhumanity to woman.

Thus, where one wife had separated from her husband and years later found another man, the husband could still get money for her; 'his name was dishonoured by her; she had (since separating) become a woman of substantial means and might have chosen to give her husband some of them.' In this case, the wife had left her husband when she was 19 and there was no evidence at all that the co-respondent had even known that she was married.

In another, a seemingly faithful wife throughout her life confessed on her death-bed to a single act of adultery, years earlier. Her widower got money for it. Yet another entrepreneur had a little capital gain from the man who had been supporting not only his wife but also his children for years.

In a few recent cases where damages have been sought the Courts have embarrassedly held that damages are for the loss of a man's wife, the injury to his feelings, the blow to his honour, and the hurt to his family life.

If her lover were a man of wealth or position, damages would be higher, though the converse would not be true: this on the hilarious premise that a man's honour is more (materially) affronted if his wife goes to bed with the boss rather than the dustman. Other relevant factors are whether the wife has helped her husband's business, 'the size of her fortune', 'her capacity as a housekeeper, and the state of her pre-marital virtue' (more for a virgin than a tart).

Where judges have ventured to defend the basis of the action (which has not been often), they have speculated that 'beneath the sordid basis of property, lay perhaps a cogent moral foundation – to maintain the purity of married life and defend the family's honour.' But its cogency was somewhat weakened by the absence of any comparable right for a wife against her husband's mistress.

In the last 30 years the Courts have increasingly been uneasy over the idea of damages. Three years ago, the Court of Appeal scathingly reviewed the authorities in a judgment which should have crushed the unfortunate husband (though he nevertheless departed £2,000 the richer). The psychology of the law, said the Court, was drawn not from reality but from the Victorian novelette. 'The concept of the reasonable common law cuckold (which they had been obliged to analyse) is needed so long as Parliament preserves a cause of action which is repugnant to modern and sensible ideas.'

Legal Curiosity

It would be comforting to assume that the action has been a mere legal curiosity. But it has not. It has evidently had public support. It is part of a wider whole, in which it is not deemed intolerable for a husband to treat his wife as a chattel during marriage as well as on divorce.

Perhaps its demise will permit a more rational approach by the Courts to what a woman must be expected to tolerate in marriage. Yet more than 100 years after Ibsen's *Doll's House*, an English High Court can say that he cannot begin to understand what Norah was making such a fuss about. And more than 50 years after Galsworthy satirised the proprietary English bourgeois family, Soames Forsyte can become a folk hero with the trendy English public.

FEMINIST CRITIQUES OF THE PUBLIC/PRIVATE DICHOTOMY

THE DISORDER OF WOMEN[49]

Carole Pateman

The dichotomy between the private and the public is central to almost two centuries of feminist writing and political struggle; it is, ultimately, what the feminist movement is about. Although some feminists treat the dichotomy as a universal, trans-historical and trans-cultural feature of human existence, feminist criticism is primarily directed at the separation and opposition between the public and private spheres in liberal theory and practice.

The relationship between feminism and liberalism is extremely close but also exceedingly complex. The roots of both doctrines lie in the emergence of individualism as a general theory of social life; neither liberalism nor feminism is conceivable without some conception of individuals as free and equal beings, emancipated from the ascribed, hierarchical bonds of traditional society. But if liberalism and feminism share a common origin, their adherents have often been opposed over the past two hundred years. The direction and scope of feminist criticism of liberal conceptions of the public and the private have varied greatly in different phases of the feminist movement. An analysis of this criticism is made more complicated because liberalism is inherently ambiguous about the 'public' and the 'private', and feminists and liberals disagree about where and why the dividing line is to be drawn between the two spheres, or, according to certain contemporary feminist arguments, whether it should be drawn at all.

Feminism is often seen as nothing more than the completion of the liberal or bourgeois revolution, as an extension of liberal principles and rights to women as well as men. The demand for equal rights has, of course, always been an important part of feminism. However, the attempt to universalise liberalism has more far-reaching consequences than is often appreciated because, in the end, it inevitably challenges liberalism itself. Liberal-feminism has radical implications, not least in challenging the separation and opposition between the private and the public spheres that is fundamental to liberal theory and practice. The liberal contrast between private and public is more than a distinction between two kinds of social activities. The public sphere, and the principles that govern it, are seen as separate from, or independent of, the relationships in the private sphere. A familiar illustration of this claim is the long controversy between liberal and radical political scientists about participation, the radicals denying the liberal claim that the social inequalities of the private sphere are irrelevant to questions about the political equality, universal suffrage and associated civil liberties of the public realm.

Not all feminists, however, are liberals: 'feminism' goes far beyond liberal-feminism. Other feminists explicitly reject liberal conceptions of the private and public and see the social structure of liberalism as the political problem, not a starting point from which equal rights can be claimed. They have much in common with the radical and socialist critics of liberalism who rely on 'organic' theories (to use Benn and Gaus's[50] terminology) but they differ sharply in their

---

49 Carole Pateman, *The Disorder of Women* (Polity Press, 1989), Chapter 6.

50 S Benn and G Gaus (eds) *Public and Private in Social Life* (Croom Helm, 1983).

analysis of the liberal state. In short, feminists, unlike other radicals, raise the generally neglected problem of the patriarchal character of liberalism.

Liberalism and Patriarchalism

Benn and Gaus's account of the liberal conception of the public and private illustrates very nicely some major problems in liberal theory. They accept that the private and the public are central categories of liberalism, but they do not explain why these two terms are crucial or why the private sphere is contrasted with and opposed to the 'public' rather than the 'political' realm. Similarly, they note that liberal arguments leave it unclear whether civil society is private or public but, although they state that in both of their liberal models the family is paradigmatically private, they fail to pursue the question why, in this case, liberals usually also see civil society as private. Benn and Gaus's account of liberalism also illustrates its abstract, ahistorical character and, in what is omitted and taken for granted, provides a good example of the theoretical discussions that feminists are now sharply criticising. The account bears out Eisenstein's claim that 'the ideology of public and private life' invariably presents 'the division between public and private life, ... as reflecting the development of the bourgeois liberal state, not the patriarchal ordering of the bourgeois state'.[51]

The term 'ideology' is appropriate here because the profound ambiguity of the liberal conception of the private and public obscures and mystifies the social reality it helps constitute. Feminists argue that liberalism is structured by patriarchal as well as class relations, and that the dichotomy between the private and the public obscures the subjection of women to men within an apparently universal, egalitarian and individualist order. Benn and Gaus's account assumes that the reality of our social life is more or less adequately captured in liberal conceptions. They do not recognise that 'liberalism' is patriarchal-liberalism and that the separation and opposition of the public and private spheres is an unequal opposition between women and men. They thus talk of 'individuals' in liberal theory at face value although, from the period when the social contract theorists attacked the patriarchalists, liberal theorists have excluded women from the scope of their apparently universal arguments. One reason why the exclusion goes unnoticed is that the separation of the private and public is presented in liberal theory as if it applied to all individuals in the same way. It is often claimed – by anti-feminists today, but by feminists in the 19th century, most of whom accepted the doctrine of 'separate spheres' – that the two spheres are separate, but equally important and valuable. The way in which women and men are differentially located within private life and the public world is, as I shall indicate, a complex matter, but underlying a complicated reality is the belief that women's natures are such that they are properly subject to men and their proper place is in the private, domestic sphere. Men properly inhabit, and rule within, both spheres. The essential feminist argument is that the doctrine of 'separate but equal', and the ostensible individualism and egalitarianism of liberal theory, obscure the patriarchal reality of a social structure of inequality and the domination of women by men.

In theory, liberalism and patriarchalism stand irrevocably opposed to each other. Liberalism is an individualist, egalitarian, conventionalist doctrine; patriarchalism claims that hierarchical relations of subordination necessarily follow from the natural characteristics of men and women. In fact, the two doctrines were successfully reconciled through the answer given by the contract

---

51   Z Eisenstein *The Radical Future of Liberal Feminism* (New York: Longman, 1981), p 223.

theorists in the 17th century to the subversive question of who counted as free and equal individuals. The conflict with the patriarchalists did not extend to women or conjugal relations; the latter were excluded from individualist arguments and the battle was fought out over the relation of adult sons to their fathers ... .[52]

... [F]eminist critiques insist that an alternative to the liberal conception must also encompass the relationship between public and domestic life. The question that feminists raise is why the patriarchal character of the separation of a depoliticised public sphere from private life is so easily 'forgotten'; why is the separation of the two worlds located within civil society so that public life is implicitly conceptualised as the sphere of men?

The answer to this question can be found only by examining the history of the connection between the separation of production from the household and the emergence of the family as paradigmatically private ... As capitalism and its specific form of sexual as well as class division of labour developed ... wives were pushed into a few, low-status areas of employment or kept out of economic life altogether, relegated to their 'natural' dependent, place in the private, familial sphere. Today, despite a large measure of civil equality, it appears natural that wives are subordinate just because they are dependent on their husbands for subsistence, and it is taken for granted that liberal social life can be understood without reference to the sphere of subordination, natural relations and women. The old patriarchal argument from nature and women's nature was thus transformed as it was modernised and incorporated into liberal-capitalism. Theoretical and practical attention became fixed exclusively on the public area, on civil society – on 'the social' or on 'the economy' – and domestic life was assumed irrelevant to social and political theory or the concerns of men of affairs. The fact that patriarchalism is an essential, indeed constitutive, part of the theory and practice of liberalism remains obscured by the apparently impersonal, universal dichotomy between private and public within civil society itself ... .[53]

Nature and Culture

Patriarchalism rests on the appeal to nature and the claim that women's natural function of child-bearing prescribes their domestic and subordinate place in the order of things ...[54]

The most thorough attempt to find a universal answer to the question of why it is that women are in subjection to men, and the most stark opposition between nature and culture, can be found in the writings of the radical feminists who argue that nature is the single cause of men's domination. The best-known version of this argument is Firestone's *The Dialectic of Sex*,[55] which also provides an example of how one form of feminist argument, while attacking the liberal separation of private and public, remains within the abstractly individualist framework which helps constitute this division of social life. Firestone reduces the history of the relation between nature and culture or private and public to an opposition between female and male. She argues that the origin of the dualism lies in 'biology itself – procreation', a natural or original inequality that is the basis of the oppression of women and the source of male power. Men, by

52 Carole Pateman, *op cit*, pp 118–20.

53 *Ibid*, p 123.

54 *Ibid*, p 124.

55 S Firestone, *The Dialectic of Sex* (New York: W Morrow, 1970).

confining women to reproduction (nature), have freed themselves 'for the business of the world' and so have created and controlled culture. The proposed solution is to eliminate natural differences (inequalities) between the sexes by introducing artificial reproduction. 'Nature' and the private sphere of the family will then be abolished and individuals, of all ages, will interact as equals in an undifferentiated cultural (or public) order.

The popular success of *The Dialectic of Sex* owes more to the need for women to continue to fight for control of their bodies and reproductive capacity than to its philosophical argument. The key assumption of the book is that women necessarily suffer from 'a fundamentally oppressive biological condition', but biology, in itself, is neither oppressive nor liberating; biology, or nature, becomes either a source of subjection or free creativity for women only because it has meaning within specific social relationships. Firestone's argument reduces the social conceptions of 'women' and 'men' to the biological categories of 'female' and 'male', and thus denies any significance to the complex history of the relationship between men and women or between the private and public spheres. She relies on an abstract conception of a natural, biological female individual with a reproductive capacity which puts her at the mercy of a male individual, who is assumed to have a natural drive to subjugate her. This contemporary version of a thorough Hobbesian reduction of individuals to their natural state leads to a theoretical dead-end, not perhaps a surprising conclusion to an argument that implicity accepts the patriarchal claim that women's subordination is decreed by nature. The way forward will not be found in a universal dichotomy between nature and culture, or between female and male individuals. Rather ... it is necessary to develop a feminist theoretical perspective that takes account of the social relationships between women and men in historically specific structures of domination and subordination; and, it might be added, within the context of specific interpretations of the 'public' and 'private'.[56]

SEXUAL DIVISIONS IN LAW[57]
Katherine O'Donovan[58]

Definition and History of Public and Private

> The realm of life and work in *Gemeinschaft* is particularly befitting to women; indeed, it is even necessary to them. For women, the home and not the market, their own or a friend's dwelling and not the street, is the natural seat of their activity.
>
> *Ferdinand Tonnies*

Liberal philosophy has developed the ideas of public and private as separate areas of life. Both concepts are used in a variety of ways. In seeking to define the private I shall concentrate on its 19th century use. Central to liberalism is the concept of privacy as a sphere of behaviour free from public interference, that is, unregulated by law. The interest of an account of traditional usage of the concept of the private is not merely definitional. It is the prelude to an explanation for the divisions between women and the men in law.

---

56   *Ibid*, pp 125–26.
57   Katherine O'Donovan, *Sexual Divisions In Law* (Weidenfeld & Nicolson, 1984).
58   Currently Professor of Law, Queen Mary and Westfield College, University of London.

In a sense the private has no history. The purpose of a chapter on her story here is not merely 'a search for origins'. It is to explain how the patriarchal family form, which flourished in medieval and early modern European culture, survives today in another guise. This is accounted for, in large part, by the unregulated private.

Dichotomies

The liberal conception of the private refers to behaviour and activities unregulated by law. For Mill, 'the only part of the conduct of any one, for which he is amenable to society, is that which concerns others. In the part which merely concerns himself, his independence is, of right, absolute. Over himself, over his own body and mind, the individual is sovereign'.[59] Mill argues for a sphere of action in which society has only an indirect interest. This 'appropriate region of human liberty' covers matters of conscience, thought, opinion, expression. It also covers 'liberty of tastes and pursuits; of framing the plan of our life to suit our own character; of doing as we like subject to such consequences as may follow'.

In liberal philosophy privacy is central to individualism as an area of life not subjected to the power of society. The importance of this area has grown in recent times, for as Benjamin Constant observed, 'nearly all the enjoyments of the moderns are in their private lives: the immense majority, forever excluded from power, necessarily take only a very passing interest in their public lives'.[60] Steven Lukes, in his review of privacy as a core idea of individualism, concludes that

> the idea of privacy refers to a sphere that is not of proper concern to others. It implies a negative relation between the individual and some wider 'public', including the state – a relation of non-interference with, or non-intrusion into, some range of his thoughts and/or action. This condition may be achieved either by his withdrawal or by the public's forbearance.[61]

An outcome of this is that law as regulator or non-regulator is a crucial expression of the limits of state intervention. Law's role in maintaining a boundary between private and public has not always been recognised by philosophers. Yet as Lukes notes: 'liberalism may be said largely to have been an argument about where the boundaries of this private sphere lie, according to what principles they are to be drawn, whence interference derives and how it is to be checked.'[62] This statement might be thought to suggest that law is discounted as a mere boundary divider. It will, however, be argued throughout this book that law is not only central to the concepts of private and public, and to the division between the two, but also plays an important part in the construction of that division.

This book uses the concepts of private and public to distinguish between areas of activity and behaviour unregulated or regulated by law, as in the classical liberal fashion. In legal discourse privacy is more often used as a concept concerned with the protection of individuals from an overly intrusive corporate state prying into personal secrets. Clearly privacy as a concept concerns itself not only with social regulation but also with data protection and evidentiary matters of access

---

59   JS Mill, *On Liberty* (London: Dent, 1910), p 9.
60   B Constant, *De L'Esprit de Conquête* (1814), cited by S Lukes, *Individualism* (Blackwell, 1973), p 65.
61   S Lukes, *ibid*, p 66.
62   *Ibid*, p 62.

to information. This relates to the boundaries of law, for in some cases law enforcement depends on evidence as to behaviour normally classified as private. Further difficulties of definition arise because in recent writings the concepts private and public stand for a variety of referents. 'Public' may be used to denote state activity, the values of the market-place, work, the male domain or that sphere of activity which is regulated by law. 'Private' may denote civil society, the values of family, intimacy, the personal life, home, women's domain or behaviour unregulated by law. The confusion is increased in legal discourse which calls legal relations between state and citizens public and those between individuals private.

If the private is identified as the unregulated zone of life this poses problems which are neither discussed nor recognised in liberal political philosophy. Those areas such as the personal, sexuality, biological reproduction, family, home, which are particularly identified socially as women's domain, are also seen as private. It can be argued that social differentiation between women and men in the gender order has its counterpart in the general social distinction between private and public. A simple summary is: 'the public sphere is that sphere in which 'history' is made. But the public sphere is the sphere of male activity. Domestic activity becomes relegated to the private sphere and is mediated to the public sphere by men who move between both. Women have a place only in the private sphere'.[63, 64]

The importance of the distinction between private and public lies in its influence on our perception of the social world and the maintenance of the distinction in law. Scholars of the medieval period agree that the pre-industrial household was a centre of production and consumption. Life was not experienced as compartmentalised into separate categories. It is true that a hierarchical order divided human beings according to status, and that gender was a crucial determinant. This was experienced as natural. Living conditions in the past, the presence of servants and kin, meant that most, if not all, behaviour was open to comment and control. With the revolution in production and the change of mentality that accompanied it, 'life would now be experienced as divided into two distinct spheres: a public sphere of endeavour governed ultimately by the Market; and a 'private' sphere of intimate relationships and individual biological existence'.[65]

In traditional sociological theory the term *Gemeinschaft* has been used to sum up the values associated today with the private sphere. The term originates with the German sociologist, Ferdinand Tonnies, writing in the late 19th century. *Gemeinschaft*, or community, is represented by pre-modern, organic, pre-capitalist societies, usually agrarian, where everything was produced within the household. Here individuals were regulated according to status but their interactions were mediated by love, duty and a common understanding and purpose. The emphasis is on regulation as expressing internalised norms, traditions and the will of the organic community. There is little or no distinction between public and private, between formal law and other forms of regulation. Social status and gender are primary determinants of the expectations of individuals for themselves and of others.

---

63 D Smith, 'Women, the Family and Corporate Capitalism', in M Stephenson (ed), *Women in Canada* (Toronto: New Press, 1974), p 6.

64 Katherine O'Donovan, *op cit*, pp 2–4.

65 B Ehrenrich and D English, *For Her Own Good* (Pluto Press, 1979), p 9.

The *Gemeinschaft* conception of justice 'elevates social harmony and subordinates both conflict resolutions and resource allocation to a conception of the total social order'.[66] It is not a description of an actual social order but rather a Weberian ideal type which enables us to understand historical ideologies of how people should live. Although *Gemeinschaft* is sometimes used as an alternative for a concept of 'the good', it has to be recognised that this type of society is status and gender-based with a consequent subordination, for the sake of the community, of women and lower-class men. That this lesser status is seen as natural and therefore internalised does not detract from the point. Modern writing which idealises the values of community often overlooks the hierarchical and dependent relationships traditionally associated with self-abnegation for the sake of others.

Tonnies contrasted *Gemeinschaft* with the modern commercial market society, the *Gesellschaft*. This represents the world of striving for profit by isolated persons. This world develops as a protest against status society and with the growth of individualism. In this atomistic marketplace the general good is seen as derived from individual competition for material advantage. A free market promoted by the liberal theory of possessive individualism enables the pursuit of self-interest through the instrument of contract. The *Gesellschaft* conception of justice emphasises formality, neutrality of adjudication, precision, rationality and predictability. Individuals are seen as abstract right- and duty-bearing entities. The distinction between law – that which is formally regulated – and the private is sharply pronounced. Contract is the model for all law, an exchange between equal individuals, the *quid pro quo* of commercial dealings.

Gesellschaft is sometimes used as a synonym for 'the bad', but it can be argued that the neutrality and equality of the market is preferable to hierarchical society. Von Ihering illustrates the advantages of contractual independence by comparing a land without hotels but general hospitality, with a land with a supply of paid accommodation. On reflection he prefers to retain his personal freedom and independence and to pay for his lodging. He argues that our moral as well as our economic independence depend on exchange.[67]

Conceptions of Privacy

Legal discussions of privacy distinguish between the definition, content and zone of privacy on the one hand, and a notion of the right to that privacy on the other. Lack of agreement about the area to he delimited has prevented a right of privacy from being enacted in English law. However, a leading American authority has shown four areas of interests in privacy that are protected by law. These are intrusion into seclusion or private affairs; public disclosure of embarrassing private facts; false publicity; appropriation of name and likeness. ...[68, 69]

An attempt to arrive at a legal definition of the area of privacy through case analysis is unsatisfactory. There are few cases and they do not make clear where the lines are drawn. Yet the idea of privacy does affect perceptions of the social world and social policy, even if not translated into legal concept. Furthermore

---

66 E Kamenka, 'What is Justice?' in E Kamenka and AES Tay (eds) *Justice* (London, E Arnold, 1979), p 7.

67 See B Rudden, 'Real Property' (1982) 2 *Oxford Journal of Legal Studies*, 238.

68 WL Prosser, 'Privacy' (1960) 48 *California Law Review*, 383.

69 Katherine O'Donovan, *op cit*, pp 4–6.

the desire for privacy has grown in the recent past, probably as a reaction to market society. As the Younger Committee pointed out:

> The modern middle class family of two parents and their children, relatively sound-proofed in their semi-detached house, relatively unseen behind their privet hedge and rose trellis, travelling with determined reserve on public transport or insulated in the family car, shopping in the supermarket and entertained by television, are probably more private in the sense of being unnoticed in all their everyday doings than any other sizeable section of the population in any other time or place.[70]

Privacy, then, has various dimensions of which being unnoticed, not having one's seclusion intruded upon, and controlling information and knowledge about oneself, are only aspects. Those instances where privacy is regarded as having been violated largely concern individuals. The issue of state intrusion is more difficult. It is for the state to decide how, where, and in what manner it will regulate individuals lives. Zones can be mapped out as being inside or outside the state's purview. The placement of an aspect of life inside or outside the law is a form of regulation. Legal acknowledgement of its existence defines and constitutes it. So regulation may take a form within or without the law.

It has already been stipulated that the term private is used in this book as synonymous with non-regulated. This requires further elaboration. There is a distinction between areas of privacy that are unrecognised and invisible and those that are specifically delimited as private. With the non-existence or invisibility model there is no public reference to the private zone. Not being referred to, it is not brought into existence, defined or constituted.[71]

A deliberate policy of non-intervention by the state may mask a passing of control to informal mechanisms. For instance the legal doctrine of the unity of spouses serves as a justification for state policy of non-intervention in marriage. As Michael Anderson observes: 'family behaviour has become the most private and personal of all areas of behaviour, almost totally free from external supervision and control.'[72] Who then controls the family? It can be argued that nonintervention by law may result in the state leaving the power with the husband and father whose authority it legitimates indirectly through public law support for him as breadwinner and household head. A deliberate policy of non-intervention does not necessarily mean that an area of behaviour is uncontrolled.

The Distinction Between Private and Public in Legal Discourse

The idea that private and public can be distinguished is imbued in legal philosophy and informs legal policy. 'One of the central goals of 19th century legal thought was to create a clear separation between constitutional, criminal, and regulatory law – public law and the law of private transactions – torts, contracts, property and commercial law.'[73] This division is not confined to distinguishing relations between individual and state from relations between individuals. It also draws a line dividing the law's business from what is called

---

70 *Report of the Committee on Privacy*, Cmnd 5012 (1972), para 78.

71 Katherine O'Donovan, *op cit*, pp 6–7.

72 M Anderson, 'The Relevance of Family History', in C Harris (ed), *The Sociology of the Family* (Keele: Soc Rev Monograph No 28, 1979), p 67.

73 M Horowitz, 'The History of the Public/Private Distinction' (1982) 130 *U Penn LR* 1423, p 1424.

private. Although this boundary between the private and public shifts over time, the existence of the distinction and the notion of boundary are rarely questioned.

The dichotomy between private and public as unregulated and regulated has its origins in liberal philosophy. The 17th century liberal tradition as represented by Locke posits a distinction between reason and passion, knowledge and desire, mind and body. This leads to a split between the public sphere in which individuals prudently calculate their own self-interest and act upon it, and a private sphere of subjectivity and desire. As Roberto Unger describes it: 'In our public mode of being we speak the common language of reason, and live under laws of the state, the constraints of the market, and the customs of the different social bodies to which we belong. In our private incarnation, however, we are at the mercy of our own sense impressions and desires.'[74] The liberal conception is of man as a rational creature making rational choices and entering the political sphere for his own ends.

Nineteenth century liberal thought, as expressed by John Stuart Mill, continued the tradition of the private/public split. In his feminist work *On the Subjection of Women* the solution for Mill was the grant to women of full equality of formal rights with men in the public sphere. From public equality, he believed, would follow a transformed family, a 'school of sympathy in equality' where the spouses live 'together in love, without power on one side or obedience on the other'. Yet he did not propose the merging of the two spheres but rather sanctioned the division of labour in which women remain in the realm of subjectivity and the private. Thus he argued: 'When the support of the family depends, not on property but on earnings, the common arrangement, by which the wife superintends the domestic expenditure, seems to me in general the most suitable division of labour between the two persons'.[75] Women's role was to remain that of loving and softening men in the domestic realm. Mill's views on household management overlooked the connection between economic power and dominance in the home. Economic inequality leads to an imbalance of power. The division of labour whereby one spouse works for earnings and the other for love encapsulates the public/private split.

The Wolfenden Committee Report on Homosexual Offences and Prostitution provides an excellent example of the implementation in law of the liberal view of the distinction between public and private. The committee accepted as unproblematic the idea of 'private lives of citizens'. It stated that the function of criminal law in relation to homosexuality and prostitution was 'to preserve public order and decency, to protect the citizen from what is offensive and injurious, and to provide sufficient safeguards against exploitation and corruption of others'.[76] Individual freedom of choice and action in 'matters of private morality' was upheld in the report:

> Unless a deliberate attempt is to be made by society, acting through the agency of law, to equate the sphere of crime with that of sin, there must remain a realm of private morality and immorality which is, in brief and crude terms, not the law's business. To say this is not to condone or encourage private immorality. On the contrary, to emphasise the personal and private nature of moral or immoral conduct is to emphasise the personal and private responsibility of the individual for his own actions, and that is a

---

74   R Unger, *Knowledge and Politics* (NY: Free Press, 1975), p 59.

75   JS Mill, *On the Subjection of Women* (London: Dent, 1929), p 263.

76   Cmnd 247 (1957), para 13.

responsibility which a mature agent can be properly expected to carry for himself without the threat of punishment from the law.[77]

This is a classic statement of liberal philosophy[78]...

The Unregulated Family

The retreat of the family from society in the 18th century has been described by Philippe Aries. A zone of private life developed, not just for the nobility, but for the middle class and eventually for all. 'The family began to hold society at a distance, to push it back beyond a steadily extending zone of private life,[79] and became a place of intimate relations, in which it was safe to be oneself, where personalities were enlarged and expressed. This development mirrored and was part of the location of paid work outside the home. In the 19th century the public sphere, which had earlier been a place in which men realised their social and cultural being, now became identified with the market for commodities. This change in the public sphere has led the family to be regarded as the last outpost of *Gemeinschaft*.

The values of *Gemeinschaft* are those of self-sacrifice in the interests of the community but the context in which these are expressed is one where social roles are ascribed according to gender. Men who pass freely between public and private, but who are primarily located in the public, are socially expected to act as rational, calculating, economic individuals, whose actions are guided by self-interest. Women, who are seen primarily in the context of reproduction, home and family are expected to retain the values of *Gemeinschaft*. The private, regarded in legal ideology as unsuitable for legal regulation is ordered according to an ideology of love.

The thesis to be elaborated in this book is that ideas of privacy established in legal decisions preclude intervention in the family. The common law assumption that 'the house of everyone is his castle'[80] is an early and useful bulwark in the defence of civil liberties. But it may also conceal a power struggle within the family. This remains unrecognised and the judicial posture is one of defence of freedom, as the following passage makes clear:

> I for one should deeply regret the day, if it ever came, when Courts of Law or Equity thought themselves justified in interfering more than is strictly necessary with the private affairs of the people of this country. Both as regards the conduct of private affairs, and domestic life, the rule is that Courts of Law should not intervene except upon occasion. It is far better that people should be left free.[81]

Free for what? is the question. Insofar as this type of rhetoric involves upholding the values of liberty and the restraint of police powers it is no doubt admirable. But it also masks physical abuse and other manifestations of power and inequality within the family.

In discussions of the privacy of marital relations or of the boundaries of state intervention, the home, the family and the married couple remain an entity that is taken for granted. The couple is a unit, a black box, into which the law does not

---

77   *Ibid*, para 61.
78   Katherine O'Donovan, *op cit*, pp 6–9.
79   P Aries, *Centuries of Childhood* (Johnathan Cape, 1973), p 385.
80   *Semayne's Case* (1604) 77 ER 194.
81   *In re Agar-Ellis* (1883) 24 Ch D 317 at 335.

purport to peer. What goes on inside the box is not perceived as the law's concern. The belief is that it is for family members to sort out their personal relationships. What this overlooks is the power inequalities inside the family which are of course affected by structures external to it. This ideology of privacy and non-intervention has been articulated by legislators, by the judiciary and by legal scholars.

The reluctance of Parliament to legislate on areas of family life denoted private can be illustrated from a wide variety of materials concerning relations between the spouses and those between parent and child. Twentieth century debates on equal ownership of the matrimonial home have foundered on Parliament's unwillingness to lay down a legislative principle of equality. In 1980 when a Law Commission Bill on co-ownership of the matrimonial home was introduced in the House of Lords, the Lord Chancellor made it clear that there was no government support.[82] Nineteenth and early twentieth century debates on child protection and incest demonstrated a great reluctance on the part of parliamentarians to legislate on 'that d——d morality' which was regarded as a private, internal and domestic affair.[83]

The judiciary also have repeatedly expressed reluctance to intervene in the private. Lord Evershed, a former Master of the Rolls, expressed his view thus:

> It was in the year 1604, not far removed from the date when Shakespeare wrote the lines from *The Taming of the Shrew* that, according to Coke's report of the judgement in *Semayne's Case*, it was judicially laid down that the house of everyone is to him as his castle and fortress. More than three centuries later Atkin LJ, in a famous judgment, said: The parties themselves are advocates, judges, courts, sheriff's officer and reporter. In respect of these promises each house is a domain into which the King's writ does not seek to run, and to which its officers do not seek to be admitted.[84]

The Shakespearian lines referred to express a husband's ownership of his wife. Petruchio: 'I will be master of what is mine own; she is my goods, my chattels; she is my house, my household stuff, my field, my barn, my horse, my ox, my ass, my anything.' The promises regarded by Atkin LJ as internal to each house were promises of financial support made by a husband to his wife. The case in question stands as legal authority for the non-enforcement of promises made by spouses, and probably by immediate members of the family, unless sealed and witnessed.[85]

This legal ideology is described as follows by a legal scholar: 'English practice has been to refrain from formulating general principles as to how families should be managed'.[86] The view is that the ongoing family and marriage should be left alone, so long as conflict does not cause breakdown. But some scholars extend their opinions to prescription:

> The normal behaviour of husband and wife or parents and children towards each other is beyond the law – as long as the family is 'healthy'. The law comes in when things go wrong. More than that, the mere hint by anyone

---

82   *Hansard* (HL), vol 405 (1980), col 147.

83   *Hansard* vol 191 (1908), col 279.

84   Lord Evershed, 'Foreword' to RH Graveson and FR Crane (eds), *A Century of Family Law*, 1957), p xv, Sweet & Maxwell.

85   *Balfour v Balfour* [1919] 2 KB 571.

86   J Eekelaar, *Family Security and Family Breakdown* (Penguin, 1971), p 76.

concerned that the law may come in is the surest sign that things are or will soon be going wrong.[87]

State Intervention

It is a standard liberal view that intervention by the state in family life is to be avoided if at all possible. The Victorians believed that 'to undermine parental responsibility was to undermine family stability and thus the stability of society itself'.[88] The 'sanctity of the domestic hearth' was not to be invaded by law or state. Family law continues to be imbued with a belief in non-intervention. But discussions of non-interference whether expressed in legal ideology or in state policy usually refer only to direct intervention. What is overlooked is that structures external to the family have a significant effect on it, and that state policy in areas such as employment, taxation and social security affects what goes on in the family. Furthermore, informal mechanisms of intervention through education, medicine, psychiatry and welfare policies have existed since the Tudor Poor Laws.

Elizabethan Poor Law legislation created a public responsibility for support of the poor which was placed on the parish as an official duty. State concern became that of minimising the cost of this expenditure to the parish. The liability of the immediate family for the maintenance of relatives was legally established and defined. This state intervention constructed new ideas about family and community responsibility. On the one hand it defined what a family is and its rights and duties of financial support. But it also changed the ideas about mutual community aid which had once devolved not only within the household but also upon a wider circle of kin and neighbours: what had been done out of sympathy and neighbourliness now became a legal duty which was resented. It has been suggested that this change symbolised a weakening of personal and kin ties outside the immediate family.[89]

This early example is intended to show that, although the state is reluctant to intervene directly, policies in areas which impinge on the family and which are expressed in legislative, judicial and administrative provisions construct a particular family form. The nuclear family in which there is a division of labour between wife and husband is an expression of these policies.

Conventional academic discussion of state intervention in family and personal life is based on the premise that legislation which directs the management of these areas is not only a problem, but the only problem. The effects of formal legal intervention are said to be the undermining of the stability of the family, the weakening of family bonds, the atomising of individual family members, and the destruction of the family as a political bulwark against excess of state power.[90] Critics of the state hold the family up as a universal good. What they overlook is that the nuclear family which they so admire reflects a particular culture within a particular set of social relations: it is the family form of the 19th century

---

87 O Kahn-Freund and KW Wedderburn, Editorial Foreword to J Eekelaar, *op cit*, p 7.

88 I Pinchbeckd and M Hewitt, *Children in English Society* vol 2 (Routledge, 1973), p 357.

89 39 Eliz I, c 3 (1597); 43 Eliz I, c 2 (1601). See J TenBroek, 'California's Dual System of Family Law' Part I (1964) 16 *Stanford Law Review*, 257.e.

90 See eg MDA Freeman, *The Rights and Wrongs of Children* (London: Frances Pinter, 1983) p 245; J Goldstein *et al*, *Beyond the Best Interests of the Child* (London: Free Press, 1973) pp 49–52.

bourgeoisie. 'People everywhere and for all time have not participated in market relations out of which they have constructed a contrastive notion of the family.'[91]

An even more serious omission in the analysis of direct state intervention as unmitigatedly bad is that it ignores the influence of state policy in areas which impinge on the private. Policies on employment, welfare, housing, education, medicine, transport, production, planning, crime, in fact on almost everything, influence family life. How could it be otherwise? The whole fabric of the personal life is imprinted with colours from elsewhere. Not to acknowledge this, and to pretend that the private is free, leads to a false analysis.

The Feminist Critique of the Private

The anthropologist Michelle Rosaldo has argued that the assignment of women to the domestic sphere and of men to the public sphere is characteristic of all societies. This provides a thread linking all known human societies, from the most primitive to the most complex, and which underlines the universal oppression of women, despite the variety of forms this takes in different societies.[92] Although Rosaldo later suggested that 'gender is not a unitary fact determined everywhere by the same sort of concerns, but, instead, the complex product of a variety of social forces,'[93] her analysis provided a universal explanation. All cultures, she argued, distinguish between male and female, and assign appropriate behaviour and tasks to each as a sexual division of labour. No matter what form this takes, men's tasks and roles are given importance, authority and value, whereas those assigned to women are of lesser significance. 'Men are the locus of cultural value.'[94]

According to Rosaldo's analysis cultural value is attached to activities in the public sphere, whereas the domestic sphere is differentiated as concerned with activities organised immediately around one or more mothers and their children. Although advanced and capitalistic societies are extreme in this regard, the dichotomy between domestic and public is found in all societies. Male authority is based partly on an ability to maintain distance from the domestic sphere. Those societies that do not elaborate the opposition of male and female seem to be the most egalitarian. 'When a man is involved in domestic labour, in child care and cooking, he cannot establish an aura of authority and distance. And when public decisions are made in the household, women may have a legitimate public role.'[95]

Although this analysis locates women's subordination in culture, it permits a foundation of that culture in an interpretation of biology. The radical feminist, Shulamith Firestone, offered 'a materialist view of history based on sex itself'.[96] Using Friedrich Engels's original insight that the first division of labour was that between men and women, and that the first expropriation of labour was by men of women's reproduction of the species, Firestone reinterpreted materialism to signify the physical realities of female and male biology. The substructure is biology, the superstructure is those political and cultural institutions which

91   J Collier, M Rosaldo and s Yanagisako, 'Is There a Family?' in B Thorne and M Yalon (eds), *Rethinking the Family* (NY: Longman, 1982), p 35.

92   M Rosaldo, 'Women, Culture and Society', in M Rosaldo and L Lamphere, *Women, Culture and Society* (Stanford UP, 1974).

93   M Rosaldo, 'The Use and Abuse of Anthropology' (1980) 5 *Signs*, p 401.

94   M Rosaldo, 'Women, Culture and Society', *op cit*, p 20.

95   *Ibid*, p 39.

96   S Firestone, *The Dialectic of Sex* (NY: Bantam Books, 1970), p 5.

ensure that biological differences determine the social order. Firestone acknowledged that these differences did not necessitate the domination of females by males but asserted that reproductive functions did. She identified four elements of biological reproduction which lead to women's subordination: childbirth, dependency of infants, psychological effects on mothers of child-dependency, division of labour between the sexes based on 'natural reproductive difference'. Her revolutionary project was to abolish current methods of biological reproduction through the substitution of artificial methods and the socialisation of childcare.

Subsequently feminist theorists criticised Firestone for misappropriating the term materialist and for failing to examine women's relationship to economic production. It is generally agreed, however, that her insistence on the ideological association of women and the private sphere as a major source of women's subordination was an unique contribution to feminist theory.

The insistence on the idea that women belong in the private sphere is part of the cultural superstructure which has been built on biological foundations. Identifying these elements and disassembling the whole gave rise to the important insight that gender is socially constructed. Conceptually the distinction between sex and gender brought out the distinction between biological sex and social and cultural expectations and roles based on gender. Feminist analysis, relying on medical research into gender identity, broke the link between biology and culture by showing that one is not necessarily connected to the other.

The focus on the social construction of women's difference from men had an immediate consequence in terms of law. Feminists and liberals were agreed in questioning differential treatment of women and men in legislation. In particular in the United States, a whole series of challenges to gender-based legislative classifications took place. Each court success, and there were many in the 1960s and 1970s, was regarded as a victory for women.[97] Since social attitudes of employers and those providing such services as credit, housing and education were perceived as denying women equal opportunity, legislation was passed in Britain and the United States making discrimination on grounds of sex illegal.[98] The aim was to eliminate women's differences as a source of subordination so far as possible by opening up the public sphere and assimilating women to men. But in their alliance with liberal reformers feminists seemed to forget that element of the analysis of difference that identified the private sphere as the location of women's oppression.

With the focus on sexual division came the celebration of women's difference. The woman-centred analysis which developed from the mid-1970s studies women's culture, held up by some as a model for all persons. This meant an examination of mothering, of women's virtues, of female sexuality, of female experience as values for the culture as a whole, and a critique of masculinity. Celebrating women's difference as a source of strength rather than of oppression became an accepted mode of analysis. Important and perhaps even essential though this stage in the development of feminist theory was, it seemed to lose

---

97   Eg *Reed v Reed* 404 US 71 (1971); *Frontiero v Richardson*, 411 US 677 (1973).

98   In Britain the Equal Pay Act 1970 and the Sex Discrimination Act 1975 made up an 'equality package'. In the US the equal protection clause of the Fourteenth Amendment to the Constitution has been the basis for court litigation. Title VII of the Civil Rights Act 1964 and the Equal Pay Act 1963 also form part of American anti-discrimination legislation.

contact with the major early feminist dissection of the myths surrounding gender.

There is a curious similarity between the positions of the feminist theorists of the 1960s and early 1970s who focused on eliminating women's differences and those from the mid-1970s onwards who celebrated difference. Both streams accepted the dichotomy between public and private. The first group favoured eliminating the differences between women and men, but not necessarily the division between private and public. The second group celebrated women's private existence.

Yet there is within feminist analysis a slogan 'the personal is political' which emphasises the falsity of the public/private dichotomy. Male hegemony has been identified as a continuum in relations between the sexes in all spheres. In the private arena, according to this analysis, relations of domination and subordination are masked by the ideology of love. In the public sphere economic and cultural factors hide the reality. Gender relationships are power relationships.

This account of the feminist critique of the private thus far is a resume of radical feminist thought since the mid-1960s. There is also within feminist theory a Marxian analysis which places class alongside gender in its account of women's oppression. This tradition has been stronger in Britain than the United States. Within Marxian feminism what I have presented as a public/private dichotomy is designated as the sexual division of labour. Relationships within the family are on a material site 'located in the relations of production of capitalism and their private, intensely individual character draws on the ideology secured by the bourgeoisie as well as pre-capitalist notions of gender and sexuality'.[99] Marxian analysis correctly identifies notions of the private with the capitalist mode of production and the separation of work and home, for as Marx said of the alienated worker: 'he is at home when he is not working, and when he is working he is not at home.'[100] Yet the historical evidence is that gender divisions pre-dated capitalism, and these were socially constructed by feudal law.

Recently a series of questions about the state have been raised by the feminist lawyer Catharine MacKinnon. Pointing out that feminism has a theory of power but no theory of the state, she argues that the 'state's formal norms recapitulate the male point of view on the level of design'.[101] Her view is that the liberal state's claim to objectivity rests on its allocation of public matters to itself to be treated objectively, and of private matters to civil society to be treated subjectively'. But feminist consciousness has exploded the private.... To see the personal as political means to see the private as public.'[102] MacKinnon criticises both Marxism and liberalism for transcending the private and for failing to confront male power and its expression in state and law.

The meaning of the slogan 'the personal is political' has not been examined in detail in relation to law. Although feminists have produced a literature depicting the relative powerlessness of women as a sex category, this insight has not been documented in relation to law, although some work has begun in the United

---

99   M Barrett, *Women's Oppression Today* (London: Verso, 1980), p 212.

100   K Marx, *Economic and Philosophical Manuscripts of 1844* (London: Lawrence and Wishart, 1973), p 110.

101   CA MacKinnon, 'Feminism, Marxism, Method, and the State: Toward Feminist Jurisprudence' (1983) 8 *Signs*, 635, at 655.

102   *Ibid*, p 656.

States.[103] Feminist legal analysis in Britain has been content with the liberal position of opening up access for women to the public sphere through sex discrimination legislation.[104] The importance of the private has not been recognised, perhaps because lawyers cannot see that not regulating is as significant as regulating. Yet we need a detailed understanding of how the particular gender/social order is constituted by law.

The Importance of law

Feminist analysis has largely succeeded in disassembling the structure of current gender arrangements, if not on a universal basis, at least in the West. What has been lacking however has been an account of how various social, economic and legal structures combine in creating, ordering and supporting the present system. In particular law has remained resistant to analysis. Because it appears immanent, that is embedded in the seemingly natural, law's role is difficult to isolate. Understanding how existing legal structures appear natural and necessary is not a process of justification; rather it is essential to a full analysis of the gender order.

Unravelling law's part is not easy. It is not just external and institutional but also has an internal aspect whereby it forms part of individual consciousness. In its external aspects law may be coercive, but legal institutions also structure, mould and constitute the external world. Law influences the world as well as responding to it. In my view law is historically and culturally contingent. The form it takes depends on the particular conditions in which it occurs. A generally accepted theory is that the law adapts to and reflects shared social values. This ignores the active part played by law in shaping perceptions of these values.

In an essay published in 1971 Professor Robert Summers identified law as a set of techniques for the discharge of social functions. He gave examples of five basic techniques used in modern law. These are the penal, 'which serves the function of crime prevention; grievance remedial, which is designed to provide compensation for injury; administrative, which is for regulation; public-benefit-conferral, which is for distributive ends; and private, which is for arranging to facilitate personal choice'.[105] Of these only the penal is obviously coercive. Summers's typology enables us to see how law is not merely coercive but takes on a number of different guises in its construction of the social order. The limitation of this account is that it takes a purely instrumental view of law. This ignores the symbolic or ideological aspect, which is also important.

The internal aspect of law is its acceptance by individuals as natural and necessary in the form it takes and the values it expresses. It is internalised and most people are unconscious of its contingency. This helps to explain why the current social/gender order is accepted by those subordinate within that order. Here law as ideology plays an important part. In using the term ideology I am referring to the symbolic statement a particular legal principle or rule makes. In popular consciousness this is generally accepted as a statement of what is fair, or

---

103 See K Powers, 'Sex Segregation and the Ambivalent Directions of Sex Discrimination Law' (1979) *Wisconsin LR*, 55; F Olsen, 'The Family and the Market: A Study of Ideology and Legal Reform' (1983) 96 *Harvard LR* 1497; N Taub and EM Schneider, 'Perspectives on Women's Subordination and the Role of Law' in D Kairys (ed), *The Politics of Law* (NY: Pantheon Books, 1983).

104 See eg Carol Smart, *The Ties That Bind* (London: Routledge, 1984).

105 RS Summers, 'The Technique Element in Law' (1971) 59 *California LR* 733.

at least what is unchangeable. Teasing out the content of a particular principle or rule is not easy. As the immanent critique of the apparently natural character of law shows, the infusion of law in the social fabric makes isolation difficult. The term ideology stands also for those beliefs that legitimate or justify legal statements of values and perspectives, and consequent practices. Making explicit the implicit content and premises is what the analysis of law as ideology attempts.

How does the imminent critique and the analysis of law as ideology relate to a dissection of current gender arrangements in Britain and the United States? In constructing legal distinctions on biological differences law constitutes both gender and the social order. In relation to the issues explored in this book law rarely shows its coercive side. Yet its external and instrumental techniques, other than coercion, order the regulation of gender categories, sexuality, marriage, taxation, social security and the mapping out of a private zone.

Although I have used the Summers typology to show how law functions, I do not share his instrumental views. For me the great significance of law is that it addresses the ineluctable problems of what people are and how they live, and it prescribes answers. These answers reveal a great deal about the kind of society prescribed. Law is not autonomous. It is part of the social order whose functions it serves. But it is also symbolic. We need to know what it means in people's lives.[106]

---

106 Katherine O'Donovan, *op cit*, pp 11–20.

CHAPTER 6

GENDER: EQUALITY/SAMENESS/DIFFERENCE

Gender, and its legal construction, is a focal point for feminist analysis. As will be seen from the case-law relating to transsexuals in the first part of this chapter, the law insists that – for certain purposes but not others – whilst medical science and technology can realign a person's physical attributes to bring them more in line with the person's psychological gender, the law will not recognise this change for the purposes of the law of marriage. Law thus *defines* gender. The manner in which law achieves this is revealed in Ormod LJ's judgment in *Corbett v Corbett*.[1] The case of *Corbett* has been followed in two cases which have come before the European Court of Human Rights under the European Convention on Human Rights and fundamental freedoms: *Rees v United Kingdom*[2] and *Cossey v United Kingdom*.[3] In the extract which follows, Professor Katherine O'Donovan examines the rationale for the decision in *Corbett v Corbett*.[4]

The gender issue is, however, far wider than the construction of gender by law. In every field of law and legal practice, the law is itself gendered. That is to say, that the law – whether developed through the courts under the common law, or enacted in legislative provisions, reflects the gender of those who have created it: men. Contract law, the criminal law, employment law, family and social welfare law, property law, the law of torts – in fact every aspect of law and legal reasoning – and jurisprudence – reflects the maleness of law.

From a feminist perspective, the law – in its predominantly male guise – excludes, marginalises and silences women. The law excludes women by adopting male standards and perceptions. For example, as will be seen from the readings, the law relating to rape, that most violative of male crimes, is cast in terms of sexual intercourse not violence. From the law's perspective what is of crucial importance in a rape trial is the conduct of the victim: did she, or did she not consent. Thus it is the victim's behaviour and personality and lifestyle which is critical to the finding of guilt or innocence. How can this be explained? Why is it that the law of rape, and the criminal proceedings related to rape, does not focus primarily on the conduct of the alleged rapist? As rape law is currently constructed, the victim of rape is very much the victim also of the legal system.[5] As another introductory example of this phenomenon, the law relating to pornography[6] is cast in terms of 'obscenity', not violence or the subordination or degradation of women or sexual harassment or sexual discrimination.

---

1   [1971] P 110; [1970] 2 All ER 654, *infra*.
2   [1986] 9 EHRR 56, *infra*.
3   [1991] 2 FLR 492, *infra*.
4   *Sexual Divisions in Law* (Weidenfeld & Nicolson, 1985), Chapter 3.
5   See further Chapter 9.
6   On which see Chapter 10.

As Lucinda Finlay's article, *Breaking Women's Silence in Law: The Dilemma of the Gendered Nature of Legal Reasoning*,[7] so cogently argues, the law is characterised by maleness: authoritative, conflictual, objective, rational and non-emotional. Law presents itself as gender-neutral, but analysis reveals that law is far from that. It is the task of feminist legal scholars to unmask the maleness of law, to attempt to break down the exclusionary and often-invisible barriers which the law creates to exclude, to ignore and to silence women.

In *The Mirror Tells Its Tale*,[8] Sheila Duncan examines the criminal law and reveals the manner in which the doctrine of consent (in relation to sexual intercourse) is overlaid with maleness. In its legal construction of consent, the law constructs sexuality and reinforces the idea that men are the true subjects of law: women merely 'the other'.

Professor Carol Gilligan's theory of moral development of boys and girls, developed in *In a Different Voice: Psychological Theory and Women's Development*,[9] is next considered. Professor Gilligan, an educational psychologist, analysed the differing moral and psychological approaches of boys and girls to problem-solving. Gilligan's studies portray girls as primarily concerned with relationships and the ethic of care, while the moral reasoning of boys is less interpersonal, more objective and logically rational. Gilligan's work has formed the focus for much debate, and disagreement, among feminist scholars, as the extracts in this chapter will reveal.

In *Portia in a Different Voice: Speculations on a Women's Lawyering Process*,[10] Carrie Menkel-Meadow provides a constructive analysis of the application of Gilligan's theory to the lawyering process, revealing the manner in which the traditionally (male) adversarial legal process might change by the greater inclusion of women's reasoning.

Leslie Bender, in *From Gender Difference to Feminist Solidarity: Using Carol Gilligan and an Ethic of Care in Law*,[11] while recognising the controversial nature of Gilligan's work for feminists, offers a constructive analysis. It is the author's belief that an ethic of care, if incorporated into the law, would transform both justice and law by lessening the 'adversarial, competitive, win-or-lose' ethos which currently characterises law.

Catharine MacKinnon's *On Sex Discrimination: Difference and Dominance*[12] represents a powerful critique of the 'sameness/equality/ difference' debate which had taken such a hold on feminist legal scholarship. For MacKinnon, a central difficulty with the debate lies in the unavoidable fact that whichever approach is postulated – sameness or difference – the referent for the analysis is always male. It is MacKinnon's thesis that the debate should be recast. Once it is recognised that the issue is one of hierarchy and (male) power, the debate can

---

7   (1989) 64 *Notre Dame Law Review*, 886, *infra*.

8   *Feminist Perspectives on the Foundational Subjects of Law* (Cavendish Publishing Ltd, 1996).

9   Harvard University Press, 1982.

10   (1985) *Berkeley Women's Law Journal* 39.

11   (1990) 15 *Vermont Law Review* 1.

12   *Feminism Unmodified* (Harvard University Press, 1987).

be reformulated in terms which explicitly recognise this in terms of male dominance and female subordination. MacKinnon's writing has mesmeric power and has attracted – perhaps more than any other feminist lawyer – both great critical acclaim and controversy even within the feminist legal movement. One critique levelled at Catharine MacKinnon's theory is that of 'essentialism'. That is to say, that it is alleged that in her writing about 'women', MacKinnon fails to acknowledge the multiciplicity of women and women's experience, as if all women are essentially white, middle-class and heterosexual.

Drucilla Cornell's book review of Catharine MacKinnon's *Toward a Feminist Theory of the State*[13] challenges MacKinnon's work on the basis that MacKinnon, in emphasising women's sexuality, portrays women as sexual objects and no more than that. In so doing, Cornell argues, MacKinnon is perpetuating the gender hierarchy which she seeks to dismantle, rather than challenging it.

In *Jurisprudence and Gender* Robin West analyses the ideas of autonomy and individualism and their conceptual counterparts, attachment and relatedness. Each of these concepts play a central role in liberal legal theory and critical legal theory.[14] Also analysed is the manner in which traditional liberal legal theory and critical legal theory, and indeed all 'traditional jurisprudence' is gendered: it is masculine and exclusionary. What is needed is a truly feminist jurisprudence and the eradication of the maleness of traditional jurisprudence in order that there may be developed a 'humanist jurisprudence' — a 'jurisprudence unmodified'.

Both Catharine MacKinnon's and Carol Gilligan's writings are critiqued in Deborah Rhode's article, *Jurisprudence and Gender*.[15] It is Rhode's contention that both authors fall into the trap of 'essentialism': MacKinnon in relation to her portrayal of women as 'one woman' and Gilligan as representing relational feminism as the predominant feminist model. Deborah Rhode calls for a more explicit recognition of women's distinctive and multifarious experience. In her view, no one theoretical stance can claim the intellectual high ground in theorising about women. What is needed is a recognition of the multiplicity and diversity within the feminist legal movement.

Angela Harris subjects Catharine MacKinnon's and Robin West's theses to critical scrutiny from the perspective of a black feminist lawyer. In *Race and Essentialism in Feminist Legal Theory*,[16] Harris argues that feminist legal theory is characterised by essentialism, a factor which causes feminist theory to be the voice of 'mostly white, straight, and socio-economically privileged', thus excluding the particular concerns of black women. Whilst white, heterosexual and economically privileged women experience discrimination from and subordination to men, black women have traditionally faced the double oppression of both sexism and racism. Harris calls for feminist jurisprudence to

13 (1990) 100 *Yale Law Journal*, 2247, *infra*.
14 On which see Chapter 8.
15 (1988) 38 *Journal of Legal Education* 38, *infra*.
16 (1990) 42 *Stanford Law Review*, 581, *infra*.

move beyond essentialism, into a theory which reflects the 'multiple consciousness' of all women.

In the extract from Patricia Cain's article, *Feminist Jurisprudence: Grounding the Theories*[17] the author approaches the gender issue from the perspective of a lesbian feminist. In Patricia Cain's analysis feminist jurisprudence has fallen into one of two traps. The first is assimilationist – that is to say the assumption that all women – irrespective of race, class or gender-orientation – can be subsumed under the label 'women'. The second is essentialism: the characterisation of all women as imbued with identical characteristics. Both approaches fail to reflect the diversity of women and women's experiences which must be incorporated within feminist jurisprudence.

In *Deconstructing Gender*,[18] Joan Williams is critical of 'difference feminism', and calls for a move away from the 'destructive debate' on difference and sameness. What is needed, the author argues is an approach which deinstitutionalises gender: which separates sex and gender and which analyses the false descriptions which are traditionally used to describe men and women, and most particularly women's employment.

GENDER DETERMINATION – BY LAW

Under English law, as currently endorsed by the European Court of Human Rights which adjudicates upon alleged violations of the European Convention on Human Rights and Fundamental Freedoms, gender is biologically determined at birth and cannot be altered subsequently. The seminal case which remains good authority for this proposition is that of *Corbett v Corbett*.[19] The parties to litigation had been through a ceremony of marriage in 1963. The issue before the court was whether the 'marriage' was legally valid. The respondent had been born male, but in 1960 had undergone a sex-change operation, since which time he/she had lived as a woman. The Court of Appeal ruled that the marriage was void; the respondent – despite the surgical treatment – remained, in law, male. Ormrod LJ delivered the leading judgment:

All the medical witnesses accept that there are at least four criteria for assessing the sexual condition of an individual. These are:

(i)   Chromosomal factors.

(ii) Gonadal factors (ie presence or absence of testes or ovaries).

(iii) Genital factors (including internal sex organs).

(iv) Psychological factors.

Some of the witnesses would add:

(v)   Hormonal factors or secondary sexual characteristics (such as distribution of hair, breast development, physique, etc. which are thought to reflect the balance between the male and female sex hormones in the body).

17   (1989) *Berkeley Women's Law Journal* 191, *infra*.
18   (1989) 87 *Michigan Law Review*, 797, *infra*.
19   [1971] P 110; [1970] 2 All ER 654.

It is important to note that these criteria have been evolved by doctors, for the purposes of systematising medical knowledge and assisting in the difficult task of deciding the best way of managing the unfortunate patients who suffer, either physically or psychologically, from sexual abnormalities. As Professor Dewhurst observed, 'we do not determine sex – in medicine we determine the sex in which it is best for the individual to live'. These criteria are, of course, relevant to, but do not necessarily decide, the legal basis of sex determination.[20]

The fundamental purpose of law is the regulation of the relations between persons and the state or community. For the limited purposes of this case, legal relations can be classified into those in which the sex of the individuals concerned is either irrelevant, relevant or an essential determinant of the nature of the relationship. Over a very large area the law is indifferent to sex. It is irrelevant to most of the relationships which give rise to contractual or tortious rights and obligations, and to the greater part of the criminal law. In some contractual relationships, eg life assurance and pensions schemes, sex is a relevant factor in determining the rate of premium or contributions. It is relevant also to some aspects of the law regulating conditions of employment and to various state run schemes such as national insurance, or to such fiscal matters as selective employment tax. It is not an essential determinant of the relationship in these cases because there is nothing to prevent the parties to a contract of insurance or a pension scheme from agreeing that the person concerned should be treated as a man or as a woman, as the case may be. Similarly, the authorities, if they think fit, can agree with the individual that he shall be treated as a woman for national insurance purposes, as in this case. On the other hand, sex is clearly an essential determinant of the relationship called marriage because it is and always has been recognised as a union of man and woman. It is the institution on which the family is built, and in which the capacity for natural heterosexual intercourse is an essential element. It has, of course, many other characteristics, of which companionship and mutual support is an important one, but the characteristics which distinguish it from all other relationships can only be met by two persons of opposite sex. There are some other relationships such as adultery, rape and gross indecency in which, by definition, the sex of the participant is an essential determinant.

Since marriage is essentially a relationship between man and women, the validity of the marriage in this case depends, in my judgment, upon whether the respondent is or is not a woman. I think, with respect, that this is a more precise way of formulating the question than that adopted in paragraph two of the petition, in which it is alleged that the respondent is a male. The greater, of course, includes the less but the distinction may not be without importance, at any rate, in some cases. The question then becomes, what is meant by the word 'woman' in the context of a marriage, for I am not concerned to determine the 'legal sex' of the respondent at large. Having regard to the essentially heterosexual character of the relationship which is called marriage, the criteria must, in my judgment, be biological, for even the most extreme degree of transsexualism in a male or the most severe hormonal imbalance which can exist in a person with male chromosomes, male gonads and male genitalia cannot reproduce a person who is naturally capable of performing the essential role of a woman in marriage. In other words, the law should adopt in the first place, the first three of the doctors' criteria, ie, the chromosomal, gonadal and genital tests, and if all three are congruent, determine the sex for the purpose of marriage

---

20 *Ibid*, p 100, D–G.

accordingly, and ignore any operative intervention. The real difficulties, of course, will occur if these three criteria are not congruent. This question does not arise in the present case and I must not anticipate, but it would seem to me to follow from what I have just said that the greater weight would probably be given to the genital criteria than to the other two. This problem and, in particular, the question of the effect of surgical operations in such cases of physical intersex, must be left until it comes for decision. My conclusion, therefore, is that the respondent is not a woman for the purposes of marriage but is a biological male and has been so since birth. It follows that the so-called marriage is void.[21]

The precedent set by *Corbett* has been followed by two cases which ultimately went to the European Court of Human Rights, following a petition under the European Convention on Human Rights and Fundamental Freedoms, alleging violation of the right to privacy (Article 8) and the right to marry and found a family (Article 12). Extracts from the judgments explain the English law and reveal the approach adopted by the European Court.

Article 8

1. Everyone has the right to respect of or his private and family life, his home and his correspondence.

2. There shall be no interference by a public authority with the exercise of this right except such as is in accordance with the law and is necessary in a democratic society in the interests of national security, public safety or the economic well-being of the country, for the prevention of disorder or crime, for the protection of health or morals, or for the protection of the rights and freedoms of others.

Article 12

Men and women of marriageable age have the right to marry and to found a family, according to the national laws governing the exercise of this right.

Rees v United Kingdom[22]

B. Compliance with Article 8

Transsexualism is not a new condition, but its particular features have been identified and examined only fairly recently. The developments that have taken place in consequence of these studies have been largely promoted by experts in the medical and scientific fields who have drawn attention to the considerable problems experienced by the individuals concerned and found it possible to alleviate them by means of medical and surgical treatment. The term 'transsexual' is usually applied to those who, whilst belonging physically to one sex, feel convinced that they belong to the other; they often seek to achieve a more integrated, unambiguous identity by undergoing medical treatment and surgical operations to adapt their physical characteristics to their psychological nature. Transsexuals who have been operated upon thus form a fairly well defined and identifiable group.

In the United Kingdom no uniform, general decision has been adopted either by the legislature or by the courts as to the civil status of postoperative transsexuals. Moreover, there is no integrated system of civil status registration, but only separate registers for births, marriages, deaths and adoption. These record the

---

21 *Ibid*, pp 105 B–106 F.
22 [1986] 9 EHRR 56.

relevant events in the manner they occurred without, except in special circumstances, mentioning changes (of name, address, etc) which in other States are registered.

However, transsexuals, like anyone else in the United Kingdom, are free to change their first names and surnames at will. Similarly, they can be issued with official documents bearing their chosen first names and surnames and indicating, if their sex is mention at all, their preferred sex by the relevant prefix (Mr, Mrs, Ms or Miss). This freedom gives them a considerable advantage in comparison with States where all official documents have to conform with the records held by the registry office.

Conversely, the drawback – emphasised by the applicant – is that, as the country's legal system makes no provision for legally valid civil status certificates, such persons have on occasion to establish their identity by means of a birth certificate which is either an authenticated copy of or an extract from the birth register. The nature of this register, which furthermore is public, is that the certificates mention the biological sex which the individuals had at the time of their birth. The production of such a birth certificate is not a strict legal requirement, but may on occasion be required in practice for some purposes.

It is also clear that the United Kingdom does not recognise the applicant as a man for all social purposes. This, it would appear that, at the present stage of the development of United Kingdom law, he would be regarded as a women, *inter alia*, as far as marriage, pension rights and certain employments are concerned. The existence of the unamended birth certificate might also prevent him from entering into certain types of private arrangements as a man.

For the applicant and the Commission this situation was incompatible with Article 8, there being in their opinion no justification for it on any ground of public interest. They submitted that the refusal of the Government to amend or annotate the register of births to record the individual's change of sexual identity and to enable him to be given a birth certificate showing his new identity cannot be justified on any such ground. Such a system of annotation would, according to the applicant, be similar to that existing in the case of adoptions. The applicant and the Commission pointed to the example of certain other Contracting States which have recently made provision for the possibility of having the original indication of sex altered from a given date. The Commission additionally relied on the fact that the United Kingdom, through its free national health service, had borne the costs of the surgical operations and other medical treatment which the applicant had been enabled to undergo. They considered that this medical recognition of the necessity to assist him to realise his identity must be regarded as a further argument for the legal recognition of the change in his sexual identity; failure to do so had the effect that the applicant was treated as an ambiguous being.

The Court is not persuaded by this reasoning.[23]

The Court accepted the Government's view that the changes necessary to respect Mr Rees' rights could not be justified in the public interest, and that given the broad band of discretion given to the State in this matter, there was no breach of Article 8. On the alleged violation of Article 12, the Court's judgment was terse:

---

23   Paras 38–42.

The applicant complained of the undisputed fact that, according to the law currently in force in the United Kingdom, he cannot marry a woman. He alleged a violation of Article 12, which provides:

> Men and women of marriageable age have the right to marry and to found a family, according to the national laws governing the exercise of this right.

The Government contested this: the Commission was divided between two conflicting views.

In the Court's opinion, the right to marry guaranteed by Article 12 refers to the traditional marriage between persons of opposite biological sex. This appears also from the wording of the Article which makes it clear that Article 12 is mainly concerned to protect marriage as the basis of the family.

Furthermore, Article 12 lays down that the exercise of this right shall be subject to the national laws of the Contracting States. The limitations thereby introduced must not restrict or reduce the right in such a way or to such an extent that the very essence of this right is impaired. However, the legal impediment in the United Kingdom on the marriage of persons who are not of the opposite biological sex cannot be said to have an effect of this kind.

There is accordingly no violation in the instant case of Article 12 of the Convention.

Cossey v United Kingdom[24]

The applicant's allegations were contested by the Government. A majority of the Commission expressed the opinion that there had been a violation of Article 12, but not of Article 8.

The Court was confronted in the *Rees* case with issues akin to those arising in the present case. It therefore has to determine whether the two cases are distinguishable on their facts, or whether it should depart from the judgment which it gave in the former case on 17 October 1986 [1987] 2 FLR 111; 'the *Rees* judgment'.

1. Is the present case distinguishable on its facts from the *Rees* case?

In the view of the applicant and certain members of the Commission, the present case was distinguishable on its facts from the *Rees* case, in that, at the time of their respective applications to the Commission, Miss Cossey had a male partner wishing to marry her whereas Mr Rees did not have a female partner wishing to marry him. Reference was also made to the ceremony of marriage between the applicant and Mr X which, although the marriage was declared void, was said to underline her wish to marry.

The Court is not persuaded that this difference is material. In the first place, the fact that Mr Rees had no such partner played no part in the Court's decisions, which were based on a general consideration of the principles involved. In any event, as regards Article 8, the existence or otherwise of a willing marriage partner has no relevance in relation to the contents of birth certificates, copies of which may be sought or required for purposes wholly unconnected with marriage. Again, as regards Article 12, whether a person has the right to marry depends not on the existence in the individual case of such a partner or a wish to marry, but on whether or not he or she meets the general criteria laid down by law.

---

24 [1991] 2 FLR 492.

Reliance was also placed by the applicant on the fact that she is socially accepted as a woman, but this provides no relevant distinction because the same was true, *mutatis mutandis*, of Mr Rees. Neither is it material that Miss Cossey is a male-to-female transsexual, whereas Mr Rees is a female-to-male transsexual: thus – the only other factual difference between the two cases – is again a matter that had no bearing on the reasoning in the *Rees* judgment.

The Court thus concludes that the present case is not materially distinguishable on its facts from the *Rees* case.

II Should the Court depart from its *Rees* judgment?

The applicant argued that, in any event, the issues arising under Articles 8 and 12 deserved reconsideration.

It is true that, as she submitted, the Court is not bounds by its previous judgments; indeed, this is borne out by r 51(1) of the Rules of Court. However, it usually follows and applies its own precedents, such a course being in the interest of legal certainty and the orderly development of the Convention case law. Nevertheless, this would not prevent the Court from departing from an earlier decision if it was persuaded that there were cogent reasons for doing so. Such a departure might, for example, be warranted in order to ensure that the interpretation of the Convention reflects societal changes, and remains in line with present day conditions.

A. Alleged violation of Article 8

The applicant asserted that the refusal to issue her with a birth certificate showing her sex as female constituted an 'interference' with her right to respect for her private life, in that she was required to reveal intimate personal details whenever she had to produce a birth certificate. In her view, the Government had not established that this interference was justified under Article 8(2).

On this point, the Court remains of the opinion which it expressed in the *Rees* judgment: refusal to alter the register of births, or to issue birth certificates whose contents and nature differ from those of the original entries, cannot be considered as an interference. What the applicant is arguing is not that the State should abstain from acting, but rather that it should take steps to modify its existing system. The question is, therefore, whether an effective respect for Miss Cossey's private life imposes a positive obligation on the United Kingdom in this regard.

As the Court has pointed out on several occasions, notably in the *Rees* judgment itself, the notion of 'respect' is not clear cut, especially as far as the positive obligations inherent in that concept are concerned: having regard to the diversity of the practices followed and the situations obtaining in the Contracting States, the notion's requirements will vary considerably from case to case. In determining whether or not a positive obligation exists, regard must be had to the fair balance that has to be struck between the general interest of the community and the interests of the individual, the search for which balance is inherent in the whole of the Convention.

In reaching its conclusion in the *Rees* judgment that no positive obligation of this kind now in issue was incumbent on the United Kingdom, the Court noted, *inter alia*, the following points: [25]

(a) The requirement of striking a fair balance could not give rise to any direct obligation on the respondent State to alter the very basis of its system for the

---

25   At pp 121–122, paras 42–44.

registration of births, which was designed as a record of historical facts, by substituting therefore a system of documentation, such as that used in some other Contracting States, for recording current civil status.

(b)   An annotation to the birth register, recording Mr Rees' change of sexual identity, would establish only that he belonged thenceforth – and not from the time of his birth – to the other sex. Furthermore, the change so recorded could not mean the acquisition of all the biological characteristics of the other sex. In any event, such an annotation could not, without more, constitute an effective safeguard for ensuring the integrity of his private life, as it would reveal the change in question.

(c)   That change, and the corresponding annotation, could not be kept secret from third parties without a fundamental modification of the existing system for maintaining the register of births, which was accessible to the public. Secrecy could have considerable unintended results and could prejudice the purpose and function of the register by, for instance, complicating factual issues arising in the fields of family and succession law. It would also take no account of the position of third parties, in that they would be deprived of information which they had a legitimate interest to receive.

The Court, having concluded that there were no material differences between the *Rees* case and the instant case, ruled that there had been no violation of Article 8. The Court proceeded, however, to make the following observation:

The Court would, however, reiterate the observations it made in the *Rees* judgment. It is conscious of the seriousness of the problems facing transsexuals and the distress they suffer. Since the Convention always has to be interpreted and applied in the light of current circumstances, it is important that the need for appropriate legal measures in this area should be kept under review.

B. Alleged violation of Article 12

In reaching its conclusion in the *Rees* judgment that there had been no violation of Article 12, the Court noted the following points:

(a)   The right to marry, guaranteed by Article 12, referred to the traditional marriage between persons of opposite biological sex. This appeared also from the wording of the article, which made it clear that its main concern was to protect marriage as the basis of the family.

(b)   Article 12 laid down that the exercise of the right to marry shall be subject to the national laws of the Contracting States. The limitations thereby introduced must not restrict or reduce the right in such a way, or to such an extent, that the very essence of the right was impaired. However, the legal impediment in the UK on the marriage of persons who were not of the opposite biological sex could not be said to have an effect of this king.

Miss Cossey placed considerable reliance, as did the Delegate of the Commission, on the fact that she could not marry at all: as a woman, she could not realistically marry another woman and English law prevented her from marrying a man.

In the latter connection, Miss Cossey accepted that Article 12 referred to marriage between a man and a woman, and she did not dispute that she had not acquired all the biological characteristics of a woman. She challenged, however, the adoption in English law of exclusively biological criteria for determining person's sex for the purposes of marriage and the Court's endorsement of that situation in the *Rees* judgment, despite the absence from Article 12 of any indication of the criteria to be applied for this purpose. In her submission, there was no good reason for not allowing her to marry a man.

As to the applicant's inability to marry a woman, this does not stem from any legal impediment and, in this respect, it cannot be said that the right to marry has been impaired as a consequence of the provisions of domestic law.

As to her inability to marry a man, the criteria adopted by English law are in this respect in conformity with the concept of marriage to which the right guaranteed by Article 12 refers.

Although some Contracting States would not regard as valid a marriage between a person in Miss Cossey's situation and a man, the developments which have occurred to date cannot be said to evidence any general abandonment of the traditional concept of marriage. In these circumstances, the Court does not consider that it is open to it to take a new approach to the interpretation of Article 12 on the point at issue. It finds, furthermore, that attachment to the traditional concept of marriage provides sufficient reason for the continued adoption of biological criteria for determining a person's sex for the purposes of marriage, this being a matter encompassed within the power of the Contracting States to regulate by national law the exercise of the right to marry.

The Court thus concludes that there is no violation of Article 12.

In spite of the decision, no fewer than eight judges issued partly or fully dissenting opinions in respect of the judgment, thus suggesting that before too much longer the court will require the United Kingdom to relax its law.

Professor Katherine O'Donovan[26] examined the issues raised in *Corbett v Corbett* in the following manner.

LEGAL CONSTRUCTION OF SEX AND GENDER[27]
Katherine O'Donovan

... Gender is the term used to denote the social meaning of sex categorisation. Sex is determined through physical assessment; gender refers to the social consequences for the individual of that assessment. Gender stereotypes embody society's view of appropriate behaviour for men and women. These take the form of gender roles, reinforced by law, thorough which individuals conform to their label and to the community's conventions. Gender identity is the psychological experience of being female or male for the individual; it is the sense of oneself as belonging to one gender category ... [28]

Legal Definitions of Sex

Legal classification of women and men as belonging to two different and separate groups follows from biological and social classifications. Biology forms the material base on which an elaborate system of social and legal distinction is built. As has already been shown, medical research no longer justifies the use of biology as support for treating the social or legal categories woman and man as opposite and closed. Nevertheless the law continues to classify human beings as if there were two clear divisions into which everyone falls on an either/or basis. In general the way in which this occurs is where legislation uses a classificatory scheme based on sex. A criminal, victim, employee, recipient of public benefit, taxpayer may be specified as belonging to one sex category only. The courts are

---

26 Currently Professor of Law, Queen Mary and Westfield College, University of London.

27 Katherine O'Donovan, *Sexual Divisions in Law* (Weidenfeld & Nicolson, 1985) Chapter 3.

28 *Ibid*, p 62.

then called upon to define legally what it means to be a woman or a man, within that legislative classification.

Two methods of approaching this judicial task of sex determination have emerged. These are the *essentialist approach* and the *cluster concept approach*. With the essentialist approach the court looks to one essential feature and assigns all individuals biologically to either the female sex or the male sex. This method is familiar to the lawyer who is continuously engaged on the task of classifying events, things, people. It is the method most used in legal reasoning. The apparent opposition of women and men leads, not surprisingly, to the logical approach in which individuals are either A or Z. The cluster concept method looks to a group of similar features which then suggest that the individual falls into one category. It is the insistence on one essential feature rather than a group of features that distinguishes essentialism from the cluster approach. Examples of the application of both methods in law will be given below, with a critique and a suggested alternative.

The essentialist approach

In the English case *Corbett v Corbett* a couple had married knowing that, whereas both had been classified as male at birth, one had undergone a sex-change operation in an attempt to move into the female category. The marriage was a failure and the male partner brought an action to have the marriage declared null and void on the ground that both parties were members of the male sex. The court agreed, taking the view that 'sex is clearly an essential determinant of the relationship called marriage because it is and always has been recognised as the union of man and woman. It is the institution on which the family is built, and in which the capacity for natural heterosexual intercourse is an essential element'.[29] Sex as a concept seems to have been used here both in the sense of biological category and in the sense of sexual intercourse.

The court went on to distinguish sex as a biological category from gender. Dealing with the argument that law permits recognition of the transsexual as a woman for national insurance purposes and that therefore it was illogical not to do the same for marriage, the court said, 'these submissions, in effect, confuse sex with gender. Marriage is a relationship which depends on sex and not on gender.'[30] Social appearance or gender identity are irrelevant in determining whether a person is male or female; the *Corbett* case makes clear that the legal test, for marriage at least, is biological.

The biological test laid down by Ormrod J in *Corbett* is the chromosomal, gonadal and genital test. If all three are congruent, they determine a person's sex. Social and psychological matters of gender identity and gender role were considered irrelevant for marriage where sex was established as 'an essential determinant of the nature of the relationship'.

It is possible to criticise this judgment on a number of grounds. At an individualistic level it may result in hardship to persons who belong neither to the male nor to the female category and who therefore cannot marry, as in the Australian case *C and D*.[31] There the husband was a genuine intersex with an ovary and a fallopian tube internally on the right side, but with nothing internally on the left. He was classified male at birth because of a small penis and

---

29 [1971] P 83, p 105.

30 *Ibid*, p 107.

31 (1979) FLC 90–636; (1975) 53 ALJ 659 (note by R Bailey).

testicle on the left side. Having grown up psychologically and socially as a male, in adulthood he sought surgical treatment for correction of the penile deformity. An article in the *Medical Journal of Australia* written soon after the decision to intervene surgically gives an account of the problem faced by the medical and surgical specialists:

> in spite of the bisexual gonadal structure, the female chromosomal arrangement, the female internal genitalia and the equivocal results of the hormonal assays, there was no doubt, in view of the assigned male sex, the male psychological orientation in a person of this age and the possibility of converting his external genitals into an acceptable male pattern, that he should continue in the sex in which he has been reared.[32]

Surgery was performed over a period of time to remove the female internal organs and breasts, and to reconstruct the penis into one of normal size and shape. The patient married, and after some years the wife sought a declaration of nullity on the ground that the husband had been unable to consummate the marriage. The Australian court held that the marriage was null because of an absence of consent on the part of the wife, who was the victim of mistaken identity. The explanation was that 'the wife was contemplating immediately prior to marriage and did in fact believe that she was marrying a male. She did not in fact marry a male but a combination of both male and female and notwithstanding that the husband exhibited as a male, he was in fact not, and the wife was mistaken as to the identity of her husband.[33]

The effect of this decision and of the *Corbett* case is that hermaphrodites cannot marry, and neither can transsexuals who have undergone surgery. A postoperative transsexual is incapable of consummating a marriage as a member of the category assigned at birth, but does not in law belong to the chosen category. On an abstract level these decisions reinforce belief in the categories woman and man as closed categories, rather than as points along a continuum. Yet to Dr Money the question whether an individual is really a woman or a man is meaningless: 'All you can say is that this is a person whose sex organs differentiated as a male and whose gender identity differentiated as a female.'[34] And in the case of hermaphrodites one cannot even make this guarded statement. The legal essentialist approach to the definition of sex is not consonant with medical research.

We are dealing with two aspects of the essentialist approach here. Firstly, there is the sense in which biology is taken to be the quintessence of the legal definition of sex. Secondly, there is the notion that certain areas of law operate on sex as a critical element. There is no doubt that Ormrod J's approach in *Corbett* is essentialist in the first sense. He said that 'the biological sexual constitution of an individual is fixed at birth (at the latest), and cannot be changed either by natural development of organs of the opposite sex or by medical or surgical means.'[35] yet the husband in *C and D*, a genuine intersex, did not belong to one sex, and there are medical records of similar patients. Even if chromosomes are taken as the *sine qua non* of a sex category, cases of XO and of XXY may cause problems. Furthermore, the objective of the medical profession has been to bring the

---

32 Fraser, Sir K, O'Reilly MJJ and Rintoul JR, 'Hermaphroditus Versus, with Report of a Case' (1966) 1 *Med J of Aus*, 1003, 1006.

33 *Op cit*, note 12, pp 78–327

34 Money J and Tucker P, *Sexual Signatures* (London: Abacus, 1977) p 69.

35 [1971] P 83, p 104.

physical appearance of patients into line with gender identity. In many cases this means confirming individuals in the sex category in which they were socialised as children. But to Ormrod J, 'a person with male chromosomes, male gonads and male genitalia cannot reproduce a person who is naturally capable of performing the essential role of a woman in marriage.'[36]

What is the essential role of a woman in marriage? It cannot be the biological reproduction of children as the inability to procreate does not render a marriage void, and neither does the unwillingness to have children. It is true that marriages which have not been sexually consummated are voidable in English law, but there have been a number of decisions holding that the use of contraceptives does not prevent consummation.[37] Biological reproduction is not essential to marriage. If procreation is not the purpose of marriage, but the law nevertheless requires the parties to belong to different biological categories, then it seems that marriage is not a private matter for the individuals concerned, but a public institution for heterosexual intercourse. It is highly unlikely that the court in *Corbett* was referring to women's social role in marriage, for the distinction between sex and gender had already been established.

This brings us to the second aspect of biological sex as the essence of the law in some areas, as in marriage. In *Corbett*, by distinguishing sex from gender, marriage law from social security law, the court implied that the law can constitute a person differently, depending on whether sex is essential or not. However, as will be shown below, this approach leads to internal incoherence in the law and may create more problems than it solves.

The cluster-concept approach

Critics of the essentialist method as exemplified in the *Corbett* case argue that the chromosome pattern which can never be changed should be ignored and that the genital test should take account of any changes that have occurred through surgery. If the genitals, gender identity and gender role are congruent, the individual should be categorised accordingly – that is, the category should be determined by apparent sex. These criticisms are based not only on compassion to individuals but also on logic. It is said in relation to adultery and rape, two areas of the law where penetration of one sexual organ by another is a necessary element, that no enquiry as to sexual identity is necessary, and that this should be the general approach. The requirement of penetration presupposes an organ capable of penetration possessed by one and an organ capable of being penetrated possessed by the other, and this establishes a sufficient degree of sexual differentiation.[38]

These critics attack the reasoning on sex determination which proceeds on the basis of either A or Z and suggest that the cluster concept form of reasoning be substituted. In looking to matters such as physical and social appearances, gender identity and gender role, the court would be looking at a cluster of concepts about what constitutes a woman or a man, rather than at one essential determinant. Compassion towards hermaphrodites and transsexuals tends to be the reason for these criticisms. Examples from other jurisdictions such as Germany, France, Switzerland and the United States, where persons are

---

36   *Ibid*, p 106.

37   *Baster v Baxter* [1948] AC 274.

38   Bartholomew, GW, 'Hermaphrodites and the Law' (1960) 2 *Univ of Malaya LJ* 83 p 108; Finlay HA, 'Sexual Identity and the Law of Nullity' (1980) 54 *Aust LJ* 115 p 125.

classified according to appearance and chosen gender, are referred to as examples for English law.[39]

The European Commission on Human Rights has held (in *Van Oosterwijck v Belgium*) that it is a violation of private and family life to require the transsexual to carry documents of identity manifestly incompatible with personal appearance. The Commission made the finding that the refusal by a signatory state to the European Declaration on Human Rights to recognise gender identity results in the treatment of the transsexual 'as an ambiguous being, an 'appearance', disregarding in particular the effects of a lawful medical treatment aimed at bringing the physical sex and the psychical sex into accord with each other'.[40]

Fair though these criticisms may be, they nevertheless accept that the law should operate on an assumption that the two sexes are distinct entities. Academic writers also accept two categories. 'As a working hypothesis this is not unreasonable, but ... it does not quite correspond with physiological reality and is therefore likely to break down from time to time.'[41] Concern is expressed because errors may be made, or because the essentialist approach is inhumane, but the premise that certain areas of the law should be organised around sexual differentiation is not queried. The cluster-concept approach may permit sex classification according to personal choice rather than by ascription. In its acknowledgement of gender in establishing apparent sex and rejection of the essentialist presupposition of two fixed and immutable categories it is preferable to essentialism. However, the cluster-concept approach has not been accepted by the courts in any jurisdiction for sex determination in relation to marriage, or other legal areas where sex has been found to be an essential element. The question remains open as to whether courts will look to apparent sex rather than biological sex in future cases.

The decision by the European Commission on Human Rights in the *Van Oosterwijck* case suggests that another way of approaching issues of sex determination might be to classify matters of gender as covered by the right to respect for private and family life. This would presumably leave states to continue to regulate areas where they considered biological sex an essential determinant. In the *Van Oosterwijck* case the right of respect for private life as laid down in Article 8 of the European Convention on Human Rights was explained as not just a right to live without publicity, for 'it comprises also to a certain degree the right to establish and to develop relationships with other human beings, especially in the emotional field for the development and fulfilment of one's own personality.[42] It was also the view of the majority of the Commission that the right to marry under Article 12 of the Convention had been violated, as

39 On Germany, see Horton KC, 'The Law and Transsexualism in West Germany' (1978) *Fam Law* 191; on France see Pace PJ, 'Sexual Identity and the Criminal Law' (1983) *Crim L Rev* 317; on Switzerland see *In re Laber*, Neuchatel Cantonal Court, 2 July 1945, cited by Kennedy I, 2 *Anglo-American L Rev* 112 (1973); on the US see Walz MB, 'Transsexuals and the Law' (1979) 5 *J of Contem L* 181.

40 (1980) 3 EHRR 557. Before the European Court of Human Rights it was held that, by reason of the failure to exhaust domestic remedies, the Court was unable to take cognisance of the merits of the case.

41 Bartholomew, *op cit*, p 84.

42 *Ibid*, p 584.

'domestic law cannot authorise states completely to deprive a person or category of person of the right to marry.'[43]

There are a number of difficulties with the separation of gender into the private sphere whilst the state continues to regulate what it defines as sex in the public sphere. From the internal viewpoint of legal reasoning, inconsistency and incoherence follow. In *Corbett* the court accepted that a person could be in the male category for marriage and in the female category for contract, employment and social security. However, subsequent legal decisions show that confusion has resulted. Other difficulties are that decision-makers use biology as the basis for gender prescription, one following 'naturally' from the other. Although sex and gender may be analytically distinguishable, social practice has been to entwine the two. And the legal construction of sex as public whilst gender was private would merely be a perpetuation of dichotomies which mask inequalities between women and men. Biology or 'nature' has a social meaning when translated into law, which itself operates on the social.[44]

BREAKING WOMEN'S SILENCE IN LAW: THE DILEMMA OF THE GENDERED NATURE OF LEGAL REASONING[45]

Lucinda Finley

Language matters. Law matters. Legal language matters. I make these three statements not to offer a clever syllogism, but to bluntly put the central thesis of this article: it is an imperative task for feminist jurisprudence and for feminist lawyers – for anyone concerned about what the impact of law has been, and will be, on the realisation and meanings of justice, equality, security, and autonomy for women – to turn critical attention to the nature of legal reasoning and the language by which it is expressed.

The gendered nature of legal language is what makes it powerful and limited.

Why Law is a Gendered (Male) Language

Throughout the history of Anglo–American jurisprudence, the primary linguists of law have almost exclusively been men – white, educated, economically privileged men. Men have shaped it, they have defined it, they have interpreted it and given it meaning consistent with their understandings of the world and of people 'other' than them. As the men of law have defined law in their own image, law has excluded or marginalised the voices and meanings of these 'others'. Law, along with all the other accepted academic disciplines, has exalted one form of reasoning and called only this form 'reason'. Because the men of law have had the societal power not to have to worry too much about the competing terms and understandings of 'others', they have been insulated from challenges to their language and have thus come to see it as natural, inevitable, complete, objective, and neutral.[46]

Thus, legal language and reasoning is gendered, and that gender matches the male gender of its linguistic architects. Law is a patriarchal form of reasoning, as

---

43 *Ibid*, p 585.

44 Katherine O'Donovan, *op cit*, pp 64–69.

45 Lucinda Finley, 'Breaking Women's Silence in Law: The Dilemma of the Gendered Nature of Legal Reasoning' (1989) 64 *Notre Dame Law Review*, 886.

46 See LM Linley, 'Transcending Equality'; and LM Finley, 'Choice and Freedom: Elusive Issues in the Search for Gender Justic' (1987) 96 *Yale Law Journal*, 914.

is the philosophy of liberalism of which law (or at least post Enlightenment Anglo-American law) is part.

The claim that legal language and reasoning is male gendered is partly empirical and historical. The legal system, and its reasoning structure and language have been framed on the basis of life experiences typical to empowered white males. Law's reasoning structure shares a great deal with the assumptions of the liberal intellectual and philosophical tradition, which historically has been framed by men. The reasoning structure of law is thus congruent with the patterns of socialisation, experience, and values of a particular group of privileged, educated men. Rationality, abstraction, a preference for statistical and empirical proofs over experiential or anecdotal evidence, and a conflict model of social life, corresponds to how these men have been socialised and educated to think, live, and work.

My claim that legal reasoning and language are patriarchal also has a normative component, in the sense that male-based perspectives, images, and experiences are often taken to be the norms in law. Privileged white men are the norm for equality law; they are the norm for assessing the reasonable person in tort law;[47] the way men would react is the norm for self-defence law; and the male worker is the prototype for labour law.[48]

Legal language is a male language because it is principally informed by men's experiences and because it derives from the powerful social situation of men, relative to women. Universal and objective thinking is male language because intellectually, economically, and politically privileged men have had the power to ignore other perspectives and thus to come to think of their situation as the norm, their reality as reality, and their wives as objective. Disempowered, marginalised groups are far less likely to mistake their situation, experience, and views as universal. Male reasoning is dualistic and polarised thinking because men have been able, thanks to women, to organise their lives in a way that enables them not to have to see such things as work and family as mutually defining. Men have acted on their fears of women and nature to try to split nature off from culture, body from mind, passion from reason, and reproduction from production.[49] Men have had the power to privilege – to assign greater value to the side of the dichotomies that they associate with themselves. Conflict oriented thinking, seeing matters as involving conflicts of interests or rights, as contrasted to relational thinking, is male because this way of expressing things is the primary orientation of more men than women. The fact that there are many women trained in and adept at male thinking and legal language does not turn it into androgynous language – it simply means that women have learned male language, as many French speakers learn English.

The claim that law is patriarchal does not mean that women have not been addressed or comprehended by law. Women have obviously been the subjects or contemplated targets of many laws. But it is men's understanding of women, women's nature. women's capacities, and women's experiences – women refracted through the male eye – rather than women's own definitions, that has informed law.

---

47 See Bender, 'A Lawyer's Primer on Feminist Theory and Tort' (1988) 38 *Journal of Legal Education* 3; LM Finley 'Break in the Silence: Including Women's Issues in a Torts Course' (1989) 1 *Yale Journal of Law and Feminism* 41.

48 See eg Conaghan, 'The Invisibility of Women in Labour Law: Gender-Neutrality in Model-Building' (1986) 14 *International Journal of Sociology of Law* 377.

49 See eg S Griffin, *Women and Nature: The Roaring Inside Her* (1978).

One notable example of a male judicial perspective characterising women as men see them is the often flayed US Supreme Court decision in *Bradwell v Illinois*,[50] in which Justice Bradley exalted the delicate timidity and biologically bounded condition of women to conclude that women were unfit for the rude world of law practice. Another example is the decision in *Geduldig v Aiello*[51] in which the Court cordoned off the female experience of pregnancy and called this experience unique, voluntary, and unrelated in any way to the workplace.

The legal definition of rape provides another example of the male judicial perspective. It is the male's view of whether the woman consented that is determinative of consent; it is men's view of what constitutes force against men and forms a resistance by men in situations other than rape that defines whether force has been used against a woman and a woman has resisted; it is men's definition of sex – penetration of the vagina by the penis – rather than women's experience of sexualised violation and violation that defines the crime. The legal view of prostitution as a crime committed by women (and more recently also committed by men playing the woman's role in a sexual encounter with men) with no 'victims' is another obvious example. The world 'family' and the area of 'family law' is yet another example. The norm of 'family', the fundamental meaning of the term embedded in and shaped by law, is of a household headed by a man with a wife who is wholly or somewhat dependent on him. Other forms of family – especially those without a man – are regarded as abnormal. To a significant extent, the purpose of the discipline of family law is to sanction the formation of ideal families and to control and limit the formation and existence of these nonideal families, and thus to control the status and lives of women.

The Power and Limitations of Male Legal Language

Analysis of the way the law structures thought and talk about social problems is necessary to understand how the law can limit our understandings of the nature of problems and can confine our visions for change. A male gendered way of thinking about social problems is to speak in terms of objectivity, of universal abstractions, of dichotomy, and of conflict. These are essentially the ways law talks about social problems.

Modern Anglo–American law talk about social problems within the individualistic framework of patriarchal Western liberalism, a theory that itself has been challenged by feminists as resting on a fundamentally male world view. This framework sees humans as self-interested, fundamentally set apart from other people, and threatened by interactions with others. To control the threat of those who would dominate you or gain at your expense, you must strive to gain power over them. This power can easily become domination because the point of its exercise is to protect yourself by moulding another to your will.

As part of this individualistic framework, law is conceptualised as a rule-bound system for adjudicating the competing rights of self-interested, autonomous, essentially equal individuals capable of making unconstrained choices. Because of the law's individualistic focus, it sees one of the central problems that it must address to be enforcing the agreements made by free autonomous individuals, as well as enforcing a few social norms to keep the battle of human life from getting out of hand. It envisions another central task to be eliminating obvious constraints on individual choice and opportunity. The constraints are thought to emanate primarily from the state or from the bad motivations of other

---

50   (1873) 83 US 442.

51   (1973) 417 US 484.

individuals. An individualistic focus on choice does not perceive constraints as coming from history, from the operation of power and domination, from socialisation, or from class, race and gender. A final key task for individualistic liberal law is to keep the state from making irrational distinctions between people, because such distinctions can frustrate individual autonomy. It is not an appropriate task to alter structures and institutions, to help the disempowered overcome subordination, to eliminate fear and pain that may result from encounters masquerading as 'freely chosen', to value nurturing connections, or to promote care and compassion for other people.

To keep its operation fair in appearance, which it must if people are to trust resorting to the legal method for resolving competing claims, the law strives for rules that are universal, objective, and neutral. The language of individuality and neutrality keeps law from talking about values, structures, and institutions, and about how they construct knowledge, choice, and apparent possibilities for conducting the world. Also submerged is a critical awareness of systematic, systemic, or institutional power and domination. There are few ways to express within the language of law and legal reasoning the complex relationship between power, gender, and knowledge. Yet in order for feminists to use the law to help effectuate change, we must be able to talk about the connection between power and knowledge. This connection must be acknowledged in order to demystify the 'neutrality' of the law, to make the law comprehend that women's definitions have been excluded and marginalised, and to show that the language of neutrality itself is one of the devices for this silencing.

The language of neutrality and objectivity can silence the voices of those who did not participate in its creation because it takes a distanced, decontextualised stance. Within this language and reasoning system, alternative voices to the one labelled objective are suspect as biased. An explicit acknowledgement of history and the multiplicity of experiences – which might help explode the perception of objectivity – is discouraged. To talk openly about the interaction between historical events, political change, and legal change is to violate neutral principles, such as adherence to precedent – and precedents themselves are rarely talked about as products of historical and social contingencies. For example, in the recent US Supreme Court decision declaring a municipal affirmative action plan unconstitutional, *City of Richmond v Croson*,[52] the majority talks in the language of neutrality, of colour-blindness, and of blind justice and it is the more classically legal voice. The dissent, which cries out in anguish about the lessons of history, power, and domination, is open to the accusation that it speaks in the language of politics and passions, not law.

In legal language, experience and perspective are translated as bias, as something that makes the achievement of neutrality more difficult. Having no experience with or prior knowledge of something is equated with perfect neutrality. This way of thinking is evident in jury selection. A woman who has been raped would almost certainly be excluded as a juror in a rape trial – it is assumed that her lived experience of rape makes her unable to judge it objectively. Legal language cannot imagine that her experience might give her a nuanced, critical understanding capable of challenging the male-constructed vision of the crime. Yet someone with no experience of rape, either as victim, perpetrator, or solacer/supporter of victim, is deemed objective, even though it may be just their lack of experience that leaves them prone to accept the biased myths about women's behaviour that surround this crime.

---

52   (1989) 109 S Ct 706.

Because it is embedded in a patriarchal framework that equates abstraction and universalisation from only one group's experiences as neutrality, legal reasoning views male experiences and perspectives as the universal norm around which terms and entire areas of the law are defined. Examples of this phenomenon abound, and exposing them has been a central project of feminist jurisprudence. Thus, for example, my previous work, as well as that of several others,[53] has examined how talk about equality, couched in comparative language of sameness/difference, requires a norm or standard for comparison – and that norm becomes white males. The more a non-white person can be talked about as the same as a white male, the more deserving she or he is to be treated equally to, or the same as, white males. This language not only uses white males as the reference point, but it also exalts them. To be the same as white males is the desired end. To be different from them is undesirable and justifies disadvantage.

Many doctrinal areas of the law are also fundamentally structured around men's perspectives and experiences. The field of labour law uses a gendered meaning of workers that which is done for wages outside your own home as its focus. Thus, any talk about reforming labour law, or regulating work, will always leave unspoken, and thus unaffected, much of what women do, even women who also 'work' in the legal conventional sense. Legal intervention in work – or the perception that no intervention is needed – assumes that workers are men with wives at home who tend to the necessities of life. It is only in this framework that we can even think of work and family as separate and conflicting spheres.

Tort law defines injuries and measures compensation primarily in relation to what keeps people out of work and what their work is worth. It is in this framework that noneconomic damages, such as pain and suffering or compensation for emotional injuries, which are often crucial founts of recovery for women, are deemed suspect and expendable. In the language of criminal law, the paradigmatic criminal is a male, and women criminals are often viewed as doubly deviant. Another example of the manifestation of the male reference points is how self-defence law looks to male notions of threat and response to assess what is reasonable. Contract law is built around the form of transactions that predominates in the male-dominated marketplace, and doctrines that are regarded as necessary to assist the weak (ie helpless women), such as reliance and restitution, are subtly demeaned by the language as 'exceptions', as deviations from the normal rules of contract. All of this suggests that for feminist law reformers, even using the terms 'equality', 'work', 'injury', 'damages', 'market', and 'contract' can involve buying into, and leaving unquestioned, the male frames of reference. It also leaves unspoken, and unrecognised, the kinds of work women do, or the kinds of injuries women suffer.

The language of law is also a language of dichotomies, oppositions, and conflict. No doubt this is partly attributable to the fact that law so frequently is invoked in situations of conflict – it is called on to resolve disputes, to respond to problems that are deemed to arise out of conflicting interests. Another reason legal language is put in terms of opposing interests is due to its place within an intellectual tradition – Western liberal thought – that orders the world in dualisms: culture/nature, mind/body, reason/emotion, public/private. Law is

---

53 See eg LM Finley, *Transcending Equality*; Littleton, 'Equality and Feminist Legal Theory' (1987) 48 *University of Pittsburgh Law Review*, 1043; M Minow, 'Learning to Live with the Dilemma of Difference: Bilingual and Special Education' (1985) 48 *Law and Contemporary Problems*, 157.

associated with the 'male' and higher valued side of each of these dualisms.[54] This means that law adopts the values of the privileged side of the dualisms, such as the self-interested, 'rational' exchange values of the marketplace, or the shunning of emotion. It also means that legal language has few terms for comprehending in a positive, valuable way the content of the devalued sides of the dualisms – or those, such as women, who are associated with the devalued sides. For example, law's operation within a perceived dichotomy of public/private, and its preference for the public as the proper area for its concern, leaves law largely ignorant of and unresponsive to what happens to women within the private realm. Thus the 'public' language of law contributes to the silencing of women.

The conflict aspect of legal language – the way it talks about situations and social problems as matters of conflicting rights or interests – fosters polarised understandings of issues and limits the ability to understand the other side. It also squeezes out of view other ways of seeing things, nonoppositional possibilities for dealing with social problems. Since a language of conflict means that one side has to be preferred, there will always be winners and losers. In a polarised language of hierarchical dualisms set within a patriarchal system, it will often be women, and their concerns, that will lose, be devalued, or be overlooked in the race to set priorities and choose sides.

Another problematic instance of the language of conflicting rights is the law's approach to issues of women's reproductive freedom. These issues are being framed by the law as conflicts between maternal rights, such as the right to privacy and to control one's body, and foetal rights, such as the right to life, or the right to be born in a sound and healthy state. They are also framed as conflicts between maternal rights and paternal rights, such as the man's interest in reproductive autonomy. To talk about human reproduction as a situation of conflict is a very troublesome way to understand this crucial human event in which the well-being, needs, and futures of all participants in the event, including other family members, are inextricably, sensitively connected. Just because everything that happens to one participant can affect the other does not mean they are in conflict. It suggests, rather, that they are symbiotically linked. The foetus is not there and cannot exist without the mother. An action taken for the sake of the mother that may, in a doctor's but not the mother's view, seem to pose a risk to the foetus, such as her decision to forego a caesarean birth, or to take medication while pregnant, may actually be necessary (although perhaps also still presenting a risk of harm) for the foetus because without an emotionally and physically healthy mother there cannot be a sustained foetus or child.[55]

If we stop talking about reproductive issues as issues of opposing interests, but discuss them as matters where the interests of all are always linked, for better or worse, then there is much less risk that one person in the equation – the woman – will drop out of the discussion. Yet that is what often happens in dualistic, win–lose conflict talk. As one commentator has said, 'respect for the foetus is purchased at the cost of denying the value of women.[56] Legal discourse is

---

54 For a discussion of the dualisms that structure liberal legal thinking see A Jagger, *Feminist Politics and Human Nature*, 1983; F Olsen, 'The Sex of Law', in Kairys, *The Politics of Law* (1990).

55 For a work that seeks to approach abortion in terms of the connections between mother and foetus, see R Goldstein, *Mother Love and Abortion: A Legal Interpretation* (1988).

56 Farrel-Smith, 'Rights-Conflict, Pregnancy and Abortion' in C Gould (ed), *Beyond Domination: New Perspectives on Women and Philosophy* (1983), p 27.

frequently guided by the male-based medical perspective, which when matched with the erasing process of win–lose legal discourse, pushes the mother further into the recesses of invisibility. Dawn Johnsen offers an insightful analysis of how this process works: '[b]y separating the interests of the foetus from those of the pregnant woman, and then examining, often *post hoc*, the effect on the foetus of isolated decisions made by the woman on a daily basis during pregnancy, the state is likely to exaggerate the potential risks to the foetus and undervalue the costs of the loss of autonomy suffered by the woman.[57] A chilling example of the process of obliterating the woman occurred in a case in which a court ordered a caesarean section performed on a woman over her religious objections. The mother virtually disappeared from the text, and certainly her autonomy was of little concern to the court, as the judge wrote that all that stood between the foetus and 'its independent existence, was, put simply, a doctor's scalpel'.[58] The court did not even say an incision in 'the mother', just 'a scalpel' – the mother was not mentioned as a person who would be cut by that scalpel, who would have to undergo risky surgery. She was not mentioned as someone whose health and existence were necessary to the child's life; she was no more than an obstacle to the foetus's life.

The legal approach to the problem of pornography as if it presented a conflict between women's and men's interests in not being objectified and degraded, and the societal interest in free speech, is another example of unproductive conflict talk which limits our understanding of a problem and of women's experiences. The equation of not being degraded and objectified with the diluted word 'interest' is troubling. The very thought that an abstract principle like free speech could be considered more important than working against domination, violence, injury, and degradation, and redressing the needs of those who have suffered from these things, is also disturbing. Talking about the pornography issue as presenting an inherent conflict with free speech, and thus simply a matter of balancing the weights of the respective interests, leaves the meaning and scope to be given to 'speech' undiscussed. The conflict talk also leaves the framework of free speech law unexamined. Yet the terms of that framework define moral harm to the consumers of pornography, and not physical harm to the people who are used to make it or are victimised by it as the appropriate focus of legal concern. The legal rhetoric also squeezes out from the debate the question whether there really is a conflict between 'free speech' and women's civil rights.

The dichotomous, polarised, either/or framework of legal language also makes it a reductionist language – one that does not easily embrace complexity or nuance. Something either must be one way, or another. It cannot be a complicated mix of factors and still be legally digestible. The law has a hard time hearing, or believing, other languages. That is part of its power.

One of the other languages that the law does not easily hear is that associated with the emotions, with expression of bursting human passion and aspirations. Law is a language firmly committed to the 'reason' side of the reason/emotion dichotomy. Indeed, the law distrusts injuries deemed emotional in character; it suspects them as fraudulent, as feigned, as not important. The inability to hear the voice of emotion to respond to thinking from the emotions, is one of the limitations of the legal voice. There are some things that just cannot be said by

---

57 Johnsen, 'The Creation of Foetal Rights: Conflicts with Women's Constitutional Rights in Liberty, Privacy and Equal Protection' (1986) 95 *Yale Law Journal* 599, p 613.

58 'In the Matter of Madyun Foetus' (1986) 114 *Daily Washington L Rep* 2233, 2240 (DC Super. Ct, July 26, 1986).

using the legal voice. Its terms, depoliticise, decharge, and dampen. Rage, pain, elation, the aching, thirsting, hungering for freedom on one's own terms, love and its joys and terrors, fear, utter frustration at being contained and constrained by legal language – all are diffused by legal language.

Examples of the 'fit' problem can be found throughout law. How can we fit a woman's experience of living in a world of violent pornography into obscenity doctrine, which is focused on moral harm to consumers of pornography? How can women fit the reality of pregnancy into equality doctrine without getting hung up on the horns of the sameness–difference dilemma? How can women fit the difference between a wanted and an unwanted pregnancy into the doctrinal rhetoric of privacy and 'choice'? This rhetoric presumes a sort of isolated autonomy alien to the reality of a pregnant woman. How can women fit the psychological and economic realities of being a battered woman into criminal law, which puts the word 'domestic' before 'violence'? This choice of terminology reduces the focus on the debilitating effects of violence and increases all supposedly free to come and go as we 'choose'. How can women fit the way incest victims repress what has happened to them until the memory is released by some triggering event in adulthood with the narrow temporal requirements of statute of limitations law? How can women fit the fact that this crime, and others of sexualised violence against women, so often happens behind closed doors with no 'objective witnesses', into the proof requirements of evidentiary law? How, as Kristin Bumiller explores in her article, *Rape as a Legal Symbol: An Essay on Sexual Violence and Racism*,[59] can we fit the experience of having what a woman thought was a pleasant social interaction but then crosses the invisible line to become threatening violence, into rape doctrine? Rape law focuses on sex, not on violence. It focuses on the woman's consent to sex, from the male point of view – and so it presumes that any indication of assent to social interaction is also assent to 'do what the man wants'. How, as Lucie White asks in her paper, *Unearthing the Barriers to Women's Speech: Notes Toward a Feminist Sense of Procedural Justice*,[60] can a black mother on welfare ever convey her world to the welfare bureaucracy that is charging her with an overpayment because she followed its erroneous advice and spent an injury insurance check? What is important to this woman is that she did nothing wrong, and that she was able to buy her children Sunday shoes. But what is relevant to the state's welfare law is not her view of right and wrong, or her own understanding of what was necessary for her family – in her world, having Sunday shoes was essential to human dignity – but whether the items she bought with the insurance check fit the state's definition of 'necessities' of life.

Legal language frames the issues, it defines the terms in which speech in the legal world must occur, it tells us how we should understand a problem and which explanations are acceptable and which are not. Since this language has been crafted primarily by white men, the way it frames issues, the way it defines problems, and the speakers and speech it credits, do not readily include women. Legal language commands: abstract a situation from historical, social, and political context; be 'objective' and avoid the lens of nonmale experience; invoke universal principles such as 'equality' and 'free choice'; speak with the voice of dispassionate reason; be simple, direct, and certain; avoid the complexity of varying, interacting perspectives and overlapping multitextured explanations;

---

59   (1988) *University of Miami Law Review* 75.

60   (1990) 38 *Buffalo Law Review* 1.

and most of all, tell it and see it 'like a man' – put it in terms that relate to men and to which men can relate.

Feminist theory, on the other hand, which is not derived from looking first to law, but rather to the multiple experiences and voices of women as the frame of reference, tells us to look at things in their historical, social, and political context, including power and gender; distrust abstractions and universal rules, because if objectivity is really perspectived and abstractions just hide the biases; question everything, especially the norms or assumptions implicit in received doctrine, question the content and try to redefine the boundaries; so distrust attributions of essential difference and acknowledge that experiences of both men and women are multiple, diverse, overlapping and thus difference itself may not be a relevant legal criterion; break down hierarchies of race, gender, or power; embrace diversity, complexity, and contradiction – give up on the need to tell 'one true story' because it is too likely that that story will be the story of the dominant group;[61] listen to the voice of 'emotion' as well as the voice of reason and learn to value and legitimate what has been denigrated as 'mere emotion'.[62]

Dealing with the dilemma of legal language

So, what's a woman do? Give up on law, on legal language entirely? Disengage from the legal arena of the struggle? Neither of these strategies is really an available option. We cannot get away from law, even if that is what we would like to do. Because law is such a powerful, authoritative language, one that insists that to be heard you try to speak its language, we cannot pursue the strategy suggested by the theorists from other disciplines such as the French feminists, of devising a new woman's language that rejects 'phallologocentric' discourses.[63]

Nor can we abandon caring whether law hears us. Whether or not activists for women look to law as one means for pursuing change, the law will still operate on and affect women's situations. Law will be present through direct regulation, through non-intervention when intervention is needed, and through helping to keep something invisible when visibility and validation are needed.[64] Law will continue to reflect and shape prevailing social and individual understandings of problems, and thus will continue to play a role in silencing and discrediting women.

Since law inevitably will be one of the important discourses affecting the status of women, we must engage it. We must pursue trying to bring more of women's experiences, perspectives, and voices into law in order to empower women and

---

61 For example, white feminists tend to tell a story of women's true situation that excludes the differing situations of poor women and women of colour and women of different ethnic backgrounds. For development of this critique of white feminism by other white feminists, see E Spelman, *Inessential Woman: Problems of Exclusion in Feminist Thought* (1989) and Kline, 'Race, Racism and Feminist Legal Theory' (1989) 12 *Harvard Women's Law Journal* 115.

62 For examples of work that seeks to value the voice of caring, see C Gilligan *In a Different Voice*; N Noddings, Caring – A Feminine Approach to Ethics and Moral Education, 1984; S Ruddick, *Maternal Thinking: Toward a Politics of Peace*, 1989; Bender, 'A Lawyer's Primer on Feminist Theory and Tort' (1989) 38 *Journal of Legal Education*; Tronto, 'Beyond Gender Difference to a Theory of Care' (1987) 12 *Signs: J. Women in Culture and Society* 644.

63 For examples of the French feminist theory, see L Irigaray, *This Sex Which is Not One* (C Porter, trans 1985), and *Speculum of the Other Woman* (G Gill, trans 1985); Cixous, *Laugh at the Medus* in *New French Feminisms*.

64 For discussion see K O'Donovan, *op cit* (1985) (extracted above); F Olsen, 'The Myth of State Intervention in the Family' (1985) 18 *University of Michigan J L Rev* 835.

help legitimate these experiences. But this is not as easy as it sounds, because there is no 'one truth' of women's experiences, and women's own understandings of their experiences are themselves affected by legal categorisations.

There have been examples of promising word changes and consequent meaning changes in legal discourse. Consider the now widespread use of the term 'sexual harassment', for what used to be considered a tort of invading individual dignity or sensibilities; the term 'battering' for domestic violence. But even these language changes get confined by the legal frameworks into which they are placed. For example, the individualistic and comparative discrimination framework now applied to sexual harassment leaves some judges wondering about bisexual supervisors as a means to deny that discrimination is what is occurring. The contract model of damages in discrimination law means that the dignity and personal identity values that tort law once recognised often go undercompensated.[65] And the use of the term 'sexual assault' in place of 'rape' in some rape reform statutes has not obviated the problems of 'objective' male perspective judgments of female sexuality and consent.

It is not my purpose to offer a simple, neat, for all times solution to the dilemma of legal language. Indeed, to even think that is possible would be contradictory to my message – it would be a capitulation to the legal ways of thinking that I seek to destabilise in order to expand. But I am not without solutions to the dilemma of the gendered nature of legal reasoning. This leads to self-conscious strategic thinking about the philosophical and political implications of the meanings and programmes we do endorse. For example, just what are the implications of arguing either sameness or difference? If both have negative implications, then this should suggest the need to reframe the issue, to ask previously unasked questions about the relevance or stability of differences, or about the role of unexamined players such as employers and workplace structures and norms. Critical thinking about norms and what they leave unexamined opens up conversations about altering the norms and thus the vision of the problem. This leads to thinking about new ways of reasoning and talking. It leads to offering new definitions of existing terms; definitions justified by explorations of context and the experiences of previously excluded voices. Or, it leads to thinking about offering wholly new terms.

In addition to critical engagements with the nature of legal language, another promising strategy is to sow the mutant seeds that do exist within legal reasoning. Because legal reasoning can be sensitive to context, we can work to expand the context that it deems relevant. By pulling the contextual threads of legal language, we can work towards making law more comfortable with diversity and complexity, less wedded to the felt need to universalising, reductive principles.

The law's oft proclaimed values of equity and fairness can also work as mutating agents. The equity side of law counsels taking individual variations and needs into account. Arguments about when this should be done in order to achieve fairness must proceed with reference to context, to differing perspectives, and to differing power positions. The more we can find openings to argue from the perspective of those often overlooked by legal language, such as the people upon whom the legal power is being exercised, or those disempowered or silenced or

---

65 See eg Schoenheider, 'A Theory of Tort Liability for Sexual Harassment in the Workplace' (1986) 134 *U of Pennsylvania Law Review* 1461.

rendered invisible by the traditional discourse, the more the opportunities to use the engine of fairness and equity to expand the comprehension of legal language.

THE MIRROR TELLS ITS TALE: CONTRUCTIONS OF GENDER IN CRIMINAL LAW[66]

Sheila Duncan[67]

... As a rape complainant, the woman is denied subjectivity, constructed as 'other' through a variety of evidential provisions. First, she has been subject to a corroboration warning which requires the judge to tell the jury that they must be careful if they are to convict on her uncorroborated testimony because she may have ulterior motives for bringing these charges.[68] Even with the abolition of this warning under s 32(1)(b) Criminal Justice and Public Order Act 1994, it may still be given in the judge's discretion. The woman is not the subject here, her truth story is undermined by these warnings.

Secondly, only in rape does the defendant – the male subject – retain his shield, his protection against the court's taking his previous convictions into account if he attacks the character of the complainant.[69] In any other offence, an attack on the character of the complainant leaves the defendant open to having his previous convictions put in evidence. In the rape trial alone, the complainant can be constructed as whore, as temptress, as liar, with impunity.

Thirdly, it is open to the defendant in the rape trial to apply to the court for the complainant's previous sexual history to be put in evidence.[70] Research shows that on a consent defence, the majority of defendants make this application and the majority of judges grant it.[71] If the complainant were present as subject, her previous sexual relationships could not possibly be relevant to whether she entered into this sexual encounter as a freely consenting and desiring subject.

The Criminal Justice and Public Order Act 1994 now extends the offence of rape to cover men who have anal intercourse forced upon them. It will be very interesting to see whether, and how, the male subject victim is subjected to these legal indignities of erased subjectivity. Will his previous sexual history be applied for or put in evidence? Will attacks on his character still leave the defendant's shield unblemished? Will the test for consent remain as honest, not necessarily reasonable, belief?[72]

---

66 *Feminist Perspectives on the Foundational Subjects of Law* (ed) Anne Bottomley (Cavendish Publishing, 1996), Chapter 9. See also Chapter 9 on victims of violence and the criminal law.

67 Lecturer in Law and Social Theory, University of Warwick.

68 It is stated in *R v Henry* and *R v Manning* (1968) 53 Cr App Rep 150 p 153 that women have a tendency to invent stories.

69 The provision that the defendant should lose his protection against his previous convictions being put in evidence where he casts imputations on the character of a prosecution witness is made under s 1(f)(ii) Criminal Evidence Act 1898. *DPP v Selvey* [1970] AC 304 provides that in rape alone the defendant does not lose his shield under these circumstances.

70 Under ss 2(1) and (2) Sexual Offences (Amendment) Act 1976 the defendant must apply for the judge's leave to cross-examine the complainant.

71 A study by Zsuzanna Adler, *Rape on Trial* (Routledge and Kegal Paul, 1987) p 73 showed that nearly 60% of defendants using the consent defence applied to put the complainant's previous sexual history in evidence: 75% of them were successful.

72 Or, most interestingly, will the male complainants with homosexual histories find themselves open to erased subjectivity and will the case of a raped heterosexual man be dealt with very differently? Will the complainant's proven heterosexuality counter any of the defendant's claims of honest belief in consent, or conversely, will his homosexuality imply ...

It is possible to see in the law of rape and prostitution how the woman is excluded from subjectivity; the mechanisms of that exclusion can be very concretely grasped by tracing the central concepts of reason and consent through aspects of the criminal law.

Notions of reason and consent

The construction of reason is central to the construction of the male subject, both in its attribution to him, and the concomitant ascription of emotionality to the female other. It is necessary now to dig more deeply into the text of criminal law to deconstruct the notions of reason that may be found there.

The criminal law's concept of consent is one of the most central constructors of gender. Its use and construction are saturated with gender. They vary across a range of offences which differentially construct the female other and the male subject and differential discipline their respective bodies.

Further, it will be argued that there is an important interplay between these notions of reason and consent, which further construct gender in the criminal legal text.

Reason

The role of reason in the rape trial can be illustrated by a deconstruction of *Morgan*,[73] the 1976 case which still provides the precedent test for consent in rape.

There are two aspects to the issue of consent in substantive rape law. The first is: was the woman consenting and the second: did the defendant believe that she was consenting? This dual aspect combined with the principle established in *Morgan* that the defendant's belief in consent only had to be honest, not necessarily reasonable, creates the space for legitimate rape. A nonconsenting woman can be subjected to sex with no legal redress if the defendant honestly believed she was consenting.[74]

What is the role of reason in the rape trial? As law's primary tool it appears in many masks in the case of *Morgan*. Defence counsel for the three younger defendants in *Morgan* argued before the House of Lords that the judgment of the reasonable man could be no guide to the beliefs of the three young men who came with *Morgan* to have sex with his wife, assured by him that she would be a willing partner albeit that they were told to expect resistance. Under these circumstances, reason could not be an appropriate test. These were reasonable men for whom, under the circumstances, reason should be suspended.

Prosecuting counsel in *Morgan* argued that reason must set the external standard for honest belief. If the belief were mistaken, then it must be reasonable, otherwise the defendant could too easily claim honest belief based on his drunkenness or his vanity. Such a test of belief in consent would have narrowed the space for the male subject's legitimate desire. In delivering their judgment on *Morgan*, the majority of the judges – Lords Cross, Hailsham and Fraser – each side-step the reasonableness test for the defendant's honest belief. Lord Cross chooses to step outside legal discourse and into popular discourse, arguing that

---

... consent and honest belief in it? For the parallels between the construction of the male homosexual and the female other see S Duncan 'Law's Sexual Discipline: Visibility, Violence and Consent' (1995) 22 *Journal of Law and Society*, p 326.

73 [1976] AC 182.

74 See S Duncan, 'Law as Literature: Deconstructing the Legal Text' in (1994) 5 *Law and Critique* p 1 for a full discussion of the case of *Morgan*.

it is necessary to consider the ordinary man's understanding of the word rape and finds that, 'according to the ordinary use of the English language, a man (cannot) be said to have committed rape if he believed that the woman was consenting to intercourse'.[75] Even if she were not, consenting.

In delivering a judgment from within legal discourse in the highest appeal court, Lord Cross finds it necessary to move from the terms of legal discourse to consider the way in which the ordinary man defines an offence and then to follow that definition. Lord Cross chooses to side-step reason and he literally invests the male subject with power to determine whether his behaviour constitutes rape.

Lords Hailsham and Fraser both concur in countering reasonable belief with intention. To intend to have intercourse with a woman who does not consent or even to be reckless as to whether she is consenting is the men's reason for rape. Such intention or recklessness side-steps the need for honest belief to be reasonable. Lord Fraser summarises their position:

> If the defendant believed (even on unreasonable grounds) that the woman was consenting to intercourse then he cannot have been carrying out an intention to have intercourse without her consent.[76]

On this basis, the legal text's own established principle that mistaken honest belief must be reasonable is jettisoned in rape, and the space is provided for the male subject to rape legitimately.

Although *Morgan* was decided in 1976 on a three to two majority judgment, it still remains the authority for the test for consent in rape. It was further shored up in the case of *Satnam and Kewal*[77] where Lord Hailsham's position on intention was quoted with approval. Public outrage after the judgment on *Morgan* led to the passing of a provision in the 1976 Sexual Offences (Amendment) Act requiring that reasonableness was one factor to be taken into account in determining whether the defendant had an honest belief in consent. A major criminal law textbook calls this a 'public relations exercise'.[78]

A further exclusion of reasonableness from rape trials occurs as a result of the decision that *Cunningham*[79] rather than *Caldwell*[80] recklessness would apply in the case of reckless rape. In *Cunningham* recklessness, the defendant simply has to know that there was a risk that the complainant was not consenting. In *Caldwell* recklessness, he would have the necessary men's reason if he failed to consider a risk which the reasonable person would have considered. Again, the rape defendant is provided with an expanded space in which to construct the consent of the female other.

Constructing consent

Two related issues flow from the construction of consent in legal discourse. First, constructions of consent construct the male as subject and the woman as other in aspects of the text of criminal law. Secondly, differential notions of consent result in differential disciplining of the male and female bodies,

---

75 *Morgan*, p 203.

76 *Ibid*, p 237.

77 *R v Satnam S and Kewal S* [1983] 78 Cr App Rep 149.

78 Smith and Hogan, *Criminal Law* (1992, 7th edn), p 452.

79 *R v Cunningham* [1981] 2 All ER 863.

80 *R v Caldwell* [1980] Cr App Rep 237, CA.

What must be focused on here is the space in which the woman is not consenting to sexual intercourse but the law does not acknowledge that what is happening is rape: the male subject's honest belief in consent where none exists. In this space, the woman is rendered powerless and unprotected; she is obliged to mirror his desires, she is constructed as other. The *Morgan* and *Caldwell* tests, the possibility of her sexual history being put in evidence, the defendant's unassailable shield, the remnants of the corroboration requirements – all these construct her as other and him as subject.

Morgan, both as precedent and as symbol, creates the possibility that even in the extremes of gang rape using all forms of resistance open to her and with her children present in the wings, the word of her husband as to her consent could have exonerated the three younger defendants and Morgan by default if only they had stuck to their story of resistance and not argued that Mrs Morgan was enjoying and participating in these activities. This is the literal and symbolic construction of the female as other and the man as desiring subject. Mrs Morgan was not consenting, the jury and both appeal courts accepted that, but the defendants were allowed to legitimately construct consent on the word of her husband and there was nothing she could do to undermine this.

The construction of the male subject's space for the legitimate expression of his sexual appetite with a nonconsenting woman extends beyond the issue of nonconsent to the issue of consent induced by fraud 'as to the nature and quality of the act'. Here there are two issues: first, the nature of sexual intercourse which was being consented to, and, secondly, consent by the female other to a nonsexual act which is sexually motivated and conducted by the male subject to the ontological degradation of the female other.

In the case of *Clarence*,[81] Mrs Clarence consented to sexual intercourse with her husband although he knew and she did not know that he suffered from venereal disease. The legal issue was whether there was fraud as to the nature and quality of the act. The court held that there was not. The act to which Mrs Clarence consented was constructed by the law as it was constructed, by the male subject. Mrs Clarence's subjectivity in consent is disregarded. She did not knowingly consent to intercourse with a diseased man. She did not consent to the grievous bodily harm which she sustained and which was foreseeable to her husband, but, although the issue here is exclusively her consent, her consent is constructed as consent to the act which he desired, ignoring the consequences of which only he was aware. Her consent has been constructed to mirror what the court established to be his primary purpose: the satiation of his desire.

Consent to nonsexual acts which are sexually motivated revolve around medical circumstances where the body of the female other, in these situations of vulnerability, is still constructed by the law for the pleasure of the male subject: through a notion of consent which denies her subjectivity.

In *Bolduc and Bird*[82] a doctor conducting a vaginal examination secured the presence of a friend by passing him off as another doctor. The court held that there was no fraud as to the nature and quality of the act. It was still a medical

---

81 *R v Clarence* (1888) 22 QBD 23.

82 *R v Bolduc and Bird* [1967] 63 CLR (2d) 82. This case arose in British Columbia, Canada. The final appeal was heard in the Supreme Court of Canada and the case is precedent in English law. The issues were whether the 'examination' was 'consented' to and whether there was fraud as to the nature and quality of the act.

examination, even if done for the prurient sexual pleasure of the doctor's friend and, possibly, the doctor himself.

In *Mobilio*,[83] the defendant penetrated a number of his female patients with an ultrasound transducer. This was for no medical purpose, without medical authorisation and entirely for the defendant's sexual gratification. Again, the court constructed consent against the female other to exonerate the male subject. There was held to be no fraud.

The male subject's legitimate space for nonconsensual sex is further underlined by the law of incest. Section 10 Sexual Offences Act 1956 forbids a man to have vaginal intercourse, irrespective of consent, with his granddaughter, daughter, sister or mother. In practice, the great majority of incest is committed by fathers with their daughters. This area of law arguably protects the girl (possibly woman) within the family. In practice it is rarely charged and, further, it only protects where there is a blood relationship between the two parties and does not protect in the event of step or adoptive relationships.[84] The rationale for the legislation has been argued to be its attempt to prevent the production of any defective resulting progeny[85] not to protect the young girl vulnerable to the power of the male subject in the family.

Technically the issue of consent does not arise because the defendant commits the offence whether or not the woman consents. However, in practice the issue does arise in two ways. First, where the girl does not consent, the man can be charged with rape but, whatever her age, she will still have to pass all the hurdles of establishing nonconsent to a rape charge.[86] It is important to stress here that for the female other in the context of the power of the male within the family, the notion of consent may be meaningless: she cannot tell her mother; her father is an all-powerful authority figure; she has nowhere else to go.

Acknowledging the space for legitimate nonconsensual sex, the law creates an offence under s 11 which can only be committed by a girl/woman over the age of 16 which is that of permitting a man in the prohibited degrees to have sexual intercourse by her consent. But it is possible for a man to have sexual intercourse with (for example) his daughter over 16 and for her not to be charged with a s 11 offence although he is not charged with rape. In other words, for the law she has not permitted intercourse to take place by her consent but neither can she establish nonconsent for the purposes of a rape charge. The space between not permitting intercourse, and the male subject's honest belief in consent, is the male subject's space for nonconsensual sex.

In his judgment in *Attorney General's Reference (No 1 of 1989)*,[87] Lord Lane gave sentencing guidelines on incest. In the first instance, he considers sex between the father and the prepubescent girl as a crime which 'falls far short of rape', although that girl may well have been coerced by fear of her father and silenced by the constellation of the family. The girl who approaches and then reaches

83   *R v Mobilio* [1991] 1 VR 339. This was an Australian case heard in the Supreme Court of Victoria and is a precedent in English law.

84   Liz Kelly states, in *Surviving Sexual Violence* (Polity, 1988), that incestuous abuse other than by a biological father is overwhelmingly likely to be by an adult male relative in a 'social father' position in relation to the victim. Quoted in N Lacey, C Wells and D Meure (eds) *Reconstructing Criminal Law* (Weidenfeld and Nicolson, 1990) p 355.

85   *R v Winch* [1974] Crim LR 487.

86   The man could be charged with indecent assault because, unlike in the case of rape, a girl under the age of 16 cannot consent. See *R v Satnam S and Kewal S* [1983] 78 Cr App Rep 149.

87   [1989] 3 All ER 571.

puberty is in this judgment increasingly constructed not merely as fully consenting but as temptress:

> The older the girl, the greater the possibility that she may have been the willing or even instigating party to the liaison, a factor which will be reflected in sentence.[88]

The equation is made between puberty and consent and the female other is constructed to mirror or even to create the desire of the male subject. Her absence of subjectivity is underlined in the case of *R v Bailie-Smith*[89] where the defendant successfully appealed against an incest conviction arguing that he mistook his 13 year old daughter for his wife. How could such a mistake have been possible? For the court this was a female body without subjectivity.

One of the biggest dichotomies in legal notions of consent arises in the distinction between consent to offences of physical violence and consent to offences of sexual violence. This distinction in itself is problematic in that sexual violence is always physical to the extent that it has a physical dimension and physical violence may also be sexual. It is easier to draw a distinction by considering specific offences which have or do not have a sexual or physical dimension to their legal definitions. Rape, indecent assault and incest all have sexual dimensions without which the offence is not committed. In the cases of rape and incest, sexual intercourse is required. The offences of common assault, assault occasioning actual bodily harm, grievous bodily harm, and grievous bodily harm with intent do not have a sexual element as part of their legal definitions, although within any one case there may be a sexual dimension. Consent is theoretically a defence in respect of all of the aforementioned offences.

The great majority of these offences of legally defined physical violence are committed by men and the great majority of them are committed against men.[90] Just as the sexual space of the male subject is constructed by the laws relating to sexual violence, so the physical space of the male subject is constructed by the law relating to physical violence. It is this space which defines the male subject's possibilities for self-expression in violence, most specifically consensual violence between men/boys.

The construction of the male subject through his participation in 'manly sports' is ensured through a line of cases from *Coney*[91] to *Attorney General's Reference (No 6 of 1980)*[92] which have preserved a space for that construction. It is possible to consent to visible violence in the case of 'properly conducted'[93] games and sports. In other areas of violent self expression, the male subject is in more difficulties. If there is no visible, physical harm, consent can be a defence but the test here will be whether the conduct of the complainant viewed as a whole could have been considered to have constituted consent[94] – a very different test from the completely subjective one in rape.

---

88 *Ibid*, p 571.

89 [1977] 64 Cr App Rep 76.

90 Patricia Mayhew, *Summary Findings British Crime Survey* (HMSO, 1994). This summary, which is based on the 1993 statistics, shows that the great majority of victims of assault crimes are males aged between 16 and 29.

91 (1882) 8 QBD 534.

92 [1981] All ER 1057.

93 *Attorney-General's Reference (No 6 of 1980)* [1980] All ER 1057, p 1059.

94 *R v Donovan* [1934] 2 KB 498. Even for common assault, consent will not be an effective defence in the case of prize fights, presumably because they are illegal in any event.

Where an intentional assault has caused visible physical harm, consent cannot be a defence unless that harm is transient or trifling or if it falls into one of the categories of exceptional circumstances as set out by case law and confirmed by *Brown*.[95] These exceptional circumstances are 'manly sports',[96] rough but innocent horseplay'[97] and where the purpose justifies the harm, most notably legitimate and authorised medical interventions.

Brown settles that: 'It is not in the public interest that people should try to cause each other actual bodily harm for no good reason' and where such good reason does not exist, consent cannot be a defence. In respect of visible violence outside of that very limited space, a male subject will not be allowed to consent, just as in the very considerable space for heterosexual male sexual violence, the law does not in its construction of rape allow the female other not to consent.

Further, the judgment in *Brown* made it clear that not only were homosexual sadomasochistic activities considered to be no good reason for the infliction of physical harm but also the House of Lords sought to extend its protection to the young men who could be 'proselytised and corrupted' by 'cult violence'. This is protection which the law does not seek to extend to young female victims of rape in general because there is no age below which the victim cannot consent. Nor was it extended to the specific 15 year old victim in *Satnam and Kewall*[98] where rape convictions against the two defendants were quashed and the court chose to reaffirm *Morgan*, leaving the honest belief test in fact and making no comment on the fact that a 15 year old can legally consent to sexual intercourse for the purposes of a rape charge although she cannot consent to indecent assault.

As willing and enthusiastic 'victim' or as protesting complainant, the male subject cannot have consent constructed against him in matters of visible physical violence.[99] Of course, the same protection is extended to the female complainant but only in matters of visible physical violence where she is much less likely to be the victim and not in sexual violence where she almost always is.

Disciplining Gendered Bodies

Legal notions of consent construct gender in the law: they assist in the construction of the male as subject and the female as other. They also differentially discipline the bodies of the male subject and the female other. The mirror – the watchful eye of disciplinary power – reflects differential norms for the male subject and the female other.

The male body is disciplined by the law through the constrictions on its capacity to exert nonconsensual violence on another male body but the capacity of the male body as political, sexual force is intensified by the space provided to the male subject in sexual offences and particularly in rape. The body of the female other is disciplined through the space which is provided to the male subject to construct her consent where none exists and by the complicity which that exacts from her in her own ontological degradation.

The very construction of sexuality creates the possibility for disciplining the body and the law constructs sexuality, particularly through its mercurial notions of

95 *R v Brown* [1992] 2 WLR 441.

96 *Coney* p 534.

97 Archbold, *Criminal Pleading and Practice* (1988, 43rd edn) paras 20–124 quoted in *R v Brown, op cit*, p 449.

98 *op cit.*

99 *R v Brown, op cit.*

consent, to provide space for the sexual expression of the male subject. The space for the female other is as mirror for that desiring male subject.

It is interesting to note that where the female other is perceived to be outside the parameters of desirable female, the law does not construct her as mirroring male desire. In the case of *Kimber*,[100] the defendant was convicted of assaulting a 56 year old mental patient, 'Betty'. Following *Morgan*, the defendant argued honest belief in consent. The court, upholding the conviction, focused on Betty's consent and Betty's desires, although, following *Morgan*, the issue was his honest belief. The space for the male subject to legitimately express his sexual desires is not extended here because those desires are constructed outside the normal and the female other is not perceived as mirroring them.

The female body is disciplined as a sexual body, disciplined to mirror the sexual desire of the male subject, to expand the space of his legitimate desire. Where her body is constructed as sexual, the space for her consent is consistently contracted; where her body is not constructed as sexual – as in the case of the ageing woman or the very young girl – that space is expanded. The criminal law disciplines the female body, as it denies subjectivity to the woman/girl.

Conclusion

It has been possible to see how the discourse of the criminal law constructs gender across a range of offences. Law's power is disciplinary – constructed around the mirror – the watchful eye of which also reflects gendered norms for the disciplined subject. In its disciplinary aspect, the law extends the power of the male subject to construct himself as desiring subject in respect of the female other who mirrors that desire. Concomitantly, it disciplines the body of the female other, subject to that power. The male physical body is itself disciplined in relation to the body of other male subjects.

The constructions of reason and consent in legal discourse are central to this process. Reason is constructed against the female other as it is ascribed to the male subject, although he is not tested by it. Differential constructs of consent create the power of the male subject for the legitimate space of the sexually constructed female other, as they limit the power of that subject's physical body. As watchful eye, as reflected norm, as refracted desire: the law's mirrors powerfully construct gender and in so doing, they gender justice.

THE EQUALITY/SAMENESS/DIFFERENCE DEBATE

Patriarchal attitudes, assumptions and labelling, discussed in Chapter 5 entails the implicit assumption that women are 'different'; that women comprise the 'other' – a species excluded from the 'natural' patriarchal ordering of society. This perception is critical for it affects in a fundamental way the manner in which civic society – and law – is viewed. Simone de Beauvoir in her seminal work *The Second Sex*[101] considered women as the 'other'. Carol Gilligan, a psychologist, in *In a Different Voice: Psychological Theory and Women's Development*[102] brought the subject of sameness versus difference centre stage with her analysis of the 'different voice' in which women appear to speak emotionally and psychologically.

---

100 [1983] 2 All ER 316.

101 (1949) Trans HM Parshley, Pan Book, 1988.

102 Harvard University Press, 1982.

THE SECOND SEX
Simone de Beauvoir[103]

Woman? Very simple, say the fanciers of simple formulas: she is a womb, an ovary; she is a female – this word is sufficient to define her. In the mouth of a man the epithet female has the sound of an insult, yet he is not ashamed of his animal nature; on the contrary, he is proud if someone says of him: 'He is a male!' The term female is derogatory not because it emphasises women's animality, but because it imprisons her in her sex: and if this sex seems to man to be contemptible and inimical even in harmless dumb animals, it is evidently because of the uneasy hostility stirred up in him by woman. Nevertheless he wishes to find in biology a justification for this sentiment. The word female brings up in his mind a saraband of imagery – a vast, round ovum engulfs and castrates the agile spermatozoon; the monstrous and swollen termite queen rules over the enslaved males; the female praying mantis and the spider, satiated with love, crush and devour their partners; the bitch in heat runs through the alleys, trailing behind her a wake of depraved odours; the she-monkey presents her posterior immodestly and then steals away with hypocritical coquetry; and the most superb wild beasts – the tigress, the lioness, the panther – bed down slavishly under the imperial embrace of the male. Females sluggish, eager, artful, stupid, callous, lustful, ferocious, abased – man projects them all at once upon woman. And the fact is that she is a female. What if we are willing to stop thinking in platitudes, two questions are immediately posed: what does the female denote in the animal kingdom? And what particular kind of female is manifest in woman?...[104]

These biological considerations are extremely important. In the history of woman they play a part of the first rank and constitute an essential element in her situation. Throughout our further discussion we shall always bear them in mind. For, the body being the instrument of our grasp upon the world, the world is bound to seem a very different thing when apprehended in one manner or another. This accounts for our lengthy study of the biological facts; they are one of the keys to the understanding of woman. But I deny that they establish for her a fixed and inevitable destiny. They are insufficient for setting up a hierarchy of the sexes; they fail to explain why woman is the Other; they do not condemn her to remain in this subordinate role forever.[105]

Carol Gilligan's research

One of the most significant catalysts in the gender debate has been the work of educational psychologist Professor Carol Gilligan, whose work *In a Different Voice: Psychological Theory and Women's Development*[106] was published in 1982. Lawrence Kohlberg had earlier established a six-stage model of human development, based on moral reasoning, which when the results of boys was compared to those of girls, showed that girls consistently underperformed.[107]

---

103 1908–86.

104 *The Second Sex*, p 3.

105 *Ibid*, p 34.

106 Harvard University Press, 1982.

107 L Kohlberg, 'Stage and Sequence: The Cognitive-Development Approach to Socialisation', in A Goslin (ed), *Handbook of Socialisation Theory and Research* (1971); 'Moral Stages and Moralisation: The Cognitive-Development Approach', in T Lichone (ed), *Moral Development and Behaviour: Theory Research and Social Issues* (1976); *The Philosophy of Moral Development* (San Francisco: Harper & Row, 1981).

Gilligan's research concerned the interpretation of the manner and extent to which girls and boys differed in their reactions to a moral dilemma. Two of the children studied, Jake and Amy, aged eleven years, were of comparable intelligence, education and social class. The problem posed concerned Heinz, a poor man whose wife required drugs in order to save her life. Heinz could not afford to pay for the drug, and the pharmacist would not lower the price. The children were asked whether, given the severity of the situation, Heinz would be morally justified in stealing the drug.

Carol Gilligan demonstrated the differing forms of reasoning undertaken by Jake and Amy. When asked whether Heinz should steal the drug, Jake answered 'yes', on the basis that, although this would amount to theft, the law itself could contain mistakes, and that if Heinz was prosecuted the judge should take this into account and give him a light sentence. Jake's reasoning followed a logical, rational pattern. Jake, Gilligan writes, considers the moral dilemma to be 'sort of like a math[s] problem with humans' (math[s] being 'the only thing that is totally logical'). Amy, on the other hand, reasoned very differently. Lacking Jake's confident, logical approach Amy first considers whether there are alternatives to stealing the drug ('a loan or something'). When asked why Heinz should not steal the drug Amy considers not the law but the effect on the relationship between Heinz and his wife (if he is caught, his wife might not get the drug and would get more sick). Amy's whole response to the dilemma revolves around a concern for relationships, a reliance on the connectedness of people rather than pure logic. Viewed from one perspective, this could be interpreted to mean that Amy's development is 'stunted by a failure of logic'. That, however, would be a false interpretation which has as its basis the assumption that boys and girls must reason to a shared standard: a standard set by the boys. In Gilligan's assessment, 'Amy's judgments contain the insights central to an ethic of care, just as Jake's judgments reflect the logic of the justice approach'. Amy's judgments are assessed by Gilligan in the following manner:

> ... the world she knows is a different world from that refracted by Kohlberg's construction of Heinz's dilemma. Her world is a world of relationships and psychological truths where an awareness of the connection between people gives rise to a recognitions of responsibility for one another, a perception of the need for response. Seen in this light, her understanding of morality as arising from the recognition of relationships, her belief in communication as the mode of conflict resolution, and her conviction that the solution to the dilemma will follow from its compelling representation seem far from naive or cognitively immature. Instead, Amy's judgements contain the insight central to an ethic of care, just as Jake's judgments reflect the logic of the justice approach.'

In the extracts which follow, the manner in which feminist scholars have reacted to Carol Gilligan's work is considered.

PORTIA IN A DIFFERENT VOICE: SPECULATIONS ON A WOMEN'S LAWYERING PROCESS[108]

Carrie Menkel-Meadow[109]

Introduction

As a scholar of the legal profession, I have asked whether the increased presence of women in the legal profession might lead to alternative ways of seeing what lawyers do and how they do it.[110] Will it be simply that more lawyers are women, or will the legal profession be transformed by the women who practice law? In recent years, two developments in feminist scholarship have offered insights which promise to shed some light on that question. This essay explores some of the potential applications to law of these two developments in feminist scholarship stated as speculative hypotheses for further study.

The first of these developments in feminist scholarship is the self-conscious observation of how women's entry into formerly male-dominated fields has changed both the knowledge base of the field[111] and the methodology by which knowledge is acquired.[112] Since our knowledge of how lawyers behave and of how the legal system functions is based almost exclusively on male subjects of study,[113] our understanding of what it means to be and act like a lawyer may be misleadingly based on a male norm. We need to broaden our enquiry to include the new participants in the profession so that we can discover whether our present understandings are accurate. With more women lawyers available for study we may learn first, whether women perform lawyering tasks in ways different from men; second, whether our descriptions of what lawyers do may have to change to reflect different goals or task orientations; and third, whether the increased presence of women in the profession may have broad institutional effects. Current studies of gender differences in other fields offer a powerful heuristic for application to our understanding of the lawyering process.

The second development is a body of theoretical and empirical research in psychology and sociology. This research has postulated that women grow up in the world with a more relational and affiliational concept of self than do men. This concept of self has important implications for the values that women develop and for the actions that are derived from those values.[114] This research

---

108 [1985] *Berkeley Women's Law Journal* 39. (Footnotes edited.)

109 At the time of writing, Professor of Law, University of California, Los Angeles.

110 Menkel-Meadow, 'Women as Law Teachers: Toward the Feminisation of Legal Education', in *Essays on the Application of a Humanistic Perspective to Law Teaching* (1981); Menkel-Meadow, 'Women in Law?' (1983) *Am B Found Research J* 189.

111 E Langland and W Gove (eds), *A Feminist Perspective in the Academy: The Difference it Makes* (1981); A Rich, 'Toward a Woman-Centred University', in *On Lies, Secrets and Silence: Selected Prose 1966-78* (1979) p 125; Abel and Nelson, 'Feminist Studies: the Scholarly is Political' (1985) 4 *The Women's Rev of Books* 10.

112 C Gilligan, *In a Different Voice: Psychological Theory and Women's Development* (1982).

113 See eg J Heinz and E Laumann, *Chicago Lawyers: The Social Structure of the Bar* (1982); J Carlin, *Lawyers on Their Own* (1962). Cf C Epstein, *Women in Law* (1981).

114 See eg C Gilligan *op cit*, N Chodorow, *The Reproduction of Mothering* (1978); D Dinnerstein, *The Mermaid and the Minotaur* (1978); J Miller, *Towards a New Psychology of Women* (1976); N Noddings, *Caring: A Feminine Approach to Ethics and Moral Education* (1974); A Schaef, *Women's Reality* (1981).

is controversial and is generating criticism from many different quarters[115] I am not unsympathetic to some of the criticism, which in part reflects a growing maturity and differentiation in feminist scholarship.[116]

I find persuasive, though not unproblematic, the notion that values, consciousness, attributes, and behaviour are gendered,[117] ie that some are identified as belonging to women and others to men. The attachment of gender labels is a product of both present empirical research[118] and social process. Thus, we may label the quality of caring a female quality, but note its presence in many men. Further, a man who exhibits many feminine qualities may be perceived as feminine, eg 'He's too sensitive to be a good trial lawyer', or alternatively, an assertive woman may be met with remarks such as, 'She's as sharp as any of the men on the team'.[119] Attributing behaviour characteristics to a particular gender is problematic, because even as we observe such generalisations to be valid in many cases, we risk perpetuating the conventional stereotypes that prevent us from seeing the qualities as qualities without their gendered context.

The process is one that most feminists deplore because what is labelled female or feminine typically is treated as inferior, and is subordinated to what is labelled male or masculine. This is particularly true if the context in which they are found is one, such as the practice of law, which has itself traditionally been labelled male. For the purpose of this essay I will assume that gender differences exist as they have been documented by such writers as Simone de Beauvoir, Carol Gilligan, Nancy Chodorow, Jean Baker Miller, Anne Schaef and others, and will leave to others the important enquiry into the origins of these differences, be they biological, sociological, political, or some combination of these. My perspective on this issue is that as long as such differences exist, studies of the world – here the legal profession – that fail to take into account women's experience of that world are incomplete, and prevent us from having a greater repertoire of societal as well as individual choices.

An important part of this enquiry is whether it is yet possible to see if women conduct themselves as lawyers differently from men. I have commented elsewhere that just because there are increasing numbers of women in the practice and teaching of law,[120] we do not yet know whether women will transform the practice or themselves when they are found in sufficient numbers. Social research has indicated that those in token numbers may feel strong pressure to conform to the already existing norms of the workplace and to minimise, rather than emphasise, whatever differences exist.[121] Thus, when we

---

115 See eg Catharine MacKinnon, 'Comments', Mitchell Lecture Series (1984) reprinted in The 1984 James McCormick Mitchell Lecture: 'Feminist Discourse, Moral Values and the Law – A Conversation' (1985) 34 *Buffalo L Rev* 11, 20.

116 For an excellent typology of the different schools within feminism, see A Jagger, *Feminist Politics and Human Nature* (1984).

117 S de Beauvoir, *The Second Sex* (1953); C Gilligan, *op cit*.

118 C Gilligan, *op cit*; E Maccoby and C Jacklin, *The Psychology of Sex Differences* (1974); Spence, 'Changing Conceptions of Men and Women: A Psychologist's Perspective', in Langland and Gove *op cit*.

119 Remarks overheard by the author by lawyers describing other lawyers.

120 Menkel-Meadow, 'Women as Law Teachers' *op cit*.

121 R Kanter, *Men and Women of the Corporation* (1977); Kanter, 'Reflections on Women and the Legal Profession: A Sociological Perspective' (1978) 1 *Harvard Women's LJ*; Spangler, Gordon and Pipkin, 'Token Women: An Empirical Test of Kanter's Hypothesis' (1978) 84 *Am J Soc* 160.

look at women who are lawyers in 1985, we may be studying those women who have been successful in assimilating to male nomns. Although there is already some evidence of Portia-like[122] dissatisfaction with the present male voice,[123] more women lawyers may be necessary to form a critical mass that will give full expression to a women's voice in law (whether expressed exclusively by women or with men in another voice).

Because our notion that women can transform a profession is quite new, I call what follows speculations on a women's lawyering process. I hope to provoke further enquiry and dialogue on this subject as we begin to include women lawyers in our studies of the legal profession and the legal system. In addition, I hope to encourage those who wish to give expression to values and behaviours in the legal profession that are currently underrepresented to do so, with the belief that this will produce a better legal system for lawyers, clients, and others who are affected by our legal institutions ...

... In conventional terms Jake would make a good lawyer because he spots the legal issues of excuse and justification, balances the rights, and reaches a decision, while considering implicitly, if not explicitly, the precedential effect of his decision. But as Gilligan argues, and as I develop more fully below, Amy's approach is also plausible and legitimate, both as a style of moral reasoning and as a style of lawyering. Amy seeks to keep the people engaged; she holds the needs of the parties and their relationships constant and hopes to satisfy them all (as in a negotiation), rather than selecting a winner (as in a lawsuit). If one must be hurt, she attempts to find a resolution that will hurt least the one who can least bear the hurt. (Is she engaged in a 'deep pocket' policy analysis?) She looks beyond the 'immediate lawsuit' to see how the 'judgment' will affect the parties. If Heinz steals the drug and goes to jail, who will take care of his wife? Furthermore, Amy is concerned with how the dilemma is resolved: the process by which the parties communicate may be crucial to the outcome. (Amy cares as much about procedure as about substance.) And she is being a good lawyer when she enquires whether all of the facts have been discovered and considered.

The point here is not that Amy's method of moral reasoning is better than Jake's, nor that she is a better lawyer than Jake. (Some have read Gilligan to argue that the women's voice is better. I don't read her that way.) The point is that Amy does some things differently from Jake when she resolves this dilemma, and these things have useful analogies to lawyering and may not have been sufficiently credited as useful lawyering skills. Jake and Amy have something to learn from one another.

Thus, although a 'choice of rights' conception (life vs property) of solving human problems may be important, it is not the only or the best way. Responsibilities to self and to others may be equally important in measuring moral, as well as legal decision-making, but have thus far been largely ignored. For example, a lawyer who feels responsible for the decisions she makes with her client may be more inclined to think about how those decisions will hurt other people and how the lawyer and client feel about making such decisions. (Amy thinks about Heinz, the druggist, and Heinz's wife at all times in reaching her decision; Jake makes a choice in abstract terms without worrying as much about the people it affects.)

---

122 W Shakespeare, *The Merchant of Venice*.

123 See eg Rifkin, 'Toward a Theory of Law and Patriarchy' (1980) 3 *Harvard Women's LJ* 83. (Extracted at p 23.)

In tracing through the sources of these different approaches to moral reasoning, Gilligan's analysis tracks that of Chodorow, Dinnerstein and Noddings. Men, who have had to separate from their differently gendered mother in order to grow, tend to see moral dilemmas as problems of separateness and individual rights, problems in which choices must be made and priorities must be ordered. Women, who need not completely separate from their same gendered mother in order to grow, see the world in terms of connections and relationships. While women thus try to change the rules in order to preserve relationships, men, in abiding by these rules, depict relationships as easily replaced. Where men see danger in too much connection or intimacy, in being engulfed and losing their own identity, women see danger in the loss of connection, in not having an identity through caring for others and by being abandoned and isolated.

Both Gilligan and Noddings see differences in the ethics men and women derive from their different experiences of the world. Men focus on universal abstract principles like justice, equality and fairness so that their world is safe, predictable and constant. Women solve problems by seeking to understand the context and relationships involved and understand that universal rules may be impossible.

The two different voices Gilligan describes articulate two different developmental processes. To the extent that we all have both of these voices within us and they are not exclusively gender based, a mature person will develop the ability to consider the implications of both an abstract rights analysis and a contextualised responsibilities analysis. For women, this kind of mature emotional and intellectual synthesis may require taking greater account of self and less account of the other, for men, the process may be the reverse. Such an integration will not resolve all issues of personal development. Those who seek inter-dependence will not necessarily find it by the individualistic integration and reciprocity of reasoning styles proposed above. And if this integration fosters equality between the sexes, there still remains the problem of equity. As one of Gilligan's subjects observed: 'People have real emotional needs to be attached to something and equality doesn't give you attachment. Equality fractures society and places on every person the burden of standing on his own two feet.'[124] The different paths toward mature moral development for men and women may give us more than one road to take to the same place, or we may find that there is more than one interesting place to go.

II. The Different Voices of Lawyering

What does moral or psychological development have to do with the law? Gilligan's observations about male-female differences in moral reasoning may have a great deal to suggest about how the legal system is structured, how law is practiced and made, and how we reason and use law in making decisions. I will speculate about each of these below but will focus primarily on the implications of these insights for the lawyering process.

Two sets of questions illustrate how we might think about the impact of two voices on our legal system as presently constituted and as it might be transformed. First, how has the exclusion, or at least the devaluation, of women's voices affected the choices made in the values underlying our current legal structures? When we value 'objectivity' or a 'right' answer, or a single winner, are we valuing male goals of victory, exclusion, clarity, predictability? What

---

124 *In A Difference Voice*, p 167.

would our legal system look like if women had not been excluded from participating in its creation? What values would women express in creating the laws and institutions of a legal system? How would they differ from what we see now? How might the different male and female voices join together to create an integrated legal system? Second, can we glimpse enclaves of another set of values within some existing legal structures? Is the judge 'male' the jury 'female'? Is the search for facts a feminine search for context and the search for legal principles a masculine search for certainty and abstract rules? It could be argued that no functional system could be either wholly masculine or wholly feminine, that there is a tendency for one set of characteristics in a system to mitigate the excesses of the other. Thus, the harshness of law produced the flexibility of equity, and conversely, the abuse of flexibility gave rise to rules of law to limit discretion. In this sense, the legal system could be seen to encompass both male and female voices already. Yet, even though our present legal structures may reflect elements of both sets of values, there is a tendency for the male-dominated or male-created forms and values to control. Thus, equity begins to develop its own harsh rules of law and universalistic regulations applied to discretionary decisions, undermining the flexibility that discretion is supposed to protect. Because men have, in fact, dominated by controlling the legal system, the women's voice in law may be present, but in a male form.

These two sets of questions explore a central issue, which is whether, to the extent that there are value choices to be made in the legal system, those choices will be differently made and with different results when the people who make decisions include a greater representation of women among their numbers. Some may prefer to see these different values as not necessarily taking gendered forms – I do. But even if the choices of values are not themselves gendered, it may be that women will favour one set of values over another in sufficient numbers, or with sufficient intensity, to change the balance at times. Although existing structures give a glimpse of what the legal system could look like, we cannot yet know what the consequences of women's participation in the legal system will be – some fear the women's voice will simply be added on and be drowned out by the louder male voice; others fear an androgynous, univoiced world with no interesting differences.

Perhaps by examining these issues in their concrete forms we can see how Portia's different voice might expand our understanding of the lawyering process. I will explore some of the tasks of the lawyer and skills that lawyers employ, and the larger adversarial system in which lawyering is embedded. The rules with which lawyers practice, which until recently have been articulated almost exclusively with male voices, will be examined so we can begin to speculate about how a woman's voice might affect the ethical rules which govern the profession and the substantive principles of the law. It is my hope that this preliminary review will spark more thorough and comprehensive research.

The Advocacy-Adversarial Model

The basic structure of our legal system is premised on the adversarial model, which involves two advocates who present their cases to a disinterested third party who listens to evidence and argument and declares one party a winner. In this simplified description of the Anglo-American model of litigation, we can identify some of the basic concepts and values which underlie this choice of arrangements: advocacy, persuasion, hierarchy, competition, and binary results (win/lose). The conduct of litigation is relatively similar (not coincidentally, I suspect) to a sporting event – there are rules, a referee, an object to the game, and a winner is declared after the play is over. As I have argued elsewhere,[125] this conception of the dispute resolution process is applied more broadly than just in the conventional courtroom. The adversarial model affects the way in which lawyers advise their clients ('get as much as you can'), negotiate disputes ('we can really get them on that') and plan transactions ('let's be sure to draft this to your advantage'). All of these activities in lawyering assume competition over the same limited and equally valued items (usually money) and assume that success is measured by maximising individual gain. Would Gilligan's Amy create a different model?

By returning to Heinz's dilemma we see some hints about what Amy might do. Instead of concluding that a choice must be made between life and property, in resolving the conflict between parties as Jake does, Amy sees no need to hierarchically order the claims. Instead, she tries to account for all the parties' needs, and searches for a way to find a solution that satisfies the needs of both. In her view, Heinz should be able to obtain the drug for his wife and the pharmacist should still receive payment. So Amy suggests a loan, a credit arrangement, or a discussion of other ways to structure the transaction. In short, she won't play by the adversarial rules. She searches outside the system for a way to solve the problem, trying to keep both parties in mind. Her methods substantiate Gilligan's observations that women will try to change the rules to preserve the relationships.

Furthermore, in addition to looking for more substantive solutions to the problem (ie not accepting the binary win/lose conception of the problem), Amy also wants to change the process. Amy sees no reason why she must act as a neutral arbiter of a dispute and make a decision based only on the information she has. She 'belie[ves] in communication as the mode of conflict resolution and [is convinced] that the solution to the dilemma will follow from its compelling representation'. If the parties talk directly to each other, they will be more likely to appreciate the importance of each other's needs. Thus, she believes direct communication, rather than third party mediated debate, might solve the problem, recognising that two apparently conflicting positions can both be simultaneously legitimate, and there need not be a single victor.

The notion that women might have more difficulty with full-commitment-to-one-side model of the adversary system is graphically illustrated by Hilary, one of the women lawyers in Gilligan's study. This lawyer finds herself in one of the classic moral dilemmas of the adversary system: she sees that her opponent has failed to make use of a document that is helpful to his case and harmful to hers. In deciding not to tell him about the document because of what she sees as her 'professional vulnerability' in the male adversary system, she concludes that 'the adversary system of justice impedes not only the supposed search for truth (the conventional criticism), but also the expression of concern for the person on the other side'. Gilligan describes Hilary's tension between her concept of rights (learned through legal training) and her female ethic of care as a sign of her socialisation in the male world of lawyering. Thus, the advocacy model, with its commitment to one-sided advocacy, seems somehow contrary to 'apprehending the reality of the other' which lawyers like Hilary experience. Even the continental inquisitorial model, frequently offered as an alternative to the adversarial model, includes most of these elements of the male system-hierarchy, advocacy, competition and binary results.

---

125 Menkel-Meadow, 'Toward Another View of Legal Negotiation: The Structure of Problem Solving' (1984) 31 *UCLA L Rev* 754.

So what kind of legal system would Amy and Hilary create if left to their own devices? They might look for ways to alter the harshness of win/lose results; they might alter the rules of the game (or make it less like a game); and they might alter the very structures and forms themselves. Thus, in a sense Amy and Hilary's approach can already be found in some of the current alternatives to the adversary model such as mediation. Much of the current interest in alternative dispute resolution is an attempt to modify the harshness of the adversarial process and expand the kinds of solutions available, in order to respond better to the varied needs of the parties. Amy's desire to engage the parties in direct communication with each other is reflected in mediation models where the parties talk directly to each other and forge their own solutions. The work of Gilligan and Noddings, demonstrating an ethic of care and a heightened sense of empathy in women, suggests that women lawyers may be particularly interested in mediation as an alternative to litigation as a method of resolving disputes.

Even within the present adversarial model, Amy and Hilary might, in their concern for others, want to provide for a broader conception of interested parties, permitting participation by those who might be affected by the dispute (an ethic of inclusion). In addition, like judges who increasingly are managing more of the details of their cases, Amy and Hilary might seek a more active role in settlement processes and rely less on court-ordered relief. Amy and Hilary might look for other ways to construct their lawsuits and remedies in much the same way as courts of equity mitigated the harshness of the law courts' very limited array of remedies by expanding the conception of what was possible.

The process and rules of the adversary system itself might look different if there were more female voices in the legal profession. If Amy is less likely than Jake to make assertive, rights-based statements, is she less likely to adapt to the male-created advocacy mode? In my experience as a trial lawyer, I observed that some women had difficulty with the 'macho' ethic of the courtroom battle. Even those who did successfully adapt to the male model often confronted a dilemma because women were less likely to be perceived as behaving properly when engaged in strong adversarial conduct. It is important to be 'strong' in the courtroom, according to the stereotypic conception of appropriate trial behaviour. The woman who conforms to the female stereotype by being 'soft' or 'weak' is a bad trial lawyer; but if a woman is 'tough' or 'strong' in the courtroom, she is seen as acting inappropriately for a woman. Note, however, that this stereotyping is contextual: the same woman acting as a 'strong' or 'tough' mother with difficult children would be praised for that conduct. Women's strength is approved of with the proviso that it be exerted in appropriately female spheres. Amy and Hilary might create a different form of advocacy, one resembling a 'conversation' with the fact finder, relying on the creation of a relationship with the jury for its effectiveness, rather than on persuasive intimidation ...

In sum, the growing strength of women's voice in the legal profession may change the adversarial system into a more co-operative, less war-like system of communication between disputants in which solutions are mutually agreed upon rather than dictated by an outsider, won by the victor, and imposed upon the loser. Some seeds of change may already be found in existing alternatives to the litigation model, such as mediation. It remains to be seen what further changes Portia's voice may make ...

Directions for New Speculations

This brief and speculative discussion of how another voice might inform the law and the lawyering process may create more problems than it illuminates. Are these different voices gender-based or just two thematically different ways of looking at the world? If these are women's voices, why haven't they been heard yet, since there are an increasing number of women in all parts of the profession? Will the new voices become assimilated to the old before they are heard in the legal system?

Have those women who have already become lawyers been socialised or self-selected to succeed with a man's voice? Have we sought to explain too much by transposing psychological observations to the legal arena? And perhaps most importantly, how will the 'women are different' argument play itself out in current legal disputes? Many of us feel the differences everyday. What we deplore is when they are used to oppress or disempower us or when they are used as immutable stereotypes that prevent recognition of individual variations. We don't yet know how many of the differences will disappear in a world socially and legally constructed so that gender is not a basis for domination. My point of view is that while we are observing the differences we might ask if we have something to learn from them. Whether or not the different voice is gendered, we might look at how our legal system might take account of a few more voices.

The new voice may create its own problems and dilemmas – the values of care, responsibility and relationship present their own difficulties. Can we care for all? How many (our client, the other client, the other lawyer, the entire system) can we be responsible for at any one time? Are all relationships good, the unequal relationships to the same extent as the equal relationships? By caring too much for others, do we lose sight of ourselves? Will too much contextualism prevent the emergence of any general principles by which we can guide ourselves? These are among the difficulties we will have to confront when and if a women's voice in the lawyering process is heard.

It is increasingly important to examine whether and how Portia might speak in a different voice and how we might try to avoid descriptions of the legal world that commit a serious fallacy by using the part (the male world of lawyers) to describe the whole. We have a demanding research agenda ahead for the study of a women's lawyering process in legal education, in the practice of law, in the structure of the profession and the legal system, and in the doctrinal and substantive values of our laws.

FROM GENDER DIFFERENCE TO FEMINIST SOLIDARITY: USING CAROL GILLIGAN AND AN ETHIC OF CARE IN LAW[126]

Leslie Bender[127]

Gilligan's work and the work of feminist gender difference theorists have generated a certain degree of controversy. Feminists who struggle against acknowledgement of sex or gender differences find Gilligan's variety of theory damagingly reminiscent of a romanticised 19th century 'separate spheres' ideology, and hence quite pernicious. Other feminists, who assert that gender relations are power hierarchies and about institutionalised privilege, consider Gilligan-type works disturbing, because they valorise 'voices' of women that are

---

126 (1990) 15 *Vermont Law Review* 1. (Footnotes edited.)

127 At the time of writing, Associate Professor, Syracuse University College of Law.

arguably results of subordination and oppression.[128] Some feminists combine both these arguments and criticise Gilligan's work for its vulnerability to cooptation, misuse, or appropriation by the conservative right.[129] Lately, another feminist critique of gender difference theories has emerged. This criticism is laced with postmodernist/poststructuralist theoretical concepts. It eschews difference theory's reliance upon a universalised liberal-humanist 'subject' or, more pointedly, on an unspoken assumption of a 'white, economically comfortable, heterosexual woman'. A similar criticism is wielded by critical race and sexuality theorists. These powerful challenges contend that gender difference theories are essentialist, ahistorical, and insensitive to differences of race, class, sexual preference, ethnicity, age, motherhood, and physical challenges.[130] Specific criticisms of Gilligan and other feminist difference theory projects are more prevalent in the non-legal literature, but they have made their way into law journals and legal conferences as well.[131] Does all this debate lead to a conclusion that although Gilligan's work provided a useful platform in the early 1980s for validating women's perspectives and knowledges (particularly when they deviated from the norms of the dominant discourses), hers is no longer a persuasive or viable theory?

I have been struggling with this idea of post-Gilliganism (not to mention postfeminism) and the imminent demise of difference theory. What is the value or 'truth' of a theory of gender differences? What is the meaning of the charge of essentialism? Does the rejection of difference theory mean that we will lose the category of women for purposes of our critiques and analyses? If so, what are the political and theoretical consequences of that move? I want to argue against critiques of feminist difference theory that lead to our inability to speak of women as a category for theorising and for political and legal struggle.

I believe it is politically and theoretically premature to give up the 'class' of women for our analysis. Differences among women based on particularised cultural, historical, and political factors ought not be ignored, but they also ought not serve to break down the category of women into infinitely smaller groups, until we end up with an analysis that can only effectively cover individuals. Real differences among women notwithstanding, there is enough that is cohesive and common about the category of women to bridge the differences for purposes of political solidarity and legal analysis. Domination, subordination, exclusion,

---

128 See, *inter alia*, Catharine MacKinnon, *Toward a Feminist Theory of the State* (1989); J Auerback, L Blum, V Smith, C Williams, 'Commentary: On Gilligan's In a Different Voice' (1985) 11 *Feminist Studies* 149; Jane Flax, 'Postmodernism and Gender Relations in Feminist Theory' (1987) 12 *Signs* 621; Joan Tronto, 'Beyond Gender Difference to a Theory of Care' (1987) 12 *Signs* 644; Martha Reineke, 'The Politics of Difference: A Critique of Carol Gilligan' (1987) 2 *Canadian Journal of Feminist Ethics* 3.

129 See eg Ann Scales, 'The Emergence of Feminist Jurisprudence: An Essay' (1986) 95 *Yale LJ* 1373. (Extracted in Chapter 4.)

130 See eg Nancy Fraser and Linda Nicholson, 'Social Criticism without Philosophy: An Encounter between Feminism and Postmodernism', in *Feminism/Postmodernism*, L Nicholson (ed) (1990); Clare Dalton, 'Where We Stand: Observations on the Situation of Feminist Legal Thought' (1989) 3 *Berkeley Women's LJ* 1; Audre Lorde, 'Age, Race, Class and Sex: Women Redefining Difference', in *Sister Outsider* (1984); Martha Minow, 'Beyond Universality' (1989) *U Chicago Legal F* 115; Elizabeth Spelman, *Inessential Woman: Problems of Exclusion in Feminist Thought* (1988).

131 See eg Angela Harris, 'Race and Essentialism in Feminist Theory (1990) 42 *Stanford LR* 581. (Extracted *infra*); D Rhode, 'The Woman's Point of View' (1988) 38 *Journal of Legal Education* 39. (Extracted *infra*); A Scales, *op cit*.

lesser status, and inter-personal care-giving responsibility infuse women's experiences and gender construction in patriarchal societies, even though these phenomena manifest themselves differently in different women's particularised lives. Yet, we can say meaningful things about women that respond to the concerns, needs and experiences of women from different economic classes, different races, different privileges and statuses. Women, with all our differences accounted for, can achieve a feminist solidarity for social and legal transformation. Gender difference theories, which investigate and work from these acknowledged commonalities among women, provide a rich vein (a motherlode) for us to tap in our reconstructive and transformative efforts.

Even though some feminist theories may be so advanced that they triumph over gender difference analysis, the historical and particularised context of the 1990s in which feminists are working for change are mirrored in the consequences and experiences of gender differences. In reflecting on feminism's contributions in the 1980s and envisioning its future for the 1990s and beyond, I want to share some of my thoughts about the continued usefulness of a theory sown in the field of gender differences. Whether we like it or not, gender is still (and historically has been) an organising concept in our society. We have no choice but to work and theorise for change from a position within a bi-polar gender system. We can challenge its dichotomised thinking and bi-polar substantive construction, but we cannot ignore its systemic, political, practical, and lived effects. Gender may not be a unified concept or separable experience, but it is a coherent, functional springboard for change. By combining what we gain from existing differences analyses with a dominance (or power) analysis and emphasising feminist methods, we can design a useful theoretical base for our next decade. I prefer to call this modification of gender difference theory by another name – feminist solidarity. My argument is that gender difference analysis can give birth to feminist solidarity. I offer these thoughts as part of an ongoing conversation.

This essay was particularly difficult for me to write, because it is part of a conversation with feminists and other progressive legal scholars about preferred strategies for social, legal, and political transformation. With trepidation, but conviction, I will explain reasons why I have concluded that we still ought to use the concept of gender difference to inform our theorising, and how some of the traits, values, and orientations that have been assigned to females through our gendered cultures are useful models for transformative arguments in law. Furthermore, I will make the more risky point that we cannot neuter the strategies and seek the transformative potential they offer by ignoring their source in women's acculturation and socialisation. Other theorists for whom I have enormous respect are highly critical of this approach and even argue that it is regressive or potentially conservative. Finding these labels attached to my theoretical understandings troubles me. I am devotedly committed to progressive ends and would be devastated if my arguments and efforts somehow undermined this struggle. But since I believe that this approach can make our feminist and progressive projects more accessible and effective, I am braving the publication of these arguments.

Overview of Gender Difference Theories

Gender difference theorists begin with the simple claim that there are behavioural, social, cultural, and psychological differences between men and women. Some argue that the differences are biologically based. Most argue that (rightly or wrongly) women and men are socialised, acculturated, or psychologically constructed differently from each other. I do not think any theorist argues that these differences hold true in every case, but all agree that gender differences are strongly linked to sex differences.

Working from this premise of difference, gender difference theorists identify the traits, characteristics, and orientations of gender construction and study how the gender woman is distinguishable from the gender man. These theorists often need to redescribe and name women's approaches and orientations, because if those characteristics had been defined at all, it was from a male observer's perspective and measured against a norm of male traits. Unlike some feminist theorists who want to eliminate gender differences once differences are redefined, difference theorists celebrate and learn from gender differences. In addition, many gender difference theorists privilege some or all of women's gender traits.

Traditional descriptions of gender difference theories end here, but I think it is unfair to assume that difference theorists are oblivious to the painful reality of gender power dynamics. Despite Professor Catharine MacKinnon's authoritative distinction between difference and dominance theories, I find that gender difference theories incorporate premises of gender dominance theory. They recognise that women have been denied political power and other significant kinds of social and inter-personal power. It is a chicken-and-egg problem whether gender differences precipitated power/treatment differences or power/treatment differences created gender differences. I maintain that this unresolvable causal problem is an incoherent enquiry in the first instance, because the phenomena are not neatly dichotomised, but inter-related and inter-active. Feminists ought not let our theory-building be immobilised by the muck of this causation quagmire. However it was that the domination of women got started, throughout our history and up to the present, women have lived in a society that treats us differently from men. Difference theorists claim that different treatment, roles, expectations, and experiences based on gender correlate with different modes of thinking, acting, inter-relating, and interpreting reality. These differences from men create issues of common concern and interest for women. Dominance theorists may even agree, but they part company on ways in which they understand and utilise these differences.

At a minimum, difference theorists clearly understand that privileging some speakers and stories (men's) excludes and marginalises others (women's). Because of those power dynamics, gender difference theories insist on uncovering the stories of people, particularly women, who traditionally have been excluded, subordinated and marginalised in the power structures of society. As difference theories have developed and as gender theorists have learned more about the structures of domination, feminists have come to understand that even people who have been excluded from power in important ways (for example, white, middle-class, heterosexual women) can unconsciously reproduce patterns of exclusion in their own theorising (by excluding women of colour, lower class and impoverished women, lesbians). This failing, to which difference theories admittedly originally fell prey, can be corrected, so that theorising can begin anew without giving up on gender difference theories entirely.

We can learn important things about the consequences of exclusion and the need for inclusion from the experience of being excluded. Women have multiple experiences of exclusion or oppression because of our sex/gender. Women's shared experiences of family and inter-personal responsibilities, of invisibility and marginality, of violence and harassment, of the limitations on our political power and public roles, and of our support systems and successes help shape a feminist solidarity. Part of feminist struggle is to name these experiences as political rather than personal.

Without a doubt, women of colour are excluded and oppressed in more complex and different ways from white women, just as poor women are oppressed and excluded in more dramatic ways than rich women. We cannot separate which parts of our oppression are gender-based and which parts are race or class-based. These dominating and oppressing forces interact synergistically. But, that does not mean that women of all races, classes, and identities cannot work together in feminist solidarity to end unjust discrimination against all women and all people. In the United States, for example, sexual difference remained a formal barrier to women's right to vote until 1920, long after formal barriers of race and property ownership had been eliminated for men. No woman – whether white or black, rich or poor, physically challenged or able-bodied, heterosexual or lesbian – was allowed to vote in federal elections. Although the Constitution was amended over a century ago in an attempt to provide equal rights and mark a formal end to race discrimination, an Equal Rights Amendment, designed to achieve a similar constitutional guarantee for women, has been repeatedly defeated. Discrimination against women because we are women continues. The Supreme Court has decided that legislatively enacted discriminations based on race are subject to the strictest scrutiny by the courts under the equal protection clause of the Fourteenth Amendment, but discriminations based on gender do not require as close attention. Furthermore, there is an underlying assumption that discriminations that disadvantage women based on their sex, as opposed to their race, may be justified on some occasions. For example, Title VII, a federally enacted equal employment law, permits sex-based discrimination in situations where sex is shown to be a bona fide occupational qualification, but contains no parallel exception for race-based discriminations. Women can work together to change these legal impediments to substantive equality for all women. Where necessary, we can treat gender separately without obscuring racial, economic, or other group struggles.

A jurisprudence that recognises gender differences seems basically correct to me, whether we like those differences or not, whether we permit courts to rely on them, or whether we believe we can change them once we figure out how they happen. My experiences, my observations of people, my intuitions, my feelings, and my studies lead me to believe that gender differences do exist. If they exist (and for as long as they do), our legal theories ought to take what we learn from gender differences analysis into consideration. Even though particularlised circumstances and other social-cultural constructs (such as race, class, and sexual orientation) may cause some women to understand themselves and their lives very differently from other women, females are still constructed as women, and as such we share something in the lived experiences of that gender construction. The gender construction of women has strong cultural meanings in patriarchies; it causes people to conceive of women as importantly different from – and often lesser than – men. As a function of being so constructed, women think and act differently from men, even men who are otherwise like us. Part of that difference has to do with power relations. Hence, at this juncture, difference theory is integrally related to – even inseparable from – dominance theory.

Finally, feminist difference theories understand gender differences as affecting or being affected by one's self-perception and one's perceptions about relationships. On this issue gender difference theories may diverge from dominance theories. Carol Gilligan suggests that many gender differences grow out of distinct conceptions of self and relations-to-others. Building on the work of Nancy

Chodorow,[132] she submits that women tend to understand people more relationally, as inter-connected and mutually dependent, whereas men tend to conceptualise people as more independent, autonomous, and ego-boundaried. According to Gilligan, these differing self-conceptions kindle gender-linked concepts of morality, human inter-personal relationships, and appropriate behaviours. Women's predominant focus for resolving ethical dilemmas is the maintenance of relationships and avoidance of hurt. This is achieved through a contextualised ethic of responsibility and care. Men focus more heavily on ordered hierarchies of principles of justice and rights (such as formal equality) to resolve moral problems. This standard stuff of Gilliganesque analysis, found in many law review articles that discuss her work, is a bit oversimplified and 'vulgarised,' but it touches on what is helpful for my argument about gender difference and legal change. Later in this essay I will explore the legal and socially transformative significance of the relational and care aspects of gender difference that Gilligan attributes, at least subtly, to women as a 'different voice' ...

... Now the question is, what to do with all of this? We could choose to follow the suggestions of gender difference theory critics and ignore gender differences, because they tend to replicate stereotypes that have been used to subordinate women. We could suppress gender differences, re-silence them, or pretend that they are not true, even if we suspect or know otherwise, in order to achieve political ends. In the alternative, we could acknowledge that gender differences exist today, but struggle not to reproduce them as gender differences in our children and their children. Or, as I prefer, we could work to use insights from and about gender cultures to improve the quality of our lives and law. If we believe that the voice of care and responsibility is an integral part of justice and being human, then we must reconstruct our legal analyses to include, value, and respond to needs for inter-personal care-giving. Women's gender cultures can be our guide.

Creating new theoretical and ethical paradigms that radiate from an appreciation of values and traits of caring, inter-personal responsibility, and co-operation, while failing to attribute them to women's cultures, devalues women's contributions once again. Law has excluded women and women's cultural differences for too long. Now that women have finally become active participants in the shaping of law, and now that legal theorists are challenging us to alter the structure of law in consideration of, or in conjunction with women's values, movements are afoot to sever these insights from their roots in women's gender cultures. Many of the transformative contributions that women have made and can make are at risk of being snatched from us. I hope that feminists will not allow fears that currently existing gender characteristics will be used as subordinating stereotypes to make us forego deserved recognition of the contributions our gender cultures will make to the enrichment of our legal system.

If stereotypes are going to be used against us, as they have been in the past, they will be so used regardless of what we say or do. Those who want to exercise their power by disadvantaging women based on stereotypes did so long before we celebrated women's cultures and will do so long after, no matter which strategy we select in our struggle for justice for women. Those who use disadvantaging stereotypes do not obtain their power by appropriating the language that we use to describe ourselves. Use of stereotypes to disadvantage groups is a matter of

132 Nancy Chodorow, *The Reproduction of Mothering* (1978).

pre-existing power, not the triumphant, persuasive or rhetorical force of alternative discourses. We ought not let others' temporary control of the dominant discourse disempower us from speaking honestly and openly about ourselves, about how we think and know, how we love and inter-relate, how we care or what we care about, how we understand justice, and how we can bring about a better life for all. Our political electivity comes from our willingness to speak our truths as we see them; not our fear of succumbing to other imposed stereotypes. If there are things about the gendered construction of women, things that have shaped our lived experiences, our relationships, and our views of the world, things that we consider good, valuable, and essential to peace, equality, and justice, then we should share them and require that they be used in reconstructing our laws. Yet, we should not be convinced to surrender them freely and without strings to the dominant powers, because they will call them 'human', discount women's contributions, and possibly distort them by partial and limited understandings. If the legal powers-that-be can decide that they know as much about 'humanism', 'care' and 'responsibility' as anyone, they can also decide that women's presence, perspectives, understandings, and experiences will not be needed to reconceptualise law with these values. We must be an integral part of this reconstruction, because our knowledges and perceptions, which we developed as gendered women, are critical to this transformative project.

Women have been students of care and care-giving, relationships and inter-personal responsibility, co-operation, and mutual dependence for a long time. Our apprenticeships give us special knowledge and insight. Careful study of women's ways of knowing and patterns of inter-relating can be illustrative for all of us in reformulating law. Women have more concrete experiences than men of integrating care and care-giving into the multiple, daily ways in which we function, work, play, and relate. We are more skillful at listening empathetically, at attending to context, and adapting appropriate 'rules' to the particularised circumstances. We tend to have better understandings of substantive equality, something that is desperately needed in law. Our gender-based perspectives and techniques must be used to shape legal culture and laws.

What does it mean to use a gendered ethic of care in law? Is it something that is already in the law in some form, as equity, as the exception, as part of 'the fundamental contradiction' of our dominant liberal legal discourse? I think not. I believe an ethic of care derived from women's cultures is a unique way to solve problems, work with people, locate truths, and foster justice that has been absent from our law.

There are so many questions to explore. Is an ethic of care just an aspect of personal morality conceived as justice, as Kohlberg has argued?[133] Does an ethic of care involve empathy,[134] compassion as sympathy, or compassion as co-feeling? Is an ethic of care a perspective that can or should inform legal processes? What difference would this difference make? Do we need rights, principles, and generalisable rules for predictability and stability? Will a care perspective lead to chaos or relativism? If not, how should we understand its application and differing results in varied situations? Furthermore, are these perspectives of care and justice in too much tension to be fruitfully combined? If

---

133 L Kohlberg, *The Psychology of Moral Development: Essays on Moral Development* (1984), pp 231–32.
134 Lynne Henderson, 'Legality and Empathy' (1987) 85 *Michigan LR* 1574.

people learn to focus on one orientation or the other, as Gilligan's studies indicate, can we ever integrate them in our thinking or in our law? How can law-makers, lawyers, judges, professors, and law students study, learn from, borrow from, and reconstitute law with a gender-based ethic of care and responsibility? Can we benefit from an ethic of care in law without limiting ourselves to either/or, dualistic thinking and dichotomous paradigms? Finally, are there only two dichotomous perspectives – care and justice – or are there multiple perspectives that intersect and combine in different ways at different times?

Gender difference theory provides a rich source for transforming law. Feminist legal theories ought to do more than expose our legal system's warts. We must supply new vocabularies, perspectives, paradigms, methodologies, and practices. Insights from difference theories about gender bias, marginality and exclusion, relationships and difference, co-operation, values of care, listening, responsibility, and solidarity can inform legal practice and jurisprudence to move us toward goals of democracy, justice, and true equality. For example, our statutory and common law legal system can develop new categories of civil law analysis (rather than criminal or regulatory law) that recognise and value relationships, inter-personal responsibility, and human needs for safety, health, education, and security, rather than its traditional focus on money and commodities.

Law can develop new methods of conflict resolution that are not premised on adversarial, competitive, win-or-lose models. An ethic of care and women's gender differences can teach us other, and perhaps better, ways to seek truth and understand justice. Law can redefine who counts as parties to controversies, reconsider what counts as relevant information, imagine new kinds of remedies to redress injuries, fulfill needs, and promote equality. Learning from feminist critiques, law can become more humble and self-critical. It can question its biases and exclusionary practices; and it can respond to what it learns by making concrete changes in perspectives, substance, and methods. Law can reformulate its understandings about power and privilege and restructure its role in eliminating hierarchy and domination. Feminist theories, and gender difference theories in particular, offer strategies and knowledges to guide this transformation of our legal system.

In my other writings I have tried to give concrete examples of how a gender-based ethic of care with its orientation toward inter-personal responsibility can be used right now to restructure important concepts in law, particularly tort law. It seems inappropriate to reproduce those arguments here, since they are otherwise available. Suffice it to say that feminist understandings of power, exclusion and alternative values derived from understandings of women's gender cultures can be used to improve our existing laws and legal practices, without compromising their simultaneous use for larger transformative efforts to shift the underlying paradigms of our legal system.

Conclusion

Gender difference and gender identity can be a starting point for feminist solidarity. Through feminist solidarity, we can transform law from its current design as a tool to preserve existing distributions of power, forms of knowledge, and hierarchies of values into a tool to empower and enable all people. Since women differ from one another by race, class, age, ethnicity, sexual preference, and physical challenges, our work to improve all women's lives will necessarily improve the lives of all people oppressed because of these identities. Our potentials for success in achieving justice are inextricably linked. Justice has been portrayed as a woman in our cultural myths for centuries. It is time we use women's gender cultures to guide the law in its quest for justice.

Carol Gilligan's work helps us understand some ways in which women's perspectives and approaches differ from men's. Relying on her insights, some feminist legal theorists have been able to show how women's differences have been left out of law. Three things have happened with Gilligan's work. First, her writings have been used as a shorthand for the idea of gender difference and the necessity to rethink the exclusionary practices that have generated existing disciplinary models. Second, they have served as a symbol of the validation of women's differences (and sometimes of their privileging, as in, 'care is better than justice' and 'relationships are better than rights'). Finally, the values of care and relational theories have provided important methodological precepts for rethinking disciplines and institutions generally, and law, in particular. I find all three moves engaging. Despite the potent and important critiques that have been wielded against Gilligan's work and gender difference theories, I have argued in this essay for the continued use of gender difference analysis as a stepping stone to feminist solidarity. A gender-based ethic of care, co-operation, and inter-personal responsibility; contextualised legal and substantive equality analyses; and feminist insights about diversity, power, privilege and exclusion are invaluable to our efforts to create a new legal regime.

Our social constructions and laws have not progressed far enough in their eradication of gender bias that we can abandon the category of gender. Maybe someday, but certainly not yet. Despite the fact that gender is not fixed, static, or 'essential,' we still need an analysis of gender to help illustrate our flaws and reconstruct our analyses. Gender is not a less valuable or transformative concept because it is fluid and subject to change under altering conditions and contexts. So long as gender power dynamics create women's cultures, gender matters for our analyses. In the 1990s, gender still matters in our social relations, and therefore must remain a central part of our dominant discourses and laws. When gender dynamics no longer teach us about power, knowledge, and values, and when gender analyses no longer offer an impetus for change, then and only then will gender be outmoded. I await the day, but I am not holding my breath. In the meantime, the law needs the transformative potential offered by gender difference analysis, and women need gender difference analysis to help build feminist solidarity. I can not refrain from acting and taking responsibility for needed changes in the law today, while waiting for us to successfully tear down the structures of gender domination. Ultimately, I believe that Gilligan's work helps us better understand gender differences and how we can improve law based on what we learn from women.

DIFFERENCE AND DOMINANCE: ON SEX DISCRIMINATION[135]
Catharine MacKinnon[136]

What is a gender question a question of? What is an inequality question a question of? These two questions underlie applications of the equality principle to issues of gender, but they are seldom explicitly asked. I think it speaks to the way gender has structured thought and perception that mainstream legal and moral theory tacitly gives the same answer to them both: these are questions of

---

135 *Feminism Unmodified* (Harvard University Press, 1987). (Footnotes edited).

136 Professor of Law, University of Michigan.

sameness and difference. The mainstream doctrine of the law of sex discrimination that results is, in my view, largely responsible for the fact that sex equality law has been so utterly ineffective at getting women what we need and are socially prevented from having on the basis of a condition of birth: a chance at productive lives of reasonable physical security, self-expression, individuation, and minimal respect and dignity. Here I expose the sameness/difference theory of sex equality, briefly show how it dominates sex discrimination law and policy and underlies its discontents, and propose an alternative that might do something.

According to the approach to sex equality that has dominated politics, law, and social perception, equality is an equivalence, not a distinction, and sex is a distinction. The legal mandate of equal treatment – which is both a systemic norm and a specific legal doctrine becomes a matter of treating likes alike and unlikes unlike; and the sexes are defined as such by their mutual unlikeness. Put another way, gender is socially constructed as difference epistemologically; sex discrimination law bounds gender equality by difference doctrinally. A built-in tension exists between this concept of equality, which presupposes sameness, and this concept of sex, which presupposes difference. Sex equality thus becomes a contradiction in terms, something of an oxymoron, which may suggest why we are having such a difficult time getting it.

Upon further scrutiny, two alternate paths to equality for women emerge within this dominant approach, paths that roughly follow the lines of this tension. The leading one is: be the same as men. This path is termed gender-neutrality doctrinally and the single standard philosophically. It is testimony to how substance gets itself up as form in law that this rule is considered formal equality. Because this approach mirrors the ideology of the social world, it is considered abstract, meaning transparent of substance; also for this reason it is considered not only to be the standard, but a standard at all. It is so far the leading rule that the words 'equal to' are codes for, equivalent to, the words 'the same as' referent for both unspecified.

To women who want equality yet find that you are different, the doctrine provides an alternate route: be different from men. This equal recognition of difference is termed the special benefit rule or special protection rule legally, the double standard philosophically. It is in rather bad odour. Like pregnancy, which always calls it up, it is something of a doctrinal embarrassment. Considered an exception to true equality and not really a rule of law at all, this is the one place where the law of sex discrimination admits it is recognising something substantive. Together with the Bona Fide Occupational Qualification (BFOQ), the unique physical characteristic exception under ERA policy, compensatory legislation, and sex-conscious relief in particular litigation, affirmative action is thought to live here.[137]

The philosophy underlying the difference approach is that sex is a difference, a division, a distinction, beneath which lies a stratum of human commonality, sameness. The moral thrust of the sameness branch of the doctrine is to make normative rules conform to this empirical reality by granting women access to what men have access to: to the extent that women are no different from men, we deserve what they have. The differences branch, which is generally seen as patronising but necessary to avoid absurdity, exists to value or compensate

---

137 See Barbara Brown, Thomas Emerson, Gail Falk and Ann Freedman, 'The Equal Rights Amendment: A Constitutional Basis for Equal Rights for Women' (1981) 80 *Yale Law Journal* 893.

women for what we are or have become distinctively as women (by which is meant, unlike men) under existing conditions.

My concern is not with which of these paths to sex equality is preferable in the long run or more appropriate to any particular issue, although most discourse on sex discrimination revolves about these questions as if that were all there is. My point is logically prior: to treat issues of sex equality as issues of sameness and difference is to take a particular approach. I call this the difference approach because it is obsessed with the sex difference. The main theme in the fugue is 'we're the same, we're the same, we're the same'. The counterpoint theme (in a higher register) is 'but we're different, but we're different, but we're different'. Its underlying story is: on the first day, difference was; on the second day, a division was created upon it; on the third day, irrational instances of dominance arose. Division may be rational or irrational. Dominance either seems or is justified. The difference is there is a politics to this. Concealed is the substantive way in which man has become the measure of all things. Under the sameness standard, women are measured according to our correspondence with man, our equality judged by our proximity to his measure. Under the difference standard, we are measured according to our lack of correspondence with him, our womanhood judged by our distance from his measure. Gender-neutrality is thus simply the male standard, and the special protection rule is simply the female standard, but do not be deceived: masculinity, or maleness, is the referent for both. Think about it like those anatomy models in medical school. A male body is the human body; all those extra things women have are studied in ob/gyn. It truly is a situation in which more is less. Approaching sex discrimination in this way – as if sex questions are difference questions and equality questions are sameness questions – provides two ways for the law to hold women to a male standard and call that sex equality.

Having been very hard on the difference answer to sex equality questions, I should say that it takes up a very important problem: how to get women access to everything we have been excluded from, while also valuing everything that women are or have been allowed to become or have developed as a consequence of our struggle either not to be excluded from most of life's pursuits or to be taken seriously under the terms that have been permitted to be our terms. It negotiates what we have managed in relation to men. Legally articulated as the need to conform normative standards to existing reality, the strongest doctrinal expression of its sameness idea would prohibit taking gender into account in any way.

Its guiding impulse is: we're as good as you. Anything you can do, we can do. Just get out of the way. I have to confess a sincere affection for this approach. It has gotten women some access to employment and education, the public pursuits, including academic, professional and blue-collar work; the military; and more than nominal access to athletics. It has moved to change the dead ends that were all we were seen as good for and has altered what passed for women's lack of physical training, which was really serious training in passivity and enforced weakness. It makes you want to cry sometimes to know that it has had to be a mission for many women just to be permitted to do the work of this society, to have the dignity of doing jobs a lot of other people don't even want to do.

The issue of including women in the military draft[138] has presented the sameness answer to the sex equality question in all its simple dignity and

138 *Rostker v Goldbert* (1981) 453 US 57. See also Lori Knornblum, 'Women Warrior in a Men's World: the Combat Exclusion' (1984) 2 *Law and Inequality: A Journal of Theory and Practice* 353.

complex equivocality. As a citizen, I should have to risk being killed just like you. The consequences of my resistance to this risk should count like yours. The undercurrent is: what's the matter, don't you want me to learn to kill ... just like you? Sometimes I see this as a dialogue between women in the afterlife. The feminist says to the soldier, 'we fought for your equality'. The soldier says to the feminist, 'oh, no, we fought for your equality'.

Feminists have this nasty habit of counting bodies and refusing not to notice their gender. As applied, the sameness standard has mostly gotten men the benefit of those few things women have historically had – for all the good they did us. Almost every sex discrimination case that has been won at the Supreme Court level has been brought by a man.[139] Under the rule of gender-neutrality, the law of custody and divorce has been transformed, giving men an equal chance at custody of children and at alimony. Men often look like better 'parents' under gender-neutral rules like level of income and presence of nuclear family, because men make more money and (as they say) initiate the building of family units.[140] In effect, they get preferred because society advantages them before they get into court, and law is prohibited from taking that preference into account because that would mean taking gender into account. The group realities that make women more in need of alimony are not permitted to matter, because only individual factors, gender-neutrally considered, may matter. So the fact that women will live their lives, as individuals, as members of the group women, with women's chances in a sex discriminatory society, may not count, or else it is sex discrimination. The equality principle in this guise mobilises the idea that the way to get things for women is to get them for men. Men have gotten them. Have women? We still have not got equal pay, or equal work, far less equal pay for equal work, and we are close to losing separate enclaves like women's schools through this approach.

Here is why. In reality, which this approach is not long on because it is liberal idealism talking to itself, virtually every quality that distinguishes men from women is already affirmatively compensated in this society. Men's physiology defines most sports, their needs define auto and health insurance coverage, their socially designed biographies define workplace expectations and successful career patterns, their perspectives and concerns define quality in scholarship, their experiences and obsessions define merit, their objectification of life defines art, their military service defines citizenship, their presence defines family, their inability to get along with each other – their wars and rulerships – defines history, their image defines god, and their genitals define sex. For each of their differences from women, what amounts to an affirmative action plan is in effect, otherwise known as the structure and values of American society. But whenever women are, by this standard, 'different' from men and insist on not having it held against us, whenever a difference is used to keep us second class and we refuse to smile about it, equality law has a paradigm trauma and it's crisis time for the doctrine.

What this doctrine has apparently meant by sex inequality is not what happens to us. The law of sex discrimination that has resulted seems to be looking only

---

139 David Cole, 'Strategies of Difference' (1984) 2 *Law and Inequality: A Journal of Theory and Practice* 33 at 34, note 4.

140 Leonore Weitzman, 'The Economic of Divorce: Social and Economic Consequences of Property, Alimony and Child Support Awards' (1982) 28 *UCLA Law Rev* 1118 at 1251, documents indicate a decline in women's standard of living of 73% and an increase of men's of 42% and within a year after divorce.

for those ways women are kept down that have not wrapped themselves up as a difference – whether original, imposed, or imagined. Start with original: what to do about the fact that women actually have an ability men still lack, gestating children in utero. Pregnancy therefore is a difference. Difference doctrine says it is sex discrimination to give women what we need, because only women need it. It is not sex discrimination not to give women what we need because then only women will not get what we need. Move into imposed: what to do about the fact that most women are segregated into low-paying jobs where there are no men. Suspecting that the structure of the marketplace will be entirely subverted if comparable worth is put into effect, difference doctrine says that because there is no man to set a standard from which women's treatment is a deviation, there is no sex discrimination here, only sex difference. Never mind that there is no man to compare with because no man would do that job if he had a choice, and of course he has because he is a man, so he won't.[141]

Now move into the so-called subtle reaches of the imposed category, the *de facto* area. Most jobs in fact require that the person, gender-neutral, who is qualified for them will be someone who is not the primary caretaker of a preschool child. Pointing out that this raises a concern of sex in a society in which women are expected to care for the children is taken as day one of taking gender into account in the structuring of jobs. To do that would violate the rule against not noticing situated differences based on gender, so it never emerges that day one of taking gender into account was the day the job was structured with the expectation that its occupant would have no child care responsibilities. Imaginary sex differences – such as between male and female applicants to administer estates or between males aging and dying and females aging and dying – I will concede, the doctrine can handle.

I will also concede that there are many differences between women and men. I mean, can you imagine elevating one half of a population and denigrating the other half and producing a population in which everyone is the same? What the sameness standard fails to notice is that men's differences from women are equal to women's differences from men. There is an *equality* there. Yet the sexes are not socially equal. The difference approach misses the fact that hierarchy of power produces real as well as fantasied differences, differences that are also inequalities. What is missing in the difference approach is what Aristotle missed in his empiricist notion that equality means treating likes alike and unlikes unlike, and nobody has questioned it since. Why should you have to be the same as a man to get what a man gets simply because he is one? Why does maleness provide an original entitlement, not questioned on the basis of *its* gender, so that it is women – women who want to make a case of unequal treatment in a world men have made in their image – (this is really the part Aristotle missed) – who have to show in effect that they are men in every relevant respect, unfortunately mistaken for women on the basis of an accident of birth?

The women that gender-neutrality benefits, and there are some, show the suppositions of this approach in highest relief. They are mostly women who have been able to construct a biography that somewhat approximates the male norm, at least on paper. They are the qualified, the least of sex discrimination's victims. When they are denied a man's chance, it looks the most like sex bias. The more unequal society gets, the fewer such women are permitted to exist. Therefore, the more unequal society gets, the *less* likely the difference doctrine is to be able to

141 Most women work at jobs mostly women do, and most of those jobs are paid less than jobs that mostly men do.

do anything about it, because unequal power creates both the appearance and the reality of sex differences along the same lines as it creates its sex inequalities.

The special benefits side of the difference approach has not compensated for the differential of being second class. The special benefits rule is the only place in mainstream equality doctrine where you get to identify as a woman and not have that mean giving up all claim to equal treatment – but it comes close. Under its double standard, women who stand to inherit something when their husbands die have gotten the exclusion of a small percentage of the inheritance tax, to the tune of Douglas J waxing eloquent about the difficulties of all women's economic situations.[142] If we're going to be stigmatised as different, it would be nice if the compensation would fit the disparity. Women have also gotten three more years than men get before we have to be advanced or kicked out of the military hierarchy, as compensation for being precluded from combat, the usual way to advance.[143] Women have also gotten excluded from contact jobs in male-only prisons because we might get raped, the court taking the viewpoint of the reasonable rapist on women's employment opportunities.[144] We also get protected out of jobs because of our fertility. The reason is that the job has health hazards, and somebody who might be a real person some day and therefore could sue – that is, a foetus – might be hurt if women, who apparently are not real persons and therefore can't sue either for the hazard to our health or for the lost employment opportunity, are given jobs that subject our bodies to possible harm.[145] Excluding women is always an option if equality feels in tension with the pursuit itself. They never seem to think of excluding men. Take combat. Somehow it takes the glory out of the foxhole, the buddiness out of the trenches, to imagine us out there. You get the feeling they might rather end the draft, they might even rather not fight wars at all than have to do it with us.

The double standard of these rules doesn't give women the dignity of the single standard; it also does not (as the differences standard does) suppress the gender of its referent, which is, of course, the female gender. I must also confess some affection for this standard. The work of Carol Gilligan on gender differences in moral reasonings[146] gives it a lot of dignity, more than it has ever had, more, frankly, than I thought it ever could have. But she achieves for moral reasoning what the special protection rule achieves in law: the affirmative rather than the negative valuation of that which has accurately distinguished women from men, by making it seem as though those attributes, with their consequences, really are somehow ours, rather than what male supremacy has attributed to us for its own use. For women to affirm difference, when difference means dominance, as it does with gender, means to affirm the qualities and characteristics of powerlessness.

Women have done good things, and it is a good thing to affirm them. I think quilts are art. I think women have a history. I think we create culture. I also know that we have not only been excluded from making what has been considered art;

---

142 *Kahn v Shevin* (1974) 416 US 351 at 353.

143 *Schlesinger v Balland* (1975) 419 US 498.

144 *Dothard v Rawlinson* (1977) 433 US 321; see also *Michael M v Sonoma County Superior Court* (1981) 450 US 464.

145 *Doerr v BF Goodrich* (1979) 484 F Supp 320 (ND Ohio); Wendy Webster Williams, 'Firing the Woman to Protect the Foetus: The Reconciliation of Foetal Protection with Employment Opportunity Goals Under Title VII' (1981) 69 *Georgetown LR* 641.

146 Carol Gilligan, *In a Different Voice* (1982).

our artefacts have been excluded from setting the standards by which art is art. Women have a history all right, but it is a history both of what was and of what was not allowed to be. So I am critical of affirming what we have been, which necessarily is what we have been permitted, as if it is women's, ours, possessive. As if equality, in spite of everything, already ineluctably exists.

I am getting hard on this and am about to get harder on it. I do not think that the way women reason morally is morality 'in a different voice'. I think it is morality in a higher register, in the feminine voice. Women value care because men have valued us according to the care we give them, and we could probably use some. Women think in relational terms because our existence is defined in relation to men. Further, when you are powerless, you don't just speak differently. A lot, you don't speak. Your speech is not just differently articulated, it is silenced. Eliminated, gone. You aren't just deprived of a language with which to articulate your distinctiveness, although you are; you are deprived of a life out of which articulation might come. Not being heard is not just a function of lack of recognition, not just that no one knows how to listen to you, although it is that; it is also silence of the deep kind, the silence of being prevented from having anything to say. Sometimes it is permanent. All I am saying is that the damage of sexism is real, and reifying that into differences is an insult to our possibilities.

So long as these issues are framed this way, demands for equality will always appear to be asking to have it both ways: the same when we are the same, different when we are different. But this is the way men have it: equal and different too. They have it the same as women when they are the same and want it, and different from women when they are different and want to be, which usually they do. Equal and different too would only be parity. But under male supremacy, while being told we get it both ways, both the specialness of the pedestal and an even chance at the race, the ability to be a woman and a person, too, few women get much benefit of either.

There is an alternative approach, one that threads its way through existing law and expresses, I think, the reason equality law exists in the first place. It provides a second answer, a dissident answer in law and philosophy, to both the equality question and the gender question. In this approach, an equality question is a question of the distribution of power. Gender is also a question of power, specifically of male supremacy and female subordination. The question of equality, from the standpoint of what it is going to take to get it, is at root a question of hierarchy, which – as power succeeds in constructing social perception and social reality – derivatively becomes a categorical distinction, a difference. Here, on the first day that matters, dominance was achieved, probably by force. By the second day, division along the same lines had to be relatively firmly in place. On the third day, if not sooner, differences were demarcated, together with social systems to exaggerate them in perception and in fact, because the systematically differential delivery of benefits and deprivations required making no mistake about who was who. Comparatively speaking, man has been resting ever since. Gender might not even code as difference, might not mean distinction epistemologically, were it not for its consequences for social power.

I call this the dominance approach, and it is the ground I have been standing on in criticising mainstream law. The goal of this dissident approach is not to make legal categories trace and trap the way things are. It is not to make rules that fit reality. It is critical of reality. Its task is not to formulate abstract standards that will produce determinate outcomes in particular cases. Its project is more substantive, more jurisprudential than formulaic, which is why it is difficult for the mainstream discourse to dignify it as an approach to doctrine or to imagine it as a rule of law at all. It proposes to expose that which women have had little choice but to be confined to, in order to change it.

The dominance approach centers on the most sex-differential abuses of women as a gender, abuses that sex equality law in its difference garb could not confront. It is based on a reality about which little of a systematic nature was known before 1970, a reality that calls for a new conception of the problem of sex inequality. This new information includes not only the extent and intractability of sex segregation into poverty, which has been known before, but the range of issues termed violence against women, which has not been. It combines women's material desperation, through being relegated to categories of jobs that pay nil, with the massive amount of rape and attempted rape – 44% of all women – about which virtually nothing is done;[147] the sexual assault of children – 38% of girls and 10% of boys – which is apparently endemic to the patriarchal family;[148] the battery of women that is systematic in one-quarter to one-third of our homes;[149] prostitution, women's fundamental economic condition, what we do when all else fails,[150] and for many women in this country, all else fails often; and pornography, an industry that traffics in female flesh, making sex inequality into sex to the tune of eight billion dollars a year in profits largely to organised crime.

These experiences have been silenced out of the difference definition of sex equality largely because they happen almost exclusively to women. Understand: for this reason, they are considered not to raise sex equality issues. Because this treatment is done almost uniquely to women, it is implicitly treated as a difference, the sex difference, when in fact it is the socially situated subjection of women. The whole point of women's social relegation – to inferiority as a gender – is that for the most part these things aren't done to men. Men are not paid half of what women are paid for doing the same work on the basis of their equal difference. Everything they touch does not turn valueless because they touched it. When they are hit, a person has been assaulted. When they are sexually violated, it is not simply tolerated or found entertaining or defended as the necessary structure of the family, the price of civilisation, or a constitutional right.

Does this differential describe the sex difference? Maybe so. It does describe the systematic relegation of an entire group of people to a condition of inferiority and attribute it to their nature. If this differential were biological, maybe biological intervention would have to be considered. If it were evolutionary, perhaps men would have to evolve differently. Because I think it is political, I think its politics construct the deep structure of society. Men who do not rape women have nothing wrong with their hormones. Men who are made sick by pornography and do not eroticise their revulsion are not underevolved. This social status in which we can be used and abused and trivialised and humiliated and bought and sold and passed around and patted on the head and put in place

---

147 Diana Russell and Nancy Howell, 'The Prevalence of Rape in the United States Revisited' (1983) 8 *Signs: Journal of Women in Culture and Society* 689.

148 Dianna Russell, 'The Incidence and Prevalence of Intrafamilial and Extrafamilial Sexual Abuse of Female Children' (1983) 7 *Child Abuse and Neglect: the International Journal* 133.

149 E Emerson Dobash and Russell Dobash, *Violence Against Wives: A Case Against the Patriarchy* (1979).

150 Kathleen Barry, *Female Sexual Slavery* (1979); Moira Griffin, 'Wives, Hookers and the Law: the Case for Decriminalising Prostitution' (1982) 10 *Student Lawyer* 18.

and told to smile so that we look as though we're enjoying it all is not what some of us have in mind as sex equality.

This second approach – which is not abstract, which is at odds with socially imposed reality and therefore does not look like a standard according to the standard for standards – became the implicit model for racial justice applied by the courts during the 1960s. It has since eroded with the erosion of judicial commitment to racial equality. It was based on the realisation that the condition of blacks in particular was not fundamentally a matter of rational or irrational differentiation on the basis of race but was fundamentally a matter of white supremacy, under which racial differences became invidious as a consequence.[151] To consider gender in this way, observe again that men are as different from women as women are from men, but socially the sexes are not equally powerful. To be on the top of a hierarchy is certainly different from being on the bottom, but that is an obfuscatingly neutralised way of putting it, as a hierarchy is a great deal more than that. If gender were merely a question of difference, sex inequality would be a problem of mere sexism, of mistaken differentiation, of inaccurate categorisation of individuals. This is what the difference approach thinks it is and is therefore sensitive to. But if gender is an inequality first, constructed as a socially relevant differentiation in order to keep that inequality in place, then sex inequality questions are questions of systematic dominance, of male supremacy, which is not at all abstract and is anything but a mistake.

If differentiation into classifications, in itself, is discrimination, as it is in difference doctrine, the use of law to change group-based social inequalities becomes problematic, even contradictory. This is because the group whose situation is to be changed must necessarily be legally identified and delineated, yet to do so is considered in fundamental tension with the guarantee against legally sanctioned inequality. If differentiation is discrimination, affirmative action, and any legal change in social inequality, is discrimination, but the existing social differentiations which constitute the inequality are not? This is only to say that, in the view that equates differentiation with discrimination, changing an unequal *status quo* is discrimination, but allowing it to exist is not.

Looking at the difference approach and the dominance approach from each other's point of view clarifies some otherwise confusing tensions in sex equality debates. From the point of view of the dominance approach, it becomes clear that the difference approach adopts the point of view of male supremacy on the status of the sexes. Simply by treating the *status quo* as 'the standard' it invisibly and uncritically accepts the arrangements under male supremacy. In this sense, the difference approach is masculinist, although it can be expressed in a female voice. The dominance approach, in that it sees the inequalities of the social world from the standpoint of the subordination of women to men, is feminist.

If you look through the lens of the difference approach at the world as the dominance approach imagines it – that is, if you try to see real inequality through a lens that has difficulty seeing an inequality as an inequality if it also appears as a difference – you see demands for change in the distribution of power as demands for special protection. This is because the only tools that the difference paradigm offers to comprehend disparity equate the recognition of a gender line with an admission of lack of entitlement to equality under law. Since equality

151 *Loving v Virginia* (1967) 388 US 1, first used the term 'white supremacy' in invalidating an anti-miscegenation law as a violation of equal protection. The law equally forbade whites and blacks to inter-marry.

questions are primarily confronted in this approach as matters of empirical fit[152] – that is, as matters of accurately shaping legal rules (implicitly modeled on the standard men set) to the way the world is (also implicitly modeled on the standard men set) – any existing differences must be negated to merit equal treatment. For ethnicity as well as for gender, it is basic to mainstream discrimination doctrine to preclude any true diversity among equals or true equality within diversity.

To the difference approach, it further follows that any attempt to change the way the world actually is looks like a moral question requiring a separate judgment of how things ought to be. This approach imagines asking the following disinterested question that can be answered neutrally as to groups: against the weight of empirical difference, should we treat some as the equals of others, even when they may not be entitled to it because they are not up to standard? Because this construction of the problem is part of what the dominance approach unmasks, it does not arise with the dominance approach, which therefore does not see its own foundations as moral. If sex inequalities are approached as matters of imposed status, which are in need of change if a legal mandate of equality means anything at all, the question whether women should be treated unequally means simply whether women should be treated as less. When it is exposed as a naked power question, there is no separable question of what ought to be. The only real question is what is and is not a gender question. Once no amount of difference justifies treating women as subhuman, eliminating that is what equality law is for.

In this shift of paradigms, equality propositions become no longer propositions of good and evil, but of power and powerlessness, no more disinterested in their origins or neutral in their arrival at conclusions than are the problems they address.

There came a time in black people's movement for equality in this country when slavery stopped being a question of how it could be justified and became a question of how it could be ended. Racial disparities surely existed, or racism would have been harmless, but at that point – a point not yet reached for issues of sex – no amount of group difference mattered anymore. This is the same point at which a groups characteristics, including empirical attributes, become constitutive of the fully human, rather than being defined as exceptions to or as distinct from the fully human. To one-sidedly measure one group's differences against a standard set by the other incarnates partial standards. The moment when one's particular qualities become part of the standard by which humanity is measured is a millenial moment.

To summarise the argument: seeing sex equality questions as matters of reasonable or unreasonable classification is part of the way male dominance is expressed in law. If you follow my shift in perspective from gender as difference to gender as dominance, gender changes from a distinction that is presumptively valid to a detriment that is presumptively suspect. The difference approach tries to map reality; the dominance approach tries to challenge and change it. In the dominance approach, sex discrimination stops being a question of morality and starts being a question of politics.

You can tell if sameness is your standard for equality if my critique of hierarchy looks like a request for special protection in disguise. It's not. It envisions a

---

152 J Tussman and J TenBroek first used the term 'fit' to characterise the necessary relation between a valued equality rule and the world to which it refers: 'The Equal Protection of the Laws' (1949) 37 *California L Rev* 341.

change that would make possible a simple equal chance for the first time. To define the reality of sex as difference and the warrant of equality as sameness is wrong on both counts. Sex, in nature, is not a bipolarity; it is a continuum. In society it is made into a bipolarity. Once this is done, to require that one be the same as those who set the standard – those which one is already socially defined as different from – simply means that sex equality is conceptually designed never to be achieved. Those who most need equal treatment will be the least similar, socially, to those whose situation sets the standard as against which one's entitlement to be equally treated is measured. Doctrinally speaking, the deepest problems of sex inequality will not find women 'similarly situated'[153] to men. Far less will practices of sex inequality require that acts be intentionally discriminatory.[154] All that is required is that the *status quo* be maintained. As a strategy for maintaining social power first structure reality unequally, then require that entitlement to alter it be grounded on a lack of distinction in situation; first structure perception so that different equals inferior, then require that discrimination be activated by evil minds who know they are treating equals as less.

I say, give women equal power in social life. Let what we say matter, then we will discourse on questions of morality. Take your foot off our necks, then we will hear in what tongue women speak. So long as sex equality is limited by sex difference, whether you like it or don't like it, whether you value it or seek to negate it, whether you stake it out as a ground for feminism or occupy it as the terrain of misogyny, women will be born, degraded, and die. We would settle for that equal protection of the laws under which one would be born, live, and die, in a country where protection is not a dirty word and equality is not a special privilege.

SEXUAL DIFFERENCE, THE FEMININE, AND EQUIVALENCY: A CRITIQUE OF MACKINNON'S TOWARD A FEMINIST THEORY OF THE STATE[155]

Drucilla Cornell[156]

Introduction

Catharine MacKinnon's *Toward a Feminist Theory of the State* is a provocative challenge to both conceptions of liberal jurisprudence and to the traditional Marxist critique of liberalism. Each stands accused of erasing the centrality of gender, sex, and sexuality in the development of a modern legal system. This erasure, MacKinnon believes, can only perpetuate injustice at its base through

---

153 *Royster Guano Co v Virginia* (1920) 253 US 412 at 415: 'A classification must be reasonable, not arbitrary, and must rest upon some ground of difference having a fair and substantial relation to the object of the legislation, so that all persons similarly circumstanced shall be treated alike.' *Reed v Reed* (1971) 404 US 71 at 76: 'Regardless of their sex, persons within any one of the enumerated classes ... are similarly situated ... By providing dissimilar treatment for men and women who are thus similarly situations, the challenged section violates the Equal Protection Clause.'

154 *Washington v Davis* (1976) 426 US 229 and *Personnel Administrator of Massachusetts v Feeney* (1979) 442 US 229 require that intentional discrimination be shown for discrimination to be shown.

155 (1990) 100 *Yale Law Journal* at 2247–75.

156 At the time of writing, Professor of Law, Benjamin Cardozo School of Law, Yeshiva University.

the pretence that equality has already been achieved – as in the case of her version of liberalism reduce it to a category of class domination which makes gender a secondary form of subordination as in the case of her interpretation of Marxism. Before turning to my critique of MacKinnon, I want to pay her the tribute she clearly deserves for her relentless insistence that any theory of equality for women will fall short of its own aspirations if it neglects the question of how sexual identity, and more specifically femininity, is constructed through a gender hierarchy in which women are subordinated and subjected. I share her insistence that we cannot begin to conceptualise a theory of equality that truly envisions the end of female domination without confronting the relationship between sex and sexuality as these have become constitutive of the gender identity imposed upon women by patriarchy. Her contribution has not been merely to criticise existing theories, she has been a proponent of specific doctrinal changes and played a key role, for example, in justifying the recognition of sexual harassment as a matter of sex discrimination and gender inequality.[157] This is one of many examples of how her understanding of the constitutive role of sexuality in the creation and perpetuation of male dominance has led to advocacy for legal and doctrinal reform.

My critique of MacKinnon, however, is that ultimately she does not fully develop her programme, which attempts to justify positive intervention by the State into current social arrangements of gender hierarchy and identity. I will argue that she cannot successfully develop her own feminist theory of the State because she is unable to affirm feminine sexual difference as other than victimisation. Of course, we need a programme that legally delegitimates the gender hierarchy and exposes the seriousness of sexual abuse. But we also need a more expansive, positive programme, for the reduction of feminine sexual difference to victimisation ultimately cannot sustain a feminist theory of the State. I propose a programme which recognises and incorporates equivalent rights.[158] Such a programme would be irreducible to an intermediary set of privileges like affirmative action – as important as these steps may be – and would go beyond addressing inequality in the name of making it possible for women to be more like men.

I do not deny the horror and the reality of the story MacKinnon tells us about the extent to which sexual abuse perpetuated against women gets taken as the way of the world, but I do want to argue against the reduction of woman to the figure of the victim. The result of this reduction is not only that MacKinnon cannot develop a useful programme of reform, but that she cannot account for the very feminist point of view that she argues must be incorporated if we are to reach for a State in which equality between the sexes would be more than mere pretense for the perpetuation of masculine privilege and female subordination.

Equivalent rights, although meant to challenge gender hierarchy, do not do so by erasing sexual difference. Further, equivalent rights should not be understood as only a means to the end of sexual difference. Instead, a programme of equivalent rights seeks to value the specificity of feminine sexual difference. MacKinnon cannot take us beyond a 'negative' programme without the affirmation of the

---

157 See CA MacKinnon, *Sexual Harassment and the Working Women: A Case of Working Women* (1984); see also *Meritor Savings Band FSB v Vinson* (1986) 477 US 57 (argued by Catharine MacKinnon).

158 See Drucilla Cornell, 'Sex Discrimination Law and Equivalent Rights' published as *Gender, Sex and Equivalent Rights* in *Feminists Theorise the Political* (eds J Butler and J Scott, 1991).

feminine difference which is irreducible to the current patriarchal trappings of her own understanding of femininity.

Crucial to my disagreement with MacKinnon is her reading of women's sexuality as constituted only by and for men and, therefore, as contrary to women's freedom from the chains of an imposed femininity, a femininity which constitutes 'our' sex and that can only justify women's domination. Thus, even if I agree with her that rape, battery, sexual abuse, and pornography must be seen not only as questions of criminal law but as barriers to the equality of women where the law has the ideological capacity to reinforce the devaluation of the feminine 'sex', I disagree with her structural analysis of feminine sexual difference and of feminine sexuality. As I already have indicated, it is not simply that MacKinnon's analysis cannot sustain a positive programme for intervention on the part of the State into gender arrangements. MacKinnon's own stance toward the feminine reflects the very 'sexual shame' of women's 'sex' that keeps the feminine from being valued and, more specifically, legally affirmed in a programme of equivalent rights. My criticism of the division she creates between freedom and sexuality assumes a conception of the self as a being of the flesh, in which sexual expression cannot be easily separated from freedom. For women, the concept of freedom cannot be separated from the struggle against the devalorisation of the feminine. Consciousness-raising, essential to fostering the dream of women's freedom, involves more than the exposure of the 'truth' of our victimisation. It demands the refiguration of what has been constituted 'to be' within patriarchy. It also demands that we think through the conditions of women's equality of well-being and capability in light of the recognition and value of feminine sexual differences.

Simply put, I will argue that women's sexuality cannot be reduced to women's 'sex', as sex has been currently defined, once we understand both the limit to institutionalised meaning and the possibility of remetaphorisation which inheres in the rule of metaphor.[159] MacKinnon's understanding of feminine sexuality accepts what Irigaray has called the 'old dream of symmetry'.[160] Irigaray uses the concept of symmetry to explain the masculine fantasy that our sexuality is symmetrical to that of men. In other words, what men fantasise women want is what they want us to want. In fact, women's sexuality is irreducible to the fantasy that we are only 'fuckees'. MacKinnon's reduction of feminine sexuality to being a 'fuckee' endorses this fantasy as 'truth' and thereby promotes the prohibition against the exploration of women's sexuality and 'sex' as we live it and not as men fantasise about it.

Men, defined by MacKinnon as sexual beings, may imagine that what they think women want, what they want women to desire, is what women desire. However, feminine writing on feminine sexuality has recognised the 'old dream of symmetry' as just that: a dream and, more specifically, a masculine dream. I want to emphasise the political and personal significance for women of challenging MacKinnon's view of feminine sexuality. The possibility of celebrating women's 'sex' and sexuality can keep us from the tragic disjuncture between sex, sexuality, and freedom that MacKinnon's analysis leads us to.

---

159 See Drucilla Cornell, 'Institutionalisation of Meaning, Recollective Imagination and the Potential for Transformative Legal Interpretation' (1988) 136 *University of Pennsylvania Law Review* 1135.

160 See Luce Irigaray, *Speculum of the Other Women*, pp 11–129, trans G Gill (1985).

In terms of a theory of equality, her critique cannot meet its own aspiration to legitimate and recognise the feminine point of view in law in the name of equality and not by appeal to special privilege. Her analysis cannot achieve this if it denies the equivalent value of the two sexes. Equivalent rights do not repeat the 'separate but equal' argument, but challenge the idea that sexual difference can or should be eradicated through the pretence that the human race is currently constituted as sex-neutral, or as if man is the equivalent of human. The view of equality I rely on to justify my understanding is Amartya Sen's equality of capability and well-being. As Sen reminds us, '[c]apability reflects a person's freedom to choose between different ways of living.[161] Sen's view of equality is valuable to feminists precisely because it allows for a 'positive' programme to guarantee women's equality of well-being and capability. Capability of well-being implies the affirmation of sex and sexuality and in the case of women more specifically, of living without shame of our sex.

The Social Construction of Women's Sexuality

Let me begin with MacKinnon's analysis of the social construction of femininity as an expression of male dominance and, more specifically, of male sexual desire. To MacKinnon: 'Male dominance is sexual. Meaning: men in particular, if not men alone, sexualise hierarchy; gender is one. As much a sexual theory of gender as a gendered theory of sex, this is the theory of sexuality that has grown out of consciousness raising.' Thus, for MacKinnon, inequality is sexual, and sexuality and the engagement in 'sex' perpetuates that inequality. An analysis of inequality that does not focus on inequality as a sexual dynamic in which male domination reduces women to their sex will ultimately 'limit' feminism to correcting sex bias by acting in theory as if male power did not exist in fact. It will 'limit' feminist theory the way sexism limits women's lives: to a response to terms men set. As a result, MacKinnon argues:

> A distinctively feminist theory conceptualises social reality, including sexual reality, on its own terms. The question is, what are they? If women have been substantially deprived not only of their own experience but of terms of their own in which to view it, then a feminist theory of sexuality which seeks to understand women's situation in order to change it must first identify and criticise the construct 'sexuality' as a construct that has circumscribed and defined experience as well as theory. This requires capturing it in the world, in its situated social meanings, as it is being constructed in life on a daily basis.[162]

The study of the construct of sexuality is, for MacKinnon, the examination of how women come to have a 'sex'. Women are, very simply put, defined as women because 'we get fucked'.

> First sexual intercourse is a commonly definitive experience of gender definition. For many women, it is a rape. It may occur in the family, instigated by a father or older brother who decided to 'make a lady out of my sister'. Women's sex gender initiation may be abrupt and anomic: 'When she was 15 she had an affair with a painter. He fucked her and she became a woman.' Simone de Beauvoir implied a similar point when she said: 'It is at her first abortion that a woman begins to 'know'. What women learn in order to 'have sex', in order to 'become women' – women as gender – comes

161 Amartya Sen, 'Inequality Reexamined: Capability and Well-Being' (unpublished).
162 *Toward a Feminist Theory of the State*, p 129.

through the experience of, and is a condition for, 'having sex' – woman as sexual object for man, the use of women's sexuality by men. Indeed, to the extent sexuality is social, women's sexuality is its use, just as femaleness is its alterity.'[163]

Femininity is the sex imposed on us by a world of male power in which men seek the fulfilment of their desire through us. Feminine gender identity is this imposed sexuality, reinforced in all gendered social arrangements and through the State, which reflects male sexual desire and legitimates sexual dominance as the rule of law. The challenge then to femininity as imposed sexuality as the subjection of our 'selves' to our 'sex,' is feminism, and ultimately this forms the basis of the feminist theory of the State.

> In feminist terms, the fact that male power has power means that the interests of male sexuality construct what sexuality as such means, including the standard way it is allowed and recognised to be felt and expressed and experienced, in a way that determines women's biographies, including sexual ones. Existing theories, until they grasp this, will not only misattribute what they call female sexuality to women as such, as if it were not imposed on women daily; they will also participate in enforcing hegemony of the social construct 'desire', hence its product sexuality, hence its construct 'woman', on the world.
>
> The gender issue, in this analysis, becomes the issue of what is taken to be 'sexuality'; what sex means and what is meant by sex, when, how, with whom, and with what consequences to whom.[164]

'Sex' difference is the consequence of this imposed sexuality. To celebrate women's difference is a form of 'false consciousness,' because women's so-called difference is only women's lives as 'fuckees,' and the affirmation of difference is only an excuse for reducing women to those who 'get fucked' in whatever way men want to do it to us. This reduction of women to 'fuckees' is what MacKinnon means when she argues that our social reality is fundamentally pornographic.

We can now begin to understand why, according to MacKinnon, pornography is absolutely central to the way in which the State enforces the male viewpoint and particularly the male vision of woman as sexual object. The representation of having men forced down women's throats is not just men's masturbatory fantasy but the truth of women's reality. 'Deep Throat', in other words, gives us a depiction of what we are forced to becomes under our current system of gender domination. This is why MacKinnon can say in all seriousness that we are all Linda Lovelace, with oral sex being the essence of women's subordination.

Yet this reality of subordination is not only ignored by the State, it is protected as a matter of right – the right of free speech under the First Amendment. Pornography, for MacKinnon, is not a matter of speech at all, but a matter of the systematic silencing of women. The image of men being shoved down women's throats is the very symbol of shutting us up.

> Thus the question Freud never asked is the question that defines sexuality in a feminist perspective: what do men want? Pornography provides an answer. Pornography permits men to have whatever they want sexually. It is their 'truth about sex'. It connects the centrality of visual objectification to both

---

163 *Toward a Feminist Theory of the State*, p 111.

164 See CA MacKinnon, *Feminism Unmodified* (Harvard University Press, 1987), pp 127, 129.

male sexual arousal and male models of knowledge and verification, objectivity with objectification. It shows how men see the world, how in seeing it they access and possess it, and how this is an act of dominance over it. It shows what men want and gives it to them. From the testimony of the pornography, what men want is: women bound, women battered, women tortured, women humiliated women degraded and defiled, women killed. Or, to be fair to the soft core, women sexually accessible, haveable, there for them, wanting to be taken and used, with perhaps just a little light bondage. Each violation of women – rape, battery, prostitution, child sexual abuse, sexual harassment – is male sexuality, made sexy, fun, and liberating of women's true nature in the pornography.[165]

That pornography is seen as the 'right to speak' is another sign of the way in which the State and the law simply reflect the male point of view and the right of men to subordinate women to their sexual desires. As MacKinnon explains:

> The State is male in the feminist sense: the law sees and treats women the way men see and treat women. The liberal State coercively and authoritatively constitutes the social order in the interest of men as a gender – through its legitimating norms, forms, relation to society, and substantive policies. The State's formal norms recapitulate the male point of view on the level of design.

The feminist point of view, on the other hand, is impossible, because, according to MacKinnon, the male 'point of view' enforces itself as true and as the totality of a pornographic social reality. As MacKinnon tells us:

> Feminism criticises this male totality without an account of women's capacity to do so or to imagine or realise a more whole truth. Feminism affirms women's point of view, in large part, by revealing, criticising, and explaining its impossibility. This is not a dialectical paradox. It is a methodological expression of women's situation, in which a struggle for consciousness is a struggle for world: for a sexuality, a history, a culture, a community, a form of power, an experience of the sacred.

For MacKinnon, the impossibility of a woman's point of view is constantly reinforced by the State, which reflects the male point of view as the rule of law and which erases what it has done in the name of neutrality. The rule of law is then transformed into ideology, further enforcing the male viewpoint not just as perspective but as the definitive interpretation of the Constitution.

Conclusion

If MacKinnon ultimately repudiates the feminine, she perpetuates rather than challenges the gender hierarchy which lies at the base of women's inequality. If the feminist point of view is to be incorporated into the State, we must have an account of its possibility. I have argued that such an account is possible once we correctly understand the role of deconstruction and, beyond this, the place of remetaphorisation and refiguration of the feminine in reinventing and thus affirming, sexual difference. This affirmation allows us to identify the wrongs to women within a context of sexual shame imposed upon women by gender hierarchy. It also allows us to challenge the idea that the human species is only one genre and therefore that the 'rights of man' give us a full conception of rights. To argue for equivalence is not to advocate special privilege once we value sexual difference as necessary for women's equality of capability and well-

---

165 *Toward a Feminist Theory of the State*, p 138.

being, and recognise sexuality itself as necessary for a creature of the flesh to enjoy a full life.

JURISPRUDENCE AND GENDER[166]
Robin West[167]

Introduction

What is a human being? Legal theorists must, perforce, answer this question: Jurisprudence, after all, is about human beings. The task has not proven to be divisive. In fact, virtually all modern American legal theorists, like most modern moral and political philosophers, either explicitly or implicitly embrace what I will call the 'separation thesis' about what it means to be a human being: A 'human being,' whatever else he is, is physically separate from all other human beings. I am one human being and you are another, and that distinction between you and me is central to the meaning of the phrase human being. Individuals are, in the words of one commentator, 'distinct and not essentially connected with one another'.[168] We are each physically 'boundaried' – this is the trivially true meaning of the claim that we are all individuals. In Robert Nozick's telling phrase, 'the 'root idea' of any acceptable moral or political philosophy is that 'there are individuals with separate lives'.[169] Although Nozick goes on to derive from this insight an argument for the minimal state, the separation thesis is hardly confined to the libertarian right. According to Roberto Unger, premiere spokesperson for the communitarian left, 'to be conscious is to have the experience of being cut off from that about which one reflects: it is to be a subject that stands over against its objects ... The subjective awareness of separation ... defines consciousness'.[170] The political philosopher Michael Sandel has recently argued that most (not all) modern political theory is committed to the proposition that 'what separates us is in some important sense prior to what connects us – epistemologically prior as well as morally prior. We are distinct individuals first, and then we form relationships and engage in co-operative arrangements with others; hence the priority of plurality over unity'.[171] The same commitment underlies virtually all of our legal theory. Indeed, Sandel's formulation may be taken as a definitive restatement of the 'separation thesis' that underlies modern jurisprudence.

The first purpose of this essay is to put forward the global and critical claim that by virtue of their shared embrace of the separation thesis, all of our modern legal theory – by which I mean 'liberal legalism' and 'critical legal theory' collectively – is essentially and irretrievably masculine. My use of 'I' above was inauthentic, just as the modern, increasing use of the female pronoun in liberal and critical legal theory, although well intended is empirically and experientially false. For the cluster of claims that jointly constitute the 'separation thesis' – the claim that human beings are, definitionally, distinct from one another, the claim that the referent of 'I' is singular and unambiguous, the claim that the word individual

---

166 (1988) 55 *University of Chicago Law Review*, 1. (Article abridged and footnotes edited.)

167 Professor of Law, University of Maryland.

168 Naomi Scheman, 'Individualism and the Objects of Psychology', in Sandra Harding and Merrill B Hintikka (eds) *Discovering Reality* (1983).

169 R Nozick, *Anarchy, State and Utopia* (1974), p 33.

170 RM Unger, *Knowledge About Politics* (1975), p 200.

171 M Sandel, *Liberalism and the Limits of Justice* (1982).

has an uncontested biological meaning, namely, that we are each physically individuated from every other, the claim that we are individuals 'first,' and the claim that what separates us is epistemologically and morally prior to what connects us – while 'trivially true' of men, are patently untrue of women ...

Masculine Jurisprudence and Feminist Theory

The by now very well publicised split in masculine jurisprudence between legal liberalism and critical legal theory[172] can be described in any number of ways. The now standard way to describe the split is in terms of politics: 'liberal legal theorists' align themselves with a liberal political philosophy which entails, among other things, allegiance to the Rule of Law and to Rule of Law virtues, while 'critical legal theorists,' typically left wing and radical, are sceptical of the Rule of Law and the split between law and politics which the Rule of Law purportedly delineates. Critical legal theorists are potentially far more sensitive to the political underpinnings of purportedly neutral legalistic constructs than are liberal legalists. I think this traditional characterisation is wrong for a number of reasons: liberal theorists are not necessarily politically naive, and critical theorists are not necessarily radical. However, my purpose is not to critique it. Instead, I want to suggest another way to understand the divisions in modern legal theory.

An alternative description of the difference (surely not the only one) is that liberal legal theory and critical legal theory provide two radically divergent phenomenological descriptions of the paradigmatically male experience of the inevitability of separation of the self from the rest of the species, and indeed from the rest of the natural world. Both schools, as we shall see, accept the separation thesis; they both view human beings as materially (or physically) separate from each other, and both view this fact as fundamental to the origin of law. But their accounts of the subjective experience of physical separation from the other – an individual other, the natural world, and society – are in nearly diametrical opposition. Liberal legalists, in short, describe an inner life enlivened by freedom and autonomy from the separate other and threatened by the danger of annihilation by him. Critical legal theorists, by contrast, tell a story of inner lives dominated by feelings of alienation and isolation from the separate other and enlivened by the possibility of association and community with him. These differing accounts of the subjective experience of being separate from others, I believe, are at the root of at least some of the divisions between critical and liberal legal theorists. I want to review each of these experiential descriptions of separation in some detail, for I will ultimately argue that they are not as contradictory as they first appear. Each story, I will suggest, constitutes a legitimate and true part of the total subjective experience of masculinity.

I will start with the liberal description of separation, because it is the most familiar and surely the most dominant. According to liberal legalism, the inevitability of the individual's material separation from the 'other' entails, first and foremost, an existential state of highly desirable and much valued freedom: Because the individual is separate from the other, he is free of the other. Because I am separate from you, my ends, my life, my path, my goals are necessarily my own. Because I am separate, I am 'autonomous.' Because I am separate, I am existentially free (whether or not I am politically free). And, of course, this is true not just of me, but of everyone: It is the universal human condition. We are each

---

172 On which see Chapter 8.

separate and we are all separate, so we are each free and we are all free. We are, that is, equally free.

This existential condition of freedom in turn entails the liberal's conception of value. Because we are all free and we are each equally free, we should be treated by our government as free and as equally free. The individual must be treated by his government and by others in a way that respects his equality and his freedom. The government must honour at the level of politics the existential claim made above: that my ends are my ends; that I cannot be forced to embrace your ends as my own. Our separation entails our freedom which in turn entails our right to establish and pursue our own concept of value, independent of the concept of value pursued or favoured by others. Ronald Dworkin puts the point in this way:

> What does it mean for the government to treat its citizens as equals? That is ... the same question as the question of what it means for the government to treat all its citizens as free, or as independent, or with equal dignity ... [To accord with this demand, a government must] be neutral on what might be called the question of the good life ... [P]olitical decisions must be, so far as is possible, independent of any particular conception of the good life, or of what gives value to life. Since the citizens of a society differ in their conceptions, the government does not treat them as equals if it prefers one conception to another, either because the officials believe that one is intrinsically superior, or because one is held by the more numerous or more powerful group.[173]

Because of the dominance of liberalism in this culture, we might think of autonomy as the 'official' liberal value entailed by the physical, material condition of inevitable separation from the other: separation from the other entails my freedom from him, and that in turn entails my political right to autonomy. I can form my own conception of the good life and pursue it. Indeed, any conception of the good which I form, will necessarily be my conception of the good life. That freedom must be respected. Because I am free, I value and have a right to autonomy. You must value it as well. The state must protect it. This in turn implies other (more contested) values, the most important of which is (or may be) equality. Dworkin continues:

> I now define a liberal as someone who holds ... [a] liberal ... theory of what equality requires. Suppose that a liberal is asked to found a new state. He is required to dictate its constitution and fundamental institutions. He must propose a general theory of political distribution ... He will arrive initially at something like this principal of rough equality: resources and opportunities should he distributed, so far as possible, equally, so that roughly the same share of whatever is available is devoted to satisfying the ambitions of each. Any other general aim of distribution will assume either that the fate of some people should be of greater concern than that of others, or that the ambitions or talents of some are more worthy, and should be supported more generously on that account.[174]

Autonomy, freedom, and equality collectively constitute what might be called the 'up side' of the subjective experience of separation. Autonomy and freedom are both entailed by the separation thesis, and autonomy and freedom both feel very good. However, there's a 'down side' to the subjective experience of

---

173 R Dworkin, *A Matter of Principle* (1985), p 191.

174 *Ibid*, pp 192–93.

separation as well. Physical separation from the other entails not just my freedom; it also entails my vulnerability. Every other discrete, separate individual – because he is the 'other' – is a source of danger to me and a threat to my autonomy. I have reason to fear you solely by virtue of the fact that I am me and you are you. You are not me, so by definition my ends are not your ends. Our ends might conflict. You might try to frustrate my pursuit of my ends. In an extreme case, you might even try to kill me – you might cause my annihilation.

Annihilation by the other, we might say, is the official harm of liberal theory, just as autonomy is its official value. Hobbes, of course, gave the classic statement of the terrifying vulnerability that stems from our separateness from the other:

> there bee found one man sometimes manifestly stronger in body, or of quicker mind then [sic] another; yet when all is reckoned together, the difference between man, and man, is not so considerable, as that one man can thereupon claim to himself any benefit, to which another may not pretend, as well as he. For as to the strength of body, the weakest has strength enough to kill the strongest, either by secret machination, or by confederacy with others, that are in the same danger with himself ... From this equality of ability, ariseth equality of hope in the attaining of our Ends. And therefore if any two men desire the same thing, which neverthelesse they cannot both enjoy, they become enemies; and in the way to their End (which is principally their owne conservation ...) endeavour to destroy, or subdue one an other. And from hence it comes to passe, that where an Invader hath no more to feare, than another mans single power; if one plant, sow, build, or possesse a convenient Seat, others may probably be expected to come prepared with forces united, to dispossesse, and deprive him, not only of the fruit of his labour, but also of his life, or liberty. And the Invader again is in the like danger of another.[175]

Thus, according to liberal legalism, the subjective experience of physical separation from the other determines both what we value (autonomy) and what we fear (annihilation). We value and seek societal protection of our autonomy: The liberal insists on my right to define and pursue my own life, my own path, my own identity, and my own conception of the good life free of interference from others. Because I am me and you are you, I value what I value, and you value what you value. The only value we truly share, then, is our joint investment in autonomy from each other: We both value our right to pursue our lives relatively free of outside control. We can jointly insist that our government grant us this protection. We also share the same fears. I fear the possibility – indeed the likelihood – that our ends will conflict, and you will frustrate my ends and in an extreme case cause my annihilation, and you fear the same thing about me. I want the right and the power to pursue my own chosen ends free of the fear that the you will try to prevent me from doing so. You, of course, want the same.

We can call this liberal legalist phenomenological narrative the 'official story' of the subjectivity of separation. According to the official story, we value the freedom that our separateness entails, while we seek to minimise the threat that it poses. We do so, of course, through creating and then respecting the state. Whether or not Robert Nozick is right that the minimal state achieves the liberal's ideal, he has nevertheless stated that liberal ideal well in the following passage:

---

175 Thomas Hobbes, *Leviathan* (1651) CB Macpherson ed (1968), pp 183–84.

The minimal state treats us as inviolate individuals; it treats us as persons having individual rights with the dignity this constitutes. [This treatment] allows us, individually or with whom we choose, to choose our life and to realise our ends and our conception of ourselves, insofar as we can, aided by the voluntary co-operation of other individuals possessing the same dignity. How dare any state or group of individuals do more. Or less [There is no *social entity* with a good that undergoes some sacrifice for its own good. There are only individual people, different individual people, with their own individual lives. Using one of these people for the benefit of the others, uses him and benefits others. Nothing more.[176]

Now, critical legal theory diverges from liberal legalism on many points, but one striking contrast is this: critical theorists provide a starkly divergent phenomenological description of the subjective experience of separation. According to our critical legal theorists, the separate individual is indeed, in Sandel's phrase, 'epistemologically prior to the collective'. Like liberal legalists, critical legal theorists also view the individual as materially separate from the rest of human life. But according to the critical theorist, what that material state of separation existentially entails is not a perpetual celebration of autonomy but, rather, a perpetual longing for community, or attachment, or unification, or connection. The separate individual strives to connect with the 'other' from whom he is separate. The separate individual lives in a state of perpetual dread not of annihilation by the other, but of the alienation, loneliness, and existential isolation that his material separation from the other imposes upon him. The individual strives through love, work, and government to achieve a unification with the other, the natural world, and the society from which he was originally and continues to be existentially separated. The separate individual seeks community – not autonomy – and dreads isolation and alienation from the other – not annihilation by him. If we think of liberalism's depiction of the subjectivity of separation as the official story, then, we might think of this alternative description of the subjectivity of separation as the unofficial story. It is the subterranean, unofficial story of the unrecognised and – at least by liberals – slightly detested subjective craving of lost individuals.

Thus, there is a vast gap, according to critical theory, between the 'official value' of liberal legalism – autonomy – and what the individual truly subjectively desires, which is to establish a true connection with the other. Similarly, there is a vast gap between the 'official harm' of liberal legalism – annihilation by the other – and what the individual truly subjectively dreads, which is not annihilation by him, but isolation and alienation from him. According to the critical theorist, while the dominant liberal culture insists we value autonomy and fear the other, what the individual truly desires, craves, and longs to establish is some sort of connection with the other, and what the individual truly dreads is alienation from him.[177]

Indeed, the individual longs to re-establish connection with the other in spite of the very real possibility (acknowledged by most if not all critical theorists) that that other might, at any moment, frustrate his ends, threaten his autonomy, or annihilate him. But this longing for community survives in the face of an even more powerful source of resistance. The longing for attachment to the other

---

176 R Nozick, *Anarchy, State and Utopia, op cit*, pp 333–34; 32–33.
177 R Unger, *Knowledge and Politics* (1975), p 201.

persists in spite of the dominant liberal culture's adamant denial of the desire's existence.[178]

In another sense, though, the longing for connection persists not so much 'in spite of the dominant culture's valuation of autonomy but because of that value. The value we place on autonomy, according to some critical legal theorists, aggravates our alienation, isolation and loneliness.[179]

The longing for connection with the other, and the dread of alienation from him, according to the critical theorists, is in a state of constant 'contradiction' with the official value and official harm that flow from separation – autonomy from the other and annihilation by him. Nevertheless, in spite of that tension, both the dread of alienation and the desire for connection are constantly there. The dominant culture insists we value autonomy from the other and fear annihilation by him, but subjectively, the individual lives with a more or less unrealised desire to connect with the other, and a constant dread or fear, of becoming permanently alienated, isolated – lost – from the other.

To summarise: According to liberal legalism, each of us is physically separate from every other, and because of that separation, we value our autonomy from the other and fear our annihilation by him. I have called these our officially recognised values and harms. Critical legal theory tells the unofficial story. According to critical legal theory, we are indeed physically separate from the other, but what that existentially entails is that we dread the alienation and isolation from the separate other and long for connection with him. While liberal culture officially and publicly claims that we love our autonomy and fear the other, subjective life belies this claim. Subjectively and in spite of the dominant culture's insistence to the contrary, we long to establish some sort of human connection with the other in order to overcome the pain of isolation and alienation which our separateness engenders.

Let me now turn to feminist theory. Although the legal academy is for the most part unaware of it, modern feminist theory is as fundamentally divided as legal theory. One way to characterise the conflict – the increasingly standard way to characterise the conflict – is that while most modern feminists agree that women are different from men and agree on the importance of the difference, feminists differ over which differences between men and women are most vital. According to one group of feminists, sometimes called cultural feminists, the important difference between men and women is that women raise children and men don't. According to a second group of feminists, now called radical feminists, the important difference between men and women is that women get fucked and men fuck: 'Women,' definitionally, are 'those from whom sex is taken,' just as workers, definitionally, are those from whom labour is taken. Another way to put the difference is in political terms. Cultural feminists appear somewhat more 'moderate' when compared with the traditional culture: From a mainstream nonfeminist perspective, cultural feminists appear to celebrate many of the same feminine traits that the traditional culture has stereotypically celebrated. Radical feminists, again from a mainstream perspective, appear more separatist and, in contrast with standard political debate, more alarming. They also appear to be more 'political' in a sense which perfectly parallels the critical theory – liberal

178 Peter Gabel, 'The Phenomenology of Rights-Consciousness and the Pact of the Withdrawn Selves' (1984) 62 *Texas L Rev* 1563, 1566–67.

179 Duncan Kennedy, 'Form and Substance in Private Law Adjudication' (1976) 89 *Harvard L Rev* 1685, 1774.

theory split described above: Radical feminists appear to be more attuned to power disparities between men and women than are cultural feminists.

I think this traditional characterisation is wrong on two counts. First, cultural feminists no less than radical feminists are well aware of women's powerlessness *vis-à-vis* men, and second, radical feminism, as I will later argue, is as centrally concerned with pregnancy as it is with intercourse. But again, instead of arguing against this traditional characterisation of the divide between radical and cultural feminism, I want to provide an alternative. My alternative characterisation structurally (although not substantively) parallels the characterisation of the difference between liberal and critical legalism. Underlying both radical and cultural feminism is a conception of women's existential state that is grounded in women's potential for physical, material connection to human life, just as underlying both liberal and critical legalism is a conception of men's existential state that is grounded in the inevitability of men's physical separation from the species. I will call the shared conception of women's existential lives the connection thesis. The divisions between radical and cultural feminism stem from divergent accounts of the subjectivity of the potential for connection, just as what divides liberal from critical legal theory are divergent accounts of the subjectivity of the inevitability of separation.

The connection thesis is simply this: Women are actually or potentially materially connected to other human life. Men aren't. This material fact has existential consequences. While it may be true for men that the individual is 'epistemologically and morally prior to the collectivity,' it is not true for women. The potential for material connection with the other defines women's subjective, phenomenological, and existential state, just as surely as the inevitability of material separation from the other defines men's existential state. Our potential for material connection engenders pleasures and pains, values and dangers, and attractions and fears, which are entirely different from those which follow, for men, from the necessity of separation. Indeed, it is the rediscovery of the multitude of implications from this material difference between men and women which has enlivened (and divided) both cultural and radical feminism in this decade (and it is those discoveries which have distinguished both radical and cultural feminism from liberal feminism). As Carol Gilligan notes, this development is somewhat paradoxical: During the same decade that liberal feminist political activists and lawyers pressed for equal (meaning same) treatment by the law, feminist theorists in nonlegal disciplines rediscovered women's differences from men.[180] Thus, what unifies radical and cultural feminist theory (and what distinguishes both from liberal feminism) is the discovery, or rediscovery, of the importance of women's fundamental material difference from men. As we shall see, neither radical feminists nor cultural feminists are entirely explicit in their embrace of the connection thesis. But both groups, implicitly if not explicitly, adhere to some version of it.

If both cultural and radical feminists hold some version of the connection thesis, then one way of understanding the issues that divide radical and cultural feminists, different from the standard account given above, is that while radical and cultural feminists agree that women's lives are distinctive in their potential for material connection to others, they provide sharply contrasting accounts of the subjective experience of the material and existential state of connection. According to cultural feminist accounts of women's subjectivity, women value

---

180 Carol Gilligan, *In a Different Voice* (1982), pp 6–8.

intimacy, develop a capacity for nurturance, and an ethic of care for the 'other' with which we are connected, just as we learn to dread and fear separation from the other. Radical feminists tell a very different story. According to radical feminism, women's connection with the 'other' is above all else invasive and intrusive: Women's potential for material 'connection' invites invasion into the physical integrity of our bodies, and intrusion into the existential integrity of our lives. Although women may 'officially' value the intimacy of connection, we 'unofficially' dread the intrusion it inevitably entails and long for the individuation and independence that deliverance from that state of connection would permit. Paralleling the structure above, I will call these two descriptions feminism's official and unofficial stories of women's subjective experience of physical connection ...

... We might summarise cultural feminism in this way: Women's potential for a material connection to life entails (either directly, as I have argued, or indirectly, through the reproduction of mothering) an experiential and psychological sense of connection with other human life, which in turn entails both women's concept of value, and women's concept of harm. Women's concept of value revolves not around the axis of autonomy, individuality, justice, and rights, as does men's but, instead, around the axis of intimacy, nurturance, community, responsibility, and care. For women, the creation of value and the living of a good life therefore depend upon relational, contextual, nurturant, and affective responses to the needs of those who are dependent and weak, while for men the creation of value and the living of the good life depend upon the ability to respect the rights of independent coequals, and the deductive, cognitive ability to infer from those rights rules for safe living. Women's concept of harm revolves not around a fear of annihilation by the other but around a fear of separation and isolation from the human community on which she depends and which is dependent upon her. If, as I have suggested, cultural feminism is our dominant feminist dogma, then this account of the nature of women's lives constitutes the official text of feminism, just as liberal legalism constitutes the official text of legalism.

These two official stories sharply contrast. Whereas according to liberal legalism, men value autonomy from the other and fear annihilation by him, women, according to cultural feminism, value intimacy with the other and fear separation from her. Women's sense of connection with others determines our special competencies and special vulnerabilities, just as men's sense of separation from others determines theirs. Women value and have a special competency for intimacy, nurturance, and relational thinking and a special vulnerability to and fear of isolation, separation from the other, and abandonment, just as men value and have a special competency for autonomy and a special vulnerability to and fear of annihilation.

Against the cultural feminist backdrop, the story that radical feminists tell of women's invaded, violated lives is 'subterranean' in the same sense that against the backdrop of liberal legalism, the story critical legal theorists tell of men's alienation and isolation from others is subterranean. According to radical feminism, women's connection to others is the source of women's misery, not a source of value worth celebrating. For cultural feminists, women's connectedness to the other (whether material or cultural) is the source, the heart, the root, and the cause of women's different morality, different voice, different 'ways of knowing,' different genius, different capacity for care, and different ability to nurture. For radical feminists, that same potential for connection – experienced materially in intercourse and pregnancy but experienced existentially in all spheres of life is the source of women's debasement, powerlessness, subjugation, and misery. It is the cause of our pain and the reason for our stunted lives. Invasion and intrusion, rather than intimacy, nurturance, and care, is the 'unofficial' story of women's subjective experience of connection.

Thus, modern radical feminism is unified among other things by its insistence on the invasive, oppressive, destructive implications of women's material and existential connection to the other. So defined, radical feminism (of modern times) begins not with the 1980s critique of heterosexuality but, rather, in the late 1960s with Shulamith Firestone's angry and eloquent denunciation of the oppressive consequences for women of the physical condition of pregnancy. Firestone's assessment of the importance and distinctiveness of women's reproductive role parallels Marilyn French's.[181] Both women view women's physical connection with nature and with the other as in some sense the 'cause' of patriarchy. But their analyses of the chain of causation sharply contrast. For French, women's reproductive role – the paradigmatic experience of physical connection to nature, to life, and to the other and thus the core of women's moral difference – is also the cause of patriarchy, primarily because of men's fear of and contempt for nature. Firestone has a radically different view. Pregnancy is indeed the paradigmatic experience of physical connection, and it is indeed the core of women's difference, but according to Firestone, it is for that reason alone the cause of women's oppression. Male contempt has nothing (at first) to do with it. Pregnancy itself, independent of male contempt, is invasive, dangerous and oppressive; it is an assault on the physical integrity and privacy of the body. For Firestone, the strategic implication of this is both clear and clearly material. The technological separation of reproduction from the female body is the necessary condition for women's liberation.[182]

In a moment, I will turn to heterosexual intercourse, for it is intercourse, rather than pregnancy, which consumes the attention of the modern radical feminism of our decade. But before doing so it's worth recognising that the original radical feminist case for reproductive freedom did not turn on rights of 'privacy' (either of the doctor-patient relationship, or of the marriage, or of the family), or rights to 'equal protection,' or rights to be free of 'discrimination.' It did not turn on rights at all. Rather, the original feminist argument for reproductive freedom turned on the definitive radical feminist insight that pregnancy – the invasion of the body by the other to which women are distinctively vulnerable – is an injury and ought to be treated as such. Pregnancy connects us with life, as the cultural feminist insists, but that connection is not something to celebrate; it is that very connection that hurts us. This argument, as I will argue later, is radically incommensurate with liberal legal ideology. There's no legal category that fits it. But it is nevertheless the radical argument – that pregnancy is a dangerous, psychically consuming, existentially intrusive, and physically invasive assault upon the body which in turn leads to a dangerous, consuming, intrusive, invasive assault on the mother's self-identity – that best captures women's own sense of the injury and danger of pregnancy, whether or not it captures the law's sense of what an unwanted pregnancy involves or why women should have the right to terminate it.

The radical feminist argument for reproductive freedom appears in legal argument only inadvertently or surreptitiously, but it does on occasion appear. It appeared most recently in the phenomenological descriptions of unwanted

---

181 M French, *Beyond Power* (1985).

182 Shulamith Firestone, *The Dialectic of Sex* (1970).

pregnancies collated in the *Thornburgh amicus brief* recently filed by the National Abortion Rights Action League (NARAL). The descriptions of pregnancy collated in that peculiarly nonlegal legal document are filled with metaphors of invasion – metaphors, of course, because we lack the vocabulary to name these harms precisely. Those descriptions contrast sharply with the 'joy' that cultural feminists celebrate in pregnancy, childbirth, and child raising. The invasion of the self by the other emerges as a source of oppression, not a source of moral value.

'During my pregnancy,' one women explains, 'I was treated like a baby machine – an incubator without feelings. 'Then I got pregnant again', another woman writes:

> This one would be only 13 months younger than the third child. I was faced with the unpleasant fact that I could not stop the babies from coming no matter what I did ....

Almost exactly a decade ago,' writes another, 'I learned I was pregnant .... I was sick in my heart and I thought I would kill myself. It was as if I had been told my body had been invaded with cancer. It seemed that very wrong.'

One woman speaks directly, without metaphor: 'On the ride home from the clinic, the relief was enormous. I felt happy for the first time in weeks. I had a future again. I had my body back.'

According to these women's self-descriptions, when the unwanted baby arrives, the injury is again one of invasion, intrusion, and limitation. The harm of an unwanted pregnancy is that the baby will elicit a surrender (not an end) of the mother's life. The fear of unwanted pregnancy is that one will lose control of one's individuated being (not that one will die). Thus, one woman writes, 'I was like any other woman who had an unintended pregnancy, I was terrified and felt as though my life was out of my control.'

This danger, and the fear of it, is gender specific. It is a fear which grips women, distinctively, and it is a fear about which men, apparently, know practically nothing. Another woman writes:

> I was furiously angry, dismayed, dismal, by turns. I could not justify an abortion on economic grounds, on grounds of insufficient competence or on any other of a multitude of what might be perceived as 'legitimate' reasons. But I kept being struck by the ultimate unfairness of it all. I could not conceive of any event which would so profoundly impact upon any man. Surely my husband would experience some additional financial burden, and additional 'fatherly' chores, but his whole future plan was not hostage to this unchosen, undesired event. Basically his life would remain the same progression of ordered events as before.

Conversely, women who had abortions felt able to form their own destiny. One woman wrote: 'Personally legal abortion allowed me the choice as a teenager living on a very poor Indian Reservation to finish growing up and make something of my life.' And another:

> I was not glad that I was faced with an unwanted, unplanned pregnancy, however I am glad that I made the decision to have an abortion. The experience was a very positive one for me. It helped me learn that I am a person and I can make independent decisions. Had I not had the abortion I would have probably ended up a single mother struggling for survival and dealing with a child that I was not ready for.

As noted above, radical feminism of the 1980s has focused more on intercourse than on pregnancy. But this may represent less of a divergence than it first appears. From the point of view of the connection thesis, what the radical feminists of the 1980s find objectionable, invasive, and oppressive about heterosexual intercourse, is precisely what the radical feminists of the 1960s found objectionable, invasive, and oppressive about pregnancy and motherhood. According to the 1980s radical critique, intercourse, like pregnancy, blurs the physical boundary between self and other, and that blurring of boundaries between self and other constitutes a profound invasion of the self's physical integrity. That invasion – the 'dissolving of boundaries' – is something to condemn, not celebrate. Andrea Dworkin explains:

> A human being has a body that is inviolate; and when it is violated, it is abused. A woman has a body that is penetrated in intercourse: permeable, its corporeal solidness a lie. The discourse of male truth – literature, science, philosophy, pornography – calls that penetration violation. This it does with some consistency and some confidence. Violation is a synonym for intercourse. At the same time, the penetration is taken to be a use, not an abuse; a normal use; it is appropriate to enter her, to push into ('violate') the boundaries of her body. She is human, of course, but by a standard that does not include physical privacy. She is, in fact, human by a standard that precludes physical privacy, since to keep a man out altogether and for a lifetime is deviant in the extreme, a psychopathology, a repudiation of the way in which she is expected to manifest her humanity.[183]

Although Dworkin herself does not draw the parallel, for both Dworkin and Firestone, women's potential for material connection with the other – whether through intercourse or pregnancy – constitutes an invasion upon our physical bodies, an intrusion upon our lives, and consequently an assault upon our existential freedom, whether or not it is also the root of our moral distinctiveness (the claim cultural feminism makes on behalf of pregnancy) or the hope of our liberation (the claim sexual liberationists make on behalf of sex). Both intercourse and pregnancy are literal, physical, material invasions and occupations of the body. The foetus, like the penis, literally occupies my body. In their extremes, of course, both unwanted heterosexual intercourse and unwanted pregnancy can be life threatening experiences of physical invasion. An unwanted foetus, no less than an unwanted penis, invades my body, violates my physical boundaries, occupies my body, and can potentially destroy my sense of self. Although the culture does not recognise them as such, the physical and existential invasions occasioned by unwanted pregnancy and intercourse are real harms. They are events we should fear. They are events which any sane person should protect herself against. What unifies the radical feminism of the 1960s and 1980s is the argument that women's potential for material, physical connection with the other constitutes an invasion which is a very real harm causing very real damage and which society ought to recognise as such.

The material, sporadic violation of a woman's body occasioned by pregnancy and intercourse implies an existential and pervasive violation of her privacy, integrity, and life projects. According to radical feminists, women's longings for individuation, physical privacy, and independence go well beyond the desire to avoid the dangers of rape or unwanted pregnancy. Women also long for

---

183 Andrea Dworkin, *Intercourse*, pp 141–42.

liberation from the oppression of intimacy (and its attendant values) which both cultural feminism and most women officially, and wrongly, overvalue. Intimacy, in short, is intrusive, even when it isn't life threatening (perhaps especially when it isn't life threatening). An unwanted pregnancy is disastrous, but even a wanted pregnancy and motherhood are intrusive. The child intrudes, just as the foetus invades.

Similarly, while unwanted heterosexual intercourse is disastrous, even wanted heterosexual intercourse is intrusive. The penis occupies the body and 'divides the woman' internally, to use Andrea Dworkin's language, in consensual intercourse no less than in rape. It pre-empts, challenges, negates, and renders impossible the maintenance of physical integrity and the formation of a unified self. The deepest unofficial story of radical feminism may be that intimacy – the official value of cultural feminism – is itself oppressive. Women secretly, unofficially, and surreptitiously long for the very individuation that cultural feminism insists women fear: the freedom, the independence, the individuality, the sense of wholeness, the confidence, the self-esteem, and the security of identity which can only come from a life, a history, a path, a voice, a sexuality, a womb, and a body of one's own. Dworkin explains:

> In the experience of intercourse, she loses the capacity for integrity because her body – the basis of privacy and freedom in the material world for all human beings – is entered and occupied; the boundaries of her physical body are – neutrally speaking – violated. What is taken from her in that act is not recoverable, and she spends her life – wanting, after all to have something – pretending that pleasure is in being reduced through intercourse to insignificance ... She learns to eroticise powerlessness and self-annihilation. The very boundaries of her own body become meaningless to her, and even worse, useless to her. The transgression of those boundaries comes to signify a sexually charged degradation into which she throws herself, having been told, convinced, that identity, for a female, is there – somewhere beyond privacy and self-respect.

Radical feminism, then, is unified by a particular description of the subjectivity of the material state of connection. According to that description, women dread intrusion and invasion and long for an independent, individualised, separate identity. While women may indeed 'officially' value intimacy, what women unofficially crave is physical privacy, physical integrity, and sexual celibacy – in a word, physical exclusivity. In the moral realm, women officially value contextual, relational, caring, moral thinking but secretly wish that everyone would get the hell out of our lives so that we could pursue our own projects – we loathe the intrusion that intimacy entails. In the epistemological and moral realms, while women officially value community, the web, the spinning wheel, and the weave, we privately crave solitude, self-regard, self-esteem, linear thinking, legal rights, and principled thought.

Finally, then, we can schematise the contrast between the description of the human being that emerges from modern legal theory and the description of women that emerges from modern feminism.

	Value	Harm		Longing	Dread
			The Official Story (Liberal legalism and cultural feminism)	The Unofficial Story (Critical legalism and radical feminism)	
Legal Theory (Human beings)	Autonomy	Annihilation; frustration		Attachment; connection	Alienation
Feminist Theory (Women)	Intimacy	Separation		Individuation	Invasion; Intrusion

As the diagram reveals, the descriptions of the subjectivity of human existence told by feminist theory and legal theory contrast at every point. First, and most obviously, the 'official' descriptions of human beings' subjectivity and women's subjectivity contrast rather than compare. According to liberal theory, human beings respond aggressively to their natural state of relative physical equality. In response to the great dangers posed by their natural aggression, they abide by a sharply anti-naturalist morality of autonomy, rights, and individual spheres of freedom, which is intended to and to some extent does curb their natural aggression. They respect a civil state that enforces those rights against the most egregious breaches, the description of women's subjectivity told by cultural feminism is much the opposite. According to cultural feminism, women inhabit a realm of natural inequality; they are physically stronger than the foetus and the infant. Women respond to their natural inequality over the foetus and infant not with aggression but with nurturance and care. That natural and nurturant response evolves into a naturalist moral ethic of care which is consistent with women's natural response. The substantive moralities consequent to these two stories, then, unsurprisingly, are also diametrically opposed. The autonomy that human beings value and the rights they need as a restriction on their natural hostility to the equal and separate other are in sharp contrast to the intimacy that women value, and the ethic of care that represents not a limitation upon, but an extension of, women's natural nurturant response to the dependent, connected other ...

Feminist jurisprudence

By the claim that modern jurisprudence is 'masculine,' I mean two things. First, I mean that the values, the dangers, and what I have called the fundamental contradiction that characterise women's lives are not reflected at any level whatsoever in contracts, torts, constitutional law, or any other field of legal doctrine. The values that flow from women's material potential for physical connection are not recognised as values by the Rule of Law, and the dangers attendant to that state are not recognised as dangers by the Rule of Law.

First, the Rule of Law does not value intimacy – its official value is autonomy. The material consequence of this theoretical undervaluation of women's values in the material world is that women are economically impoverished. The value women place on intimacy reflects our existential and material circumstance; women will act on that value whether it is compensated or not. But it is not. Nurturant, intimate labour is neither valued by liberal legalism nor compensated by the market economy. It is not compensated in the home, and it is not compensated in the workplace – wherever intimacy is, there is no compensation.

Similarly, separation of the individual from his or her family, community, or children is not understood to be a harm, and we are not protected against it. The Rule of Law generally and legal doctrine in its particularity are coherent reactions to the existential dilemma that follows from the liberal's description of the male experience of material separation from the other: The Rule of Law acknowledges the danger of annihilation, and the Rule of Law protects the value of autonomy. Just as assuredly, the Rule of Law is not a coherent reaction to the existential dilemma that follows from the material state of being connected to others, and the values and dangers attendant to that condition. It neither recognises nor values intimacy and neither recognises nor protects against separation.

Nor does the Rule of Law recognise, in any way whatsoever, muted or unmuted, occasionally or persistently, overtly or covertly, the contradiction which characterises women's, but not men's, lives: while we value the intimacy we find so natural, we are endangered by the invasion and dread the intrusion in our lives which intimacy entails, and we long for individuation and independence. Neither sexual nor foetal invasion of the self by the other is recognised as a harm worth bothering with. Sexual invasion through rape is understood to be a harm, and is criminalised as such, only when it involves some other harm: Today, when it is accompanied by violence that appears in a form men understand (meaning a plausible threat of annihilation); in earlier times, when it was understood as theft of another man's property. But marital rape, date rape, acquaintance rape, simple rape, unaggravated rape, or as Susan Estrich wants to say 'real rape'[184] are either not criminalised, or if they are, they are not punished – to do so would force a recognition of the concrete, experiential harm to identity formation that sexual invasion accomplishes.

Similarly, foetal invasion is not understood to be harmful, and therefore the claim that I ought to be able to protect myself against it is heard as nonsensical. The argument that the right to abortion mirrors the right of self-defence falls on deaf ears for a reason: The analogy is indeed flawed. The right of self-defence is the right to protect the body's security against annihilation literally understood, not invasion. But the danger an unwanted foetus poses is not to the body's security at all but, rather, to the body's integrity. Similarly, the woman's fear is not that the she will die but that she will cease to be or never become a self. The danger of unwanted pregnancy is the danger of invasion by the other, not of annihilation by the other. In sum, the Rule of Law does not recognise the danger of invasion, nor does it recognise the individual's need for, much less entitlement to, individuation and independence from the intrusion which heterosexual penetration and foetal invasion entails. The material consequence of this lack of recognition in the real world is that women are objectified – regarded as creatures who can't be harmed.

The second thing I mean to imply by the phrase masculine jurisprudence is that both liberal and critical legal theory, which is about the relation between law and life, is about men and not women. The reason for this lack of parallelism, of course, is hardly benign neglect. Rather, the distinctive values women hold, the distinctive dangers from which we suffer, and the distinctive contradictions that characterise our inner lives are not reflected in legal theory because legal theory (whatever else it's about) is about actual, real life, enacted, legislated, adjudicated law, and women have, from law's inception, lacked the power to make law)

---

184 Susan Estrich, *Real Rape*.

protect, value, or seriously regard our experience. Jurisprudence is masculine because jurisprudence is about the relationship between human beings and the laws we actually have, and the laws we actually have are masculine both in terms of their intended beneficiary and in authorship. Women are absent from jurisprudence because women as human beings are absent from the law's protection: Jurisprudence does not recognise us because law does not protect us. The implication for this should be obvious. We will not have a genuinely ungendered jurisprudence (a jurisprudence 'unmodified,' so to speak) until we have legal doctrine that takes women's lives as seriously as it takes men's. We don't have such legal doctrine. The virtual abolition of patriarchy is the necessary political condition for the creation of nonmasculine feminist jurisprudence.

It does not follow, however, that there is no such thing as feminist legal theory. Rather, I believe what is now inaccurately called feminist jurisprudence consists of two discrete projects. The first project is the unmasking and critiquing of the patriarchy behind purportedly ungendered law and theory, or, put differently, the uncovering of what we might call patriarchal jurisprudence from under the protective covering of jurisprudence. The primary purpose of the critique of patriarchal jurisprudence is to show that jurisprudence and legal doctrine protect and define men, not women. Its second purpose is to show how women – that is, people who value intimacy, fear separation, dread invasion, and crave individuation – have fared under a legal system which fails to value intimacy, fails to protect against separation, refuses to define invasion as a harm, and refuses to acknowledge the aspirations of women for individuation and physical privacy.

The second project in which feminist legal theorists engage might be called reconstructive jurisprudence. The last twenty years have seen a substantial amount of feminist law reform, primarily in the areas of rape, sexual harassment, reproductive freedom, and pregnancy rights in the workplace. For strategic reasons, these reforms have often been won by characterising women's injuries as analogous to, if not identical with, injuries men suffer (sexual harassment as a form of 'discrimination'; rape as a crime of 'violence'), or by characterising women's longing as analogous to, if not identical with, men's official values (reproductive freedom – which ought to be grounded in a right to individuation – conceived instead as a 'right to privacy,' which is derivative of the autonomy right). This misconceptualisation may have once been a necessary price, but it is a high price and, as these victories accumulate, an increasingly unnecessary one. Reconstructive feminist jurisprudence should set itself the task of rearticulating these new rights in such a way as to reveal, rather than conceal, their origin in women's distinctive existential and material state of being ...

Reconstructive jurisprudence

The goal of reconstructive feminist jurisprudence is to render feminist reform rational. We must change the fact that from a mainstream point of view, arguments for feminist legal reform efforts are (or appear to be) invariably irrational. The moral questions feminist reforms pose are always incommensurable with dominant moral and legal categories. Let me put it this way: Given present moral categories, women's issues are crazy issues. Arguments for reproductive freedom, for example, are a little insane: Prochoice advocates can't explain the difference between reproductive freedom and infanticide, or how this right can possibly be grounded in the Constitution, or how it is that women can claim to be 'nurturant' and at the same time show blatant disregard for the rights and feelings of foetuses. In fact, my sense, drawn from anecdotal evidence only, is that the abortion issue is increasingly used in ethics as well as constitutional law classrooms to exemplify the 'irrationality' of individual moral commitment. Rape reform efforts that aim to expand the scope of the defined harm are also perceived, I believe, as insane. Why would anyone possibly object to nonviolent sex? Isn't sex always pleasurable? Feminist pornography initiatives are viewed as irrational, and the surrogate motherhood issue is no better. There's an air of irrationality around each of these issues.

That air of irrationality is partly real and partly feigned. The reason for the air of irrationality around particular, substantive feminist legal reform efforts, I believe, is that feminist legal reforms are by necessity advocated in a form that masks rather than reflects women's true subjective nature. This is hardly surprising: Language, of course, constrains our descriptive options. But whether or not surprising, the damage is alarming, and we need to understand its root. Arguments for reproductive freedom, for example, are irrational because the categories in which such arguments must be cast are reflective of men's, not women's, nature. This culture thinks about harm and violence and therefore self-defence in a particular way, namely, a Hobbesian way, and a Hobbesian conception of physical harm cannot possibly capture the gender-specific subjective harm that constitutes the experience of unwanted pregnancy. From a subjective, female point of view, an abortion is an act of self-defence (not the exercise of a 'right of privacy'), but from the point of view of masculine subjectivity, an abortion can't possibly be an act of self-defence: The foetus is not one of Hobbes's 'relatively equal' natural men against whom we have a right to protect ourselves. The foetus is unequal and above all else dependent. That dependency and inequality is the essence of foetushood, so to speak. Self-defence doctrine, with its Hobbesian background and overlay, simply doesn't apply to such dependent and unequal 'aggressors'; indeed, the notion of aggression itself does not apply to such creatures.

Rape reform efforts to criminalise simple rape are also irrational, as Susan Estrich has discovered, and for the same reason: Subjectively, 'simple rapes' are harms, but from the point of view of masculine subjectivity, nonviolent acts that don't threaten annihilation or frustration of projects can't possibly be 'harmful'. In both cases, we have tried to explain feminist reform efforts through the use of analogies that don't work and arguments that are strained. The result in both cases is internally inconsistent, poorly reasoned, weak, and ultimately vulnerable legal doctrine.

'Reconstructive feminist jurisprudence,' I believe, should try to explain or reconstruct the reforms necessary to the safety and improvement of women's lives in direct language that is true to our own experience and our own subjective lives. The dangers of mandatory pregnancy, for example, are invasion of the body by the foetus and the intrusion into the mother's existence following childbirth. The right to abort is the right to defend against a particular bodily and existential invasion. The harm the unwanted foetus does is not the harm of annihilation nor anything like it: It is not an assault or a battery or a breached contract or an act of negligence. A foetus is not an equal in the state of nature, and the harm a foetus can do is not in any way analogous to that harm. It is, however, a harm. The foetus is an 'other,' and it is perfectly sensible to seek a liberal sounding 'right' of protection against the harm the foetus does.

We need, though, to be more accurate in our description of the harm. Unwanted intercourse is 'harmful' because it is invasive, not because it is (necessarily) violent. For that reason alone, the harm of intercourse is descriptively incommensurate with liberal concepts of harm. But it is not incommensurate with women's lives. The goal of reconstructive feminist jurisprudence should be to provide descriptions of the 'human being' underlying feminist legal forms that will be true to the conditions of women's lives. Our jurisprudential construct – liberalism and critical theory – might then change as well to account for true descriptions of women's subjectivity.

Conclusion: Toward a Jurisprudence Unmodified

The separation thesis, I have argued, is drastically untrue of women. What's worth noting by way of conclusion is that it is not entirely true of men either. First, it is not true materially. Men are connected to another human life prior to the cutting of the umbilical cord. Furthermore, men are somewhat connected to women during intercourse, and men have openings that can be sexually penetrated. Nor is the separation thesis necessarily true of men existentially. As Suzanna Sherry has shown, the existence of the entire classical republican tradition belies the claim that masculine biology mandates liberal values.[185] More generally, as Dinnerstein, Chodorow, French, and Gilligan all insist, material biology does not mandate existential value: Men can connect to other human life. Men can nurture life. Men can mother. Obviously, men can care and love and support and affirm life. Just as obviously, however, most men don't. One reason that they don't, of course, is male privilege. Another reason, though, may be the blinders of our masculinist utopian visionary. Surely one of the most important insights of feminism has been that biology is indeed destiny when we are unaware of the extent to which biology is narrowing our fate, but that biology is destiny only to the extent of our ignorance. As we become increasingly aware, we become increasingly free. As we become increasingly free, we, rather than biology, become the authors of our fate. Surely this is true both of men and women.

On the flip side, the connection thesis is also not entirely true of women, either materially or existentially. Not all women become pregnant, and not all women are sexually penetrated. Women can go through life unconnected to other human life. Women can also go through life fundamentally unconcerned with other human life. Obviously, as the liberal feminist movement firmly established, many women can and do individuate, speak the truth, develop integrity, pursue personal projects, embody freedom, and attain an atomistic liberal individuality. Just as obviously, most women don't. Most women are indeed forced into motherhood and heterosexuality. One reason for this is utopian blinders: Women's lack of awareness of existential choice in the face of what are felt to be biological imperatives. But that is surely not the main reason. The primary reason for the stunted nature of women's lives is male power.

Perhaps the greatest obstacle to the creation of a feminist jurisprudence is that feminist jurisprudence must simultaneously confront both political and conceptual barriers to women's freedom. The political barrier is surely the most pressing. Feminists must first and foremost counter a profound power imbalance, and the way to do that is through law and politics. But jurisprudence – like law – is persistently utopian and conceptual as well as apologist and political: Jurisprudence represents a constant and at least at times a sincere attempt to articulate a guiding utopian vision of human association. Feminist jurisprudence must respond to these utopian images, correct them, improve upon them, and participate in them as utopian images, not just as apologies for patriarchy. Feminism must envision a postpatriarchal world, for without such a vision we have little direction. We must use that vision to construct our present

185 Sherry (1986) 72 *Virginia Law Review*, p 584.

goals, and we should, I believe, interpret our present victories against the backdrop of that vision. That vision is not necessarily androgynous; surely in a utopian world the presence of differences between people will be cause only for celebration. In a utopian world, all forms of life will be recognised, respected, and honoured. A perfect legal system will protect against harms sustained by all forms of life and will recognise life affirming values generated by all forms of being. Feminist jurisprudence must aim to bring this about, and to do so, it must aim to transform the images as well as the power. Masculine jurisprudence must become humanist jurisprudence, and humanist jurisprudence must become a jurisprudence unmodified.

THE 'WOMAN'S POINT OF VIEW'[186]
Deborah L Rhode

For many women, the request for the 'woman's point of view' provokes an ambivalent response. On one level, it is an improvement over all those circumstances and all those years in which no one thought to ask and no one was available to respond. On another level, the request, which often proceeds from feminist sympathies, risks perpetuating attitudes at odds with feminist commitments. What follows are a few cautionary remarks on the issue of perspective, on the implications of 'woman's point of view' for legal, social, and feminist theory.

One reason for ambivalence on the subject stems from its historical legacy. For most of American history, emphasis on women's distinctive perspective has worked against women's distinctive interests. An obvious example involves the legal profession's traditional response to female entrants. What is perhaps most striking about this response is the utter lack of self-consciousness with which exclusively male decision-makers have coped with challenges to male exclusivity.

Although women occasionally acted as attorneys during the Colonial period, the formalisation of entry standards during the post-Revolutionary period prevented further participation. Despite the laxity of screening procedures during the Jacksonian era, females and felons remained two groups subject to categorical exclusions.[187] The reasons for resistance to women entrants varied, but what bears emphasis is the presumed difference in the sexes' capacity for legal work. In the view of many 19th century jurists, the 'Law of the Creator' decreed that women's nature was to nurture.[188] Divine inspiration revealed that domesticity was destiny; the 'peculiar qualities of womanhood, its gentle graces, its quick sensibility, its tender susceptibility', were not qualities for 'forensic strife'.[189]

Long after women gained formal admission to the Bar, many educators, employers, and bar associations continued to resist the 'clack of ... possible Portias'.[190] The stated concerns were manifold, ranging from the risks of unchaperoned intellectual intercourse in libraries to the seemingly insurmountable difficulties of constructing separate lavatory facilities. At least

---

186 (1988) 38 *Journal of Legal Education* at 38–46.

187 See Deborah L Rhode, 'Moral Character as a Professional Credential' (1985) 94 *Yale LJ* 491.

188 *Bradwell v State* (1872) 83 US (16 Wall) 130, 141-42 (Bradley J concurring).

189 *In Re Motion to Admit Goodell* (1875) 39 Wis 232, 245.

190 Jannette Barnes, 'Women and Entrance to the Legal Profession' (1970) 23 *Journal of Legal Education* 276, 283.

some of the resistance, however, rested on women's presumed intellectual incapacity and emotional instability. A prevailing assumption was that females were less adept at 'thinking like a lawyer', whatever exactly that meant. Such attitudes were plainly apparent in hiring, promotion, and academic policies. Leading law schools, law firms, and law associations excluded women entirely or relegated them to subordinate roles. In many classrooms, the 'female point of view' was welcome only on special 'ladies' days' or on special issues (eg hypotheticals involving domestic skills or sexual relationships).[191] Employers similarly restricted women practitioners to specialties in which their 'nurturing qualities' were thought particularly appropriate (eg family and estate work) and in which their status, financial compensation, and professional influence were likely to remain limited. Minority women were doubly disadvantaged and significantly underrepresented at all professional levels.

This is familiar history. However, more subtle forms of bias remain. Although the last decade has witnessed substantial improvement in the demographic and cultural landscape of the profession, the rhetoric of gender equality does not yet match the reality of women's experience.

Against this historical backdrop, contemporary discussions of the 'woman's point of view' mark an important advance. The phrase has taken on new meanings that reflect broader changes in the landscape of the law and in other disciplines from which it draws. Feminist perspectives are helping to reshape not only legal doctrine and legal education but also their deeper intellectual foundations. Over the last two decades, the number of courses in women's studies has grown from a few hundred to well over 30,000, and related scholarship has increased at a comparable pace. The result has been not only to increase knowledge about women's experience but also to challenge what counts as knowledge. Informed by other developments in critical social theory, feminist scholarship has drawn attention to the biases of traditional paradigms and to the way that data has been constructed, not simply collected. Together with other activists from the contemporary women's movement, feminist academics have helped to alter the categories and consequences of legal decision-making. While much remains to be done, the increasing influence of 'woman's point of view' has advanced our thinking about the premises and processes of the law. It should not in any sense detract from that achievement to raise certain concerns about its future direction. The concerns are not unique to law, but because they have not been aired as fully in legal arenas as in other contexts, a few general observations bear emphasis, first about 'woman' and second about 'point of view'.

Over the last century, American feminists have centred theoretical and political attention on issues related to differences between men and women. Over the last decade, feminists have increasingly realised the importance of focusing also on differences among women. A crucial contribution of recent theory has been its emphasis on diversity of race, class, age, ethnicity, and sexual orientation. Requests for 'the woman's perspective' tend to obscure that diversity, and risk perpetuating a homogenised view of women's identity and a reductive analysis of women's interests. Such requests point up a central paradox for contemporary feminism. Much of the theoretical and political force of the feminist movement stems from its aspiration to identify values and perspectives that grows out of women's distinctive experience. Yet one of the critical lessons of that experience is its diversity, which demands attention to differences as well as commonalities.

---

191 See Epstein, *Women in Law* (New York, 1976) pp 101–11.

Requests for a single and singular 'point of view' raise related difficulties. To assume that feminism offers one theoretical stance is to miss a central point of recent feminist theory. Drawing on postmodernist analysis, contemporary feminists stress the inability of any single overarching framework, including a feminist one, to provide an adequate account of social experience. Theoretical approaches claiming such adequacy have often proved too broad and abstract to explain particular ideological, material, and historical relationships. Alternatively, such approaches have been too grounded in specifics to yield generalisable insights and illumine larger cultural patterns. These limitations have encouraged feminists not to renounce theory but rather to emphasise the need for theories for multiple accounts from multiple disciplines at multiple levels that will avoid privileging any single methodological approach.

Yet the importance of such diversity is too often obscured by the popularisation of one strand of contemporary feminist research. This strand encompasses a range of methodologies and perspectives that do not co-exist peacefully under any single label. For present purposes, however, it makes sense to borrow the generic term 'relational feminism' which stresses the importance of relationships in explaining attributes historically linked with women. Theorists such as Nancy Chodorow, Dorothy Dinnerstein, Jean Bethke Elshtain, Carol Gilligan, Susan Griffin, Alice Rossi, and Sarah Ruddick all emphasise certain caretaking traits and values predominantly associated with women. Despite the diversity among such scholars, their work is often presented as emblematic of the 'woman's point of view'.

The usefulness of relational feminism for legal analysis has been explored at length elsewhere and need not be rehearsed here. Most important, this body of work insists that values associated with women be valued and stresses the need for altering existing structures, not just assimilating women within them. It also provides theoretical foundations for legal reforms necessary to accommodate caretaking interests. Yet the contributions of this scholarly framework have not come without cost, particularly given the unqualified way such perspectives have often emerged in contemporary legal and popular publications.

The problem stems partly from limitations in the theories themselves. An obvious example involves Carol Gilligan's *In a Different Voice*, which, of all relational work, has attracted the greatest following in legal circles. Drawing from psychological theory and empirical research on moral reasoning, Gilligan argues that women are more likely than men to use a 'different voice', ie a voice unlike the one that prominent theorists have generally associated with the highest stage of ethical development. In Gilligan's terms, this different, predominantly female voice stresses concrete responsibilities and relationships rather than abstract principles of rights and justice. For purposes of legal analysis, her conclusion is that conventional approaches place excessive weight on rights rather than relationships.

Like other relational work, Gilligan's makes important contributions. It also requires qualifications that are too often overlooked. In part, the difficulties are methodological, and stem from her work's inattention to differences in women's experiences across culture, class, race, ethnicity, and so forth. Related limitations involve the lack of focus on historical, social, and economic forces that mediate these experiences. Such limitations assume greater significance in light of a substantial body of other research that casts doubt on how different the different voice really is. For example, a review of some 60 recent empirical studies involving moral reasoning finds that most reveal no significant gender differences. So too, much contemporary research on leadership styles and political values discloses less substantial variations between men and women than relational theory would suggest.

In any event, the most critical issue is not empirical or methodological but normative. The extent to which women and men exhibit different values or reasoning styles is far less important than the consequences of stressing such differences in particular contexts. In assessing those consequences, a number of concerns require attention. On a theoretical level, an emphasis on difference risks oversimplifying and overclaiming. Males' association with abstract nationality and females with inter-personal nurturing reflects longstanding dichotomies that have restricted opportunities for both sexes. The celebration of women's maternal instincts by some relational feminists bears striking resemblance to the assertions of anti-feminists over the last several centuries. The claim that women's liberation does not lie in 'formalistic' equality but in 'the recognition of that specific thing in the feminine personality the vocation of a woman to become a mother' reflects the phrasing of Pope Paul VI, but it could as readily be drawn from work of the New Right or the feminist left.

These different constituencies do, of course, offer different explanations and draw different political conclusions from their points of common emphasis. At least some relational feminists, however, including those with leftist backgrounds, advocate women's retention of primary caretaking roles or emphasise the physiological roots of caretaking capacities. Yet much of this work obscures the extent to which ostensibly female characteristics are socially constructed and constrained. Sex-linked traits and values are profoundly affected by forces that are culturally contingent, not biologically determined. If women do sometimes speak in a different voice, it may be one that is more ascribed than intrinsic.

It is, moreover, a voice that speaks in more than one register. Missing from many relational accounts, particularly in popular and legal circles, is any attention to the dark side of difference, to the less benign aspects of women's caretaking roles and values. Mother-child relationships can involve physical abuse and psychological impairment as well as care and commitment. In addition, women's disproportionate family responsibilities may encourage forms of dependence, sex-role socialisation, and parochialism that carry heavy costs. Yet the tendency in too much relational work has been to ignore the downside of difference or assume that its negative aspects will vanish automatically as structures of subordination erode.

That tendency is understandable. Much of what is theoretically and politically empowering about relational feminism comes from its insistence on the positive attributes of women's experience. But that emphasis carries a price, one that escalates when rhetoric outruns experience. Certain strands of relationalism present the same risk of overclaiming that marred the suffrage campaign. Just as some late 19th and early 20th century activists claimed that woman's involvement would purify politics, some contemporary theorists have assumed that her participation will of itself totally reshape the structure and substance of public decision-making. That assumption is problematic on several levels. It finesses the difficult question of how 'woman's voice' will attain such influence. And it ignores the possibility that what will be reshaped is the voice rather than the context in which it is heard. An add-woman-and-stir approach does not of itself ensure transformation of the existing social order.

From a legal perspective, the simple dichotomies between rights and responsibilities that emerge in some relational feminist work present further difficulties. Rights can impose responsibilities and responsibilities can imply rights. Often the concepts serve identical ends; ie a right to freedom from intentional discrimination imposes a responsibility not to engage in it. The converse is also true, and privileging one form of discourse over the other is unlikely to reshape the foundations of American law. Our problems stem less from a jurisprudential focus than from an absence of effective strategies for accommodating the needs of independence and inter-dependence.

The 'woman's point of view' can play an important role in developing such strategies, but not if it is equated with some single theoretical stance or perspective. In certain contexts the risks of such reductionism are especially acute. A common example involves circumstances in which females remain significantly underrepresented, and those in positions of power are more concerned about remedying the appearance than the fact of underrepresentation. In such settings, the request for a 'woman's perspective' is best understood as a request for a woman. It just looks unseemly to leave half the race absent from committees, councils, conferences, boards, panels, etc. And it looks equally unseemly, and indeed ungrateful, for the chosen woman to decline, no matter how belated the invitation, how far removed from her interests or expertise, or how overcommitted her schedule. After all, such requests are clearly preferable to the traditional alternative. As Barbara Babcock once noted, when asked how she felt about being appointed an assistant attorney general because she was a woman: 'It's better than not being appointed because I'm a woman.' Those should not be the only alternatives.

Not all attempts to broaden representation fall into the 'oh my God we've got to have a woman' category. Many requests stem from the well-meant desire for more inclusive perspectives. But in too many circumstances, the real desire is not for a female, let alone feminist, participant, but for an honorary male, for someone who is too acculturated, assimilated, or simply polite to draw attention to her gender or to the selection processes that make gender so apparent. The additional irony is that, in such contexts, it is women who end up feeling uncomfortable, rather than the men whose prior decisions have contributed to that discomfort. Under these circumstances, any response is on some level unsatisfying; token participation risks legitimating a selection process that is anything but legitimate, while exclusion risks perpetuating the patterns that perpetuate exclusivity.

Similar conflicts arise when the request is for a point of view, but the motive springs more from intellectual voyeurism than intellectual curiosity. A representative illustration is the academic who is well versed in political and jurisprudential theory but is unacquainted with feminist work and would like a five-minute summary over lunch. The subtle or not so subtle implication is that he has heard 'you girls think differently' and he is interested in knowing a little about why. And a little is what he has in mind. Bibliographic suggestions will not suffice. A condensed version is what he is after, and again it is something of a no-win situation. A little knowledge is a dangerous thing, but the alternative is hardly better. To offer some reductive account that will be interpreted as the feminist perspective does violence to feminist premises. But it does not advance feminist politics to pass up opportunities to arouse curiosity. After all, sometimes one thing does lead to another.

A variation on this theme emerges when somewhat more knowledgeable colleagues become hell-bent on new footnote fodder. The problem comes if they are interested less in feminism than in feminist chic, ie in the latest intellectual fashions. The most obvious example involves individuals who want to keep up with what is being read by the 'in crowd,' not because they intend to read it but because they are intent on citing it. All too often the end product has a disturbingly *deus ex machina* flavour. Women's 'different voice' arrives just in time to supply whatever dimensions the author finds important and undervalued in contemporary legal discourse. These dimensions could often just as easily be associated with humanism, socialism, or critical legal theory. The feminism comes largely in the footnotes, in the choice of citations. Instead of famous dead Europeans, these colleagues often want obscure living feminists, and the request for sources often comes attached with a request for a brief overview of the works suggested; eg one-sentence wrap-ups of the positions of Helene Cixous, Luce Irigaray, and Julia Kristeva and their relevance for modern legal theory. Usually this is all needed by yesterday. And frequently the request comes from colleagues who are most sympathetic in principle but least committed in practice to feminist premises. Once again, the situation is not lacking in irony, particularly when the scholarly emphasis on relational values emerges from an individual who often ignores them in collegial relations.

If these sketches have a familiar resonance, it is perhaps because few of us, least of all this author, are entirely free of such patterns in our own interactions with members of underrepresented groups. To break these patterns, we need to acknowledge the importance of 'the woman's (or minority's) point of view' without homogenising or essentialising its content. When a request comes for that perspective, we must offer a response, but not in the form the invitation assumes. The opportunity to provide a point of view is an opportunity to challenge the assumption that any single stance can adequately capture the diversity of our experiences and interests. Only by entering the debate about 'women's views' can we challenge the terms on which it has traditionally proceeded.

RACE AND ESSENTIALISM IN FEMINIST LEGAL THEORY[192]
Angela P Harris[193]
Methodology

... In this article, I discuss some of the writings of feminist legal theorists Catharine MacKinnon and Robin West. I argue that their work, though powerful and brilliant in many ways, relies on what I call gender essentialism – the notion that a unitary, 'essential' women's experience can be isolated and described independently of race, class, sexual orientation, and other realities of experience. The result of this tendency toward gender essentialism, I argue, is not only that some voices are silenced in order to privilege others (for this is an inevitable result of categorisation, which is necessary both for human communication and political movement) but that the voices that are silenced turn out to be the same voices silenced by the mainstream legal voice of 'We the People' – among them, the voices of black women.

This result troubles me for two reasons. First, the obvious one: As a black woman, in my opinion the experience of black women is too often ignored both in feminist theory and in legal theory, and gender essentialism in feminist legal theory does nothing to address this problem. A second and less obvious reason for my criticism of gender essentialism is that, in my view, contemporary legal theory needs less abstraction and not simply a different sort of abstraction. To be

---

192 (1990) 42 *Stanford Law Review* 581.
193 At the time of writing, Acting Professor, University of California at Berkeley.

fully subversive, the methodology of feminist legal theory should challenge not only law's content but its tendency to privilege the abstract and unitary voice, and this gender essentialism also fails to do ...

... In feminist legal theory, however, the move away from univocal toward multivocal theories of women's experience and feminism has been slower than in other areas. In feminist legal theory, the pull of the second voice, the voice of abstract categorisation, is still powerfully strong. 'We the People' seems in danger of being replaced by 'We the Men'. And in feminist legal theory, as in the dominant culture, it is mostly white, straight, and socio-economically privileged claim to speak for all of us.[194] Not surprisingly, the story they tell about 'women' despite its claim to universality, seems to black women to be peculiar to women who are white, straight, and socio-economically privileged – a phenomenon Adrienne Rich terms 'white solipsism'.[195] Elizabeth Spelman notes:

> [T]he real problem has been how feminist theory has confused the condition of one group of women with the condition of all ... A measure of the depth of white middle-class privilege is that the apparently straightforward and logical points and axioms at the heart of much of feminist theory guarantee the direction of its attention to the concerns of white middle-class women.[196]

The notion that there is a monolithic 'women's experience' that can be described independent of other facets of experience like race, class, and sexual orientation is one I refer to in this essay as 'gender essentialism'. A corollary to gender essentialism is 'racial essentialism' – the belief that there is a monolithic 'Black Experience', or 'Chicano Experience'. The source of gender and racial essentialism (and all other essentialisms, for the list of categories could be infinitely multiplied) is the second voice, the voice that claims to speak for all. The result of essentialism is to reduce the lives of people who experience multiple forms of oppression to addition problems: 'racism + sexism = straight black women's experience,' or 'racism + sexism homophobia = black lesbian experience'.[197]

Thus, in an essential world, black women's experience will always be forcibly fragmented before being subjected to analysis, as those who are 'only interested in race' and those who are 'only interested in gender' take their separate slices of our lives.

Moreover, feminist essentialism paves the way for unconscious racism. Spelman puts it this way:

> [T]hose who produce the 'story of woman' want to make sure they appear in it. The best way to ensure that is to be the storyteller and hence to be in a position to decide which of all the many facts about women's lives ought to go into the story, which ought to be left out. Essentialism works well in behalf of these aims, aims that subvert the very process by which might come to see where and how they wish to make common cause. For essentialism invites me to take what I understand to be true of me 'as a women' for some

---

194 See eg Catharine MacKinnon, 'On Collaboration', in *Feminism Unmodified* (1987) at pp 198, 204.

195 Rich defines white solipsism as the tendency to 'think, imagine, and speak as if whiteness described the world.' Adrienne Rich, 'Disloyal to Civilisation: Feminism, Racism, Gynephobia' in *On Lies, Secrets and Silence* (1979) at pp 275, 299.

196 E Spelman, *op cit* at p 4.

197 See Deborah King, 'Multiple Jeopardy, Multiple Consciousness: The Context of a Black Feminist Idelogy' (1988) 14 *Signs* at 42, 51.

golden nugget of womenness all women have as women; and it makes the participation of other women inessential to the production of the story. How lovely: the many turn out to be one, and the one that they are is me.[198]

In a racist society like this one, the storytellers are usually white, and so 'woman' turns out to be 'white woman.'

Why, in the face of challenges from 'different' women and from feminist method itself, is feminist essentialism so persistent and pervasive? I think the reasons are several. Essentialism is intellectually convenient, and to a certain extent cognitively ingrained. Essentialism also carries with it important emotional and political payoffs. Finally, essentialism often appears (especially to white women) as the only alternative to chaos, mindless pluralism, and the end of the feminist movement. In my view, however, as long as feminists, like theorists in the dominant culture, continue to search for gender and racial essences, black women will never be anything more than a crossroads between two kinds of domination, or at the bottom of a hierarchy of oppressions; we will always be required to choose pieces of ourselves to present as wholeness ...

> Our future survival is predicated upon our ability to relate within equality. As women, we must root out internalised patterns of oppression within ourselves if we are to move beyond the most superficial aspects of social change. Now we must recognise differences among women who are our equals, neither inferior nor superior, and devise ways to use each others' difference to enrich our vision and our joint struggles.[199]

Audre Lorde

In this part of the article, I want to talk about what black women can bring to feminist theory to help us move beyond essentialism toward multiple consciousness as feminist and jurisprudential method. In my view, there are at least three major contributions that black women have to offer post-essentialist feminist theory: the recognition of a self that is multiplicitous, not unitary; the recognition that differences are always relational rather than inherent; and the recognition that wholeness and commonality are acts of will and creativity, rather than passive discovery ...

The Abandonment of Innocence

Black women experience not a single inner self (much less one that is essentially gendered), but many selves. This sense of a multiplicitous self is not unique to black women, but black women have expressed this sense in ways that are striking, poignant, and 'potentially' useful to feminist theory. bell hooks describes her experience in a creative writing programme at a predominantly white college, where she was encouraged to find 'her voice' as frustrating to her sense of multiplicity.

> It seemed that many black students found our situations problematic precisely because our sense of self, and by definition our voice, was not, 'lateral, monologist, or static but rather multi-dimensional'. We were as at home in dialect as we were in standard English. Individuals who speak languages other than English, who speak patois as well as standard English, find it a necessary aspect of self-affirmation not to feel compelled to choose one voice over another, not to claim one as more authentic, but rather to

---

198 E Spelman, *op cit*, p 159.
199 A Lorde, *op cit*, p 122.

construct social realities that celebrate, acknowledge, and affirm differences, variety.[200]

This experience of multiplicity is also a sense of self-contradiction, of containing the oppressor within oneself. In her article *On Being the Object of Property*,[201] Patricia Williams writes about herself writing about her great-great-grandmother, 'picking through the ruins for my roots'.[202] What she finds is a paradox: she must claim for herself 'a heritage the weft of whose genesis is [her] own disinheritance.' Williams's great-great-grandmother, Sophie, was a slave, and at the age of about 11 was impregnated by her owner, a white lawyer named Austin Miller. Their daughter Mary, Williams's great-grandmother, was taken away from Sophie and raised as a house servant.

When Williams went to law school, her mother told her: 'The Millers were lawyers, so you have it in your blood.' Williams analyses this statement as asking her to acknowledge contradictory selves:

> [S]he meant that no one should make me feel inferior because someone else's father was a judge. She wanted me to reclaim that part of my heritage from which I had been disinherited, and she wanted me to use it as a source of strength and self-confidence. At the same time, she was asking me to claim a part of myself that was the dispossessor of another part of myself, she was asking me to deny that disenfranchised little black girl of myself that felt powerless, vulnerable and, moreover, rightly felt so.[203]

The theory of black slavery, Williams notes, was based on the notion that black people are beings without will or personality, defined by 'irrationality, lack of control, and ugliness'. In contrast, 'wisdom, control, and aesthetic beauty signify the whole white personality in slave law'. In accepting her white self, her lawyer self, Williams must accept a legacy of not only a disinheritance but a negation of her black self. To the Millers, her forebears, the Williams, her forebears, did not even have selves as such.

Williams's choice ultimately is not to deny either self, but to recognise them both, and in so doing to acknowledge guilt as well as innocence. She ends the piece by invoking 'the presence of polar bears': bears that mauled a child to death at the Brooklyn Zoo and were subsequently killed themselves, bears judged in public debate as simultaneously 'innocent, naturally territorial, unfairly imprisoned, and guilty'.

This complex resolution rejects the easy innocence of supposing oneself to be an essential black self with a legacy of oppression by the guilty white other. With such multilayered analyses, black women can bring to feminist theory stories of how it is to have multiple and contradictory selves, selves that contain the oppressor as well as the oppressed.

Strategic Identities and Difference

A post-essentialist feminism can benefit not only from the abandonment of the quest for a unitary self, but also from Martha Minow's realisation that difference – and therefore identity – is always relational, not inherent. Zora Neale Hurston's work is a good illustration of this notion.

---

200 B Hooks, *Talking Back* (1989) at 122.
201 (1988) 14 *Signs* 5.
202 *Ibid*, p 5.
203 *Ibid*.

In an essay written for a white audience, *How It Feels to Be Me*,[204] Hurston argues that her colour is not an inherent part of her being, but a response to her surroundings. She recalls the day she 'became coloured' – the day she left her home in an all-black community to go to school: 'I left Eatonville, the town of the oleanders, as Zora. When I disembarked from the river-boat at Jacksonville, she was no more. It seemed that I had suffered a sea change. I was not Zora of Orange County any more, I was now a little coloured girl.'[205] But even as an adult, Hurston insists, her coloured self is always situations 'I'd not always feel coloured. Even now I often achieve the unconscious Zora of Eatonville before the Hegira. I feel most coloured when I am thrown against a sharp white background.'[206]

As an example, Hurston describes the experience of listening to music in a jazz club with a white male friend:

> My pulse is throbbing like a war drum. I want to slaughter something – give pain, give death to what, I do not know. But the piece ends. The men of the orchestra wipe their lips and rest their fingers. I creep back slowly to the veneer we call civilisation with the last tone and find the white friend sitting motionless in his seat, smoking calmly.

> 'Good music they have here,' he remarks, drumming the table with his fingertips.

> Music. The great blobs of purple and red emotion have not touched him. He has only heard what I felt. He is far away and I see him but dimly across the ocean and the continent that have fallen between us. He is so pale with his whiteness then and I am so coloured.[207]

In reaction to the presence of whites – both her white companion and the white readers of her essay – Hurston invokes and uses the traditional stereotype of black people as tied to the jungle, 'living in the jungle way'. Yet in a later essay for a black audience, *What White Publishers Won't Print*,[208] she criticises the white 'folklore of reversion to type':

> This curious doctrine has such wide acceptance that it is tragic. One has only to examine the huge literature on it to be convinced. No matter how high we may seem to climb, put us under strain and we revert to type, that is, to the bush. Under a superficial layer of western culture, the jungle drums throb in our veins.[209]

The difference between the first essay, in which Hurston revels in the trope of black person as primitive, and the second essay, in which she deplores it, lies in the distinction between an identity that is contingent, temporary, and relational, and an identity that is fixed, inherent, and essential. Zora as jungle woman is fine as an argument, a reaction to her white friend's experience; what is abhorrent is the notion that Zora can always and only be a jungle woman. One image is in flux, 'inspired' by a relationship with another; the other is static, unchanging, and ultimately reductive and sterile rather than creative.

---

204 In *I Love Myself When I Am Laughing – And Then Again when I Am Looking Mean and Impressive,* A Walker (ed) (1979), p 152.

205 *Ibid,* p 153.

206 *Ibid,* p 154.

207 *Ibid*.

208 In *I Love Myself When I am Laughing, op cit,* p 169.

209 *Ibid,* p 172.

Thus, 'how it feels to be coloured Zora' depends on the answer to these questions: 'Compared to what? As of when? Who is asking? In what context? For what purpose? With what interests and presuppositions?' What Hurston rigorously shows is that questions of difference and identity are always functions of a specific interlocutionary situation – and the answers, matters of strategy rather than truth.[210] Any 'essential self' is always an invention; the evil is in denying its artificiality.

To be compatible with this conception of the self, feminist theorising about 'women' must similarly be strategic and contingent, focusing on relationships, not essences. One result will be that men will cease to be a faceless 'Other' and reappear as potential allies in political struggle. Another will be that women will be able to acknowledge their differences without threatening feminism itself. In the process, as feminists begin to attack racism and classism and homophobia, feminism will change from being only about 'women as women' (modified women need not apply), to being about all kinds of oppression based on seemingly inherent and unalterable characteristics. We need not wait for a unified theory of oppression; that theory can be feminism.

Integrity as Will and Idea

> Because each had discovered years before that they were neither white nor male, and that all freedom and triumph was forbidden to them, they had set about creating something else to be.[211]
>
> *Toni Morrison*

Finally, black women can help the feminist movement move beyond its fascination with essentialism through the recognition that wholeness of the self and commonality with others are asserted (if never completely achieved) through creative action, not realised in shared victimisation. Feminist theory at present, especially feminist legal theory, tends to focus on women as passive victims. For example, for MacKinnon, women have been so objectified by men that the miracle is how they are able to exist at all. Women are the victims, the acted-upon, the helpless, until by radical enlightenment they are somehow empowered to act for themselves. Similarly, for West, the 'fundamental fact' of women's lives is pain – 'the violence, the danger, the boredom, the ennui, the non-productivity, the poverty, the fear, the numbness, the frigidity, the isolation, the low self-esteem, and the pathetic attempts to assimilate.[212]

This story of woman as victim is meant to encourage solidarity by emphasising women's shared oppression, thus denying or minimising difference, and to further the notion of an essential woman – she who is victimised. But as bell hooks has succinctly noted, the notion that women's commonality lies in their shared victimisation by men 'directly reflects male supremacist thinking. Sexist ideology teaches women that to be female is to be a victim.[213] Moreover, the story of woman as passive victim denies the ability of women to shape their own lives, whether for better or worse. It also may thwart their abilities. Like Minnie Bruce Pratt, reluctant to look farther than commonality for fear of jeopardising the comfort of shared experience, women who rely on their victimisation to

---

210 Barbara Johnson, 'Thresholds of Difference', in *Race, Writing and Difference, op cit*, pp 323–24.
211 Toni Morrison, *Sula* (1974) p 52.
212 R West, 'Jurisprudence and Gender' (1987) 3 *Wisconsin Women's LJ* 81. (Extracted at p 227.)
213 B Hooks, *Feminist Theory, op cit*, p 45.

define themselves may be reluctant to let it go and create their own self-definitions.[214]

At the individual level, black women have had to learn to construct themselves in a society that denied them full selves. Again, Zora Neale Hurston's writings are suggestive. Though Hurston plays with being her 'coloured self' and again with being 'the eternal feminine with its string of beads',[215] she ends *How It Feels to Be Coloured Me* with an image of herself as neither essentially black nor essentially female, but simply:

> a brown bag of miscellany propped against a wall. Against a wall in company with other bags, white, red and yellow. Pour out the contents, and there is discovered a jumble of small things priceless and worthless. A first-water diamond, an empty spool, bits of broken glass, lengths of string, a key to a door long since crumbled away, a rusty knife-blade, old shoes saved for a road that never was and never will be, a nail bent under the weight of things too heavy for any nail, a dried flower or two still fragrant. In your hand is the brown bag. On the ground before you is the jumble it held – so much like the jumble in the bags, could they be emptied, that all might be dumped in a single heap and the bags refilled without altering the content of any greatly. A bit of coloured glass more or less would not matter. Perhaps that is how the 'Great Stuffer of Bags' filled them in the first place, who knows?[216]

Hurston thus insists on a conception of identity as a construction, not an essence – something made of fragments of experience, not discovered in one's body or unveiled after male domination is eliminated.

This insistence on the importance of will and creativity seems to threaten feminism at one level, because it gives strength back to the concept of autonomy, making possible the recognition of the element of consent in relations of domination, and attributes to women the power that makes culpable the many ways in which white women have actively used their race privilege against their sisters of colour. Although feminists are correct to recognise the powerful force of sheer physical coercion in ensuring compliance with patriarchal hegemony, we must also come to terms with the ways in which women's culture has served to enlist women's support in perpetuating existing power relations.

However, at another level, the recognition of the role of creativity and will in shaping our lives is liberating, for it allows us to acknowledge and celebrate the creativity and joy with which many women have survived and turned existing relations of domination to their own ends. Works of black literature like *Beloved*, *The Colour Purple*, and *Song of Solomon*, among others, do not linger on black women's victimisation and misery; though they recognise our pain, they ultimately celebrate our transcendence.

Finally, on a collective level this emphasis on will and creativity reminds us that bridges between women are built, not found. The discovery of shared suffering is a connection more illusory than real; what will truly bring and keep us together is the use of effort and imagination to root out and examine our differences, for only the recognition of women's differences can ultimately bring feminist movement to strength. This is hard work, and painful work; but it is also radical

---

214 Minnie Bruce Pratt, *Identity: Skin Blood Heart* in MB Pratt and B Smith, *Yours in Struggle: Three Feminist Perspectives on Anti-Semitism and Racism* (1984).

215 Z Hurston, *op cit*, p 155.

216 *Ibid*.

work, real work. As Barbara Smith has said, 'What I really feel is radical is trying to make coalitions with people who are different from you. I feel it is radical to be dealing with race and sex and class and sexual identity all at one time. I think that is really radical because it has never been done before.'[217]

FEMINIST JURISPRUDENCE: GROUNDING THE THEORIES[218]
Patricia A Cain[219]

Introduction

This essay originates from my participation in a workshop of the same title at the 20th National Conference on Women and the Law, held in Oakland, California in Spring 1989. The workshop focused on the following two questions: (1) to what extent is feminist theoretical scholarship in the field of law actually grounded in the experience of women (ie based on feminist method); and (2) to the extent that the theory is grounded in women's experience, does it reflect the diversity of women's experience?

Because I had recently been struggling with both of these issues, I readily accepted the invitation to participate. At the time, I hoped that my preparation for the workshop would help clarify my own thinking about the connections between feminist method and theory. My particular concern was that feminist legal theorists often ignore, or at best marginalise, lesbian experience. I call this the problem of the invisible lesbian. It is a problem that has serious consequences for the building of feminist legal theory.

What makes any theory particularly feminist is that it is derived from female experience, from a point of view contrary to the dominant male perception of reality. If feminist legal theory is derived from a feminist method uninformed by critical lesbian experience, the theory will be incomplete. Lesbian experience is essential to the formation of feminist theory because it stands in opposition to the institution of heterosexuality, which is a core element of male-centred reality. To the extent feminist legal theory seeks to challenge the male view of reality, it cannot afford to ignore lesbian experience.

The invisibility (or marginalisation) of lesbian experience in feminist legal theory calls for further scrutiny. First of all, we ought to question why the invisibility is so prevalent. Second, we ought to consider what difference an eradication of that invisibility might make.

During the workshop at the Women and the Law Conference, my aim was to explore the fact of lesbian invisibility. I hoped to engage the audience in a form of consciousness-raising (CR) that would deepen their understanding of the invisibility problem and then lead to a discussion of feminist legal theory in which the centrality of lesbian experience was assumed. I was committed to consciousness-raising as my means of communication because I believe CR is an example of genuine feminist method.

I think of CR as a process that occurs whenever women come together to share experiences that produce a new critical understanding of what it means to be a woman. Normally CR occurs when women gather and talk in a space that feels safe enough to explore topics that are private, topics that are rarely discussed.

---

217 Barbara Smith and Beverly Smith, 'Across the Kitchen Table: A Sister-to-Sister Dialogue', in *This Bridge Called My Back*, *op cit*, p 126.

218 (1989) *Berkeley Women's Law Journal* 191. (Footnotes edited.)

219 Professor of Law, University of Texas.

One does not usually think of a speech to a crowded room of 300 women as CR. Nonetheless, by telling my own and others' personal stories, followed by an invitation for critical self-reflection, my hope was to cause a shift in the level of consciousness of many women in the room. I think we succeeded. The response to my presentation, as I experienced it, was a resounding silence – a silence that I now interpret positively. Valid self-reflection, I was told by women in the audience, requires some separate space, some silence.

Feminist Jurisprudence, Feminist Method, and Feminist Legal Scholarship

A. Feminist Jurisprudence

The first recorded use of the phrase 'feminist jurisprudence' occurred in 1978 at a conference celebrating the 25th anniversary of women graduates of the Harvard Law School. Professor Ann Scales, then a Harvard student, moderated a panel of feminist lawyers, legal educators, and judges. The question for debate was whether there was in fact, or should be, such a thing as a feminist jurisprudence. As I understand it from Professor Scales, the consensus was that there should not be.

Professor Scales, unwilling to abide by the consensus, entitled her first scholarly article *Towards a Feminist Jurisprudence*.[220] She admitted that the risk of calling her project 'feminist jurisprudence' was that the work might be misunderstood as a politically-motivated argument for special laws favouring women. Actually, she intended to question, from a feminist perspective, the completeness of a jurisprudence that is not responsive to specifically female concerns (eg pregnancy).

More recently, Professor Robin West has claimed that 'feminist jurisprudence is a conceptual anomaly'.[221] Existing jurisprudence is masculine, according to West, because it is about the connection between patriarchal laws and human beings, who are presumed by those laws to be male. Feminist jurisprudence cannot exist until patriarchy is abolished.

I understand Professor West to be saying that we cannot create a complete theory of law (a jurisprudence) that is truly feminist until conditions are such that we can build the theory authentically. So long as patriarchal dominance continues, female authenticity is presumably impossible. As Catharine MacKinnon keeps reminding us, she (the 'female') cannot articulate her own definitions now 'because his foot is on her throat'.[222]

Without fully accepting the West/MacKinnon thesis (I believe we have glimpses of our own authenticity even within the patriarchy), I do agree that we do not now have a feminist jurisprudence. We do have (and West agrees) feminist legal theory. That is, we have feminist critiques of existing (masculine) jurisprudence.[223] We have examples of feminist deconstruction that uncover the male bias in the existing legal system. And we have feminist litigation that strives to restructure the existing system. Thus we are moving 'towards a

---

220 (1981) 56 *Indiana LJ* 375. (Extracted in Chapter 4.)

221 'Jurisprudence and Gender' (1988) 55 *U Chi L Rev* 1 at 4. (Extracted, *supra*.)

222 DuBois, Dunlap, Gilligan, MacKinnon, Menkel-Meadow, 'Feminist Discourse: Moral Values and the Law – A Conversation' (1985) 34 *Buffalo L Rev* at 11, 74–75.

223 See eg M Minow, 'Forward: Justice Engendered' (1987) *Harv L Rev* 10; Resnik, 'On the Bias: Feminist Reconsiderations of the Aspirations for Our Judges' (1988) 61 *S Cal L Rev* 1877; Scales, 'The Emergence of Feminist Jurisprudence' (1986) 95 *Yale LJ* 1373. (Extracted in Chapter 4.); West *op cit*.

feminist jurisprudence', because the critiques and the litigation have challenged the strength of the patriarchy.

B. Feminist Method

Recent feminist legal scholarship emphasises the importance of feminist method'. While it is not clear whether feminist method is, in fact, limited to consciousness-raising,[224] nor whether it should be,[225] there does appear to be general agreement that feminist method begins with the primacy of women's experience. Listening to women and believing their stories is central to feminist method. If we are careful to listen to women when they describe the harms they experience as women, we are likely to get the legal theory right (ie perceive the problem correctly and propose the right solutions).

Consider Carol Gilligan's pathbreaking work in psychology.[226] Feminist method led Gilligan to suggest new theories regarding women's moral development. Gilligan's method was to listen to female experience as female experience and not merely as other-than-male experience. Gilligan listened to women tell their own stories. She did not force the stories into preformed male categories. Because she really listened, she uncovered a 'different voice' than that heard by her male colleagues.

Theories about women, however, are not always grounded on feminist method. Theories about women, even if developed by a woman, are not necessarily based on women's experience. For example, women law professors are confined to an academic environment that is particularly male. There is no guarantee that those of us who focus our scholarship on legal issues of concern to women will necessarily build theories based on women's experience. Indeed, unless we take pains to seek out women's communities, empirical data about women, and other sources of female experience, there is every risk that we will do just the opposite.

Catharine MacKinnon may be the feminist legal scholar who has most consistently focused on the importance of feminist method.[227] Feminist method, for MacKinnon, means women listening to other women.[228] Women, as they listen to each other, tend to discover a commonality of experiences. Uncovering the fact of women's common experiences creates new knowledge.

MacKinnon listened to women's common experience of sexual harassment and built a legal theory that reflected that experience. In May, 1975, Working Women United held a 'Speak-Out' on sexual harassment. Women told their stories of being treated as sex objects at work. They spoke of the unarticulated job requirements for women, requirements regarding physical attractiveness and sexual availability. The organisation reported that 70% of the women who responded to their survey had experienced some sexual harassment on the job.[229] During this part of the 1970s, individual women also began to bring their claims regarding sexual harassment to the courts.

---

224 See L Bender, 'A Lawyer's Primer on Feminist Theory and Tort' (1988) 38 *J Legal Educ* 3.

225 See Bottomley, Givson and Meteyard, 'Dworkin, Which Dworkin? Taking Feminism Seriously' (1987) 14 *Brit J L and Society* at 47, 56.

226 *In a Different Voice: Psychological Theory and Women's Development* (1982).

227 *Feminism Unmodified* (Harvard UP, 1987).

228 See CA MacKinnon, *Toward a Feminist Theory of the State* (Harvard UP, 1989), Chapters 5 and 6.

229 Silverman, *Sexual Harassment: Working Women's Dilemma in Building Feminist Theory* (Longman, 1981), p 84.

MacKinnon, beginning with the data of real women's experience,[230] and building on the arguments put forth by feminist litigators, developed a legal theory that characterised sexual harassment as a form of sex discrimination that ought to be covered by Title VII. A theory was necessary because existing jurisprudence did not recognise sexual harassment as a harm which the law should remedy. The theory revealed the male bias of the law (ignoring harms that only occur to women) and proposed a revision: a remedy for sexual harassment harms under Title VII.

C. Feminist Legal Scholarship

To be classified as feminist, legal scholarship should be based on women's experience. My particular concern is whether the 'women's experience' that informs feminist legal theory excludes lesbian experience. I will briefly discuss what I consider to be the three stages of feminist legal scholarship' and will review what impact, if any, lesbian experience has had on the development of each of these stages ...

The author then considers the achievements of the women's movement in the United States of America in the 1960s, which she labels the 'second wave' of feminism. In that period, Cain writes, the Equal Pay Act of 1963 and Title VII[231] which prohibited sex discrimination in employment exhibited a 'commitment to the principle of equal opportunity'. In 1966 the National Organisation for Women was founded: focusing on formal equality in the public arena, but initially avoiding contentious issues such as abortion and sexual and reproductive freedom. Lesbian feminists, she writes, were 'disinherited' by the mainstream feminist movement of this time.

In 'Stage Two' — the period in which feminist theory centred on the equality/sameness/difference issue — also ignored lesbian experience. In Patricia Cain's analysis, the work of both cultural feminists, such as Carol Gilligan and Robin West, and dominance theorists such as Catharine MacKinnon, fail to acknowledge lesbian feminists. Cultural feminists concentration on women as nurturers of and carers for children and women's greater connectedness to others, presupposes female heterosexuality, to the exclusion of lesbian women. Catharine MacKinnon's insistence of recasting the sameness/difference debate in the language of dominance and subordination is equally premised on heterosexuality, again to the exclusion of lesbian feminists.

On MacKinnon's views Cain writes:

To the claim that lesbian experience is different, that lesbians are not subordinate to men, that their care is not male-directed, MacKinnon appears to have two different responses. Her first response is that exceptions do not matter. MacKinnon's intent is to offer a critique of the structural condition of women as sexual subordinates and not to make existential claims about all women. It does not affect her theory that all women are not always subordinated to men. Thus, for MacKinnon, lesbian experience of non-subordination is simply irrelevant.

---

230 See CA MacKinnon, *Sexual Harassment of Working Women* (1979).
231 Civil Rights Act 1964, 42 USC 1981 (1982).

Her second response is more troubling. It goes beyond the assertion that lesbian experience is irrelevant; it denies the claim that lesbian experience is free from male domination.

> Some have argued that lesbian sexuality – meaning here simply women having sex with women, not with men – solves the problem of gender by eliminating men from women's voluntary sexual encounters. Yet women's sexuality remains constructed under conditions of male supremacy; women remain socially defined as women in relation to men; the definition of women as men's inferiors remains sexual even if not heterosexual, whether men are present at the time or not.[232]

I find this passage objectionable for several reasons. My primary objection is that MacKinnon has defined lesbian sexuality to suit her purposes ('simply women having sex with women' – ie with nothing else changed except that a woman replaces a man). Although I do not dispute that lesbian couples can sometimes escape their heterosexual counterparts, I am infuriated by MacKinnon's silencing of the rest of lesbian experience. Where is MacKinnon's feminist method? To whom does she choose to listen? Would it not enrich her theory to recognise the reality of non-subordination that some lesbians claim as their experiential reality and ask about its relevance to her underlying theory? And yet, because her theory is premised on a single commonality among women, sexual subordination, MacKinnon fails to see the relevance of the lesbian claim to non-domination, even when it stands – literally – in front of her.

The exclusion of lesbian experience from feminist legal theory is also documented in Clare Dalton's recent summary of feminist legal thought.[233] Dalton describes present aspirations to feminist jurisprudence as falling within two camps: 'woman as mother' theories and 'woman as sexual subordinate' theories. Neither camp embraces lesbian experience as central to the formation of theory. I suspect Professor Dalton's description is accurate. I can find no major 'theory piece' by a legal scholar that focuses on the experience of adult women loving each other as the core experience for building a legal theory premised on caring and connections. And although 'woman as sexual subordinate' theorists are more likely to acknowledge the fact of lesbian existence, they focus on a critique of male dominance rather than on lesbian bonding as a possible alternative to male dominance.

3. Stage Three: Postmodernism

Borrowing from Clare Dalton, I call the third stage of feminist legal theory postmodernism. Postmodern thought challenges notions such as objectivity and universality. The postmodern 'knowing self' is subjective, concrete and particular, constructed through the lived experiences of the subject.

Postmodern feminism is generally associated with French feminists, such as Helene Cixous, Luce Irigaray, and Julia Kristeva.[234] The influence of Simone de Beauvoir's work[235] on these theorists is evident. Beauvoir's existential analysis of woman as 'other' is conceived by postmodern feminists as enabling women to

---

232 CA MacKinnon, *Feminist Theory of State*, at pp 141–42.

233 C Dalton, 'Where We Stand: Observations on the Situation of Feminist Legal Thought' (1988) 3 *Berkeley Women's LJ* 1.

234 For an excellent overview of postmodern feminism, and of these three French theorists in particular, see R Tong, *Feminist Thought: A Comprehensive Introduction* (1989), pp 217–33.

235 S de Beauvoir, *The Second Sex* (1952).

critique the dominant culture. Being 'other' allows women to understand 'plurality, diversity, and difference'.

From a postmodern perspective, feminist theory is inadequate when limited by the perception that there is one essential commonality among all women. Cultural feminists who focus on 'woman' solely as mother (actual or cultural) do not speak to the full complexity of female experience. Radical feminists, such as MacKinnon, who focus on 'woman' solely as 'sexual subordinate' also speak limited truths. Good feminist theory ought to reflect the real differences in women's realities, in our lived experiences. These include differences of race,[236] class, age, physical ability, and sexual preference.

Postmodern legal theorists will want to reject the limitations caused by any categorisation. Although they will want to listen to the reality of lesbian experience, these theorists will not be inclined to build a grand theory based on the concept of 'woman' as 'lesbian'. In the final part of this essay, I offer some thoughts about the potential relevance of lesbian experience to the postmodern development of feminist legal theory.

The Retelling

I believe that current feminist legal theory is deficient and impoverished because it has not paid sufficient attention to the real life experiences of women who do not speak the 'dominant discourse'. Elsewhere I have urged that feminist law teaching ought to include 'listening to difference' and 'making connections'.[237] Here I urge the same for feminist legal scholarship.

Most feminist legal theorists, by focusing on sameness and difference, have fallen into either the assimilationist trap (all women are the same as men/all women are the same) or the essentialist trap (all women are different from men in one essential way/all women are different, but what counts is their essential commonality). The only difference between assimilationists and essentialists is that the former ignore the reality of differences whereas the latter say that differences generally do not matter. The two concepts, assimilationism and essentialism, collapse into each other to the extent they treat women as a single class that is essentially the same.

Elizabeth Spelman describes the essentialist's solution to the 'differences' problem in feminist theory: 'The way to give proper significance to differences among women is to say that such differences simply are less significant than what women have in common. This solution is very neat, for it acknowledges differences among women only enough to bury them.'[238] The difficulty arises when an individual essentialist theorist must determine the content of this commonality which is so significant that it trumps differences. When white, straight, economically privileged feminists name the commonality, and ignore differences, the result may be that all women are assimilated into a single class of white, straight, middle-class women.

It is not enough to name the differences of race, class, and sexuality. The differences need to be understood. Much recent feminist legal scholarship

---

236 For an especially good critique of the failure of feminist legal theorists to acknowledge and understand the difference that race makes, see A Harris, 'Race and Essentialism in Feminist Legal Theory' (1990) 42 *Stanford L Rev* 581. (Extracted, *supra*.)

237 See P Cain, 'Teaching Feminist Theory at Texas: Listening to Difference and Exploring Connections' (1988) 38 *J of Legal Educ* 165.

238 See E Spelman, *Inessential Woman: Problems of Exclusion in Feminist Thought* (1988), p 3.

includes the perfunctory footnote, dropped the first time the essential category 'woman' is mentioned, which acknowledges the differences of race and class, and sometimes of sexual preference. Such politically correct footnotes name the differences, but I see no evidence in the accompanying texts that the differences matter. Scholarship that nominally recognises differences, but still categorises 'woman' from a single perspective is stuck in the assimilationist/essentialist trap.

I do not mean to ignore the importance of our commonalities. It is valuable to identify the similarities among all women. When we identify what we have in common, we begin to build bridges and connections. Yet if we ignore the differences, we risk distorting those connections, because any connection that fails to recognise differences is not a connection to the whole of the other self. A normative principle that honours only what I have in common with each of you fails to respect each of you for the individual woman that you are. To respect you, despite your difference, is an insult. Such respect is not respect for your difference, but only for our sameness. Such respect belittles your difference and says it does not matter. Such 'respect' falls into the assimilationist/essentialist trap.

Let me give you an example. A white law professor says to her black female colleague: 'Sometimes I forget that you are black. Sometimes I think of you as white.' The comment is meant as a compliment, but it denies the real life experience of the black woman to whom it is addressed. It says, ultimately, 'what I respect in you is only what you have in common with me'.

Now let me give you an example out of lesbian experience. A lesbian college teacher proposes a course entitled *The Outsider in 20th Century American Literature*. The course is to include writings of lesbians and gay men, as well as other outsiders, such as persons who have been in mental institutions or prisons. In discussing the potential course, the teacher's (presumably) heterosexual colleagues dismiss the notion that an author's sexuality might be an important aspect of her or his writing, claiming that sexuality is no different from 'a thousand other things' that might influence the writer'. None of the teacher's colleagues considers having to live as a 'different' person in a heterosexist culture as a factor important to one's writing.

Adrienne Rich, a lesbian poet, echoes the same theme in the following story:

> Two friends of mine, both artists, wrote me about reading the *Twenty-One Love Poems* with their male lovers, assuring me how 'universal' the poems were. I found myself angered, and when I asked myself why, I realised that it was anger at having my work essentially assimilated and stripped of its meaning, 'integrated' into heterosexual romance. That kind of 'acceptance' of the book seems to me a refusal of its deepest implications. The longing to simplify ... to assimilate lesbian experience by saying that 'relationship' is really all the same, love is always difficult – I see that as a denial, a kind of resistance, a refusal to read and hear what I've actually written, to acknowledge what I am.[239]

There is a commonality between Adrienne Rich and her heterosexual artist friends. They all experience love and relationship. Yet even if some portion of the love experience is universal, the heterosexual world will never understand the gay and lesbian world if we all focus on the commonality, the universal. To claim that lesbians are the same as heterosexual women or that black women are the

---

239 An interview with Adrienne Rich.

same as white women is to fall into the assimilationist/essentialist trap. Such claims deny the reality of our differences by ignoring or discounting them. Yet it is not enough to recognise and name the differences among us as women. We must also understand those differences.

I ask those of you in the audience who are heterosexual to focus on an important love relationship in your life. This could be a present relationship or a past one, or even the relationship you hope to have. I ask you: how would you feel about this relationship if it had to be kept utterly secret? Would you feel 'at one with the world' if a slight mistake in language ('we' instead of 'I') could lead to alienation from your friends and family, loss of your job? Would you feel at one with your lover if the only time you could touch or look into each other's eyes was in your own home – with the curtains drawn? What would such self-consciousness do to your relationship?

I use the following exercise to demonstrate to my students our different points of view. First I ask each student to write down three self-descriptive nouns or adjectives, to name three aspects of her (or his) personal self. When they have finished writing, we go around the room and each student reads the three choices aloud. For my women students, the list almost always includes either the word woman or female. Thus, we share a perception of self as female. The meaning of female may vary, but it is significant that we all view the fact that we are women as one of the three most important facts about ourselves.

As to the rest of the list, there are important differences. For example, no white woman ever mentions race, whereas every woman of colour does. Similarly, straight women do not include 'heterosexual' as one of the adjectives on their lists, whereas lesbians, who are open, always include 'lesbian' as one of the words on their lists. The point is, not only are we different from each other in such obvious ways as race and sexuality, but we perceive our differences differently.

The results of my exercise are not surprising. Because of the pervasive influences of sexism, racism, and heterosexism, white, heterosexual women think of gender as something that sets them apart, as something that defines them, whereas neither race nor sexuality seems to matter much. Yet if neither race nor sexuality matters much to a white, heterosexual woman, how can she begin to understand the ways in which it matters to others who are different from her in these dimensions?

I wonder sometimes whether heterosexual women really understand the role that heterosexuality plays in the maintenance of patriarchy. Indeed, I sometimes wonder whether lesbians really understand. And yet, if feminist legal theory is to provide meaningful guidance for the abolition of patriarchy, feminist theorists must understand heterosexuality as an institution and not merely as the dominant form of sexuality.

Adrienne Rich illuminated the problem years ago in her brilliant critique of heterosexuality:

> [I]t is not enough for feminist thought that specifically lesbian texts exist. Any theory or cultural/political creation that treats lesbian existence as a marginal or less 'natural' phenomenon, as mere 'sexual preference,' or as the mirror image of either heterosexual or male homosexual relations, is profoundly weakened thereby ...[240]

240 A Rich, 'Compulsory Heterosexuality and Lesbian Existence' (1980) 5 *Signs* 631.

Feminist research and theory that contributes to lesbian invisibility or marginality is actually working against the liberation and empowerment of woman as a group.[241]

Adrienne Rich encourages us to look at heterosexuality from a new perspective, from the perspective of the 'lesbian possibility'. The invisibility of lesbian existence, however, removes the lesbian possibility from view. If there are no lesbians, the only possibility is heterosexuality. Men will assume all women are equally available as sex partners. Women will choose men and never question that choice.

If the choice is never questioned, can it be an authentic choice? Do heterosexual women really choose men or are they victims of false consciousness? And if they are victims of false consciousness, then how do we know that most women are heterosexual? Might they not choose otherwise if they were truly free to choose?

Marilyn Frye offers a challenge to feminist academics and I want to echo her in repeating it here for feminist legal theorists:

> I want to ask heterosexual academic feminists to do some hard analytical and reflective work. To begin with, I want to say to them:
>
> I wish you would notice that you are heterosexual.
>
> I wish you would grow to the understanding that you choose heterosexuality.
>
> I would like you to rise each morning and know that you are heterosexual and that you choose to be heterosexual – that you are and choose to be a member of a privileged and dominant class, one of your privileges being not to notice.
>
> I wish you would stop and seriously consider, as a broad and long-term feminist political strategy, the conversion of women to a woman-identified and woman-directed sexuality ...[242]

Frye reports that a typical response by heterosexual women to such enquiries is that, although they may understand what she is saying, they cannot just up and decide to be lesbian. I, too, have women colleagues and friends who similarly respond, with a shake of the head, that they are hopelessly heterosexual, that they just are not sexually attracted to women.

Frye says that she wants to ask such women (and so do I), 'Why not? Why don't women turn you on? Why aren't you attracted to women?' These are serious questions. Frye encourages heterosexual women to consider the origins of their sexual orientation:

> The suppression of lesbian feeling, sensibility, and response has been so thorough and so brutal for such a long time, that if there were not a strong and widespread inclination to lesbianism, it would have been erased from human life. There is so much pressure on women to be heterosexual, and this pressure is both so pervasive and so completely denied, that I think heterosexuality cannot come naturally to many women; I think that widespread heterosexuality among women is a highly artificial product of the patriarchy ... I want heterosexual women to do intense and serious

---

241 *Ibid* at pp 632, 647–48.
242 Frye, 'A Lesbian Perspective on Women's Studies', in M Cruikshank (ed), *Lesbian Studies* (1982), pp 194, 196.

consciousness-raising and exploration of their own personal histories and to find out how and when in their own development the separation of women from the erotic came about for them. I would like heterosexual women to be as actively curious about how and why and when they became heterosexual as I have been about how and why and when I became lesbian.[243]

Silence

Engage in self-reflection. Did she really mean that? Am I supposed to sit here and consider lesbianism as a possibility? Why not? And if I do consider it, but choose men anyway, is my choice more authentic? What about tomorrow? Do I choose again? She doesn't understand. I did choose. Twenty years ago I chose for the children. Does that make my choice inauthentic? What does my choice mean for me today? What about those of us who choose to live alone, who reject intimacy altogether? Am I choosing to be lesbian if I reject men or only if I choose women? As a woman alone, how am I perceived? To take lesbianism seriously, do I have to reject men? Can I choose both women and men? What is all this about choice? I've been a lesbian all my life. I never chose it. I've just lived my life as it was.

Connections

The most consistent feminist claim, at least since the publication of Simone de Beauvoir's *The Second Sex*, is that knowledge of reality has been constructed from a male-centred standpoint. From their position as outsider, women have questioned that reality, because women's life experiences differ – often dramatically – from those of men. The most cohesive and challenging critiques of male-centred reality have been made by women from standpoints that are exactly opposite, experientially, from those of men'. One such critique is made by cultural feminists from the 'woman as mother' standpoint. Another is made by other radical feminists from the 'woman as sexual subordinate' standpoint.

The fact that so many women can identify common life experiences that are ignored by the male version of reality makes any critique based on such common experiences compelling and powerful. But theorists ought to resist transforming a critical standpoint into a new all-encompassing version of reality. Indeed, my fear is that what started as a useful critique of one privileged (male) view of reality may become a substitute claim for a different privileged (female) view of reality.

Catharine MacKinnon, for example, critiques the patriarchy from a 'woman as sexual subordinate' standpoint. As compelling as her critique is, it should not be viewed as the one and only existential reality for women. And yet MacKinnon herself is so committed to this standpoint that she sometimes seems to claim it as the only reality for women.[244]

MacKinnon's theory is that woman's subordination is universal and constant, but not necessarily inevitable. She cautions against building theory on the basis of Carol Gilligan's discovery of woman's 'different voice' because the women Gilligan listened to were all victims of the patriarchy. Thus, MacKinnon is wary of assigning value to their moral voice. As she explains:

> [By] establishing that women reason differently from men on moral questions, [Gilligan] revalues that which has accurately distinguished women from men by making it seem as though women's moral reasoning is somehow women's, rather than what male supremacy has attributed to

---

243 *Ibid* at pp 196–97.
244 CA MacKinnon, *Feminist Theory of the State*, p 116.

women for its own use. When difference means dominance as it does with gender, for women to affirm differences is to affirm the qualities and characteristics of powerlessness ... To the extent materialism means anything at all, it means that what women have been and thought is what they have been permitted to be and think. Whatever this is, it is not women's, possessive.[245]

When MacKinnon espoused these beliefs regarding women's subordination and inauthenticity in a dialogue with Gilligan at the now somewhat infamous 'Mitchell Lecture' at Buffalo, Mary Dunlap (a lesbian), who was also a speaker at the event, interrupted. Dunlap said: 'I am speaking out of turn. I am also standing, which I am told by some is a male thing to do. But I am still a woman standing.'

> I am not subordinate to any man! I find myself very often contesting efforts at my subordination – both standing and lying down and sitting and in various other positions – but I am not subordinate to any man! And I have been told by Kitty MacKinnon that women have never not been subordinate to men. So I stand here an exception and invite all other women here to be an exception and stand.

MacKinnon has subsequently described this event as 'a stunning example of the denial of gender',[246] claiming that Dunlap was saying, 'that all women who are exempt from the condition of women, all women who are not women, stand with me'. I believe MacKinnon misinterpreted Dunlap's reaction. Dunlap's claim that her experiential reality is often free of male domination was not a denial of the existence of male power, nor a statement that she had risen above other women. It was merely a statement of fact about her reality, a statement she felt compelled to make because MacKinnon's description of 'what is' had continued to exclude Dunlap's reality.

Dunlap's reality is not irrelevant to feminist theory. Mary Dunlap, and I, and other lesbians who live our private lives removed from the intimate presence of men do indeed experience time free from male domination. When we leave the male-dominated public sphere, we come home to a woman-identified private sphere. That does not mean that the patriarchy as an institution does not exist for us or that the patriarchy does not exist during the time that we experience freedom from male domination. It means simply that we experience significant periods of non-subordination, during which we, as women, are free to develop a sense of self that is our own and not a mere construct of the patriarchy.

Nor do we work at this experience of non-subordination and creation of authentic self to set ourselves apart from other women. We are not asserting a 'proud disidentification from the rest of [our] sex and proud denial of the rest of [our] life'.[247] The struggle is to make non-subordination a reality for all women, and the reality of non-subordination in some women's lives is relevant to this struggle. The reality of non-subordination in lesbian lives offers the 'lesbian possibility' as a solution.

At the same time, I believe MacKinnon's claim that all women are subordinate to men all the time is a fair claim upon which to critique the male version of reality, because subordination is such a pervasive experience for women. Her claim

---

245 *Ibid*, p 51.

246 *Feminism Unmodified*, pp 305–06, n 6.

247 *Feminism Unmodified*, pp 305–06.

gives her a valid standpoint for her critique even though it is not experientially true for all women. Similarly, I believe Robin West's claim that all women are 'connected' to life is a fair claim upon which to critique the male version of the 'separation thesis'. But I do not believe that the 'connection thesis' is true of all women'. Feminist legal theorists must be careful not to confuse 'standpoint critiques' with existential reality. And the theorist who has not confused the two must also be careful to prevent her readers from making the confusion.

The problem with current feminist theory is that the more abstract and universal it is, the more it fails to relate to the lived reality of many women. One problem with much feminist legal theory is that it has abstracted and universalised from the experience of heterosexual women. Consider again Marilyn Frye's challenge to heterosexual academic feminists: 'I wish you would notice that you are heterosexual. I wish you would grow to the understanding that you choose heterosexuality ... that you are and choose to be a member of a privileged and dominant class, one of your privileges being not to notice.'[248]

Marilyn Frye's challenge was specifically addressed to heterosexual women. When I elected to adopt her challenge at the Women and the Law Conference (and in this essay), I was choosing a 'lesbian standpoint' to critique the dominant reality in the same way that some cultural feminists have chosen a 'mother standpoint' to critique patriarchy. My intent was not to convert a roomful of women to lesbianism. It was to raise everyone's self-consciousness about our different 'standpoints'. Feminist legal theory must recognise differences in order to avoid reinforcing lesbian invisibility or marginality, ie impeding 'the liberation and empowerment of woman as a group'.

My 'lesbian standpoint' enables me to see two versions of reality. The dominant reality, which I experience as 'theirs' includes the following: lesbians are not mothers, all women are dominated by men, male relationships are valuable and female relationships are not, lesbian is a dirty word, lesbians are sick, women who live alone desire men, women who live together desire men, no one knows a lesbian, lesbians don't have families, all feminist legal theorists are heterosexual, all women in this room are heterosexual, lesbians are sex, most women are heterosexual and not lesbian.

By contrast, the reality that I live, the reality I call 'mine' includes the following: some mothers are lesbian, many women are lesbian, many lesbian women are not dominated by men, many women do not desire men, lesbian is a beautiful word, lesbians are love, love is intimacy, the heterosexual/lesbian dichotomy is false, all lesbians are born into families, lesbians are family, some feminist legal theorists are lesbian, lesbians are brave.

Why is the lesbian so invisible in feminist legal theory? Why is 'my reality' so different from 'their reality?' And which reality is true? For the postmodernist, the last question is meaningless. But the first two are not.

---

248 Frye, *op cit.*

DECONSTRUCTING GENDER[249]
Joan C Williams[250]

Introduction

I start out, as have many others, from the deep split among American feminists between 'sameness' and 'difference.' The driving force behind the mid-20th century resurgence of American feminism was an insistence on the fundamental similarity of men and women and, hence, their essential equality. Betty Friedan comes to mind as an enormously influential housewife whose focus on men and women as individuals made her intensely hostile to gender stereotyping.[251] Mid-century feminism, now often referred to somewhat derisively as assimilationism, focused on providing opportunities to women in realms traditionally preserved for men. In the 1980s two phenomena have shifted feminists' attention from assimilationists' focus on how individual women are like men to a focus on gender differences, on how women as a group differ from men as a group. The first is the feminisation of poverty, which dramatises the chronic and increasing economic vulnerability of women. Feminists now realise that the assimilationists' traditional focus on gender-neutrality may have rendered women more vulnerable to certain gender-related disabilities that have important economic consequences. The second phenomenon that plays a central role in the current feminist imagination is that of career women 'choosing' to abandon or subordinate their careers so they can spend time with their small children. These phenomena highlight the fact that deep-seated social differences continue to encourage men and women to make quite different choices with respect to work and family. Thus, 'sameness' scholars are increasingly confronted by the existence of gender differences.

Do these challenges to assimilationism prove that we should stop trying to kid ourselves and admit the 'real' differences between men and women, as the popular press drums into us day after day and as the 'feminism of difference' appears to confirm? Do such phenomena mean that feminists' traditional focus on gender-neutrality is a bankrupt ideal? I will argue no on both counts, taking an approach quite different from that ordinarily taken by feminists on the sameness side of the spectrum. 'Sameness' feminists usually have responded to the feminists of difference by reiterating their basic insight that individual men and women can be very similar. While true this is not an adequate response to the basic insight of 'difference' feminists: that gender exists, that men and women differ as groups. In this chapter I try to speak to feminists of difference on their own terms. While I take gender seriously, I disagree with the description of gender provided by difference feminists ...

Refocusing the Debate

This section pursues two themes that will be crucial in refocusing the debate within feminism away from the destructive battle between 'sameness' and 'difference' toward a deeper understanding of gender as a system of power relations. I first argue that despite the force of Catharine MacKinnon's insight that gender involves disparities of power, her rejection of the traditional feminist ideal of gender-neutrality rests on misconceptions about this traditional goal,

---

249 (1989) 87 *Michigan Law Review* 797.

250 At the time of writing, Associate Professor of Law, Washington College of Law, American University.

251 B Friedan, *The Feminine Mystique* (1963).

whose core aim is to oppose rules that institutionalise a correlation between gender and sex. Thus the traditional goal is not one of gender blindness; the goal instead is to deinstitutionalise gender, a long and arduous process that first requires us to see through the seductive descriptions of men and women offered by domesticity. I conclude the chapter by arguing that to the extent these descriptions offer an accurate description of gender differences, they merely reflect the realities of the oppressive gender system. Beyond that, the description is unconvincing.

From Gender-neutrality to Deinstitutionalising Gender

'Sameness' feminists' focus on the similarities between individual men and individual women led them to advocate 'gender-neutral' categories that do not rely on gender stereotypes to differentiate between men and women. Recent feminists have challenged the traditional goal of gender-neutrality on the grounds that it mandates a blindness to gender that has left women in a worse position than they were before the 20th century challenge to gender roles.

This argument has been made in two different ways. Scholars such as Martha Fineman have argued that liberal feminists' insistence on gender-neutrality in the formulation of 'no-fault' divorce laws has led to courts' willful blindness to the ways in which marriage systematically helps men's, and hurts women's, careers.[252] Catharine MacKinnon has generalised this argument. She argues that because women are systematically disadvantaged by their sex, properly designed remedial measures can legitimately be framed by reference to sex.[253]

MacKinnon's 'inequality approach' would allow for separate standards for men and women so long as 'the policy or practice in question [does not] integrally contribute to the maintenance of an underclass or a deprived position because of gender status'. The strongest form her argument takes is that adherence to gender roles disadvantages women: Why let liberal feminists' taboo against differential treatment of women eliminate the most effective solution to inequality?

This debate is graced by a core truth and massive confusion. The core truth is that an insistence on gender-neutrality by definition precludes protection women victimised by gender.

The confusion stems from the use of the term gender-neutrality. One could argue that problems created by the gendered structure of wage labour, or other aspects of the gender system, should not be remedied through the use of categories that identify the protected group by reference to the gender roles that have disadvantaged them. For example, one could argue that workers whose careers were disadvantaged by choices in favour of child care should not be given the additional support they need to 'catch up' with their former spouses, on the grounds that the group protected inevitably would be mostly female, and this could reinforce the stereotype that women need special protections. Yet I know of no feminist of any stripe who makes this argument, which would be the position of someone committed to gender-neutrality.

Traditionally, feminists have insisted not upon a blindness to gender, but on opposition to the traditional correlation between sex and gender. MacKinnon's

252 Fineman, 'Implementing Equality: Ideology, Contradiction and Social Change' (1983) *Wis L Rev* at 789, 791.

253 *Sexual Harassment* at pp 100–41 (discussing *Phillips v Martin Marietta Corp* 400 US 542 (1971)); *Feminism Unmodified* at pp 35–36.

crucial divergence is that she accepts the use of sex as a proxy for gender. Thus MacKinnon sees nothing inherently objectionable about protecting workers who have given up ideal worker status due to child care responsibilities by offering protections to women. Her inequality approach allows disadvantages produced by gender to be remedied by reference to sex. This is in effect an acceptance and a reinforcement of the societal presumption that the social role of primary caretaker is necessarily correlated with possession of a vagina.

MacKinnon's approach without a doubt would serve to reinforce and to legitimise gender stereotypes that are an integral part of the increasingly oppressive gender system. Let's focus on a specific example. Scholars have found that the abolition of the maternal presumption in child custody decisions has had two deleterious impacts on women.[254] First, in the 90% of the cases where mothers received custody, mothers often find themselves bargaining away financial claims in exchange for custody of the children. Even if the father does not want custody, his lawyer often will advise him to claim it in order to have a bargaining chip with which to bargain down his wife's financial claims. Second, the abolition of the maternal preference has created situations where a father who wants custody often wins even if he was not the primary caretaker prior to the divorce – on the grounds that he can offer the children a better life because he is richer than his former wife. In these circumstances, the ironic result of a mother's sacrifice of ideal worker status for the sake of her children is that she ultimately loses the children.

While these results are no doubt infuriating, do they merit a return to a maternal presumption, as MacKinnon's approach seems to imply? No: the deconstruction of gender, by highlighting the chronic and increasing oppressiveness of the gender system, demonstrates the undesirability of the inequality approach, which would reinforce the gender system in both a symbolic way and a practical one. On a symbolic level, the inequality approach would reinforce and legitimise the traditional assumption that childrearing is naturally the province of women. MacKinnon's rule also would reinforce gender mandates in a very concrete way. Say a father chose to give up ideal worker status in order to undertake primary child care responsibility. MacKinnon's rule fails to help him because the rule is framed in terms of biology, not gender. The result: a strong message to fathers that they should not deviate from established gender roles. MacKinnon's rule operates to reinforce the gender system.

What we need, then, is a rule that avoids the traditional correlation between gender and sex, a rule that is sex- but not gender-neutral. The traditional goal, properly understood, is really one of sex neutrality, or, more descriptively, one of deinstitutionalising gender. It entails a systematic refusal to institutionalise gender in any form. This approach mandates not an enforced blindness to gender but, rather, a refusal to reinforce the traditional assumption that adherence to gender roles flows 'naturally' from biological sex. Reinforcing that assumption reinforces the grip of the gender system as a whole. For an example that highlights the distinction between gender-neutrality and deinstitutionalisation, let us return to our 'divorce revolution' example. It is grossly unfair for the courts suddenly to pretend that gender roles within marriage do not exist once a couple enters the courtroom, and the deinstitutionalisation of gender does not require it. What is needed is not a

---

254 See Polikoff, 'Why Mothers are Losing: A Brief Analysis of Criteria Used in Child Custody Determinations' (1982) 7 *Women's Rts L Rep* 235.

gender-neutral rule but one that avoids the traditional shorthand of addressing gender by reference to sex.

This analysis shows that the traditional commitment, which is really one to deinstitutionalising gender rather than to gender-neutrality, need not preclude rules that protect people victimised by gender. People disadvantaged by gender can be protected by properly naming the group: in this case, not mothers but anyone who has eschewed ideal worker status to fulfill child care responsibilities. One court, motivated to clear thinking by a legislature opposed to rules that addressed gender disabilities by reference to sex, has actually framed child custody rules in this way.[255]

The traditional goal is misstated by the term gender-neutrality. The core feminist goal is not one of pretending gender does not exist. Instead, it is to deinstitutionalise the gendered structure of our society. There is no reason why, people disadvantaged by gender need to be suddenly disowned. The deconstruction of gender allows us to protect them by reference to their social roles instead of their genitals.

Deconstructing Difference

How can this be done? Certainly the hardest task in the process of deconstructing gender is to begin the long and arduous process of seeing through the descriptions of men and women offered by domesticity. Feminists need to explain exactly how the traditional descriptions of men and women are false. This is a job for social scientists, for a new Carol Gilligan in reverse, who can focus the massive literature on sex stereotyping in a way that dramatises that Gilligan is talking about metaphors, not actual people. Nonetheless, I offer some thoughts on Gilligan's central imagery: that women are focused on relationships, while men are not. As I see it, to the extent this is true, it is merely a restatement of male and female gender roles under the current gender system. Beyond that, it is unconvincing.

This is perhaps easiest to see from Gilligan's description of men as empty vessels of capitalist virtues – competitive and individualistic and espousing liberal ideology to justify this approach to life. Gilligan's description has an element of truth as a description of gender: it captures men's sense of entitlement to ideal worker status and their gendered choice in favour of their careers when presented with the choice society sets up between childcare responsibilities and being a 'responsible' worker.

Similarly, Gilligan's central claim that women are more focused on relationships reflects gender verities. It is true in the sense that women's lives are shaped by the needs' of their children and their husbands – but this is just a restatement of the gender system that has traditionally defined women's social existence in terms of their husbands' need to eliminate child care and other responsibilities that detract from their ability to function as ideal workers. And when we speak of women's focus on relationships with men, we also reflect the underlying reality that the only alternative to marriage for most women – certainly for most mothers – has traditionally been poverty, a state of affairs that continues in force to this day.

The kernel of truth in Gilligan's 'voices,' then, is that Gilligan provides a description of gender differences related to men's and women's different roles

---

255 See *Garska v McCoy* (W Va 1981) 278 SE 2d 357 at 360–63, cited in Williams, 'The Equality Crisis: Some Reflections on Culture, Courts, and Feminism' (1982) 7 *Women's Rts L Rep* at 175, 190, n 80.

with respect to wage labour and childcare under the current gender regime. Yet we see these true gender differences through glasses framed by an ideology that distorts our vision. To break free of traditional gender ideology, we need at the simplest level to see how men nurture people and relationships and how women are competitive and powerful. This is a task in which we as feminists will meet considerable resistance, both from inside and outside the feminist movement.

Our difficulty in seeing men's nurturing side stems in part from the word nurture. Although its broadest definition is 'the act of promoting development or growth', the word derives from nursing a baby, and still has overtones of 'something only a mother can do'.[256] Yet men are involved in all kinds of relationships in which they promote another's development in a caring way: as fathers, as mentors, as camp counsellors, as boy scout leaders. These relationships may have a somewhat different emotional style and tone than do those of women and often occur in somewhat different contexts: that is the gender difference. But a blanket assertion that women are nurturing while men are not reflects more ideology than reality.

So does the related claim that women's voice involves a focus on relationships that is lacking in men. Men focus on relationships, too. How they can be said not to in a culture that deifies romantic love as much as ours does has always mystified me. Perhaps part of what resonates in the claim that men do not focus on relationships is that men as a group tend to have a different style than do women: whereas women tend to associate intimacy with self-disclosure, men tend not to.[257] This may be why women forget about the role that relationships play in men's lives, from work relationships, to solidarity based on spectator sports, to time spent 'out with the boys'. These relationships may not look intimate to women, but they are often important to men.

Ideology not only veils men's needy side, it also veils the competitive nature of many women who want power as avidly as men.

Feminists have long been fiercely critical of male power games, yet we have often ignored or concealed our own conflicts over money, control, position, and recognition ... It is time to end the silence.[258] The first step, as these authors note, is to acknowledge the existence of competition in women's lives. Women's desire for control may be exercised in running 'a tight ship' on a small income, in tying children to apron strings, or in nagging husbands – the classic powerplay of the powerless. Note how these examples tend to deprecate women's desire for power. These are the stereotypes that come to mind because they confirm the ideology that 'real' women don't need power. These are ways women's yearning for power has been used as evidence against them, as evidence they are not worthy as wives, as mothers, or as women. Feminists' taboo against competition has only reinforced the traditional view that real women don't need power. Yet women's traditional roles have always required them to be able to wield power with self-confidence and subtlety. Other cultures recognise that dealing with a two-year-old is one of the great recurring power struggles in the cycle of human life. But not ours. We, are too wrapped up in viewing childrearing as nurturing, as something opposed by its nature to authoritative wielding of power, to see

---

256 William Morris (ed), *The American Heritage Dictionary* (1970).

257 See Rubin and Shenker, 'Friendship, Proximity, and Self-disclosure' (1978) 46 J *Personality* at 1–22.

258 V Miner and H Longino (eds), *Competition: A Feminist Taboo?* (1987).

.

that nurturing involves a sophisticated use of power in a hierarchical relationship. The differences between being a boss and a mother in this regard are differences in degree as well as in kind.

Moving ever closer to the bone, we need to reassess the role of power in relationships based on romantic love. The notion that a marriage involves complex ongoing negotiations over power may seem shocking. But if we truly are committed to a deconstruction of traditional gender verities, we need to stop blinding ourselves to nurturing outside the home and to power negotiations within it.

Conclusion

The first message of this chapter is that feminists uncomfortable with relational feminism cannot be satisfied with their conventional response: 'When we get a voice, we don't all say the same thing.' The traditional focus on how individuals diverge from gender stereotypes fails to come to terms with gender similarities of women as a group. I have tried to present an alternative response. By taking gender seriously, I have reached conclusions very different from those of the relational feminists. I have not argued that if gender differences do not exist; only that relational feminists have misdescribed them.

Relational feminism, I have argued, can best be understood as encompassing two critiques: the critique of possessive individualism and the critique of absolutes. Both are better stated in non-gendered terms, though for different reasons. Feminists are simply incorrect when they claim the critique of absolutes as women's voice, since that critique has been developed by men and its ideal is different from the traditional stereotype of women as emotional and illogical.

Relational feminism's linkage of women to the critique of possessive individualism is trickier. If all relational feminists claim is that elite white men are disproportionately likely to buy more completely into the ideology that controls access to wealth, in one sense this is true. I would take it on faith that a higher proportion of elite white males buy into possessive individualism than do black males, working-class and poor males, or women of all groups. Indeed, in the last 20 years writers have documented that these marginalised groups have developed their own cultures that incorporate critiques of mainstream culture. 'One very important difference between white people and black people is that white people think you are your work', a black informant told an anthropologist in the 1970s. 'Now a black person has more sense than that.'[259] Marginalised groups necessarily have maintained a more critical perspective on possessive individualism in general, and the value of wage labour in particular, than did white males who had most to gain by taking the culture's dominant ideology seriously. Moreover, the attitude of white women towards wage labour reflects their unique relationship with it. Traditionally, married white women, even many working-class women, had a relationship to wage, labour that only a very few leisured men have ever had. These women viewed wage labour as something that had to prove its worth in their lives because the option not to work remained open to them psychologically (if, at times, not economically).

Fewer blacks and women have made the virtues of possessive individualism a central part of their self-definition, and this is a powerful force for social change.

---

259 JL Gwaltney, *Drylongsoul: A Self-Portrait of Black America* (1981) pp 173–74, quoted in S Harley, 'When Your Work is Not Who You Are', paper given at the Conference on Women in the Progressive Era, sponsored by the American Historical Association in conjunction with the National Museum of American History (1988).

But blacks as a group and women as a group have these insights not because they are an abiding part of 'the' black family or of women's 'voice'. These are insights black culture and women's culture bring from their history of exclusion. We want to preserve the insights but abandon the marginalisation that produced them: to become part of a mainstream that learns from our experience. The *Sears case* shows how these insights transformative potential can easily backfire if the critiques can be marginalised as constitutive of a semi-permanent part of the black or female personality.[260]

Relational feminists help diffuse the transformable potential of the critique of possessive individualism by championing a gendered version of that critique. The simple answer is that they should not say they are talking about women if they admit they aren't. Once they admit they are talking about gender, they have to come to terms with domesticity's hegemonic role in enlisting women in their own oppression.

The approach of deconstructing gender requires women to give up their claims to special virtue. But it offers ample compensation. It highlights the fact that women will be vulnerable until we redesign the social ecology, starting with a challenge to the current structure of wage labour. The current structure may not have been irrational in the 18th century, but it is irrational today. Challenging it today should be at the core of a feminist programme.

The message that women's position will remain fundamentally unchanged until labour is restructured is both a hopeful and a depressing one. It is depressing because it shows that women will remain economically vulnerable in the absence of fundamental societal change. Yet it is hopeful because if we heed it, we may be able to unite as feminists to seize the opportunity offered by mothers' entry into the work force, instead of frittering it away rediscovering traditional (and inaccurate) descriptions of gender differences.

---

260 *EEDC v Sears, Roebuck & Co*, 628 F Supp 1264 (ND 1ll 1986), aff'd, 839 F 2d 302 (7th Cir 1988).

PART III

WOMEN IN POLITICAL AND LEGAL THEORY

CHAPTER 7

ANCIENT POLITICAL THOUGHT

The patriarchal tradition, the origins of which lie in nature and culture, became firmly established in early political thought. The writings of Plato[1] and Aristotle,[2] which have so influenced later political and legal thought, reveal deep ambivalences regarding the position of women in society. The question of gender difference, analysed in Chapter 6, has its seeds of origin in ancient Greek thought. In this chapter, extracts from these philosophers' works will be presented, together with a critique from a feminist perspective.

In Plato's writings, a deep uncertainty exists regarding women. In *The Republic* for example is to be found the clearest expression of equality between the sexes and the irrelevance of biological differences between men and women. Later, however, Plato appears to change his mind: when it comes to the power to be allocated in civic society, only women of the highest class are to be entrusted with responsibility. The remainder – the largest sector – are to be relegated to the private domain. The class structure runs through Plato's work as a common theme. The highest class – the guardians – are to be regulated in a different manner from the masses. In relation to the guardians, Plato distrusted both private property and the family; the former for its tendency to distract man from his civic responsibilities, the latter for its tendency to isolate individuals and bind them in a particular affective unit. His responses are radical: abolish both private property and the family. Women would be freed from the duties of the private family and thus gain full civic equality. However, the task of childbearing remained of fundamental importance, and to accommodate society's needs, Plato envisaged a system whereby male and female guardians would mate under carefully monitored conditions in order to ensure the production of the most talented of children.

In the dialogue which follows, Socrates discusses the role of women with Glaucon.

THE REPUBLIC[3]
Plato

'We can, I think, only make satisfactory arrangements for the possession and treatment of women and children by men born and educated as we have described, if we stick to the course on which we started; our object you remember, was to make them like watchdogs guarding a flock.'

'Yes.'

'Let us, then, proceed to arrange for their birth and upbringing accordingly. We can then see if it suits our purpose.'

'How do you mean?'

'What I mean is this. Ought female watchdogs to perform the same guard-duties as male, and watch and hunt and so on with them? Or ought they to stay at

---

1   C 427–347 BC.

2   384–322 BC.

3   Trans D Lee (Penguin Classics, 2nd edn, 1974).

home on the grounds that the bearing and rearing of their puppies incapacitates them from other duties, so that the whole burden of the care of the flocks fall on the males?'

'They should share all duties, though we should treat the females as the weaker, the males as the stronger.'

'And can you use any animal for the same purpose as another', I asked, 'unless you bring it up and train it in the same way?'

'No.'

'So if we are going to use men and women for the same purposes, we must teach them the same things.'

'Yes.'

'We educated the men both physically and mentally.'

'Yes.'

'We shall have to train the women also, then, in both kinds of skill, and train them for war as well, and treat them in the same way as the men.'

'It seems to follow from what you said', he agreed.

'I dare say', I rejoined, 'that their novelty would make many of our proposals seem ridiculous if they were put into practice.'

'There's no doubt about that,' he said.

'And won't the most ridiculous thing of all be to see the women taking exercise naked[4] with the men in the gymnasium? It won't only be the young women; there will be elderly women too, just as there are old men who go on with their exercises when they are wrinkled and ugly to look at.'

'Lord!' he said, 'that's going to be a funny sight by present standards.'

'Still,' I said, 'now we've launched out on the subject we must not be afraid of the clever jokes that are bound to be made about all the changes that follow in the physical training and education of women, and above all about them being trained to carry arms and ride.'

'You are quite right.'

'So having started off, we must go on to legislate for the real difficulties.'[5]

Socrates then considers whether natural differences should translate into differing responsibilities:

'Well,' he [an imaginary critic] will continue, 'isn't there a very great natural difference between men and women?' And when we admit that too, he will ask us whether we ought not to give them different roles to match these natural differences. When we say yes, he will ask, 'Then aren't you making a mistake and contradicting yourselves, when you go on to say that men and women should follow the same occupations, in spite of the great natural difference between them?' What about that? Are you clever enough to answer him?'

'It's not easy to answer on the spur of the moment,' he replied. 'I can only turn to you and ask you to explain our case in reply, whatever it is.'[6]

---

4   The Greeks always exercised naked, and the nakedness is merely the consequence of the proposal that women should take part in athletics at all.

5   *The Republic*, Book Five, 451e–452e.

6   *Ibid*, Book Five, 453b–453c.

'Well, let's see if we can find a way out. We admit that different natures ought to have different kinds of occupation, and that men and women have different natures; and yet we go on to maintain that these admittedly different natures ought to follow the same occupations. That is the charge we have to meet, isn't it?'

'That is it.' ...[7]

... 'We are sticking obstinately to the verbal debating point that different natures should not be given the same occupations; but we haven't considered what kind of sameness or difference of nature we mean, and what our intention was when we laid down the principle that different natures should have different jobs, similar natures similar jobs.'

'No, we've not taken that into consideration.'

'Yet we might just as well, on this principle, ask ourselves whether bald men and long-haired men are of the same or opposite natures, and, having agreed that they are opposite, allow bald men to be cobblers and forbid long-haired men to be, or vice versa.'

'That would be absurd.'

'But the reason why it is absurd,' I pointed out, 'is simply that we never meant that natures are the same or different in an unqualified sense, but only with reference to the kind of sameness or difference which is relevant to various employments. For instance, we should regard a man and a woman with medical ability as having the same nature. Do you agree?'

'Yes.'

'But a doctor and a carpenter we should reckon as having different natures.'

'Yes, entirely.'

'Then if men or women as a sex[8] appear to be qualified for different skills or occupations,' I said, 'we shall assign these to each accordingly; but if the only difference apparent between them is that the female bears and the male begets, we shall not admit that this is a difference relevant for our purpose, but shall still maintain that our male and female Guardians ought to follow the same occupations.'

'And rightly so,' he agreed. ...[9]

... 'Then is there any human activity at which men aren't far better in all these respects than women? We need not waste time over exceptions like weaving and various cooking operations, at which women are thought to be experts, and get badly laughed at if a man does them, better.'

'It's quite true,' he replied, 'that in general the one sex is much better at everything than the other. A good many women, it is true, are better than a good many men at a good many things. But the general rule is as you stated it.'

'There is therefore no administrative occupation which is peculiar to woman as woman or man as man; natural capacities are similarly distributed in each sex, and it is natural for women to take part in all occupations as well as men, though in all women will be the weaker partners.'

---

7   *The Republic*, Book Five, 454b.

8   *Genos*: natural kind.

9   *The Republic*, Book Five, 454e.

'Agreed.' ...[10]

... 'Do you agree, then, that the best arrangement is for our men and women to share a common education, to bring up their children in common and to have a common responsibility, as guardians, for their fellow-citizens, as we have described? That women should in fact, so far as possible, take part in all the same occupations as men, both in peace within the city and on campaign in war, acting as guardians and hunting with the men like hounds, that this is the best course for them, and that there is nothing unwomanly[11] in this natural partnership of the sexes?'[12]

In *Symposium*, Plato considers the nature of love. Here is found his true view of women – as inferior beings tinged with 'lewdness'. Plato's misogyny shines clearly through in the following passage. The discussion takes place at a dinner; the first speaker is Pausanias:

SYMPOSIUM[13]
Plato

Now you will all agree, gentlemen, that without Love there could be no such goddess as Aphrodite. If, then, there were only one goddess of that name, we might suppose that there was only one kind of Love, but since in fact there are two such goddesses there must also be two kinds of Love. No one, I think, will deny that there are two goddesses of that name – one, the elder, sprung from no mother's womb but from the heavens themselves, we call the Uranian, the heavenly Aphrodite, while the younger, daughter of Zeus and Dione, we call Pandemus, the earthly Aphrodite. It follows, then, that Love should be known as earthly or as heavenly according to the goddess in who company his work is done. And our business, gentlemen – I need hardly say that every go must command our homage – our business at the moment is to define the attributes peculiar to each of these two.

Now it may be said that any kind of action that the action itself, as such, is neither good nor bad. Take, for example, what we are doing now. Neither drinking nor singing nor talking has any virtue in itself, for the outcome of each action depends upon how it is performed. If it is done rightly and finely, the action will be good; if it is done basely, bad. And this holds good of loving, for Love is not of himself either admirable or noble, but only when he moves us to love nobly.

Well then, gentlemen, the earthly Aphrodite's Love is a very earthly Love indeed, and does his work entirely at random. It is he that governs the passions of the vulgar. For, first, they are as much attracted by women as by boys; next, whoever they may love, their desires are of the body rather that of the soul; and, finally, they make a point of courting the shallowest people they can find, looking forward to the mere act of fruition and careless whether it be a worth or unworthy consummation. And hence they take their pleasures where they find them, good and bad alike. For this is the Love of the younger Aphrodite, whose nature partakes of both male and female.

---

10   *Ibid*, Book Five, 455c–455d.
11   More fully, 'nothing against the nature of woman as compared with man'. (Translator.)
12   *The Republic*, Book Five, 466c–466d.
13   Trans M Joyce, in *Plato: the Collected Dialogues*, eds E Hamilton and H Cairns (Princeton University Press, 1963), p 526.

But the heavenly Love springs from a goddess whose attributes have nothing of the female, but are altogether male, and who is also the elder of the two, and innocent of any hint of lewdness.[14]

In *Laws*,[15] Plato makes it clear that men and women are not to be treated equally in matters of succession. In the passage which follows, Athenian is discussing the matter with Clinias:

Our statute shall be to this effect. A person making written testamentary disposition of his effects, shall, if he have issue, first set down the name of such son as he judges proper to inherit. If he have another son whom he offers for adoption by a fellow citizen, he shall set his name down also. If there be still a son left, not already adopted as heir to any patrimony, who may expect in course of law to be sent to some overseas settlement, it shall be free to him to bequeath to such son such of his goods as he sees fit, other than his patrimonial estate and its complete plenishing. If there be more such sons than one, the father shall divide his possessions, other than his patrimony, among them in such proportions as he pleases. But if a son already possess a house, no portion of such goods shall be bequeathed to him, and the same shall hold in the case of a daughter; a daughter not contracted to a husband shall receive her share, but a daughter already so contracted shall receive none. If a son or daughter be found to have come into possession of an allotment of land subsequent to the date of the will, such party shall leave the bequest in the hands of the testator's heir. If the testator leave only female issue without male, he shall by will provide one daughter, selected at his pleasure, with a husband and himself with a son, and shall name such husband as his heir. If a man's son, naturally begotten or adopted, die in infancy before reaching the age of manhood, the testator shall further make provision for this contingency by naming a child to succeed such son with happier omens. If the party making his testament is absolutely childless, he may set aside one-tenth part of his acquired possessions for the purpose of legacies to any persons he pleases; all else shall be left to the adopted heir whom he shall make his son, in all integrity on the one part and gratitude on the other, with the law's approval.[16]

Aristotle adopts a very different stance from that of Plato, who in *The Republic* argues for the abolition of private property and the family – at least in relation to the 'upper classes', or Guardians. In *The Politics*, Aristotle starts with an enquiry:

THE POLITICS[17]

Aristotle

In a State, either all the citizens share all things, or they share none, or they share some but not others. It is clearly impossible that they should have no share in anything; at the very least, a constitution being a form of association, they must share in the territory, the single territory of a single State, of which single State the citizens are sharers. The question then becomes twofold: if a city is to be run well, is it better that all the citizens should share in all things capable of being

---

14 *Symposium*, 180d–181d.

15 Trans AE Taylor, in *Plato: the Collected Dialogues, op cit*, p 1225.

16 *Laws*, Book XI, 923d, e, 924a.

17 Trans TA Sinclair, revised TJ Saunders (Penguin Classics, 1981).

shared, or only in some of them and not in others? It is certainly quite possible for citizens to go shares with each other in children, in wives, and in pieces of property, as in *The Republic* of Plato. For in that work Socrates says that children, wives, and property ought to be held in common.[18] We ask, therefore, is it better to do as we now do, or should we adopt the law proposed in *The Republic*?[19]

Aristotle's first objection to Plato's proposal relates to Socrates wish that the State 'should be as much of a unity as possible.'[20] This, argues Aristotle is unrealistic: 'the State consists not merely of a plurality of men, but of different kinds of men; you cannot make a State out of men who are all alike.'[21] Extreme unity, according to Aristotle, as hypothesised by Plato, is unrealistic. Aristotle also recognises the strong desire which humans have for their own 'possessions':

THE POLITICS

So, taken all round, the results of putting such laws as these in practice would inevitably be directly opposed to the results which correct legislation ought to bring about, and moreover to those that Socrates regards as the reason for ordering matters in this way for children and wives. For we believe that the existence of affectionate feelings in states is a very great boon to them: it is a safeguard against faction. And Socrates is emphatic in his praise of unity in the State, which (as it seems, and as he himself says) is one of the product of affection. In another of Plato's dialogues, one which treats of love, we read[22] that Aristophanes said that lovers because of the warmth of their affection are eager to grow into each other and become one instead of two. In such an event one or other must perish, if not both. But in a State in which there exists such a mode of association[23] the feelings of affection will inevitably be watery, father hardly ever saying 'my son', or son 'my father'. Just as a small amount of sweetening dissolved in a large amount of water does not reveal its presence to the taste, so the feeling of relationship implied in these terms become nothing; and in a State organised like this there is virtually nothing to oblige fathers to care for their sons, or sons for their fathers, or brothers for each other. There are two impulses which more than all others cause human beings to cherish and feel affection for each other: 'this is my own', and 'this is a delight'. Among people organised in this manner no one would be able to say either.

Turning now to the good man, we find the same two qualities.[24] And this is true even though the self-control and justice exercised in ruling are not the same in kind.[25] For clearly the virtue of the good man, who is free but governed, for example, his justice will not be always the same: it will take different forms according to whether he is to rule or be ruled, just as self-control and courage vary as between men and women. A man would seem a coward if he had only

---

18 *Republic*, Book Four, 427c ff.

19 *The Politics*, Book II, 1260b.

20 *Republic*, Book Four, 422 ff, Book Five, 462a ff.

21 *The Politics*, Book IIii, 1261a22.

22 *Symposium*, 191a and 192d, e. On which see above at p 280.

23 Ie one like *The Republic*'s, which, by holding wives and children in common, aims at excessive unity, as in the *Symposium*.

24 The knowledge and ability both to rule and be ruled.

25 Ie not the same as the self-control and justice exercised in being ruled.

the courage of a woman, a woman a chatterbox if she were only as discreet as a good man. Men and women have different parts to play in managing the household: his to win, hers to preserve. But the only virtue special to a ruler is practical wisdom; all the others must be possessed, so it seems, both by rulers and by ruled. The virtue of a person being ruled is not practical wisdom but correct opinion; he is rather like a person who makes the pipes, while the ruler is the one who can play them.[26]

Aristotle makes it clear that in his view women are naturally inferior to men. Aristotle regards the 'household' as a crucial element within a State, and argues that as with the State, there must be a ruler – a master of the household. Moreover, it is clear that reproduction is the most important function assigned to wives.

THE POLITICS

The Two 'Pairs'

We shall, I think, in this as in other subjects, get the best view of the matter if we look at the natural growth of things from the beginning. The first point is that those which are incapable of existing without each other must be united as a pair. For example, (a) the union of male and female is essential for reproduction; and this is not a matter of choice, but is due to the natural urge, which exists in the other animals too and in plants, to propagate one's kind. Equally essential is (b) the combination of the natural ruler and ruled, for the purpose of preservation. For the element that can use its intelligence to look ahead is by nature ruler and by nature master, while that which has the bodily strength to do the actual work is by nature a slave, one of those who are ruled. Thus there is a common interest uniting master and slave.

Formation of the Household

Nature, then, has distinguished between female and slave: she recognises different functions and lavishly provides different tools, not an all-purpose tool like the Delphic knife,[27] for every instrument will be made best if it serves not many purposes but one. But non-Greeks assign to female and slave exactly the same status. This is because they have nothing which is by nature fitted to rule; their association[28] consists of a male slave and a female slave. So, as the poets say, 'It is proper that Greeks should rule non-Greeks,'[29] the implication being that non-Greek and slave are by nature identical.

Thus it was out of the association formed by men with these two, women and slaves, that a household was first formed; and the poet Hesiod was right when he wrote, 'Get first a house and a wife and an ox to draw the plough'.[30] (The ox is the poor man's slave.) This association of persons established according to nature for the satisfaction of daily needs, is the household, the members of which

---

26   *The Politics* trans TA Sinclair (Penguin Books, 1981), Book IIIiv, 1277b16, p 182.
27   Evidently a knife capable of more than one mode of cutting, and not perfectly adapted to any one of them.
28   That is, of marriage.
29   Euripides, Iphigeneia in Aulis 1400.
30   *Works and Days* 405.

Charondas calls 'bread-fellows', and Epimenides the Cretan 'stable-companions'.[31, 32]

When the allocation of roles within the household – that fundamental unit of the State – is considered, Aristotle is clear that the husband is 'the ruler' within the household:

THE POLITICS

There are, as we say, three parts of household-management, one being the rule of a master,[33] which has already been dealt with, next the rule of a father, and a third which arises out of the marriage relationship. This is included because rule is exercised over wife and children – over both of them as free persons, but in other respects differently: over a wife, rule is as by a statesman; over children, as by a king. For the male is more fitted to rule than the female, unless conditions are quite contrary to nature; and the elder and fully grown is more fitted than the younger and undeveloped. It is true that in most cases of rule by statesmen there is an interchange of the role of ruler and ruled, which aims to preserve natural equality and non-differentiation; nevertheless, so long as one is ruling and the other is being ruled, the ruler seeks to mark distinctions in outward dignity, in style of address, and in honours paid. (Witness what Amasis said about his foot-basin.)[34] As between male and female this kind of relationship is permanent. Rule over children is royal, for the begetter is ruler by virtue both of affection and of age, and this type of rule is royal. Homer therefore was right in calling Zeus 'father of gods and men',[35] as he was king over them all. For a king ought to have a natural superiority, but to be no different in birth; and this is just the condition of elder in relation to younger and of father to son.[36]

For Aristotle, women's role was primarily that of marriage, procreation and rearing of the healthiest possible future citizens. In this cause, Aristotle considers the regulation of sexual intercourse, reproduction and envisages abortion on eugenic grounds, in the interests of the State.

Now as it is a law-giver's duty to start from the very beginning in looking for ways to secure the best possible physique for the young who are reared, he must consider first the union of their parents, and ask what kind of people should come together in marriage, and when. In making regulations about this partnership he should have regard both to the spouses themselves and to their length of life, in order that they may arrive at the right ages together at the same time, and so that the period of the father's ability to beget and that of the mother's to bear children may coincide. A period when one of the two is capable and the other not leads to mutual strife and quarrels. Next, as regards the timing of the children's succession,[37] there should not be too great a gap in age between

---

31 Charondas was a law-giver of Catana, in Sicily, probably of the 6th century: Aristotle refers to him several times. Epimenides was a Cretan seer and wonder-worker of about 600.

32 *The Politics*, Book III, 1252a24–1252b9.

33 Over slaves.

34 Herodotus (II 172) relates how King Amasis of Egypt (6th century), being reproached for his humble origins, had a foot-basin refashioned into a statue of a god, which the Egyptians then worshipped – the moral being that it is what one is now that matters.

35 *Iliad* I, 144.

36 *The Politics*, Book I xii, 1259a37.

37 Ie, at their parents' death, to their estate – the culmination of a period of mutual service as between them and the children, facilitated by an age-gap neither too wide nor too narrow.

father and children; for then there is no good that the young can do by showing gratitude to elderly parents, and their fathers are of no help to them. Nor should they be too close in age, for this causes the relationship to be strained: like contemporaries, people in such a position feel less respect, and the nearness in age leads to bickering in household affairs. And further, to go back to the point we started from, one should ensure that the physique of the children that are produced[38] shall be in accordance with the wishes of the legislator.

All these purposes can be fulfilled, or nearly so, if we pay sufficient attention to one thing. Since, generationally speaking, the upper limit of age for the begetting of children is for men seventy years and for women fifty, the beginning of their union should be at ages such that they will arrive at this stage of life simultaneously. But the intercourse of a very young couple is not good for childbearing. In all animals the offspring of early unions are defective, inclined to produce females, and diminutive; so the same results are bound to follow in human beings too. And there is evidence that this is so: in States where early unions are the rule, the people are small in stature and defective. A further objection is that young women have greater difficulty in giving birth and more of them do. (Some say that here we have also the reason for the oracle given to the people of Troezen:[39] there is no reference to the harvesting of crops, but to the fact that the marrying of girls at too young an age was causing many deaths.) It is also more conducive to restraint that daughters should be no longer young when their fathers bestow them in marriage, because it seems that women who have sexual intercourse at an early age are more likely to be dissolute. On the male side too it is held that if they have intercourse while the seed is just growing, it interferes with their bodily growth; for the seed is subject to a fixed limit of time, after which it ceases to be replenished except on a small scale. Accordingly we conclude that the appropriate age for the union is about the eighteenth year for girls and for men thirty to seventy. With such timing, their unions will take place when they are physically in their prime, and it will bring them down together to the end of procreation at exactly the right moment for both.[40]

Further, it is important that women should look after their bodies during pregnancy. They must not relax unduly, or go on a meagre diet. It is easy for a legislator to ensure this by making it a rule that they shall each day take a walk, the object of which is to worship regularly the gods whose office is to look after children. But while the body should be exercised, the intellect should follow a more relaxed regime, for the unborn infant appears to be influenced by her who is carrying it as plants are by the earth.[41]

With regard to the choice between abandoning an infant or rearing it, let there be a law that no cripple child be reared. But since the ordinance of custom forbids the exposure of infants on account of their numbers, there must be a limit to the production of children. If contrary to these arrangements copulation does take place and a child is conceived, abortion should be procured before the embryo

---

38 *Ta gennomena*, 'the children being produced'. In the first paragraph, probably of both born and unborn children; in the third, probably of born children only; in the fourth, of the unborn only (*cf* Plato *Laws*, 788c ff).

39 'Do not cut (ie plough) a new (ie young) furrow.'

40 *The Politics*, Book VII xvi, 1334b29–13335a6.

41 *Ibid* at Book VII xvi, 1335b12.

has acquired life and sensation; the presence of life and sensation will be the mark of division between right and wrong[42] here.[43]

Since we have already decided the beginning of the period of life at which male and female should enter their union, we must also decide upon the length of time during which it is proper that they should render the service of producing children. The offspring of elderly people, like the offspring of the unduly young, are imperfect both in intellect and in body; and those of the aged are feeble. We should therefore be guided by the highest point of intellectual development, and this in most cases is the age mentioned by certain poets who measure life by periods of seven years, that is to say about the fiftieth year of life.[44] Thus anyone who has passed this age for four or five years ought to give up bringing children into the world. But provided it is clearly for the sake of health or other such reason intercourse may continue.[45]

As for extra-marital intercourse, it should, in general, be a disgrace to be detected in intimacy of any kind whatever, so long as one is a husband and so addressed. If anyone is found to be acting thus during the period of his begetting of children, let him be punished by such measure of disgrace as is appropriate to his misdemeanour.[46]

WOMEN IN WESTERN POLITICAL THOUGHT

Philosopher Queens and Private Wives[47]

Susan Moller Okin[48]

The aim of the true art of ruling, as Plato conceives of it, is not the welfare of any single class or group, but the greatest possible happiness of the entire community.[49] 'Happiness', however, can be a misleading word, for if it leads us to thoughts of freedom, individual rights, or equality of opportunity, we are far from Plato's idea of happiness (eudaimonia). Neither equality nor liberty nor justice in the sense of fairness were values for Plato. The three values on which both his ideal and his second-best cities are based are, rather, harmony, efficiency and moral goodness: the last is the principal key to his entire political philosophy. Because of his belief in the intrinsic value of the soul, and the consequent importance of its health, Plato does not think that happiness results from the freedom to behave just as one wants; it is regarded as in no way attainable independently of virtue. Statesmen, therefore, should 'not only preserve the lives of their subjects but reform their characters too, so far as human nature permits of this'.[50] Though the ultimate aim of the true ruler is the happiness of all his subjects, the only way he can attain this is by raising them all, by means of education and law, to the highest possible level of wisdom and virtue.

---

42 *To hosion kai to me* – literally 'that which is holy/lawful/permitted, and that which is not'.
43 *Ibid* at 1335b19.
44 Ie the husband's.
45 *The Politics*, Book VII xvi, 1335b26.
46 *Ibid*, Book VII xvi, 1335b38.
47 *Women in Western Political Thought* (Princeton University Press, 1979), Chapter 2.
48 At the time of writing, Professor of Political Science at Stanford University.
49 *The Republic* at 420b.
50 *Statesman* at 297b; cf *Laws* at 630c, 644– 645; 705d–706a, 707d; *Euthydemus*, 292b–c; see also Sheldon Wolin, *Politics and Vision* (London, 1961), pp 34–36.

The gravest of all human faults, however, is considered by Plato to be one that is inborn in most people – that 'excessive love of self' which is 'the cause of all sins in every case'.[51] 'Worse still, whereas the soul, and next the body, should take priority, the all too prevalent tendency is to give one's property – in truth the least valuable of possessions – one's greatest attentions.[52] Thus the ruler's task in promoting his subjects' virtue is two-fold. He must aim to overcome both their extremes of self-love and also their fatal preference for material possessions over the welfare of their souls. A person who is to be virtuous and great must be able to transcend his own interests, but above all to detach himself from the passion to acquire. As Glenn Morrow has noted, there is abundant evidence in both the *Republic* and the *Laws* that Plato regarded the maintenance of a temperate attitude toward property as essential for the security and well-being of a State.[53] It was acquisitiveness, after all, that had led the first city Socrates depicted – the simple, 'true' and 'healthy' city – into war with its neighbours and all the complications which this entailed. Again, the recurrent theme of Book VIII of the *Republic*, in which the process of political degeneration is analysed, is the corruption that results from increasing possessiveness.[54]

The Republic is an extremely radical dialogue. In his formulation of the ideal state, Plato is prepared to question and challenge the most sacred contemporary conventions. The solution he proposes for the problem of selfishness and divisive interests is for private property and hence private interests to be abolished, to the greatest possible extent. For in this city, not just the harmony but the unity of interest is the objective. 'Have we any greater evil for a city', asks Socrates, 'than what splits it and makes it many instead of one? Or a greater good than what binds it together and makes it one?' He concludes that the best-governed city is that 'which is most like a single human being'.[55] Nothing can dissolve the unity of a city more readily than for some of its citizens to be glad and others to grieve because of the same happening, so that all do not work or even wish in concert. The way to achieve the highest possible degree of unity is for all the citizens to feel pleasure and pain on the same occasions, and this 'community of pleasure and pain' will occur only if all goods are possessed in common. The best-governed city will be that 'in which most say 'my own' and 'not my own' about the same thing, and in the same way'.[56]

We need have no doubt that, if he had thought it possible, Plato would have extended the communal ownership of property to all the classes of his ideal city. The first of the 'noble lies', according to which all the citizens are to be told that they are one big family, can be read as the complete expression of an ideal which can unfortunately be met only in part. It is because of his belief in the tendency of most human beings to selfishness that Plato considers the renunciation of private property to be something that can be attained only by the best of persons. This is made clear in the *Laws*, where he rejects the possibility of eliminating ownership for the citizens of his projected 'second-best' city, since tilling the soil in common is 'beyond the capacity of people with the birth, rearing and training we

---

51   *Laws*, 731e.

52   *Laws*, 743d–e.

53   Morrow, *Plato's Cretan City: A Historical Interpretation of the Laws* (Princeton, 1960), p 101; see also *Laws* at 736e cite.

54   *Republic*, 372e–373e, and viii passim.

55   *Republic*, 462a–e.

56   *Republic*, 462a–e.

assume'.[57] What is impossible for the citizens of the second-best city, with all their carefully planned education, must regretfully be regarded as beyond the capacity of the inferior classes in the ideal city. Thus it is the guardian class alone which is to live up to the ideal of community of property and unity of interests.[58]

The overcoming of selfish interests is regarded as most necessary for those who are to have charge of the welfare and governance of all the other citizens, quite apart from the fact that they are the best equipped to overcome them. Since a person will always take care of what he loves, the guardians, especially, must love the whole community, and have no interests other than its welfare. For them above all, then, the permitted property arrangements must be 'such as not to prevent them from being the best possible guardians and not to rouse them up to do harm to the other citizens'.[59] The possession by the rulers of private lands and wealth would, Plato argues, inevitably lead to the formation of factions, and make of the rulers 'masters and enemies instead of allies of the other citizens'.[60] The combination of wealth and private interests with political power is intolerable and can lead only to the destruction of the city.

Plato's ideal for the guardians is expressed by the proverb, 'friends have all things in common'.[61] But if communal ownership of inanimate property is a great aid to the required unity of the city, it appears to follow that communal ownership of women and children will conduce to even greater unity. It is quite clear from the way Plato argues that he regards the communalisation of property as implying the simultaneous abolition of the family. He does not regard the two as distinct innovations requiring independent justifications. In fact, the first mention of the abolition of the family is slid over, almost as a parenthesis,[62] and both in the *Republic* and the brief summary that is presented in the *Laws*, the two proposals are justified by the same arguments and frequently at the same time. In the *Laws*, especially, in the passages where Plato looks back to the institutions of the ideal city, the classification of women and children together with other possessions occurs frequently. Thus he talks of 'community of wives, children, and all chattels', and later, by contrast, of that less desirable state of affairs in which 'women and children and houses remain private, and all these things are established as the private property of individuals'.[63]

Thus women are classified by Plato, as they were by the culture in which he lived, as an important subsection of property. The very expression, 'community (or common having) of women and children', which he uses to denote his proposed system of temporary matings, is a further indication of this, since the phenomenon could just as accurately be described as 'the community of men', were it not for its inventor's customary way of thinking about such matters'.[64]

Just as other forms of private property were seen as destructive of society's unity, so the concept of 'private wives' is viewed by Plato as divisive and subversive in the same way. Thus, in contrast to the unified city he is proposing, he points to

57 *Laws*, 739c–740a.
58 *Republic*, 416c–417b.
59 *Republic*, 416c–d.
60 *Republic*, 417a–b.
61 *Republic*, 423e; *Laws*, 739c.
62 *Republic*, 423e.
63 *Republic*, 423e, 462, 464; *Laws*, 739c, 807b.
64 *cf* Grube, *Plato's Thought* (London, 1935), p 89.

those institutional arrangements which foster the ascendance of particularism and factionalism, with 'one man dragging off to his own house whatever he can get his hands on apart from the others, another being separate in his own house with separate women and children, introducing private pleasures and grieves of things that are private'.[65] Again, in the *Laws*, he strikes out at the same time against Athenian practices with regard both to private property and to women: 'we huddle all our goods together, as the saying goes, within four walls, and then hand over the dispensing of them to the women'.[66] It is clear that conventional marriage and woman in her traditional role as guardian of the private household were seen by Plato as intimately bound up with that whole system of private possessions which separated citizens from each other, made them hostile and envious, and was the greatest impediment to the unity and well-being of the city.

It is in Book VIII of the *Republic*, however, as Plato reviews the successively degenerate forms of the political order, that we can see his association of the private possession of women with corruption at its most graphic. Just as women were communalised at the same time as other property, so are they now, without separate explanation, made private at the same time as other property, as the course of the city's degeneration is described. Once private, moreover, women are depicted as hastening the course of the decline, due to their exclusive concern with the particular interests of their families. First, when the rulers begin to want to own land, houses and money, and to set up domestic treasuries and private lovenests, they will fail as guardians of the people, and the city will start to degenerate. Thereafter, the private possession of women is depicted as a major cause of further corruption. The mother's complaints that her husband's lack of concern for wealth and public prestige disadvantages her among the other women make the timocratic youth begin to despise his worthy father and to feel challenged into showing that he is more of a man. The wife, then, with her selfish concerns, who 'chants all the other refrains such as women are likely to do in cases of this sort', is, like Pandora, the real originator of the evils that follow.[67]

The fact that Plato identifies the abolition of the family so closely with the communalisation of property, and does not appear to regard the former as an emotional deprivation of any more severity than the latter, must be understood in the context of the functions and status of the family in contemporary upper-class Athenian life. In view of the chattel status of Athenian women, and the 'peculiarly close relation thought to hold between a family and its landed property', Plato's intertwining of two issues which appear to us to be much more distinct is not hard to explain. As we have seen, it was almost impossible for husbands and wives to be either day-to-day companions or emotional and intellectual intimates. Consequently, as recent scholars of Greek life agree, 'the family does not bulk large in most Greek writing, its affective and psychological sides hardly at all', and 'family life, as we understand it, hardly existed' in late fifth century Athens.[68] The prevailing bisexuality meant that 'two complementary institutions coexisted, the family taking care of what we may call

---

65 *Republic*, 464c–d.

66 *Laws*, 805e.

67 *Republic*, 547b, 548a.

68 MI Finley, *The Ancient Greeks* (New York, 1963), pp 123–24; Ehrenberg, *Society and Civilization in Greece and Rome* (Cambridge: Mass, 1964), p 59.

the material side, pederasty (and the courtesan) the affective, and to a degree the intellectual, side of a man's intimate life'.[69]

On the other hand, while the family was certainly no centre of the upper-class Greek's emotional life, it did function in ways that the modern family does not – ways which rendered it potentially far more socially divisive. The single-family household had emerged from the clan in comparatively recent times, and it was only gradually that the polis was gaining the loyalty that had previously belonged to the once autonomous clan. Antigone represents the paradigm of this conflict of loyalties, and there were in fact various areas of life where it had not yet become clear whether family or civic obligations should prevail. The extent to which the victim's kin, rather than the rulers, were responsible for ensuring that crime was properly avenged is well documented in the *Laws*.[70] Again, the predominance of duties to parents over any notion of legal justice is clearly indicated in the *Euthyphro*, where Socrates is incredulous that a man could even think of prosecuting his own father for the murder of anyone who was not a relative.[71] Despite its minimal functioning as an emotional base, then, the Athenian family of the early fourth century, as a firm economic entity and the focus of important duties, constituted an obviously divisive force and potential threat to civic loyalty.

Those Plato scholars who have expressed profound horror at the idea that the family be abolished and replaced by those mating arrangements designed to produce the best offspring seem to have treated the issue anachronistically, by neglecting to consider the function of the family in Athenian life. When Grube, for example, objects to the system of temporary matings advocated for the guardians as 'undesirable because it does violence to the deepest human emotions' and 'entirely ignores the love element between the 'married' pair,'[72] he seems to forget that at the time the family was simply not the locus for the expression of the deepest human emotions. Even a cursory knowledge of the *Symposium*, with its deprecating comparison of those who turn their love toward women and raise families with those whose superior spiritual love is turned toward boys and philosophical searching, reveals that Plato and his audience would not have regarded the abolition of the family as a severe limitation of their intimate lives. Stranger still is the attitude taken by Leo Strauss, who not only assumes that the family is 'natural' and any move to abolish it 'convention', but makes the issue of whether the abolition of the family is possible or not into an acid test for determining the feasibility of the entire ideal State.[73] Those passages of *The Republic* to which he refers in order to demonstrate the supposed 'fact that men seem to desire naturally to have children of their own' are quite remarkably inadequate to prove his point. Moreover, his objection that Plato's controls on heterosexual behaviour means that 'the claims of eros are simply silenced' implies a complete denial of the prevailing homosexual ethos of the time. It is in fact very probable that Plato's audience would have regarded the ideal State's restrictions on their homosexual behaviour as far more repressive of their sexual feelings than the abolition of the family and the controls placed on heterosexual intercourse.

69 Finley, *The Ancient Greeks*, p 124.
70 *Laws*, eg 866 and 873e.
71 *Euthyphro*, 4a–b.
72 *Plato's Thought, op cit*, p 270; see also AE Taylor, *Plato, the Man and his Work* (London, 1926; 7th ed, 1960), p 278.
73 On Plato's *Republic*, in *The City of Man*, p 117.

The same scholars – Grube, Taylor and Strauss – who reject the abolition of the family as impossible, are those most intolerant of the proposed alternative, in which partners are chosen for each other supposedly by lot but, in fact, for eugenic purposes. Those who reject such proposals as quite impracticable, given human nature, because of their 'intolerable severity'[74] would do well to consider the position of respectable Greek women. For they were just as controlled and deprived with respect to their sexual lives as both sexes of guardians were to be in the ideal city, and without having available to them the compensations of any participation in life outside the domestic sphere. The Greek woman was not permitted to choose her sexual partner, any more than Plato's guardians were. Moreover, in her case the partner had not only the absolute right to copulate with and reproduce via her for the rest of her life, but also all the powers which her father had previously wielded over her. Once married, a woman had no condoned alternative sexual outlets, but was entirely dependent on a husband who might have any number of approved hetro or homosexual alternatives, for any satisfaction that he might choose to give her. The extent of the double standard is clearly brought into relief by the fact that the Greek word for adultery meant nothing but sexual intercourse between a married woman and a man who was not her husband. Needless to say, the punishments were very severe. Even if her husband died, a woman had no control over her life or her body, since she was returned to the custody of her father or guardian, who could remarry her at his pleasure. Alternatively to marriage, a citizen could give his sister or daughter into concubinage, whence she could be sent to a brothel, without any reproach to her owner.[75]

If Athenian women of the highest class, living in one of the most highly cultured societies the world has known, could be controlled and deprived to this extent, it is hardly arguable that the exigencies of human nature render the Platonic mating system, with its requirement of supposedly 'unnatural continence',[76] impossible to enact. Women's sexual lives have been restricted throughout the greater part of world history, just as rigidly as Plato proposes to control the intimate lives of his guardians. 'The claims of eros' have been 'simply silenced' in women with considerable success. It is apparent from much of the history of the female sex that, with a suitable indoctrination and the backing of strong sanctions, human beings can be conditioned to accept virtually any extent of control on their sexual and emotional lives. The point is, of course, that the scholars concerned have used the terms 'human emotions' and 'human nature' to refer only to men. What seems really horrific to Grube, Taylor and Strauss is that whereas the Greeks, like many other peoples, merely reserved women for the production of legitimate issue and controlled their lives accordingly, Plato has dared to suggest that the sexual lives of both male and female guardians should be controlled for the purpose of producing the best possible off-spring for the community.

The significance of Plato's abolition of the family is profound, and the proposal has been echoed by a number of subsequent theorists or rulers of Utopian societies that depend to a very high degree on cohesion and unity. As Stanley Diamond has asserted, in an illuminating essay which analyses the significance

---

74 Taylor, *op cit*, p 278; see also Grube, *op cit*, p 270, and L Strauss, *The City of Man* (Chicago, 1964), p 117.

75 J Ithurriague, *Les Idées de Platon sur la condition de la femme au regard des traditions antiques* (Paris, 1931), p 53.

76 Grube, *op cit*, p 270.

of Plato's treatment of the family: 'The obvious aim is to disengage (the guardians) from all connections and motives which might diminish their dedication to the State ... Plato clearly sensed the antagonism between State and family, and in order to guarantee total loyalty to the former, he simply abolished the latter'.[77] Moreover, it is important to notice that Plato's revolutionary solution to the conflict was not simply to obliterate the primary ties of kinship, but to extend them throughout the entire ruling class. The guardians were in fact 'to imagine that they were all one family',[78] and it is stressed in many ways that the formation of the rulers into one family is to be no mere formality. Not only are they all to address each other as brother, parent, and so on, but 'it would be ridiculous', Glaucon agrees, 'if they only mouthed, without deeds, the names of kinship'.[79] Thus, the fear and shame associated with violence toward a parent will operate as an unusually strong sanction against attack on anyone at all of the older generation. Likewise, lawsuits and factional disputes will be no more common than they would be within a family, and the city's success in war will be in large part due to the fact that soldiers will be no more likely to desert their comrades than to abandon members of their own families.[80] Indeed, as Gregory Vlastos has concisely stated, 'The ideal society of *The Republic* is a political community held together by bonds of fraternal love'.[81]

For the purposes of this study, the most important consequence of Plato's transformation of the guardian class into a single family is the radical implication it has for the role of women. Jean-Jacques Rousseau, in the course of bitterly attacking Plato both for doing away with the family and for giving equal opportunities to women, reveals in spite of his hostility a very perceptive understanding of the connection between the two innovations. 'I am well aware that in *The Republic* Plato prescribes the same exercises for women as for men,' he says. 'Having dispensed with the individual family in his system of government, and not knowing any longer what to do with women, he finds himself forced to turn them into men.'[82] If we substitute the word 'people' for 'men', since for Rousseau, as we shall see, in many important ways only men were people, Rousseau appears to be right. Scholars who have considered the connection between the first two 'waves of paradox' of Book V – the granting of equal opportunities to women and the abolition of the family – do not, however, agree. Some have stressed the independence of the two proposals, some have maintained that there is probably a causal link between them but have been unwilling to commit themselves on its direction, and at least one has rather dogmatically asserted, without giving any reasons, that it is the emancipation of women which leads to the abolition of the family. For a number of reasons, however, it seems that to the extent that a causal relationship exists between the two paradoxes, its direction is as Rousseau states it.

In the ideal city, since there is no private wealth or marriage for those in the guardian class and living arrangements are communal, there is no domestic role

---

77 S Diamond, 'Plato and the Definition of the Primitive', in *Culture in History*, S Diamond (ed) (New York, 1960) p 126.

78 Timaeus, 18c–e.

79 *The Republic*, 463c–e.

80 *The Republic* 1, 464d–e, 465a–b, 471c–d.

81 Vlastos, *The Individual as an Object of Love*, p 11.

82 Rousseau, Emile, *Oeuvres Complètes* (Paris, Pleiade Edition, 1909), Vol 4, pp 699–700 (author's translation).

such as that of the traditional housewife. Since planned breeding and communal childrearing minimise the unpredictability of pregnancy and the time demands made on mothers, maternity is no longer anything approaching a full-time occupation. Thus, women can no longer be defined by their traditional roles. However, every person in the ideal city is defined by his or her function; the education and working life of each citizen is dedicated totally to the optimal performance of a single craft.[83] If for the female guardians the relationship to particular men, children and households has ceased to be crucial, there seems to be no alternative for Plato but to consider women as persons in their own right. If they are to take their place as members of the guardian class, each must necessarily share in the functions of that class. Thus Plato had to convince his disbelieving audience that women were indeed able to perform tasks very different from those that society had customarily assigned to them. Since the general climate of opinion was so hostile to this way of thinking, the Socratic assertions that woman's nature is not inferior to man's, and that male and female virtue are the same, must undoubtedly have paved the way for the arguments Plato proceeds to put forward.

The arguments of *Republic* about the nature of women will be analysed in more detail in Chapter 3, but the main points need to be summarised here. Socrates first reminds his audience that they have all firmly agreed that each individual should be assigned work that is suited to his or her nature. But, he says, since no one will claim that there is no difference of nature between the male and the female, they are now in danger of contradicting themselves, if they argue that the female guardians should do the same work as the male. There are, however, we are reminded, many ways in which human beings can differ in their natures, and we by no means regard all of them as relevant in assigning different functions to different persons. Up to this point, Socrates asserts, we have not considered 'what form of different and same nature, and applying to what, we were distinguishing when we assigned different practices to a different nature and the same ones to the same'.[84] But, he continues, is it not reasonable to consider only those differences and similarities that have some bearing on the activity in question? We do not, for example, worry about whether a man is bald or long-haired when assessing his capability to be a good shoemaker. There seems, therefore, to be no reason to consider the difference between the sexes with regard to their procreative function – 'that the female bears and the male mounts' – as relevant in deciding whether they should play equal roles in the ruling class. Socrates lays the burden of proof firmly on whoever should claim that it is. He argues, rather, that since it is the characteristics of the soul that determine whether a person has the requisite nature for a certain pursuit, and since sex is no more related to the soul than the presence or absence of hair, members of both sexes will be skilled in all the various arts, depending on the nature of their individual souls. Thus, though he asserts that women in general are not as capable as men in general, especially in physical strength, individual members of both sexes will be capable of performing all the functions needed by the city, including guardianship and philosophy. The only way to ensure that persons are assigned the jobs for which they are best suited is to assess the merits of each, independently of sex.

---

83 *Republic* at 370; this is graphically illustrated by the assertion at 406d–407a, that if one can no longer perform one's task, it is worthless to go on living.

84 *Republic* at 454b, and see 454–456 in general for source of this paragraph.

This argument, simple as it seems, is unique among political philosophers in their assessments of the role of women. It has revolutionary implications. Plato's bold suggestion that perhaps there is no difference between the sexes apart from their roles in procreation is possible only because the requirement of unity within the ruling class, and the consequent abolition of private property and the family, entail the abolition of wifehood and the minimisation of the role of motherhood. Once the door is open, moreover, the possibilities for women are acknowledged to be boundless. The abandonment of traditional sex roles among the guardians is total – even caring for the youngest children is prescribed as work for men as well as women.[85] Plato concludes that, though females as a group are less able, the best of women can share with the best of men in the most elevated of functions involved in ruling the city. The 'philosopher monarchs', as they should always have been called, were to include both sexes .[86]

The overwhelming hostility from male scholars to Plato's first wave of paradox is discussed in an Appendix. However, one charge that has been laid against him must be dealt with here. Leo Strauss and Allan Bloom have claimed that Plato's arguments for the equality of women depend on his 'abstracting from' or 'forgetting' the body, and particularly his 'abstracting from the difference between the sexes with regard to procreation'.[87] Clearly they do not. Plato is very careful to take into account those differences between the sexes that are palpably biological and therefore inevitable – pregnancy, lactation and a degree of difference in physical strength. The mistake these scholars, in the company of millions of other people, make is that of assuming, as Plato very rationally does not, that the entire conventional female sex role follows logically from the single fact that women bear children. The real significance of the treatment of the subject of women in Book V of the *Republic* is that it is one of the very few instances in the history of thought when the biological implications of femaleness have been clearly separated out from all the conventional, institutional, and emotional baggage that has usually been identified with them. Plato's abolition of the private sphere of the guardians' lives entailed as a corollary the radical questioning of all the institutionalised differences between the sexes.

During the course of the argument about the proper education and role of women, Socrates twice indicates that these and the abolition of the family are really parts of the same issue. He talks, first, of the 'right acquisition and use of children and women' and later of 'the law concerning the possession and rearing of the women and children'.[88] In addition, the way the question of the emancipation of the female guardians is raised is in itself significant. Having introduced in an aside the proposal that the guardians will have women and children in common as well as their other possessions, Socrates is challenged, at the beginning of Book V, to justify this important decision. In answer, he embarks on his discussion, first, of the equal education and treatment of women, and second, of the communal breeding and rearing arrangements. It seems, then, that having decided to do away with the conventional role of women by doing away with the family, he feels impelled to make the proposal seem more feasible by demonstrating that, indeed, women are capable of filling many other roles and can be well utilised outside of their traditional sphere. A brief passage from

---

85 *Republic* at 460b.

86 *Republic* at 540c.

87 Strauss, On Plato's *Republic, op cit.* Part 2 of *The City and Man*, pp 116–117; Allan Bloom, *Interpretive Essay to the Republic of Plato*, pp 382–83.

88 *Republic* at 451c and 453d.

the *Laws* suffices to indicate how aware Plato was of the danger of freeing women from their confined, domestic role without giving them any alternative function. The example of the Spartans ought, he thought, to be enough to discourage any legislator from 'letting the female sex indulge in luxury and expense and disorderly ways of life, while supervising the male sex'.[89] Thus it was his dismantling of the family which not only enabled Plato to rethink the question of woman's role and her potential abilities but, more accurately, forced him to do so.

Two additional arguments strengthen the case that it is the abolition of the family which leads Plato into emancipating the female guardians rather than vice versa. First, no mention is made of the women of the inferior classes. We are told that among these householders and farmers, private land, houses and other property are to be preserved. The close connection between these things and the private ownership of women and children implies, though we are not specifically told this, that the family, too, is preserved for the lower classes.[90] Moreover, we can have no doubt that one of Plato's primary aims in the organisation of the artesans is maximum efficiency, which presumably implies the best possible use of all members of these classes. In spite of this objective, however, and although the argument in Book V concerning women's talents is applicable just as much to the other crafts as to that of governing the city, there is no suggestion of applying it to any class of women but the guardians. The only possible explanation of this seems to be that, where the family is retained, and women are private wives and functional mothers, their equality with men in other roles is not considered to be an open issue.

Second, as we shall now see, what happens to women in Plato's second-best city – as described in the *Laws* – overwhelmingly confirms our hypothesis. On the subject of women, Plato in the *Laws* shows a marked ambivalence. His dilemma results from his inability to reconcile his increasingly firm beliefs about the potential capabilities of the female sex with the reintroduction of private property and the family into the social structure of his city. On the one hand, having once thought about women as individuals, and as half of society with vast unused talents, Plato seems to have become more convinced than ever, by the time he wrote the *Laws*, that existing practice with regard to women was foolish, and that they should be educated and used, like men, to their greatest capacity. In theory, the radical statements about women from *Republic* V are carried in the *Laws* to new extremes. On the other hand, the *Laws* is a considerably less revolutionary document than the *Republic*; far from being 'a pattern laid up in heaven', whose realisation on earth is so remote a possibility that it is immaterial whether it could exist or not, the second-best city is presented as a much less Utopian construct.[91] The very title of the dialogue, usually translated '*Laws*', is in fact more accurately rendered as 'Tradition'. A significant casualty of this 'realism' is Plato's conception of the role of women. What is proposed for them in general terms is simply not carried out in the detailed institutions of the society, in which they are again private wives and the functioning mothers of particular children.

As we shall presently see, Plato's arguments and conclusions in the *Laws* about the natural potential of women are far more radical than those put forward in the

---

89 *Laws* at 806a–c.

90 *Republic* at 417a–b.

91 *Republic* at 592b, *Laws* at 739.

Republic. He appears, in fact, to attribute to the different rearing and education afforded the two sexes practically all of the differences in their subsequent abilities and achievements. Pointing to the example of the Sarmatian women, who participate in warfare equally with the men, as proof of the potential of the female sex, he argues that the Athenian practice of maintaining rigid sex roles is absurd. Only a 'surprising blunder' of a legislator could allow the waste of half the State's available resources, by prescribing that 'most irrational' practice – 'that men and women should not all follow the same pursuits with one accord and with all their might'.[92]

However, having made the general proclamation that the law should prescribe the same education and training for girls as for boys, and that 'the female sex must share with the male, to the greatest extent possible, both in education and in all else'; should 'share with men in the whole of their mode of life',[93] Plato's Athenian legislator fails to apply these precepts in many of the most crucial instances. In order to understand the inconsistency between the general statements about women and the very different detailed specifications that are set out with regard to the most important of civic duties, we must consider the effects on women of the reinstatement of the family.

Though it is clearly a source of regret to Plato, he reconciles himself to the fact that the citizens of the second-best city, not being gods or sons of gods, are not capable of holding their property in common. Moreover, the reinstatement of private property, one of the most far-reaching differences between the *Laws* and the *Republic*, brings with it in the same paragraph the reintroduction of marriage and the family.[94] It is clear from the context that it is primarily the need for a property-holding man to have an heir that necessitates the disappearance of the communal ownership of women and children simultaneously with that of other property. However, the identification of women and children together with other possessions was so natural to the Greek mind that no special justification is felt to be necessary. The failure to achieve communism of property means, it seems, that women, too, become private possessions.

The family, moreover, is the very basis of the polity planned in the *Laws*. As Glenn Morrow has noted, 'The State is a union of households or families, not a collection of detached citizens', and 'The vitality of the family in Plato's State is evident at many points in his legislation'.[95] The existence of family shrines, the complex and detailed marriage and inheritance laws, the family's crucial role in the prosecution of criminal justice, and the denial to sons of the right to defend themselves against their fathers – all these provisions indicate the central and authoritative position of the family.[96] The marriage laws are the first to be drawn up, and their implications for the position of women are immediate and extensive. In contrast to the temporary mating system of the *Republic*, in which neither sex had any more freedom to choose or right to refuse a mate than the other, with the reintroduction of permanent marriage, the matter of choosing a spouse is, without any explanation, quite different for women than for men. Marriage is indeed compulsory for all, since procreation is regarded as a universal duty. But whereas a man decides whom he will marry, provided he

---

92 *Laws* at 805a–b.
93 *Laws* at 805c–d.
94 *Laws* at 740a–c.
95 *Plato's Cretan City, op cit*, pp 118–19.
96 *Laws* at 866a, 868b–c, 871b, 879c. See G Morrow, *op cit*, pp 120–121.

seeks a partnership that will result in the best offspring for his society, a woman is 'given' in marriage.[97] The 'right of valid betrothal' of a woman belongs in turn to a long succession of male kindred, and only if she has no close male relatives at all is she to have any say in choosing her husband. Ironically, considering this pre-emption of women's choice, Plato refuses to enforce legally the prohibition of unsuitable marriages, since he considers that to do so 'besides being ridiculous, would cause widespread resentment' ...[98] Apparently what was customary for women was considered intolerable control if applied to the choices made by men.

The status of women as determined by the marriage laws is closely related to the fact that women are also virtually excluded from the ownership of property. Even if she has no brothers, a daughter may participate in the inheritance of the family estate only by serving as the instrument through which the husband chosen for her by her father can become her father's heir.[99] The *Laws*, in fact, provides very clear documentation of the essential linkage of property and inheritance to the marriage system and position of women. When a man owns inheritable property, he must own a wife too, in order to ensure a legitimate heir. The fact that women thereby become private wives means that in many ways they are treated as property rather than as persons. They themselves cannot inherit real property, which to a large extent defines personhood within the society (a disinherited son must leave the city unless another citizen adopts him as his heir),[100] and they are treated as commodities to be given away by their male relatives. Given these basic features of the social structure of the city, it is not surprising that Plato, in spite of general pronouncements to the contrary, is not able to treat or use women as the equals of his male citizens. Their status as property seems to pre-empt the execution of his declared intentions.

Although the legal status of women in Plato's second-best city is an improvement on that in contemporary Athens, it is not at all one of equality with men. Glenn Morrow has said that 'it is certainly Plato's expressed intention (though not fully carried out) to give women a more equal status under the law'.[101] The proposed divorce laws, unlike the marriage laws, treat women considerably more equally than did those of contemporary Athens. The criminal statutes enforce the same punishments for the wounding or murder of wives as of husbands, and are generally applied without discrimination according to the sex of either plaintiff or defendants. The most striking instance of equal treatment before the law is in the case of extra-marital intercourse, where the same penalties are extended to offenders of both sexes.[102] This unusual departure from the double moral standard that one might expect to find in a society so firmly based on monogamy and inheritance can probably be explained by Plato's aim to make all the members of his city as virtuous and temperate as possible. It is not that the standards are relaxed for women, after all, but that they are considerably tightened up for men. However, the Athenian concept of women as legal minors is still present in significant ways in the *Laws*. Besides not being eligible to own property, they are not allowed until the age of 40 to give

97 *Laws* at 772d–773e, 774e.
98 *Laws* at 773c.
99 *Laws* at 923e.
100 *Laws* at 928e–929a.
101 Morrow, *op cit*, p 113.
102 *Laws* at 784b, 929e, 930b, 882c. See Morrow, p 121.

evidence in a court of law or to support a plea, and only if unmarried are they ever allowed to bring an action.[103] Women, then, especially if married, are still to a large extent *femmes couvertes*.

What begins to be revealed through the denial to women of certain important civil and legal rights is strongly confirmed by the roles they are allotted within the official governmental sphere. In the *Republic*, once we have been told that the women of the guardian class are to share with the men in every aspect of ruling and guarding, they are not specifically mentioned as eligible for certain offices, with the implication that they are ineligible for others. The only case where women are specifically mentioned as being eligible for office is at the end of Socrates' account of the philosophers' education. Here, presumably because the very idea must have seemed so outrageous, Plato finds it necessary to remind his audience that everything he has been saying applies equally to all those women who have the necessary abilities.[104] It is most unlikely that the guardian women, if allowed to compete for the highest rank of all, would be excluded from any other office.

In the *Laws*, by contrast, in spite of the general pronouncements cited above, Plato both specifies when a certain function, such as the priesthood, is to be performed by persons of both sexes, and makes particular mention of certain offices being filled by women, frequently with the strong implication that only women are eligible for them.[105] Thus, it is women who supervise married couples, who look after infants, whose role in the educational system is to provide the children's meals and oversee their games – in short, who perform, in positions not of the highest rank, all those domestic, nurturing, child-oriented tasks to which women have traditionally been assigned. On the other hand, there is no suggestion of any women participating in the ranks of the magistracy, or the 'divine nocturnal synod', whose role parallels that of the philosophers in the *Republic*.[106] The children are given their lessons by male educational officers; as for the post of supervisor of education, which is 'by far the most important ... of the highest offices of State' and must be filled by 'that one of the citizens who is in every way the most excellent', it is explicitly laid down that its occupant be male, for he must be 'the father of legitimate children'. This specification adds weight to what is implied throughout the work – that in the second-best city, unless the eligibility of women is plainly mentioned, most offices, and especially high ones, are reserved for men. Moreover, even for those positions for which a woman is eventually eligible, she does not become so until aged 40, whereas a man is eligible from the age of 30.[107]

In spite of the controversial proposal in the *Laws* that, in the interests of order and discipline, even married women should take their meals communally, though segregated from the men, it is clear that Plato was ambivalent about the wisdom, or perhaps the feasibility, of bringing wives out of their domestic seclusion. Thus, for example, when he describes the funeral processions that are to be held for distinguished citizens, women of childbearing age are noticeably omitted from a list in which every other class of citizen has its place. They are

---

103 *Laws* at 937a–b.

104 *Republic* at 540c. the fact that Plato's rulers have always been referred to as philosopher kings tends to suggest that the reminder indeed was, and still is, necessary.

105 *Laws* at 741c, 759b, 764c–d, 800b, 813c, 828b, 784a–c, 790a, 794a–b, 795d, 930.

106 *Laws* at 961.

107 *Laws* at 1, 785b.

similarly omitted from the choral competitions.[108] Most remarkable, however, given Plato's previous insistence that neither gymnastics nor riding are improper for women, and that trained women can perform in the military sphere equally as well as men,[109] is the fact that, in detailing the regulations, he proceeds to exempt women almost entirely from military service. From the very beginning, girls are to learn the military arts only 'if they agree to it', whereas such instruction is obligatory for boys.[110] Then, although Plato makes the general provision that men, women and children are all to participate in military training at least one day a month, when the details are spelled out, women after the age of marriage (20 at the latest) are again noticeably absent. They are not included either in races or in wrestling, both of which sports are presented as integral parts of the training. As for horsemanship, it is decreed that 'it is not worthwhile to make compulsory laws and rules about their taking part in such sports', but that women may do so 'without blame', if they like.[111] It should be noted that Plato was certainly not in the habit of making aspects of his educational systems optional – particularly those relating to the defence of the State.

Finally, the term of military service for men is from the age of 20 to 60; 'for women they shall obtain what is possible and fitting in each case, after they have finished bearing children, and up to the age of fifty, in whatever kind of military work it may be thought right to employ their services'.[112] This means that for all the grand assertions about the necessity and rationality of training women equally with men to share in the defence of the State, women are in fact allowed, not compelled, to train up to the age of, at latest, 20, are then excluded from most military activity until they are past childbearing, and are subsequently exempted again at 50. Since in Plato's proposed society men were to have no other condoned sexual outlet than their wives, and since contraception was hardly in an advanced state, this could well mean an expectation of five years of military service from adult women. Surely this was no way to produce Amazons.

Despite Plato's professed intention to have the women of the second-best city share equally with the men in carrying out all the duties of citizenship, the fact that they are private wives curtails their participation in public life for three major reasons. The first is the practical matter of pregnancy and lactation, which is not controlled and predictable as in the *Republic*, where the guardians mate only at the behest of the rulers. The women in the *Laws*, since as permanent wives they are far less able to time or limit their pregnancies, cannot be held liable on a continuous basis for public and especially, military duties. Secondly, the reinstitution of the private household makes each wife into the mistress responsible for its welfare, and it is clear that in the *Laws* a mother is to participate far more in early child care than does the female guardian, who is not even to know which child is hers.[113]

The third reason is that it is clearly inconceivable to Plato that women who are 'private wives' – the private property of the male citizens – should play the same kind of public, and especially military, roles, as the female guardians, who are

108 *Laws* at 947b–d, 764e.
109 *Laws* at 804e–805a, 806b.
110 *Laws* at 794c–d.
111 *Laws* at 833c–d, 834a, 834d.
112 *Laws* at 785b.
113 *Laws* at 808a, 808e.

not defined in terms of a traditional relationship to a man. Whereas the female guardians can, like the male, exercise naked, the young girls in the *Laws*, must be 'clad in decent apparel', as a maiden who was shortly to become the respectable wife and private property of a citizen could hardly be allowed to be seen naked by the world at large.[114] In fact, Plato expresses at least as much expectation of ridicule for his suggestion in the *Laws* that wives should dine in public, though at segregated tables, as he had expressed in the *Republic* for his proposal that all the guardians of both sexes should exercise together naked.[115] Although he regarded it as even more dangerous to leave women undisciplined than to neglect men, and insisted that women, too, should dine in public, he was well aware that in the kind of society he was planning, there would be enormous resistance to such an idea. Consequently, although he deplored the fact that even the supposedly trained women of Sparta had panicked and run when an enemy invaded their city, and thought it folly that so important a potential for defence as the entire female sex should be neglected, he seems to have found it impossible to hold consistently to his original proposal that women should participate in military activities equally with men. If merely the segregated public dining of private wives could cause a general outcry, there was no knowing what revolutions might be provoked by the proposal that men should mingle with other men's private wives on the battlefield. Despite all his professed intentions in the *Laws* to emancipate women and make full use of the talents that he was now convinced they had, Plato's reintroduction of the family has the direct effect of putting them firmly back into their traditional place.

114 *Laws* at 1, 833d.
115 Compare *Laws* at 781c–d with *Republic* at 1, 452a–b.

CHAPTER 8

'TRADITIONAL' JURISPRUDENCE

'Traditional' jurisprudential theories are male theories of and about law, and about law's relationship to society. In this chapter these 'traditional' theories are subjected to feminist critical analysis. In the first part of this chapter, positivist legal theory is considered by feminist scholars Ngaire Naffine and Margo Stubbs. In the paper which follows, Nicola Lacey submits the common assumptions made by positivistic legal scholarship to feminist analysis. Attention is then turned to social contract theories. John Locke, writing in the seventeenth century provides one analysis of the basis of the relationship between citizens and the state. The more recent *Theory of Justice* of John Rawls is also analysed from a feminist perspective. Marxist theory has long occupied both traditional jurisprudence and feminist scholars. In the third part of this chapter Engels' work on the source of women's oppression is considered and critically analysed.

Contemporary jurisprudence is considered in the fourth and final part of this chapter. In the post modern age – characterised by uncertainty and diversity – the 'Grand Theory' has fallen into disfavour. Critical Legal Studies (CLS), the movement which characterises dissatisfaction with past theorising, is considered here. One of the tenets of CLS is its suspicion of rights-based theories. From a feminist perspective this has considerable implications as will be discussed in this part of the chapter.

POSITIVIST LEGAL THEORY

Positivist scholarship became dominant in the 19th century. Fuelled by the perceived need to identify the characteristics of law and legal systems, positivist scholars seek to portray law in a scientific manner. Natural law thinking, so influential from ancient times, was perceived to cloud people's thinking about law by insisting on lofty moral notions of 'right' and 'good' law.[1] From a positivist perspective, it is not primarily the 'rightness' or 'goodness' of a legal system which is of central importance, but rather the identification of the central concepts in the law as laid down by 'political superiors' to citizens. While John Austin,[2] Hans Kelsen[3] and HLA Hart[4] offer differing analyses of positivism, the central objective is shared. From a feminist perspective, however, positivism has been found wanting.

In *Law and the Sexes*[5] Ngaire Naffine turns attention to legal positivism:

---

1   See AP d'Entrèves, *Natural Law;* JM Finnis, *Natural Law and Natural Rights* (Clarendon, 1980).
2   *The Province of Jurisprudence Determined* (London, 1832).
3   See, *The General Theory of Law and State* (Harvard University Press, 1946).
4   *The Concept of Law* (Oxford University Press, 1961).
5   Allen & Unwin, 1990.

LAW AND THE SEXES
Ngaire Naffine[6]

Legal Positivism

Legal positivism represents the official version of law – law's explanation of itself. It is the dominant model of the legal process in the Anglo-American and Australian legal world, 'the typical outlook of the legal profession [which] informs most legal scholarship and teaching ...'.[7]

Legal positivism is fundamental to the constitution of legal thought. It is a key reason why lawyers come to accept the official version of law as legal reality, why lawyers tend not to question the nature and purpose of law but take it as a given. It also helps to explain why the law comes to assume the status of objectivity and why judges become the seekers of truth.

Positivism is a philosophical position. According to Flew's *A Dictionary of Philosophy*,[8] its exponents use the term 'positive' in a very particular sense, to indicate 'that which is laid down, that which has to be accepted as we find it and is not further explicable'. Positivists are committed to the scientific method. They believe that 'all genuine human knowledge is contained within the boundaries of science [and that] whatever questions cannot be answered by scientific methods we must be content to leave permanently unanswered'.

To the positivist, what matters, scientifically, is what we are able to observe. It follows that moral issues, questions of judgment and belief, are rendered extraneous. The positivist invokes a rigid separation of facts and beliefs and exalts the value-free nature of the scientific method. Science, it is thought, should refrain from making value-judgments about the matters it observes and it should not enquire into the values held by those paced under the microscope.[9]

Transposed to the legal context, a positivist outlook interprets law as a collection of rules which can be authenticated as valid law by the application of certain formulaic tests. These tests are intended to indicate whether any given rule has issued from a recognised law-maker. If it has, that rule becomes part of 'the data' of law 'which it is the lawyer's task to analyse and order'.[10] Put differently, law is that, and only that, which has been laid down or 'posited', as John Austin put it, by an appropriate source. Thus to Cross, a rule derived from precedent was a proper rule 'because it was made by the judges, and not because it originated in common usage, or the judges' idea of justice and public convenience'. And to Kelsen, 'law is always positive law, and its positivity lies in the fact that it is created and annulled by acts of human beings, thus being independent of morality and other norm systems'.[11]

In the view of legal positivists, it is not the lawyer's job to look behind the laws for the values which might inform them. The justice or fairness of any particular

---

6   At the time of writing, Research Fellow, University of Adelaide and Visiting Scholar, Australian National University.
7   RBM Cotterrell, *The Sociology of Law: An Introduction* (Butterworths, 1984), p 10.
8   London: Pan Books, 1979.
9   RBM Cotterrell, *op cit*, p 10.
10 RBM Cotterrell, *op cit*, p 10.
11 All quoted in B Simpson, 'The Common Law and Legal Theory', in W Twining (ed), *Legal Theory and Common Law* (Basil Blackwell, 1986).

law is simply not essential to its understanding and certainly beyond the interest of the lawyer. What matters is that it has gone through the necessary processes to function as official, usable legal material.

In his analysis of law and modern society, the British jurist PA Atiyah offers a useful summary of the key propositions which comprise the positivist approach to law:

> First, laws are commands of human being addressed to other human beings; second, there is no necessary connection between law and morals; third, the analysis of law and legal concepts is a true 'scientific' enquiry which is concerned with the formal requirements of valid law, and not with its content; and fourth, judges, when deciding new points of law, must confine themselves to 'legal' arguments and not to moral or policy issues.[12]

Atiyah blames the positivist tradition in law for what he sees as the impoverishment of legal theory and English law. He believes that positivism has contributed to an unwillingness on the part of lawyers to address the moral and political components of law. Positivism may also be seen to legitimate the refusal of most judges to consider the extent to which their particular approach to the world informs their decisions, that is, it lends support to the formalist position that what is being dispensed is always a politically neutral type of justice.

According to the Australian legal critic Margot Stubbs,[13] (see below) legal positivism is a highly convenient approach to the law from the point of view of the legal professions. Its doctrine that law is 'an autonomous, self-contained system' renders the perceptions and the methods of lawyers as neutral, value-free and independent of politics. Lawyers are untainted by passions; they rise above commitments to any particular ideology in their disinterested pursuit of their client's interests.[14]

FEMINISM AND LEGAL POSITIVISM[15]
Margot Stubbs

Introduction

It is a timely observation that the development of a feminist critique of law has failed to keep pace with feminist enquiry in other disciplines. The purpose of this paper is to focus attention on why this is so. It aims to illustrate how the conceptual framework of legal positivism (a doctrine that constitutes the methodological infrastructure of Western legal discourse) has very effectively constrained the development of a feminist critique of law. Further, the article will proceed to a consideration of the direction that a 'jurisprudence' that is properly feminist in character should take, suggesting a framework within which the fundamental connections between patriarchy and law can be constructively addressed.

It needs to be made quite clear at the outset that the point of this paper is not to overview the literature on legal positivism, or focus on variations on its basic themes from Bentham through to Austin and Hart, as this has been more than

---

12   PS Atiyah, *Law and Modern Society* (Oxford University Press, 1983), p 103.

13   M Stubbs, 'Feminism and Legal Positivism' (1986) 3 *Australian Journal of Law and Society* at 63.

14   N Naffine, *Law and the Sexes*, pp 34–36.

15   (1986) 3 *Australian Journal of Law and Society* at 63.

adequately addressed in mainstream legal enquiry and, as Simon notes, even the rigour and elegance of the above expositions are insufficient to overcome the fundamental problems in positivist theory, which are as equally fatal in their most elaborate, as in their most simple, statements.[16] Rather, this paper has a more fundamental purpose, and that is to extract the basic definition or understanding of what law is which is implicit in positivist jurisprudence, and to examine, from a feminist perspective, the conceptual and political imperatives that flow from it. This paper postulates that the development of a theory of law which is properly feminist in character must necessarily transcend positivism's claim to trans-historicity and universality, and should articulate the functional and ideological role of legal positivism in the reproduction of the sex and economic class relations of capitalist society. It is proposed to draw attention to the conceptual limitations of legal positivism, and to show that it is a doctrine based on an understanding of 'the law' as being an autonomous, self-contained system, one that is supposedly uninvolved in the process of class production and reproduction. It will illustrate how a positivist understanding of law has a conservative political consequence, as it effectively separates critical analysis of the law from broader sociological enquiry into the nature of capitalism when in actual fact 'the law' (as we shall see) is intimately involved in the process of reconstituting the relations of capitalism, and, as an institution, plays a crucial role in the class subordination of women.

The key reason why it has been so observably difficult to develop a feminist critique of law relates directly to the conceptual limitations of the definition of law provided in the legal-positivist tradition. A feminist critique of law cannot be expressed within a framework that is predicated on the autonomy of the law – that is, one based on an understanding of law as a neutral and independent structure that is supposedly uninvolved as an institution in the repression of women. The corollary of this approach is that women's problems with the law are thus only problems with particular legal rules or, at the most, particular areas of the law. A feminist critique of law must reject this view of the legal systems, and should be predicated on an understanding of law as praxis – that is, as Klare defines the term, as being a form of 'practice' through which the social order is defined.[17] As will be illustrated, a feminist analysis of the law must clearly reject the central tenet of legal positivism – that is, that law is external to the question of class – for such a position by definition renders it impossible to develop a political critique of the legal system. A feminist critique of law, in other words, must recognise and transcend the 'mind-forged manacles'[18] of positivist jurisprudence, for this, it is contended, is the first and necessary step in developing a politically meaningful line of enquiry into the relation between law and the subordination of women. It is absolutely crucial that feminists unravel the role the law plays in maintaining and reproducing the sex and economic divisions in our society, for capitalism has a class structure that is innately patriarchal.[19]

---

16 WH Simon, 'The Ideology of Advocacy: Procedural Justice and Professional Ethics' (1978) *Wisconsin Law Review* 29.

17 K Klare, 'Law-Making as Praxis' (1979) 40 *Telos* 123.

18 D Hay, 'Authority and the Criminal Law', in *Albion's Fatal Tree: Crime and Society in 18th Century England* (New York: Allen Lane, 1975), pp 48–49.

19 *Feminism and Legal Positivism*, pp 63–64.

To start with: what is legal positivism? There has been a great deal written on this topic, characteristically in supportive (and generally abstruse) terms. HLA Hart succinctly outlines a set of five propositions usually associated with the positivist tradition in law that well illustrate its analytical tenor.[20] In overview, these are: firstly, that all laws are the command of human beings, (ie emanating from a sovereign). Secondly, the contention that there is no necessary connection between law and morals – that is, law as it is and law as it should be. Thirdly, the analysis of legal concepts should be distinguished from historical enquiry into the causes and origins of law, and should be separated from sociological enquiry into the relationship between law and other social phenomena. Fourthly, positivism contends that the legal system is a closed, logical system, in which correct legal decisions can be deduced by logical means from predetermined legal rules, without reference to social aims, policies or moral standards. Finally, that moral judgments are unable to be established or defended – as can statements of fact – by rational argument, evidence or proof.

As Hart's summary adverts to it, legal positivism is concerned with abstract notions of sovereignty, hierarchy and command as the intrinsic condition of the law. It defines law simply as a set of rules carried from the sovereign to 'subject', that is processed through a legal system that is held out to be primarily administrative in character. Legal positivism presents us with a model of the legal process: the courts, the styles of consciousness with which lawyers perceive and 'resolve' problems,[21] the way in which they interact between client and system, and the role of the judiciary, which is supposedly separate from politics and which is presented as intrinsically neutral and value-free.

Feminist legal enquiry to date has generally been expressed within this conceptual tradition, as it has focused primarily on the function of the law at those points where it directly intersects the social experience of women. For example, there have been extensive feminist critiques of the law relating to rape, abortion, criminal and family law and so forth, but there has been comparatively little attention directed to the broader question as to how the very structure of the legal order in contemporary capitalist society – its structural qualities of 'formality, generality and autonomy'[22] – serve to reinforce and reproduce existing sex and economic class relationships.

Feminist enquiry should appreciate that the distinguishing attributes of the Western legal order – its 'generality, uniformity, publicity and coercion'[23] – perform an express political function in the reproduction of class relationships, and ideologically find their expression in a particular legal philosophy – legal positivism – that animates and legitimates capitalist society.[24] Positivism in law is structurally connected to a deeper set of presuppositions about society that are expressed under the rubric of 'liberalism'. Liberal philosophy embraces legal positivism in the way it presents the legal system as a neutral, independent and apolitical mechanism for resolving social tension. This presentation of law is given its political expression in the notion of the 'rule of law' – that is, the legal doctrine that all people are equal under the law and can expect from it a neutral

20 HLA Hart, 'Positivism and the Separation of Morals' (1958) 71 *Harvard Law Review* at 601–02.

21 K Klare, *Law-Making as Praxis, op cit*, p 124.

22 I Balbus, 'Legal Form and Commodity Form: An Essay on the Relative Autonomy of the Law' (1977) 11 *Law and Society Review* 71.

23 RM Unger, *Law in Modern Society* (New York: The Free Press, 1976), pp 72–73.

24 J Sklar, *Legalism* (1964).

and unbiased determination of their rights.[25] The 'rule of law' in fact, is widely accepted as the lynchpin of individual liberty and justice in liberal-democratic society. Indeed, the very legitimacy of the modern state hinges on this 'reification' of the law – that is, in obscuring the role the law as an institution plays in the reconstitution of class relationships. In fact, far from recognising the role the law plays of the individual (positivist's subjectivity of values), a legal epistemology that separates fact from value (the formal rule) and a rationalisation of practice which accords legal validity only to rule-dictated outcomes.

It stands to reason that positivism in law should thus be subjected to the same criticisms that have been directed at liberalism – namely that it provides us with a largely artificial understanding of the way modern society works. Legal positivism, however, has not been subjected to as incisive or developed a criticism as has liberal philosophy. This is no doubt due to the ideological importance of the law in legitimating the modern state, and the fact that the study and practice of 'the law' have been so 'professionalised' in character. That is, that legal education has been largely left in the control of that group of people, middle-class male lawyers, who have a vested interest in maintaining its existing form and the class structure it reinforces.

Legal positivism presents us with a highly formalistic and apolitical understanding of the law. The legal system as defined in this tradition is not part of 'the problem' and 'reforming the law' has, even from a feminist perspective, become almost synonymous with changing the content of particular rules or areas of the law. This, of course, has an important place in feminist political strategy, but if we are to understand the way in which the legal system reinforces the class oppression of women, we must look beyond the largely artificial way law is defined in the positivist tradition. Feminist legal enquiry needs, in short, a different starting point if it is to understand the specific way in which law mediates class relations,[26] specifically the class relations of sex. From a feminist perspective, 'the law' must be understood not as autonomous from society, but as being a form of practice through which existing sex and economic class relations are reproduced. This involvement can be described in shorthand by approaching the legal system as a form of 'praxis' – henceforth to be understood as connoting human activity through which people define or change their world. Thus an acceptance of the understanding of the law presented in mainstream Western jurisprudence (as defined by the 'science of legal positivism') limits the development of a political critique of law as it presents the law as an autonomous, self-contained system, fuelled by its own logic, which is supposedly uninvolved in the processes of class production and reproduction, simply to the positivist 'constituting conventions which set the boundaries among particular interests so that the interests' will not destroy each other.[27]

The consequence of legal positivism is, in short, to set up a theoretical schism between law and other social phenomena, conceptually separating it from the capitalist whole of which it is, in reality, a fundamental part. Legal positivism developed at the same historical conjuncture as liberal philosophy, and we must appreciate that it serves the same ideological function – and that is, taking some

---

25   AV Dicey, *Law of the Constitution* (New York: St Martin's Press, 1958), pp 202–03.

26   S Picciotto, 'The Theory of the State, Class Struggle and the Rule of Law', in *Capitalism and the Rule of Law: From Deviance Theory to Marxism* (Academic Press, 1979), p 165.

27   RM Unger, *Knowledge and Politics* (New York: The Free Press, 1975), p 72.

licence with Poulantzas, 'to hide the real contradictions, [and] reconstitute at an imaginary level a relatively coherent discourse which serves as the horizon of agents' experience'.[28] Indeed, it is not overstating the case to argue that the veneer of legal positivism is the cornerstone of legitimacy in the capitalist social order, which is unable to countenance even the suggestion that 'the courts' or 'the judiciary' are anything other than autonomous and 'politically neutral' arbiters of social tension. The rejection of the schema of law provided by liberal positivism, however, does not propel us into a crude Marxist instrumentalism – that is, the approach that conceptualises 'the law' as simply an instrument of social control of the bourgeoisie. In its own way, this is as artificial an understanding of the function of the law as is found in liberal legalism, as it is also predicated on a concept or understanding of 'law' that has a strong epistemologically positivist flavour, as still presented in terms of 'rules' or 'commands'. Indeed, the critique of law[29] makes the point that both liberal pluralist and vulgar Marxist analyses both posit law as an 'instrument' – the two views differing simply on the empirical point of whose interest it expresses – in the former, that of a (generally democratically elected sovereign) and in the latter, the naked class interests of the bourgeoisie. These approaches are both inadequate as they allow no dynamism to the structure of the legal system in the production and reproduction of class relations – as Balbus notes, that is, for the way in which 'this form [of law] articulates the overall requirements of the capitalist system in which these social actors function'.[30]

As suggested, a feminist analysis of law must address the significance of the form of law in regulating the oppression of women in capitalist society. That is, a necessary element of any feminist critique of law must be the examination of the way in which the structural characteristics of the Western legal system – its formality, its generality, its autonomy and its professionalism – function to mediate social tension in the political interests of capital, an interest that we have seen is necessarily predicated upon the political, sexual and economic subordination of women.

Our critique of law – a feminist critique of law – needs to be developed within a theory of social reproduction; it is only by transcending the positivist conceptual framework of both liberal legalism and Marxist instrumentalism that we can make the conjunction between 'the woman question' and 'the law' – and thus articulate the crucial role the law plays in the production (and, importantly, the reproduction) of the iniquitous class relationships of capitalist society.

Beyond Positivism – Law and Social Reproduction

This article proposes to offer a way to approach the fundamental connections between patriarchy and law[31] by showing how our legal system presents us with a dispute resolution process that has (ideological claims to neutrality and impartiality aside) the express insignificance, any claims for social justice made upon it by women. Although it is true, as Thompson[32] notes, that the ideological function of the law requires that it occasionally give substantive effect to its claims to equity and justice (which the women's movement has, it is

---

28 N Poulantzas, *Political Power and Social Classes* (New Left Books, 1978), p 207.
29 1978.
30 *Op cit*, p 572.
31 J Rifkin, 'Toward a Feminist Jurisprudence' (1983) *Harvard Women's Law Journal* 83 at 84.
32 EP Thompson, *Whigs and Hunters: Origins of the Black Acts* (Penguin, 1977), pp 257–67.

acknowledged, had past cause to be thankful for) its general function is to structurally frustrate the attainment of sexual liberation through the legal process.

These structural features collapse together to constitute a form of practice through which the social order of capitalism is reproduced across time; serving to maintain and perpetuate and, indeed, legitimate patriarchal domination under its veneer of formal justice, procedural equity, neutrality and judicial impartiality. Expressed within such a framework, it is hardly surprising that feminist litigators have not, as observed by Rifkin, 'challenged the fundamental patriarchal social order'[33] in spite of the fact that the practice of law now includes experienced and talented feminist litigators and academics. Rather than reflecting some sex-typed lack of legal ability, feminist difficulties in engaging the law in the struggle against patriarchy are attributable to the structure of liberal legalism – a form of law which for women (to borrow a term used by Connell in another context) effectively constitutes a 'praxis trap' – that is, it is 'a situation in which people (ie feminist litigators and academics) do things for good reasons and skilfully, in situations that turn out to make their original purpose difficult to achieve'.[34] Feminists will continue to find the pursuit of 'justice' (as we understand the term) within the parameters of legalism to be a chimera – always promised, never realised – for we are attempting to employ in our interests a legal framework that has the express political function of perpetuating the powerlessness of women, and which institutionally reinforces the patriarchal logic of capital accumulation.

The purpose of this article has been to suggest a framework within which the fundamental connections between culture, patriarchy and law can be constructively addressed. It is contended that the lacunae in feminist scholarship in relation to law seriously impairs the feminist political project: for, as we have seen, 'the law' plays a key institutional role in both reinforcing and reproducing the class subordination of women to men. I have argued that it simply incorrect to 'dismiss' the law from feminist scholastic and strategic enquiry as some 'inert' mechanism for giving effect to 'male' interests. It is, rather, an organic social relation that is actively involved in mediating and controlling the tensions engendered in a class-structured society. 'The law' is intimately involved in structuring every aspect of women's lives. It stands at the very centre of the 'arena of social struggle' and is of fundamental significance to the very legitimacy of the capitalist State and, by implication, the legitimacy of sexual subordination. I believe that a reorientation of the 'feminist' approach to law is long overdue: for as it is politically central to patriarchal domination, we simply cannot afford to keep it at the penumbra of our political project.

Our task, as I perceive it, is to 'crack open' law to politics: to reject the conceptual framework of positivist jurisprudence, and to approach the law as a form of praxis, for only then can we unveil its particular function in the process of reproducing the exploitative sexual and economic class structures of capitalist society.

---

33 J Rifkin, 'Toward a Feminist Jurisprudence' (1983) *Harvard Women's Law Journal* 83 at 87.

34 R Connell, *Which Way is Up?* (Sydney: Allen & Unwin, 1983), p 156.

FEMINISM AND THE TENETS OF CONVENTIONAL LEGAL THEORY

Nicola Lacey[35]

In this paper, I shall explore the argument that there is something not about particular *laws* or sets of laws, but rather, and more generally, about the very structure or methodology of modern law, which is hierarchically gendered. To most lawyers this is a far more counter-intuitive claim than, say, feminist allegation of bias in particular laws. It is, however, absolutely central to any strong feminist theory of law. In what follows, therefore, my main concerns will be to clarify the ways in which feminist legal theory differs from and challenges the understandings of law which inform conventional legal theory; to explore the continuities between feminist and other critical approaches to the study of law; and to identify some of the difficult questions still confronting feminist analyses.

To speak of 'feminist legal theory' is, of course, to gather together a set of heterogeneous approaches. In this paper, I shall not be concerned with these important differences. I shall simply set out from an inclusive conception of feminist legal theory as proceeding from two foundational claims. First, at an analytical and indeed sociological level, and on the basis of a wide range of research in a number of disciplines, feminist legal theorists take sex/gender to be one important social structure or discourse. We hence claim that sex/gender characterises the shape of law as one important social institution. Secondly, at a normative or political level, feminist legal theorists claim that the ways in which sex/gender has shaped the legal realm are presumptively politically and ethically problematic, in that sex/gender is an axis not merely of differentiation but also of discrimination, domination or oppression. At a methodological level, feminist legal theorists are almost universally committed to a social constructionist stance: in other words to the idea that the power and meaning of sex/gender is a product not of nature but of culture. Feminist legal theorists are hence of the view that gender relations are open to revision through the modification of powerful social institutions such as law.

Within this broad conception, it is probably worth distinguishing two main schools of feminist legal thought. The first, which might be called liberal feminism, is committed, as is mainstream legal theory, to the ideals of gender neutrality and equality before the law. Its focus is primarily instrumental, seeing law as a tool of feminist strategy, and the impact of law as basis for feminist critique. By contrast the second approach, which I shall label difference feminism, is sceptical about the possibility of neutrality; it has an implicit commitment to a more complex idea of equality which accommodates and values, whilst not fixing, women's specificity 'as women'; and it has a focus on the symbolic and dynamic aspects of law and not just on its instrumental aspects.[36] In what follows, I shall concentrate on the implications of this more radical approach to feminist legal theory – difference feminism – for the tenets of conventional legal scholarship and theory.

I shall approach this question by singling out a number of assumptions common to positivistic legal scholarship which are the target of feminist critique of the

---

35 Professor of Law, Birkbeck College, University of London; Visiting Professor in Feministrechtwissenschaft, Humboldt University, 1996.

36 For more detailed discussion see Nicola Lacey, 'Feminist Legal Theory: Beyond Neutrality' [1995] *Current Legal Problems* p 1.

gender bias of legal method. These various points are closely interwoven, but I think that it is useful to separate them out to get a sense of the range of arguments which have been influential in the development of feminist legal thought.

1. The neutral framework of legal reasoning

A central tenet of both positivistic scholarship and of the liberal rule of law ideal is that laws set up standards which are applied in a neutral manner to formally equal parties: the questions of inequality and power which may affect the capacity of those parties to engage effectively in legal reasoning has featured little in mainstream legal theory. These questions have, on the other hand, always been central to critical legal theory, and they now find an important place within feminist legal thought. In particular, recent work by Carol Gilligan[37] on the varying ways of constructing moral problems, and their relationship to gender, has opened up a very striking argument about the possible 'masculinity' of the very process of legal reasoning.

As is widely known, Gilligan's research was motivated by the finding of psychological research that men reach a 'higher' level of moral development than do women. Gilligan set out to investigate the neutrality of the tests being applied: she also engaged in empirical research designed to illuminate the ways in which different people construct moral problems. Her research elicited two main approaches to moral reasoning. The first, which Gilligan calls the ethic of rights, proceeds in an essentially legalistic way: it formulates rules structuring the values at issue in a hierarchical away, and then applies those rules to the facts. The second, which Gilligan calls the ethic of care or responsibility, takes a more holistic approach to moral problems, exploring the context and relationships, as well as the values, involved, and producing a more complex, but less conclusive, analysis. The tests on which assessments of moral development have conventionally been made by psychologists were based on the ethic of rights: analyses proceeding from the ethic of care were hence adjudged morally under-developed. It was therefore significant that Gilligan's fieldwork suggested that these two types were gender-related, in that women tended to adopt the care perspective, whilst men more often adopted the rights approach.

Gilligan's assertion of the relationship between the two models and gender is a controversial one. Nonetheless, her analytical distinction between the two ethics is of great significance for feminist legal theory. The idea that the distinctive structure of legal reasoning may systematically silence the voices of those who speak the language of relationships is a potentially important one for all critical legal theory. The rights model is, as I have already observed, reminiscent of law: it works from a clear hierarchy of sources which are reasoned through in a formally logical way. The more contextual, care or relationship-oriented model would, by contrast, be harder to capture by legal frameworks, within which holistic or relationally oriented reasoning tends to sound 'woolly' or legally incompetent, or to be rendered legally irrelevant by substantive and evidential rules. Most law students will be familiar with the way in which intuitive judgments are marginalised or disqualified in legal education, which proceeds precisely by imbuing the student with a sense of the exclusive relevance of formal legal sources and technical modes of reasoning.

---

37   Carol Gilligan, *In a Different Voice* (Harvard University Press, 1982). (See further Chapter 6.)

There are, however, several important pitfalls for feminist legal theory in some of the arguments deriving from Gilligan's research.[38] One way of reading the implications for law of Gilligan's approach is that legal issues, indeed the conceptualisation of legal subjects themselves, should be recast in less formal and abstract terms. But such a strategy of recontextualisation may obscure the (sometimes damaging) ways in which legal subjects are already contextualised. In the sentencing of offenders, or in the assumptions on which victims and defendants are treated in rape cases, for example, we have some clear examples of effective contextualisation which cuts in several political directions – not all of them appealing to feminists. In certain areas, it may be that legal reasoning is already 'relational' in the sense espoused by many feminists, but that it privileges certain kinds of relationships: ie proprietary, object relations.[39] A general call for 'contextualisation' may also be making naive assumptions about the power of such a strategy to generate real change given surrounding power relations: as the case of rape trials shows all too clearly, the framework of legal doctrine is not the only formative context shaping the legal process. The important project, I would argue, is that of recontextualisation understood not as reformist strategy but rather as critique: in other words, the development of a critical analysis which unearths the logic, the substantive assumptions, underlying law's current contextualisation of its subjects, and which can hence illuminate the interests and relationships which these arrangements privilege.[40]

2. Law's autonomy and discreteness

Another standard assumption of mainstream legal scholarship is that law is a relatively autonomous social practice, discrete from politics, ethics, religion. An extreme expression of this assumption is found in Hans Kelsen's 'pure' theory of law,[41] but weaker versions inform the entire positivist tradition. Indeed, this is what sets up one of positivism's recurring problems – that is, the question of foundations, of the boundaries between the legal and the non-legal; of the source of legal authority, and the relation between law and justice.

This mainstream assumption, like the idea that legal method is discrete or distinctive, is challenged by feminist legal theory. Feminist theory seeks to reveal the ways in which law reflects, reproduces, expresses, constructs and reinforces power relations along sexually patterned lines: in doing so, it questions law's claims to autonomy and represents it as a practice which is continuous with deeper social, political and economic forces which constantly seep through its supposed boundaries. Hence the ideals of the Rule of Law call for modification and reinterpretation. There are obvious, and strong, continuities here between the feminist and the Marxist traditions in legal thought.

3. Law's neutrality and objectivity

As I have already mentioned, difference feminism has developed a critique of the very idea of gender neutrality, of gender equality before the law, in a sexually

---

38   For a useful discussion, see Mary Joe Frug, *Postmodern Legal Feminism* (Routledge, 1992), Chapter 3.

39   For further discussion see Jennifer Nedelski,' Reconceiving Rights as Relationship' [1993] *Review of Constitutional Studies*, 1; Luce Irigaray, *I Love to You* (trans Alison Martin) (Routledge, 1996).

40   See further Nicola Lacey, 'Normative Reconstruction in Socio-Legal Theory' (1996) 5 *Social and Legal Studies*, 131.

41   H Kelsen, *The Pure Theory of Law* (University of California Press, 1967).

patterned world. Feminist legal theory deconstructs law's claims to be enunciating Truths, its pretension to neutral or objective judgement, and its constitution of a field of discrete and hence unassailable knowledge.

This argument takes a number of forms in contemporary feminist legal theory. One derives from the Foucaultian critique of feminist writers such as Smart.[42] The argument is that law, by policing its own boundaries via its substantive rules and rules of evidence, constitutes itself as self-contained, as a self-reproducing system. There is, hence, a certain 'truth' to this aspect of law. But by standing back so as to cast light on the point of view from which law's truth is being constructed, we can undermine law's claims to objectivity. Another, rather different, example is Catharine MacKinnon's well known epistemological argument.[43] In MacKinnon's view, law constructs knowledge which claims objectivity, but objectivity in fact expresses the male point of view. Hence 'objective' standards in civil and criminal law – the 'reasonable person' – in fact represents a position which is specific in not only gender but also class, ethnic and other terms. The epistemological assertion of 'knowledge' or 'objectivity' disguises this process of construction, and writes sexually specific bodies out of the text of law. The project of feminism is to replace them. The difficult trick is to do so without fixing their shape and identity within received categories of masculine and feminine. Hence not all feminists endorse the idea of abandoning 'reasonableness' tests or the appeal to otherwise universal standards.[44]

4. Law's centrality

In stark contrast to not only a great deal of positivist legal scholarship but also much 'law and society' work, feminist writers have often questioned law's importance or centrality to the constitution of social relations and the struggle to change those relations. Clearly feminist views diverge here. Catharine MacKinnon, for example, is optimistic about using law for radical purposes; but many other feminists – notably British feminist Carol Smart – have questioned the wisdom of placing great reliance on law and of putting law too much at the centre of our critical analysis. Perhaps this is partly a cultural difference: the British women's movement has typically been relatively anti-institutional and appositional. Yet even in the USA, where there is a stronger tradition of reformist legal activism, feminists associated with critical legal studies have been notably more cautious about claims advanced in some critical legal scholarship[45] about law's central role in constituting social relations. Feminists have thus tended further towards a classical Marxist orientation on this question than have their non-feminist critical counterparts. In terms of analytic focus, however, this has led feminists to address a range of social institutions – the family, sexuality, the political realm, bureaucracies – well beyond the Marxist terrain of political economy. Feminists writers continue to be ambivalent about whether and how law ought to be deployed as a tool of feminist action, practice and strategy. To the extent that feminist critique identifies law as implicated in the construction of existing gender relations, how far can it really be used to change them, and do strategic attempts to use law risk the danger of reconfirming law's power?

---

42 See Carol Smart, *Feminism and the Power of Law* (Routledge, 1989); Michel Foucault, *Discipline and Punish* (Penguin, 1977).

43 Catharine MacKinnon, *Toward a Feminist Theory of the State* (Harvard University Press, 1989).

44 See for example Drucilla Cornell, *The Imaginary Domain* (Routledge, 1995), Chapter 1.

45 See for example, Roberto Unger, 'The Critical Legal Studies Movement in America' (1983) 99 *Harvard Law Review*, 561.

5. Law as a system of enacted norms or rules

Typically, feminist legal theory reaches beyond a conception of law as a system of norms or rules – statutes, constitutions, cases – and beyond 'standard' legal officials, such as judges – to encompass other practices which are legally relevant or 'quasi-legal'. For example, the Oslo school of Women's Law had a main focus on administrative and regulatory bodies such as social welfare agencies, the medical system and the family.[46]

This institutional refocusing is also connected with poststructuralist ideas, and notably with Michel Foucault's reconceptualisation of power, and the implications of this reconceptualisation for law.[47] Foucault distinguished between sovereignty power – power as a property or possession; and disciplinary power – the relational power which inheres in particular practices and which flows unseen throughout the 'social body'. His basic argument was that the later modern world was gradually seeing the growth of subtle, intangible, disciplinary power, at the expense of the old sovereignty power. Since Foucault associated legal power with sovereignty power, he also tended to think that law was waning in importance. Smart, however, uses his argument about power in a different way in relation to law: she points out that law itself has not only sovereignty but disciplinary power. For one of the distinguishing features of disciplinary power is its subtly normalising effect, and as soon as we look beyond a narrow stereotype of law as a system of rules backed up by sanctions, we begin to see that one of law's functions is precisely to distribute its subjects with disciplinary precision around a mean or norm. For example, the way in which legal rules distribute social welfare benefits or allocate custody of children (on divorce or via adoption) reflects judgements about the right way to live; it expresses assumptions about 'normality'. A yet more spectacular example is that of the construction of gay and straight sexualities in criminal laws and in family and social welfare legislation. These 'normalising' assumptions have a pervasive power which also structures the administration of laws – eg of social welfare benefits and policing policies – at the bureaucratic level, generating phenomena such as reluctance to prosecute in 'domestic violence' cases, the oppressive policing of gay sexuality, and the discriminatory administration of welfare benefits. Feminist (like other critical) analyses are interested here in not just legal doctrine but also legal discourse – ie how differently sexed legal subjects are constituted by and inserted within legal categories via the mediation of judicial, police or lawyers' discourse. The feminist approach therefore mounts a fundamental challenge to the standard ways of conceptualising law and the legal, and moves to a broader understanding of legally relevant spheres of practice.[48]

6. Law's unity and coherence

Readers of both student texts and legal cases will be familiar with the very high importance attached by lawyers and legal commentators to the idea (perhaps the ideal) of law as a unitary and a coherent system of rules or norms. It is an idea which informs legal theory in a number of ways. Once again, Kelsen provides a

---

46 See Tove Stang Dahl, *Women's Law* (Norwegian University Press, 1986).

47 Michel Foucault, *The Archaeology of Knowledge* (Tavistock Press, 1972); *Discipline and Punish* (Penguin, 1977); Carol Smart, *Feminism and the Power of Law* (Routledge, 1989).

48 For further discussion, see Nicola Lacey, 'Normative Reconstruction in Socio-Legal Theory' (1996) 5 *Social and Legal Studies*, 131.

spectacular example[49] his *Grundnorm* had to be hypothesised precisely because otherwise it would have been impossible to interpret law as a coherent, non-contradictory normative field of meaning. As a law student, one of the first things one is taught to do is to hone in on contradictory or inconsistent arguments. The idea of coherence as the idea(l) which lies at the heart of law finds its fullest expression in Ronald Dworkin's idea of 'law as integrity',[50] but it also finds some support in procedurally oriented ethical and political theories, notably in critical theory of the Frankfurt School.[51]

Feminist scholarship, like much other critical legal theory, is concerned to unsettle this belief in law's coherence and rather to reconstruct the pretension to coherence as part of the ideology of both law and jurisprudence: as part of what helps to represent law as authoritative; adjudication as democratically legitimate and so on. The search for contradictions, and the unearthing of what have been called 'dangerous supplements' and hidden agendas, takes place both at the level of doctrine and at that of discourse.[52]

To take some specific examples, the assertion within legal doctrine of particular questions or issues as within public or private spheres is contradictory, question-begging, under-determined: sexuality, for example, is public for some purposes and private for others[53] the idea of the legal subject as rational and as abstracted from its social context is undermined by exceptions such as defences in criminal law, shifts of time frame in the casting of legal questions, and an arbitrary division of issues pertaining to conviction and those pertaining to sentence.[54] In contract law, one could cite shifts between a freedom of contract model and a model which views contract as a long term relationship within which, for example, loss occasioned by contracting parties' general reliance upon the contractual relationship can be recognised and compensated.[55] Nor are these incoherencies confined to the doctrinal framework: they mark also the discourse through which human subjects are inserted into that structure. For example, the rational and controlled male of legal subjectivity is, after all, also the rape defendant who is subject to feminine wiles and incapable of telling yes from no. The unearthing of such contradictions is not just a matter of 'trashing': it forms part of an intellectual and political strategy – of exposing law's indeterminacy, of emphasising its contingency, and of finding resources for its reconstruction in those doctrinal principles and discursive images which are less dominant yet which fracture and complicate the seamless web imagined and created by orthodox legal scholarship.

---

49 H Kelsen, *The Pure Theory of Law, op cit.*

50 R Dworkin, *Law's Empire* (Fontana, 1986).

51 See Jurgen Habermas, *Faktizitat und Geltung* (Suhrkamp Verlage, 1992).

52 Roberto Unger, *The Critical Legal Studies Movement in America* (1983) 99 *Harvard Law Review* 561.

53 See Frances Olsen, 'The Family and the Market' (1983) 96 *Harvard Law Review*, 1497; Nicola Lacey, 'Theory into Practice: Pornography and the Public/Private Dichotomy' (1993) 20 *Journal of Law and Society*, 93.

54 See Mark Kelman, 'Interpretive Construction in the Substantive Criminal Law' (1981) 33 *Stanford Law Review* 181; Nicola Lacey, 'Feminist Legal Theory: Beyond Neutrality' (1995) *Current Legal Problems*, 1.

55 See Hugh Collins, *The Law of Contract* (Butterworths, 2nd edn, 1993).

7. Law's rationality

Perhaps most fundamentally of all, it is argued that contradictions and indeterminacy in legal doctrine undermine law's supposed grounding in reason, just as the smuggling in of contextual and affective factors undermines law's apparent construction of the subject as rational, self-interested actor. Furthermore, in so far as law is successful in maintaining its self-image as a rational enterprise, this is because the emotional and affective aspects of legal practice are systematically repressed in orthodox representations. Once one reads cases and other legal texts not only for their formal meaning but also as rhetoric, one sees how values and techniques which are not acknowledged on the surface of legal doctrine are in fact crucial to the way in which cases are decided.[56]

Conclusion

These, then, are the principal ways in which feminist legal theory has challenged the tenets of conventional jurisprudence. It will be apparent that feminist method shares certain conceptual tools with other critical approaches, including Marxist theory and American critical legal theory. Clearly, these ambitious arguments of a general theoretical nature raised by feminist legal scholars raise a number of difficult questions with which those scholars are still coming to terms. Equally, it should be apparent that the feminist challenge to conventional legal theory is of considerable intellectual power and ethical importance. It is a challenge which the legal academy can no longer afford to ignore.

SOCIAL CONTRACT THEORY

Theories of social contract and the rights of man derive in large measure from the political upheavals of the 18th century, and the American War of Independence[57] and the French Revolution.[58] The writings of John Locke,[59] Jean-Jacques Rousseau[60] and Thomas Paine[61] are all infused with the doctrine of the inalienability of individual human rights – rights which transcend the law of the State, which cannot be overridden by the State, and which affirm the supremacy of the law of the State with the important proviso that the law of the State is in compliance with individual rights. The questions which arise from a feminist jurisprudential perspective is whether the social contract as originally hypothesised by Locke, Paine and Rousseau and later interpretations – between government and citizen – is a contract in which women participate, or whether the 'social contract' is a male construct established to serve the needs of men to the exclusion – intentional or unintentional – of female participation in civic life.

Feminist scholars have examined the works of the social contractarian writers – most particularly those of John Locke, writing in the 18th century, and of John Rawls, a 20th century exponent of social contract theory.

---

56 See Mary Joe Frug, *Postmodern Legal Feminism* (Routledge, 1991); Peter Goodrich, *Reading the Law* (Blackwell, 1986).

57 1775–83.

58 1789.

59 *Two Treatises on Government* (1690).

60 *The Social Contract* (1762).

61 *The Rights of Man* (1791).

Early conceptions of limited governmental power

John Locke

In *Two Treatises of Government*,[62] John Locke claimed that sovereign power was limited and that the people had the right to resort to revolution against the sovereign if power was abused. Such writing was both revolutionary and seditious – challenging the very basis of state authority. Locke went into exile in 1683.[63] With the accession of William of Orange to the throne in 1689, Locke returned to England and his work – previously unpublished – reached the light of day, albeit anonymously. The timing of publication could not have been more forceful. An historic settlement between parliament and Crown had finally and recently been reached – resulting in the Bill of Rights 1689, thus ending centuries of conflict. However, Locke's writing presented a theory which asserted the rights of man against the sovereign power. Much of the first *Treatise* is an argument directed against absolute monarchical power and the use of the prerogative. By insisting that government held its power on trust Locke was indirectly asserting the sovereignty of the people over the sovereignty of government. Government had a legitimate right to rule, and to use the law for the good of the people; but that right was conditional and limited by the ultimate power of the people to overthrow a government which violated its trust. As Locke observed:

> ... acting for the preservation of the community, there can be but one supreme power, which is the legislative, to which all the rest are and must be subordinate, yet the legislative being only a fiduciary power to act for certain ends, there remains still in the people a supreme power to remove or alter the legislative, when they find the legislative act contrary to the trust reposed in them. For all power given with trust for the attaining an end being limited by that end, whenever that end is manifestly neglected or opposed, the trust must necessarily be forfeited, and the power devolve into the hands of those that gave it, who may place it anew where they shall think best for their safety and security. And thus the community perpetually retains a supreme power of saving themselves from the attempts and designs of anybody, even of their legislators, whenever they shall be so foolish or so wicked as to lay and carry on designs against the liberties and properties of the subject. For no man or society of men having a power to deliver up their preservation, or consequently the means of it, to the absolute will and arbitrary dominion of another, whenever any one shall go about to bring them into such slavish condition, they will always have a right to preserve what they have not a power to part with, and to rid themselves of those who invade this fundamental, sacred, and unalterable law of self-preservation for which they entered into society. And thus the community may be said in this respect to be always the supreme power, but not as considered under any form of government, because this power of the people can never take place till the government be dissolved.[64]

---

62 Assumed to have been in manuscript form by 1683.

63 Whilst in exile Locke wrote the essay *Concerning Human Understanding* and the *Letter on Toleration*.

64 *Two Treatises of Government*, Book II, Chapter XIII, para 149.

Despite the intuitive attraction of Locke's writing, when viewed from a feminist perspective, the question arises as to whether Locke would accord equal rights to women in civil society. Melissa Butler analyses the work of John Locke in the following manner.

EARLY LIBERAL ROOTS OF FEMINISM: JOHN LOCKE AND THE ATTACK ON PATRIARCHY[65]

Melissa Butler[66]

Social Relations in the Second Treatise

... From the very outset of the discussion of the parent-child relation, Locke rejected the terminology of patriarchy, claiming that:

> [paternal power] seems so to place the Power of Parents over their Children wholly in the Father, as if the Mother had no share in it whereas if we consult Reason or Revelation, we shall find she hath an equal Title ... For whatever obligation Nature and the Right of Generation lays on Children, it must certainly find them equal to both the concurrent Causes of it.[67]

The basic argument at the root of his terminological objection was one familiar from the *First Treatise*. Patriarchal theory could not stand if power were shared by husband and wife. As Locke argued in the *Second Treatise*, 'it will but very ill serve the turn of those Men who contend so much for the Absolute Power and Authority of the Fatherhood, as they call it, that the Mother should have any share in it'.[68]

Locke's examination of the conjugal relationship demanded a more extensive analysis of the roles and status of women in society. He described conjugal society as follows:

> Conjugal Society is made by a voluntary Compact between Man and Women: tho' it consist chiefly in such a Communion and Right in one another's Bodies, as is necessary to its chief End, Procreation; yet it draws with it mutual Support and Assistance, and a Communion of Interest too, as necessary not only to unite their Care, and Affection, but also necessary to their common Off-spring, who have a Right to be nourished and maintained by them, till they are able to provide for themselves.[69]

Conjugal society existed among human being as a persistent social relationship because of the long term of dependency of the offspring and further because of the dependency of the women who is 'capable of conceiving, and *de facto* is commonly with Child again, and Brings forth too a new Birth long before the former is out of a dependency'.[70] Thus the father is obliged to care for his children and is also 'under an Obligation to continue in Conjugal Society with the same Woman longer than other creatures'.[71]

---

65 Mary Lyndon Shanley and Carole Patemen (eds), *Feminist Interpretations and Political Theory* (Polity Press, 1991).

66 At the time of writing, Associate Professor of Political Science at Wabash College.

67 Locke, *Two Treatises*, II, 52.

68 *Ibid* at II, 53.

69 *Ibid* at II, 78.

70 *Ibid* at II, 80.

71 *Ibid*.

Though the conjugal relationship began for the sake of procreation, it continued for the sake of property. After praising God's wisdom for combining in man an acquisitive nature and a slow maturing process, Locke noted that a departure from monogamy would complicate the simple natural economics of the conjugal system.[72] Though conjugal society among human beings would be more persistent than among other species, this did not mean that marriage would be indissoluble. Indeed Locke wondered:

> why this Compact where Procreation and Education are secured, and Inheritance taken care for, may not be made determinable, either by consent or at a certain time, or upon certain Conditions, as well as any other voluntary Compacts, there being no necessity in the nature of the thing, nor to the ends of it, that it shall always be for life.[73]

Locke's tentative acceptance of divorce brought him criticism over 100 years later. Thomas Elrington commented that 'to make the conjugal union determinable by consent, is to introduce a promiscuous concubinage'. Laslett notes that Locke was prepared to go even further and suggested the possibilities of lefthand marriage.[74] In Locke's view, the actual terms of the conjugal contract were not fixed and immutable:

> Community of Goods and the Power over them, mutual Assistance and Maintenance, and other things belonging to Conjugal Society, might be varied and regulated by that Contract, which united Man and Wife in that society as far as may consist with Procreation and the bringing up of Children.[75]

Nevertheless, Locke described what he took to be the normal distribution of power in marital relationships:

> The Husband and Wife, though they have but one common Concern, yet having different understandings will unavoidably sometimes have different wills, too; it therefore being necessary, that the last Determination, ie the Rule, should be placed somewhere, it naturally falls to the Man's share, as the abler and the stronger.[76]

Clearly all forms of patriarchalism did not die with Filmer and his fellows. Here, the subjection of women is not based on Genesis, but on natural qualifications. Nature had shown man to be the 'abler and stronger'. Locke's patriarchy was limited though. The husband's power of decision extended only to those interests and properties held in common by husband and wife. Locke spelled out the limits on the husband's power:

> [His power] leaves the Wife in the full and free possession of what by Contract is her Peculiar Right, and gives the Husband no more power over her Life, than she has over his. The Power of the Husband being so far from that of an absolute monarch that the Wife has, in many cases, a Liberty to separate from him; where natural Right or their Contract allows it, whether that Contract be made by themselves in the state of Nature or by the Customs

---

72 *Ibid.*

73 *Ibid*, II, 81.

74 *Ibid* Laslett (ed) at p 364n.

75 *Ibid*, II, 83.

76 *Ibid*, II, 82.

or Laws of the Country they live in; and the Children upon such Separation fall to the Father or Mother's lot, as such contract does determine.[77]

In addition, Locke distinguished between the property rights of husband and wife. All property in conjugal society was not automatically the husband's. A wife could have property rights not subject to her husband's control. Locke indicated this in a passage on conquest: 'For as to the Wife's share, whether her own Labour or Compact gave her a Title to it, 'tis plain, her Husband could not forfeit what was hers.'[78]

There were several similarities between the conjugal and the political relationship. Both were grounded in consent. Both existed for the preservation of property. Yet conjugal society was not political society because it conferred no power of the life and death of its members. In addition, political society could intervene in the affairs of conjugal society. Men and women in the state of nature were free to determine the terms of the conjugal contract. But in civil society these terms could be limited or dictated by the 'Customs or Laws of the Country'.

The extent to which the participants in the parental and conjugal relationships could also participate in the political relationship remains to be considered. We may gain some insight into the matter by following Locke's route, that is, by tracing the origins of political power from the state of nature.

To Locke, the state of nature was a 'state of perfect Freedom' for individuals 'to order Actions and dispose of their Possessions, and Persons, as they think fit'. Furthermore, Locke also described the state of nature as:

A State also of Equality, wherein all the Power and Jurisdiction is reciprocal, no one having more than another: there being nothing more evident, than that Creatures of the same species and rank promiscuously born to all the same advantages of Nature and the use of the same faculties should also be equal one amongst another without Subordination or Subjection, unless the Lord and Master of them all should by any manifest Declaration of his Will set one above another.[79]

Because of certain inconveniences, men quit the state of nature to form civil society through an act of consent. It was in criticising the formation of society by consent that Filmer's theory was most effective. Indeed, Locke found it difficult to show how free and equal individuals actually formed civil society. Ultimately he was forced to admit that the first political societies in history were probably patriarchal monarchies. He described the historic origins as follows:

As it often happens, where there is much Land and few People, the Government commonly began in the Father. For the Father having by the Law of Nature, the same Power with every Man else to punish his transgressing Children even when they were Men, and out of their Pupilage; and they were very likely to submit to his punishment, and all join with him against the Offender in their turns, giving him thereby power to Execute his Sentence against any transgression [the] Custome of obeying him, in their Childhood made it easier to submit to him rather than to any other.[80]

---

77 *Two Treatises*, II, 82.
78 *Ibid*, II, 183.
79 *Ibid*, II, 4.
80 *Ibid*, II, 105.

In this passage, Locke lumped paternal power and natural power together, allowed for the slightest note of consent, and – presto – civil society emerged. Even in a Lockean state of nature, paternal (parental?) power could be effective. Children growing up in the state of nature were under the same obligations to their parents as children reared in civil society ...[81]

... But what of women? Locke remained silent on the specific question of their participation in the founding of political society. Of course, it is possible Locke referred to the role of women in the lost section of the *Treatises*. Or, perhaps Locke understood that explicit exclusion of women seriously weakened a theory grounded in the natural freedom of mankind. Yet Locke was also a good enough propagandist to have realised how deeply ingrained patriarchalism was in everyday life. Locke had criticised Filmer's use of the fifth commandment – 'Honour thy father' – as a basis for political obligation. If the command were taken seriously, he charged, then 'every Father must necessarily have Political Dominion, and there will be as many Sovereigns as there are Fathers'. But the audience Locke was addressing was essentially an audience of fathers, household heads and family sovereigns. Locke had freed them from political subjection to a patriarchal superior – the king. He did not risk alienating his audience by clearly conferring a new political status on their subordinates under the patriarchal system, that is, on women. Nevertheless, despite the absence of any sustained analysis of the problem of women, we may draw some conclusions from an examination of Locke's scattered thoughts on women.

Though Locke gave the husband ultimate authority within conjugal society, this authority was limited and nonpolitical. Yet when Locke's account of the husband's conjugal authority was combined with his account of the historical development of political society, several questions occur which were never adequately resolved in Locke's moral theory. Did not the award of final decision-making power to the father and husband (in conjugal society) transform 'parental power' into 'paternal power'? Was the subsequent development of political power based on paternal power a result of that transformation? What was woman's role in the establishment of the first political society? Since her husband was to be permitted final decisions in matters of their common interest and property, and since political society, obviously, was a matter of common interest, would her voice simple by 'concluded' in that of her husband? If so, then Filmer's question recurs – what became of her rights as a free individual? Did she lose her political potential because she was deemed not as 'able and strong' as her husband? If this were the case, Locke would have had to introduce new qualifications for political life.

Locke portrayed political society as an association of free, equal, rational individuals who were capable of owning property. These individual came together freely, since none had any power or jurisdiction over others. They agreed to form a civil society vested with power to legislate over life and death, and to execute its decisions in order to protect the vital interests of its members, that is, their lives, liberties and estates. Yet John Locke was certainly no believer in the absolute equality of human beings. Indeed, on that score, he was emphatic:

> Though I have said ... That all Men by Nature are equal, I cannot be supposed to understand all sorts of quality; Age or Virtue may give Men a just Precedency: Excellence of Parts and Merit may place others above the Common Level; Birth may subject some and Alliance or Benefits other, to pay

---

81   *On Locke*, pp 84.

an Observance to those whom Nature, Gratitude, or other Respects may have made it due.[82]

But these inequalities in no way affect an individual's basic freedom or political capacity, for Locke continued in the same passage:

> ... yet all this consists with the Equality which all Men are in, in respect of Jurisdiction or Dominion one over another, which was the Equality I there spoke of, as proper to the Business in hand, being that equal Right every Man hath, to his Natural Freedom, without being subjected to the Will or Authority of any other Man ...[83]

If 'Man' is used as a generic term, then woman's natural freedom and equality could not be alienated without her consent. Perhaps a marriage contract might be taken for consent, but this is a dubious proposition. Locke had indicated that a marriage contract in no way altered the political capacity of a queen regnant. While the decision-making power over the common interests of a conjugal unit belonged to the husband, Locke admitted that the wife might have interests apart from their shared interests. Women could own separate property not subject to her husbands' control. If a husband forfeited his life or property as a result of conquest, his conquerors acquired no title to his wife's life or property.

Did these capacities entitle women to a political role? Locke never directly confronted the question; nevertheless, it is possible to compare Locke's qualifications for political life with his views of women. Locke used the Genesis account to show that women possessed the name natural freedom and equality as men. Whatever limitations had been placed on women after the Fall could conceivable be overcome through individual effort or scientific advance. Furthermore, women were capable of earning through their own labour, of owning property and of making contracts.

Locke and the Rational Women

The one remaining qualification for political life is rationality. For Locke's views on the rationality of women it will be necessary to turn to his other writings, notably his *Thoughts on Education*.

In the published version of his advice on education, Locke mentioned that the work had been originally intended for the education of boys; but he added that it could be used as a guide for raising children of either sex. He noted that 'where difference of sex requires different Treatment, 'twill be no hard Matter to distinguish'.

Locke felt that his advice concerning a gentleman's education would have to be changed only slightly to fit the needs of girls. However, in a letter to a friend, Mrs Edward Clarke, Locke tried to show that his prescriptions were appropriate for her daughter and not unnecessarily harsh. On the whole, Locke believed that except for 'making a little allowance for beauty and some few other considerations of the s[ex], the manner of breeding of boys and girls, especially in the younger years, I imagine should be the same'...[84]

The differences which Locke thought should obtain in the education of men and women amounted to slight differences in physical training. While Locke thought that 'meat, drink and lodging and clothing should be ordered after the same

---

82 *Two Treatises*, II, 54.

83 *Ibid*.

84 Locke to Mrs Clarke, 1 January 1685, in *Correspondence*, Rand (ed).

manner for the girls as for the boys', he did introduce a few caveats aimed at protection the girls' complexions.

Locke introduced far fewer restriction in his plan for a young lady's mental development. In a letter to Mrs Clarke he wrote: 'Since therefore I acknowledge no difference of sex in your mind relating ... to truth, virtue and obedience, I think well to have no thing altered in it from what is [right for the son]'. Far from advocating a special, separate and distinct form of education for girls, Locke proposed that the gentleman's education should more closely resemble that of young ladies. For example, he favoured the education of children at home by tutors. Modern languages learned through conversation should replace rote memorisation of classical grammars. In addition, Locke suggested that young gentlemen as well as young ladies might profit from a dancing master's instruction.

Taken as a whole, Locke's thought on education clearly suggest a belief that men and women could be schooled in the use of reason. The minds of both men and women were blank slates to be written on by experience. Women had intellectual potential which could be developed to a high level.

Locke's educational process was designed to equip young men for lives as gentlemen. Since the gentleman's life certainly included political activity, a young man's education had to prepare him for political life. If a young lady were to receive the same education, it should be expected that she, too, would be capable of political activity.

Finally, 300 years ago, Locke offered a 'liberated' solution to a controversy which still rages in religious circles – the question of the fitness of women to act as ministers. In 1696 Locke, together with King William, attended a service led by a Quaker preacher, Rebecca Collier. He praised her work and encouraged her to continue it, writing: 'Women, indeed, had the honour first to publish the resurrection of the Lord of Love; why not again the resurrection of the Spirit of Love?' It is interesting to compare Locke's attitude here with the famous remark made by Samuel Johnson on the same subject in the next century: 'Sir, a woman's preaching is like a dog walking on his hindlegs. It is done well; but you are surprised to find it done at all.'[85]

Perhaps a similar conclusion might be reached about the roots of feminism in Lockean liberalism. In a world where political anti-patriarchalism was still somewhat revolutionary, explicit statements of more far-reaching forms of anti-patriarchalism were almost unthinkable. Indeed, they would have been considered absurdities. Thus, while Filmer had presented a comprehensive and consistent patriarchal theory, many of his liberal opponents rejected political patriarchalism by insisting on the need for individual consent in political affairs but shied away from tampering with patriarchal attitudes where women were concerned. John Locke was something of an exception to this rule. Though his feminist sympathies certainly did not approach the feminism of Mill writing nearly two centuries later, in view of the intense patriarchalism of 17th century England, it should be surprising to find such views expressed at all.[86]

85 EL McAdam and G Milne (eds), *A Johnson Reader* (New York: Pantheon Books, 1964), p 464.
86 *On Locke*, p 88.

John Rawls's *Theory of Justice*[87]

In 1972 John Rawls's *Theory of Justice* was published to much critical acclaim. Hailed as the most comprehensive contemporary exposition of the social contract, Rawls elaborates on the ideas of earlier writers such as Locke, Paine and Rousseau. The result is a painstakingly worked and reworked calculation of the criteria for a 'nearly just society'. The formula to which Rawls works is to hypothesise about placing representative people from differing walks of life in a society behind a 'veil of ignorance'. This veil prevents individuals from knowing their personal characteristics, including, inter alia, their intelligence, wealth, class or position in society. Only by stripping people of their individuality does Rawls consider that the principles on which society – and hence laws – should be based can be reached. Rawls does not envisage that everyone in a society at any point in time will go behind this 'veil of ignorance'. Rather the original position (under the veil of ignorance) is a mental construct to be used for the determination of rational principles for the ordering of society. Rawls writes:

> ... the original position is not to be thought of as a general assembly which includes at one moment everyone who will live at some time; or, much less, as an assembly of everyone who could live at some time. It is not a gathering of all actual or possible persons. To conceive of the original position in either of these ways is to stretch fantasy too far; the conception would cease to be a natural guide to intuition ...[88]

Rather than an assembly of all persons, those in the original position are viewed as being 'representatives' of a class of persons.

Knowledge and ignorance behind the 'veil of ignorance'

In order to maximise the rationality and disinterest in decision-making about society and laws, Rawls denies the respresentatives in the veil of ignorance certain knowledge. Such persons do not know:

> ... his place in society, his class position or social status; nor does he know his fortune in the distribution of natural assets and abilities, his intelligence and strength, and the like. Nor, again does anyone know his conception of the good, the particulars of his rational plan of life, or even the special feature of his psychology such as his aversion to risk or liability to optimism or pessimism. More than this, I assume that the parties do not know the particular circumstances of their own society. They do not know its economic or political situation, or the level of civilisation and culture it has been able to achieve.

On the other hand, representatives do know 'general facts' about human society. For example:

> They understand political affairs and the principles of economic theory: they know the basis of social organisation and the laws of human psychology. Indeed the parties are presumed to know whatever general facts affect the choice of the principles of justice.[89]

---

87 Oxford University Press, 1973.

88 *A Theory of Justice*, p 139.

89 *Ibid*, p 137.

By denying parties any particular knowledge of their personal situation, Rawls considers that the parties will be unable to bargain to reach decisions about justice from a self-interested position. Rather, parties – who will have a general desire to achieve their 'life plan' and to participate as fully as possible in the good of society – will adopt an attitude to decision-making which, should they end up as less advantages than others, will protect their position as far as possible. The parties behind the veil of ignorance are vaguely pessimistic about their own end-position, and as a result, will always gear their decisions towards the 'worst off' position in society.

The principles of justice

The principles which would be chosen by this representative congress of people are explained to be as follows. First: each person is to have an equal right to the most extensive basic liberty compatible with a similar liberty for others. Second: social and economic inequalities are to be arranged so that they are both (a) reasonably expected to be to everyone's advantage, and (b) attached to positions and offices open to all.

The principles are ordered lexically – that is to say the first principle is 'prior to the second',[90] and accordingly no departure from the first principle is justified by any greater social or economic advantages which might flow from such a departure. Rawls reworks this explanation to provide a more comprehensive account of the two principles of justice.

First principle: each person is to have an equal right to the most extensive total system of equal basic liberties compatible with a similar system of liberty for all. Second principle: social and economic inequalities are to be arranged so that they are both: (a) to the greatest benefit of the least advantaged, consistent with the just savings principle, and (b) attached to offices and positions open to all under conditions of fair equality of opportunity.

First priority rule (the priority of liberty)

The principles of justice are to be ranked in lexical order and therefore liberty can be restricted only for the sake of liberty. There are two cases: (a) a less extensive liberty must strengthen the total system of liberty shared by all; (b) a less than equal liberty must be acceptable to those with the lesser liberty.

Second priority rule (the priority of justice over efficiency and welfare)

The second principle of justice is lexically prior to the principle of efficiency and to that of maximising the sum of advantages; fair opportunity is prior to the difference principle. There are two cases:

(a) an inequality of opportunity must enhance the opportunities of those with the lesser opportunity;

(b) an excessive rate of saving must on balance mitigate the burden of those bearing this hardship.

As a general conception, Rawls provides that:

---

90   *A Theory of Justice*, p 61.

All social primary goods – liberty and opportunity, income and wealth, and the bases of self-respect – are to be distributed equally unless an unequal distribution of any or all of these goods is to the advantage of the least favoured.[91]

From a feminist perspective a number of large questions loom out of Rawls's conception of the criteria for selecting principles of justice in society, and *A Theory of Justice* has been submitted to feminist scrutiny.[92] Amongst other matters, the question of the gender of Rawls's 'representative persons' arises. Also central to the analysis is Rawls's attitude to the reality of equality in a just society. Extracts from the writings of Mari Matsuda and Carole Pateman are presented here to elucidate the perceived strengths and weaknesses of Rawls's theory.

Rawls's methodology is subject to scrutiny by Mari J Matsuda who argues, inter alia, that Rawls's abstractions are unhelpful.

LIBERAL JURISPRUDENCE AND ABSTRACTED VISIONS OF HUMAN NATURE: A FEMINIST CRITIQUE OF RAWLS'S THEORY OF JUSTICE[93]

Mari J Matsuda[94]

To argue at the level of abstraction proves nothing and clouds our vision. What we really need to do is to move forward through Rawls's veil of ignorance, losing knowledge of existing abstractions. We need to return to concrete realities, to look at our world, rethink possibilities, and fight it out on this side of the veil, however indelicate that may be. By ignoring alternative visions of human nature, and by limiting the sphere of the possible, Rawls creates a gridlock in which escape from liberalism is impossible, and dreams of the seashore futile.[95]

Having considered the 'facts' which persons in the original position do and do not know, Mari Matsuda writes:

Feminist theory suggests alternative conceptions that, while like Rawls's are not provable, show how Rawls made some determinative choices in describing the original position.

Feminist theory suggests that we can achieve identity of interest on the real-life side of the veil. In that world, people would not be moved solely by self-interest, but also by feelings of love, intimacy, and care for others. They would be in a perpetual state of mutual concern. Rawls begins to consider this possibility when he discusses families and social unions, but his dominant idea is that it is personally advantageous for individuals to join social unions. Feminist experience suggests there is something beyond personal advantage – a collectivist way of thinking that presume it natural, joyful, and easy to care for

---

91 *Ibid*, pp 302–03.

92 M Matsuda, 'Liberal Jurisprudence and Abstracted Visions of Human Nature: A Feminist Critique of Rawls's Theory of Justice' (1986) 16 *New Mexico Law Review* at 613; SM Okin, *Women in Western Political Thought* (Virago, 1980); 'Justice and Gender' (1987) 16 *Philosophy and Public Affairs* 42; D Kearns, 'A Theory of Justice – and Love: Rawls on the Family' in M Simms (ed), *Australian Women and the Political System* (Melbourne: Longman, 1984).

93 (1986) 16 *New Mexico Law Review* 613.

94 At the time of writing, Assistant Professor of Law, University of Hawaii.

95 *Ibid*, p 624.

others. There is an element of self-interest in this proposition, but it is not a dismal struggle for individual advantage within the merely convenient context of social union that Rawls proposes.

Another counter-assumption is that this may not be a world of an endless mad grab for limited goods. First, it may be possible for all of us to achieve happiness by deciding we don't want the goods anymore. The desire for wealth and property may be the product of false consciousness and consumerist, patriarchal traditions. The desire for power and achievement may be a product of never learning to rejoice at the excellence of others, of never learning to play for the sake of playing rather than winning. Second, the scarcity of goods may be an illusion. Science and technology, good fortune and good weather, cooperation and creativity, may change the availability of most of the goods we covet. This leaves the problem of distribution of such Rawlsian goods as self-respect and excellences, or natural talents and assets. The whole concept of self-respect presumes that others will try to interfere with our plans. Self-respect is defined by Rawls as being left alone to pursue one's own ends. Again, this is a nonsensical concept unless one presumes that individualism is the only possible creed of human conduct. Similarly, excellences are the subject of envy only if it is presumed that we can't rejoice at the gifts of others, and that they won't rejoice in the use of their gifts to help us without some *quid pro quo*.

This leads to another counter-assumption, one that challenges Rawls's stern view of what feels good. Achievement, carrying out a plan, excellence feel good to him. Feminist thought, derived through consciousness raising, considers the possibility that humour, modesty, conversation, spontaneity, laziness, and enjoying the talents and differences of others also feel good. Because Rawls imposes a limited view of what feels good upon the deliberators in the original position, they adopt a limited formula for redistribution. This ignores the possibility that we can take collective pleasure in knowing that there is some rare and fine advantage that only a few can have, and that we can all celebrate when those few are chosen. Sports fans might understand this.

It seems that what really hurts, and this Rawls seeks to avoid, is when those rare and fine advantages are distributed not by grace, but by arbitrary privilege. If this is the real problem, then perhaps justice requires elimination of class differences. My purpose here is not to construct or prove true other theories of justice, but only to point out that Rawls's theory arises from Rawls's unproven premises, and that different premises suggest different results.

Conclusion

There are many hopeful counter-premises that Rawls ignores, and the method of abstraction allows him to do this. Rawls might characterise the counter-assumptions suggested here as alternative conceptions of the good that will be considered in the abstract in the original position. That response is not good enough. It doesn't explain why the presumptions of self-interest and mutual disinterest are not abstracted out, but taken as given, while the possibility of collectivisim is just another possibility that saints may choose on the real-life side of the veil.

Rawls's technique may have value, but it is unfair to achieve consensus by fiat. What we really have to do is to leave the original position, and argue on the common ground of this planet earth. We have to consider the possibility that we can all choose to be saints and that we can set up institutions that allow us to do this. Once we have explored the real-life potential of humankind in the concrete context, it may then be valuable to go back behind the veil and work the theory with a set of general facts about human nature that are more fairly derived. I suspect, however, that once we have the answers on this side of the veil, we won't need to resort to abstraction. The proof will lie in the lives we will live.

This essay has criticised in particular Rawls's quickness to use abstraction. This is not to suggest that theory and abstraction are without value. The suggestion made here is a more modest one. Theory has value, as long as we remember that real people create theory and that real people live their lives in worlds affected by theory. Half of those people are women, and their experiences can teach us something about justice.[96]

THE SEXUAL CONTRACT[97]
Carole Pateman[98]

In *A Theory of Justice*, the parties in the original position are purely reasoning entities. Rawls follows Kant on this point, and Kant's view of the original contract differs from that of the other classic contract theorists, although in some other respects his arguments resemble theirs. Kant does not offer a story about the origins of political right or suggest that, even hypothetically, an original agreement was once made. Kant is not dealing in this kind of political fiction. For Kant the original contract is 'merely an idea of reason, an idea necessary for an understanding of actual political institutions'. Similarly, Rawls writes in his most recent discussion that his own argument 'tries to draw solely upon basic intuitive ideas that are embedded in the political institutions of a constitutional democratic regime and the public traditions of their interpretation'. As an idea of reason, rather than as a political fiction, the original contract helps us 'work out what we now think'. If Rawls is to show how free and equal parties, suitably situated, would agree to principles that are (pretty near to) those implicit in existing institutions, the appropriate idea of reason is required. The problem about political right faced by the classic contract theorists has disappeared. Rawls's task is to find a picture of an original position that will confirm 'our' intuitions about existing institutions, which include patriarchal relations of subordination.

Rawls claims that his parties in their original position are completely ignorant of any 'particular facts' about themselves. The parties are free citizens, and Rawls states that their freedom is a 'moral power to form, to revise, and rationally to pursue a conception of the good', which involves a view of themselves as sources of valid claims and as responsible for their ends. If citizens change their idea of the good, this has no effect on their 'public identity', that is, their juridical standing as civil individuals or citizens. Rawls also states that the original position is a 'device of representation'. But representation is hardly required. As reasoning entities, the parties are indistinguishable one from another. One party can 'represent' all the rest. In effect, there is only one individual in the original position behind Rawls's 'veil of ignorance'. Rawls can, therefore, state that 'we can view the choice [contract] in the original position from the standpoint of one person selected at random'.

Rawls's parties merely reason and make their choice – or the one party does this as the representative of them all – and so their bodies can be dispensed with. The

---

96 *Ibid*, pp 626–29.
97 Polity Press, 1988.
98 At the time of writing, Professor of Political Science, University of California.

representative is sexless. The disembodied party who makes the choice cannot know one vital 'particular fact', namely, its sex. Rawls's original position is a logical construction in the most complete sense. It is a realm of pure reason with nothing human in it – except that Rawls, of course, like Kant before him, inevitably introduces real, embodied male and female beings in the course of his argument. Before ignorance of 'particular facts' is postulated, Rawls has already claimed that parties have 'descendants' (for whom they are concerned), and Rawls states that he will generally view the parties as 'heads of families'. He merely takes it for granted that he can, at one and the same time, postulate disembodied parties devoid of all substantive characteristics, and assume that sexual difference exists, sexual intercourse takes place, children are born and families formed. Rawls's participants in the original contract are, simultaneously, mere reasoning entities, and 'heads of families', or men who represent their wives.

Rawls's original position is a logical abstraction of such rigour that nothing happens there. In contrast, the various states of nature pictured by the classic social contract theorists are full of life. They portray the state of nature as a condition that extends over more than one generation. Men and women come together, engage in sexual relations and women give birth. The circumstances under which they do so, whether conjugal relations exist and whether families are formed, depends on the extent to which the state of nature is portrayed as a social condition.[99]

FEMINISM AND MARXISM

Marxism has long been a site of special research interest for feminist scholars. The writings of Karl Marx[100] and Friedrich Engels[101] concerning the structure and evolution of society, the fundamental importance of the economic base as the determinant of social relations and class structures in society, and the ideological function of law in supporting the economic base, represented a startling philosophical challenge to all political and legal thinkers. For jurists trained in classical Western political thought, Marx offered a strong challenge, for an essential feature of all Marxist thought is that law – far from being the central feature of society – is but a reflection of, and supporter of, the economic base, the *infrastructure*. Law is thus part of the *superstructure*: but part of those features of society – religion, politics, history and philosophy, which are secondary – in terms of the unfolding of society – to the economic base. As a result Marxists are not primarily interested in law, but rather in demonstrating the unfolding of society in a manner analogous to Hegel's dialectical, and natural, process. For Marx, the dialectical process is that of the material – or economic – base. Society evolves through differing stages, essentially from feudalism, to capitalism, to socialism and finally to communism.

In the section which follows Hugh Collins first explains the limited role which law plays in Marxist theory. Next considered is Friedrich Engels' analysis of the evolution of the family and the role of women. It is Engels' thesis that in

99 At pp 41–43
100 1818–83.
101 1820–95.

early times succession came about through the female line. This 'mother right' had to be early overthrown if men were to gain the economic ascendency in the family.

Engels' analysis is subjected to criticism by Simone de Beauvoir. In the extract from *The Second Sex*[102] the author is critical of an explanation which has as its basis the assumption that history may be explained by historical materialism alone. Private property as the 'enslaving' construct does not, without more, explain women's subordination.

In *Looking Again at Engels' 'Origins of the Family, Private Property and the State'*[103] Rosalind Delmar explains Engels' analysis of the means by which women will be emancipated: through their inclusion in socially productive work outside the family. This solution, the author argues, is insufficient so long as women remain primarily responsible for domestic and child care responsibilities within the home.

In *The Sexual Contract*,[104] Carole Pateman criticises Engels' over-reliance, in her view, on a class analysis to explain female subordination, and for women's emancipation. Engles argued that women in the family were analogous to the proletariat, whereas the husband assumed the role of the bourgeoisie. Thus woman was the slave, the husband the owner. Where this analysis breaks down, Pateman argues, is in ignoring the husband's sexual interest. Engels' assumption that the 'social contract' is blind to sexual difference and is akin to the gender-neutral relations in the capitalist market, misses the real dimension which explains women's subordination.

MARXISM AND LAW[105]

Hugh Collins[106]

Marxism is a theory about the meaning of history. However aimless the wanderings of mankind may have seemed to others, Marxists have discerned a regular evolutionary pattern controlling the human condition. Behind the complexity and particularity of isolated events human civilisation has been gradually moving towards the goal of history. Once the direction of this progress and the reasons for social change are perceived, then the secrets of the future can be glimpsed. According to Marxism the meaning of history is that man's destiny lies in the creation of a Communist society where men will experience a higher stage of being amounting to the realisation of true freedom ...[107]

Is there a Marxist Theory of Law?

It has often been remarked that there is no Marxist theory of law. At first sight this is a strange assertion for it is in the nature of Marxism as a general theory of the evolution of societies that it will pass comment on significant institutions such as the law. Admittedly the main thrust of Marxist analysis is directed

---

102 1949.

103 In *The Rights and Wrongs of Women* (eds) J Mitchell and A Oakley (Penguin, 1976).

104 Polity Press, 1988.

105 Oxford University Press, 1982.

106 University of Oxford.

107 *Marxism amd Law*, p 2.

towards the economic infrastructure and the organisations of power in a community. That emphasis stems naturally from Marx's insight that the source of social change and the revelation of the destiny of man can only be discovered from the material circumstances of life and how man has responded to them. It follows that law is not a central focus of concern for Marxists. Neither is law a prominent analytical concept of comparable importance to social class or capitalism for example ...[108]

... To demand a general theory of law from a Marxist is to ask him to run the risk of falling prey to what can be termed the fetishism of law. What is meant by the term 'fetishism of law'? In simple terms it is the belief that legal systems are an essential component of social order and civilisation. This belief is a pervasive feature of social and political theories outside the Marxist tradition. It serves as the foundation for most liberal political theory. In addition, this notion underlies all the important general theories of law which are in currency today. Because Marxism does not subscribe to the fetishism of law it also resists the directions of speculative thought which seek to provide a general theory of law. We can understand this point more clearly if the attributes of legal fetishism are examined in greater detail.

There are three features of legal fetishism which should be highlighted. In the first place there is the thesis that a legal order is necessary for social order: unless there is a system of laws designed to ensure compliance with a set of rules which define rights and entitlements then no civilisation is possible; if laws and legal institutions were abolished anarchy would immediately break out. HLA Hart expresses this idea with his claim that there must be a minimum content of law. Unless there are rules governing ownership of property and enforcing prohibitions against physical violence, he says, society would be impossible. If a legal system, or at least some kind of coercive system failed to provide such rules, the community would disintegrate. For those who fetishise law, legal rules are at the centre of social life, forming the basis for peaceful social intercourse ...[109]

... A second contention of legal fetishism is that law is a unique phenomenon which constitutes a discrete focus of study. Legal systems are not simply types of a broader species of systems of power, but they possess distinctive characteristics. In particular, modern jurisprudence identifies three exclusive features of legal systems. First, there are regular patterns of institutional arrangements associated with law such as the division between a legislature and a judiciary. Second, lawyers communicate with each other through a distinctive mode of discourse, though the exact nature of legal reasoning remains controversial. Third, legal systems are distinguished from simple exercises of force by one group over another; for legal rules also function as normative guides to behaviour which individuals follow regardless of the presence or absence of officials threatening to impose sanctions for failing to comply with the law. Together these three features of law, its institutional framework, its methodology, and its normativity, are considered to make law a unique phenomenon. They constitute the background for the whole enterprise of modern jurisprudence which seeks to provide a general theory of law. Whereas the first thesis of legal fetishism encouraged us to believe that law contains the answers to the problem of the origin of civilisation and thus made a general theory of law of interest, the second feature of legal fetishism, a belief in the

---

108 *Ibid*, p 9.
109 *Ibid*, pp 10–11.

uniqueness of law, suggests that it is possible to isolate legal phenomena and to study their nature. A final aspect of legal fetishism makes a general theory of law not only interesting and possible but also crucial to political theory.

This third feature is the doctrine of the rule of law. The meaning of this idea is complex. For the time being a crude approximation to its meaning will suffice to demonstrate its link to legal fetishism. The core principle of the doctrine is that political power should be exercised according to rules announced in advance ...[110]

... Marxists have rejected these three aspects of legal fetishism. To begin with, the notion that society rests on law is too simplistic ...[111]

... Equally Marxists deny that there is a special and distinctive phenomenon which we can term law. Because Marxism has approached law tangentially, treating it as one aspect of a variety of political and social arrangements concerned with the manipulation of power and the consolidation of modes of production of wealth, there has been no commitment towards an identification of the unique qualities of legal institutions. What is more important for a Marxist is to notice how laws or law-like institutions serve particular functions within a social formation. The focus is switched from proposing a definition and drawing up of lists of functions of law to devising an explanation of the functions which laws together with other social institutions help to perform in particular historical contexts. Guided by the emphasis upon materialism, Marxists avoid assumptions about the uniqueness of legal phenomena or their essence, and so they rarely offer a general theory of law.

The final aspect of legal fetishism, the doctrine of the rule of law, illustrates one of the functions which laws help to perform, and as such it has been of great interest to Marxists. Since legal rules can inhibit the arbitrary exercise of power, even if their control is precarious, law can contribute an important dimension to political philosophies seeking to explain or justify the existing structures of political domination on the ground that the powerful are constrained by the demands of due process of law. The ideal of the rule of law encapsulates this legitimising function of legal systems. The bulk of Western jurisprudence uses the rule of law doctrine as a standard by which to judge the success of desirability of a general theory of law. It is crucial for these legal philosophers to demonstrate the superiority of their approach towards the problem of the identification of the laws of a particular legal system because they can then argue that they have proved the coherence of the predominant legitimating ideology of power in liberal society. Marxists, however, are obviously uninterested in putting forward a theory of their own, for their purpose is to challenge rather than defend the present organisation of power. Accordingly you will not find here those elaborate analyses of the structures of legal systems which parade as legal theory in the law schools. Nevertheless, the rule of law and the function of law in modern theories of the legitimation of power remain of vital interest to Marxists in their search for a critical understanding of the complexities of modern social system. Therefore a general theory of law in the conventional mode would be an anathema to Marxism, though legal phenomena must constitute a central focus of enquiry ...[112]

---

110 *Ibid*, pp 11–12.
111 *Ibid*, pp 12–13.
112 *Ibid*, pp 13–14.

Engels on Women and the Family

Friedrich Engels subjected the family – and the position of women within the family – to a critical Marxist analysis. Before considering feminist responses to Engel's thought, it is necessary to consider, in outline, the original work. Engels, relying on the empirical research conducted in Lewis Morgan,[113] traces the evolution of the family unit from earliest times.

In *The Origin of the Family, Private Property and the State*,[114] Engels stresses that social structures are determined by the stage of development of both labour and the family. Engels – relying on the research of Morgan and others – recounts the changing pattern of the family, demonstrating the changing regulation of the family. From early societies it is clear that rules against sexual intercourse between close family members existed. At the same time, the line of descent – for the purposes of proof of parenthood and inheritance – was in early times through the mother, not the father. In essence, such an approach was necessitated by the simple fact of the proof of parenting was conclusive in relation to the mother through the fact of giving birth, but not necessarily so conclusive in relation to the paternity of the child. However, as societies progressed and private property entered into social relations, this dominance of the mother, and inheritance being determined through the mother's 'gens' (genus: group based on descent through a particular line) the effect was the disinheritance of the father's sons, for – as Engels explains – the chain of inheritance would go 'first to his brothers and sisters and to his sister's children, or to the issue of his mother's sisters. But his own children were disinherited'.[115] Thus it was necessary to overthrow the 'mother right'. It was the destruction of mother-right and the establishment of male power which, Engels explains, represented the world historical defeat of the female sex. Not only did the male assume economic power within the family but he also subordinated the woman who, became 'a slave of his lust and a mere instrument for the production of children. Thus was the patriarchal family born.

Shortly after the destruction of mother-right, monogamous marriage became the norm, for the male was determined to assure the fidelity of his wife, and hence the legitimacy of his children. The evolution of family forms passed through three stages: 'for the period of savagery, group marriage; for barbarism, paring marriage; for civilisation, monogamy supplemented by adultery and prostitution. Only with the overthrow of the capitalist mode of production will the slavery into which monogramy has cast women be overthrown.

Marxist theory has been much criticised by feminist writers. The principal objection is to the equation of women with class, and the argument that the woman is in the same position as her husband in terms of that class. In the following extracts these arguments are considered.

---

113 *Ancient Society, or Researches in the Lines of Human Progress from Savagery, through Barbarism to Civilisation* (Macmillan and Co, 1877).

114 1884 (Lawrence and Wishart Ltd, 1940).

115 *The Origin of the Family*, pp 57–58.

THE SECOND SEX[116]

Simone de Beauvoir

Although the chain of thought as outlined by Engels marks an advance upon those we have been examining, we find it disappointing – the most important problems are slurred over. The turning-point of all history is the passage from the regime of community ownership to that of private property, and it is in no wise indicated how this could have come about. Engels himself declares in *The Origin of the Family* that 'at present we know nothing about it'; not only is he ignorant of the historical details: he does not even suggest any interpretation. Similarly, it is not clear that the institution of private property must necessarily have involved the enslavement of women. Historical materialism takes for granted facts that call for explanation: Engels assumes without discussion the bond of interest which ties man to property; but where does this interest, the source of social institutions, have its own source? Thus Engels's account remains superficial, and the truths that he does reveal are seemingly contingent, incidental. The fact is that we cannot plumb their meaning without going beyond the limits of historical materialism. It cannot provide solutions for the problems we have raised, because these concern the whole man and not that abstraction: *Homo oeconomicus.*

It would seem clear, for example, that the very concept of personal possession can be comprehensible only with reference to the original condition of the existent. For it to appear, there must have been at first an inclination in the subject to think of himself as basically individual, to assert the autonomy and separateness of his existence. We can see that this affirmation would have remained subjective, inward, without validity as long as the individual lacked the practical means for carrying it out objectively. Without adequate tools, he did not sense at first any power over the world, he felt lost in nature and in the group, passive, threatened, the plaything of obscure forces; he dared think of himself only as identified with the clan: the totem, *mana*, the earth were group realities. The discovery of bronze enabled man, in the experience of hard and productive labour, to discover himself as creator; dominating nature, he was no longer afraid of it, and in the fact of obstacles overcome he found courage to see himself as an autonomous active force, to achieve self-fulfilment as an individual. But this accomplishment would never have been attained had not man originally willed it so; the lesson of work is not inscribed upon a passive subject: the subject shapes and masters himself in shaping and mastering the land.

On the other hand, the affirmation of the subject's individuality is not enough to explain property: each conscious individual through challenge, struggle, and single combat can endeavour to raise himself to sovereignty. For the challenge to have taken the form of potlatch or ceremonial exchange of gifts – that is, of an economic rivalry – and from this point on for first the chief and then the members of the clan to have laid claim to private property, required that there should be in man another original tendency. As we have seen in the preceding chapter, the existent succeeds in finding himself only in estrangement, in alienation; he seeks through the world to find himself in some shape, other than himself, which he makes his own. The clan encounters its own alienated existence in the totem, the mana, the terrain it occupies; and when the individual becomes distinguished from the community, he requires a personal incarnation.

---

116 (1949) (Everyman's Library, 1993).

The *mana* becomes individualised in the chief, then in each individual; and at the same time each person tries to appropriate a piece of land, implements, crops. Man finds himself in these goods which are his because he has previously lost himself in them; and it is therefore understandable that he places upon them a value no less fundamental than upon his everyday life. Thus it is that man's interest in his property becomes an intelligible relation. But we see that this cannot be explained through the tool alone: we must grasp in its entirely the attitude of man wielding the tool, an attitude that implies an ontological substructure, a foundation in the nature of his being.

On the same grounds it is impossible to deduce the oppression of woman from the institution of private property. Here again the inadequacy of Engels's point of view is obvious. He saw clearly that women's muscular weakness became a real point of inferiority only in its relation to the bronze and iron tool; but he did not see that the limitations of her capacity for labour constituted in themselves a concrete disadvantage only in a certain perspective. It is because man is a being of transcendence and ambition that he projects new urgencies through every new tool: when he had invented bronze implements, he was no longer content with gardens – he wanted to clear and cultivate vast fields. And it was not from the bronze itself that this desire welled up. Woman's incapacity brought about her ruin because man regarded her in the perspective of his project for enrichment and expansion. And this project is still not enough to explain why she was oppressed; for the division of labour between the sexes could have meant a friendly association. If the original relation between a man and his fellows was exclusively a relation of friendship, we could not account for any type of enslavement; but no, this phenomenon is a result of the imperialism of the human consciousness, seeking always to exercise it sovereignty in objective fashion. If the human consciousness had not included the original category of the Other[117] and an original aspiration to dominate the Other, the invention of the bronze tool could not have caused the oppression of woman.

Nor does Engels account for the peculiar nature of this oppression. He tried to reduce the antagonism of the sexes to class conflict, but he was halfhearted in the attempt; the thesis is simply untenable. It is true that division of labour according to sex and the consequent oppression bring to mind in some ways the division of society by classes, but it is impossible to confuse the two. For one thing, there is no biological basis for the separation of classes. Again, the slave in his toil is conscious of himself as opposed to his master; and the proletariat has always put its condition to the test in revolt, thereby going back to essentials and constituting a threat to its exploiters. And what it has aimed at is its own disappearance as a class. I have pointed out in the 'Introduction' how different woman's situation is, particularly on account of the community of life and interests which entails her solidarity with man, and also because he finds in her an accomplice; no desire for revolution dwells within her, nor any thought of her own disappearance as a sex – all she asks is that certain sequels of sexual differentiation be abolished.

What is still more serious, woman cannot in good faith be regarded simply as a worker; for her reproductive function is as important as her productive capacity, no less in the social economy than in the individual life. In some periods, indeed, it is more useful to produce offspring than to plough the soil. Engels slighted the problem, simply remarking that the socialist community would abolish the

---

117 On Simone de Beauvoir's explanation of the Other, see Chapter 6.

family – certainly an abstract solution. We know how often and how radically Soviet Russia has had to change it policy on the family according to the varying relation between the immediate needs of production and those of repopulation. But for that matter, to do away with the family is not necessarily to emancipate woman. Such examples as Sparta and the Nazi regime prove that she can be none the less oppressed by the males, for all her direct attachment to the State.

A truly socialist ethics, concerned to uphold justice without suppressing liberty and to impose duties upon individuals without abolishing individuality, will find most embarrassing the problems posed by the condition of woman. It is impossible simply to equate gestation with a task, a piece of work, or with a service, such as military service. Woman's life is more seriously broken in upon by a demand for children than by regulation of the citizen's employment – no State has ever ventured to establish obligatory copulation. In the sexual act and in maternity not only time and strength but also essential values are involved for woman. Relationalist materialism tries in vain to disregard this dramatic aspect of sexuality; for it is impossible to bring the sexual instinct under a code of regulation. Indeed, as Freud said, it is not sure that it does not bear within itself a denial of its own satisfaction. What is certain is that it does not permit of integration with the social, because there is in eroticism a revolt of the instant against time, of the individual against the universal. In proposing to direct and exploit it, there is risk of killing it, for it is impossible to deal at will with living spontaneity as one deals at will with inert matter; and no more can it be obtained by force, as a privilege may be.[118]

LOOKING AGAIN AT ENGELS'S ORIGINS OF THE FAMILY, PRIVATE PROPERTY AND THE STATE[119]

Rosalind Delmar

According to the materialistic conception, the determining factor in history is, in the last resort, the production and reproduction of immediate life. But this itself is of a two-fold character. On the one hand, the production of means of subsistence, of food, clothing and shelter and the tools requisite therefore; on the other, the production of human beings themselves, the propagation of the species. The social institutions under which men of a definite country live are conditioned by both kinds of production: by the stage of development of labour, on the one hand, and of the family on the other. The less the development of labour, and the more limited its volume of production and, therefore, the wealth of society, the more preponderantly does the social order appear to be dominated by ties of sex. However, within this structure of society based on ties of sex, the productivity of labour develops more and more; with it, private property and exchange, differences in wealth, the possibility of utilising the labour power of others and thereby the basis of class antagonisms: new social elements, which strive in the course of generations to adapt the old structure of society to the new conditions until finally the incompatibility of the two leads to a complete revolution. The old society based on sex groups bursts asunder in the collision of the newly developed social classes; in its place a new society appears, constituted in a State, the lower units of which are no longer sex groups but territorial groups, a society in which the family system is entirely dominated by the

---

118 *Ibid*, pp 56–61.
119 Juliet Mitchell and Ann Oakley (eds), *The Rights and Wrongs of Women* (Penguin, 1976), Chapter 9.

property system and in which the class antagonisms and class struggles, which make up the content of all hitherto written history now freely develop.[120]

It is thus that Engels summarises the main argument of his *Origins of the Family, Private Property and the State*, a text based on Lewis Morgan's *Ancient Society*.[121]

...

... Division of labour in the family had regulated the distribution of property between man and wife. This division of labour remained unchanged, and yet it now put the former domestic relationship topsy-turvy, simply because the division of labour outside the family had changed. The very cause that had formerly made the woman supreme in the house, namely, her being confined to domestic work, now assured supremacy in the house for the man: the woman's housework lost its significance compared with the man's work in obtaining a livelihood ...[122]

... It was this new economic power, according to Engels, which gave men the strength to institute a political revolution against women, and overturn mother-right, replacing it with father-right. 'The reckoning of descent through the female line and the right of inheritance through the mother were hereby overthrown and male lineage and right of inheritance from the father-instituted.'[123] What was thereby also instituted was the right to undisputed paternity. He adds that 'as to how and when this revolution was effected among the civilised peoples we know nothing', and depends for proof that such an upheaval did take place on both Morgan's demonstration of the existence of matrilineality and Bachofen's cultural researches into Greek myth and drama.[124] Bachofen had found, in the *Oresteia*, for example, an acting out of the rights of mother, father and son which culminated in an affirmation of the law of the father, and had interpreted in this the drama of a struggle between the old order and the new. With this political revolution came a new form of family, the patriarchal family, tied to agriculture, which incorporates bondsmen into its structure, as a transitional form before the appearance of the monogamous family. The imposition of the patriarchy meant that women lost any right to separation. Leaving to one side for the moment Engels's characterisation of the monogamous family, it is instructive to compare his hypothesis of the transition with that of the future liberation of women, in order to bring out what they have in common.

> The emancipation of women and their equality with men are impossible and must remain so as long as women are excluded from socially productive work and restricted to housework, which is private. The emancipation of women becomes possible only when women are enabled to take part in production on a large, social scale, and when domestic duties require attention only to a minor degree. And this has become possible only as a result of modern large-scale industry, which not only permits the participation of women in production in large numbers, but actually calls for it and, moreover, strives to convert private domestic work also into a more public industry.[125]

120 *Origins of the Family, Private Property and the State* (hereinafter Origins), pp 25–26.

121 Lewis Morgan, *Ancient Society* (Macmillan, 1877).

122 *Ibid*, p 521.

123 *Origins*, p 67.

124 Johann Jacob Bachofen, *Myth, Religion and Mother-Right, Selected Writings* (Routledge and Kegal Paul, 1967).

125 *Origins*, p 152.

This is the kernel of Engels's conspectus of the future emancipation of women. Economic emancipation in socially organised production and the liberation of women from restriction to housework are the keys to sexual emancipation. On this all else rests.

Just as the subjugation of women coincided with the subjugation of one section of humanity into slavery, so women's future liberation will coincide with the abolition of wage slavery, for only when that happens will women finally have full freedom in marriage and regain the lost rights of separation: 'full freedom in marriage can become generally operative only when the abolition of capitalist production and of the property relations created by it, has removed all those secondary economic considerations which still exert so powerful an influence on the choice of partner'.[126]

Engels thus locates women's oppression at the level of participation in production, links the conflict between the sexes to the appearance of private ownership of wealth, and posits the reconciliation of the sexes as possible only when private property has been abolished. The fortunes of women and of oppressed classes are intimately connected: neither can be free until economic formations based on private property have been abolished ...

The Division of Labour

Marx and Engels conceived of a spontaneous sexual division of labour arising out of physiological difference and carried over into the social world: 'The first division of labour is that between man and woman for childbreeding.'[127] And again, writing of the American Indian organisations, Engels remarks that 'the division of labour was a pure and simple outgrowth of nature: it existed only between the sexes'.[128]

In *The Origins of the Family* Engels sees the division of labour as 'women in the home, men outside the home', a separation reflected in the division of property: men control the instruments of labour used outside the home, women those within it. But later anthropological findings have made it clear that there are no grounds for assuming such a clear and spontaneous division of labour, property and tasks of the kind Engels predicted, although a division of labour often of the most intricate kind, always does occur. This division, however, does not appear to be a 'simple outgrowth of nature', but rather, an element of the process of the transformation from nature to culture.

Engels's work does not contain any criticism of the sexual division of labour. Indeed this form of separation of responsibility is for him a question entirely outside of the problems of women's oppression. 'The division of labour is determined by entirely different causes than those which determine the status of women'.[129] His criticism is focused on the relative economic weighting which these forms of labour acquire, and the privatisation of domestic labour. Whilst he envisages a future society where such labour will be transformed from private service into public industry, and where child will be socialised, there is no hint that in this future state of affairs such collective labour might cease to be performed exclusively by women.

---

126 *Ibid*, p 88.
127 *Ibid*, p 75.
128 *Ibid*, p 149.
129 *Ibid*, p 61.

This failure to criticise the sexual division of labour marks the break between Engels's analysis (and that of classical socialism) and the feminist perspective. Modern feminism implies a demand for reciprocity. Not only 'anything a man can do a woman can do', but also 'anything a woman can do a man can do'.

The argument that the main focus of women's oppression lies in women's confinement within a privatised domestic economy seems valid. But at the same time it is difficult to believe that work-sharing within the home (the abolition of housework as a category of labour performed by one person or by one sex) can be achieved if, in the social sphere, socialised domestic services and child care continue to be performed exclusively by women.

The feminist critique of the division of labour between the sexes comes from the experience, of women living within monopoly capitalist and imperialist countries. In these societies technology has developed to such an extent that any physiological difference between women and men (such as physical strength) can be rendered irrelevant by labour-saving machinery. At the same time the 'feminine' qualities of the heart, like nurturing and caring, have been recorded as cultural qualities rather than natural phenomena, and are not necessarily restricted to women alone. The recourse to arguments about an immutable female nature is often a defence of the *status quo*. Feminists question not only women's place in the social order, but that of men too.

Socialist feminists have developed a new analysis of the economic importance of women's work in the reproduction of labour power, and in the main have concentrated on the political economy of housework. More attention is now being paid to the implications and development of the sexual division in the world of employment. And various tendencies in the women's movement have encouraged the involvement of men in the care and education of small children. Both the emphasis on the economic and ideological importance of the reproduction of labour power and the demand that this cease to be women's work signal a radical shift from the socialist perspective.

If it is over the issues of the critique of monogamy and the division of labour that modern feminism goes beyond Engels, at the same time Engels did point his finger at some crucial questions which remain to be solved. First, Engels demonstrated that once capitalism is established, the contradiction arises for women between their work in social production and their work in the home. But although the attempted resolutions are different, this contradiction has appeared in socialist countries as well as in capitalist ones. Second, the *Origins of the Family* represents a sustained effort to demonstrate that the existence of sex conflict was bound up with particular historical phases in the development of the family. Such a perspective makes an appraisal of family organisation central to an understanding of women's oppression. This is not to imply that Engels thought that the family was a totally autonomous structure. However, he does imply that the family has a relative autonomy, and that this family does not only inherit 'superstructures' (in the notable case of kinship relations), but also produces its own 'superstructures' – juridical relations (marriage and family law) and social sexual mores. The terms of Engels's analysis are thus: (1) the mode of production, (2) the form of family, (3) the kinship system, (4) juridical relations, and (5) social-sexual mores. What a revolutionary transformation of the form of family thus requires is, in the first place, the revolutionary transformation of the mode of production, a new set of legal guarantees, and the continuous transformation of social-sexual mores and kinship systems. The latter two require as a condition of their success a developed practice of ideological struggle.

Last, we should consider the step forward Engels's work represented. If the *Origins of the Family* constituted an achievement it was this – that it asserted women's oppression as a problem of history, rather than of biology, a problem which it should be the concern of historical materialism to analyse and revolutionary politics to solve.

THE SEXUAL CONTRACT[130]

Carole Pateman

The *locus classicus* for the argument that wives are like workers is, of course, Engels' conjectural history of *The Origin of the Family, Private Property and the State*. Engels argues that 'the first class oppression' was that of male oppression of the female sex, and he states that 'within the family [the husband] is the bourgeois and the wife represents the proletariat'. However, he also claims that in the monogamous family the wife became 'the head servant', and that 'the modern individual family is founded on the open or concealed domestic slavery of the wife'. Engels' famous statement about the oppression of wives thus uses all three feminist terms of comparison; the upper servant, the slave and the worker. Despite his references to the slave and the servant, Engels treats all subordination as class subordination; all 'workers' lack freedom in the same way whether they are located in public workplace or the private workplace of the home, whether they receive protection or the token of free exchange, the wage. Sex is irrelevant to subordination, and the position of wives is best understood as exactly like that of proletarians. Thus, Engels argued that the solution to the subordination of wives in the home was 'to bring the whole female sex back into public industry'. If wives became public workers like their husbands, the married couple would stand together as equals against capitalism, and the husband would have lost the means through which he could control his wife's labour power in the home.

Engels' solution assumes that the original contract was purely a social contract that the terms of the social contract are universal; conjugal relations in the family are like those in the market. That is to say, he assumes that men have no stake as men in their power over women; a husband's interest in his wife's subordination is exactly like that of any capitalist who has another man labour for him. Engels also assumes that sexual difference is irrelevant in the capitalist market. Once women enter into paid employment then, as workers, they become their husbands' equals. The category of 'worker' is universal and applicable to all who enter the capitalist market and sell their labour power.

Contemporary feminists soon ran into difficulties with these assumptions. When the current revival of the organised feminist movement focused attention on housework, many socialists and feminists assumed initially that what became called 'domestic labour' could be brought within the orthodox Marxist critique of capitalism.[131] This approach led to a series of dead-ends; little insight could be gained into the subordination of a wife by seeing her merely as another (unpaid) worker in the interest of capital. The theoretical impasse in the domestic labour debate provoked new interest in the concept of patriarchy. Once it was apparent that the subjection of wives could not be subsumed directly under class subordination, the way was opened for new theoretical categories to be used to

---

130 Polity Press, 1988.
131 The domestic labour debate can be followed in E Malos (ed), *The Politics of Housework* (London: Alison and Busby, 1980).

understand conjugal power. However, as the 'dual systems' account of the relationship between capitalism and patriarchy illustrates, patriarchy is all too frequently merely joined to existing analyses of class. The model of bourgeois and proletarian is still seen as appropriate for marriage, even though the husband's appropriation of his wife's labour is also seen as patriarchal power. That the wife's subjection derives from the fact that she is a woman has received acknowledgment, but the full political implications of patriarchal right remain obscured.

The dual systems argument assumes that patriarchy is a feudal relic, part of the old world of status, and that feminist criticism of this relic must be added to the existing socialist critique of capitalism. But 'class' and the 'worker' can wear the trousers (to borrow a formulation that philosophers are fond of using) in the 'partnership' between capitalism and patriarchy only because half the original contract is ignored. No hint is given that capitalism and class have been constructed as modern patriarchal categories. The social contract is about the origins of the civil sphere and capitalist relations. Without the sexual contract there is no indication that the 'worker' is a masculine figure or that the 'working class' is the class of men. The civil, public sphere does not come into being on its own, and the 'worker', his 'work' and his 'working class' cannot be understood independently of the private sphere and his conjugal right as a husband. The attributes and activities of the 'worker' are constructed together with, and as the other side of, those of his feminine counterpart, the 'housewife'. A (house)wife, a woman, naturally lacks the capacities required of a participant in civil life, and thus she cannot participate as a worker on the same basis as her husband. Women have now won civil and juridical standing almost equal to men's, but they are not incorporated into workplaces on the same basis as male workers. The story of the original contract shows how sexual difference gives rise to a patriarchal division of labour, not only in the conjugal home between the (house)wife and her husband, but in the workplaces of civil society.

A (house)wife is not a worker who happens to be located outside the workplace and who is subject to her husband; she is not a 'worker' at all. The work of a housewife – housework – is the work of a sexually subject being who lacks jurisdiction over the property in her person, which includes labour power. But sale of labour power, in contrast to sale of labour or the person, is what makes a man a free worker; the ability to contract out a piece of property in exchange for a wage is, it is held, what distinguishes the worker, the wage labourer, from unfree labourers and slaves. A (house)wife does not contract out her labour power to her husband. She is not paid a wage – there is no token of free exchange – because her husband has command over the use of her labour by virtue of the fact that he is a man. The marriage contract is a labour contract in a very different sense from the employment contract. The marriage contract is about women's labour; the employment contract is about men's work.

The connection between the sexual division of labour and the subordination of wives was emphasised in various radical circles in the early 19th century, especially by the Owenite co-operative socialists, including William Thompson. They attacked 'single family arrangements' and, in their model communities established between the 1820s and 1840s, they attempted (not altogether successfully) to combat marital subjection through communal forms of housework.[132] If Marx and Engels had not dismissed their predecessors so

132 See B Taylor, *Eve and the New Jerusalem* (Virago Press, 1983), esp Chapter VIII.

summarily and scathingly as utopians, they would have found it far harder to forget the sexual contract, and to treat the private sphere as the politically irrelevant, natural basis from which the worker emerges to contract out his labour power and engage in political struggle in the workplace. Socialist criticism of the employment contract might then have continued to be informed by feminist criticisms of the marriage contract and an appreciation of the mutual dependence of conjugal rights and civil equality.[133]

FEMINISM AND CRITICAL LEGAL STUDIES

The contemporary jurisprudential feminist debate is characterised by diversity. As current social and political theory reflects the uncertainties of the postmodern era, so too feminist jurisprudence questions its orientation and scope. If 'modernity' suggested that social and legal theory could be constructed as some universal truth – some form of certifiable absolute – the postmodern condition implies uncertainty, fragmentation and a distrust of Grand Theory.

Part of this broad movement in social and political theory is reflected in the Critical Legal Studies (CLS) movement. 'Critical Legal Studies' as a broad movement – or a reaction against, traditional jurisprudential thought – which has much affected feminist thought, emerged in the 1980s. CLS has been described by Professor Alan Hunt as the 'enfant terrible of contemporary legal studies'. CLS scholars – while adopting differing approaches – are united in their rejection of traditional legal thought and legal theory. Given the diversity of approach and the rejection of Grand Theory, CLS cannot itself be regarded as 'a theory' or 'a school'. Critical legal scholarship has been applied to feminist jurisprudence, as Professor Deborah Rhode explains in the following passage:[134]

> Critical feminism, like other critical approaches, builds on recent currents in social theory that have made theorising increasingly problematic. Postmodern and poststructural traditions that have influenced left legal critics presuppose the social construction of knowledge.[135] To varying degrees, critics within these traditions deny the possibility of any universal foundations for critique. Taken as a whole, their work underscores the cultural, historical, and linguistic construction of human identity and social experience.[136]

---

133 *The Sexual Contract*, pp 133–36.

134 In 'Feminist Critical Theories' (see further below).

135 For discussion of postmodernism's denial that categorical, non-contingent, abstract theories derived though reason or human nature can serve as the foundation for knowledge, see JF Lyotard, *The Postmodern Condition* (1984); J Rajchmand and C West (eds), *Psycho-Analytic Philosophy* (1985); Nancy Fraser and Linda Nicholsen, 'Social Criticism Without Philosophy: An Encounter Between Feminism and Postmodernism', in A Ross (ed), *Universal Abandon?: The Politics of Postmodernism* (1988), p 83; Sandra Harding, 'The Instability of the Analytical Categories of Feminist Theory' (1986) 11 *Signs* 645; David Luban, 'Legal Modernism' (1986) 84 *Michigan Law Review* 1656; Robin West, 'Feminism, Critical Social Theory and Law' (1989) *U Chi Legal F* 59.

For a useful overview, see Christopher Norris, *Deconstruction: Theory and Practice* (1982); P Fitzpatrick and A Hunt, 'Critical Legal Studies: Introduction' (1987) 14 *J Law and Society* 1; David Kennedy, 'Critical Theory, Structuralism and Contemporary Legal Scholarship' (1986) 231 *New England L Rev* 209.

136 See, for example, JF Lyotard above; Jane Flax, 'Postmodernism and Gender Relations in Feminist Theory' (1987) 12 *Signs* 621. Critical legal studies scholars have responded in varying ways, …

Critics such as Francois Lyotard invoke the term postmodernism to describe the present age's collapse of faith in traditional Grand Narratives. Since the Enlightenment, these metanarratives have sought to develop principles of objective science, universal morality, and autonomous art.

Poststructuralism, which arises from and contributes to this postmodern tradition, refers to the theories of interpretation that view meaning as a cultural construction mediated by arrangements of language or symbolic form. What distinguishes poststructuralism from other interpretive schools is the premise that these arrangements are unstable and contradictory, and that readers create rather than simply discover meaning.

FEMINISM AND CRITICAL LEGAL THEORY: AN AMERICAN PERSPECTIVE[137]

Frances Olsen

Liberal Dualisms

Since the rise of classical liberal thought, and perhaps since the time of Plato, most of us have structured our thinking around a complex series of dualisms, or opposing pairs: rational/irrational; active/passive; thought/feeling; reason/emotion; culture/nature; power/sensitivity; objective/subjective; abstract/contextualised; principled/personalised. These dualistic pairs divide things into contrasting spheres or polar opposites.

This system of dualisms has three characteristics that are important to this discussion. Firstly, the dualisms are sexualised. One half of each dualism, is considered masculine, the other half feminine. Secondly, the terms of the dualism are not equal, but are thought to constitute a hierarchy. In each pair, the term identified as 'masculine' is privileged as superior, while the other is considered negative, corrupt, or inferior. And thirdly, law is identified with the 'male' side of the dualism.

Sexualisation

The division between male and female has been crucial to this dualistic system of thought. Men have identified themselves with one side of the dualisms and have projected the other side upon women. I have listed each dualism in the same order, with the term associated with men on the left: rational, active, thought, reason, culture, power, objective, abstract, principled. The terms associated with women are on the right side: irrational, passive, feeling, emotion, nature, sensitivity, subjective, contexualised, personalised.

    rational/irrational
    active/passive
    thought/feeling
    reason/emotion
    culture/nature
    power/sensitivity
    objective/subjective
    abstract/contextualised
    principled/personalised

... ranging from Roberto Unger's and Jurgen Habermas's continued embrace of universalist claims, to Duncan Kennedy's reliance on deconstructive technique. *Cf* Roberto Mangabeira Unger *Knowledge and Politics* (1975) and Jurgen Habermas *Legitimation Crisis* (1975) with Peter Gabel and Duncan Kennedy, 'Roll Over Beethoven' (1984) 36 *Stanford L Rev* 1.

137 (1990) 18 *International Journal of the Sociology of Law* 199–215.

The sexual identification of the dualism has both a descriptive and a normative element. Sometimes it is said that men are rational, active etc and at other times it will be said that men should be rational, active etc. Similarly, the claim about women is sometimes considered to be descriptive: women simply are irrational, passive etc. A lot of people used to believe that this was an inevitable immutable fact about women – that women were unable to become rational, active etc. Another kind of claim is that women should be irrational, passive etc or at least that they should not become rational, active etc – either because it is important that women remain different from men, or because irrational, passive etc are good traits as applied to women.

Hierarchisation

The system of dualisms is hierarchised. The dualisms do not just divide the world between two terms; the two terms are arranged in a hierarchical order. Just as men dominate and define women, one side of the dualism dominates and defines the other. Irrational is the absence of rational; passive is the failure of active; thought is more important than feeling; reason takes precedence over emotion.

This hierarchy has been somewhat obscured by a complex and often insincere glorification of women and the feminine. While men have oppressed and exploited women in the real world, they have also placed women on a pedestal and treasured them in a fantasy world. And just as men simultaneously exalt and degrade women, so, too, do they simultaneously exalt and degrade the concepts on the 'feminine' side of the dualisms. Nature, for example, is glorified as something awesome, a worthy subject of conquest by male heroes, while it is simultaneously degraded as inert matter to be exploited and shaped to men's purpose. Irrational subjectivity and sensitivity are similarly treasured and denigrated at the same time. However much they might romanticise the womanly virtues, most men still believe that rational is better than irrational, objectivity is better than subjectivity, and being abstract and principled is better than being contextualised and personalised. It is more complicated than this, however, because no one would really want to eliminate irrational, passive etc from the world altogether. But men usually want to distance themselves from these traits; they want women to be irrational, passive, and so forth. To women, this glorification of the 'feminine' side of the dualisms seems insincere.

Law as Male

Law is identified with the hierarchically superior, 'masculine' sides of the dualisms. 'Justice' may be depicted as a woman but, according to the dominant ideology, law is male, not female. Law is supposed to be rational, objective, abstract and principled, like men; it is not supposed to be irrational, subjective, contextualised or personalised, like women.

The social, political and intellectual practices that constitute 'law' were for many years carried on almost exclusively by men. Given that women were long excluded from the practice of law, it is not surprising that the traits associated with women are not greatly valued in law. Moreover, in a kind of vicious cycle, this presumed 'maleness' of law used to provide justification for excluding women from practising law. While the number of women in law has been rapidly increasing, the field continues to be heavily male-dominated. In a similar vicious cycle, law is considered rational and objective in part because it is highly valued, and it is highly valued in part because it is considered rational and objective.[138]

---

138 *Ibid*, pp 200–01.

Feminist Strategies

Feminist strategies for attacking the dominant dualistic system of thought fall into three broad categories. The first category consists of strategies that oppose the sexualisation of the dualism and struggle to identify women with the favoured side, with rational, active, and so forth. Strategies in the second category reject the hierarchy men have established between the two sides of the dualisms. This second category accepts the identification of women with irrational, passive etc but proclaims the value of these traits; they are as good or better than rational, active, and so forth. The third category rejects both the sexualisation and the hierarchisation of the dualisms. Strategies in this third category question and disrupt the differences asserted between men and women, and they deny the hierarchy of rational, active etc over irrational, passive, and so forth. Rational, active etc and irrational, passive etc are not polar opposites, and they do not and cannot divide the world into contrasting spheres.[139]

Olsen then analyses the differing approaches taken by feminists in relation to the first two categories she identifies, namely those who oppose the 'sexualisation of the dualisms', and those who reject the hierarchical nature that men assert characterises the dualisms – in men's favour. Attention is then turned to the third category, which rejects both sexualisation and hierarchalism.

Critical Legal Theory

The third category of feminist criticisms of law rejects the hierarchy of rational, objective etc over irrational, subjective etc and denies that law is or could be rational, objective, abstract and principled. The feminists who endorse this third category agree in part and disagree in part with the first two categories of criticism.

These feminists do not belittle the benefits obtained by the legal reform feminists in the name of women's rights, but remain unconvinced by their claims about the role of abstract legal theory in obtaining these benefits. Legal reasoning and legal battles are not sharply distinguishable from moral and political reasoning, and moral and political battles.

Similarly, feminists of the third category agree that law is often ideologically oppressive to women. They disagree, however, that law is male; law has no essence or immutable nature. Law is a form of human activity, a practice carried on by people – predominantly men. The men who carry on this activity make claims about what they are doing that are just not true and could not be true. While it is true that law has been dominated by men, the traits associated with women have been only obscured, not eliminated. Law is not male. Law is as irrational, subjective, concrete and contextualised as it is rational, objective, abstract and principled.

Law is not all one side of the dualisms

Law is not now, and could not, consistent with what we believe, become principled, rational, and objective.

(1) *Law not principled.* The claim that law is principled is based upon the belief that law consists of a few rules or principles and that these general rules provide a principled basis for deciding individual cases. But instead of this, law is actually made up of an agglomeration of lots of specific rules and some very general standards.

---

139 *Ibid*, pp 201–02.

The rules are too specific, definite, and contextualised to count as principles. The existence of these rules is what gives law the degree of predictability that it has – but no rules are too detailed and each rule covers too few cases to make the law principled. For example, in the United States there is at present a rule which allows for States to use gender-based statutory rape laws to try to reduce the incidence of teenage pregnancy, and there is another rule which states that the age of majority for purposes of terminating parental support may not be gender-based. In *Michael M v Sonoma County* (1981), the United States Supreme Court let stand a gender-based statutory rape law that the California Supreme Court said was intended to reduce the incidence of teenage pregnancy. In *Stanton v Stanton* (1975), the Supreme Court struck down a Utah law that required a parent to support his son until age 21 but allowed him to stop supporting his daughter at age 18. My point is not that these two rules conflict or that the cases cannot be reconciled with one another. Rather, each of these two rules apply in two few circumstances to provide any principled answer to the questions of when States may use gender-based laws.

The standards, on the other hand, are too vague and indeterminate to decide cases. In each interesting disputed case, you can find at least two different broad, general standards, that could apply to the case and that would lead to different results. For example, American courts have a long tradition of respecting family autonomy and not intervening in the family; they have an equally long tradition of protecting the welfare of children. Often, in particular cases, the standard of non-interference in the family will support one outcome, while the standard of protecting children will support the opposite outcome. Just as rules apply to too few cases, standards apply to too many. The legal system fluctuates between being based on rules and being based on standards, but its aspiration to be principled is not achieved. Law is no more abstract and principled than it is personalised and contextualised.

(2) *Law is not rational.* Nor is law rational. The efforts by American feminists to work out a rational elaboration of equal rights of human beings in order to achieve rights for women has not worked and it will not work. The classic conflicts between equality of opportunity and equality of result, between natural rights and positive rights, and between rights-as-a-guarantee-of-security and rights-as-a-guarantee-of-freedom, render rights analysis incapable of settling any meaningful conflict. More specifically, if one outcome will protect the plaintiff's right to freedom of action, the opposite outcome will often protect the defendant's right to security. If one outcome will protect a women's right to formal equality of treatment, her right to substantive equality of result may seem to require a different outcome. This conflict explains, for example, why American feminists argued opposite sides in *California Federal v Guerra* (1987), in which the United States Supreme Court upheld a State maternity leave provision. Some feminists argued that formal equality requires that the law treats pregnancy just like any other temporary disability. Other feminists maintained that substantive equality requires that women be able to give birth to children without losing their jobs – even if no other temporary absence from work is excused. Therefore some feminists argued that women should insist on formal equality and reject any form of special maternity leave; while other feminists argued that working women need adequate maternity leave, even if no similar leave of absence are given to men or other people who are not pregnant. The law does not provide a rational basis for choosing which right to recognise and protect in any particular case. Rights analysis cannot settle these conflicts, but merely restates them in a new – at most somewhat obscured – form.

(3) Law is not objective. Further, law is not objective. The idea that law is objective is refuted by the gradual recognition that policy issues appear everywhere. Every time a choice is made, every legal decision that is not obvious and uncontroversial, is a decision based on policy – which cannot be objective. Thus, it is simply a mistake to say that law is or could become rational, principled and objective. Law is not all one side of the dualisms.

Law cannot be segregated

Sometimes dominant legal theory recognises that law is not principled, rational and objective. The dominant ideology does recognise the so-called 'female' traits – indeed it celebrates them – but only on the periphery, or in their own 'separate sphere'. For example, family law may be subjective, contextual and personalised, but commercial law is thought to be principled, rational and objective. It is important for feminists to correct this misperception, to dissolve the ghettos of law, and to show that you cannot exclude the personalised, irrational, and subjective from any part of law.

(1) *Dissolve law's irrational, subjective ghettos.* One way that dominant ideology makes law seem principled, rational, and objective is by banishing to the periphery of law those fields believed to be tainted by unruly, discretionary standards – fields such as family law, trust law, and the law of fiduciary obligations in general. The core subjects or the important fields of law are said to remain male. We can show, however, that in banishment, family law, trusts, and fiduciary obligations continue to influence the rest of law – including those fields that were supposed to be the bastion of the so-called 'male' principles of law. For example, the ideology of the market-place depends upon the ideology of the family, and commercial law can be understood adequately only by recognising the inter-relationship between it and family law.

(2) *Reconceive the core and periphery.* Another technique by which the dominant ideology tries to make the law seem rational and objective is by separating each field between, on the one hand, a set of basic rules, or a 'male' core that is principled, rational and objective and, on the other hand, a periphery of exceptions that can contain irrational and subjective elements. For example, contract law is frequently conceptualised as a set of rational, consistent, individualist rules, softened by somewhat subjective, variable, 'altruistic' exceptions, such as promissory estoppel. Therefore the basic core of contract law remains male. Feminists can disrupt this by showing that the conflict between the individualistic 'rule' and the altruistic 'exception' reappears in every doctrine. Every doctrine is a choice or compromise of sorts between the individualistic and altruistic impulses. This feminist analysis also problematises what should be considered the rule and what the exception. It is not possible to separate any field of law into a core and a periphery and the traits associated with women cannot be excluded from law.

Conclusion

As I have said, the feminist strategies for attacking legal theory are analogous to feminist strategies for attacking male dominance in general. The 'reject sexualisation' position resonates with the 'legal reformist' position, the 'reject hierarchisation' with the 'law as patriarchy' and the 'androgyny' with 'critical legal theory'. But I do not want to claim that the relationship is anything more than this – an analogy or a resonance. The sets of categories are not identical, and no strategy from one set requires or entails any strategy from the other set.

First, there is no necessary relationship between a feminist's attitude towards the sexualisation of the dualisms and her attitude toward the identification of law as rational, objective, and principled. Moreover, a feminist can accept the hierarchisation for some purposes – for example, can believe that it is better for law to be rational, objective, and principled – but still reject the hierarchisation in general. Some feminists support androgyny but still claim that law is patriarchal. Similarly, one can support critical legal theory and still believe either that women are inherently or morally superior to men or that women should be rational, active etc like men.

My support for androgyny would not require me to support critical legal theory or vice versa, but both are related to my values and vision of the universe and both inform my political activity. Nothing in either theory will provide easy answers to concrete questions – such as 'Would women really benefit from more State regulation of the family?' or 'Could revised statutory rape laws protect young females without oppressing and demeaning them?'. What I do hope is that by improving the theories upon which we operate we can understand better what is at stake in questions like these. I hope that by recognising the impossibility of easy, logical answers we can free ourselves to think about the questions in a more constructive and imaginative manner. Law cannot be successfully separated from politics, morals, and the rest of human activities, but is an integral part of the web of social life.[140]

FEMINIST CRITICAL THEORIES[141]
Deborah L Rhode

Heidi Hartmann once described the relation between Marxism and feminism as analogous to that of husband and wife under English common law: 'Marxism and feminism are one, and that one is Marxism.' In Hartmann's view: 'Either we need a healthier marriage or we need a divorce.'[142] Responding to that metaphor, Gloria Joseph underscored the exclusion of black women from the wedding and redescribed the interaction between Marxist, feminist, and minority perspectives as an 'incompatible *ménage à trois*'.[143]

The relations between Critical Legal Studies (CLS) and feminism have provoked similar concerns. The origins of this article are a case in point. The piece has grown out of an invitation to offer a feminist perspective for an anthology on critical legal studies. Such invitations are problematic in several respects. Almost any systematic statement about these two bodies of thought risks homogenising an extraordinarily broad range of views. Moreover, providing some single piece on the 'women question' perpetuates a tradition of tokenism that has long characterised left political movements.

Whatever the risks of other generalisations, one threshold observation is difficult to dispute: feminism takes gender as a central category of analysis, while the core texts of critical legal studies do not. To be sure, many of these texts make at least some reference to problems of sex-based subordination and to the existence (if not the significance) of feminist scholarship. Yet most critical legal theory and the traditions on which it relies have not seriously focused on gender inequality.

---

140 *Ibid*, pp 208–11.

141 (1990) 42 *Stanford Law Review* 617.

142 Heidi Hartmann, 'The Unhappy Marriage of Marxism and Feminism: Toward a More Progressive Union', in L Sargent (ed), *Woman and Revolution* (1981).

143 Gloria Joseph, 'The Incompatible Menage a Trois: Marxism, Feminism and Racism' in *Women and Revolution*, p 91.

Why then should feminists continue participating in enterprises in which their perspectives are added but not integrated, rendered separate but not equal?

Efforts to provide the 'woman's point of view' also risk contributing to their own marginalisation. In effect, feminists are invited to explain how their perspectives differ from others associated with critical legal studies or with more mainstream bodies of legal theory. Such invitations impose the same limitations that have been characteristic for women's issues in conventional legal ideology. Analysis has fixated on how women are the same or different from men; men have remained the unstated standard of analysis.

In recent years, these concerns have increasingly emerged within the critical legal studies movement. During the last decade issues of gender as well as race and ethnicity dominated the agendas of several national CLS conferences and feminist theorists organised regional groups around common interests. A growing body of feminist and critical race scholarship also developed along lines that paralleled, intersected, and challenged critical legal theory.[144]

This chapter charts relationships among these bodies of work. Although no brief overview can adequately capture the range of scholarship that co-exists under such labels, it is at least possible to identify some cross-cutting objectives, methodologies, and concerns. The point of this approach is neither to develop some unifying Grand Theory nor simply to compare feminism with other critical frameworks. Rather, it is to underscore the importance of multiple frameworks that avoid universal or essentialist claims and that yield concrete strategies for social change.

The following discussion focuses on a body of work that may be loosely identified as feminist critical theories. Although they differ widely in other respects, these theories share three central commitments. On a political level, they seek to promote equality between women and men. On a substantive level, feminist critical frameworks make gender a focus of analysis, their aim is to reconstitute legal practices that have excluded, devalued, or undermined women's concerns. On a methodological level, these frameworks aspire to describe the world in ways that correspond to women's experience and that identify the fundamental social transformations necessary for full equality between the sexes. These commitments are, for the most part, mutually reinforcing, but they occasionally pull in different directions. This essay explores various ways that feminists have sought to fuse a political agenda that is dependent on both group identity and legalist strategies with a methodology that is in some measure sceptical of both.

What distinguishes feminist critical theories from other analysis is both the focus on gender equality and the conviction that it cannot be obtained under existing ideological and institutional structures. This theoretical approach partly overlaps and frequently draws upon other critical approaches, including CLS and critical race scholarship. At the most general level, these traditions share a common goal: to challenge existing distributions of power. They also often employ similar deconstructive or narrative methodologies aimed at similar targets – certain organising premises of conventional liberal legalism. Each tradition includes both internal and external critiques. Some theorists focus on the inadequacy of conventional legal doctrine in terms of its own criteria for coherence, consistency,

---

144 See C Menkel-Meadow, 'Feminist Legal Theory – Critical Legal Studies: Minority Critiques of the Critical Legal Studies Movement' (1987) 22 *Harv CR-CLL Rev* 297; 'Voices of Experience: New Responses to Gender Discourse' (1989) 24 *Harv CR-CLL Rev* 1.

and legitimacy. Other commentators emphasise the role of legal ideology in legitimating unjust social conditions. Yet these traditions also differ considerably in their theories about theory, in their critiques of liberal legalism, in their strategies for change, and in their alternative social visions.

1. Theoretical Premises

Critical feminism like other critical approaches, builds on recent currents in social theory that have made theorising increasingly problematic. Postmodern and poststructural traditions that have influenced left legal critics presuppose the social construction of knowledge.[145] To varying degrees, critics within these traditions deny the possibility of any universal foundations for critique. Taken as a whole, their work underscores the cultural, historical, and linguistic construction of human identity and social experience.[146]

Yet such a theoretical stance also limits its own aspirations to authority. For feminists, this postmodern paradox creates political as well as theoretical difficulties. Adherents are left in the awkward position of maintaining that gender oppression exists while challenging our capacity to document it.[147] Such awkwardness is, for example, especially pronounced in works that assert as unproblematic certain 'facts' about the pervasiveness of sexual abuse while questioning the possibility of any objective measure.[148]

To take an obvious illustration, feminists have a stake both in quantifying the frequency of rape and in questioning the conventional definitions on which rape statistics are based. Victims of sexual assault by acquaintances often respond to questions such as, 'Have you ever been raped?' with something like, 'Well ... not exactly'. What occurs in the pause between 'well' and 'not exactly' suggests the gap between the legal understanding and social experience of rape, and the ways in which data on abuse are constructed, not simply collected.

Although responses to this dilemma vary widely, the most common feminist strategies bear mentioning. The simplest approach is to decline to address the problem – at least at the level of abstraction at which it is customarily formulated. The revolution will not be made with slogans from Lyotard's *Postmodern Condition*, and the audiences that are most in need of persuasion are seldom interested in epistemological anxieties. Critiques of existing ideology and institutions can proceed under their own standards without detailed discussions of the philosophy of knowledge. Yet even from a purely pragmatic view, it is helpful to have some self-consciousness about the grounding for our claims about the world and the tensions between our political and methodological commitments.

Critical feminism's most common response to questions about its own authority has been reliance on experiential analysis. This approach draws primarily on

---

145 See J-F Lyotard, *The Postmodern Condition* (1984); *Post-Analytic Philosopy*, J Rajchmand and C West (eds) (1985).

146 See Jane Flax, 'Post Moderism and Gender Relations in Feminist Theory' (1987) 12 *Signs* 621.

147 As Nancy Cott notes, 'in deconstructing categories of meaning, we deconstruct not only patriarchal definitions of 'womanhood' and ' truth' but also the very categories of our own analysis – 'women' and 'feminism' and 'oppression'. (Quoted in France E Macia-Lees, Patricia Sharpe and Colleen Ballerino Cohen, 'The Postmodernist Turn in Anthropology: Cautions from a Feminist Perspective' (1989) 15 *Signs* 7 at 27.)

148 Compare CA MacKinnon, *Feminism Unmodified* (1987), pp 81–92 (discussing the social construction of rape and sexual violence) with *ibid*, p 23 (asserting 'facts' about its prevalence). See also CA MacKinnon, *Toward a Feminist Theory of the State* (1989), p 100 (acknowledging without exploring the difficulty).

techniques of consciousness raising in contemporary feminist organisations but also on pragmatic-philosophical traditions. A standard practice is to begin with concrete experiences, integrate these experiences into theory, and rely on theory for a deeper understanding of the experiences. One distinctive feature of feminist critical analysis is, as Katharine Bartlett emphasises, a grounding in practical problems and a reliance on 'practical reasoning'.[149] Rather than working deductively from abstract principles and overarching conceptual schemes such analysis builds from the ground up. Many feminist legal critics are also drawn to narrative styles that express the personal consequences of institutionalised injustice.[150] Even those commentators most wedded to broad categorical claims usually situate their works in the lived experience of pornography or sexual harassment rather than, for example, in the deep structure of Blackstone's *Commentaries* or the fundamental contradictions in Western political thought.[151]

In part, this pragmatic focus reflects the historical origins and contemporary agenda of feminist legal theory. Unlike critical legal studies, which began as a movement within the legal academy and took much of its inspiration from the Grand Theory of contemporary Marxism and the Frankfurt school, feminist legal theories emerged against the backdrop of a mass political movement. In America, that struggle has drawn much of its intellectual inspiration not from overarching conceptual schemes but from efforts to provide guidance on particular substantive issues. As Carrie Menkel-Meadow has argued the strength of feminism 'originates' in the experience of 'being dominated, not just in thinking about domination' and in developing concrete responses to that experience.[152] Focusing on women's actual circumstances helps reinforce the connection between feminist political and analytic agendas, but it raises its own set of difficulties. How can critics build a unified political and analytical stance from women's varying perceptions of their varying experiences? And what entitles that stance to special authority?

The first question arises from a long-standing tension in feminist methodology. What gives feminism its unique force is the claim to speak from women's experience. But that experience counsels sensitivity to its own diversity across such factors as time, culture, class, race, ethnicity, sexual orientation and age. As Martha Minow has noted, 'cognitively we need simplifying categories, and the unifying category of 'woman' helps to organise experience, even at the cost of denying some of it'.[153] Yet to some constituencies, particularly those who are not white, heterosexual, and economically privileged, that cost appears prohibitive, since it is their experience that is most often denied.

---

149 See, for example, the work of Amelie Rorty, discussed in Katharine Bartlett, 'Feminist Legal Methods' (1990) 103 *Harvard L Rev* 829. (Extracted in Chapter 4.) Margaret Jane Radin, 'The Pragmatist and the Feminist' (1990) 63 *S Cal L Rev* 1699.

150 See eg Patricia Williams, 'Spirit Murdering the Messenger: The Discourse of Fingerpointing as the Law's Response to Racism' (1987) 42 *U Miami L Rev* 127; Mari J Matsuda, 'Public Response to Racist Speech: Considering the Victim's Story' (1989) 87 *Michigan L Rev* 2320; Robin West, 'The Difference in Women's Hedonic Lives: A Phenomenological Critique of Feminist Legal Theory' (1987) 3 *Wisconsin Women's Law Journal* 81.

151 See Duncan Kennedy, 'The Structure of Blackstone's Commentaries' (1979) 28 *Buffalo L Rev* 205.

152 Menkel-Meadow, *op cit*, p 61.

153 Martha Minow, 'Feminist Reason: Getting It and Losing It' (1988) 38 *J Legal Education* 47, 51.

A variation of this problem arises in discussions of 'false consciousness'. How can feminists wedded to experiential analysis respond to women who reject feminism's basic premises as contrary to their experience? In an extended footnote to an early article, Catharine MacKinnon noted:

> Feminism aspires to represent the experience of all women as women see it, yet criticises anti-feminism and misogyny, including when it appears in female form. [Conventional responses treat] some women's views as unconscious conditioned reflections of their oppression, complicitous in it. [This approach] criticises the substance of a view because it can be accounted for by its determinants. But if both feminism and anti-feminism are responses to the condition of women, how is feminism exempt from devalidation by the same account? That feminism is critical and anti-feminism is not, is not enough, because the question is the basis on which we know something is one or the other when women, all of whom share the condition of women, disagree.[154]

Yet having raised the problem, MacKinnon declined to pursue it. As a number of feminist reviewers have noted, MacKinnon has never reconciled her unqualified condemnation of opponents with her reliance on experiential methodology.[155]

The issue deserves closer attention, particularly since contemporary survey research suggests that the vast majority of women do not experience the world in the terms that most critical feminists describe. Nor do these feminists agree among themselves about which experiential accounts of women's interests should be controlling in disputes involving, for example, pornography, prostitution, surrogate motherhood, or maternity leave.

A related issue is how any experiential account can claim special authority. Most responses to this issue take one of three forms. The first approach is to invoke the experience of exclusion and subordination as a source of special insight. According to Menkel-Meadow the 'feminist critique starts from the experiential point of view of the oppressed, dominated, and devalued, while the critical legal studies critique begins – and, some would argue, remains – in a male-constructed, privileged place in which domination and oppression can be described and imagined but not fully experienced'.[156] Yet such 'standpoint' theories, if left unqualified, present their own problems of privilege. There remains the issue of whose standpoint to credit, since not all women perceive their circumstances in terms of domination and not all who share that perception agree on its implications. Nor is gender the only source of oppression. Other forms of subordination, most obviously class, race, ethnicity, and sexual orientation, can yield comparable and, in some instances competing, claims to subjugated knowledge. To privilege any single trait risks impeding coalitions and understating other forces that constitute our identities.

A second feminist strategy is to claim that women's distinctive attributes promote a distinctive form of understanding. Robin West has argued, for example, that –

> there is surely no way to know with any certainly whether women have a privileged access to a way of life that is more nurturant, more caring, more natural, more loving, and thereby more moral than the lives which both men

---

154 CA MacKinnon, 'Feminism, Marxism and State' (1982) 7 *Signs* at 637, n 5.

155 See West, *op cit*, pp 117–18.

156 Menkel-Meadow, *op cit*, p 61.

and women presently pursue in the public sphere, including the legal sphere of legal practice, theory, and pedagogy. But it does seem that whether by reason of sociological role, psychological upbringing or biology, women are closer to such a life.[157]

Such claims occur in more muted form in much of the legal scholarship that draws on relational strands of feminist theory. This line of analysis, popularised by Carol Gilligan, argues that women tend to reason in 'a different voice'; they are less likely than men to privilege abstract rights over concrete relationships and are more attentive to values of care, connection, and context.[158] The strength of this framework lies in its demand that values traditionally associated with women be valued and that legal strategies focus on altering societal structures, not just assimilating women within them. Such an approach can yield theoretical and political cohesiveness on initiatives that serve women's distinctive needs.

Yet such efforts to claim an authentic female voice illustrate the difficulty of theorising from experience without essentialising or homogenising it. There is no 'generic woman',[159] or any uniform 'condition of women'.[160] To divide the world solely along gender lines is to ignore ways in which biological constraints are experienced differently by different groups under different circumstances. If, as critical feminists generally maintain, women's experience has been shaped through culturally contingent patterns of subordination, no particular experience can claim universal authentic status. Moreover, to emphasise only the positive attributes traditionally associated with women is to risk overclaiming and oversimplifying their distinctive contributions. Most empirical work on moral reasoning and public values discloses less substantial gender differences than relational frameworks generally suggest.[161] These frameworks also reinforce dichotomous stereotypes – such as males' association with abstract rationality and females' with empathetic nurturance – that have restricted opportunities for both sexes.

Such concerns underpin those strands of critical feminism that focus on challenging rather than celebrating sex-based difference. The virtue of their approach lies in revealing how legal ideology has misdescribed cultural constructions as biological imperatives. Yet the strengths of this framework also suggest its limitations. Affirmations of similarity between the sexes may inadvertently institutionalise dominant social practices and erode efforts to build group solidarity. Denying difference can, in some contexts, reinforce values that critics seek to change.

A more promising response to the 'difference dilemma' and to more general questions about feminist epistemology is to challenge the framework in which these issues are typically debated. The crucial issue becomes not difference, but the difference that difference makes. In legal contexts, the legitimacy of sex-based

---

157 West, *op cit*, p 48.

158 See Carol Gilligan, *In a Different Voice* (1982); Mary Field Belenky, Blythe McVickar Clinchy, Nancy Rule Goldberger and Jill Mattuck Tarule, *Women's Ways of Knowing* (1986); Carrie Menkel-Meadow, 'Portia in a Different Voice: Speculations on a Woman's Lawyering Process' (1985) 1 *Berkeley Women's LJ* 39. (Extracted in Chapter 6.)

159 The phrase is Elizabeth Spelman's in *Inessential Woman: Problems of Exclusion in Feminist Thought* (1988), p 188. See also Adrenne Rich, 'Disloyal to Civilisation: Feminism, Racism, Gynephobia' in *On Lies, Secrets and Silence* (1979), p 275.

160 CA MacKinnon, *op cit*, p 637, n 5.

161 D Rhode, *Justice and Gender*, pp 311–12.

treatment should not depend on whether the sexes are differently situated. Rather, analysis should turn on whether legal recognition of gender distinctions is likely to reduce or reinforce gender disparities in power, status, and economic security. Since such issues cannot be resolved in the abstract, this strategy requires contextual judgments, not categorical choices. It asks which perspective on difference can best serve particular theoretical or practical objectives and recognises that there may be trade-offs between them. Such an approach demands that feminists shift self-consciously among needs to acknowledge both distinctiveness and commonality between the sexes and unity and diversity among their members.

On the more general question of what validates any particular feminist claim, the first step is to deconstruct the dualistic framework of truth and falsehood in which these issues are often discussed. As postmodernist theorists remind us, all perspectives are partial, but some are more incomplete than others. To disclaim objective standards of truth is not to disclaim all value judgments. We need not become positivists to believe that some accounts of experience are more consistent, coherent, inclusive, self-critical, and so forth. Critical feminism can illuminate the process by which claims about the world are constituted as well as the effects of marginalising women and other subordinate groups in that process. Such a framework can subject traditional forms of argument and criteria of relevance to sustained scrutiny. It can challenge exclusionary institutions in which knowledge is constructed. And it can press for social changes that would encourage deeper understanding of our experience and the forces that affect it.

Although critical feminists by no means speak with one voice on any of these issues, part of our strength lies in building on our differences as well as our commonalities. Precisely because we do not share a single view on this, or other more substantive concerns, we need theories but not a Theory. Our objective should be multiple accounts that avoid privileging any single universalist or essentialist standpoint. We need understandings that can resonate with women's shared experience without losing touch with our diversity. The factors that divide us can also be a basis for enriching our theoretical perspectives and expanding our political alliances. Any framework adequate to challenge sex-based oppression must simultaneously condemn the other forms of injustice with which it intersects.

What allies this method with other critical accounts is its scepticism toward everything, including scepticism. Critical feminist theories retain a commitment to locate judgment within the patterns of social practice, to subject that judgment to continuing critique, and to promote gender equality as a normative ideal. Those commitments may take us in multiple directions, but as Martha Minow maintains, they are unifying commitments nonetheless.[162]

2. Liberal Legalism

For CLS theorists, the most frequent unifying theme is opposition to a common target: the dominance of liberal legalism and the role law has played in maintaining it.[163] On this issue, critical feminism offers more varied and more ambivalent responses. This diversity in part reflects the diversity of perspectives within the liberal tradition. The target appearing in many critical legal studies

---

162 Martha Minow, 'Beyond Universality' (1989) *U Chi Legal F* 115.

163 Robert W Gordon, 'New Developments in Legal Theory', in *The Politics of Law: A Progressive Critique*, p 281; A Hutchinson, 'Introduction to Critical Legal Studies', in A Hutchinson (ed) (1989).

accounts and in some critical feminist analyses is only one version of liberal legalism, generally the version favoured by law and economics commentators. Under a more robust framework, many inequalities of greatest concern to feminists reflect limitations less in liberal premises than in efforts to realise liberalism's full potential.

From both a philosophical and pragmatic standpoint, feminist legal critics have less stake in the assault on liberalism than CLS. Their primary target is gender inequality, whatever its pedigree, and their allies in many concrete political struggles have come as often from liberal as from radical camps. Thus, when critical feminist theorists, join the challenge to liberal legalism, they often do so on somewhat modified grounds. Their opposition tends to focus on the particular form of liberalism embodied in existing legal and political structures and on the gender biases it reflects.

Although they differ widely in other respects, liberal theorists generally begin from the premise that the State's central objective lies in maximising individuals' freedom to pursue their own objectives to an extent consistent with the same freedom for others. Implicit in this vision are several assumptions about the nature of individuals and the subjectivity of values. As conventionally presented, the liberal State is composed of autonomous, rational individuals. Their expressed choices reflect a stable and coherent understanding of their independent interests. Yet while capable of full knowledge of their own preferences, these liberal selves lack similar knowledge about others. Accordingly, the good society remains as neutral as possible about the meaning of the good life: it seeks simply to provide the conditions necessary for individuals to maximise their own preferences through voluntary transactions. Although liberal theorists differ widely about what those background conditions entail, they share a commitment to preserving private zones for autonomous choices, free from public intervention.[164]

Critical feminist theorists have challenged this account along several dimensions. According to theorists such as West, these liberal legalist selves are peculiarly masculine constructs – peculiarly capable of infallible judgments about their own wants and peculiarly incapable of empathetic knowledge about the wants of others.[165] Classic liberal frameworks take contractual exchanges rather than affiliative relationships as the norm. Such frameworks undervalue the ways social networks construct human identities and the ways individual preferences are formed in reference to the needs and concerns of others. For many women, a nurturing, giving self has greater normative and descriptive resonance than an autonomous, egoistic self.[166]

Critical feminists by no means agree about the extent, origins, or implications of such gender differences. Some concept of autonomy has been central to the American women's movement since its inception, autonomy from the constraints of male authority and traditional roles. How much emphasis to place on values

164 See John Rawls, *A Theory of Justice* (1971); Ronald Dworkin, 'Liberalism in Public Morality', in S Hampshire (ed) (1978), p 113; Bruce Ackermanm, *Social Justice in the Liberal State* (1980). See generally Steven Shiffrin, 'Liberalism, Radicalism and Legal Scholarship' (1983) 30 *UCLA L Rev* 1103.

165 Robin West, 'Economic Man and Literary Women: One Contrast' (1988) 39 *Mercer L Rev* 867.

166 A Jaggar, *op cit*, pp 21–22; Virginia Held, 'Feminism and Moral Theory', in E Kittay and D Meyers (eds), *Women and Moral Theory* (1987), p 111; Susan Moller Okin, 'Humanist Liberalism' in N Rosenblum (ed), *Liberalism and the Moral Life* (1989), p 39; Robin West, 'Jurisprudence and Gender' (1988) 55 *U Chi L Rev* 1 (extracted in Chapter 6).

of self-determination and how much to place on values of affiliation have generated continuing controversies that cannot be resolved at the abstract level on which debate has often foundered. Even critical feminists who agree about the significance of difference disagree about its causes and likely persistence. Disputes centre on how much importance is attributable to women's intimate connection to others through childbirth and identification with primary caretakers, how much to cultural norms that encourage women's deference, empathy, and disproportionate assumption of nurturing responsibilities and how much to inequalities in women's status and power.

Yet despite these disagreements, most critical feminists share an emphasis on the importance of social relationships in shaping individual preferences. From such a perspective, no adequate conception of the good society can be derived through standard liberal techniques, which hypothesise social contracts among atomistic actors removed from the affiliations that give meaning to their lives and content to their choices.

This feminist perspective points up a related difficulty in liberal frameworks, which critical theorists from a variety of traditions have noted. The liberal assumption that individuals' expressed preferences can be taken as reflective of genuine preferences is flatly at odds with much of what we know about human behaviour. To a substantial extent, our choices are socially constructed and constrained; the desires we develop are partly a function of the desires our culture reinforces. As long as gender plays an important role in shaping individual expectations and aspirations, expressed objectives cannot be equated with full human potential. Women, for example, may 'choose' to remain in an abusive relationship, but such choices are not ones most liberals would want to maximise. Yet a liberal legalist society has difficulty distinguishing between 'authentic' and 'inauthentic' preferences without violating its own commitments concerning neutrality and the subjectivity of value.

Similar problems arise with the legal ideology that underpins contemporary liberal frameworks. In its conventional form, liberal legalism assumes that appropriate conduct can be defined primarily in terms of adherence to procedurally legitimate and determinate rules, that law can be separated from politics, and that spheres of private life can be insulated from public intrusion.[167] Critical feminism challenges all of these assumptions on both empirical and normative levels.

The feminist critique joins other CLS work in denying that the rule of law in fact offers a principled, impartial, and determinate means of dispute resolution. Attention has centred both on the subjectivity of legal standards and the gender biases in their application. By exploring particular substantive areas, feminists have underscored the law's fluctuation between standards that are too abstract to resolve particular cases and rules that are too specific to result in principled, generalisable norms.[168] Such explorations have also revealed sex-based assumptions that undermine the liberal legal order's own aspirations.

These limitations in conventional doctrine are particularly apparent in the law's consistently inconsistent analysis of gender difference. Decision-makers have often reached identical legal results from competing factual premises. In other

---

167 See Judith N Schklar, *Legalism* (1964); Duncan Kennedy, 'Legal Formality' (1973) 2 *J Legal Stud* at 351, 371–72; Karl Klare, 'Law-Making as Praxis' (1970) 40 *Telos* pp 123, 132.

168 See Clare Dalton, 'An Essay in the Deconstruction of Contact Doctrine' (1985) 95 *Yale LJ* pp 997, 1106–08.

cases, the same notions about sexual distinctiveness have yielded opposite conclusions. Identical assumptions about woman's special virtues or vulnerabilities have served as arguments for both favoured and disfavoured legal treatment in criminal and family law and for both including and excluding her from public roles such as professional occupations and jury service. For example, although courts and legislatures traditionally assumed that it was 'too plain' for discussion that sex-based distinctions in criminal-sentencing statutes and child custody decisions were appropriate, it was less plain which way those distinctions cut. Under different statutory schemes, women received lesser or greater punishments for the same criminal acts and in different historical periods were favoured or disfavoured as the guardians of their children.[169]

The law's traditional approach to gender-related issues has not only yielded indeterminate interpretations; it has allowed broad mandates of formal equality to mask substantive inequality. Part of the problem with 'difference' as an organising principle is that legal decision makers do not always seem to know it when they see it. One of the most frequently noted illustrations is the Supreme Court's 1974 conclusion that pregnancy discrimination did not involve gender discrimination or even 'gender as such'; employers were simply distinguishing between 'pregnant women and non-pregnant persons'.[170] So too, although most contemporary divorce legislation promises 'equal' or 'equitable' property distributions between spouses, wives have in practice received neither equality nor equity. In the vast majority of cases, women end up with far greater caretaking responsibilities and far fewer resources to discharge them.[171]

Such indeterminacies and biases also undermine the liberal legalist distinction between public and private spheres. From a critical feminist view, the boundary between State and family is problematic on both descriptive and prescriptive grounds. As an empirical matter, the State inevitably participates in determining what counts as private and what forms of intimacy deserve public protection. Governmental policies concerning child care, tax, inheritance, property, welfare, and birth control have all heavily influenced family arrangements. As Fran Olsen and Clare Dalton have noted, the same legal decisions regarding intimate arrangements often can be described either as intervention or non-intervention, depending on the decision-makers' point of view. For example, a refusal to enforce unwritten co-habitation agreements can be seen as a means of either preserving or intruding on intimate relationships.[172]

Conventional public/private distinctions present normative difficulties as well. Contrary to liberal legalist assumptions, the State's refusal to intervene in private matters has not necessarily expanded individual autonomy; it has often simply substituted private for public power. The courts' failure to recognise unwritten agreements between co-habitants or to enforce support obligations and rape

---

169 See Frances Olsen, 'The Politics of Family Law' (1984) 2 *Law and Inequality* at 1, 12–19.

170 *Geduldig v Aiello* 417 US 484 at 497, n 20 (1974); see also *General Electric Co v Gilbert* 429 US 125 (1976).

171 Lenore J Weitzman, *The Divorce Revolution* (1985); Herma Hill Kay, 'Equality and Difference: A Perspective on No-Fault Divorce and Its Aftermath' (1987) 56 *U Cin LR* at 1, 60–65; Deborah Rhode and Martha Minow, 'Reforming the Questions, Questioning the Reforms: Feminist Perspectives on Divorce Reform', in S Sugarman and H Kay (eds), *Divorce Reform at the Crossroads* (1990).

172 Dalton, at 1107; Frances Olsen, 'The Myth of State Intervention in the Family' (1985) 18 *U Mich J L Ref* 835.

prohibitions in ongoing marriages has generally enlarged the liberties of men at the expense of women.[173]

Critical feminism does not, however, categorically renounce the constraints on the State power that liberal legalism has secured. Rather, it denies that conventional public/private dichotomies provide a useful conceptual scheme for assessing such constraints. As the following discussion of rights suggests, judgments about the appropriate scope of State intervention require a contextual analysis, which takes account of gender disparities in existing distributions of power. In this, as in other theoretical contexts previously noted, we need less reliance on abstract principles and more on concrete experience.

A similar point emerges from one final challenge to liberal legalism. Building on the work of moral theorists such as Carol Gilligan, Annette Baier, and Sarah Ruddick, some commentators have questioned the primacy that this culture attaches to formal, adversarial, and hierarchical modes of dispute resolution.[174] A legal system founded on feminist priorities – those emphasising trust, care, and empathy – should aspire to less combative, more conciliatory, procedures.

Yet as other feminist critics have noted, an appeal to empathetic values leaves most of the difficult questions unanswered. With whom should legal decision making empathise when individual needs conflict?[175] And what procedural protections should be available to monitor those judgments? One risk is that conciliation between parties with unequal negotiating skills, information, and power can perpetuate those inequalities. Judicial systems that have aspired to a more nurturing processes, such as juvenile and family courts, have often reinforced patriarchal assumptions and sexual double standards.[176] Norms appropriate to our vision of justice in an ideal state may not be the best way to get us there.

Here again, a critical feminist approach to procedural values demands contextual judgment to further the substantive objectives that critical feminism seeks. Its greatest challenge lies at the pragmatic level; its task is to design frameworks more responsive to the experiences of subordinate groups. A crucial first step is to deconstruct the apparent dichotomy between formalism and informalism that has traditionally structured debate over alternative dispute resolution processes. Since neither approach has adequately responded to women's experiences and concerns, we cannot rest with debunking both possibilities or choosing the least objectionable alternative. Rather, as is true with debates over substantive rights, we need to re-imagine the range of procedural options and to challenge the broader system of sex-based subordination that constrains their exercise.

One central difference between critical feminism and other critical legal theory involves the role of rights. Although both bodies of work have challenged liberal legalism's reliance on formal entitlements, feminist accounts, like those of

---

173 See MDA Freeman and Christina Lyon, *Cohabitation Without Marriage: An Essay in Law and Social Policy* (1983); Diana EH Russel, *Rape in Marriage* (1982), pp 17–24; F Olsen, *op cit*, pp 843–58; Marjorie Maguire Shultz, 'Contractual Ordering of Marriage: A New Model for State Policy' (1982) 70 *Calif L Rev* 204.

174 C Gilligan; Annette Baier, 'Trust and Antitrust' (1986) 96 *Ethics* at 231, 247–53; Sara Ruddick, 'Maternal Thinking' (1980) 6 *Feminist Studies* 3342; see Lynne Henderson, 'Legality and Empathy' (1987) 85 *Michigan L Rev* 1574; C Menkel-Meadow *op cit*.

175 Toni Masaro, 'Empathy, Legal Storytelling, and the Rule of Law' (1989) 87 *Michigan L Rev* 2104.

176 Judith Resnik, 'On the Bias: Feminist Reconsiderations of the Aspirations for Judges' (1988) 61 *S Cal L Rev* 1877, 1926–33.

minority scholars, have tended more toward contextual analysis than categorical critique.

Most CLS scholarship has viewed rights-based strategies as an ineffective and illusory means of progressive social change. While sometimes acknowledging the importance of basic political liberties in preserving opportunities for dissent, critical legal theorists have generally presented the liberal rights agenda as a constraint on individual consciousness and collective mobilisation. Part of the problem arises from the indeterminacy noted earlier. Feminist commentators such as Fran Olsen have joined other critical theorists in noting that rights discourse cannot resolve social conflict but can only restate it in somewhat abstract, conclusory form. A rights-oriented framework may distance us from necessary value choices and obscure the basis on which competing interests are accommodated.[177]

According to this critique, too much political energy has been diverted into battles that cannot promise significant gains. For example, a decade's experience with State equal rights amendments reveals no necessary correlation between the standard of constitutional protection provided by legal tribunals and the results achieved. It is unlikely that a federal equal rights amendment would have ensured the vast array of substantive objectives that its proponents frequently claimed. Supporters' tendencies to cast the amendment as an all-purpose prescription for social ills – the plight of displaced homemakers, the feminisation of poverty, and the gender gap in earnings – have misdescribed the problem and misled as to the solution.[178]

A related limitation of the liberal rights agenda involves its individualist premises and restricted scope. A preoccupation with personal entitlements can divert concern from collective responsibilities. Rights rhetoric too often channels individuals' aspirations into demands for their own share of protected opportunities and fails to address more fundamental issues about what ought to be protected. Such an individualistic framework ill serves the values of cooperation and empathy that feminists find lacking in our current legal culture.

Nor are mandates guaranteeing equality in formal rights adequate to secure equality in actual experience as long as rights remain restricted to those that a predominately white upper-middle-class male judiciary has been prepared to regard as fundamental. No legal structure truly committed to equality for women would end up with a scheme that affords extensive protection to the right to bear arms or to sell violent pornography but not to control our reproductive lives.

In a culture where rights have been defined primarily in terms of 'freedoms from' rather than 'freedoms to', many individuals lack the resources necessary for exercising rights to which they are formally entitled. Such problems are compounded by the costs and complexities of legal proceedings and the maldistribution of legal services available to enforce formal entitlements or prevent their curtailment. By channelling political struggles into legal disputes,

---

177 F Olsen, 'Statutory Rape: A Feminist Critique of Rights' (1984) 63 *Texas L Rev*; see Peter Gabel, 'The Phenomenology of Rights-Consciousness and the Pact of the Withdrawn Selves' (1984) 62 *Texas L Rev* 1563; Mark Tushnet, 'An Essay on Rights' (1984) 62 *Texas L Rev* at 1363, 1382–84.

178 See D Rhode, *Justice and Gender*, p 16; Catharine A MacKinnon, 'Unthinking ERA Thinking' (Book Review) (1987) 54 *U Chi L Rev* 759.

rights-based strategies risk limiting aspirations and reinforcing dependence on legal decision makers.

Yet while acknowledging these limitations, critical feminism has also emphasised certain empowering dimensions of rights strategies that other CLS work discounts. As theorists including Kimberly Crenshaw, Christine Littleton, Elizabeth Schneider, and Patricia Williams have argued, legal rights have a special resonance in our culture.[179] The source of their limitations is also the source of their strength. Because claims about rights proceed within established discourse, they are less readily dismissed than other progressive demands. By insisting that the rule of law make good on its own aspirations, rights-oriented strategies offer a possibility of internal challenge that critical theorists have recognised as empowering in other contexts.

So too, critiques that focus only on the individualist premises of rights rhetoric obscure its collective dimensions. The dichotomies often drawn between rights and relationships or rights and responsibilities are highly exaggerated. Rights not only secure personal autonomy; they also express relationships between the individual and the community. Just as rights can impose responsibilities, responsibilities can imply rights. Often the concepts serve identical ends: a right to freedom from discrimination imposes a responsibility not to engage in it. Discarding one form of discourse in favour of another is unlikely to alter the foundations of our legal culture. Moreover, for subordinate groups, rights-based frameworks have supported demands not only for individual entitlements but also for collective self-hood. For example, women's right to reproductive autonomy is a prerequisite to their social equality; without control of their individual destinies, women cannot challenge the group stereotypes and role constraints that underpin their subordinate status. Claims of right can further advance collective values by drawing claimants within a community capable of response and demanding that its members take notice of the grievances expressed.[180]

For critical feminism, the most promising approach is both to acknowledge the indeterminate nature of rights rhetoric and to recognise that in particular circumstances, such rhetoric can promote concrete objectives and social empowerment. Too often, rights have been abstracted from their social context and then criticised as abstract. Yet however manipulable, the rubric of autonomy and equality have made enormous practical differences in the lives of subordinate groups. Undermining the conceptual foundations of rights like privacy, on which women's reproductive choice has depended, involves considerable risks. Even largely symbolic campaigns, such as the recent ERA struggle, can be highly important, less because of the specific objective they seek than because of the political mobilisation they inspire. Like the suffrage movements half a century earlier, the contemporary constitutional battle offered women invaluable instruction in both the limits of their own influence and the strategies necessary to expand it.

---

179 Kimberley Williams Crenshaw, 'Race, Reform and Retrenchment: Transformation and Legitimation in Anti-discrimination Law' (1988) 101 *Harv L Rev* 1331 at 1366–69; Schneider, 'The Dialictic of Rights and Politics' (1986) 61 *NYU L Rev* 589; Patricia J Williams, 'Alchemical Notes: Reconstructing Ideals from Deconstructed Rights' (1987) 22 *Harv CR-CLL Rev* 401.

180 See Schneider; Marth Minow, 'Interpreting Rights: An Essay for Robert Cover' (1987) 96 *Yale LJ* 1860 at 1875–77.

Whatever its inadequacies, rights rhetoric has been the vocabulary most effective in catalysing mass progressive movements in this culture. It is a discourse that critical feminists are reluctant to discard in favour of ill-defined or idealised alternatives. The central problem with rights-based frameworks is not that they are inherently limiting but that they have operated within a limited institutional and imaginative universe. Thus, critical feminism's central objective should be not to delegitimate such frameworks but, rather, to recast their content and recognise their constraints. Since rights-oriented campaigns can both enlarge and restrict political struggle, evaluation of their strategic possibilities requires historically situated contextual analysis.

On this point, feminists join other critical theorists in seeking to build on the communal, relational, and destabilising dimensions of rights-based arguments.[181] Claims to self-determination can express desires not only for autonomy but also for participation in the communities that shape our existence. If selectively invoked, the rhetoric of rights can empower subordinate groups to challenge the forces that perpetuate their subordination.

Alternative Visions

One final issue on which critical feminism often parts company with other critical theory involves the construction of alternative visions of the good society. Although both traditions reflect considerable ambivalence about the value of such projects, the focus of concern varies. Most critical theory that has attempted to construct alternative visions assumes away the problems with which feminists have been most concerned or opens itself to the same challenges of indeterminacy that it has directed at other work. Partly for these reasons, feminist legal critics have devoted relatively little attention to idealised programmes. Rather, their efforts have centred on identifying the values that must be central to any affirmative vision and the kinds of concrete legal and institutional transformations that such values imply.

A recurrent problem with most progressive Utopian frameworks involves their level of generality. Objectives are often framed in terms of vague, seemingly universal aspirations – such as Roberto Unger's appeal to a world free 'from deprivation and drudgery, from the choice between isolation from other people and submission to them'.[182] Such formulations leave most of the interesting questions unanswered. How are such ideals to be interpreted and implemented under specific circumstances, how are interpretive disputes to be resolved; and how are gender relations to be reconstructed?

In response to such questions, a standard critical strategy is to specify conditions under which answers would be generated. Habermas's ideal speech situation has been perhaps the most influential example. Under his theory, beliefs would be accepted as legitimate only if they could have been acquired through full uncoerced discussion in which all members of society participate. Some critical feminists, including Drucilla Cornell and Seyla Benhabib, draw on similar conversational constructs.[183]

---

181 See Staughton Lynd, 'Communal Rights' (1984) 62 *Texas L Rev* 1417; Roberto M Unger, 'The Critical Legal Studies Movement' (1983) 96 *Harv L Rev* 561 at 612–16.

182 See Unger, p 651; see also R Unger, pp 18, 24.

183 See Seyla Benhabib, 'The Generalised and the Concrete Other', in J Benhabib and D Cornell (eds), *Feminism as Critique* (1987), pp 92–94; see also J Habermas, Richard J Bernstein, 'Philosophy', in R Hollinger (ed), *The Conversation of Mankind in Hermaneutics and Praxis* (1985), pp 54, 82.

Such strategies are, however, problematic on several levels. One difficulty involves the level of abstraction at which the ideals are formulated. It is not self-evident how individuals with diverse experiences, interests, and resources will reach consensus or how their agreements can be predicted with enough specificity to provide adequate heuristic frameworks. Strategies emphasising uncoerced dialogue have often assumed away the problems of disparate resources and capacities that parties bring to the conversation. Given the historical silencing of women's voices, many critical feminists have been unsatisfied by approaches that are themselves silent about how to prevent that pattern from recurring.

A related difficulty stems from idealists' faith in dialogue as the primary response to social subordination. Alternative visions that proceed as if the central problem were our inability to imagine such alternatives often understate the material conditions that contribute to that inability. Many feminists have no difficulty imagining a world without pervasive sexual violence or the feminisation of poverty; the difficulty lies in commanding support for concrete strategies that would make that vision possible. It is, of course, true that we cannot be free from coercive institutional structures as long as we retain an ideology that legitimates them. But neither can we rid ourselves of that ideology as long as such structures limit our ability to challenge it.

In response to this dilemma, critical feminism has tended to focus on particular issues that implicate both material and ideological concerns. Rather than hypothesising some universal Utopian programme, feminist legal critics have generally engaged in more concrete analysis that challenges both structural inequalities and the normative assumptions that underlie them. In evaluating particular strategies, critical feminism focuses on their capacity to improve women's social and economic status; to reach those women most in need; and to enhance women's self-respect, power, and ability to alter existing institutional arrangements.

For example, the struggle for comparable pay for jobs of comparable worth presents direct opportunities to increase women's financial security. The campaign has helped reveal the cultural undervaluation of 'women's work' has exposed gender and racial bias in employers' own criteria for compensation, and has aided workplace organising efforts.[184] Pay equity initiatives have also raised broader questions about market principles and social priorities. How should we reward various occupational and worker characteristics and how should those decisions be made? Are we comfortable in a society that pays more to parking attendants than child care attendants, whatever the gender composition of those positions? The struggle for comparable worth could spark a rethinking of the scope of inequality and the ideologies that sustain it.

The feminist focus on concrete issues has avoided an idealised vision that must inevitably change in the course of change. Feminist legal critics have been less interested in predicting the precise role that gender would play in the good society than in undermining its role in this one. Whether sex would ultimately become as unimportant as eye colour or whether some sex-linked traits and affiliations would endure is not an issue on which more speculation seems fruitful. Since what is now problematic about gender relations is the disparity in power, we cannot fully anticipate the shape of those relations in an ideal world

---

184 See D Rhode, *Justice and Gender*, pp 368–69. See generally *Comparable Worth: New Directions for Research* (H Hartmann (ed), 1985).

where, by definition, such disparities do not exist. At Utopian as well as practical levels, critical feminism is unwilling to remain trapped in debates about women's commonality with or difference from men. Its commitment is neither to embrace nor to suppress difference but to challenge the dualism and make the world safe for differences.

Although we cannot know *a priori* what the good society will be, we know more than enough about what it will not be to provide a current agenda. It will not be a society with sex-based disparities in status, power, and security. Nor will it be a society that denies many of its members substantial control over the terms of their daily existence. To realise its full potential, feminism must sustain a vision concerned not only with relations between men and women, but also with relations among them. The commitment to sexual equality that gave birth to the women's movement is necessary but not sufficient to realise the values underlying it. Those values place critical feminism in both tension and alliance with aspirations that other critical legal theory expresses.

DECONSTRUCTING THE CLS-FEM SPLIT[185]
Robin West[186]

Legal theorists within the critical legal studies movement have appropriated from literary theory some of the insights of the deconstruction movement, and as a result of that appropriation the Critical Legal Studies (CLS) school has made the rest of us more aware, I believe, than we would have been otherwise, of what people with legal power do with the words they use, and how those words at the same time mask what legally empowered people do. Deconstruction has found a natural home in legal theory. But the usefulness of 'deconstruction' is surely not limited to law, or to the unmasking of legal power, or to the workings of legal institutions, any more than it should be limited to literature, to the unmasking of literary power, or to the workings of subcommittees within English departments. Deconstruction at its most broadly conceived is simply a way to examine the verbal masks constructed by groups of powerful people. At its best, deconstruction is a tool of analysis for the benefit of the relatively disempowered in any given hierarchical institution.

One such group of relatively powerful people are the tenured male law professors who are members of the CLS conference, and one such group of relatively powerless people are the untenured, feminist and female law professors who are members of that same institution. Relative to the larger society, of course, female law professors are quite powerful. But relative to the institutions that structure the work lives of legal-academics we are not, and one such institution is the conference on CLS itself – the very 'institution' which more than any other has facilitated deconstructionist analysis. But no matter how much gratitude we might feel toward institutional CLS for the insights it has offered, it is nevertheless an institution within which we work from a position of relative disempowerment. Therefore, if deconstruction is as essential to an understanding of power as its proponents profess, then it is surely important, perhaps imperative, for feminists in CLS (or who pay attention to its literature) to begin to deconstruct their words. We must understand what men with power within CLS are doing, with words and to women – and how they use words to mask what it is they do.

185 [1985] *Wisconsin Women's Law Journal* 85.
186 At the time of writing, Assistant Professor University of Maryland Law School.

Towards that end, these comments offer a brief deconstruction of part of a short piece by Duncan Kennedy entitled *Psycho-Social CLS*,[187] which chronicles among other things the troubled relationship between feminists in CLS and non-feminists, particularly men. In that piece, Kennedy first issues a complaint, follows the complaint with a promise, and ends with a warning. The complaint is about the behaviour of women in the CLS movement. Women in CLS do several things that annoy Kennedy, but at the top of the list is that CLS women deny men visual access to women's sexuality. To quote: 'there sometimes seems to arise ... a feminist taboo on seductive self-presentation and on competition with other women [for men's favours] one that applies even where such behaviour looks appropriate [in my eyes].'[188] The promise is that if women would break the taboo and willingly be more sexually giving, love and equality might be the reward. To quote Kennedy: 'There is also the possibility that the eroticisation of [the relationship of domination between male mentor and female mentee] will be the route through to equality and love.'[189] The warning Kennedy issues is that unless CLS women give more of their sexuality to CLS men, the women will not 'get' from their male CLS mentors everything there is to get. 'When the mentor is a man and the mentee is a feminist, it seems likely she will ... apply the feminist taboo against seductive self-presentation and competition for men's favours. Yet it is very difficult to get what is to be gotten from a mentor if one is seriously inhibited from entering his or her universe.'[190]

In this brief space I want to argue that Kennedy's complaint, warning, and promise are all grounded in an 'interpretation' of a 'social text'. The 'social text' that Kennedy is interpreting is CLS women's refusal to engage in seductive self-presentation. The 'interpretation' that Kennedy offers of this text is that the reason women refuse to engage in seductive self-presentation is the presence of a 'feminist taboo' against that kind of behaviour. This interpretation, I will argue, rests on a partly explicit and partly implicit account of the way people just naturally are. My claim is that to even understand – much less criticise – how Kennedy arrives at his dangerously anti-feminist interpretation of women's behaviour within the CLS movement, we must first deconstruct its motivating vision. That is: we must first clearly see the vision for what it is – namely, a commitment to a particular prescriptive claim about how women might be, not how we naturally and ultimately are – and then come to grips with the empowered choices – not observations – that have rendered this vision so pervasive and familiar as to be virtually invisible. That vision has two parts. The first is a set of claims and values that emanate from the larger heterosexual culture to which CLS belongs. The second is a set of beliefs that emanate from the CLS subculture. Both claims have to do with the nature of desire – the first with sexual desire, the second with desire itself.

1. The Nature and Politics of Heterosexual Desire

The first part of the vision – borrowed from the larger culture – concerns the nature of heterosexual desire. Here, Kennedy is very explicit. He spells the vision out in some detail:

---

187 D Kennedy, 'Psycho-Social CLS: A Common on the Cardozo Symposium' (1985) 6 *Cardozo Law Review* 1013.

188 *Ibid*, p 1021. Kennedy notes that his judgment of 'appropriateness' may be biased by his 'ruling class, straight, white, male' identity.

189 *Ibid*, p 1022.

190 *Ibid*, p 1023.

There are three crucial aspects of the sexual politics of CLS. First, there is
desire – between men and women and also between men and between
women ... Second, there is the historical fact of the oppression of women by
men ... Oppression on the basis of gender is the actual context within which
CLS came into being – 'it's no accident that the mentors are men' – and CLS
has never been a counter-sphere within which it was absent. [T]he internal
structure of the conference is unmistakably reflective of the larger patriarchy.
Men have much more power than women ... (My emphasis.)[191]

Combining claims one and two – the presence of sexual desire between men and
women, with the historical oppression of women, yields the sum: powerful men
in CLS desire powerless women and disempowered, oppressed women sexually
desire powerful men. Kennedy's belief that sexual desire between disempowered
women and powerful men is reciprocal and symmetrical, despite the asymmetry
of the hierarchy on which they find themselves, is reflected in word choice,
grammar and style: sexual desire exists between men and women, women and
women, and men and men. Oppression, by contrast, is not symmetrical, it is
hierarchical: men have power, women are powerless, men are on top, women on
bottom. The conjunction of these two claims, it is important to emphasise, is not
simply that men desire women and women desire men, and that men happen to
have more power. Their conjunction is that empowered men desire
disempowered women, and that disempowered women desire empowered men.

Kennedy's choice of grammar, placement, word choice and style also reveal his
(unstated) belief that sexual desire between men and women in CLS is natural,
while the oppression of women by men – both within and outside of CLS – is
'contingent' and historical. Look at the first short sentence: 'First, there is desire
...' Desire is unmodified in this sentence – it just is. There are no qualifying
adjectives. Now note its placement: the desire is prior to oppression. 'First,'
Kennedy intones, 'there is desire.' The naturalness of sexual desire between men
and women thus immediately implies the interpretation of texts (such as
behaviour) which might suggest to the contrary: the reluctance of CLS women to
give expression to those natural desires. Or as Kennedy puts it in another
passage, women's reluctance to give expression to their 'strong emotions' –
evidenced by their refusal to act seductively – must be because of an artificial,
political, consciously imposed 'taboo.' Like all taboos, this taboo against
seductive behaviour inhibits what is natural sexual seduction.

Against the backdrop of natural, prior, heterosexual desire, is the 'second aspect'
of sexual politics in CLS: the 'historical fact' of gendered oppression. 'Second,'
Kennedy teaches, 'there is the historical fact of oppression ...'. The oppression of
women by men is factual, contingent, historical, and, of course, hierarchical –
men on top; women on bottom – while the desire of men for women and *vice
versa* is natural, universal, symmetrical and prior to the factual oppression. To be
more precise, then, the conjunction of claims one and two recited above is this:
contingently powerful men naturally desire contingently disempowered women,
and contingently disempowered women naturally desire contingently powerful
men.

Finally, Kennedy makes clear that in his view the historical and contingent
oppression of women is a very bad thing, and he accordingly aligns himself with
what he perceives to be feminism's definitive commitment to resist it. 'Third',
Kennedy intones, 'there is feminism, a self-conscious reaction against the

oppression of women', with which Kennedy professes to feel 'undiluted enthusiasm, at the conscious level ...'. He is equally clear (although not so explicit) that the sexual desire of the disempowered women for the powerful men and *vice versa* – is as good as it is natural and can lead to good things. It can, for example, free what the mentors have to give, and at least on occasion it might lead to equality and love. Therefore, like all taboos, the feminist political taboo against expressing natural sexual desire, while understandable, is unfortunate: it leads to 'rough sledding'. Kennedy complains it inhibits the mentor; and it prevents the mentee from entering the mentor's universe and from getting all the mentor has to give.

Kennedy's total vision, then, of sexual politics in CLS can be summed as follows. Contingently disempowered women naturally desire contingently empowered men, and while the oppression which yields the power disparity is bad, the natural heterosexual desire between the differently empowered is good.

I want to make only one point regarding this picture, and it is the deconstructionist's: the source of this vision of sexual desire is not our human nature or anything like it. The source of this vision is the empowered institutions of the larger heterosexual society, namely marriage and the family, and the institutions which derivatively support them – including law, courts, and the popular media. The societal and institutional commitment to the notion that powerless women naturally desire powerful men – that heterosexual desire is reciprocal, symmetrical and natural even though it is between concededly unequal partners – accounts for this society's inability to 'see' marital rape as rape rather than as 'bad sex'. It accounts for the societal belief that women who do not desire men are 'frigid'. It accounts for the societal inability to see that sexual harassment in the workplace is indeed harassment rather than the soft 'personal' touch of an office. It accounts for the societal inability to even consider the possibility that teenage pregnancy is a function of teenage male coercion rather than a breaking of societal 'taboos' against 'natural' promiscuity. It accounts for the belief that rape victims asked for it. It accounts for the belief that pornography causes no harm other than an imagined and illusory offence to a Victorian sensibility. It accounts for the belief that wolf whistles and sexual jeers on the streets are compliments rather than assaults. In Kennedy's essay, it accounts for his belief that the powerless women in CLS desire the powerful men as much as the men desire the women, and for his interpretive claim that the reason that women do not behave as though this were true is that they have imposed upon themselves an artificial, unnatural, political taboo against their 'powerful emotions' to the contrary.

The value judgments reflected in Kennedy's piece – that the natural sexual desire between the disempowered and the empowered is good, even if the inequality itself is bad – are also derived from the larger culture. Those judgments account in the larger culture for the societal approval of the romantic liaisons and the marriages that evolve from hierarchies of sexual inequality, even while condemning the inequality itself. Thus, the romantic attachments and marriages between female secretaries and male executives or female students and male teachers, are applauded – viewed as loving and equal – even by those who generally disparage the disparity in power and income between secretaries and executives, and students and teachers. The fruit is treasured even though the vine is rotten. In Kennedy's piece, the same values account for his promise that eroticisation of the dominance between male mentor and female mentee in CLS may have within it seeds of equality and love. Oppression is bad and equality is good, as is natural sexual desire. Therefore, eroticisation of bad hierarchy is the route to good equality. Through natural sexual desire, inequality becomes purity. Through natural sexual desire the inequality between women and men becomes equality.

Now the core contention of modern radical feminism is that Kennedy's heterosexual vision is simply wrong both as description and prescription. Heterosexual desire of disempowered women for empowered men (and *vice versa*) is not reciprocal, it is not symmetrical, and it is not 'natural'. Eroticisation of hierarchical, dominating relationships is not the route to 'equality' and 'love', it is the route to unequal marriages, low female self-esteem, boredom, inactivity, unemployment and a devastating waste of female talent. It might indeed lead to what we have grown used to calling love, but what we call love actively embraces, does not dissolve, the dominance from which Kennedy claims it can evolve. Women love powerful men more often than not because we have been told to, not because they give pleasure, and unless they give pleasure – since they do not yield equality – we have no business applauding them as good. Thus, it is Kennedy's endorsement of the imperative judgment of the larger heterosexual culture – that powerless women will sexually desire powerful men – and his mistaking that imperative judgment for an empirical truth about women's nature, which accounts for his inability to grasp the fundamental insight of radical feminism, both legal and otherwise. That is, that heterosexual desire is a socially imposed, rather than naturally imposed, imperative.

Kennedy's commitment to the 'naturalness' of heterosexual desire, in short, is why 'he doesn't get it'. It is his insistence that heterosexual desire is natural rather than contingent that dictates the categories in which he sees the social world: polar camps of male and female, and straight and gay. It is thus not surprising that Kennedy cannot come to grips with a feminist analysis that insists that all four of these poles are socially constructed, not naturally created, categories. Similarly, it is Kennedy's endorsement of the imperative judgment of the larger heterosexual culture that leads him to affirm what is not the case – that natural heterosexual desire, reciprocal and symmetrical, can dissolve the asymmetrical, non-reciprocal, contingent hierarchy that constitutes gendered mentor/mentee relationships. It is his alignment with that heterosexual imperative that leaves him free to warn CLS women that unless they drop their unnatural 'taboo' against their 'natural sexual desire' they will not get what can be gotten from their male mentors. It is his acquiescence with the beliefs and values of the larger heterosexual culture that allows Kennedy, in the pages of the Cardozo Law Review, to bemoan the demise of behaviour which many feminists and many more women now understand to be sexual harassment on the job, plain and simple.

2. The Nature and Politics of Desire

Desire, for Kennedy, is as immutable as it is natural. The desire for powerful men by powerless women is 'first' prior, a given, and is accordingly frustrated by feminist politics. If the politics are right, then the frustration of sexual, natural desire is a necessary evil; a casualty to a good cause. It is this perceived conflict between the immutability of heterosexual desire and the political correctness of feminist ideals that accounts for the hint of a tragic tone in Kennedy's piece. For although the piece is not overtly anti-feminist (or not intentionally so), Kennedy does not present himself as a feminist fellow-traveller; far from it. He endorses the feminist resistance to oppression, while at the same time willingly expresses his fears of its consequences. He thinks there's something right about feminism, but he fears he will lose, should it prove successful. Thus the following contradiction:

So long as women seem to be mainly interested in participating through CLS in an attack on patriarchy in the outside world, we men feel undiluted enthusiasm ... infected only by anxiety about what will happen to our own patriarchal privileges after the revolution. For the internal challenge, there is much more intense ambivalence, all the syndrome of defensiveness and rage against the feminist critique, a deep sense of guilt [and] fear of feminist power ...

One can hardly imagine the same ambivalence so freely expressed over a left-wing class or race triumph. Both the ambivalence Kennedy feels regarding feminist triumph and the apparent permissibility of the expression and publication of that ambivalence are reflections of the conflict he sees between his (and other's) immutable given 'first' heterosexual desire, and the political, contingent, historical, egalitarian ideal, an ideal to which he at least nominally subscribes. Yet this conflict is nonsense. Our desires, sexual or otherwise, and whatever their source, are not immutable. They are no more immutable than they are natural. Neither men nor women have to eroticise the dominance that permeates male mentor/female mentee relationships. The alternative is not loneliness, coldness, isolation or despair. We can, after all, eroticise other things. We can eroticise mountains, trees, men, women, equality, or, yes, dominance itself, so long as we do so in safe and undamaging circumstances. The mentor/mentee relationship is not such a circumstance, so look elsewhere. I am not, but I strongly doubt that the relationships in CLS are, as shot through with eroticism – whether or not censored by feminist political taboos – as Kennedy would hope. But to whatever extent they are, they need not be. The self-pity in this piece is silly because it is false. It is as false as the immutable vision of our sexual nature from which it draws.

Conclusion

I will conclude with three points. First, men in CLS should eroticise something other than the relationships of dominance that are mentor/mentee relationships. Second, unless they do so, CLS is not a congenial atmosphere for feminist work, nor is it a healthy environment for women, and women should therefore get out. But third, feminists cannot afford to lose the audience of the CLS movement, even if we must forego their mentorship. The commitment to deconstruction, if its dictates are consistently followed, should make CLS members willing, even if unhappy, listeners of feminist claims. Deconstruction commits the theorist to at least the coherency of the claim that what a culture or institution has defined as natural is in fact a social, cultural or institutional imperative. The core radical-feminist claim that 'heterosexuality is compulsory' – a socially rather than naturally imposed imperative – badly needs the deconstructionist's commitment for its minimal coherency. Feminists now need listeners as well as participants, an audience as well as adherents. By virtue of its commitment to deconstruction, and in spite of its present anti-feminist bias, the CLS members are surely the logical audience to cultivate.

PART IV

KEY ISSUES IN FEMINIST JURISPRUDENCE

CHAPTER 9

WOMEN, VIOLENCE AND THE LEGAL SYSTEM

Patriarchal attitudes pervade the legal system. Whether the enquiry is into the personnel of the legal profession, or attitudes towards female victims of crime or defendants in the criminal process, the legal system reveals itself as still steeped in the patriarchal, exclusionary, tradition. Before considering the manner in which the law responds to female victims of violence, the personnel of the legal profession is considered. In the first extract, recent data on access to the legal profession is outlined. There follows an extract from Albie Sachs and Joan Hoff Wilson's seminal work on sexism and the law, which traces the early attempts by women to enter the legal profession, and details the resistances which were then faced. These resistances, whilst ostensibly now eliminated, continue to have depressing relevance to the opportunities for women in the legal profession – a matter which, whilst difficult to quantify in precise terms, has an inevitable and direct bearing on the manner in which the law continues to treat the victims of violence and rape and those women who, having suffered violence for protracted periods of time, respond with violence against their partners.

THE PERSONNEL OF LAW[1]

Access to Legal Education and the Profession

1. Access to legal education

Factors of gender, race and ethnicity and social class raise common concerns both in relation to access to legal education and in relation to access to the legal profession. The following data provide an outline summary of relevant changes over time in respect of these factors.

(a) Gender

In Australia in 1960 women comprised to 11.4% of the law student cohort: by 1984 the proportion had increased to 41%,[2] although in 1986 only 17.2% of all lawyers engaged in practice were women.[3] In Ontario,[4] in 1978, women comprised 31% of all law undergraduates; in 1987 this proportion had increased to 42.5%. Nationally by 1989 this figure was 48%, and women engaged in legal

---

1   Extracted from Hilaire Barnett, 'The Province of Jurisprudence Determined – Again!' [1995] *Legal Studies* p 88.
2   D Weisbrot, 'Access to Legal Education in Australia', in R Dhavan, N Kibble, W Twining (eds), *Access to Legal Education and the Legal Profession* (Butterworths, 1989), p 85.
3   Australian Bureau of Statistics National Census cited in D Weisbrot, *Australian Lawyers* (Longman, 1990).
4   National figures unavailable for that time.

practice amounted to only 22%.[5] In the United Kingdom in 1990 52.1% of admissions to universities for law were women.[6]

(b) Race and ethnicity

In Australia special preparatory courses for Aboriginal students are offered at Monash, Queensland and the University of New South Wales.[7] In 1987 the Pearce Committee, in its nationwide review of legal education at the tertiary level,[8] reported that in 1986 just six Aboriginal lawyers had been admitted to practice. In Canada, by contrast, a 'Programme of Legal Studies for Native People' was established in 1973 at the University of Saskatchewan Native Law Centre in an attempt to increase the disproportionately low number of native Canadian lawyers. Between 1973 and 1985 202 of the 302 students registered on this course were recommended for admission to law school.[9] Four-fifths of all native Canadian law school applicants go through the Saskatchewan programme: each year 200 to 250 apply for admission to law school; of this number between 40 and 50 actually register – a five-fold increase within a decade.[10] Canadian universities adopt discretionary admissions policies and may specifically use the successful completion of the Programme of Legal Studies as a criterion for entry to law school.[11] In England, by way of comparison, the Law Society's 1994 survey of student characteristics concludes that 'some ethnic minority groups are very well represented among students doing law degrees'.[12] Students of Indian, Pakistani and African-black origins are well represented; Bangladeshis and Afro-Caribbeans are not. The same report reveals that ethnic minority students are most likely to study law at the 'new' universities (where they represent 26% of students reading law). In older universities the corresponding proportion figure is 20% of the total and at Oxbridge 12%.[13]

(c) Socio-economic Background

Research in Australia shows that the majority of law students come from a high socio-economic background.[14] Professor D Weisbrot states that 'the social background of young lawyers is, if anything, more elite than in previous

---

5   DAA Stager and HW Arthurs, *Lawyers in Canada* (University of Toronto Press, 1990).

6   45% at 'old', 55% at 'new' universities. Admissions for the CPE course were 50%. See D Halpern, 'Entry into the Legal Professions' *The Law Society Research and Policy Planning Unit Study No 15* (1994).

7   In 1986 the Aboriginal and Torres Strait Islands population amounted to 1.43% of the total national population: D Weisbrot *op cit*, n 6.

8   *Australian Law Schools, A Discipline Assessment for the Commonwealth Tertiary Education Commission* (Canberra, 1987).

9   BM Mazer, 'Access to Legal Education and the Profession in Canada', in *Access to Legal Education and the Legal Profession, op cit*, n 6.

10 *op cit*, n 9.

11 See eg the *University of Toronto Faculty of Law Calendar 1993–94*, p 60.

12 D Halpern *op cit*, n 10; but *cf* N Kibble, 'Access to Legal Education and the Legal Professions in England', in *Access to Legal Education and the Profession, op cit*, n 6.

13 *Ibid*, p 19.

14 Pearce, Appendix 4.

generations'.[15] Moreover, with the increasing numbers of women being admitted to legal education – the majority of whom come from the same social class as the majority of men – coupled with the decreasing availability of alternative qualifying routes into the profession, there are correspondingly fewer opportunities for those from lower socio-economic backgrounds to gain entry to legal education. In Canada socio-economic data relating to law students has until recently been unavailable. Professor Brian Mazer has commented that '[the] dearth of demographic information is of concern, if one is of the opinion that the legal profession may not be representative, in any significant way, of the Canadian population'. It is nevertheless recognised that the Programme for Native People and the increasing admission of mature students have extended the range of backgrounds from which law students are drawn.[16] Professors Stager and Arthurs have observed that in Canada there has been a slight increase in the proportion of lawyers from minority ethnic groups.[17]

In England and Wales in the late 1970s it is reported that 50% of 20–24 year olds in full-time education had professional or managerial fathers (compared with approximately 20% of the general population, but that among law students 54% had professional or managerial fathers and only 16% working class fathers.[18] David Halpern's survey for the Law Society in 1993 reveals that even today only 23% of law students are drawn from working class backgrounds and that the figures vary widely according to the type of institution attended. Working class parentage accounts for 25% of law students at new universities, 16% at 'old' universities and 9% at Oxbridge.[19] Moreover, it seems that the Common Professional Examination course, in attracting candidates from disproportionately higher socio-economic backgrounds, has not achieved its intended goal of broadening the social background of entrants to the legal profession but has restricted further the socio-economic base of future lawyers.[20]

The broad picture of the legal profession in each jurisdiction is one of a primarily male, white, middle class institution. In England, constructive – if belated – attempts are being made to redress the imbalance in gender and race. The Policy Studies Institute undertook research in 1995 on behalf of the Law Society's research and policy planning unit. The latest research confirms that sexual and racial discrimination remains rife. In 1995, of 63,628 practising solicitors in England and Wales, a mere 18,417 were women, and only 70 practising solicitors were from ethnic minorities. When figures for partnerships are examined, the Young Women Lawyers group have found that only 25% of new partners in 1995 were women; a drop from 1985 when 44% of new

---

15 *op cit*, n 6.

16 *op cit*, p 129 at n 13.

17 *op cit*, n 9.

18 *Royal Commission on Legal Services 1979* (Cmnd 7648), cited in D Halpern *op cit*, n 10 at para 5.1.

19 'Entry Into the Legal Profession', *op cit* n 10, p 22.

20 *op cit*, p 23, n 10.

partnerships were granted to women. At the bar, the Bar Council has endorsed a new 'equality code' which is aimed at tackling discrimination within the profession.[21]

The absence of a profession which is balanced on gender and racial lines has inevitable consequences for women who find themselves dealing with law. The continued dominance of the profession by middle-class, middle-aged white males – the majority of whom it may reasonably be assumed are conservative in outlook (even if not political party) ensures a continuance of the traditional stereotypical attitudes to women. With this background in mind, attention can now be turned to the manner in which the legal system is imbued with patriarchal attitudes.

In the following extract from Albie Sachs and Joan Hoff Wilson's now seminal work on gender-based discrimination in the law, the authors explain the obstacles which women have faced when attempting to enter the legal profession.

SEXISM AND THE LAW[22]
Albie Sachs and Joan Hoff Wilson
Britain: Barristers and Gentlemen

A major reason for the obdurate resistance by judges and lawyers to the entry of women into the professions was simply their determination to exclude competitors seeking to participate in a lucrative monopoly activity. The feminists themselves had no doubt that this was a prime consideration, though only two of the many judgments referred to earlier alluded directly to this point. In one case a Scottish judge relatively sympathetic to Sophia Jex-Blake's claim went out of his way to emphasise that the exclusion of women from medical practice was not, as alleged, due to economic jealousy, but a leading South African judge openly stated that the choice was between denying women the right to economic independence and increasing the ranks of an already overcrowded profession.

In general, however, the exclusion of females was justified on the basis of maintaining professional standards. Maleness was converted into one of the attributes of professionalism (just as the capacity to be professional, that is, intellectually detached and emotionally uninvolved, became one of the attributes of the middle-class male). The professions, like clubs and elite schools, were not simply institutions from which women happened to be absent. Their maleness became part of their character, so that the admission of women was seen as not merely adding to their number or introducing some novelty, but as threatening the very identity of the institutions themselves.

Whereas the medical profession expressly set out to take healing away from women – many female folk-healers being condemned on the testimony of professional male doctors as witches – the legal profession established a monopoly of litigation and conveyancing that only incidentally excluded females. The procedures designed to protect the income and status of the professional lawyers from the competition of unregistered scribes and other unqualified persons were not specifically anti-female, but their consequences

---

21   *The Times*, 14 November, 1995.
22   (Martin Robertson, 1978) Chapter 5.

were such as to make it impossible for women to practise law. Once this exclusion of women had been established, however, maleness became part of the ethos of the profession, and male-exclusiveness was elevated to the level of a principle. A legal profession centralised around the courts in London, as opposed to community lawyers dispersed through the population, favoured the exclusion of women. The monopoly established by the profession over litigation and later over transfers of land, defined the function and the style of the profession from the first, and tied it in firmly with landed and commercial interests, creating what to this day has become the model of lawyers' work. In the neighbourhoods there were of course wise women as well as wise men who were consulted and asked to arbitrate informally on local disputes, but since they did not work for a fee in association with the courts they were not regarded as lawyers.

Incidentally, it is interesting to note that the professions were almost invariably described as 'overcrowded'. It is in the nature of professions dependent on fees from private clients to be permanently 'overcrowded', just as it is in the nature of publicly funded professions to be perpetually 'short-staffed'. It would seem that public funding through such agencies as the National Health Service and the Legal Aid Fund has played a major role in weakening the opposition of males to the entry into the professions of females. Public funding, however, makes specialisation and progress through a career structure the crucial determinants of income and status, and it is suggested that males have shifted their control away from the point of entry towards the routes of advancement. To say this is not to suggest that men conspire as a secret brotherhood to exclude women – though male condescension may well be nearly universal and male hostility fairly common – or even that individual male bigotry is the dominant bar to female advancement. Institutions tend to have machinery for their self-perpetuation, and all professions are structurally organised so as to maintain male domination and female subordination. This is most noticeable in areas such as health, education, and the social services, where men are in a small minority as far as all occupations are concerned, but grossly over-represented in the highest echelons. The social services have been built up by women and are largely staffed by women, but nine out of ten top posts are held by men.[23] And anyone who doubts the special role of professionalism in maintaining male privilege need merely to look at what professionalism has meant in relation to the kitchen. Women do the cooking in almost every home – men are at pains to perpetuate their inferiority here – but women are almost entirely excluded from the well-paid and prestigious activity of professional chef.

Women have been struggling for at least a century to find a place in the legal profession. just over a 100 years ago 92 women signed a petition requesting permission to attend lectures in Lincoln's Inn, a preliminary step to being called to the Bar. The Benchers (leaders) of the Inn regretted that this was 'not expedient'.[24]

Although there appear to have been examples in the distant past of women acting as attorneys in England, the first application in modern times for a woman to be enrolled as a solicitor seems to have been made in 1876, which was seven years after Arabella Mansfield had become the first woman to be admitted to legal practice in the United States. The English application was rejected by the

23 *House of Lords Select Committee Report on Anti-Discrimination Bill* (HL 104), House of Lords 1972–73, Vol VIII.
24 Helena Kennedy, in Robert Hazel (ed), *The Bar on Trial* (Quarter Books, 1978), p 148.

Law Society and when six years later a male solicitor proposed to offer employment to female clerks, the *Solicitors' Journal* treated the suggestion as a huge joke.[25] In fact it was the typewriter rather than the law degree that opened the way for women to enter legal offices. Initially, all important documents were handwritten by male clerks, and typing was regarded as a form of copying appropriate for inferior materials only, fit to be done by women at low rates of pay. The subordinate status of women typists continued even after they became responsible for the preparation of important documents. Lawyers in fact long resisted the entry of both typewriters and women into their offices, but eventually gave way to economic pressures that favoured the replacing of male clerks by machines and by women.

In his study of the black-coated worker, David Lockwood points out that in the century 1851 to 1951 clerical workers increased from one in 100 of the general labour force to one in ten, and that the proportion of women clerks during this period rose from less than one in 1000 to nearly two out of three.[26] Clerical work thus became largely feminised, which acted to the advantage rather than the disadvantage of male clerks in that they tended to be the ones who offered themselves or were preferred for promotion. The characteristic office situation was thus of the supervisor or manager being an older man and his assistants being younger women, the men exercising discipline through personal contact, 'whether the ensuing relationship [was] paternalistic, petty tyrannical or sexually exploitive'. The lawyers' office, it should be mentioned, tended to take on a three-tiered structure, with men occupying virtually all of the top or professional sector, as well as most of the middle or managing layer, while women filled almost all of the bottom or clerical zone.

There were, however some women who from the 1880s onwards practised neither as clerks nor as qualified lawyers, but as legal workers dealing directly with the 'public' or else giving assistance to solicitors and barristers. The admission of women to the universities in the last quarter of the century led to a number of women receiving law degrees, a state of affairs which was not objected to by the profession as long as it led nowhere. But, as has been seen, when in 1903 Bertha Cave brought a test application on behalf of herself and other recent graduates, including Christabel Pankhurst, seeking admission to the Bar, both the Bar and the judges insisted that the profession be confined to men only. It is interesting to speculate what the result on the suffrage movement would have been had women been admitted to legal practice at that time. If many leading rebels and revolutionaries have been lawyers, few leading lawyers have been rebels, and it is highly likely that even the spirited Christabel Pankhurst would have been totally contained by the Bar. As it was, 'the hot strife at the Bar', which allegedly was too much for women, appealed to her temperament, and in her capacity as a defendant she manifested such forensic brilliance that it was the male witnesses, magistrates and lawyers who found the combat too intense, not her. The courtroom became an arena in which she was far more effective as a feminist law-breaker than she would have been as a female barrister, and the occasion when she humiliated Lloyd George in the witness box – a government minister, solicitor and orator of note – stands, out as one of the notable pieces of cross-examination of her era.

---

25 Abel-Smith and Stevens, *Lawyers and the Courts*, p 193, give a brief history of attempts by women to enter the profession.

26 Lockewood's study, *The Black-Coated Worker* (London, 1958) was unusual for its period in that it focused on gender relationships at work.

Not all the women rejected by the Bar followed her example of embarking on full-time political activity. Ivy Williams, who 18 years later was to be the first woman to be called to the Bar in England, declared in 1903 that women holding University law degrees could set up practice outside of the profession without being trammelled by the lawyers' trade union rules. The *Law Journal* countered what it called 'these threats which have been added to the weapons with which women are assailing the legal fortress', by reporting the comforting news that women had not been triumphant rivals in countries where the profession had been opened to them, quoting as evidence a letter from a member of the American Bar.[27]

The Bar and the Law Society were not merely unhelpful to women, they resolutely set their organisations against women, fighting tenaciously both inside and out of Parliament to maintain their male-exclusive character. To the extent that they bothered to argue the matter at all, male lawyers insisted on evaluating possible female lawyers against the stereotype woman rather than the stereotype lawyer – either they suborned male judges and juries with feminine wiles, or else they became 'un-sexed'.[28] Even after women won the vote at the end of the First World War, the professions hoped to uphold a legal barrier to women entering practice, but once women had the franchise, Members of Parliament were not willing to risk their seats in order to support a male monopoly in which they no longer participated. The Sex Disqualification Removal Act 1919 expressly authorised what the profession had expressly resisted, namely the right of women to set up as barristers and solicitors.

By 1921 there were 20 women barristers listed, and by 1929 the number had grown to 77.[29] By 1955 the total had actually declined to 64 (3.2%) and ten years later it had grown only to 99 (4.6%). By 1970 the increase had been rather more rapid and the total stood at 147 (5.7%) while by 1976 it had reached 313 (8.1%). In that year only four out of 370 practising Queen's Counsel (senior barristers) were female. As one female barrister recently put it:

> The successful jealously guard their right to remain overworked, and junior tenants who have only just got on to the bottom rung of the ladder are frequently the least sympathetic to the plight of those waiting below ... Females become a luxury the profession cannot afford.[30, 31]

VIOLENCE AGAINST WOMEN

Violence, in general, of course takes many varied forms. Physical violence specifically directed against women includes domestic violence, rape committed against a stranger, acquaintance or family member – including wives and daughters. Violence may also be more broadly defined to include harassment – sexual or other – whether private or public. Violence may also be defined to include violence against women's images, represented in the form of

---

27 (1904) 39 *Law Journal*.

28 *Cf* Holdord Knight (1913) *Times*, 4 July.

29 Figures from Vera Brittain, *Women's Work in Modern England* (London, 1928); Ruth Miller in (1973) *Times*, 1 January; *Legal Action Group Bulletin* (December 1975); H Kennedy, *op cit*, p 153.

30 Helena Kennedy, *op cit*, p 153.

31 *Sexism and the Law*, pp 170–74.

pornography. Because pornography raises a number of specific and difficult issues for feminist jurisprudence, it is considered separately in Chapter 10.

It is important to recognise the seemingly intractable problem of eradicating violence against women. As was seen in Chapter 2, historically there is a broad, ill-defined, movement from nature to culture, and from culture to law. Implicitly and explicitly, this movement incorporates at each stage of societal development the 'distinctive', 'special', 'separate', domain of women – with women being confined, as a result of her physical vulnerability in times of childbearing and child-rearing, to the private domain under the suzerainty of her patriarchal kin. Not only is woman relegated to the private domain, but she is kept there – excluded from the public, civic world of politics, government and power. The 'patriarchal society', however, is not merely protective and benevolent, it also includes *control of women*. This control is, from the point of view of the patriarch, essential to the maintenance of several features of his society. Firstly, it is a feature of all societies that there are taboos against incest within family groups – whether defined by consanguinity or affinity. This taboo is explainable on two bases. In the first place there exist eugenic justifications against incestuous relationships. It is scientifically established that there are risks involved in sexual relationships between closely related family members. Children born of closely related family members may result in mental and/or physical sub-normality. As important for the patriarchal society is the continuation of the legitimate line of succession of power and property. It is for this reason that under English law from the sixteenth century, at least, there have been punitive laws penalising the woman who bore a child outside wedlock, and the woman who committed adultery. The patriarchal society has a vested proprietorial interest in legitimacy. For this reason, the patriarch insisted on the right of *physical control* over women. This control – this dominium – is both physical and non-physical. It is from the claimed right of physical control over women that, it is submitted, the seeds for violence are sown. Woman is relatively physically weak and at times physically vulnerable. Her 'special' position as the bearer of legitimate – and only legitimate – children with the right to succeed to the property of the male, requires her protection against weakness, whether emotional, psychological or sexual in order that the line of legitimate succession be ensured. Thus, a right to correction was implied in the relationship between the patriarch and women. This right of 'protection' – which in fact means 'correction' becomes recognised in law, in the progression from nature to culture to law, as demonstrated in the selected extracts.

Other forces are also at work. Whilst immunity from the law of rape for husbands – on which see further below – had long been 'justified' under English law under the doctrine of 'one flesh' – similar arguments cannot prevail in relation to rape between unmarried persons, whether strangers or acquaintances.

RAPE WITHIN MARRIAGE

Prior to 1991, under English law, a husband had immunity from rape within marriage. The governing doctrine was that of implied consent to sexual intercourse by virtue of entering marriage. Accordingly, unless husband and wife were living apart under an order of the court,[32] no wife could complain that forced sexual intercourse amounted to rape. In addition, where a couple had agreed to live apart, or were in fact living apart, the court might hold that consent to intercourse was thereby revoked. The immunity from rape within marriage stems from the opinion of Sir Matthew Hale, expressed in *History of the Pleas of the Crown* (1736) in the following manner:

> But the husband cannot be guilty of a rape committed by himself upon his lawful wife, for by their mutual matrimonial consent and contract the wife hath given herself up in this kind unto her husband which she cannot retract.[33]

This immunity from prosecution for rape, deriving from the fictitious 'deemed consent' of a wife[34] had long been abolished in other common law jurisdictions – for example Canada, New Zealand, Victoria, New South Wales, Western Australia, Queensland, Tasmania, the Republic of Ireland,[35] and Israel had all abandoned the doctrine. Reform of the law of England was to be brought about only in 1991 with the case of *R v R*.[36]

In *Woman and the Law* (1984), Susan Atkins and Brenda Hoggett considered the question of marital rape, and the traditional – masculine – objections raised to criminalising rape within marriage.

WOMEN AND THE LAW[37]
Susan Atkins and Brenda Hoggett

Far and away the most important remaining aspect of a wife's legal subjection to her husband is that he cannot be prosecuted for raping her. He may be prosecuted for any accompanying assault, even if this was no more than necessary to achieve his object,[38] but unless he causes her actual bodily harm apart from the intercourse itself and its effects,[39] she would have to bring a private prosecution for the minor offence of common assault. The statutory definition of rape refers only to 'unlawful' (that is, extramarital) intercourse, but it is assumed that earlier cases hold good. These remove the husband's

---

32 Orders of Judicial Separation, non-molestation, personal protection or ouster orders made in relation to domestic violence, all of which are deemed to revoke the wife's consent to sexual intercourse.

33 *History of the Pleas of the Crown* (1736), Vol 1, Chapter 58, p 629.

34 See *R v Clarence* [1888] 22 QBD 12, [1886–90] All ER 113. See also *R v Clarke* [1949] 2 All ER 448; *R v Miller* [1954] 2 All ER 529; *R v Reid* [1972] 2 All ER 1350; *R v O'Brien* [1974] 3 All ER 663; *R v Steele* [1976] 65 Cr App Rep 22; *R v Roberts* [1986] Crim LR 188.

35 Where doubt existed as to whether the supposed immunity had survived the adoption of the Constitution of 1937.

36 [1991] 2 WLR 1065 (Court of Appeal); [1991] 3 WLR (House of Lords). Subsequently, an application was lodged under the European Convention on Human Rights alleging that the United Kingdom had infringed the provisions against retrospectivity (Article 7). The Court of Human Rights ruled unanimously that there had been no violation: see *CR v United Kingdom* (48/1994/495/577), judgment 22 November 1995.

37 Basil Blackwell, 1984.

38 *R v Miller* [1954] 2 QB 282.

39 See *R v Clarence* (1888) 22 QBD 23, in which the husband infected the wife with the venereal disease from which he knew that he was suffering.

protection once there has been a decree of judicial separation,[40] decree nisi of divorce[41] or anti-molestation injunction[42] or agreement. The same would probably apply to a magistrates' order excluding the husband from the home but not to a personal protection order which prohibits only violence or the threat of violence. But there is no protection for the wife who is living apart from her husband under some other form of order or without any order at all, still less for the wife who is still living with him.

The arguments which are advanced against a change in the law are curiously weak.[43] Two of them are inconsistent. On the one hand it is said that marital rape will be difficult to prove, while on the other it is said that the threat of unjustified proceedings may be used by a wife to blackmail her husband into a favourable settlement at the ending of their marriage. The difficulties of proving rape are indeed formidable, particularly where the woman knows her assailant well; and if they are likely to deter her from prosecuting, they are equally likely to deter her from threatening it improperly or her husband from succumbing to such threats. There is no reason why the difficulties of proving antisocial behaviour should make us any less ready to acknowledge it as a crime. Two other objections assert that the criminal law should not intervene in marital relationships and that the wife will be adequately protected by her matrimonial remedies. The second cannot be right for, as the Criminal Law Revision Committee (CLRC) itself points out,[44] matrimonial remedies no longer depend upon considerations of conduct alone, even if all courts could be relied upon to regard a single act of marital rape in the same serious light. Even if they could, the damage would already have been done (as the CLRC again realised, this was an insuperable objection to its proposed replacement of criminal with civil sanctions against intercourse with severely mentally handicapped people).[45] The belief that the criminal law has no place in family relationships could equally be applied to familial violence. At bottom, it is a plea to the wife to put her responsibility to preserve the family unit above her wish to preserve the integrity of her person:

> Spouses have responsibilities towards one another and to any children there may be as well as having rights against each other. If a wife could invoke the law of rape in all circumstances in which the husband forced her to have sexual intercourse without her consent, the consequences for any children could be grave, and for the wife too.[46]

The fact that the victim may suffer as much as, if not more than, the aggressor does not normally inhibit the criminal law from condemning antisocial behaviour, and it will certainly be another factor deterring her from the hasty action which is so much feared. But although hasty action is deplored, so also is the risk that the victim may change her mind, which again has been much favoured as a reason for failing to respond to violence against women in their homes. the evidence on this is debatable, but in any event the fact that some may

---

40 *R v Clarke* [1949] 2 All ER 448.

41 *R v O'Brien* [1974] 3 All ER 663.

42 *R v Steel* (1976) 65 Cr App R 22.

43 See MDA Freeman, 'But if You Can't Rape Your Wife, Whom Can You Rape?: the Marital Rape Exemption Re-examined' (1981) 15 *Family Law Quarterly* pp 1–29.

44 *Sexual Offences* (1984), para 2.79.

45 *Ibid*, para 9.3.

46 *Sexual Offences* (1980), para 33.

withdraw is no reason to deny the law's protection to those who continue to want it or to the much greater number whose husbands may be deterred by the knowledge that raping their wives would be a crime.

The real reason for opposing a change in the law is the difficulty which many seem to find in believing that it is indeed so dreadful for a husband to rape his wife that he should be called a criminal for doing it.[47] After all, she did once wish to have intercourse with him and may do so again. If they are still living together and sharing a bed, can he not be allowed to use a little persuasion upon her for the sake of their marriage? In the nullity case of G v G,[48] Lord Dunedin permitted himself to wish that the husband had used some 'gentle violence' instead of acquiescing in his wife's refusals. In Baxter v Baxter[49] the Court of Appeal actually refused a decree because the husband had not insisted, although the House of Lords disagreed.[50]

This argument appears to have caused the CLRC to change its mind between working paper and report. In 1980 a majority thought that wives should no longer be so subject to their husbands or in a position less favourable than that of unmarried cohabitants. Nevertheless, they believed that the consent of the Director of Public Prosecutions (DPP) should be required as check upon prosecutions which were 'not desirable in the public interest'.[51] What they meant by this was not explained. By 1984 all were agreed that the husband's exemption should go once the couple were no longer living together; but as they could not find an acceptable definition of this, they were divided as to whether the law should stay as it is or whether the exemption should be abandoned altogether. A narrow majority favoured leaving it as it is, and even most of those who wished it to go would have required the consent of the DPP to prosecution.

The majority view is clearly based on the perceived need to preserve the unique character of the 'true rape'. Although the Committee will happily contemplate an offence of indecent assault ranging from a small stroke to violent oral intercourse, it finds it hard to contemplate an offence of rape which includes intercourse between husband and wife. Yet if, as the Committee elsewhere asserts, the unique gravity of rape lies in the risk of pregnancy and childbirth, the most serious objection to the marital rape exemption ought to have been apparent. Before the advent of reliable contraception, it could effectively force a wife to bear her husband's children. Even today, unless she is a suitable candidate for oral contraceptives or an intra-uterine device, it allows him to proceed without waiting for her to take the precautions which are safest for women but which he may dislike. This objection may carry little weight with people who see a woman's prime vocation as bearing children, and particularly her husband's children. From the women's point of view, she may indeed have the same ambitions, but she might prefer it if the law left to her the decision as to whether and when. As with the decision to prosecute, however, the law remains curiously reluctant to allow women to take responsibility for their own lives.[52]

---

47   See Criminal Law Revision Committee, *Sexual Offences* (1980), para 42.

48   [1924] AC 349.

49   [1948] AC 274.

50   See also N Morris and AL Turner, 'Two Problems in the Law of Rape', *University of Queensland Law Journal*, vol 1, 1952–55, pp 247–63, quoted with apparent approval in JC Smith and B Hogan *Criminal Law* (Butterworths, 1978, 4th edn), pp 40–43.

51   *Sexual Offences* (1980), para 42.

52   *Women and the Law*, pp 71–73.

Sourcebook on Feminist Jurisprudence

In *R v R* the wife had left the family home and informed the husband that she intended to seek a divorce. While the wife was staying with her parents, the husband forced his way into the house and had nonconsensual sexual intercourse with the wife. The wife alleged rape. The Court of Appeal (Criminal Division) upheld the conviction for rape; a decision which was affirmed by the House of Lords. Lord Keith of Kinkel, having referred to Sir Matthew Hale's opinion, stated:

> For over 150 years after the publication of Hale's work there appears to have been no reported case in which judicial consideration was given to his proposition. The first such case was *R v Clarence* (1888) 22 QBD 23, to which I shall refer later. It may be taken that the proposition was generally regarded as an accurate statement of the common law of England. The common law is, however, capable of evolving in the light of changing social, economic and cultural developments. Hale's proposition reflected the state of affairs in these respects at the time it was enunciated. Since then the status of women, and particularly of married women, has changed out of all recognition in various ways which are very familiar and upon which it is unnecessary to go into detail. Apart from property matters and the availability of matrimonial remedies, one of the most important changes is that marriage is in modern times regarded as a partnership of equals, and no longer one in which the wife must be the subservient chattel of the husband. Hale's proposition involves that by marriage a wife gives her irrevocable consent to sexual intercourse with her husband under all circumstances and irrespective of the state of her health or how she happens to be feeling at the time. In modern times any reasonable person must regard that conception as quite unacceptable.

Following *R v R* the Law Commission reviewed the state of the law.[53] Having considered Hale's opinion, and the exceptions to the exemption from prosecution for rape, the Commission recommended that the immunity should be formally abolished. The Commission reasoned in the following manner:

> We think that the principal matter to be considered in deciding whether the present marital immunity is supportable on grounds of policy and principle, as opposed to history, is whether non-consensual intercourse by a husband with his wife is sufficiently different from non-consensual intercourse by a man with a women to whom he is not married, or with his wife when a non-molestation or personal protection order is in existence, as to justify giving the husband immunity from the law of rape. That in its turn involves consideration of the nature of, and justification for the existence of, the crime of rape.
>
> The reasons for the existence of a separate crime of rape, and for that crime being regarded as of a particularly serious nature, are in our view best expressed by the Criminal Law Revision Committee's Policy Advisory Committee, in a passage specifically approved by the CLRC itself –
>
>> Rape involves a severe degree of emotional and psychological trauma; it may be described as a violation which in effect obliterates the personality of the victim. Its physical consequences equally are severe: the actual physical harm occasioned by the act of intercourse; associated violence or force and in some cases degradation; after the event, quite apart from the woman's continuing

---

53   *Rape Within Marriage*, Working Paper No 116 (HMSO, 1990).

insecurity, the fear of venereal disease of pregnancy. We do not believe this latter fear should be underestimated because abortion would usually be available. That is not a choice open to all women and it is not a welcome consequence of any. Rape is also particularly unpleasant because it involves such intimate proximity between the offender and the victim. We also attach importance to the point that the crime of rape involves abuse of an act which can be a fundamental means of expressing love for another; and to which as a society we attach considerable value.[54]

The (narrow) majority of the CLRC did not, however, agree that those considerations operate where the non-consensual intercourse is by a husband with his wife –

> The majority of us, who would not extend the offence of rape to married couples cohabiting at the time of the act of sexual intercourse, believe that rape cannot be considered in the abstract as merely 'sexual intercourse without consent'. The circumstances of rape may be peculiarly grave. This feature is not present in the case of a husband and wife cohabiting with each other when an act of sexual intercourse occurs without the wife's consent. They may well have had sexual intercourse regularly before the act in question and, because a sexual relationship may involve a degree of compromise, she may sometimes have agreed only with some reluctance to such intercourse. Should he go any further and force her to have sexual intercourse without her consent, this may evidence a failure of the marital relationship. But it is far from being the 'unique' and 'grave' offence described earlier. Where the husband goes so far as to cause injury, there are available a number of offences against the person with which he may be charged, but the gravamen of the husband's conduct is the injury he has caused not the sexual intercourse he has forced.

Like the minority of the CLRC, we find that view hard to accept. The minority were, in our view, right to say that 'a woman, like a man, is entitled on any particular occasion to decide whether or not to have sexual intercourse, outside or inside marriage'. The question is, therefore, whether, as the minority thought, she is entitled to be protected in both situations, inside and outside marriage, by the law of rape. We have quoted ... above the grounds advanced by the majority of the CLRC for distinguishing the two cases. We see the following difficulties in the distinction that they made.

First, and most fundamentally, if the rights of the married and the non-married woman are in this respect the same, those rights should be protected in the same way, unless there are cogent reasons of policy for taking a different course.

Second, it is by no means necessarily the case that non-consensual intercourse between spouses has less serious consequences for the woman, or is physically less damaging or disturbing for her, than in the case of non-consensual intercourse with a stranger. Depending on the circumstances the wife whose husband thrusts intercourse upon her may suffer pain from the act of intercourse itself; or the fear or the actuality of venereal or other disease; or the fear or the actuality of an unwanted pregnancy if because of the suddenness of the attack she has taken no contraceptive precautions or such precautions are unacceptable or impossible for medical reasons; and in the event of actual pregnancy a termination may be unavailable or morally offensive to her. All of these hazards may apply equally in the case of marital as of non-marital rape.

---

54 Fifteenth Report, at para 2.2.

Third, we think that there is a danger that the CLRC underestimated the emotional and psychological harm that a wife may suffer by being subjected by her husband to intercourse against her will, even though on previous occasions she has willingly participated in the same act with the same partner. In Kowalski[55] the Court of Appeal approved the trial judge's ruling, in respect of an act of fellatio that the husband compelled the wife to perform on him, that she was entitled to say –

> I agree I have done that with you before. I agree I did not find it indecent when we did it as an act of love, but I now find it indecent; I find it repellent; I find it abhorrent.

It is well recognised that unwanted sexual intercourse can be a particularly repellent and abhorrent experience for a woman: that is one main justification for the existence of the offence of rape. We see no reason why a wife cannot say that she feels that abhorrence for such intercourse with her husband, whether or not she has willingly participated on previous occasions.

Fourth, for a man to oblige his wife to have intercourse without her consent may be equally, or even more, 'grave' or serious as when that conduct takes place between non-spouses. We quoted above the CLRC's own view, that it was important that 'the crime of rape involves abuse of an act which can be a fundamental means of expressing love for another; and to which as a society we attach considerable value'. In the case of the husband, however, he abuses not merely an act to which, as a matter of abstract principle, society attaches value, but the act that has been or should have been his means of expressing his love for his wife. There seems every reason to think that that abuse can be quite as serious on the part of the husband, and quite as traumatic for the wife, as is rape by a stranger of casual acquaintance.

Fifth, in many cases where the husband forces intercourse on his wife they will be living in the same household, or at least she will be in some sort of dependent relationship with him. It is likely to be harder, rather than easier, for such a woman to avoid her husband's insistence on intercourse, since to do so she may for instance have to leave the matrimonial home. That is a further respect in which non-consensual intercourse by a husband may be a particular abuse.

Our view, as at present advised, is therefore, that there are no good grounds of principle for distinguishing between marital and other types of rape.[56]

The Law Commission's Report[57] endorsed the conclusions reached in the Working Paper, and the law of rape was statutorily reformed in the Criminal Justice and Public Order Act 1994, which provides that:

s142   For section 1 of the Sexual Offences Act 1956 (rape of a woman) there shall be substituted the following section–

1.–(1) It is an offence for a man to rape a woman or another man.

(2) A man commits rape if –

(a) he has sexual intercourse with a person (whether vaginal or anal) who at the time of the intercourse does not consent to it; and

(b) at the time he knows that the person does not consent to the intercourse or is reckless as to whether that person consents to it.

---

55   (1987) 86 Cr App R 339.

56   Paras 4.16–4.25.

57   *Criminal Law: Rape Within Marriage*, No 205 (HMSO, 1992).

(3) A man also commits rape if he induces a married woman to have sexual intercourse with him by impersonating her husband.

Ngaire Naffine analysed the now reformed common law of immunity for marital rape in the following manner:

POSSESSION: EROTIC LOVE IN THE LAW OF RAPE[58]
Ngaire Naffine

English common law prescribed a certain form of female sexuality in which women were positively required to assume a particular part – that of the possessed. And there was a certain part prescribed for the man: to possess her. In the sex prescribed and proscribed by law, the sexual natures of men and women were made to correspond with nature. Within marriage, the common law spelled out the obligation of the wife to renounce her subjectivity to her husband. In his *Commentaries on the Laws of England*, William Blackstone (now famously) explained the legal status of the married woman. 'By marriage, the husband and wife are one person in law: that is, the very being or legal existence of the woman is suspended during the marriage, or at least is incorporated into that the husband: under whose wing, protection, and cover, she performs every thing'.[59]

In marriage, the law specifically countenanced the use of a reasonable measure of force by a husband in order to keep the unaccommodating wife in line: she who was not true to her own nature could be bent to his will with a rod no bigger than his thumb. In his exposition of the legal relations between husband and wife, Blackstone asserted the husband's right of 'domestic chastisement, in the same moderation that a man is allowed to correct his apprentices or children'.[60] Marriage law also deprived a woman of the sort of economic independence needed to mount an effective challenge to male authority. Upon marriage, her property effectively passed into the hands of her husband. She was also deprived of her ability to function as an independent political and economic citizen in the public realm. The married woman was coerced by her husband in more than one way. More than one violence was done to her: one was physical, another was economic, a third was explicitly sexual.

All three forms of violence could be seen to operate implicitly within the law of primogeniture – the law which ensured the passage of property to the eldest son of the marriage upon the death of the husband and father. The concern of primogeniture was with 'posterity and the family lineage, but it also enabled the accumulation of wealth'.[61] For this law to work, for a husband to secure his future through his son and his son's son, it was vital that the law recognise the male right of control over (the fertility of) his wife. The husband had to have access to her reproductive body as well as the right to exclude all others from her body (for he had to know that his sons were his).

The law of primogeniture presupposed the right of the husband to obtain sex from his wife. The legal fiction employed to guarantee this right was to treat a woman's consent to marriage as much the same thing as consent to intercourse (with her husband). That is to say, consent to marriage also meant ongoing consent to sex – for the life of that marriage. Once married, the wife was

---

58 [1994] 57 *Modern Law Review*, p 10.
59 Blackstone, *Commentaries on the Laws of England* (New York: Garland, 1978) vol 1, p 442.
60 *Ibid*, p 444. On more modern expressions of this 'right' see further below.
61 Katherine O'Donovan *Sexual Divisions in Law* (Weidenfeld and Nicolson, 1985), p 22.

therefore presumed to have consented to every act of intercourse with her husband: a married woman had no right to refuse the proposal to be possessed. Sir Matthew Hale, English Chief Justice in the seventeenth century, still provides an authoritative word on the legal attitude to rape in marriage. To Hale, 'the husband cannot be guilty of a rape committed by himself upon his lawful wife, for by their mutual matrimonial consent and contract the wife hath given up herself in this kind unto her husband, which she cannot retract'.[62] Thus Hale expounded unambiguously the traditional possessive form of sex reflected in the law of rape. The wife was required by law to give herself up to her husband: the husband had the lawful right to take her.[63]

In certain circumstances, the husband's proprietorial right of the sex of his wife was one he could also claim and exercise against other men. Indeed, a line of men held right in her body. As Hale explains:

> If the woman consented not at the time of the rape committed, but consented after, she shall not have an appeal of rape ... but yet the king shall have the suit by indictment, and ... if she have a husband, he shall have an appeal, and if she have none, then her father or other next of blood shall have an appeal of such rape.[64]

Outside marriage, the possessory rights of the man were more limited (though intercourse was cast in the same form). The unmarried woman (of good reputation) had the legal right not to be possessed (in that she could complain of rape). She had the right to save her chastity for a husband who could then possess her with a legal right. Indeed, a woman already sexually possessed was of little value to the man who might possess her as a husband. No longer could she be exclusively possessed and so he was dispossessed. Again, Hale tells us of the sort of woman whom the law protected. She was a woman 'of good fame', who revealed the injury immediately: otherwise 'the strong presumption [was] that her testimony [was] false or feigned'.[65]

The sexual paradigm of law, the naturalised sex of law, invariably cast the man (never the woman) in the role of initiator (never the negotiator) of a sexual act (a singular, never a plural, thing which never took the form of an engagement) which always entailed the thrusting of the penis into the vagina (never the lips of a woman on the lips of another, to think of just one of the many other forms that 'the act' might have taken). Other female orifices (where his seed would not flourish) were outlawed as unnatural whether or not the act took place with the consent of the woman. If we return to Hale this all becomes plain. 'Rape' in the view of Hale was 'the carnal knowledge of any woman above the age of ten years against her will'. He was, in Hale's words, the 'ravished', she was 'ravished'. So obvious to Hale was the male subjectivity of the sexual act(or) that he was not concerned to spell it out. He does not tell us that 'carnal knowledge' is always the man's knowledge because the subjective role of the man is axiomatic: literally, it goes without saying. The sex of law involves the man's 'knowledge' of the woman, never the woman's knowledge of the man, never the woman's knowledge of another woman, never the woman's knowledge of herself – all unthinkable relations. She is necessarily the object of his knowledge,

---

62 Hale, *The History of the Pleas of the Crown* (London: Professional Books, 1971), p 629.
63 Though, of course, when a husband had intercourse with his wife by force, it was not rape as the law defined it.
64 Hale, *op cit*, p 631.
65 Hale, *op cit*, p 633.

he the knowing subject. The woman, then, was always the respondent to the man's proposal and it was a proposal leading to her ultimate pleasure. He was expected to persuade, using reasonable force if necessary; but eventually she was to capitulate (ultimately with pleasure as she realised her sexual fulfilment in her possession by him). As we saw, Hale explicitly recognised that consent could come after rape, in effect, that a rape could produce a woman's consent, making her the assenting 'ravished'.

The Death of Hale?

Hale's *Pleas* should now have the ring of antiquity, as should the writings of Blackstone. We know that law and society have undergone dramatic change in their understandings of the sexes and so we are surely now at a great remove from the lives and crimes so eloquently depicted by these two 'great men' of law. Surely it is an odd thing to do, to exhume these Englishmen of centuries past and yet we find this is not so. The possessive ideal of sexuality described by our legal forbears persists, both in English and Australian law and society, though it has assumed new and mystifying forms.

While the general movement of English law in this century has been towards formal sex equality (usually interpreted as treating the sexes the same, as gender-neutrality), this shift has been uneven. English men and women may now be (formally) equal subjects before the law, but rape is still 'the most gender specific of all crimes', as Temkin reminds us.[66] '[O]nly a man .... can be the actual perpetrator, only a woman the victim'.[67] The possessive idea of male sexuality also remains within the modern crimes of incest. In the relevant provisions of the Sexual Offences Act 1956, we see explicitly repeated the idea that it is the man who has the woman and the woman who is had. Thus, it is an offence 'for a man to have sexual intercourse with a woman whom he knows to be his grand-daughter' and 'for a woman ... to permit a man whom she knows to be her grandfather [etc] ... to have sexual intercourse with her by consent. As Lacey, Wells and Meure observe, 'the "natural" mode is subtly portrayed as vaginal sexual intercourse with the woman as the passive partner'.[68]

Debates leading up to, and surrounding, the abolition of the husband's common law immunity from prosecution for rape of his wife also suggest that many jurists still favour the possessive ideal of heterosexuality. In the landmark decision of *R v R*, the House of Lords condemned as anachronistic the common law view of rape in marriage and declared that now the 'husband and wife are for all practical purposes equal partners to a marriage'.[69] In the opinion of the Court, the reference to rape as '*unlawful* intercourse' in the Sexual Offences (Amendment) Act 1976 posed no obstacle to this interpretation of the law. The

---

66 Jennifer Temkin *Rape and the Legal Process* (Sweet & Maxwell, 1987), p 7.

67 Section 1 of the Sexual Offences Act 1956 states that 'It is a felony for a man to rape a woman'. 'Rape' us ten defined by the Sexual Offences (Amendment) Act 1976:
A man commits rape if –
(a) he has unlawful sexual intercourse with a woman who at the time of the intercourse does not consent to it;
(b) and at the time he knows that she does not consent to the intercourse or he is reckless as to whether she consents to it.

68 *Reconstructing Criminal Law: Critical Perspectives on Crime and the Criminal Process* (Weidenfeld and Nicolson, 1990), p 355.

69 [1991] 3 WLR 767, at 771.

word 'unlawful' was mere 'surplusage' and was not intended to confine the crime of rape to incidents occurring outside marriage.

In her commentary on *R v R*, Vanessa Laird questions this reading of the Act. She maintains that the retention of the term 'unlawful intercourse' in the Act was really an expression of Parliamentary ambivalence about 'the politically troublesome issue of marital rape'.[70] In 1976, Parliament lacked the resolve to remove the husband's immunity, preferring to leave the matter to the forthcoming Criminal Law Revision Committee. When in 1984 that Committee produced its final report on the law of rape in marriage, however, it affirmed the right of an Englishman to have intercourse with his wife. The majority of the Committee said that when a man forced his wife to have intercourse with him, and it did not result in overt injury, this was merely 'evidence of the failure of the marital relationship', not of rape.[71] It might be a problem for social workers, but it was not the province of the criminal law.[72] The Committee stressed that the 'gravamen of the husband's conduct is the injury he has caused not the sexual intercourse he has forced'.[73]

By 1990 legal opinion had changed dramatically. In its Working Paper on Rape within Marriage, the Law Commission recommended, provisionally that the husband's immunity be lifted.[74] It said that there were 'no valid reasons for distinguishing between non-consensual sexual intercourse within marriage' and without it.[75] In 1991 the House of Lords abolished the immunity at common law and in 1992 the Final Report of the Law Commission recommended that 'the law should continue to be that there is no immunity in the crime of rape'.[76] The legal community, however, remains divided on the issue, with Professor Glanville Williams perhaps the most vocal critic of the new approach. In his response to the provisional recommendations of the Working Paper, Professor Williams did not mince words. He asked:

> Why is rape an inappropriate charge against the cohabiting husband? The reasons should be too obvious to need spelling it out. We are speaking of a biological activity, strongly baited by nature, which is regularly and pleasurably performed on a consensual basis by mankind ... Occasionally some husband continues to exercise what he regards as his right when his wife refused him ... What is wrong with his demand is not so much the act requested but its timing, or the manner of the demand. The fearsome stigma of rape is too great a punishment for husbands who use their strength in these circumstances.[77]

However, there is reason to believe that Williams should not be too concerned about the ill-fated possessing husband. As Vanessa Laird explains, *R v R* generates the false impression that 'inequalities between husband and wife have been resolved', thus obscuring 'the social conditions that shape women's consent'. That is, many women still do not feel they have the right or the capacity

---

70 'Reflections on *R v R*' (1991) 55 *Modern Law Review*, 386, 391.

71 *Sexual Offences* (HMSO, 1984) Cmnd 9213.

72 *Ibid*, para 2.64.

73 *Ibid*.

74 Working Paper No 116, *op cit*.

75 *Ibid*, p 83.

76 The Law Commission (Law Com No 205) *Criminal Law: Rape Within Marriage* (1992), p 18, *supra*.

77 Williams 'The Problem of Domestic Rape', 15 February 1991, *New Law Journal* 205, 206.

to say 'no' to a husband. The simple assertion of the equal sexual rights of wives by the House of Lords does not make it so.[78]

RAPE

In the passage which follows Professor Susan Estrich examines the differing approaches of American and English courts to the issue of rape. Neither approach, in the author's view, satisfies the requirements of justice and the protection of women. The law and legal process, Professor Estrich argues, in effect places women on trial – not the male rapist.

RAPE[79]

Susan Estrich[80]

The Definition of Rape: The Common Law Tradition

The traditional way of defining a crime is by describing the prohibited act (*actus reus*) committed by the defendant and the prohibited mental state (*mens rea*) with which he must have done it. We ask: What did the defendant do? What did he know or intend when he did it?

The definition of rape stands in striking contrast to this tradition, because courts, in defining the crime, have focused almost incidentally on the defendant – and almost entirely on the victim. It has often been noted that traditionally at least, the rules associated with the proof of a rape charge – the corroboration requirement, the requirement of cautionary instructions, and the fresh complaint rule – as well as the evidentiary rules relating to prior sexual conduct by the victim, placed the victim as much on trial as the defendant. Such a reversal also occurs in the course of defining the elements of the crime. *Mens rea*, where it might matter, is all but eliminated; prohibited force tends to be defined according to the response of the victim; and non-consent – the *sine qua non* of the offence – turns entirely on the victim's response.

But while the focus is on the female victim, the judgment of her actions is entirely male. If the issue were what the defendant knew, thought, or intended as to key elements of the offence, this perspective might be understandable; yet the issue has instead been the appropriateness of the woman's behaviour, according to male standards of appropriate female behaviour.

To some extent, this evaluation is but a modern response to the long-standing suspicion of rape victims. As Matthew Hale put it three centuries ago: 'Rape is ... an accusation easily to be made and hard to be proved, and harder to be defended by the party accused, tho never so innocent'.

But the problem is more fundamental than that. Apart from the women's conduct, the law provides no clear, working definition of rape. This rather conspicuous gap in the law of rape presents substantial questions of fair warning for men, which the law not so handily resolves by imposing the burden of warning them on women.

At its simplest, the dilemma lies in this: If non-consent is essential to rape (and no amount of force or physical struggle is inherently inconsistent with lawful

---

78 *Possession: Erotic Love in the Law of Rape*, pp 18–23.
79 95 *Yale Law Journal* 1087.
80 Robert Kingsley Professor of Law and Political Science, University of Southern California.

sex), and if no sometimes means yes, and if men are supposed to be aggressive in any event, how is a man to know when he has crossed the line? And how are we to avoid unjust convictions?

This dilemma is hardly inevitable. Partly it is a product of the way society (or at least a powerful part of it) views sex. Partly it is a product of the lengths to which the law has gone to enforce and legitimise those views. We could prohibit the use of force and threats and coercion in sex, regardless of 'consent'. We could define consent in a way that respected the autonomy of women. Having chosen neither course, however, we have created a problem, of fair warning, and force and consent have been defined in an effort to resolve this problem.

Usually, any discussion of rape begins (and ends) with consent. I begin instead with *mens rea*, because if unjust punishment of the blameless man is our fear (as it was Hale's), then *mens rea* would seem an appropriate place to start addressing it. At least a requirement of *mens rea* would avoid unjust convictions without adjudicating the 'guilt' of the victim. It could also be the first step in expanding liability beyond the most traditional rape.

Without *mens rea*, the fair warning problem turns solely on the understanding of force and consent. To the extent that force is defined apart from a women's reaction, it has been defined narrowly, in the most schoolboyish terms. But most of the time, force has been defined according to the woman's will to resist, judged as if she could and should fight like a man. Thus defined, force serves to limit our understanding of rape even in cases where a court might be willing to say that this woman did not consent.

Rape is not a unique crime in requiring non-consent. But it is unique in the definition given to non-consent. As it has been understood, the consent standard denies female autonomy; indeed, it even denies that women are capable of making decisions about sex, let alone articulating them. Yet consent, properly understood, has the potential to give women greater power in sexual relations and to expand our understanding of the crime of rape,. That is, perhaps, why so many efforts have been made to cabin the concept.

A. Mens Rea

It is difficult to imagine any man engaging in intercourse accidentally or mistakenly. It is just as difficult to imagine an accidental or mistaken use of force, at least as force is conventionally defined. But it is not at all difficult to imagine cases in which a man might claim that he did not realise that the woman was not consenting to sex. He may have been mistaken in assuming that no meant yes. He may not have bothered to inquire. He may have ignored signs that would have told him that the woman did not welcome his forceful penetration.

In doctrinal terms, such a man could argue that his mistake of fact should exculpate him because he lacked the requisite intent or *mens rea* as to the woman's required non-consent. American courts have altogether eschewed the *mens rea* or mistake inquiry as to consent, opting instead for a definition of the crime of rape that is so limited that it leave little room for men to be mistaken, reasonably or unreasonably, as to consent. The House of Lords, by contrast, has confronted the question explicitly and, in its leading case has formally restricted the crime of rape to men who act recklessly, a state of mind defined to allow even the unreasonably mistaken man to avoid conviction.

This section argues that the American courts' refusal to confront the *mens rea* problem works to the detriment of the victim. In order to protect men from unfair convictions, American courts end up defining rape with undue restrictiveness. The English approach, while doctrinally clearer, also tends toward an unduly restricted definition of the crime of rape.

While the defendant's attitude toward consent may be considered either an issue of *mens rea* or a mistake of fact, the key question remains the same. In *mens rea* terms, the question is whether negligence suffices, that is, whether the defendant should be convicted who claims that he thought the woman was consenting, or didn't think about it, in situations where a 'reasonable man' would have known that there was not consent. In mistake-of-fact terms, the question is whether a mistake as to consent must be reasonable in order to exculpate the defendant.

In defining the crime of rape, most American courts have omitted *mens rea* altogether. In Maine, for example, the Supreme Judicial Court has held that there is no *mens rea* requirement at all for rape.[81] In Pennsylvania, the superior court held in 1982 that even a reasonable belief as to the victim's consent would not exculpate a defendant charged with rape.[82] In 1982 the Supreme Judicial Court of Massachusetts left open the question whether it would recognise a defence of reasonable mistake of fact as to consent, but it rejected the defendant's suggestion that any mistake, reasonable or unreasonable, would be sufficient to negate the required intent to rape; such a claim was treated by the court as bordering on the ridiculous.[83] The following year the court went on to hold that a specific intent that intercourse be without consent was not an element of the crime of rape,[84] that decision has since been construed to mean that there is no intent requirements at all as to consent in rape cases.[85]

To treat what the defendant intended or knew or even should have known about the victim's consent as irrelevant to his liability sounds like a result favourable to both prosecution and women as victims. But experiences makes all too clear that it is not. To refuse to inquire into *mens rea* leaves two possibilities: turning rape into a strict liability offence where, in the absence of consent, the man is guilty of rape regardless of whether he (or anyone) would have recognised non-consent in the circumstances; or defining the crime of rape in a fashion that is so limited that it would be virtually impossible for any man to be convicted where he was truly unaware or mistaken as to non-consent. In fact, it is the latter approach which has characterised all of the older, and many of the newer, American cases. In practice, abandoning *mens rea* produces the worst of all possible worlds: the trial emerges not as in inquiry into the guilt of the defendant (Is he a rapist?) but of the victim (Was she really raped? Did she consent?). The perspective that governs is therefore not that of the woman, nor even of the particular man, but of a judicial system intent upon protecting against unjust conviction, regardless of the dangers of injustice to the woman in the particular case.

The requirement that sexual intercourse be accompanied by force or threat of force to constitute rape provides a man with some protection against mistakes as to consent. A man who uses a gun or knife against his victim is not likely to be in serious doubt as to her lack of consent, and the more narrowly force is defined, the more implausible the claim that he was unaware of non-consent.

But the law's protection of men is not limited to a requirement of force. Rather than inquire whether the man believed (reasonably or unreasonably) that his victim was consenting, the courts have demanded that the victim demonstrate

---

81 *State v Reed*, 479 A.2d 1291, 1296 (me. 1984).

82 *Commonwealth v Williams* 294 a Super 93, 99–1000, 439 A 2d 765, 769 (1982).

83 *Commonwealth v Sherry* 437 NE 2d 224, 386 Mass 682 (1982).

84 *Commonwealth v Grant* 391 Mass 645, 464 NE 2d 33 (1984).

85 *Commonwealth v Lefkowitz* 20 Mass App Ct 513, 481 NE 2d 227, 230, review denied. 396 Mass 1103, 485 NE 2d 224 (1985).

her non-consent by engaging in resistance that will leave no doubt as to non-consent. The definition of non-consent as resistant – in the older cases, as utmost resistance,[86] while in some more recent ones, as 'reasonable' physical resistance[87] – functions as a substitute for *mens rea* to ensure that the man has notice of the woman's non-consent.

The choice between focusing on the man's intent or focusing on the woman's is not simply a doctrinal flip of the coin.

First, the inquiry into the victim's non-consent puts the woman, not the man, on trial. Her intent, not his, is disputed, and because her state of mind is key, her sexual history may be considered relevant (even though utterly unknown to the man).[88] Considering consent from *his* perspective, by contrast, substantially undermines the relevance of the woman's sexual history where it was unknown to the man.

Second, the issue for determination shifts from whether the man is a rapist to whether the woman was raped. A verdict of acquittal thus does more than signal that the prosecution has failed to prove the defendant guilty beyond a reasonable doubt; it signals that the prosecution has failed to prove the woman's sexual violation – her innocence – beyond reasonable doubt. Thus, as one dissenter put it in disagreeing with the affirmance of a conviction of rape: 'the majority today ... declares the innocence of an at best distraught young woman'.[89] Presumably, the dissenter thought the young woman guilty.

Third, the resistance requirement is not only ill conceived as a definition of non-consent but is an overbroad substitute for *mens rea* in any event. Both the resistance requirement and the *mens rea* requirement can be used to enforce a male perspective on the crime, but while *mens rea* might be justified as protecting the individual defendant who has not made a blameworthy choice, the resistance standard requires women to risk injury to themselves in cases where there may be no doubt as to the man's intent or blameworthiness. The application of the resistance requirement has not been limited to cases in which there was uncertainty as to what the man thought, knew or intended; it has been fully applied in cases where there can be no question that the man knew that intercourse was without consent.[90] Indeed, most of the cases that have dismissed claims that *mens rea* ought to be required have been cases where both force and resistance were present and where there was danger of any unfairness.

Finally, by ignoring *mens rea*, American courts and legislators have imposed limits on the fair expansion of our understanding of rape. As long as the law holds that *mens rea* is not required and that no instructions on intent need to be given, pressure will exist to retain some form of resistance requirement and to insist on force as conventionally defined in order to protect men against

---

86   See *King v State* 210 Tenn 150, 158, 357 SW 2d 42, 45 (1962); *Moss v State* 208 Miss 531, 536, 45 So 2d 125, 126 (1950) *Brown v State*, 127 Wis 193, 199, 106 NW 536, 538 (1906); *People v Dohring* 59 NY 374, 386 (1874).

87   See eg *Satterwhite v Commonwealth* 210 Va 478, 482, 111 SE 2d 820, 823 (1960); *Goldberg v State* 41 Md App 58, 68, 395 A 2d 1213, 1218–19 (1979); *State v Lima* 64 Hawaii 470, 476–77, 643 P.2d 536, 540 (1982).

88   See eg *Government of the Virgin Islands v John* 447 F 2d 69 (3d Cir 1971) (holding victim's reputation for chastity relevant to consent); *Packineau v United States* 202 F 2d 681, 687.

89   *State v Rusk* 289 Md 230, 256, 424 A 2d 720, 733 (1981) (Cole J, dissenting).

90   See eg *Goldberg v State* 41 Md App 58, 68, 395 A 2d 1213 (1979). See also *State v Lima* 64 Hawaii 470, 643 P 2d 536 (1982).

conviction for 'sex'. Using resistance as a substitute for *mens rea* unnecessarily and unfairly immunises those men whose victims are afraid enough, or intimidated enough, or, frankly, smart enough, not to take the risk of resisting physically. In doing so, the resistance test may declare the blameworthy man innocent and the raped woman guilty.

While American courts have unwisely ignored the entire issue of *mens rea* or mistake of fact, the British courts may have gone too far in the other direction. To their credit, they have squarely confronted the issue, but their resolution suggests a highly restrictive understanding of criminal intent in cases of sexual assault. The focal point of the debate in Great Britain and the Commonwealth countries was the House of Lords' decision in *Director of Public Prosecutions v Morgan*,[91] in which the certified question was: 'whether in rape the defendant can properly be convicted, notwithstanding that he in fact believed that the woman consented, if such belief was not based on reasonable grounds'.[92] The majority of the House of Lords answered the question in the negative.

The Heilbron Committee was created to review the controversial *Morgan* decision. The committee's recommendation ultimately enacted in 1976, retained the *Morgan* approach in requiring that at the time of intercourse the man knew or at least was aware of the risk of non-consent but provided that the reasonableness of the man's belief could be considered by the jury in determining what he in fact knew.[93] In situations where a 'reasonable man' would have known that the woman was not consenting, most defendants will face great difficulty in arguing that they were honestly mistaken or inadvertent as to consent. Thus, in *Morgan* itself, the House of Lords, although holding that negligence was not sufficient to establish liability for rape, upheld the convictions on the ground that no properly instructed jury, in the circumstances of that case, could have concluded that the defendants honestly believed that their victim was consenting. Still, in an English case decided shortly after *Morgan*, on facts substantially similar (a husband procuring a buddy to engage in sex with his crying wife), an English jury concluded that the defendant had been negligent in believing, honestly but unreasonably, in the wife's consent. On the authority of *Morgan*, the court held that the defendant therefore deserved acquittal.[94]

My view is that such a 'negligent rapist' should be punished, albeit – as in murder – less severely than the man who acts with purpose or knowledge, or even knowledge of the risk. First, he is sufficiently blameworthy for it to be just to punish him. Second, the injury he inflicts is sufficiently grave to deserve the law's prohibition.

The traditional argument against negligence liability is that punishment should be limited to cases of choice, because to punish a man for his stupidity is unjust and, in deterrence terms, ineffective. Under this view, a man should only be held responsible for what he does knowingly or purposely, or at least while aware of the risks involved. As one of *Morgan*'s most respected defenders put it:

---

91 [1976] AC 182; [1976] 2 All ER 347; [1975] 2 WLR 913.

92 *Ibid* at 205; [1975] 2 All ER at 354.

93 The Sexual Offences (Amendment) Act, s 1. See generally Smith, *The Heilbron Report* 1976 Criminal Law Review 97, 98–105.

94 The most striking difference between that case, *R v Cogan* [1975] 3 WLR 316 (CA) and *Morgan* is the number of 'buddies' involved. In the law of rape, numbers often assume major significance in a court's approach to the facts.

To convict the stupid man would be to convict him for what lawyers call inadvertent negligence – honest conduct which may be the best that this man can do but that does not come up to the standard of the so-called reasonable man. People ought not to be punished for negligence except in some minor offences established by statute. Rape carries a possible sentence of imprisonment for life, and it would be wrong to have a law of negligent rape.[95]

If inaccuracy or indifference to consent is 'the best that this man can do' because he lacks capacity to act reasonably, then it might well be unjust and ineffective to punish him for it. But such men will be rare, and there was no evidence that the men in *Morgan* were among them, at least as long as voluntary drunkenness is not equated with inherent lack of capacity. More common is the case of the man who could have done better but didn't; could have paid attention, but didn't; heard her say no, or saw her tears, but decided to ignore them. Neither justice nor deterrence argues against punishing this man.

Certainly, if the 'reasonable' attitude to which a male defendant is held is defined according a 'no means yes' philosophy that celebrates male aggressiveness and female passivity, there is little potential for unfairness in holding men who fall below that standard criminally liable. Under such a low standard of reasonableness, only a very drunk man could honestly be mistaken as to a woman's consent, and a man who voluntarily sheds his capacity to act and perceive reasonably should not be heard to complain here – any more than with respect to other crimes – that he is being punished in the absence of choice.

But even if reasonableness is defined – as I argue it should be – according to a rule that 'no means no', it is not unfair to hold those men who violate the rule criminally responsible, provided that there is fair warning of the rule. I understand that some men in our society have honestly believed in a different reality of sexual relations and that because men and women may perceive these situations differently and because the injury to women stemming from the different male perception may be grave that it is necessary and appropriate for the law to impose a duty upon men to act with reason and to punish them when they violate that duty.

In holding a man to such a standard of reasonableness, the law signifies that it considers a woman's consent to sex to be significant enough to merit a man's reasoned attention. In effect the law imposes a duty on men to open their eyes and use their heads before engaging in sex – not to read a woman's mind but to give her credit for knowing her own mind when she speaks it. The man who has the inherent capacity to act reasonably but fails to do so has made the blameworthy choice to violate this duty. While the injury caused by purposeful conduct may be greater than that caused by negligent acts, being negligently sexually penetrated without one's consent remains a grave harm, and being treated like an object whose words or actions are not even worthy of consideration adds insult to injury. This dehumanisation exacerbates the denial of dignity and autonomy which is so much a part of the injury of rape, and it is equally present in both the purposeful and negligent rape.

By holding out the prospect of punishment for negligence, the law provides an additional motive for men to 'take care before acting, to use their faculties and draw on their experience in gauging the potentialities of the contemplated

---

95 Professor Glanville Williams in a letter to *The Times* (London) 8 May 1975, p 15, col 6.

conduct'.[96] We may not yet have reached the point where men are required to ask verbally. But if silence does not negate consent, at least the word no should, and those who ignore such an explicit sign of non-consent should be subject to criminal liability.[97]

Professor Estrich then analyses the use of force in relation to rape and further examines the question of consent or non-consent as revealed in American caselaw. Her conclusions as to the appropriate approach to rape is set out below.

RAPE

Susan Estrich

Conclusion

The conduct that one might think of as 'rape' ranges from the armed stranger who breaks into a woman's home to the date she invites in who takes silence for assent. In between are literally hundreds of variations: the man may be a stranger, but he may not be armed; he may be armed, but he may not be a stranger; he may be an almost, rather than a perfect, stranger – a man who gave her a ride or introduced himself through a ruse; she may say yes, but only because he threatens to expose her to the police or the welfare authorities; she may say no, but he may ignore her words.

In 1985, the woman raped at gunpoint by the intruding stranger should find most of the legal obstacles to her complaint removed. That was not always so: as recently as ten years ago, she might well have faced a corroboration requirement, a cautionary instruction, a fresh complaint rule, and a searing cross-examination about her sexual past to determine whether she had nonetheless consented to sex. In practice, she may still encounter some of these obstacles, but to the extent that the law communicates any clear message, it is likely to be that she was raped.

But most rapes do not as purely fit in the traditional model, and most victims do not fare as well. Cases involving men met in bars (*Rusk*) or at work (*Goldberg*) or in airports (*Evans*), let alone cases involving ex-boyfriends (*Alston*) still lead some appellate courts to enforce the most traditional view of women in the context of the less traditional rape. And in the system, considerations of prior relationship and the circumstances of the initial encounter, as well as force and resistance and corroboration, seem to reflect a similarly grounded if not so clearly stated view of the limits of rape law.

In thinking about rape, it is not as difficult to decide which rapes are more serious or which rapists deserving of more punishment: weapons, injury, and intent – the traditional grading criteria of the criminal law – are all justifiable answers to these questions. Most jurisdictions that have reformed their rape laws in the last ten years have focused on creating degrees of rape – aggravated and unaggravated – based on some combination of the presence of weapons and injury. While *mens rea* or mistake needs to be addressed more clearly in some

---

96 Model Penal Code, s 2.02 comment at 126–127 (Tent. draft No 4, 1955). The Model Penal Code commentators thus recognised the deterrence rationale of negligence liability in justifying its inclusion as a potential basis for criminal liability (albeit for a limited number of crimes, not including rape).

97 *Rape*, pp 162–67.

rape laws, and bodily injury more carefully defined in others, these are essentially problems of draftsmanship which are hardly insurmountable.

The more difficult problem comes in understanding and defining the threshold for liability – where we draw the line between criminal sex and seduction. Every statute still uses some combination of 'force', 'threats', and 'consent' to define the crime. But in giving meaning to those terms at the threshold of liability, the law of rape must confront the powerful norms of male aggressiveness and female passivity which continue to be adhered to by many men and women in our society.

The law did not invent the 'no means yes' philosophy. Women as well as men have viewed male aggressiveness as desirable and forced sex as an expression of love, women as well as men have been taught and have come to believe that when a women 'encourages' a man, he is entitled to sexual satisfaction. From the sociological surveys to prime time television, one can find ample support in society and culture for even the most oppressive views of women and the most expansive notions of seduction enforced by the more traditional judges.

But the evidence is not entirely one sided. For every prime time series celebrating forced sex, there seems to be another true confession story in a popular magazine detailing the facts of a date rape and calling it 'rape'. College men and women may think that the typical male is forward and primarily interested in sex, but they no longer conclude that he is the desirable man. The old sex manuals may have lauded male sexual responses as automatic and uncontrollable, but some of the new ones no longer see men as machines and even advocate sensitivity as seductive.

We live, in short, in a time of changing sexual mores – and we are likely to for some time to come. In such times, the law can cling to the past, or help move us into the future. We can continue to enforce the most traditional views of male aggressiveness and female passivity, continue to adhere to the 'no means yes' philosophy and to the broadest understanding of seduction, until and unless change overwhelms us. That is not a neutral course, however; in taking it, the law (judges, legislators, or prosecutors) not only reflects (a part of) society but legitimates and reinforces those views.

Or we can use the law to move forward. It may be impossible – and even unwise – to try to use the criminal law to change the way people think, to push progress to the ideal. But recognition of the limits of the criminal sanction need not be taken as a justification for the status quo. Faced with a choice between reinforcing the old and fuelling the new in a world of changing norms, it is not necessarily more legitimate or neutral to choose the old. There are lines to be drawn short of the ideal: the challenge we face in thinking about rape is to use the power and legitimacy of law to reinforce what is best, not what is worst, in our changing sexual mores.

In the late eighteenth and early nineteenth centuries, the judges of England waged a successful campaign against duelling. While 'the attitude of the law' was clear that killing in a dual was murder, the problem, was that for some, accepting a challenge remained a matter of 'honour', and juries would therefore not convict. 'Some change in the public attitude toward duelling, coupled with the energy of judges in directing juries in strong terms, eventually brought about convictions, and it was not necessary to hang many gentlemen of quality before the understanding became general that duelling was not required by the code of honour'.[98]

98 Williams, 'Consent and Public Policy' [1962] 9 *Criminal Law Review*, 74, 154 (pts I and II); at 77.

There has been 'some change in the public attitude' about the demands of manhood in heterosexual relations, as in duelling. If the 'attitude of the law' is made clearer – and that is, in essence, what this chapter is about – then it may not be necessary to prosecute too many 'gentlemen of quality' before the understanding becomes general that manly honour need not be inconsistent with female autonomy.

In a better world, I believe that men and women would not presume either consent or non-consent. They would ask, and be certain. There is nothing unromantic about showing the kind of respect for another person that demands that you know for sure before engaging in intimate contact. In a better world, women who said yes would be saying so from a position of equality, or at least sufficient power to say no. In a better world, fewer women would bargain with sex because they had nothing else to bargain with; they would be in at least as good a position to reject demands for sexual access as men are to reject demands for money.

If we are not at the point where it is appropriate for the law to presume non-consent from silence, and the reactions I have received to this chapter suggest that we are not, then at least we should be at the point where it is legitimate to punish the man who ignores a woman's explicit words of protestations. I am quite certain that many women who say yes – whether on dates or on the job – would say no if they could; I have no doubt that women's silence is sometimes the product not of passion and desire but of pressure and pain. But at the very least the criminal law ought to say clearly that women who actually say no must be respected as meaning it; that non-consent means saying no; that men who proceed nonetheless, claiming that they thought no meant yes, have acted unreasonably and unlawfully.

So, too, for threats of harm short of physical injury and for deception and false pretences as methods of seduction. The powerlessness of women and the value of bodily integrity are great enough to argue that women deserve more comprehensive protection for their bodies than the laws of extortion or fraud provide for money. But if going so far seems too complicated and fraught with difficulty, as it does to many, then we need not. For the present, it would be a significant improvement if the law of rape in any state prohibited exactly the same threats as that state's law of extortion and exactly the same deceptions as that state's law of false pretences or fraud.

In short, I am arguing that 'consent' should be defined so that 'no means no'. And the 'force' or 'coercion' that negates consent ought [to] be defined to include extortionate threats and deceptions of material fact. As for *mens rea*, unreasonableness as to consent, understood to mean ignoring a woman's words, should be sufficient for liability: reasonable men should be held to know that no means no, and unreasonable mistakes, no matter how honestly claimed, should not exculpate. Thus, the threshold of liability – whether phrased in terms of 'consent, force', or 'coercion', or some combination of the three, should be understood to include at least those nontraditional rapes where the woman says no or submits only in response to lies or threats which would be prohibited were money sought instead. The crime I have described would be a lesser offence than the aggravated rape in which life is threatened or bodily injury inflicted, but it is, in my judgment, 'rape'. One could, I suppose, claim that as we move from such violent rapes to 'just' coerced or nonconsensual sex, we are moving away from a crime of violence toward something else. But what makes the violent rape different – and more serious – than an aggravated assault is the injury to personal integrity involved in forced sex. That same injury is the reason that forced sex should be a crime even when there is no weapon or no beating. In a very real sense, what does make rape different from other crimes, at every level of the offence, is that rape is about sex and sexual violation. Were the essence of the crime the use of the gun or the knife or the threat, we wouldn't need – and wouldn't have – a separate crime.

Crime is labelled as criminal 'to announce to society that these actions are not to be done and to secure that fewer of them are done'.[99] As a matter of principle, we should be ready to announce to society our condemnation of coerced and nonconsensual sex and to secure that we have less of it. The message of the substantive law to men, and to women, should be made clear.

That does not mean that this crime will, or should, be easy to prove. The constitutional requirement of proof beyond a reasonable doubt may well be difficult to meet in cases where guilt turns on whose account is credited as to what was said. If the jury is in doubt, it should acquit. If the judge is uncertain, he should dismiss.

The message of the substantive law must be distinguished from the constitutional standards of proof. In this as in every criminal case, a jury must be told to acquit if it is in doubt. The requirement of proof beyond reasonable doubt rests on the premise that it is better than ten guilty should go free than that one innocent man should be punished. But if we should acquit ten, let us be clear that we are acquitting them not because they have an entitlement to ignore a woman's words, not because what they allegedly did was right or macho or manly, but because we live in a system that errs on the side of freeing the guilty.[100]

AGAINST OUR WILL: MEN, WOMEN, AND RAPE[101]
Susan Brownmiller

Evan Connell, a novelist of some repute, wrote a *tour de force* some years ago entitled *The Diary of a Rapist*. Connell's protagonist, Early Summerfield, was a timid, white, middle-class civil-service clerk, age twenty-seven, who had an inferiority complex, delusions of intellectual brilliance, a wretched, deprived sex life, and an older, nagging, ambitious, 'castrating' wife. Connell's book made gripping reading, but the portrait of Earl Summerfield was far from an accurate picture of an average real-life rapist. In fact, Connell's *Diary* contains almost every myth and misconception about rape and rapists that is held in the popular mind. From the no-nonsense FBI statistics and some intensive sociological studies that are beginning to appear, we can see that the typical American rapist is no weirdo, psycho schizophrenic beset by timidity, sexual deprivation, and a domineering wife or mother. Although the psycho rapist, whatever his family background, certainly does exist, just as the psycho murderer certainly does exist, he is the exception and not the rule. The typical American perpetrator of forcible rape is little more than an aggressive, hostile youth who chooses to do violence to women.

---

99 HLA Hart *Punishment and Responsibility* (Oxford University Press, 1968), p 6.

100 *Rape*, pp 179–82.

101 New York: Simon & Schuster 1975; Reprint Fawcett 1993, Chapter 6.

We may thank the legacy of Freudian psychology for fostering a totally inaccurate popular conception of rape. Freud himself, remarkable as this may seem, said nothing about rapists. His confederates were slightly more loquacious, but not much. [Carl] Jung mentioned rape only in a few of his mythological interpretations. Alfred Adler, a man who understood the power thrust of the male and who was a firm believer in equal rights for women, never mentioned rape in any of his writings. [Helene] Deutsch and [Karen] Horney, two brilliant women, looked at rape only from the psychology of the victim.

In the nineteen fifties a school of criminology arose that was decidedly pro-Freudian in its orientation and it quickly dominated a neglected field. but even among the Freudian criminologists there was a curious reluctance to tackle rape head on. The finest library of Freudian and Freudian-related literature, the AA Brill Collection, housed at the New York Psychoanalytic Institute, contains an impressive number of weighty tomes devoted to the study of exhibitionism (public exposure of the penis) yet no Freudian or psychoanalytic authority has ever written a major volume on rape. Articles on rape in psychology journals have been sparse to the point of nonexistence.

Why Freudians could never come to terms with rape is a puzzling question. It would not be too glib to suggest that the male bias of the discipline, with its insistence on the primacy of the penis, rendered it incapable of seeing the forest for the trees. And then, the use of the intuitive approach based largely on analysis of idiosyncratic case studies allowed for no objective sampling. But perhaps most critically, the serious failure of the Freudians stemmed from their rigid unwillingness to make a moral judgment. The major psychoanalytic thrust was always to 'understand' what they preferred to call 'deviant sexual behaviour' but never to condemn.

'Philosophically', write Dr Manfred Guttmacher in 1951, 'a sex offence is an act which offends the sex mores of the society in which the individual lives. And it offends chiefly because it generates anxiety among the members of that society. Moreover, prohibited acts generate the greatest anxiety in those individuals who themselves have strong unconscious desires to commit similar or related acts and who have suppressed or repressed them. These actions of others threaten our ego defences'.

This classic paragraph, I believe, explains most clearly the Freudian dilemma.

When the Freudian-orientated criminologists did attempt to grapple with rape they lumped the crime together with exhibitionism (their hands-down favourite!), homosexuality, prostitution, pyromania, and even oral intercourse, in huge, indigestible volumes that sometimes bore a warning notice on the flyleaf that the material contained herein might advisably be restricted to adults. Guttmacher's *Sex Offences* and Benjamin Karpman's *The Sexual Offender and His Offences* were two such products of the 'fifties. Reading through these and other volumes it is possible to stumble on a nugget of fact or a valuable insight, and we ought to keep in mind, I guess, how brave they must have seemed at the time. After all, they were dealing not only with s-e-x, but with aberrant s-e-x, and in their misguided way they were attempting to forge a new understanding. 'Moral opprobrium has no place in medical work', wrote Karpman. A fine sentiment, indeed, yet for one hundred pages earlier this same Karpman in this same book defined perversity as 'a sexual act that defies the biological goal of procreation'.

By and large the Freudian criminologists, who loved to quibble with one another, defined the rapist as a victim of an 'uncontrollable urge' that was 'infantile' in nature, the result of a thwarted 'natural' impulse to have intercourse with his mother. His act of rape was 'a neurotic overreaction' that stemmed from his 'feelings of inadequacy'. To sum up in the Freudian's favourite phrase, he was a 'sexual psychopath'. Rapists, wrote Karpman, were 'victims of a disease from which many of them suffer more than their victims'.

This, I should amend, was a picture of the Freudian's favourite rapist, the one they felt they might be able to treat. Dr Guttmacher, for one, was aware that other types of rapists existed but they frankly bored him. Some, he said, were 'sadistic', imbued with an exaggerated concept of masculine sexual activity, and some seemed 'like the soldier of a conquering army'. 'Apparently', he wrote, 'sexually well-adjusted youths have in one night committed a series of burglaries and, in the course of one of them, committed rape – apparently just as another act of plunder'.

Guttmacher was chief medical officer for the Baltimore criminal courts. His chilling passing observation that rapists might be sexually well-adjusted youths was a reflection of his Freudian belief in the supreme rightness of male dominance and aggression, a common theme that runs through Freudian-orientated criminological literature. But quickly putting the 'sexually well-adjusted youths' aside, Guttmacher dove into clinical studies of two rapists put at his disposal who were more to his liking. Both were mail-biters and both had 'nagging mothers'. One had an undescended testicle. In his dreary record of how frequently they masturbated and wet their beds, he never bothered to write down what they thought of women.

Perhaps the quintessential Freudian approach to rape was a 1954 Rorschach study conducted on the *wives* of eight, count 'em eight, convicted rapists, which brought forth this sweeping indictment from one of the authors, the eminent psychoanalyst and criminologist Dr David Abrahamsen:

> The conclusions reached were that the wives of the sex offenders on the surface behaved towards men in a submissive and masochistic way but latently denied their femininity and showed an aggressive masculine orientation; they unconsciously invited sexual aggression, only to respond to it with coolness and rejection. They stimulated their husbands into attempts to prove themselves, attempts which necessarily ended in frustration and increased their husband's own doubts about their masculinity. In doing so, the wives unknowingly continued the type of relationship the offender had with his mother. There can be no doubt that the sexual frustration which the wives caused is one of the factors motivating rape, which might be tentatively described as a displaced attempt to force a seductive but rejecting mother into submission.

In the nineteen-sixties, leadership in the field of criminology passed to the sociologists, and a good thing it was. Concerned with measuring the behaviour of groups and their social values, instead of relying on extrapolation from individual case studies, the sociologists gave us charts, tables, diagrams, theories of social relevance, and, above all, hard, cold statistical facts about crime. (Let us give credit where credit is due. The rise of computer technology greatly facilitated this kind of research.)

In 1971 Menachem Amir, an Israeli sociologist and a student of Marvin E Wolfgang, America's leading criminologist, published a study of rape in the city of Philadelphia, begun ten years before. *Patterns of Forcible Rape*, a difficult book for those who choke on methodological jargon, was annoyingly obtuse about the culturally conditioned behaviour of women in situations involving the threat of force, but despite its shortcomings the Philadelphia study was an eye-opener. It was the first pragmatic, in-depth statistical study of the nature of rape and rapists. Going far beyond the limited vision of the police and the [FBI's] *Uniform Crime Reports*, or the idiosyncratic concerns of the Freudians, Amir fed his computer such variables as *modus operandi*, gang rape versus individual rape, economic class, prior relationships between victim and offender, and both racial and interracial factors. For the first time in history the sharp-edged profile of the typical rapist was allowed to emerge. It turned out that he was, for the most part, an unextraordinary, violence-prone fellow.

Marvin Wolfgang, Amir's mentor at the University of Pennsylvania's school of criminology, deserves credit for the theory of the 'sub-culture of violence', which he developed at length in his own work. An understanding of the subculture of violence is critical to an understanding of the forcible rapist. 'Social class', wrote Wolfgang, 'looms large in all studies of violent crime'. Wolfgang's theory, and I must oversimplify, is that within the dominant value system of our culture there exists a subculture formed of those from the lower classes, the poor, the disenfranchised, the black, whose values often run counter to those of the dominant culture, the people in charge. The dominant culture can operate within the laws of civility because it has little need to resort to violence to get what it wants. The subculture, thwarted, inarticulate and angry, is quick to resort to violence; indeed, violence and physical aggression become a common way of life. Particularly for young males.

Wolfgang's theory of crime, and unlike other theories his is soundly based on statistical analysis, may not appear to contain all the answers, particularly the kind of answers desired by liberals who want to excuse crimes of violence strictly on the basis of social inequities in the system, but Wolfgang would be the first to say that social injustice is one of the root causes of the subculture of violence. His theory also would not satisfy radical thinkers who prefer to interpret all violence as the product of the governmental hierarchy and its superstructure of repression.

But there is no getting around the fact that most of those who engage in antisocial, criminal violence (murder, assault, rape and robbery) come from the lower socio-economic classes; and that because of their historic oppression the majority of black people are contained within the lower socio-economic classes and contribute to crimes of violence in numbers disproportionate to their population ratio in the census figures *but not disproportionate* to their position on the economic ladder.

We are not talking about Jean Valjean, who stole a loaf of bread in *Les Miserables*, but about physical aggression as 'a demonstration of masculinity and toughness' – this phrase is Wolfgang's – the prime tenet of the subculture of violence. Or, to use a current phrase, the *machismo* factor. Allegiance or conformity to machismo, particularly in a group or gang, is the *sine qua non* of status, reputation and identity for lower-class male young. Sexual aggression, of course, is a major part of *machismo*.

The single most important contribution of Amir's Philadelphia study was to place the rapist squarely within the subculture of violence. The rapist, it was revealed, had no separate identifiable pathology aside from the individual quirks and personality disturbances that might characterise any single offender who commits any sort of crime.

The patterns of rape that Amir was able to trace were drawn from the central files of the Philadelphia police department for 1958 and 1960, a total of 646 cases and 1,292 offenders.[102] One important fact that Amir' study revealed right off the bat was that in 43% of the Philadelphia cases, the rapists operated in pairs or groups, giving the lie to one of the more commonly held myths that the rapist is a secretive, solitary offender.

The median age of the Philadelphia rapist was twenty-three, but the age group most likely to commit rape was the fifteen to nineteen bracket. A preponderant number of the Philadelphia rapists were not married, a status attributable to their youthful age. Ninety per cent of the Philadelphia rapists 'belonged to the lower part of the occupational scale', in descending order 'from skilled workers to the unemployed'. Half of the Philadelphia rapists had a prior arrest record, and most of these had the usual run of offences, such as burglary, robbery, disorderly conduct and assault. Only 9% of those with prior records had been previously arrested for rape. In other words, rapists were in the mould of the typical youthful offender ...

'Contrary to past impression', Amir wrote, 'analysis reveal that 71% of the rapes were planned'. This observation was another of Amir's most significant contributions to the study of rape. Far from being a spontaneous explosion by an individual with pent-up emotions and uncontrollable lusts, he discovered the act was usually planned in advance and elaborately arranged by a single rapist of a group of buddies. In some cases the lone rapist or the gang had a particular victim in mind and coolly took the necessary steps to lure her into an advantageous position. In other cases the decision to rape was made in advance by a gang, a pair of cohorts, or a lone-wolf rapist, but selection of the female was left to chance. Whoever happened by and could be seized, coerced or enticed to a favourable place became the victim. As might be expected, almost all group rapes in Philadelphia police files were found to have been planned. As a matter of fact, advance planning and coordination proved absolutely essential to the commission of gang rape. A 'secure' place had to located; precautions had to be taken to guarantee that the rape-in-progress would remain undetected by passers-by, police or neighbours; and selection of the victim had to be agreed upon by the group.

Group rape may be defined as two or more men assaulting one women. As I have mentioned, Amir found that in 43% of his Philadelphia cases the female victim had two or more assailants. A Toronto survey came up with a figure of 50%. A Washington, DC, study reported 30%. In Toronto and Philadelphia, rapists who operated in groups accounted for 71% of the total number of offenders.

'Whatever may be the causal explanation, these results are amazing', wrote Amir, a man not given to hyperbole. The sociologist expressed this astonishment because psychiatric literature on rape had treated the phenomenon of group rape 'with silence'. Police departments, as a rule, do not tally group-rape statistics for public consumption and the FBI's *Uniform Crime Reports* do not analyse such information.

When men rape in pairs or in gang, the sheer physical advantage of their position is clear-cut and unquestionable. No simple conquest of man over

---

102 Amir's data was based on statistical information about all reported rapes that the police felt were founded'. Amir did not include cases of attempted rape, but he did include profiles of 'known' offenders who were never apprehended. The sociologist used 'known' to mean 'undeniably existing', not necessarily 'known to the police'. Of the 1,292 offenders that form the basis of Amir's study, only 845 men were actually arrested.

women, group rape is the conquest of men over Woman. It is within the phenomenon of group rape, stripped of the possibility of equal combat, that the male ideology of rape is most strikingly evident. Numerical odds are proof of brutal intention. they are proof, too, of male bonding, to borrow a phrase made popular by Lionel Tiger, and proof of a desire to humiliate the victim beyond the act of rape through the process of anonymous mass assault ...

... Amir deals with what he politely calls 'sexual humiliation' in his Philadelphia study. Ignoring such acts as urination, ejaculation into the victim's face and hair, and other defilements – perhaps they did not appear in the Philadelphia police reports – he does deal with the incidence of forced cunnilingus, fellatio and 'pederasty' or 'sodomy'. By these two last imprecise terms I think he was referring to anal penetration He concludes that 'these are not the acts of an "impotent", which the psychiatric school so emphatically suggests'.

Including repeated intercourse in his definition of 'sexual humiliation' Amir found that in more than one-quarter of his cases the victim was subjected to some form of extra insult beyond the simple rape. Sexual humiliation ran higher in group rapes than in individual rapes, and the most common form of extra insult in group rape was repeated intercourse. Amir remarked, 'Taking repeated turns is part of what group rape can "offer" to the participants'.

As the act of intercourse itself is deliberately perverted in rape by forcing it on an unwilling participant, so, too, the purpose of any sidebar activity is to further humiliate and degrade, and not to engage in sophisticated erotics. (The purpose is never to satisfy the victim). At best, fringe defilements can be in the nature of clinical experiments performed by initiates who are convinced that all sex is dirty and demeaning. Not surprisingly in Amir's study, when it came to oral sex, few rapists showed interest in cunnilingus. What they demanded was fellatio done on them. What these rapists were looking for was another avenue or orifice by which to invade and thus humiliate their victim's physical integrity, her private inner space ...

... As ... defined by the statistical profiles of the sociologists and the FBI, America's police-blotter rapists are dreary and banal. To those who know them, no magic, no mystery, no Robin Hood bravura, infuses their style. Rape is a dull, blunt, ugly act committed by punk kinds, their cousins and older brothers, not by charming, witty, unscrupulous, heroic, sensual rakes, or by timid souls deprived of a 'normal' sexual outlet, or by *super-menschen* possessed of uncontrollable lust. And yet, on the shoulders of these unthinking, predictable, insensitive, violence-prone young men there rests an age-old burden that amounts to an historic mission: the perpetuation of male domination over women by force.

The Greek warrior Achilles used a swarm of men descended from ants, the Myrmidons, to do his bidding as hired henchmen in battle. Loyal and unquestioning, the Myrmidons served their master well, functioning in anonymity as effective agents of terror. Police-blotter rapists in a very real sense perform a myrmidon function for all men in our society. Cloaked in myths that obscure their identity, they, too, function as anonymous agents of terror. Although they are the ones who do the dirty work, the actual *attentat*, to other men, their superiors in class and station, the lasting benefits of their simple-minded evil have always accrued.

A world without rapists would be a world in which women moved freely without fear of men. That *some* men rape provides a sufficient threat to keep all women in a constant state of intimidation, forever conscious of the knowledge that the biological tool must be held in awe, for it may turn to weapon with sudden swiftness born of harmful intent. Myrmidons to the cause of male dominance, police-blotter rapists have performed their duty well, so well in fact that the true meaning of their act has largely gone unnoticed. Rather than society's aberrants or 'spoilers of purity', men who commit rape have served in effect as front-line masculine shock troops, terrorist guerrillas in the longest sustained battle the world has ever known.

DOMESTIC VIOLENCE

While domestic violence may of course include rape, which has been considered above, in this section we examine the broader problem of occasional and/or systematic sustained physical or psychological violence within the home. As with other instances of domination and subordination between the sexes, the cultural, historical and now traditional explanations for such conduct must be borne in mind. Domestic violence – whether physical or psychological – manifests itself most frequently and regularly as violence against women. Domestic violence, whilst undoubtedly existing from time immemorial, became recognised by law as a problem to be addressed only in the 1970s, with the raising of women's consciousness and the movement for freedom from sexual, patriarchal, oppression. In large measure the work of Erin Pizzey, author and founder of the Chiswick Women's Refuge, was responsible for much of the legislative and other activity in the 1970s in England. Her book, *Scream Quietly or the Neighbours Will Hear*, represented a chilling account of the experiences of women in dealing with violent partners, and also revealed starkly the inadequacies of the avenues of legal redress and protection from such conduct.

Domestic violence is not, of course, confined to Western society – as a phenomenon it is as timeless and universal as patriarchy and society itself. The United Nations' 1990 Report, *The World's Women: Trends and Statistics*,[103] states that:

> Domestic violence, the dark side of family life, is inflicted on a family's weakest members – women, children, the very old and the disabled. It manifests itself in habitual physical abuse, psychological torture, deprivation of basic needs and sexual molestation. Secrecy, insufficient evidence and social and legal barriers continue to make it difficult to acquire accurate data on domestic violence against women, which many criminologists believe to be the most underreported crime. Most data on violence against women are compiled from small studies, giving only a glimpse of what is assumed to be a world-wide phenomenon. They can not be used to provide precise indicators on the extent of violence against women, but they do show that violence in the home is common and that women are most frequently the victims.

> Domestic violence against women exists in all regions, classes and cultures. the United Nations Secretariat's Division for the Advancement of Women compiled available information of domestic violence in 36 countries in the mid-1980s:

> • In Austria in 1985, domestic violence against the wife was cited as a contributing factor to the breakdown of the marriage in 59% of 1,500 divorce cases. Of those instances, 38% of working-class wives called the police in

---

103 HMSO, 1990. See also Chapter 12 for further statistics on the response of the United Nations towards gender-based violence.

response to battering, while only 13% of middle-class women and 4% of upper-class women did.

- In Colombia during 1982 and 1983, the Forensic Institute of Bogota found that of 1,170 cases of bodily injuries, one of five was due to conjugal violence – and 94% of those hospitalised were battered women.

- India had 999 registered cases of dowry deaths in 1985, 1,319 in 1986 and 1,786 in 1987.[104]

- Of 153 Kuwaiti women asked if they had ever been assaulted, a third answered yes. Asked if they knew of friends or relatives who had been victims of such violence, 80% responded yes.

- In Thailand, 25% of the malnourished children at a Bangkok rehabilitation centre treated during the first half of 1985 were from families where the mother was regularly beaten by her spouse. More than 50% of married women studied from Bangkok's biggest slum and construction sites were beaten regularly by their husbands.

- In the United States of America in 1984, 2,928 people were killed by a family members. Of female homicide victims alone, nearly a third died at the hands of a husband or partner. Husbands were responsible for 20% of women killed in 1984, while boyfriends were the offenders in 10% of the cases.[105]

Susan Atkins and Brenda Hoggett explain the legal position regarding domestic violence in England:

WOMEN AND THE LAW[106]

The Breadwinner's Lawful Authority

Where two people are one in the eyes of the law, whatever the degree of formal authority enjoyed by one over the other there can be no remedy between them should a husband abuse it. The secular courts began to allow a wife to 'swear the peace' against her husband early in the seventeenth century. Originally, as with child-beating today, there was an exception for *moderate castigation*, but towards the end of the century it was held that this meant not beating but only admonition and confinement in cases of extravagance.[107] It was still admitted that 'where a wife makes undue use of her liberty, either by squandering her husband's estate or going into lewd company, it is lawful for the husband to preserve his honour and estate to lay her under restraint.'[108] A similar view appears in Blackstone.[109] But the 1832 edition of Bacon's *Abridgement* was still quoting the earlier statements allowing moderate punishment, along with the right of restraint. It is scarcely surprising that courts and people alike were confused as to the extent to which husbands could enforce their commands.[110]

There was no doubt during most of the nineteenth century that a husband could use self-help to enforce his wife's primary obligations towards him. In *Re*

---

104 On which see further Chapter 2.

105 United Nations, *The World's Women*, pp 19–20.

106 Basil Blackwell, 1984.

107 *Lord Leigh's Case* (1674) 3 Keb 433.

108 *R v Lister* (1723) 1 Strange 478.

109 Sir W Blackstone *Commentaries on the Laws of England* (Clarendon Press, 1765), p 445.

110 M Ma, 'Violence in the Family: an Historical Perspective', in JP Martin (ed), *Violence and the Family* (Chichester: Wiley, 1978).

Cochrane[111] a wife was refused *habeas corpus* to enable her to escape from a husband who trapped her in his apartment and confined her there in order to prevent her living separately from him. Courts had earlier refused to grant *habeas corpus* to two husbands who wished to force their wives to return, but in each case the wife had some excuse for her departure. One husband had agreed to her living apart in consideration of a large sum from her separate property.[112] Another had treated her with cruelty.[113] Not until *R v Leggatt ex parte Sandilands*[114] was *habeas corpus* refused to a husband on the clear ground that he had no right to the custody of his wife, so that even if she had no good cause for living apart, his remedy was in the ecclesiastical or matrimonial courts rather than at common law, and in *R v Jackson*[115] the court took away the husband's right of self-help and granted *habeas corpus* to release a wife whose husband had behaved in almost exactly the same way as had Mr Cochrane half a century earlier. Even then the court reserved the possibility that restraint might be lawful in extreme situations, as where she was just about to leave him for another man. The best part of another century elapsed before a husband who behaved as Mr Cochrane and Mr Jackson had done was convicted of the common law offence of kidnapping and sentenced to three years' imprisonment.[116] There are still circumstances in which a husband is entitled to use self-help to enforce the wife's duty to have sexual intercourse with him.[117]

Thus the husband's rights of coercion went hand in hand with his rights of possession. A striking feature of many of the reported cases in criminal and family law is the continuing desire of the husband to possess a wife who has made it quite clear that she wants nothing more to do with him. Where they were still together, Dobash and Dobash found that 44% of the arguments which preceded a violent attack were triggered by the husband's jealousy.[118]

Husband and wife remain under a mutual duty to live together unless released. Although the strict scheme of matrimonial rights and duties has now been abandoned, a wife's reasons for wanting to live apart from her husband will be relevant to the regulation of their rights to occupy the matrimonial home, to any claim for financial relief or personal protection and to the ground for divorce. Hence it is one thing to deny the husband the right to coerce his wife and another thing to grant her the right to escape from him. As Mill commented, 'it is contrary to reason and experience to suppose that there can be any real check to brutality, consistent with leaving the victim in the power of the executioner.'[119] Thus, although physical violence has long been a valid excuse for the wife to leave and a good ground for obtaining relief, the courts' approach to its interpretation may still be relevant.[120]

---

111 (1840) 8 Dowl PC 630.

112 *R v Mead* (1758) 1 Burr 542.

113 *R v A Brooke and Thomas Fladgate* (1766) 4 Burr 1991.

114 (1852) 18 QB 781.

115 [1891] 1 QB 671.

116 *R v Reid* [1973] QB 299.

117 But see now the revised position regarding rape within marriage, discussed above.

118 Dobash and Dobash, *Violence Against Wives*, p 245.

119 JS Mill *The Subjection of Women* (1869), p 251.

120 *Women and the Law*, pp 127–28.

Female victims and the legal process

Consistent with the treatment of woman as the 'other', as 'different', 'unequal' and subordinated in society, the legal process itself reveals evidence of bias which is reflected in legal judgments; in defences which the law permits to be advanced for certain crimes, and in the sentencing of women. In this section the evidence is examined.

In the case of a man on trial for alleged murder of a woman, the conduct, lifestyle and personality of the woman are central to the question of the guilt or innocence of the man. However, when women are on trial for the alleged murder of their male partner, the same consideration apply in relation to the women, but not to the male victim. Two, now seminal cases, will be considered here in order to reveal the difficulties under which female defendants labour in establishing a defence to murder of their male partners. In the case of *R v Ahluwalia* the defendant had suffered years of violent abuse at the hands of her husband. Rather than striking back when attacked, however, she bided her time and only when he was asleep did she attack and kill him.[121] In the later case of *R v Thornton*[122] a similar factual situation existed. Sara Thornton had again endured years of violence at the hands of her husband. When ultimately her ability to cope with the sustained abuse snapped, Sara Thornton waited until her husband had fallen asleep and then stabbed him to death. She was convicted of murder and sentenced to life imprisonment, the court ruling that the defence of provocation was unavailable by virtue of the fact that Sara Thornton had not reacted instantly to the provocation of her husband. 'Cumulative provocation' under English law, unlike Australian law, has not yet been recognised.

The deficiency of English criminal law in relation to victims of domestic violence is all too apparent from the cases of Kimaljit Ahluwalia and Sara Thornton. The refusal of the law to recognise the physical and psychological inability for an immediate provoked response to violence, led, in these and other cases, to the victim being cast into jail for murder. In both cases, the victims were ultimately released. In *Ahluwalia*'s case, Kimaljit Ahluwalia's conviction was reduced to manslaughter and she was released, having served at adequate period of imprisonment. In *Sara Thornton*'s case, however, events have taken a different course, which may possibly have a constructive outcome for the victims of domestic violence. The Secretary of State for the Home Department referred the matter to the Court of Appeal. The Court of Appeal quashed Thornton's conviction for murder and has ordered a retrial, on the basis that in the absence of full medical evidence as to Thornton's 'personality disorder' and suffering caused by 'battered women's syndrome',[123] the decision of the jury could not be regarded as 'safe and satisfactory'.

If the legal system has hitherto been either blind or unsympathetic to the problems of women trapped into violent and ultimately fatal relationships, the

---

121 In May 1989.

122 1990.

123 On which see below.

system demonstrates an unremitting harshness when the issue of liability for rape and violence is considered. As with victims of 'ordinary', 'domestic' violence, rape victims are themselves on trial in the courtroom. Moreover, judicial reactions to rape victims has included breathtaking illustrations of traditional patriarchal attitudes, which indicate that the male personnel of the legal system are far from the required rational objectivity required of the judiciary where sexual offences are concerned. Helena Kennedy QC has examined such attitudes.[124] the author cites Sir Melford Stevenson being lenient in sentencing a rapist on the basis that the victim, a sixteen year old, had been hitch-hiking; Mr Justice Jupp in 1990 passing a suspended sentence on a husband who had twice raped his wife on the basis of some (curious) distinction between rape within the home and rape by a stranger; Mr Justice Leonard passing a reduced sentence on the perpetrators of a violent multiple rape on the basis that the victim had made a 'remarkable recovery'.[125] Perhaps most notorious of all are the words of Judge Wile, in his directions to a jury in 1982:

> Women who say no do not always mean no. It is not just a question of how she says it, how she shows and makes it clear. If she doesn't want it she only has to keep her legs shut and she would not get it without force and then there would be the marks of force being used.[126]

In the case of a man on trial for alleged murder of a woman, the conduct, lifestyle and personality of the woman are central to the question of guilt or innocence of the man, as the extract above demonstrates. However, when women are on trial for the alleged murder of their male partner, the same considerations apply in relation to the woman, but not to the male victim.

In the article which follows, which was written before Sarah Thornton's successful appeal, Susan Edwards analyses the traditional attitude of the English courts to battered women's syndrome.

BATTERED WOMAN SYNDROME[127]

Susan Edwards

On Friday, September 25, 1992, Kiranjit Ahluwalia, a battered wife serving life for murder, was freed after the prosecution accepted her plea to diminished responsibility following new evidence. The judge, Mr Justice Hobbouse, imposed a prison sentence of three years and four months, exactly the length of time she had already served. This new evidence detailed the effects of long term battering, a condition known and accepted in legal circles in the USA, Canada and Australia as the battered woman syndrome. The syndrome is something akin to a state of fear, trauma and shock, characterised by anxiety and depression, a perception that death is likely, a total inability to escape and a feeling of helplessness.

This recognition by the Court of Appeal of such a state of mind in women who have been subject to battering will have three consequences. First, in future cases

---

124 See Helena Kennedy, *Eve Was Framed* (Vintage, 1993).

125 See *ibid*, pp 120–21.

126 *Ibid*, p 110.

127 (1992) *New Law Journal*, 1350.

coming before the courts, expert testimony on the long term psychological effects of battering will now be admissible, and as a result such 'offenders' will pursue a defence of diminished responsibility rather than attempting to advance a defence under provocation.

Secondly, in future cases the defence may wish to pursue a defence of diminished responsibility and provocation together given that the presence of the battered woman syndrome may well influence her response to the last act of provocation, however slight.

Thirdly, the acceptance of this new evidence will now make it essential that battered women currently serving prison sentences who have killed, such as Sara Thornton, be allowed the same opportunity to have expert opinion on the battered woman syndrome put before the court in assessing whether their responsibility was diminished in this same way. Under s 17 of the Criminal Appeal Act 1968, referrals via the Home Secretary back to the Court of Appeal on the grounds of fresh evidence must now be inevitable in such cases. During the last few months none of the appeals on behalf of battered women convicted of the murder have challenged the very bedrock of the common law on provocation in the way Lord Gifford and Geoffrey Robertson in *Thornton* and *Ahluwalia* in the appeal court succeeded in doing. In these cases, counsel sought to interpret the definition of provocation beyond the immediacy principle, introducing under certain circumstances the concept of the 'slow burn'. In *Ahluwalia*, counsel proposed that experience of battering so characterised the accused that it should be adduced as a 'notional characteristic'.

In *Thornton*,[128] Lord Gifford QC was unable to persuade the Court of Appeal of the slow burn and the earlier failure to convince the trial jury of evidence of diminished responsibility meant that a conviction for murder was upheld. Lord Gifford raised three grounds of appeal. He contended that the judge had misdirected the jury on the issue of provocation. On this point Gifford sought to argue that the court had interpreted her delay in reacting as a 'cooling off' period when it should have regarded this apparent delay as one of 'chronic boiling over'. The defence of provocation he said:

'... is apt to describe the sudden rage of a male, but not the slow burning emotion suffered by a woman driven to the end of her tether.'

He went on to argue that the Homicide Act s 3, when read together with the judgment in *DPP v Camplin*,[129] *per* Lord Morris, meant that Devlin's interpretation in *Duffy*[130] did not have to be slavishly followed (at 313 g). Secondly, Gifford contended that the trial judge had misdirected the jury on diminished responsibility. Thirdly, that the conviction of the appellant was unsafe and unsatisfactory because counsel at the trial failed to advance the defence of provocation as an alternative to, or in addition to, the defence of diminished responsibility.[131]

Beldam LJ delivering the judgment of the court did not accede to this argument on provocation.[132]

---

128 *R v Thornton* [1992] 1 All ER 306–317, 29 July 1991.

129 [1978] 2 All ER at 721.

130 [1949].

131 At p 308 f–g.

132 At 313 j.

However, the court held that domestic violence '... might be considered by the jury as part of the context or background against which the accused's reaction to provocative conduct had to be judged'.[133] Accordingly, the judge had not misdirected the jury and the decision of her legal advisers to concentrate on diminished responsibility did not raise a lurking doubt.

Some saw *Thornton* as a setback since the court dug its heels in and was determined not to retreat from the immediacy principle in *Duffy*. But there was some small progress made nonetheless. The interpretation of provocation brought from the background into the foreground the history of battering, and where such a history of battering was present – when taken together with other similar provocative acts over a period of time – would allow from thenceforward a defence of provocation, however slight the last provocative act, and therefore had consequences for reasonableness. But it was the case of Kiranjit Ahluwalia, convicted of murder on December 7, 1989 which was to become a legal landmark in the evolution of principles relating to provocation and diminished responsibility.

Subjected to years of abuse by her husband Deepak, she 'set fire to the bedding', so that he could not run after her and hurt her again. She said, 'I didn't intend to kill him or cause him really serious injury'. She was convicted of murder; a defence of provocation having failed. At the appeal hearing Geoffrey Robertson QC raised three grounds, The first two related to the trial judge's direction to the jury on provocation. Mr Robertson, like Lord Gifford in *Thornton*, argued that the *Duffy* direction is wrongly based upon a failure to understand and comprehend the true meaning and impact of s 3 as explained by the House of Lords in *DPP v Camplin*,[134] where Lord Diplock referred to that section as abolishing'... all previous rules of what can or cannot amount to provocation'.

Relying on expert evidence not before the trial judge, it was argued that women who have been subjected over a long period to violent treatment may react to the final act or words by a 'slow burn' reaction (cumulative provocation) rather than by an immediate loss of self control (NLJ p 1159). The second ground of appeal raised the question of the treatment of the appellant's characteristics, that is the 'notional characteristic'.

The judge's direction to the jury contained this passage:

> 'The only characteristics of the defendant about which you know specifically that might be relevant are that she is an Asian woman, married, incidentally to an Asian man, the deceased, living in this country.'

This ground of appeal turned on the very characteristic the judge ignored, that is, the evidence of battering in the battered woman syndrome as a 'notional characteristic. within the meaning of Lord Diplock's formulation. The third ground of appeal related to diminished responsibility and new, evidence based on psychiatric reports and expert evidence. The Court rejected the first two grounds although the third ground was considered sufficient to order a retrial, an unprecedented step since there have been no retrials in the years 1987–1990.[135] At the Old Bailey before Mr Justice Hobhouse, the prosecution

---

133 At 307 c.

134 [1978] 2 All ER 168.

135 Criminal Statistics, Supplementary Tables Vol 4.

accepted the plea to diminished responsibility on the grounds of the presence of the battered woman syndrome. What makes this case a landmark?

For the first time, in a case where a battered woman kills her husband the court has taken on board as of legal relevance evidence of the psychological effects on her state of mind of living in a battering relationship. This is not the first time, however, that evidence of battered woman syndrome has been put before the court. It has always been difficult for jurors and for the court to understand how a woman can apparently stand by whilst the child in her care is being physically or sexually abused by her partner or by the child's father.

There has been a catalogue of such cases from Kimberley Carlisle onwards. In January 1992, Sally Emery stood trial with her boyfriend for the ill treatment of her child, who died as a result. Helena Kennedy QC, counsel for Emery in her defence introduced expert testimony evidence of battered woman syndrome to assist the court in comprehending her incapacity to act and paralysis in the protection of her own daughter. She was sentenced to four years for failure to protect.

Similarly, in the USA the trial of *People v Steinberg*[136] where a middle class lawyer physically abused his lover's child resulting in her death left the public and the jury horrified by the mother's incapacity to prevent her own child from harm. The jury were to learn that the mother was horrifically physically abused and totally under his will to such a degree that she was incapable of independent action.

Whilst the decision in *Ahluwalia* is a landmark and a personal triumph, there are problems in setting up a battered woman's defence along these lines. For women in similar circumstances can it really be said that they are suffering from diminished responsibility within the meaning of the Homicide Act? Alternatively, as Geoffrey Robertson tried to argue, is evidence of battering over a long period a 'notional characteristic' within a defence of provocation?

Either way, the effects of battering do not fit squarely in either legal camp. And, if we listen to the vocabulary of motives and justifications of battered women who kill, they talk in language of self defence, not cumulative provocation and not of mental impairment. Sara Thornton clearly perceived imminent danger. Thornton: 'Do you know what he has done to me in the past?', Investigator: 'Did he beat you up tonight?' Thornton: 'No'. Investigator: 'Did he threaten to?' Thornton: 'He would have'. And later in the interview, Thornton: 'I'll kill you before you ever get a chance to kill me'. Helena Kennedy QC in *Eve Was Framed*[137] writes,

> Women invoke self defence or provocation defences infrequently, and the reason is that the legal standards were constructed from a male perspective and with men in mind ... women have a problem fulfilling the criteria.

The acknowledgement by the courts of the battered woman syndrome is one thing, but the direction of the step taken by the Court of Appeal is another. But there is no doubt that the 'syndrome' will continue in some shape or form to influence the development of legal principles in such cases.

In the Canadian case of *Lavallee v R*,[138] heard before the Supreme Court in Canada, the accused was tried for second degree murder of her common law

---

136 1989.

137 1992.

138 [1990] SCR 852, reversing (1988) 52 ManR (2d) 274, 44 CCC (3d) 113, 65 CR (3d) 387 (CA) (expert opinion).

spouse. At trial the defence of self defence was raised. A psychiatrist testified that when she committed the homicide she had a reasonable apprehension of death or grievous bodily harm because she was a battered woman and because her action was characteristic of the battered wife syndrome. She was acquitted. The Crown appealed to the Manitoba Court of Appeal and a new trial was ordered. On a further appeal to the Supreme Court, the court allowed the appeal and restored the jury's verdict of acquittal. The Supreme Court acceded that expert evidence was necessary:

'How can the mental state of the applicant be appreciated without it? The average member of the public (or of the jury) can be forgiven for asking: Why would a woman put up with this kind of treatment? Why should she continue to live with such a man? How could she love a partner who beat her to the point of requiring hospitalisation? We would expect the woman to pack her bags and go. Where is her self respect? Why does she not cut loose and make a new life for herself. Such is the reaction of the average person confronted with the so called battered wife syndrome'.[139]

Mme Wilson J stated:

> Where evidence exists that an accused is in a battering relationship, expert testimony can assist the jury in determining whether the accused has a reasonable apprehension of death when she acted by explaining the heightened sensitivity of a battered woman to her partner's acts. Without such testimony I am sceptical that the average fact finder would be capable of appreciating why her subject fear may have been responsible in the context of the relationship. The jury is not compelled to accept the opinions preferred by the expert without the effects of battering on the mental state of victims generally or on the mental state of the accused in particular. But fairness and integrity of the trial process demands that the jury have the opportunity to hear them.

However unsatisfactory the concept – and contradictions abound – since evidence of battering has been used to argue that women are immobilised, paralysed, unable to act and that women after a long course of conduct finally act and take positive steps where 'the worm turns', the matter of how the courts are to treat the battered woman who kills, in her words, in self defence is far from being resolved. The condition now recognised as battered woman syndrome gives women a voice, a language and legal recognition, but such women are far from being impaired in the manner the Homicide Act requires. The necessity to abolish the mandatory life sentence remains as urgent and pressing now as it has ever been, if justice is to be just and if punishment is to fit the crime.

IN DEFENCE OF BATTERED WOMEN WHO KILL[140]

Aileen McColgan[141]

Over the last number of years the commonplace nature of physical and sexual abuse within families has been increasingly brought into the public gaze. Women are much more likely to experience violence at the hands of their partners than from the strangers they are taught to fear, and many women who are killed are

---

139 At 112.
140 [1993] 13 *Oxford Journal of Legal Studies* 508. (Footnotes edited.)
141 At the time of writing Lecturer in Law, King's College, London.

killed by their husbands or lovers.[142] While the extent of private violence continues to be overlooked by measures such as the Child Support Act, the increasing recognition of its existence and, to a lesser extent perhaps, of the difficulties experienced by women who attempt to escape it, has focused attention upon the legal plight of battered women who kill their abusers.

One such woman was Sara Thornton. Her conviction for murder in February 1990, and more especially the rejection of her appeal,[143] caused a great deal of public unease. The apparent injustice of her plight was highlighted by the two-year suspended sentence imposed on Joseph McGrail two days after the rejection of her appeal. Freeing McGrail, who had kicked to death his alcoholic wife as she lay drunk, Popplewell J declared that she would have tried the patience of a saint. The law has been accused of sexism before and the *Thornton* case was far from unique. It seised the public imagination, however, led to as – yet unsuccessful attempts by Labour MPs Jack Ashley and Harry Cohen to alter the law on provocation, and has continued to resonate through media coverage of similar cases since. In doing so it has drawn attention to the apparently haphazard quality of justice experienced by battered women who kill: Sara Thornton received a life sentence for murder when she stabbed her violent, alcoholic husband after an argument during which he told her that he would kill her as she slept; Jane Scotland received a non-custodial sentence for man-slaughter when she bludgeoned her husband to death after 22 years of mental torture, physical ill-treatment and the sexual abuse of their daughter,[144] and Pamela Sainsbury received a two-year suspended sentence for manslaughter on the ground of diminished responsibility from a trial judge who took the view that her violent and jealous husband had psychologically paralysed her. More recently Kiranjit Ahluwalia's appeal against her murder conviction was allowed by the Court of Appeal on the ground that the trial judge had refused to admit evidence of the defendant's endogenous depression, presumably the result of continued battering.[145] A retrial was ordered and, her plea of diminished responsibility having been accepted by the prosecution on the grounds that she was suffering from battered woman syndrome , she was sentenced to three years and four months imprisonment, which time she had already served.[146]

In many cases there appears to be little to distinguish between killings which lead to non-custodial penalties and those which result in the mandatory life sentence for murder. While this is to a certain extent inevitable in a jury-based criminal justice system, the problem is aggravated in the context of battered women who kill by the inherent unsuitability of the partial defences of provocation and diminished responsibility upon which they presently rely.[147] Not all battered women who kill their abusers do so under the same circumstances: some strike back in the midst of physical attack; some in response

142 Home Office Statistics for 1990 show that, in 43% of UK homicides where the victim was female, the principal suspect was a partner. This figure was comparable with the figures for 1983–89, and can be contrasted with the 5% of male homicides where the principal suspect fell into this category.

143 *R v Thornton* [1992] 1 All ER 306.

144 (1992) *Independent*, 24 March.

145 *Ahluwalia* [1992] 4 All ER 889.

146 See discussion of *Ahluwalia* in Edwards, 'Battered Woman Syndrome' [1992] *NLJ* 1350, *supra*.

147 See A Ashworth, 'Sentencing in Provocation Cases' [1985] *Crim LR* 553 at 561 and J Horder, 'Sex, Violence and Sentencing in Domestic Provocation Cases' [1989] *Crim LR* 566.

to verbal threats – some use force in the aftermath of an attack or in anticipation of one; and others perhaps are motivated by feelings of revenge. This together with the very small number of defendants concerned makes generalisations difficult, and the nature of the defence or partial defence most appropriately pleaded by each will depend on the exact circumstances of her case. This paper will seek to argue, however, that self-defence (whether at common law or under s 3 of the Criminal Law Act 1967) should be more often considered as a possible defence even in those cases whose facts do not correspond with the traditional model of self-defence.

Proposals for improving the defence of battered women who kill in the UK tend to focus on the modification or re-interpretation[148] of the provocation defence, and a new approach to provocation would be of assistance to some battered women who kill. It will, however, be argued that self-defence more adequately reflects the facts of many cases and that, properly understood and applied, it may be more likely to result in an acquittal than either provocation or diminished responsibility would be to avoid a murder conviction. A movement towards the use of self-defence in situations other than those which involve traditionally paradigmatic applications of its principles would continue a trend started about ten years ago in the United States1[149] and which has also found favour more recently with the Supreme Court of Canada in *Lavallee*.[150] In some respects the current UK law of self-defence avails itself more readily to such an application than does the law in Canada or in many US jurisdictions, but such a movement involves a rethinking of the traditional view of self-defence and consideration of the possible use of expert evidence in the defence of battered women who kill. This latter point is particularly important in the light of the recent acceptance by the Court of Appeal of the admissibility of expert psychiatric evidence of the effects of continued battering. An attempt will be made here to transpose some of the Canadian and US reasoning into the UK context, to review the problems that have arisen, and to suggest how their repetition could be avoided here. Before turning to a discussion of self-defence and its potential for the defence of battered women who kill, however, the failure of the present law to provide even a partial defence for many such defendants will be briefly discussed.

The problems incurred by battered women killers who attempt to plead provocation have been documented elsewhere,[151] and this paper shall do no more than point to a few recent cases in which the defence has failed in order to illustrate its unsuitability for many women who kill abusive partners. The rule in *Duffy*[152] that the defendant's loss of self-control must be sudden and temporary in order to found the defence led to an unfavourable jury direction in *Thornton* where the defendant had left the scene of provocation and fetched a knife before returning and stabbing her husband.

---

148 S Yeo, 'Provocation Down Under' [1991] *NLJ* 1200; S Edwards, 'Battered Women who Kill' [1990] *NLJ* 1380; *cf* C Wells, 'Domestic Violence and Self-defence' [1990] *NLJ* 127.
149 See *People v Diaz No 2714* (Supreme Court Bronx Co, New York 1983), but *cf State v Stewart* 243 Kan 639.
150 [1990] 1 SCR 852. See J Castel in 'Discerning Justice for Battered Women who Kill' 48 *Toronto Faculty of Law Review* 229 at 231.
151 See S Edwards, *supra*; L Taylor, 'Provoked Passion in Men and Women: Heat-of-Passion Manslaughter and Imperfect Self-Defence' 33 *UCLA LR* 679.
152 [1949] 1 All ER 932.

In *Duffy*, a case itself concerned with homicide by a battered woman, the Court of Appeal approved the statement of Devlin J (as he then was) that a long course of conduct causing suffering and anxiety are not by themselves sufficient to constitute provocation, and that circumstances (such as a history of abuse) which induce a desire for revenge are inconsistent with provocation.[153] While the judge's power to determine the sufficiency of the provocation has since been removed by s 3 of the Homicide Act 1957 the Court of Appeal in *Thornton* expressed the view that the sudden and temporary requirement was particularly important in cases involving cumulative provocation in order to distinguish those who killed in the heat of passion from those who had time to reflect and regain control before killing deliberately. In *Ahluwalia* too, the Court of Appeal refused to jettison the sudden and temporary rule. Lord Taylor CJ ruled that the defence would not as a matter of law be negatived simply because of the delayed reaction in cases of women subjected frequently over a period to violent treatment, provided that at the time of the killing there was a sudden and temporary loss of self-control, but stated that it remained open to the judge to draw the attention of the jury to forward the position that the reasons for which they kill must be taken seriously in the determination of their criminal liability, that the traditional view of self-defence must not be allowed to prevent the application of its principles to appropriate cases where battered women kill, and that misinformed assumptions about women's responsibility in their own abuse must not be allowed to deny them justice.[154]

Pleading Self-Defence

Given the current ideal model of self-defence, it is clear that attention has to be drawn to its inequitable application to women who kill to protect themselves, in order that they may successfully plead self-defence in response to murder charges. In the absence of challenges to the common assumptions about when force is necessary in response to actual or threatened violence, and about the level of force which a woman might reasonably use against an unarmed man, such women will be unable to successfully plead self-defence. Judicial resistance to acquitting women in these circumstances is evident from US cases such as *State v Stewart* where the court ruled that, as a matter of law, the defendant could not plead self-defence when she killed her sleeping husband, taking the view that to allow such a plea would be to leap into the abyss of anarchy;.[155] from remarks made by UK judges which have illustrated an apparently wilful blindness to the realities of private violence;[156] and from the Australian development of the partial defence of provocation to cover typical cases of battered women killers. Julia Tolmie argues that the reluctance of the courts to categorise battered women's killings as self-defence is rooted partly in the ideology of family life:

> To recognise that women may be trapped and justified in fighting for their lives within the most intimate relationship validates many women's experiences in a way which threaten the ideology of familiness. The characterisation of the family as private can be seen instead to have operated to create a sphere in which women are isolated, rendered invisible and placed beyond the protection of the legal system. Recognising that many

---

153 See M Wasik, 'Cumulative Provocation and Domestic Killing' [1982] *Crim LR* 29.

154 *'In Defence of Battered Women Who Kill*, pp 508–14.

155 Note 64.

156 Note 65.

women find family life threatening also necessitates examining deep social structures and attitudes by which violence against women is institutionalised throughout our society ...[157]

This reluctance is all the more understandable in view of the fact that, in the words of Wilson J in *Lavallee*:

> Far from protecting women from it the law historically sanctioned the abuse of women within marriage as an aspect of the husband's ownership of his wife and his right to chastise her. One need only recall the centuries old law that a man is entitled to beat his wife with a stick no thicker than his thumb. ... One consequence of this attitude was that wife battering was rarely spoken of, rarely reported, rarely prosecuted, and even more rarely punished. Long after society abandoned its formal approval of spousal abuse tolerance of it continued and continues in some circles to this day.[158]

It was not until 1991 that the English courts, arguably contrary to the intention of legislation passed as recently as 1976, removed husbands' freedom to rape their wives[159] and the financial dependency historically forced upon women by their husbands automatic ownership of their goods still finds its existence in women's loss of entitlement upon cohabitation or marriage to most social security benefits. It is therefore essential, where women kill in response to a perceived threat from an abusive partner to their life or the lives of their children, that juries are made aware of the circumstances of the case, including the history of violence and its effects on the woman's perceptions of the threat violence, as well as to the effect of the relative disadvantages of many women in terms of passive socialisation and physical size, strength and training. This approach would not afford women defendants favourable legal treatment; it would, rather, go some way to addressing the prejudice against them that is built into the system by virtue of its development through typically male cases of self-defence. In the context of self-defence, then, the male standards of necessity and proportionality, together with the current failure adequately to address the reality of extreme violence under which many women exist, must be recognised and compensated for in the application of the self-defence standard to battered women who kill.

The decision of the Court of Appeal in *Ahluwalia* establishes that battered women may be able to adduce expert evidence of the psychiatric effects of continued abuse, but a successful plea of self-defence requires the recognition that a battered woman's perceptions of danger may be affected by her situation, rather than that that situation has rendered her psychiatrically abnormal. The difficulty lies in the refusal of the UK courts, following *Turner*,[160] to admit expert psychiatric evidence relating to defendants who were not suffering from an abnormal mental condition at the time of the alleged offence. In *Turner*, Lawton LJ stated that:

> If on the proven facts a judge or jury can form their own conclusion, then the opinion of an expert is unnecessary ... The fact that an expert witness has impressive qualifications does not by that fact alone make his opinion on matters of human nature and behaviour within the limits of normality any

---

157 J Tomie, 'Provocation or Self-Defence for Battered Women who Kill', in Yeo (ed), *Partial Excuses to Murder* (1991).

158 [1990] 1 SCR 852.

159 In *R v R* [1994] 4 All ER 481.

160 [1975] QB 834 at 841.

more helpful than that of the jurors themselves; but there is a danger that they may think it does.

The principle in *Turner* was applied to expert psychological evidence in *Neeson*, where the trial judge refused to admit evidence of the effects of mob hysteria on human behaviour (the defendants were charged with a number of offences arising out of the killing of two British Army officers at the funeral of an IRA man who had himself been assassinated at an earlier funeral). McCullom J ruled that the evidence, which was intended to explain the behaviour that might be engaged in by, or reactions that might occur in, unusual situations was inadmissible on the grounds that the jury were capable of forming their own conclusions about matters which are part of the sum of human experience and knowledge and are readily recognisable by ordinary people.[161]

If the reactions of a funeral crowd driven towards at speed several days after the person they had assembled to bury had himself been assassinated at another funeral is seen as being part of the sum of human experience and knowledge, it is unlikely that a court would accept that the same is not true of the reactions of a battered woman to the use or threat of physical force. Short of claiming that the battering has produced psychiatric abnormality sufficient to amount to diminished responsibility under s 2 of the Homicide Act, it is unlikely that defence counsel could persuade the courts that expert evidence of the effect of such abuse has anything to add to jurors understanding of a woman s perceptions of danger and the reasonableness of her response to it. Further, an examination of the US experience calls into doubt the potential value of such evidence even if it were to be deemed admissible by the UK courts in an extension of *Ahluwalia*.

Early US theorists such as Elizabeth Schneider argued that evidence of the psychological effects of repeated assaults could be utilised, together with lay evidence about the history of defendant and deceased, in order to combat the prejudice inherent in the traditionally male model of self-defence, to equalise the positions of male and female defendants by recognising their differences and to allow the question of reasonableness to be assessed in the light of all the circumstances relevant to the defendant.[162] In the event, however, decisions about whether or not to admit such evidence have often been based on the court's assessment of the reasonableness of the defendant's actions, testimony often being excluded in the non-traditional confrontation cases on the basis that the battered woman's behaviour was unreasonable.

In cases where the battered woman's act of self-defence took place in the context of actual physical assault, the US courts have admitted expert evidence of the effects of prolonged abuse apparently because they doubt the reasonableness of a battered woman's perception of danger.[163] Where such evidence has been admitted it has frequently been used to construct a stereotypical battered woman, rather than to counter the male perceptions of danger, immediacy and harm (which) inform the perception of what constitutes a reasonable physical response and to explain why a battered woman might reasonably perceive danger, use a deadly weapon, or fear bodily harm under circumstances in which

---

161 (1990) Belfast Crown Court, unreported. See Mackay and Colman, 'Excluding Expert Evidence: A Tale of Ordinary Folk and Common Experience' [1991] *Crim LR* 800.

162 E Schneider, note 55.

163 See *Smith v State* [1981] 247 Ba 612; *Strong v State* 251 Ga 540; *State v Borders* [1983] 433 So 2d 1325.

a man or non-battered woman might not. When women failed to fit the stereotype (where for example they had fought back before) the evidence would often then be put to one side and their conduct judged against the standard of the reasonable man without consideration of the fact that a woman's, especially a battered woman's, perceptions of danger might reasonably differ from those of a man.[164]

The focus on whether a defendant conforms or fails to conform to the stereotypical model of the battered woman is perhaps inevitable when reliance is placed on an expert's evidence of the effects of such abuse. In any case, the usefulness of any such evidence is questionable given the fact that the defendant, by virtue of having killed her abuser, has behaved in contradiction to the stereotypical battered woman's characteristic passivity. Even if such evidence, were to be admitted by the UK courts, it might serve only to distract jurors' attention from the question of whether or not the defendant's use of violence in the immediate situation was reasonable given her size, strength and perception of danger, and cause them instead to base their decision on their assessment of the reasonableness of the defendant's failure to leave the abuser, a failure for which she is not officially on trial. Although someone who seeks out violence deliberately will not be able to plead self-defence if she later uses force to defend herself from it, English law creates no duty in the defendant to avoid places where she may lawfully be, and she may arm herself against an anticipated attack. If a defendant will not be prevented from pleading self-defence where he walks down a street where he knows he may be attacked, or makes and stores petrol bombs in anticipation of an attack on his shop, it is inappropriate that a woman's failure to leave her own home should be used to cast doubt on her plea of self-defence. This was explicitly recognised by the Supreme Court of Canada in *Lavallee* where Wilson J, delivering the unanimous decision of that court, stated:

> ... it is not for the jury to pass judgement on the fact that an accused battered woman stayed in the relationship. Still less is it entitled to conclude that she forfeited her right to self-defence for having done so ... the traditional self-defence doctrine does not require a person to retreat from her home instead of defending herself. A man's home may be his castle but it is also the woman's home even if it seems to her more like a prison in the circumstances. If, after hearing the evidence ... the jury is satisfied that the accused had a [reasonable] apprehension of death or grievous bodily harm and felt incapable of escape, it must ask itself what the reasonable person would do in such a situation.[165]

Where a battered woman reacts to an actual attack by her abuser, or where she is given the opportunity to express her perception of anticipated danger in the light of the deceased's previous behaviour towards her, it is questionable whether expert opinion on the psychological effects of abuse would be of much assistance to the defence. This is all the more true in view of the fact that a mistaken belief in the existence of a threat need not be reasonable in the UK in order to found a claim of self-defence. If the defendant creates some doubt in the minds of the jurors that she believed herself to be under threat of imminent attack, the fact that a reasonable onlooker would not have realised the significance of a movement or threat from the deceased that the defendant knew had preceded

164 *Browne* [1973] NI 96.
165 [1990] 1 SCR 852 at 888–89.

serious violence in the past, should have no bearing on their assessment of her actions. The test of whether her response to that perceived attack was reasonable is an objective question only to the extent that her views of the necessity for force, and of the level of force required in response to the perceived attack, are not conclusive, but are nevertheless, according to Lord Morris in *Palmer*, the most potent evidence of the reasonableness of such force.[166]

Where the defendant does not claim that she foresaw violence as an immediate possibility, it will still be possible in many cases, even in the absence of expert evidence of 'learned helplessness' to explain why her use of force was nevertheless necessary. In many of the US cases the defendant had on one or more previous occasions attempted to leave her partner, but had been sought out and forced to return by his threats of further harm to herself or her children if she did not. There is no reason to suppose that the situation would be found to be that different here. In other cases the attack which ended with the death of the abuser will have occurred after the defendant has left the shared home or involved the police or both, in which case the threatening presence of the abuser will constitute evidence that action beyond flight or police involvement is necessary effectively to safeguard her life and safety, or the lives and safety of her children. In other cases the defendant will have been prevented from leaving by the knowledge or belief that her abuser will track her down and kill her if she does. The need for secrecy as to the whereabouts of women's refuges illustrates the dangers experienced by battered women who leave, and it is virtually impossible for women to disappear completely from their abusers. Many will have common acquaintances or friends, and the situation is not assisted by she potential leverage given to abusing men by the emphasis of the Children Act 1989 on dual parenting even after divorce. Women are pursued and attacked sometimes long after they leave their abusive partner, having spent years in fear of retaliation, never fully setting down new roots but attempting to remain always one step ahead of their pursuer. Police action is ineffective against such determined pursuit: a court order cannot physically restrain a man from the exercise of deadly force and, once broken, it may be too late for the woman to complain of the breach.

Conclusion

The application of self-defence to many battered women who kill does not involve any alteration or extension of the defence, rather a rethinking of the way in which the requirement that the defendant's use of force be reasonable is applied to cases other than those involving the traditional model of a one-off adversarial meeting between strangers. Self-defence is frequently regarded as a justificatory defence, and it is this aspect of it perhaps which underlies the unease which is expressed about its application in cases other than those in which it has traditionally been accepted. One judge felt obliged to warn, while directing the acquittal of a woman who killed her rapist while defending herself from further attack, that his ruling was not to be regarded in any way as a 'charter for ... rape victims, to kill their assailants'.[167]

JC Smith, too, while arguing that the analysis of duress in terms of justification leads to the conviction of defendants who might be acquitted if duress was viewed as an excuse, states nevertheless that even if it is true that the remedies

---

166 *Palmer v R (Privy Council)* [1971] AC 814, 831–32 *per* Lord Morris of Barth-y-Gest.

167 Judge Hazan in *Clugstone* (1987) *Times*, October. The decision is discussed in JC Smith, *Justification and Excuse in the Criminal Law*, p 109.

available are inadequate, to hold that the deliberate killing of a sleeping or unconscious man is justified or even excused would be, in effect, to give his victim the right to execute him; and that, surely, cannot be right.[168] To acquit a defendant who has killed, however, is not, in the words of Lord Edmund-Davies in *Lynch*,[169] to express approval of the action of the accused but only to declare that it does not merit condemnation and punishment. Even if self-defence were properly categorised as a justification, a resulting acquittal amounts to an admission by the court that the defendant's use of force was the lesser of two evils. In *Lavallee* Wilson J expressed the view that the defendant had had to choose between using force against her partner when he was vulnerable or 'accepting murder by instalment' by postponing any use of force until an attack upon her was already under way. 'Society gains nothing' from 'requiring such a delay except perhaps the additional risk that the battered woman will herself be killed'.[170]

In any case, the acceptance by the Privy Council in *Beckford* that the threat to the defendant, and the reasonableness of her reaction to it, must be judged on the facts as she saw them makes impossible any analysis of self-defence purely in terms of justification. Further, as Marianne Giles points out,[171] even where a defendant's perception of the facts is correct, the approach of the Privy Council in *Palmer*, and of the Court of Appeal in *Shannon*[172] and *White*,[173] have so emphasised her honest and instinctive belief in the necessity for the use of force and in the level of force required as to render the test of reasonableness almost subjective. The House of Lords established in *Camplin* that the reasonableness of a defendant's reaction to provocation could not be determined without consideration of her characteristics, and in *Ahluwalia* Lord Taylor CJ stated that the reasonableness of the defendant's reactions fell to be considered in the light of the history of '[her] marriage, the misconduct and ill-treatment of the appellant by her husband'. So, too, in the context of self-defence, the reasonableness of the defendant's conduct cannot be assessed in a vacuum. The jury's assessment of whether she believed that she was under threat of attack and of the seriousness of an anticipated attack will clearly be influenced by evidence of the abuser's past conduct. Many women experience abuse as a cyclical occurrence where a period of increasing tension is followed by physical abuse which is in turn followed by remorse on the part of the abuser. A battered woman might anticipate an impending attack from signals which have in the past marked the transition from the period of tension-building to the battering phase. Under such circumstances, evidence of the cyclical pattern as it has affected the defendant herself, rather than generalised expert evidence about the nature of woman-battering, can enable the jury to appreciate her apprehension of danger even where no threat is apparent to an onlooker.

Equally, abuse often escalates in seriousness between one battering episode and the next, and many women who kill do so when they fear that they will be

168 *Ibid*, p 117.

169 [1975] AC 643 at 716.

170 Adopting the reasoning of M Willoughby, 'Rendering Each Woman Her Due: Can a Battered Woman Claim Self-defence When She Kills Her Sleeping Batterer?' (1989) 38 *Kansas Law Review* 170 at 194.

171 M Giles, 'Self-Defence and Mistake: A Way Forward' (1990) 53 *MLR* 187.

172 (1980) Cr App Rep 192.

173 [1987] 3 All ER 416.

unable to survive the next episode. Again, it is vital that jurors are made aware of the history in order that they may understand the nature of the threat which the defendant feared. Even where a woman kills a sleeping partner, evidence of her circumstances may allow a jury to appreciate the absence of alternatives open to her, so that they may consider the reasonableness of her actions as they might those of a hostage who sees no alternative to the proactive use of force against a threat which may be rendered insurmountable if he waits to be attacked.

Self-defence exists in order to allow citizens to take steps to protect themselves where circumstances render it necessary for them so to do. Many battered women are faced with no realistic alternative to the use of force against abusive partners. The construction of the family as private and the resulting societal blindness to violence within it, the power inequalities which result from men's greater earning potential and the resulting economic dependency of many women, the isolation of many women within their homes and their subsequent alienation from formal and informal support structures, the unavailability of decent alternative accommodation for women who leave their abusers, the fear of pursuit and greater injury or death; these factors render many women hostages of domestic violence and make invisible any escape from that violence except by the force. The way to prevent battered women killing is to provide them with adequate alternative means of escape from violence, and perhaps then to condemn those who choose to use violence instead. Such a course of action would have the effect of saving the lives of battered women as well as those of their abusers. It is however a long-term solution, and one which requires the commitment of government rather than the law alone. In the meantime, society's failure to protect women from violence within their homes must be brought to the fore by defence lawyers and taken into account by those whose task it is to allocate blame.[174]

FEMALE VICTIMS IN THE CRIMINAL LAW[175]
Sheila McLean[176]

There is no obvious reason why females should be victims in the general criminal law any more often than males. Indeed, in certain offences, there is little doubt that males are more highly represented in the victim group.[177] It may, therefore, seem unnecessary to treat females as a special category of victim, since liability to become a victim seems rather randomly spread, and is, apparently, not gender-specific. However, gender does have a relevance to the criminal law, not only in the methods by which female offenders are treated but also in certain types of offences – notably those involving sexual activities. Of obvious importance in such offences are the crimes of rape and incest which have, by definition in the case of rape, and by practice in the case of incest, a predominantly female victim group.

The contention in this chapter will be that the definition of rape whilst designed to offer protection to females and apparently importing no gender assumptions –

---

174 *In Defence of Battered Women who Kill*, pp 521–29.

175 Sheila McLean and Noreen Burrows (eds), *The Legal Relevance of Gender* (Macmillan Press, 1988), Chapter 10.

176 At the time of writing, Lecturer, Institute of Law and Ethics, University of Glasgow.

177 For discussion, see M Hindelang, M Gottfredson and J Carofalo, *Victims of Personal Crime* (Cambridge, Mass: Ballinger Publishing, 1978); M Hough and P Mayhew, *The British Crime Survey* (HMSO, 1983).

none the less, by its concentration on certain types of forced sexual behaviour, and by defining rape in purely heterosexual terms,[178] has contributed to the generation of a sexual mythology which makes care and sympathy for victims less than readily available. Moreover, it will be contended that where rape is thus defined, the terminology itself perpetuates the view that rape is essentially a sexual offence, again contributing to the perpetuation of unhelpful (and unacceptable) stereotypes. Thus, the victim specificity of the crime allows for the varieties in victims to be ignored. It is well acknowledged that:

> ... women of all ages, lifestyles, or economic status are victimised by sexual assault. Nuns, grandmothers, toddlers, prostitutes, married, divorced or single women working outside or inside the home have experienced sexual assault from strangers, fathers, uncles, friends, husbands – men known and unknown to them .[179]

However, the one characteristic which all of these people share is their sex, a factor which should be irrelevant but which does, in fact, facilitate, if not encourage, the making of assumptions about victims and their aggressors.

Nor is the problem confined to rape cases. Since the contention is that it is the 'femaleness' of victims which plays a significant role in their admittedly harsh treatment, then this implies that the law and its enforcers are prepared to entertain certain disvaluing and insulting presumptions about gender, which are sufficiently powerful and ingrained to override anticipated concern for the victims of violent and degrading offences. There are groups other than rape victims who then become vulnerable to the importation of similar prejudice, again because of the fact that they are female. Most significantly, this will affect the victims of incest, who are predominantly female. It will be concluded, therefore, that the unreasonable prejudice attached to the female victim in crimes which are perceived as sexual, stems primarily from something to do with the combination of this perception and the fact of being female.[180] Regardless of the circumstances, therefore, and however many symbolic expressions of abhorrence society makes in respect of these offences, even children who are sexually molested may find that it is assumptions about female sexuality which predict the level of care and concern which they can expect when they become victims. The example of rape will predominate in this chapter. However, the victims of incest will often find themselves viewed in much the same way as the victims of rape, and indeed their treatment draws heavily on the attitudes generated and reinforced by the assumptions made about the one crime which, in many jurisdictions, remains exclusively the province of males to inflict on females.[181]

Moreover, in failing to recognise the true character of rape – its basis in aggression and in the struggle for domination over the 'weak' and the vulnerable – other groups who are also vulnerable are generally excluded from even the symbolic impact of the rape charge.[182] Furthermore, victim precipitation and

---

178 See L Snider, 'Legal Reform and Social Control: the Dangers of Abolishing Rape' (1985) 13 *International Journal of the Sociology of Law* at 337–56.

179 Hanmer and Stanki, 'Stripping Away the Rhetoric of Protection' (1985) 13 *International Journal of the Sociology of Law* at 357–74.

180 For discussion of incest and its impact, see KC Meiselman, *Incest* (Jossey-Bass Publishers, 1979); S Forward and C Buck, *Betrayal of Innocence: Incest and its Devastation* (Pelican, 1981).

181 Sexual Offences Act 1956 (England); Sexual Offences (Scotland) Act 1976. See now s 142 of the Criminal Justice and Public Order Act 1994.

182 See Snider, *op cit*; see also (1986) *Guardian*, 22 January, for discussion of male 'rape'.

participation have become well used 'explanations' for unjustifiable behaviour. In other words, if rape is seen solely or primarily as an act designed (with or without encouragement) to achieve the sexual gratification of the offender, and for as long as it remains tied to heterosexual intercourse (which could otherwise be a pleasurable experience) then fantasies that the victim 'seduced' the attacker or 'enjoyed' the experience can be maintained, and the sexual rather than the violent motivation for the crime is rendered more credible.

This is not to suggest that there is no sexual element in rape, but, such as there is, it is 'sexual' in a manner somewhat different from that which is often presumed. In all rape, the use of sex as a weapon is significant as a means of manifesting the inherent violence of the crime and achieving dominance. The fact that rape involves vandalising the human sexual organs does not deny that sex is a significant aspect of the crime. If anything, it reinforces the significance of sex to all human beings. The ultimate degradation inherent in such violence lies in turning what could be a good and pleasurable act into a nightmare – by abusing these particular parts of the human physiology and psyche, total insult is achieved.

Legal management of rape

The law and its agents inevitably play a highly significant role in crime and its management. It has already been suggested that the terminology of the law in many jurisdictions can unwittingly import gender assumptions which are irrelevant to the fact of violence. Moreover, the attitudes of the law enforcer will have a major impact on the reporting of crime, on detection rates and on conviction rates, all of which are important if the system of justice is to operate in the desired fashion. Whilst most victims of, for example, assault or theft will report that they have been the victims of an offence, and can expect the instigation of certain procedures by the police and the courts, the victims of rape (and incest) cannot guarantee this, nor can they even be sure that they will be treated politely – far less with compassion. Thus, '[the] problems of victims of sexual assault who are courageous enough to identify themselves as such are notorious'.[183]

The initial question to be answered, therefore, is, why is this so? The answer is complicated and concerns the victim as much as it does the law. For example, in an increasingly violent world it is relatively common to read or see statements from the police to the effect that a particular person whom they are seeking is known to be violent and should not be approached by the public if sighted. Bank tellers are warned merely to hand over the money in the event of a robbery – resistance is seen as neither necessary nor sensible. The life of the individual takes precedence. However, if a woman is raped by this same dangerous individual, she is required to establish that she did resist him in order to prove that the intercourse was not consensual. The bank teller need not establish that he resisted the robber in order for it not to be assumed that he was complicit in the offence. The victim of a rape, however, must show this, otherwise a conviction will not be secured, and institutional abuse will be added to the physical and emotional violence of the initial attack.

Of course, there are differences in the nature of the offences which, at first sight, might seem to be so significant as to render the analogy unhelpful. In particular, it might be said, such examples have no relevance to the crime of rape, because in this case – unlike the others – consent is actually central to the offence itself.

---

183 E Hilberman, *The Rape Victim* (Basic Books, 1976) Introduction.

The fact that a person intended to rob a bank will still render him or her guilty of the offence, even if the bank teller waives every assistance, and is actually hoping that the bank will be robbed. If a woman encourages or consents to intercourse, then there is no crime.

However, when considering the treatment of the victim, the real interest is not in whether there are differences in the nature of the crimes (which admittedly there are), but rather in the approach to their victims. For example, except in unusual cases, it will not routinely be the assumption of the police that the bank teller – or the bank itself, whichever is deemed to be the victim – was a participant in the commission of the offence, whereas in the case of rape it often seems that there is a clear presumption by the administrators of justice that an element of complicity or actual willing submission was present or likely. In practice, this is often the first assumption made when rape is reported, and its implications linger insidiously throughout the whole treatment of the victim. The fact that consent is central to the crime of rape, and not to the other used in the illustration, is, paradoxically, precisely what makes them useful comparisons. In the interests of crime detection, if the police can justify the presumption of consent in the rape victim as a useful device in identifying 'real' crime, then why is it confined in its use to rape? The bank teller who actually is complicit – and this must happen – might equally be treated with suspicion, since, if he or she is complicit then he or she is personally guilty of a crime, and the interests of justice would be served by detecting this. It appears, however, that assumptions about victim participation are only, or predominantly, made when the crime alleged falls into particular categories.

There are, therefore, problems for the victims of rape which do not exist in other cases, not least the attitudes of those with the responsibility for pursuing justice disinterestedly. Again, the differential treatment seems to be based not only, or even substantially, on the consent requirement in rape, but on assumptions about the victim herself. Is it really reasonable to assume that women hitch-hikers are likely to welcome intercourse with complete strangers? Is it rational to presume that women enjoy sex only if they are badly beaten by strangers (or 'friends')? Does the woman walking down a street really hope that she will be accosted by a stranger, and does she have no higher aspiration than to be abused by him? These questions may seem extreme, but they reflect the reality of the basis of prejudicial treatment of rape victims. However different those acting on these sorts of assumptions may regard their particular attitudes as being, it is factors like them which lie at the root of the mistreatment of victims of rape. Assumptions about the victim inform the attitudes of law enforcers to many aspects of the situation, not least the credibility of the victim's statement. As has been noted:

> Whereas testing the validity of a victim's story is agreed to be a legitimate police function, the criteria by which validity is determined and the means employed by the police in so doing [in rape cases] are both open to question.[184]

The significance of the heterosexual terms of the crime itself is equally apparent. The assumptions which have been given as examples are derivative from the fact that heterosexual intercourse is, in most experience, an enjoyable activity. Therefore, and without any logic, it must always be desirable. Thus the victim

---

184 TW McCahill, LC Meyer and AM Fischman, *The Aftermath of Rape* (Lexington Books, 1979), p 103.

must have wanted or enjoyed it. Since women are also often seen as passive sexually, then it should come as no surprise that they are seen as having enjoyed the experience of being 'taken' against their expressed will, or without regard to it. The emphasis on sexuality which this definition perpetuates, permits the traditional (male) views of female sexuality to be neatly incorporated into the treatment of the victim. Women are passive (and therefore, being ladylike, do not want to admit that they want sex), and dependent on male sexual recognition (therefore they tease or encourage male sexual activity). This is perhaps a convenient, but nonetheless unacceptable, manner in which to dismiss the claims of victims that they are indeed victims. It is here, too, that the significance of the female – only victim group, based on legal definition, can be seen. As Hilberman says: 'The profound impact of the rape stress is best understood in the context of rape as a crime against the person and not against the hymen.'[185]

However, since the common characteristic among the totality of raped women is their gender, it becomes apparently more tempting to make generalisations about the group, based on this factor. The characteristic which makes them a group – since it is not yet established that they also share the common characteristic of being a victim – is that they are female. By implication, their involvement in the alleged rape will have something to do with this characteristic. When this implication is combined with the assumption that rape is a sexual offence – implying sexual gratification – the door is wide open to stereotyping victims on the irrelevant criterion of gender, including the presumed sexuality of females as a group. Moreover, discrimination is completed by the failure to individualise – the group insult to all women which such stereotypes create and perpetuate completes the process of disvaluation and abuse.

This is not insignificant as a conclusion, since it seems that gender differentiation is common in legal process, however irrelevant or degrading it may be. As Edwards notes, for example:

Instances of sex-gender division, that is occasions of the disparate treatment of 'men' and 'women' in their particular sex roles and the accommodation of men and women in their social and gender roles are readily observable features in both criminal law and the operation of the legal justice process.[186]

This does not merely mean that the law recognises men and women as biologically different – in itself not necessarily discriminatory – unacceptable. Rather, it permits of the incorporation as fact into the legal process of arguable, prejudicial and often degrading assumptions about the nature of males and females, and of role stereotyping based on simplistic presumptions about gender and its impact on behaviour. In particular, female victims of 'sexual' crimes are vulnerable to the application of these unreasonable presumptions. Myths about female behaviour and sexuality inform the treatment of both the victim and the offender.[187]

The mythology of 'sexual' offences

The sexual explanation of rape remains predominant, and is incorporated into the very definition of the crime. Myths about the victim are perpetuated and a relevant response to the situation rendered more difficult. As has been noted, in

---

185 Hilberman, *The Rape Victim*, Introduction.
186 SSM Edwards, *Women on Trial* (Manchester University Press, 1984), p 4.
187 *Female Victims in the Criminal Law*, pp 195–200.

the case of rape, these myths inevitably centre on the common element in the victim – that is the fact that she is female. Victimologists may use this common characteristic to define or explain the victim in ways which stereotype both her and her sexuality, and expectations of the behaviour typically associated with males and females inform the explanation of the crime. For example, women may be seen as sexual teases, inflaming men to a point at which they cannot control themselves. This, of course, is not an uncommon 'explanation', and it is impressive in its cleverness, since it achieves two objects simultaneously.

The first is that it suggests that the intercourse in question is neither morally nor legally culpable. The man is, therefore, the victim of female stimulation of his sexuality, and entitled to the gratification which he seeks. However, if that line is a little lacking in credibility, the second strand of the 'explanation' can serve to isolate the man in question. Thus, if it cannot be accepted that all women are teases in this way, at least it is possible to concentrate on the outrageous sexual appetite of the offender, thereby distinguishing him from 'normal' men who would, of course, never do such a thing. Criminologists and others can then explain the offender in such cases as 'over-sexed' and, therefore, more susceptible of treatment than punishment, whilst at the same time distinguishing this group of men from the rest. As Illich has pointed out, in another context,[188] there is great value in this kind of approach, since every society seems to need people it can label as 'strange' or 'different' in order to reaffirm its own normality. So efficient is this 'explanation' of rape that it may seem scarcely surprising that it has retained a dominance in current thought (at least current male thought).

However, victims in these cases may find this 'explanation' less than satisfactory – not to say, offensive. In legal terms it also is significant, since it and related presumptions present a hurdle for the victim of rape (and of other offences classed as sexual) which does not exist for victims of other crime. Again it seems likely that there is something about the nature of the offence, or the nature of the victim, which stimulates this differential treatment. It has already been suggested that the categorisation of the offence as sexual leads to problems. But what of the victim?

One obvious distinction between the victims of rape and those of other crimes is, as has been noted, their gender. Indeed, any other similarity in rape victims is difficult, if not impossible, to find. However, unless gender is being used *per se* as a characteristic which leads to suspicion, mistrust and hostility, it is difficult, at first sight, to understand why it should be seen as relevant at all in a legal context. It would be good to think, then, that it cannot be this common factor which leads to the unusually harsh treatment of victims in these cases, but, unfortunately, to believe this is to demonstrate excessive naïveté. The history of the crime of rape and the treatment of victims, coupled with the extensive discrimination against females which exists even in so-called civilised communities, suggest that mere membership of the female sex is sufficient reason to restrict rights and freedoms, to disvalue contributions and to minimise autonomy.

The suspicion of the law and its enforcers towards (female) victims of rape, is encapsulated in resistance to legal reform. Suggestions that the corroboration requirement is a major hindrance to the effective safeguarding of women, since it renders conviction very difficult, are met (reasonably) with fears that the legal

---

188 I Illich, *The Expropriation of Health: Medical Nemesis* (Penguin, 1977).

process is thereby rendered more susceptible to abuse and unsoundness. This is a major concern, but arguments based on it lose some of their credibility when one considers that the present system can scarcely claim to be any better – merely it seems to favour one group (the male attacker) over the other group (the female victim). In any event, as has already been suggested, it may be that compassionate treatment of victims would lead to a situation where alternative corroborative details might become available. Equally, were the assumptions that women consent to intercourse with strangers in bizarre situations to be removed, then the circumstances of the offence might themselves provide an element of probity.

Unfortunately, another commonly held myth comes into the arena at this stage. Resistance to legal reform is not merely based on the difficulties of maintaining legal principle, but also – sometimes quite overtly – on the further fantasy that women routinely 'cry rape'. Convictions based solely on their evidence, and with no proof of force to provide corroboration, are, therefore, instantly suspect. Given the assumptions about male sexual gratification and female sexuality, this barrier to reform of the law – or of attitudes – is scarcely surprising, and heralds the emergence of yet further problems for the rape victim.

It is, as Toner cogently points out, no longer rape which is under consideration, but 'real' rape. As she says:

> Rape occurs when a woman's consent to intercourse is disregarded but the more closely it resembles seduction the more easily it is forgiven. Any indication of sexual aggression on the part of the victim – in her dress, her language, even in her failure to remove herself from the threat in time – mitigates the offence. She will be judged to have stepped out of line and to have forfeited her victim status ... The clearer her sexual neutrality, the more violent her assault, the 'truer' a victim she is seen to be.[189]

The assumption that females are only truly raped when they can prove their innocence of this 'sexual aggression', is both generated and reflected by viewing rape as a sexual offence. If it is a crime of violence, then the attitude, sexuality or sexual attractiveness of the victim are all irrelevant. Failure to remove yourself from the scene of a possible assault – for whatever reason – does not render the intention of the assailant less culpable. Studies have shown that many rapes are accompanied by threats of the use of weapons which would make flight dangerous or impractical.[190] Nonetheless, the victim of rape is obliged to attempt escape or violence, or run the risk of being disbelieved. Moreover, failure to do so may well influence the assessment by the law enforcer, either as to the victim's willingness, or the reasonableness of the assailant's belief that she consented.

If rape continues to be viewed as a sexual offence, then the failure of the victim to maintain permanent suspicion – of all men in the street, in her home, on the bus and at work – can be – and is – interpreted as a covert and unspoken acceptance of sexual advances. Such an approach is almost too outrageous to have credibility, but the overtones of sexual mythology (about females and males) which remain inherent in both the historical and the contemporary views of rape, make it apparently acceptable. Thus the view of the victim as precipitator or participator is reinforced and the behaviour of the male who 'just got carried away' is explained and decriminalised. Indeed, it is bereft even of more

---

189 Toner, *The Facts of Rape* (Arrow Books, 1982), p 108.
190 Walker and Brodsky, *Sexual Assault* (Lexington, Mass: DC Heath & Co, 1976), p 50.

opprobrium. And, of course, in those situations which cannot be neatly fitted into this latter explanation, then the man who behaves in this way can conveniently be separated from the 'normal' man, and his behaviour explained away in other terms. Moreover, such perceptions seem often to have influenced what should otherwise be informed comment on the crime itself. As Toner says:

> In identifying victims and rapists, researchers concern themselves with the contribution of the victims to the crime and the motives of the men who commit them. Undoubtedly these are important questions. Those who seek to answer them satisfactorily, however, are apparently hampered by an unhappy predilection to apportion blame to the victim and find excuses for the rapists – succumbing to the always popular belief that men are driven to rape women who lead them on.[191]

Rape and incest

Many of the comments about rape and its victims also apply to those who are the victims of incest. Although rape and incest are often considered as separate offences, the differences between the crimes are not necessarily major. Of course, some incest is clearly rape, but much of it is apparently consensual. However, even a moment's consideration of 'consensual' incest will show that the pressures on children to participate in sexual activity of this sort may often be similar to those on adult women not to resist a rapist. In other words, the quality of compliance should be considered, rather than the lack of apparent resistance. Both sets of victims share a number of common characteristics which are significant both to the contention that such offences are power and violence motivated rather than the outcome of sexual desire, and to the argument that gender may significantly affect the quality of treatment of the victim.

Furthermore, evidence of the way in which incest victims are treated shows such clear parallels with the treatment of rape victims that it is difficult not to conclude that the experience of the rape victim has significantly affected that of the incest victim. At first sight, however, it might seem difficult to explain such apparent similarities since, even if the view of adult females already described is unacceptable, at least the person is adult, and might be expected to be able to take care of herself. However, in the standard case of incest (at least as far as incomplete statistics can show) the victim is often young, and it might, therefore, be expected that the specially protected status usually accorded to children would lead to the victims being dealt with compassionately and with great concern in the face of the traumatic effects of another's behaviour. Society's concern for children – concern which is used to limit their rights in potentially exploitative situations – could be expected to move into top gear in situations of this sort. However, the evidence does not suggest that this is routinely the case. The incest victim may run the same gauntlet of hostility which is the lot of the rape victim. It has been suggested that apparent vulnerability marks certain groups out for potential victim status. Whilst it might not be obvious why adult, sane, fully fledged human beings should be regarded as inherently vulnerable, as is apparently the case with the female of the species, there may seem to be good reasons for regarding children in this way. However, as with adult females, vulnerability – an apparent predictor of the likelihood of abuse in a power relationship – should result in additional protection, if it is indeed such a predictor. Given the treatment of rape victims, it is clear that if vulnerability pure and simple were what made them victims, then it certainly does not lead to

---

191 Toner, *The Facts of Rape*, p 108.

protection. Rather, vulnerability makes them exploitable, whilst at the same time they are deemed to be fully fledged participants when that is convenient in explaining this exploitation away.

This is no less true of the victims of incest, even although they are often children. The question, therefore, is, what is it about the victims of incest which provokes society into rejecting its otherwise benevolent stance in their respect? Why should the child victim of incest be subjected to the institutional abuse which seems to be built in to the treatment of rape victims, in addition to the trauma of involvement in the offence itself?

The answer to these questions may not be so difficult as at first sight appears. The treatment of the rape victim and the incest victim shows similarities for two very obvious reasons. Firstly, that the offence is categorised as sexual rather than violent, and assumptions about the sexuality of the participants can therefore be built-in to the treatment of the offender and the victim alike. Secondly, and crucially, the average victim of incest shares what has been claimed to be a fundamental predictor of treatment by the legal process, that is, the female sex.

Although males may be the victims of incest, it remains the case that – as far as the, admittedly incomplete, figures can show – vast majority of incest is father-daughter incest.[192] As with rape, the aggressor is male and the victim female. Moreover, in incest cases the power struggle involved in the deliberate abuse of another's sexuality is even more clear than it is in cases of rape. That fathers use their daughters in this way seems to demonstrate that the concept of property (including the capacity to use property) which so bedevilled attempts at female emancipation, is alive and well and living in the nuclear family. Despite the powerful emotional mysticism surrounding both sex and the family unit, the privacy and sanctity of the female participants are regularly, and often violently, disregarded and abused.

Nor does the pattern of abuse stop there. As with the victim of rape, the incest victim will often find her allegations treated with suspicion, and the evidential requirements are equally problematic. The sex of the victim permits of perpetuation of theories about their behaviour, which bear striking resemblances to those used to stigmatise the victim, and to explain the offender, in rape cases. In showing that incest may be generated by a need for affection on the part of the aggressor, by showing that sexual feelings between adults and children are normal, the fundamental point is missed.

Moreover, the former of these also may serve to implicate the wife in the offence, thereby doubling the female guilt in the process. As with explanations and theories about offender and victim in rape cases, it is of course important that sound theoretical views are stated and tested. However, the crucial question of why, in the case of incest, the aggressor turns to the particular victim is often lost in a morass of conflicting and confusing emotions.

It has been claimed that vulnerability is not *per se* a sufficient explanation for the abuse of women or other groups. Nor is the sexual drive of the aggressor either an explanation or an excuse. Indeed the emphasis on such explanations fails to challenge the apparent assumption that sexual gratification or solace can be achieved by non-consensual intercourse. In fact, what seems to be crucial in the treatment of victims is the sexual stereotyping which their gender routinely seems to import. The dangers of such assumptions can be clearly seen when such

---

192 See S Forward and C Buck, *Betrayal of Innocence*; Meiselman, *Incest.*

stereotypes are translated into the case of incest. In fact, in this case, the element of power or domination can be seen most starkly. Indeed, in the case of incest, the very factors used to explain the choice of victim, might equally have been expected to be the crucial elements which would prevent its occurrence – that is, the proximity of the victim and the relationship of trust which is thought to exist between, for example, fathers and their daughters. Even if convenience is an explanation for the choice of victim, it is not convenience pure and simple. The taboo surrounding incest is powerful in many societies, and generally must be overridden. Is it not more likely that the explanation relates rather to the control which fathers perceive themselves as having in respect of their daughters, and the assumption that female sexuality is there for male enjoyment – factors which are evident in the history of male treatment of females in general? Nor can sexual deprivation explain the offence in the face of these other considerations, unless the assumption that male sexual desires take precedence over those of females – which was evident in the case of rape – is also imported into thinking about incest and its victims.

The conclusion that incest, like rape, is an act of male domination and a demonstration of power and aggression, is again forced into the forefront. It may be concluded that '[to] rape is not a fundamental instinct, nor is it a sexual act. It is an act of aggression and hostility and it flourishes where cultures encourage it'.[193] Sexually to use your daughter shows characteristics of striking similarity.

Conclusions

Whilst it may be true that '[all] democratic countries have as one of their highest aspirations the attaining of equality among their citizens'[194] it is also true that 'in no democratic country in the world do women have equal rights with men'.[195] Thus, although adult females may be formally accorded full citizenship of a country, and female children may apparently be equal members of the family unit, they remain second-class citizens in many vital ways – not least, in their rights to freedom of choice in sexual matters. Their freedom in this vitally important area is, and will remain, limited, for as long as men continue to view women as sex objects, and the enforcers of the law remain predominantly male.

An overview of the crimes which are characteristically inflicted by males on females, and which are completed by sexual violence highlights a number of troubling, but important factors. First, that non-consensual sexual activity is very much a part of the history of most cultures, and, even more strikingly, that the victims of such abuses are predominantly those who can be characterised as weaker, more vulnerable or subject to the power of those who represent society's dominant norm – that is, the heterosexual male. This is a damning, but unavoidable, conclusion.

Moreover, there is a major paradox in the fact that laws expressly designed to protect those groups which are most commonly abused have succeeded – through their terminology, interpretation or enforcement – in perpetuating and reinforcing the problems which make these groups vulnerable. The terminology of rape ensures a tightly defined victim group, around whom fantasies degrading to all women can be spun. Furthermore, these same fantasies lend themselves to other situations where females form the vast proportion of the

---

193 Toner, *The Facts of Rape*, p 50.

194 J Mitchell, 'Women and Equality', in J Mitchell and A Oakley (eds), *The Rights and Wrongs of Women* (Penguin, 1976), p 381.

195 *Ibid*.

victim group. Whilst gender may be a relevant factor in certain situations, as indeed it was in the development of the outlawing of rape – expressly designed to protect one gender group – it is an irrelevant factor in the treatment of victims of violent and traumatic abuse. The conclusion that the fact that a victim is female explains the hostility, aggression and disbelief with which the victims of rape and incest are treated, is one which right-minded citizens would hope not to have to reach. Yet there is no other factor which obviously links them. The violence inherent in these crimes is thus disguised, both by the concentration on sex and sexuality which is contained in their definitions, and by the theories offered to explain the offender, or to justify caution in believing the victim.

Clearly, however, improvements in the treatment of victims cannot be achieved by legal change alone. Although the definition of rape may have contributed to the problems of the victim, and the consequent treatment of female victims may have had significant impact on the victims of incest (at least where they are also female), there is clearly much more at stake than mere legal terminology. When flatly stated, the assumptions about female sexual behaviour, which generate maltreatment and hostility, seem so ridiculous as to defy belief. They are, nonetheless, deeply rooted in the treatment of women in general, and the victims of 'sexual' offences in particular. To discriminate against females seems so endemic to society that mere legal rules or legal change cannot bring about the emotional and intellectual revolution which would be required to change the situation, although they may go some way towards improving it.

However, for as long as societies do not question the assumptions on the basis of which members of a particular sex are treated, and do not challenge the relevance of gender in these matters, the pattern of abuse is complete and seemingly permanent. Not only will females be vulnerable to abuse and attack, but the acceptance that gender is relevant imports into the management of victims – inferences – degrading both individually and collectively – which preclude compassionate and effective treatment. Gender may make females vulnerable, but it is irrelevant to the fact of abuse, and should be seen as such in the treatment of victims.

CHAPTER 10

PORNOGRAPHY

INTRODUCTION

Obscenity and pornography raise difficult questions for jurisprudence, both for traditional male jurisprudence and feminist theorists. Each topic involves a mixture of competing questions and philosophies. Each may be viewed as matters in which individual freedom should reign supreme, and accordingly from a traditional liberal political perspective, participants and consumers should be free to engage in the activities, and market forces should rule. It would follow from this (liberal) standpoint – most clearly expressed in the writing of John Stuart Mill – that the role of the law should be confined to that of preventing any harm to persons. Unless, it can be proven that harm is resulting from pornography, there should be no legal restriction. From the perspective of radical feminists this proposition is both fallacious and dangerous. As will be seen below, while women ostensibly participate freely in pornography the reality of the situation is much different. The pornography industry – for industry it undeniably is – is controlled by men for the benefit and profit of men. Those in control, whether photographic or film producers exercise control over individual women's minds and bodies and also maintain and encourage the now well-documented phallocentric hierarchical power of men over women, thereby simultaneously both denying women true equality and further denigrating women in the eyes of society.

The competition between 'male' liberalism and equality requires examination in this regard. For radical feminists, the tenets of liberalism become dangerous weapons which are employed to defeat true quality which can only be realised when the mask of liberalism is uncovered and understood for what it represents to both men and women: freedom for men, inequality for women. For feminists Andrea Dworkin and Catharine MacKinnon the solution to the 'pornography problem' lies in campaigning for civil remedies to be available to female victims of pornography.[1] An alternative approach – which is generally favoured by the 'Moral Right' – is that of censorship: the prohibition of the production and distribution of pornography. This approach, however, contains inherent problems. For this reason, as will be seen below, there are good arguments for not pursuing the prohibition of pornography, but rather using legal means by which to restrict access to pornography, or alternatively, as advocated by radical feminists, namely, the provision of remedies under civil law.

In this chapter, these approaches to pornography are considered, in order that readers may both appreciate the breadth of the debate, the intractable nature of the problem of pornography, and reach their own preferred solution to the issue.

Pornography represents a graphic and powerful representation of the subordination and in equality of women, and the correlative power and control

---

1   See pp 441–42 below.

of men. As such pornographic representations may be argued to lie at the heart of the debate on gender equality and continue to raise complex issues for feminist scholars as to the appropriate role of law.

DEFINITIONS

'*Pornography*' –

> begins with a root 'porno', meaning 'prostitution' or 'female captives', thus letting us know that the subject is not mutual love, or love at all, but domination and violence against women ... It ends with a root 'graphos', meaning 'writing about' or 'description of', which puts still more distance between subject and object, a replaces a spontaneous yearning for closeness with objectification and voyeurism.[2]

'Erotica', on the other hand, stems from 'eros' or passionate love and 'thus in the idea of positive choice, free will, the yearning for a particular person'.[3] Under English law, legal regulation is concerned neither with 'erotica', nor with pornography, *per se*, but rather with obscene materials. An article[4] is 'obscene' if:

> ... its effect ... is ... such as to tend to deprave and corrupt persons who are likely, having regard to all relevant circumstances, to read, see or hear the matter contained or embodied in it.[5]

An article will be 'published', according to s 1(3) of the Obscene Publications Act 1959, if a person:

(a)   distributes, circulates, sells, lets on hire, gives, or lends it, or who offers it for sale or for letting on hire; or

(b)   in the case of an article containing or embodying matter to be looked at or a record, shows, plays or projects its.

Alternatively, as defined by s 163(8) of the Canadian Criminal Code:

> For the purposes of this Act, any publication a dominant characteristic of which is the undue exploitation of sex, or of sex and any one or more of the following subjects, namely, crime, horror, cruelty and violence, shall be deemed to be obscene.[6]

Or according to the Supreme Court of the United States in *Roth v United States* 'material which deals with sex in a manner appealing to prurient interest' where the prurient interest refers to 'having a tendency to excite lustful thoughts [or as a] shameful and morbid interest in sex' which is 'utterly without redeeming social importance'.[7]

---

2   *Ibid.*

3   Gloria Steinem, 'Erotica and Pornography: A Clear and Present Difference' in S Dwyer, *The Problem of Pornography* (Wadsworth, 1995), p 31, and see Andrea Dworkin, *infra.*

4   Which covers books, pictures, films, records and video cassettes.

5   Section 1(1).

6   See Legal Appendix in S Dwyer *op cit*, p 240.

7   354 US 476.

LEGAL REGULATION OF PORNOGRAPHY IN ENGLAND

The Obscene Publications Act 1959

The Obscene Publications Act 1959 creates the offence of publication of an obscene article, whether or not for gain. Further it is an offence to have such articles in ownership, possession or control for the purpose of publication for gain or with a view to publication.[8]

The tendency to 'deprave and corrupt'

It is not sufficient that an article disgusts or is 'filthy', 'loathsome' or 'lewd'.[9] What must be established is that the article will 'deprave or corrupt'.[10] Nor is it sufficient that the article is capable of depraving or corrupting one person: the test is whether or not a significant proportion of persons likely to read or see the article would be depraved or corrupted by it.[11] The fact that the persons likely to read the article regularly read such materials is irrelevant to whether or not the material can deprave or corrupt (one can be corrupted more than once)[12] although the same argument may not hold if the likely audience is to be police officers experienced with dealing with pornography.[13]

The defence of public good

The defence of public good[14] was originally interpreted narrowly. In *DPP v Jordan*[15] where the defendant argued the psychotherapeutic benefit of 'soft-porn' the judge rejected the defence, holding that what was for the public good was art, literature or science. However, the tide turned when, in 1968 the trial of *Last Exit to Brooklyn*[16] established the right of authors to 'explore depravity and corruption explicitly described'.[17] In 1976 *Inside Linda Lovelace* was acquitted, despite the judge directing the jury that: 'If this isn't obscene, members of the jury, you may think that nothing is obscene.'[18] In 1979 the Williams Committee

---

8   Section 2(1) as amended.
9   *R v Anderson* [1972] 1 QB 304.
10 *R v Martin Secker and Warburg* [1954] 2 All ER 683.
11 *DPP v Whyte* [1972] AC 849 at 860 *per* Lord Wilberforce.
12 *Shaw v DPP* [1962] AC 220.
13 *R v Clayton and Halsey* [1963] 1 QB 163.
14 Section 4.
15 [1977] AC 699 and see *Attorney General's Reference (No 3 of 1977)* [1978] 3 All ER 1166.
16 *R v Calder and Boyars Ltd* [1969] 1 QB 151.
17 G Robertson, *Freedom, the Individual and the Law* (Penguin, 6th edn, 1989), p 183.
18 Cited by G Robertson *op cit*, p 189.

recommended that all restrictions on the written word should be lifted.[19] Since that time the use of the criminal law to restrict pornographic literature has largely been abandoned.[20]

Theatre, cinematic regulation and the licensing of sex shops

The Theatres Act 1968 introducing censorship in the theatre stems from 1551. The sole basis for censorship of the theatre is obscenity. The Indecent Displays (Control) Act 1981 placed sex shop proprietors under a duty to regulate window displays, to restrict entry to persons over 18 and to put warning notices in their windows. The Local Government (Miscellaneous Provisions) Act 1982 enabled local authorities to licence shops 'used for a business which consists to a significant degree of selling books, magazine, films, videos and artefacts which portray, encourage or are otherwise used in connection with sexual activity'.[21]

Conspiracy to Corrupt Public Morals

Under the common law, publishers may be caught by the offence of conspiracy to corrupt public morals. In *Shaw v DPP*,[22] Shaw, the publisher of a 'directory' giving the names and details of prostitutes was prosecuted for conspiracy to corrupt public morals.[23] The House of Lords (Lord Reid dissenting) held that the courts have a 'residual power to enforce the supreme and fundamental purpose of the law, to conserve not only the safety and order but also the moral welfare of the State'.[24] *Shaw v DPP* was upheld in *Knuller Ltd v DPP*.[25] The publishers had produced a magazine containing advertisements of male homosexuals. The House of Lords upheld *Shaw* rejecting as a defence the fact that the Sexual Offences Act 1967 provided that homosexual acts between adult males, in private, were no longer an offence. The use of this common law offence is rare; nevertheless it remains an available offence which enables the State to avoid statutory offences which provide defences such as that of the 'public good'.[26]

19 *Committee on Obscenity and Film Censorship* (Cmnd 7772) (London: HMSO).
20 Although jury trial can be avoided by the use of s 3 'forfeiture orders' which results in the destruction of works without a trial.
21 G Robertson *op cit*, p 200.
22 [1961] AC 220.
23 Shaw was also found guilty of an offence under the Obscene Publication Act 1959. See further below.
24 [1962] AC 220 at 268. See JE Hall Williams (1961) 24 *MLR* 626; D Seaborne Davies (1962) 6 JSPTL 104; G Robertson *Obscenity*.
25 [1973] AC 435.
26 Section 4 of the Obscene Publication Acts 1959.

Legal regulation of obscenity in Australia, Canada and the United States of America

Different constitutional arrangements lead to very differing results. In both Canada and the United States pornography and obscenity are clear constitutional issues. The First Amendment to the US Constitution provides that:

Congress shall make no law respecting an establishment of religion, or prohibiting the free exercise thereof; or abridging the freedom of speech, or of the press; or the right of the people peaceably to assemble, and to petition the Government for a redress of grievances.[27]

Section 2 Canadian Charter of Rights and Freedoms provides:

Everyone has the following rights and freedoms:

(a)   the freedom of conscience and religion;

(b)   the freedom of thought, belief, opinion and expression, including freedom of the press and other media of communication;

(c)   freedom of peaceful assembly; and

(d)   freedom of association.

However, this provision is not absolute since s 1 provides that:

The Canadian Charter of Rights and Freedoms guarantees the rights and freedoms set out in it subject to reasonable limits prescribed by law as can be demonstrably justified in a free and democratic society.[28]

In Australia, having a written constitution but no Canadian-style Charter of Rights, pornography is largely regulated by State, rather than Federal, law. Exceptions to this lie in the area of customs and excise prohibitions on importing pornographic material and also in the regulation of films and computer games where the State have given power to the Federal Government under 'cross vesting' legislation. In the absence of entrenched freedom of expression legislation, pornography has not become a battleground for litigation as it has become in the United States of America.

THE SCALE OF 'THE PROBLEM' OF PORNOGRAPHY

Pornography is largely a creature of technology. In earlier times, aside from pictorial pornographic images, pornography's existence was dependent upon both printing technology and levels of literacy in society, the scale of pornography was small (if significant). Nowadays, pornography is available in books, magazines, film, video, television, computer software and via the internet. Internationally the pornography business is estimated to amount annually to billions of US dollars. The materials may be generalised or specialised. There is growing lesbian and male homosexual pornography. Paedophiles, fetishists, sadomasochists: all are catered for.[29]

---

27   See *ibid*, p 235.

28   *Ibid*, p 236.

29   See S Dwyer, *The Problem of Pornography* (Wadsworth, 1995) Chapter 1.

Possible approaches to the pornography 'problem'

1   Pornography offends society's morality: accordingly the law must protect society against pornography.

2   Pornography is an aspect of freedom of expression. In the absence of clear evidence of 'harm' pornography cannot be restricted.

3   Pornography is a manifestation of freedom of expression. However, access to pornography may be restricted to reflect the preferences of society, provided that the restrictions are reasonable and do not place too great an inconvenience etc on those wishing to have access to it.

4   Pornography is outside the boundaries of freedom of expression: it is accordingly not protected by 'free speech' constitutional guarantee.

5   Pornography is an aspect of sexual discrimination and sexual hatred (or incitement thereto). As a central tenet of male supremacy and female subordination, those harmed by pornography should have access to (civil) legal remedies.

Pornography has represented a site of conflict amongst legal scholars. Liberal feminists argue that pornography is in some sense freedom of expression, or alternatively is unproblematical for women in the sense that it is not a causal factor in sexual discrimination or sexual hatred.[30] Alternatively it is argued by liberal scholars, such as Ronald Dworkin, that whatever the possible harm caused by pornography, that harm is overshadowed by the constant and pervasive presentation of women in the media and arts in traditional, subservient, domestic roles or in the portrayal of women – subtle or not – as sexual objects which 'sell' products in advertising.

For radical feminist scholars, such 'defences' of pornography, or the minimising of pornography's damaging effects represents, to adopt Catharine MacKinnon's phrase 'collaboration'.[31]

The enforcement of morals argument

Lord Devlin is the leading exponent of the right – indeed duty – of the law to protect morality within society. Protection of morality is as important as protection against subversion of the State.[32] However, this should not be taken to imply that there should be no toleration. As Devlin states:

> the first factor ... is that there must be toleration of the maximum individual freedom that is consistent with the integrity of society ... the judgment which the community passes on a practice which it dislikes must be calm and dispassionate and ... mere disapproval is not enough to justify interference.[33]

---

30   See for an example of a feminist anti-anti-pornography approach, Alison Assiter and Avedon Carol (eds), *Bad Girls and Dirty Pictures: The Challenge to Radical Feminism* (Pluto Press, 1993).

31   See CA MacKinnon, *On Collaboration* in *Feminism Unmodified: Discourses on Life and Law* (Harvard University Press, 1987).

32   *The Enforcement of Morals* (1965), p 14.

33   *Ibid*, Preface ix.

Thus what is punishable by law must be something 'which lies beyond the limits of tolerance'. For Devlin it is not enough that 'a majority dislike a practice; there must be a real feel of reprobation ...'. [34] The judgment as to whether such an effect has been caused by the material is to be made by the 'man in the jury box'. [35] If 12 jurymen come to the unanimous conclusion that something is 'injurious to society' and beyond the limits of tolerance, the law has a right to regulate the matter. This is the view given judicial expression in *Shaw v DPP*: [36]

> There remains in the courts of law a residual power to enforce the supreme and fundamental purpose of the law, to conserve not only the safety and order but also the moral welfare of the State. [37]

Professor HLA Hart observes that morality represents a 'seamless web' within society which binds it together. Without the protection of law, from Devlin's point of view, this 'seamless web' would cease to exist: society would 'disintegrate'. [38] There is little evidence that this is the case – again, as Hart observes – moral values in society shift over time: any rigorous enforcement of moral standards today would not necessarily 'freeze' morality. Society must evolve in its own way.

The liberal's dilemma

John Stuart Mill: *On Liberty*

John Stuart Mill, writing in 1869, argued for the sovereignty of the free individual exercising freedom of conscience, thought and expression 'without impediment from our fellow-creatures, so long as what he does not harm them, even though they should think our conduct foolish perverse, or wrong'. [39] Mill's view, ie that the role of the law should be confined to the prevention of harm to others raises the issue of liberalism and equality, can be stated as follows:

> [T]hat principle is, that the sole end for which mankind are warranted, individually or collectively, in interfering with the liberty of action of any of their number, is self-protection. That the only purpose for which power can be rightfully exercised over any member of a civilised community, against his will, is to prevent harm to others. His own good, either physical or moral, is not a sufficient warrant. [40]

On this basis, without clear proof of harm, there could be no justified legal restriction. Without proof of harm we are free to educate, to criticise, but not to infringe another's liberty by legislating. The inescapable difficulty in relation to pornography is evaluating the harm it causes in a meaningful manner. As seen below, the empirical evidence as to harm is equivocal. From a radical feminist

---

34 *Ibid*, p 17.

35 *Ibid*, p 15.

36 [1962] AC 220.

37 At p 267.

38 *Law, Liberty and Morality* (1963).

39 *On Liberty* (Cambridge University Press), p 15.

40 *Ibid*, p 13.

perspective, however, the issue of harm is less whether, and the extent to which, there can be proven to be a specific cause and effect relationship, and rather more the idea that it is pornography, in its often sadistic depiction of women generally degraded, hurt and violated, and always submitting to male domination, which of itself – without more – is the harm. For the harm from this perspective, as argued by Andrea Dworkin and Catharine MacKinnon, is to all women, the image of all women, and not only those participating in the acts portrayed.

Empirical evidence concerning pornography[41]

The question – from a liberal perspective – is whether restrictions on freedom of expression should be allowed on the basis that it causes 'harm' to others. This 'harm' principle was adopted by the Williams' Committee in its review of obscenity and censorship.[42] The problem with the 'harm' principle in relation to pornography lies in establishing whether harm is caused, and to whom. The evidence itself is equivocal and provides no clear basis on which to draw conclusions.[43] Thus, for example, the United States Commission on Obscenity and Pornography concluded (by a majority) in 1970, that the evidence was insufficient to establish that 'pornography is a central causal factor in acts of sexual violence.'[44] Conversely the Canadian Attorney General's Commission on Pornography, reporting in 1986, concluded that:

> The available evidence strongly supports the hypothesis that substantial exposure to sexually violent materials as described here bears a causal relationship to antisocial acts of violence and, for some subgroups, possibly to unlawful acts of sexual violence.[45]

The efficacy of the pornography debate which focuses on the 'cause and effect' construction has been examined by Deborah Cameron and Elizabeth Frazer, who argue for a rejection of the 'simplistic' linkage between pornography and sexual violence.[46] Notwithstanding that, the authors argue that the pornography debate must be advanced – albeit with a different focus. Basing their argument on the idea that pornography is a form of representation,[47] the writers argue that while in their view it cannot be proven to cause sexual

---

41 See, *inter alia*, Edna F Einsiedel, 'The Experimental Research Evidence: Effect on Pornography on the Average Individual'; Diana Russell, 'Pornography and Rape: A Causal Model'; James Check, 'The Effects of Violent Pornography, Non-Violent Dehumanising Pornography', and 'Erotica: Some Legal Implications from a Canadian Perspective', all reproduced in Catherine Itzin, *Pornography: Women, Violence and Civil Liberties* (Oxford University Press, 1992).

42 *Report of the Committee on Obscenity and Film Censorship* (Cmnd 7772) (London: HMSO, 1979).

43 D Howitt and G Cumberbatch, *Pornography: Impacts and Influences* (London: Home Office, 1990).

44 See Legal Appendix *op cit*, p 241.

45 *Ibid*, p 245.

46 See D Cameron and E Fraser, 'On the Question of Pornography and Sexual Violence: Moving Beyond Cause and Effect' in C Itzin (ed), *Pornography: Women, Violence and Civil Liberties* (Oxford University Press, 1992).

47 On which see, Susanne Keppeler, *The Pornography of Representation* (Polity Press, 1986).

violence, pornography plays a role in 'shaping certain forms of desire'. These forms, they argue, are essentially transgressive (ie it is 'illicit, forbidden, a dirty secret'): that is to say, that pornographic representations transgress the boundaries of acceptable sexual behaviour and practices and establish in the minds of its consumers, some normative standard to be achieved.[48] The harm caused by pornographic representations lies in the portrayal of men in a position of 'transcendence and mastery' over women. Women, conversely, are portrayed as the 'Other', the (submissive) object of desire of the male consumer. In moving beyond a debate focussing on the cause and effect relationship between pornography and sexual violence, the authors argue that feminists need to develop further an understanding of the effects of pornographic representation and sexual practices with a view to 'shaping alternative' visions of sexual practices which celebrate neither mastery nor submission.

Feminist legal theorists Catharine MacKinnon[49] and Andrea Dworkin[50] argue the case against pornography on the basis that it demeans women by 'objectifying' them – portraying women as merely objects to be used by men:[51]

> Pornography, in the feminist view, is a form of forced sex, a practice of sexual politics, an institution of gender inequality. In this perspective, pornography, with the rape and prostitution in which it participates, institutionalises the sexuality of male supremacy, which fuses the erotisation of dominance and submission with the social construction of male and female. Gender is sexual. Pornography constitutes the meaning of that sexuality. Men treat women as they see women as being. Pornography constructs who that is. Men's power over women means that the way men see women defines who women can be. Pornography is that way. In this light, obscenity law can be seen to treat morals from the male point of view, meaning the standpoint of male dominance. The feminist critique of pornography, by contrast, proceeds from women's point of view, meaning the standpoint of the subordination of women to men.[52]

The Dworkin and MacKinnon Civil Rights' Ordinances

It is for reasons such as those expressed above that Catharine MacKinnon and Andrea Dworkin drafted, in 1983, the amendment to the Minneapolis Civil Rights Ordinance.[53] The amendment both defines what is to be regarded as pornography and also defines pornography as 'a form of discrimination of the basis of sex' which is actionable in law. In 1984 the Indianapolis City and

---

48 See L Kelly, *Surviving Sexual Violence* (Polity Press, 1989).

49 *Feminism Unmodified* (Harvard University Press, 1987).

52 *Pornography: Men Possessing Women* (Women's Press, 1981).

51 The literature is now extensive. See A Dworkin, *Pornography* (Women's Press, 1981); 'Against the Male Flood'; E Wolgast, 'Pornography' in *Feminist Jurisprudence* (ed) P White. Catharine MacKinnon: see *Feminism Unmodified* (Harvard University Press, 1987); *Towards a Feminist Theory of State* (Harvard University Press); *Only Words* (1993). See also C Smart, *Feminism and the Power of Law* (London: Routledge 1989), especially Chapter 6; C Itzin (ed), *Pornography: Women, Violence and Civil Liberties* (Oxford University Press, 1992).

52 C MacKinnon, *Toward a Feminist Theory of State* (Harvard University Press, 1989) Chapter 11, p 197.

53 On which see further below.

County Council adopted a modified version of the Dworkin-MacKinnon *Model Anti-Pornography Ordinance*. The Indianapolis Ordinance prohibited any 'production, sale, exhibition, or distribution' of the material defined as pornographic. Pornography is defined in the Minneapolis Civil Rights Ordinance as:

> Pornography is the sexually explicit subordination of women, graphically depicted, whether in pictures or in words, that also includes one or more of the following:
>
> (i)   women are presented dehumanised as sexual objects, things or commodities; or
>
> (ii)   women are presented as sexual objects who enjoy pain or humiliation; or
>
> (iii) women are presented as sexual objects who experience sexual pleasure in being raped; or
>
> (iv) women are presented as sexual objects tied up or cut up or mutilated or bruised or physically hurt; or
>
> (v)   women are presented in postures of sexual submission; or
>
> (vi) women's body parts – including but not limited to vaginas, breasts, and buttocks – are exhibited, such that women are reduced to those parts; or
>
> (vii) women are presented as whores by nature; or
>
> (viii) women are presented as being penetrated by objects or animals; or
>
> (ix) women are presented in scenarios of degradation, injury, abasement, torture, shown as filthy or inferior, bleeding, bruised, or hurt in a context that makes those conditions sexual.

In addition the ordinance provided that:

> The use of men, children, or transsexuals in the place of women in ... (i)-(ix) above is pornography ...

Rather than seeking to prohibit the production and distribution of pornography, a solution which is favoured by right-wing moralists, the Ordinances provided not for prohibition and enforcement thereof through the criminal law agencies, but by using the civil law to provide remedies for those harmed by pornography – either directly or indirectly. The Ordinances cannot therefore be seen as attempted censorship, but rather the provision of civil remedies for those harmed by pornography.[54] How have the Ordinances fared? They have, in short, been declared unconstitutional on the basis of violating the First Amendment to the US Constitution: the right to freedom of speech.[55] In *American Booksellers Association Inc v Hudnut*, the Circuit Court for the Seventh Circuit upheld the District Court's ruling and the Supreme Court summarily refused to review that decision. Judge Easterbrook in the Circuit Court ruled that nothing must be censored 'because the message it seeks to deliver is a bad one, or because it expresses ideas that should not be heard at all'.[56]

---

54 For an analysis of the strengths and weaknesses of the campaign, see Mary Joe Frug, *The Politics of Postmodern Feminism: Lessons from the Anti-Pornography Campaign in Postmodern Legal Feminism* (Routledge, 1991) Chapter 8.

55 *American Booksellers Association Inc v Hudnut* 771 F 2d aff'd S Ct 1172 [1986].

56 Cited in R Dworkin, *Liberty and Pornography*, p 117, *The Problem of Pornography, op cit*.

In the first extract in this Chapter, feminist writer Andrea Dworkin[57] defines pornography from a radical feminist perspective. In *Whores* Andrea Dworkin analyses pornography. Women are defined by pornographic representations and by prostitution – women become defined as little more than sexual objects. For the author, as will be seen, there is a politics to pornography: both left and right, which together collude to mask the real meaning of pornography.

In *Francis Biddle's Sister*, feminist lawyer Professor Catharine MacKinnon argues that pornography constructs the social reality of gender – the subordination and inequality of women. Pornography defines women. Pornography's effect is to make the twin relationships of male domination and female subordination into the reality of sex. Pornography is the practice of sexual discrimination.

In the Preface to *Only Words*,[58] Catharine MacKinnon advances the feminist analysis of the potentiality of law for the control of pornography. If, the author argues, individuals may be prosecuted for standing by and actively encouraging a murder, why should not the same argument be made for those active in the pornography industry: do not they also participate in the violation and abuse of women?

Elizabeth Wolgast analyses the traditional liberal tradition in relation to pornography. In *Pornography and the Tyranny of the Majority*,[59] the author considers liberalism as characterised by John Stuart Mill. Would Mill, despite his clear injunction regarding the use of law to intervene in matters of private morality in the absence of proof of clear harm? Should the First Amendment of the United States' Constitution be employed to protect pornography as an incident of free speech. The author analyses that there are reasons why it should not do so. For Wolgast, the issue is one of respect for women versus their continued inferiority which is promoted by pornography.

Emily Jackson, in *The Problem with Pornography: A Critical Survey of the Current Debate*,[60] considers the difficulties in defining pornography; the differing interpretations of pornography; the opposing analyses of 'what to do about' pornography and the role of law in its regulation.

PORNOGRAPHY: MEN POSSESSING WOMEN[61]
Andrea Dworkin

The word 'pornography', derived from the ancient Greek '*porne*' and '*graphos*', means 'writing about whores'. '*Porne*' means 'whore', specifically and exclusive the lowest class of whore, which in ancient Greece was the brothel slut available to all male citizens. The *porne* was the cheapest (in the literal sense), least regarded, least protected of all women, including slaves. She was, simply and clearly and absolutely, a sexual slave. '*Graphos*' means 'writing, etching, or drawing'.

---

57 In *Pornography: Men Possessing Women* (The Women's Press, 1981).
58 Harper Collins, 1994.
59 *The Grammar of Justice* (Ithica: Cornell, 1987).
60 [1995] *Feminist Legal Studies* 49.
61 Women's Press, 1981.

The word 'pornography' does not mean 'writing about sex' or 'depictions of the erotic' or 'depictions of sexual acts' or 'depictions of nude bodies' or 'sexual representations' or any other such euphemism. It means the graphic depiction of women as vile whores. In ancient Greece, not all prostitutes were considered vile: only the *porneia*. Contemporary pornography strictly and literally conforms to the word's root meaning: the graphic depiction of vile whores, or, in our language, sluts, cows (as in: sexual cattle, sexual chattel), cunts. The word has not changed its meaning and the genre is not misnamed. The only change in the meaning of the word is with respect to its second part, graphos: now there are cameras – there is still photography, film, video. The methods of graphic depiction have increased in number and in kind: the content is the same; the meaning is the same; the purpose is the same; the status of the women depicted is the same; the sexuality of the women depicted is the same; the value of the women depicted is the same. With the technologically advanced methods of graphic depiction, real women are required for the depiction as such to exist.

The word pornography does not have any other meaning that the one cited here, the graphic description of the lowest whores. Whores exist to serve men sexually. Whores exist only within a framework of male sexual domination. Indeed, outside the framework the notion of whores would be absurd and the usage of women as whores would be impossible. The word whore is incomprehensible unless one is immersed in the lexicon of male domination. Men have created the group, the type, the concept, the epithet, the insult, the industry, the trade, the commodity, the reality of woman as whore. Woman as whore exists within the objective and real system of male sexual domination. The pornography itself is objective and real and central to the male sexual system. The valuation of women's sexuality in pornography is objective and real because women are so regarded and so valued. The force depicted in pornography is objective and real because force is so used against women. The debasing of women depicted in pornography and intrinsic to it is objective and real in what women are so debased. The uses of women depicted in pornography are objective and real because women are so used. The women used in pornography are used in pornography. The definition of women articulated systematically and consistently in pornography is objective and real in that real women exist within and must live with constant reference to the boundaries of this definition. The fact that pornography is widely believed to be 'sexual representations' or 'depictions of sex' emphasises only that the valuation of women as low whores is widespread and that the sexuality of women is perceived as low and whorish in, and of itself. The fact that pornography is widely believed to be 'depictions of the erotic' means only that the debasing of women is held to be the real pleasure of sex. As Kate Millett wrote, women's sexuality is reduced to the only essential: 'cunt ... our essence, our offence.' The idea that pornography is 'dirty' originates in the conviction that the sexuality of women is dirty and is actually portrayed in pornography; that women's bodies (especially women's genitals) are dirty and lewd in themselves. Pornography does not, as some claim, refute the idea that female sexuality is dirty: instead, pornography embodies and exploits this idea; pornography sells and promotes it.

In the United States, the pornography industry is larger than the record and film industries combined. In a time of widespread economic impoverishment, it is growing: more and more male consumers are eager to spend more and more money on pornography – on depictions of women as vile whores. Pornography is now carried by cable television; it is now being marketed for home use in video machines. The technology itself demands the creation of more and more *porneia* to meet the market opened up by the technology. Real women are tied up, stretched, hanged, fucked, gang-banged, whipped, beaten and begging for more. In the photographs and films, real women are used as *porneia* and real women are depicted as *porneia*. To profit, the pimps must supply the *porneia* as the technology widens the market for the visual consumption of women being brutalised and loving it. One picture is worth a thousand words. The number of pictures required to meet the demands of the marketplace determines the number of *porneia* required to meet the demands of graphic depiction. The numbers grow as the technology and its accessibility grow. The technology by its very nature encourages more and more passive acquiescence to the graphic depictions. Passivity makes the already credulous consumer more credulous. He comes to the pornography a believer; he goes away from it a missionary. The technology itself legitimises the uses of women conveyed by it.

In the male system, women are sex; sex is the whore. The whore is *pornê*, the lowest whore, the whore who belongs to all male citizens: the slut, the cunt. Buy her is buying pornography. Having her is pornography. Seeing her is pornography. Seeing her sex, especially her genitals, is seeing pornography. Seeing her in sex is seeing the whore in sex. Using her is using pornography. Wanting her means wanting pornography. Being her means pornography.[62]

WHORES[63]

Andrea Dworkin

> The best houses do not exhibit the women in cages. (The Nightless City or the History of the Yoshiwara Yukwaku, 1899 report on a red-light district in Japan.)

Male sexual domination is a material system with an ideology and a metaphysics. The sexual colonialisation of women's bodies is a material reality: men control the sexual and reproductive uses of women's bodies. The institutions of control include law, marriage, prostitution, pornography, health care, the economy, organised religion, and systematised physical aggression against women (for instance, in rape and battery). Male domination of the female body is the basic material reality of women's lives; and all struggle for dignity and self-determination is rooted in the struggle for actual control of one's own body, especially control over physical access to one's own body. The ideology of male sexual domination posits that men are superior to women by virtue of their penises; that physical possession of the female is a natural right of the male; that sex is, in fact, conquest and possession of the female, especially but not exclusively phallic conquest and phallic possession; that the use of the female body for sexual or reproductive purposes is a natural right of men; that the sexual will of men properly and naturally defines the parameters of a woman's sexual being, which is her whole identity.

The metaphysics of male sexual domination is that women are whores. This basic truth transcends all lesser truths in the male system. One does not violate something by using it for what it is: neither rape nor prostitution is an abuse of the female because in both the female is fulfilling her natural function; that is why rape is absurd and incomprehensible as an abusive phenomenon in the male system, and so is prostitution, which is held to be voluntary even when the prostitute is hit, threatened, drugged, or locked in. The woman's effort to stay

---

62 *Pornography: Men Possessing Women*, pp 199–202.
63 Andrea Dworkin, *Pornography: Men Possessing Women* (Women's Press, 1981), Chapter 7.

innocent, prove innocence, her effort to prove in any instance of sexual use that she was used against her will, is always and unequivocally an effort to prove that she is not a whore. The presumption that she is a whore is a metaphysical presumption: a presumption that underlies the system of reality in which she lives. A whore cannot be raped, only used. A whore by nature cannot be forced to whore – only revealed through circumstance to be the whore she is. The point is her nature, which is a whore's nature. The word 'whore' can be construed to mean that she is a cunt with enough gross intelligence to manipulate, barter, or sell. The cunt wants it; the whore knows enough to use it. 'Cunt' is the most reductive word; whore adds the dimension of character – greedy, manipulative, not nice. The word whore reveals her sensual nature (cunt) and her natural character.

'No prostitute of anything resembling intelligence', writes Mencken, 'is under the slightest duress ...'.[64] 'What is a prostitute?' asks William Acton in his classic work on prostitution. 'she is a woman who gives for money that which she ought to give only for love ...'[65] Jane Addams, who worked against the so-called white slave trade, noted that '[t]he one impression which the trial [of procurers] left upon our minds was that all the men concerned in the prosecution felt a keen sense of outrage against the method employed to secure the girl [kidnapping] but took for granted that the life she was about to lead was in the established order of things, if she had chosen it voluntarily'.[66] Only the maternal can mitigate the whorish, an opposition more conceptual than real, based on the assumption that the maternal or older woman is no longer desired. Freud writes to Jung that a son approaching adulthood naturally loses his incestuous desires for the mother 'with her sagging belly and varicose veins'.[67] Rene Guyon, who argued for male-defined sexual liberation, writes that '[w]oman ages much sooner. Much earlier in life she loses her freshness, her charm, and begins to look withered or overripe. She ceases to be an object of desire'.[68] The mother is not the whore only when men have stopped desiring her.

Guyon, in whose name societies for sexual freedom exist today, held that women were defined exclusively by their sexuality, which was essentially and intrinsically the sexuality of the prostitute. 'Womens sexual parasitism', writes Guyon, 'is innate. She has a congenital tendency to rely on man for support, availing herself of her sexual arts, offering in return for maintenance (and more, if she can get it) the partial or complete possession of her person'.[69] This propensity for exchanging her body for material goods is her sexuality, her purpose, her passion, and consequently '[s]ale or contract, monogamy or harem – these words mean little to her in comparison with the goal'.[70] For this reason, Guyon contends that even the so-called white slave trade – the organised abduction of lone or young or destitute women for the purposes of prostitution – cannot be construed as forcible prostitution:

64 HL Mencken, *In Defence of Women* (Garden City Publishing Co, 1922), p 187.
65 William Acton, *Prostitution* (New York: Frederick A Praeger, 1969), p 118.
66 Jane Addams, *A New Conscience and An Ancient Evil* (New York: Macmillian, 1914), p 40.
67 Sigmund Freud, *The Freud/Jung Letters*, ed William McGuire, trans Ralph Manheim and RFC Hull (Princeton University Press, 1974), p 503.
68 R Guyon, *Sexual Freedom*, trans Eden and Cedar Paul (New York: Alfred A Knopf, 1958), p 239.
69 *Ibid*, p 198.
70 *Ibid*, p 200.

> How hypocritical it is to speak of the White [*sic*] Slave Trade only as a means
> for recruiting the ranks of prostitution. The White [*sic*] Slave Trade is
> universal, being carried on with the consent of the 'slaves', since every
> woman has a specific sexual value. She must sell herself to the highest bidder,
> even though she cheat as to the quality of the goods.[71]

Like most male advocates of sexual freedom (the unrestrained expression of male
sexuality) Guyon theoretically and repeatedly deplores the use of force; he
simply never recognises its existence in the sexual use of women.

Typically, every charge by women that force is used to violate women – in rape,
battery, or prostitution – is dismissed by positing a female nature that is
essentially fulfilled by the act of violation, which in turn transforms violation into
merely using a thing for what it is and blames the thing if it is not womanly
enough to enjoy what is done to it.

Sometimes 'consent' is construed to exist. More often, the woman is perceived to
have an active desire to be used by the male on his terms. Great Britain's
Wolfenden Report, renowned for its recommendation that legal persecution of
consenting male homosexuals cease, was also a report on female prostitution.
The report stressed that 'there are women who, even when there is no economic
need to do so, choose this form of livelihood'.[72] It recommended increasing legal
penalties against prostitutes and argued for more stringent enforcement of laws
aimed at prostitutes. Male sexual privilege was affirmed both in the vindication
of consensual male homosexuality and in the advocacy of greater persecution of
female prostitutes. At the same time, women's degraded status was affirmed.
The whore has a nature that chooses prostitution. She should be punished for her
nature, which determines her choice and which exists independent of any social
or economic necessity. The male homosexual also has a nature, for which he
should not be punished.

This desire of the woman to prostitute herself is often portrayed as greed for
money or pleasure or both. The natural woman is a whore, but the professional
prostitute is a greedy whore: greedy for sensation, pleasure, money, men.
Novelist Alberto Moravia, like many leftist writers seemingly obsessed with the
prostituted woman, writes in an assumed first-person female voice to convey the
woman's pleasure in prostitution:

> The feeling I experienced at that moment bewildered me and, no matter how
> or when I have received money from men since, I have never again
> experienced it so clearly and so intensely. It was a feeling of complicity and
> sensual conspiracy ... It was a feeling of inevitable subjection which showed
> me in a flash an aspect of my own nature I had ignored until then. I knew, of
> course, that I ought to refuse the money, but at the same time I wanted to
> accept. And not so much from greed, as from a new kind of pleasure which
> this offering had afforded me.[73]

The pleasure of the prostitute is the pleasure of any woman used in sex – but
heightened. The specific – the professional whore – exists in the context of the
general – women who are whores by nature. There is additional pleasure in

---

71 *Ibid*, p 204.

72 John Wolfenden, *Report of the Committee on Homosexual Offences and Prostitution* (London:
    HMSO, 1957), p 80.

73 Alberto Moravia, *The Woman of Rome*, trans Lydia Holland (New York: Manor Books, 1974),
    p 88.

being bought because money fixes her status as one who is for sex, not just woman but essence of woman or double-woman. The professional prostitute is distinguished from other women not in kind but by degree. 'There are certainly no women absolutely devoid of the prostitute instinct to covet being sexually excited by any stranger',[74] writes Weininger, emphasising both pleasure and vanity. 'If a woman hasn't got a tiny streak of a harlot in her', writes DH Lawrence, 'she's a dry stick as a rule'.[75] The tininess of Lawrence's 'streak' should not be misunderstood: 'really, most wives sold themselves, in the past, and plenty of harlots gave themselves, when they felt like it, for nothing.'[76] The 'tiny streak' is her sexual nature: without a streak of whore, 'she's a dry stick as a rule.'

There is a right-wing ideology and a left-wing ideology. The right-wing ideology claims that the division of mother and whore is phenomenologically real. The virgin is the potential mother. The left-wing ideology claims that sexual freedom is in the unrestrained use of women, the use of women as a collective natural resource, not privatised, not owned by one man but instead used by many. The metaphysics is the same on the left and on the right: the sexuality of the woman actualised is the sexuality of the whore; desire on her part is the slut's lust; once sexually available, it does not matter how she is used, why, by whom, by how many, or how often. Her sexual will can exist only as a will to be used. Whatever happens to her, it is all the same. If she loathes it, it is not wrong, she is.

Within this system, the only choice for the woman has been to embrace herself as whore, as sexual wanton or sexual commodity within phallic boundaries, or to disavow desire, disavow her body. The most cynical use of women has been on the left – cynical because the word 'freedom' is used to capture the loyalties of women who want, more than anything, to be free and who are then valued and used as left-wing whores: collectivised cunts. The most cynical use of women has been on the right – cynical because the word good is used to capture the loyalties of women who want, more than anything, to be good and who are then valued and used as right-wing whores: wives, the whores who breed. As Kate Millett writes: '... the great mass of women throughout history have been confined to the cultural level of animal life in providing the male with sexual outlet and exercising the animal functions of reproduction and care of the young.'[77]

Men of the right and men of the left have an undying allegiance to prostitution as such, regardless of their theoretical relationship to marriage. The left sees the prostitute as the free, public woman of sex, exciting because she flaunts it, because of her brazen availability. The right sees in the prostitute the power of the bad woman of sex, the male's use of her being his dirty little secret. The old pornography industry was a right-wing industry: secret money, secret sin, secret sex, secret promiscuity, secret buying and selling of women, secret profit, secret pleasure not only from sex but also from the buying and selling. The new pornography industry is a left-wing industry: promoted especially by the boys of the 1960s as simple pleasure, lusty fun, public sex, the whore brought out of the bourgeois (sic) home into the streets for the democratic consumption of all men; her freedom, her free sexuality, is as his whore – and she likes it. It is her political

74 Otto Weininger, *Sex and Character* (New York: GP Putman's Sons, 1975), p 219.
75 DH Lawrence, *Sex, Literature and Censorship*, ed Harry T Moore (New York: Twayne Publishers, 1953), p 69.
76 *Ibid*.
77 Kate Millett, *Sexual Politics* (New York: Avon Books, 1971), p 119.

will as well as her sexual will; it is liberation. The dirty little secret of the left-wing pornography industry is not sex but commerce.

The new pornography industry is held, by leftist males, to be inherently radical. Sex is claimed by the left as a leftist phenomenon; the trade in women is most of sex. The politics of liberation are claimed as indigenous to the left by the left; central to the politics of liberation is the mass-marketing of material that depicts women being used as whores. The pimps of pornography are hailed by leftists as saviours and savants. Larry Flynt has been proclaimed a saviour of the counter-culture, a working-class hero, and even, in a full-page advertisement in the *New York Times* signed by distinguished leftist literati, an 'American Dissident' persecuted as Soviet dissidents are. Hugh Hefner is viewed as a pioneer of sexual freedom who showed, in the words of columnist Max Lerner, 'how the legislating of sexuality could be fought, how the absurd anti-play and anti-pleasure ethic could be turned into a stylish hedonism and a lifeway which includes play and playfulness along with work'.[78] Lerner also credits Hefner with being a precursor of the women's movement.

On the left, the sexually liberated woman is the woman of pornography. Free male sexuality wants, has a right to, produces, and consumes pornography because pornography is pleasure. Leftist sensibility promotes and protects pornography because pornography is freedom. The pornography glut is bread and roses for the masses. Freedom is the mass-marketing of woman as whore. Free sexuality for the woman is in being massively consumed, denied an individual nature, denied any sexual sensibility other than that which serves the male. Capitalism is not wicked or cruel when the commodity is the whore. Profit is not wicked or cruel when the alienated worker is a female piece of meat. Corporate bloodsucking is not wicked or cruel when the corporations in question organised crime syndicates selling cunt. Racism is not wicked or cruel when the black cunt or yellow cunt or red cunt or Hispanic cunt or Jewish cunt has her legs splayed for any man's pleasure. Poverty is not wicked or cruel when it is the poverty of dispossessed women who have only themselves to sell. Violence by the powerful against the powerless is not wicked or cruel when it is called sex. Slavery is not wicked or cruel when it is sexual slavey; torture is not wicked or cruel when the tormented are women, whores, cunts. The new pornography is left-wing; and the new pornography is a vast graveyard where the left has gone to die. The left cannot have its whores and its politics too ...[79]

... In the system of male sexual domination explicated in pornography, there is no way out, no redemption: not through desire, not through reproduction. The woman's sex is appropriated, her body is possessed, she is used and she is despised: the pornography does it and the pornography proves it. The power of men in pornography is imperial power, the power of the sovereigns who are cruel and arrogant, who keep taking and conquering for the pleasure of power and the power of pleasure. Women are the land, as Marcuse wrote. He did not write the rest: men are the army; penises and their symbolic representations are the weapons; terror is the means; violence is the so-called sex. And inside this system, women are porn, in our real live bodies the graphic depictions of whores, used as whores are used, valued as whores are valued.

78 Max Lerner, 'Playboy: An American Revolution of Morality' (1979) *New York Post*, 10 January.

79 Andrea Dworkin, *Pornography, op cit*, pp 203–09.

... We will know that we are free when the pornography no longer exists. As long as it does exist, we must understand that we are the women in it: used by the same power, subject to the same valuation, as the vile whores who beg for more. The boys are betting on our compliance, our ignorance, our fear. We have always refused to face the worst that men have done to us. The boys count on it. The boys are betting that we cannot face the horror of their sexual system and survive. The boys are betting that their depictions of us as whores will beat us down and stop our hearts. The boys are betting that their penises and fists and knives and fucks and rapes will turn us into what they say we are – the compliant women of sex, the voracious cunts of pornography, the masochistic sluts who resist because we really want more. All the boys are betting. The boys are wrong.[80]

FRANCIS BIDDLE'S SISTER: PORNOGRAPHY, CIVIL RIGHTS, AND SPEECH[81]

Catharine MacKinnon[82]

I will first situate a critique of pornography within a feminist analysis of the condition of women. I will speak of what pornography means for the social status and treatment of women. I will briefly contrast that with the obscenity approach, the closest this government has come to addressing pornography. Next I will outline an argument for the constitutionality of the ordinance Andrea Dworkin and I conceived, in which we define pornography as a civil rights violation. Here I will address what pornography does as a practice of sex discrimination, and the vision of the First Amendment with which our law is consistent. Evidence, much of it drawn from hearings on the ordinance in Minneapolis, supports this argument. The Supreme Court has never considered this legal injury before, nor the factual support we bring to it. They have allowed the recognition of similar injuries to other people, consistent with their interpretation of the First Amendment. More drastic steps have been taken on a showing of a great deal less harm, and the courts have allowed it. The question is: will they do it for women? ...[83]

... My formal agenda has three parts. The first treats pornography by connecting epistemology – which I understand to be about theories of knowing – with politics – which I will take to be about theories of power. For instance, Justice Stewart said of obscenity, 'I know it when I see it'.[84] I see this as a statement connecting epistemology – what he knows through his way of knowing, in this case, seeing – with the fact that his seeing determines what obscenity is in terms of what he sees it to be, because of his position of power. To wonder if he and I know the same things from what we see, given what's on the newsstand, is not a personal query about him.

Another example of the same conceptual connection is this. Having power means, among other things, that when someone says, 'This is how it is' it is taken as being that way. When this happens in law, such a person is accorded what is

---

80 *Pornography*, p 224.
81 *Feminism Unmodified: Discourses on Life and Law* (Harvard University Press, 1987). Footnotes edited.
82 At the time of writing, Professor of Law, University of Michigan.
83 *Francis Biddle's Sister*, p 163.
84 *Jocobellis v Ohio* 378 US 184 at 197 (1964).

called credibility. When that person is believed over another speaker, what was said becomes proof. Speaking socially, the beliefs of the powerful become proof, in part because the world actually arranges itself to affirm what the powerful want to see. If you perceive this as a process, you might call it force, or at least pressure or socialisation or what money can buy. If it is imperceptible as a process, you may consider it voluntary or consensual or free will or human nature, or just the way things are. Beneath this, though, the world is not entirely the way the powerful say it is or want to believe it is. If it appears to be, it is because power constructs the appearance of reality by silencing the voices of the powerless, by excluding them from access to authoritative discourse. Powerlessness means that when you say 'this is how it is', it is not taken as being that way. This makes articulating silence, perceiving the presence of absence, believing those who have been socially stripped of credibility, critically contextualising what passes for simple fact, necessary to the epistemology of a politics of the powerless.

My second thematic concern is jurisprudential. It is directed toward identifying, in order to change, one dimension of liberalism as it is embodied in law: the definition of justice as neutrality between abstract categories. The liberal view is that abstract categories – like speech or equality – define systems. Every time you strengthen free speech in one place, you strengthen it everywhere. Strengthening the free speech of the Klan strengthens the free speech of blacks. Getting things for men strengthens equality for women. Getting men access to women's schools strengthens women's access to education. What I will be exploring is the way in which substantive systems, made up of real people with social labels attached, are also systems. You can reverse racism abstractly, but white supremacy is unfudgeably substantive. Sexism can be an equal abstraction, but male supremacy says who is where. Substantive systems like white supremacy do substantively different things to people of colour than they do to white people. To say they are also systems is to say that every time you score one for white supremacy in one place, it is strengthened every place else. In this view, the problem with neutrality as the definition of principle in constitutional adjudications is that it equates substantive powerlessness with substantive power and calls treating these the same, 'equality.' The neutrality approach understands that abstract systems are systems, but it seems not to understand that substantive systems are also systems ...[85]

... The *Lochner* line of cases[86] created concern about the evils of their substance, which, as women were erased, came to stand for the evils of substantivity as such. There has been correspondingly little discussion, with the partial exception of the debate on affirmative action,[87] on the drawbacks of abstraction as such. Granted, trying to do anything on a substantive basis is a real problem in a legal system that immediately turns everything into an abstraction. I do hope to identify this as something of a syndrome, as a risk of abuse. Considering it the definition of principle itself ensures that nothing will ever basically change, at least not by law.

---

85 *Francis Biddle's Sister*, p 164.

86 See *Lochner v New York* 198 US 45 (1905); *Allgeyer v Louisiana* 165 US 578 (1897) (invalidating maximum hours restrictions on the ground of liberty to freely contract).

87 See eg *Regents of the University of California v Bakke* 438 US 265 (1978); John Ely, *Democracy and Distrust: A Theory of Judicial Review* (1981), pp 54–55. But see Laurence Tribe, 'Speech as Power: Swastikas, Spending, and the Mask of Neutral Principles', in *Constitutional Choices* (1985).

When these two frames converge – epistemology and politics on the one hand with the critique of neutrality on the other – they form a third frame: one of political philosophy. Here is how they converge. Once power constructs social reality, as I will show pornography constructs the social reality of gender, the force behind sexism, the subordination in gender inequality, is made invisible; dissent from it becomes inaudible as well as rare. What a woman is, is defined in pornographic terms; this is what pornography does. If the law then looks neutrally on the reality of gender so produced, the harm that has been done will not be perceptible as harm. It becomes just the way things are. Refusing to look at what has been done substantively institutionalises inequality in law and makes it look just like principle.

In the philosophical terms of classical liberalism, an equality-freedom dilemma is produced: freedom to make or consume pornography weighs against the equality of the sexes. Some people's freedom hurts other people's equality. There is something to this, but my formulation, as you might guess, comes out a little differently. If one asks whose freedom pornography represents, a tension emerges that is not a dilemma among abstractions so much as it is a conflict between groups. Substantive interests are at stake on both sides of the abstract issues, and women are allowed to matter in neither. If women's freedom is as incompatible with pornography's construction of our freedom as our equality is incompatible with pornography's construction of our equality, we get neither freedom nor equality under the liberal calculus. Equality for women is incompatible with a definition of men's freedom that is at our expense. What can freedom for women mean, so long as we remain unequal? Why should men's freedom to use us in this way be purchased with our second-class civil status?

Substantively considered, the situation of women is not really like anything else. Its specificity is not just the result of our numbers – we are half the human race – and our diversity, which at times has obscured that we are a group with an interest at all. It is, in part, that our status as a group relative to men has almost never, if ever, been much changed from what it is. Women's roles do vary enough that gender, the social form sex takes, cannot be said to be biologically determined. Different things are valued in different cultures, but whatever is valued, women are not that. If bottom is bottom, look across time and space, and women are who you will find there. Together with this, you will find, in as varied forms as there are cultures, the belief that women's social inferiority to men is not that at all but is merely the sex difference.

Doing something legal about a situation that is not really like anything else is hard enough in a legal system that prides itself methodologically on reasoning by analogy. Add to this the specific exclusion or absence of women and women's concerns from the definition and design of this legal system since its founding, combined with its determined adherence to precedent, and you have a problem of systemic dimension. The best attempt at grasping women's situation in order to change it by law has centred on an analogy between sex and race in the discrimination context. This gets a lot, since inequalities are alike on some levels, but it also misses a lot. It gets the stigmatisation and exploitation and denigration of a group of people on the basis of a condition of birth. It gets that difference, made an issue of, is an excuse for dominance, and that if forced separation is allowed to mean equality in a society where the line of separation also divides top from bottom in a hierarchy, the harm of that separation is thereby made invisible. It also gets that defining neutrality as principle, when reality is not neutral, prevents change in the guise of promoting it. But segregation is not the central practice of the inequality of the sexes. Women are as often forcibly integrated with men, if not on an equal basis. And it did help the struggle against white supremacy that blacks had not always been in bondage to white people.

Most important, I think it never was a central part of the ideology of racism that the system of chattel slavery of Africans really was designed for their enjoyment and benefit. The system was defended as an expression of their true nature and worth. They were told to be grateful for good treatment and kind masters. Their successful struggle to organise resistance and avoid complicity while still surviving is instructive to all of us. But although racism has been defended by institutionalising it in law, and then calling that legal; although it has been cherished not just as a system of exploitation of labour but as a way of life; and although it is based on force, changes in its practices are opposed by implying that they are really only a matter of choice of personal values. For instance: 'you can't legislate morality.'[88] And slave owners did say they couldn't be racist – they loved their slaves. Nonetheless, few people pretended that the entire system existed because of its basis in love and mutual respect and veneration, that white supremacy really treated blacks in many cases better than whites, and that the primary intent and effect of their special status was and is their protection, pleasure, fulfilment, and liberation. Crucially, many have believed, and some actually still do, that Black people were not the equals of whites. But at least since *Brown v Board of Education*,[89] few have pretended, much less authoritatively, that the social system, as it was, was equality for them.[90]

Looking at the world from this point of view, a whole shadow world of previously invisible silent abuse has been discerned. Rape, battery, sexual harassment, forced prostitution, and the sexual abuse of children emerge as common and systematic. We find that rape happens to women in all contexts, from the family, including rape of girls and babies, to students and women in the workplace, on the streets, at home, in their own bedrooms by men they do not know and by men they do know, by men they are married to, men they have had a social conversation with, and, least often, men they have never seen before. Overwhelmingly, rape is something that men do or attempt to do to women (44% of American women according to a recent study)[91] at some point in our lives. Sexual harassment of women by men is common in workplaces and educational institutions. Based on reports in one study of the federal workforce, up to 85% of women will experience it, many in physical forms.[92] Between a quarter and a third of women are battered in their homes by men. Thirty-five per cent of little girls are sexually molested inside or outside the family. Until women listened to women, this world of sexual abuse was not spoken of. It was the unspeakable. What I am saying is, if you are the tree falling in the epistemological forest, your demise doesn't make a sound if no one is listening. Women did not 'report' these events, and overwhelmingly do not today, because no one is listening, because no one believes us. This silence does not mean nothing happened, and it does not mean consent. It is the silence of women of which Adrienne Rich has written, 'Do not confuse it with any kind of absence'.[93]

---

88   See eg Derrick Bell, *Race, Racism and American Law* (1972), pp 1–85.

89   347 US 483 (1954).

90   *Francis Biddle's Sister*, p 168.

91   See Diana Russell, 'The Prevalence of Rape in United States Revisited' (1983) 8 *Signs: Journal of Women in Culture and Society* 689.

92   *US Merit Systems Protections Board, Sexual Harassment in the Federal Workplace: is it a Problem?* (US Government Printing Office, 1981).

93   Adrienne Rich, 'Cartographies of Silence', in *The Dream of a Common Language* (1978).

Believing women who say we are sexually violated has been a radical departure, both methodologically and legally. The extent and nature of rape, marital rape, and sexual harassment itself, were discovered in this way. Domestic battery as a syndrome, almost a habit, was discovered through refusing to believe that when a woman is assaulted by a man to whom she is connected, that it is not an assault. The sexual abuse of children was uncovered, Freud notwithstanding, by believing that children were not making up all this sexual abuse.[94] Now what is striking is that when each discovery is made, and somehow made real in the world, the response has been: it happens to men too. If women are hurt, men are hurt. If women are raped, men are raped. If women are sexually harassed, men are sexually harassed. If women are battered, men are battered. Symmetry must be reasserted. Neutrality must be reclaimed. Equality must be re-established ...[95]

... Men are damaged by sexism (by men I mean the status of masculinity that is accorded to males on the basis of their biology but is not itself biological). But whatever the damage of sexism to men, the condition of being a man is not defined as subordinate to women by force. Looking at the facts of the abuses of women all at once, you see that a woman is socially defined as a person who, whether or not she is or has been, can be treated in these ways by men at any time, and little, if anything, will be done about it. This is what it means when feminists say that maleness is a form of power and femaleness is a form of powerlessness.

In this context, all of this 'men too' stuff means that people don't really believe that the things I have just said are true, though there really is little question about their empirical accuracy. The data are extremely simple, like women's pay figure of 59 cents on the dollar. People don't really seem to believe that either. Yet there is no question of its empirical validity. This is the workplace story: what women do is seen as not worth much, or what is not worth much is seen as something for women to do. Women are seen as not worth much, is the thing. Now why are these basic realities of the subordination of women to men, for example, that only 7.8% of women have never been sexually assaulted, not effectively believed, not perceived as real in the face of all this evidence? Why don't women believe our own experiences? In the face of all this evidence, especially of systematic sexual abuse – subjection to violence with impunity is one extreme expression, although not the only expression, of a degraded status – the view that basically the sexes are equal in this society remains unchallenged and unchanged. The day I got this was the day I understood its real message, its real coherence: this is equality for us.

I could describe this, but I couldn't explain it until I started studying a lot of pornography. In pornography, there it is, in one place, all of the abuses that women had to struggle so long even to begin to articulate, all the unspeakable abuse: the rape, the battery, the sexual harassment, the prostitution, and the sexual abuse of children. Only in the pornography it is called something else: sex, sex, sex, sex, and sex, respectively. Pornography sexualises rape, battery, sexual harassment, prostitution, and child sexual abuse; it thereby celebrates, promotes, authorises, and legitimises them. More generally, it eroticises the dominance and submission that is the dynamic common to them all. It makes hierarchy sexy and

---

94 See Florence Rush, *The Best-Kept Secret: Sexual Abuse of Children* (1980). See also Jeffrey Masson, *The Assault on Truth: Freud's Suppression of the Seduction Theory* (1983).

95 *Francis Biddle's Sister*, p 170.

calls that 'the truth about sex'[96] or just a mirror of reality. Through this process pornography constructs what a woman is as what men want from sex. This is what the pornography means.

Pornography constructs what a woman is in terms of its view of what men want sexually, such that acts of rape, battery, sexual harassment, prostitution, and sexual abuse of children become acts of sexual equality. Pornography's world of equality is a harmonious and balanced place. Men and women are perfectly complementary and perfectly bipolar. Women's desire to be fucked by men is equal to men's desire to fuck women. All the ways men love to take and violate women, women love to be taken and violated. The women who most love this are most men's equals, the most liberated; the most participatory child is the most grown-up, the most equal to an adult. Their consent merely expresses or ratifies these pre-existing facts.

The content of pornography is one thing. There, women substantively desire dispossession and cruelty. We desperately want to be bound, battered, tortured, humiliated, and killed. Or, to be fair to the soft core, merely taken and used. This is erotic to the male point of view. Subjection itself, with self-determination ecstatically relinquished, is the content of women's sexual desire and desirability. Women are there to be violated and possessed, men to violate and possess us, either on screen or by camera or pen on behalf of the consumer. On a simple descriptive level, the inequality of hierarchy, of which gender is the primary one, seems necessary for sexual arousal to work. Other added inequalities identify various pornographic genres or subthemes, although they are always added through gender: age, disability, homosexuality, animals, objects, race (including anti-semitism) and so on. Gender is never irrelevant.

What pornography does goes beyond its content: it eroticises hierarchy, it sexualises inequality. It makes dominance and submission into sex. Inequality is its central dynamic; the illusion of freedom coming together with the reality of force is central to its working. Perhaps because this is a bourgeois culture, the victim must look free, appear to be freely acting. Choice is how she got there. Willing is what she is when she is being equal. It seems equally important that then and there she actually be forced and that forcing be communicated on some level, even if only through still photos of her in postures of receptivity and access, available for penetration. Pornography in this view is a form of forced sex, a practice of sexual politics, an institution of gender inequality.

From this perspective, pornography is neither harmless fantasy nor a corrupt and confused misrepresentation of an otherwise natural and healthy sexual situation. It institutionalises the sexuality of male supremacy, fusing the erotisation of dominance and submission with the social construction of male and female. To the extent that gender is sexual, pornography is part of constituting the meaning of that sexuality. Men treat women as who they see women as being. Pornography constructs who that is. Men's power over women means that the way men see women defines who women can be. Pornography is that way. Pornography is not imagery in some relation to a reality elsewhere constructed. It is not a distortion, reflection, projection, expression, fantasy, representation, or symbol either. It is a sexual reality.

In Andrea Dworkin's definitive work, *Pornography: Men Possessing Women*, sexuality itself is a social construct gendered to the ground. Male dominance here

---

96   Foucault, 'The West and the Truth of Sex' (1978) 20 *Substance* 5.

is not an artificial overlay upon an underlying inalterable substratum of uncorrupted essential sexual being. Dworkin presents a sexual theory of gender inequality of which pornography is a constitutive practice. The way pornography produces its meaning constructs and defines men and women as such. Gender has no basis in anything other than the social reality its hegemony constructs. Gender is what gender means. The process that gives sexuality its male supremacist meaning is the same process through which gender inequality becomes socially real.

In this approach, the experience of the (overwhelmingly) male audiences who consume pornography is therefore not fantasy or simulation or catharsis but sexual reality, the level of reality on which sex itself largely operates. Understanding this dimension of the problem does not require noticing that pornography models are real women to whom, in most cases, something real is being done. Nor does it even require enquiring into the systematic infliction of pornography and its sexuality upon women, although it helps. What matters is the way in which the pornography itself provides what those who consume it want. Pornography *participates* in its audience's eroticism through creating an accessible sexual object, the possession and consumption of which is male sexuality, as socially constructed; to be consumed and possessed as which, *is* female sexuality, as socially constructed; pornography is a process that constructs it that way.

The object world is constructed according to how it looks with respect to its possible uses. Pornography defines women by how we look according to how we can be sexually used. Pornography codes how to look at women, so you know what you can do with one when you see one. Gender is an assignment made visually, both originally and in everyday life. A sex object is defined on the basis of its looks, in terms of its usability for sexual pleasure, such that both the looking – the quality of the gaze, including its point of view – and the definition according to use become eroticised as part of the sex itself. This is what the feminist concept 'sex object' means. In this sense, sex in life is no less mediated than it is in art. Men have sex with their image of a woman. It is not that life and art imitate each other; in this sexuality, they are each other.

To give a set of rough epistemological translations, to defend pornography as consistent with the equality of the sexes is to defend the subordination of women to men as sexual equality. What in the pornographic view is love and romance looks a great deal like hatred and torture to the feminist. Pleasure and eroticism become violation. Desire appears as lust for dominance and submission. The vulnerability of women's projected sexual availability, that acting we are allowed (that is, asking to be acted upon) is victimisation. Play conforms to scripted roles. Fantasy expresses ideology and is not exempt from it. Admiration of natural physical beauty becomes objectification. Harmlessness becomes harm. Pornography is a harm of male supremacy made difficult to see because of its pervasiveness, potency, and, principally, because of its success in making the world a pornographic place. Specifically, its harm cannot be discerned, and will not be addressed, if viewed and approached neutrally, because it is so much of 'what is'. In other words, to the extent pornography succeeds in constructing social reality, it becomes invisible as harm. If we live in a world that pornography creates through the power of men in a male-dominated situation, the issue is not what the harm of pornography is, but how that harm is to become visible.

Obscenity law provides a very different analysis and conception of the problem of pornography. In 1973 the legal definition of obscenity became that which the average person, applying contemporary community standards, would find that, taken as a whole, appeals to the prurient interest. That is, that which depicts or describes in a patently offensive way – you feel like you're a cop reading someone's *Miranda* rights – sexual conduct specifically defined by the applicable State law; and that which, taken as a whole, lacks serious literary, artistic, political or scientific value.[97] Feminism doubts whether the average person gender-neutral exists; has more questions about the content and process of defining what community standards are than it does about deviations from them; wonders why prurience counts but powerlessness does not and why sensibilities are better protected from offence than women are from exploitation. It defines sexuality, and thus its violation and expropriation, more broadly than does State law; and questions why a body of law that has not in practice been able to tell rape from intercourse should be entrusted, without further guidance, with telling pornography from anything less.

Taking the work 'as a whole' ignores that which the victims of pornography have long known: legitimate settings diminish the perception of injury done to those whose trivialisation and objectification they contextualise. Besides, and this is a heavy one, if a woman is subjected, why should it matter that the work has other value? Maybe what redeems the work's value is what enhances its injury to women, not to mention that existing standards of literature, art, science, and politics, examined in a feminist light, are remarkably consonant with pornography's mode, meaning, and message. And finally – first foremost, actually – although the subject of these materials is overwhelmingly women, their contents almost entirely made up of women's bodies, our invisibility has been such, our equation as a sex with sex has been such, that the law of obscenity has never even considered pornography a women's issue.

Obscenity, in this light, is a moral idea, an idea about judgments of good and bad. Pornography, by contrast, is a political practice, a practice of power and powerlessness. Obscenity is ideational and abstract; pornography is concrete and substantive. The two concepts represent two entirely different things. Nudity, excess of candour, arousal or excitement, prurient appeal, illegality of the acts depicted, and unnaturalness or perversion are all qualities that bother obscenity law when sex is depicted or portrayed. Sex forced on real women so that it can be sold at a profit and forced on other real women; women's bodies trussed and maimed and raped and made into things to be hurt and obtained and accessed, and this presented as the nature of women in a way that is acted on and acted out, over and over; the coercion that is visible and the coercion that has become invisible – this and more bothers feminists about pornography. Obscenity as such probably does little harm. Pornography is integral to attitudes and behaviours of violence and discrimination that define the treatment and status of half the population.

At the request of the city of Minneapolis, Andrea Dworkin and I conceived and designed a local human rights ordinance in accordance with our approach to the pornography issue. We define pornography as a practice of sex discrimination, a violation of women's civil rights, the opposite of sexual equality. Its point is to hold those who profit from and benefit from that injury accountable to those who are injured. It means that women's injury – our damage, our pain, our enforced

---

97 *Miller v California* 413 US 15 at 24 (1973).

inferiority – should outweigh their pleasure and their profits, or sexual equality is meaningless.

We define pornography as the graphic sexually explicit subordination of women through pictures or words that also includes women dehumanised as sexual objects, things, or commodities; enjoying pain or humiliation or rape; being tied up, cut up, mutilated, bruised, or physically hurt; in postures of sexual submission or servility or display; reduced to body parts, penetrated by objects or animals, or presented in scenarios of degradation, injury, torture; shown as filthy or inferior; bleeding, bruised, or hurt in a context that makes these conditions sexual. Erotica, defined by distinction as not this, might be sexually explicit materials premised on equality.[98] We also provide that the use of men, children, or transsexuals in the place of women is pornography. The definition is substantive in that it is sex-specific, but it covers everyone in a sex-specific way, so is gender-neutral in overall design.

There is a buried issue within sex discrimination law about what sex, ie gender, is. If sex is a difference, social or biological, one looks to see if a challenged practice occurs along the same lines; if it does, or if it is done to both sexes, the practice is not discrimination, not inequality. If, by contrast, sex has been a matter of dominance, the issue is not the gender difference but the difference gender makes. In this more substantive, less abstract approach, the concern with inequality is whether a practice subordinates on the basis of sex. The first approach implies that marginal correction is needed; the second requires social change. Equality, in the first view, centres on abstract symmetry between equivalent categories; the asymmetry that occurs when categories are not equivalent is not inequality, it is treated unlikes differently. In the second approach, inequality centres on the substantive, cumulative disadvantagement of social hierarchy. Equality for the first is non-differentiation; for the second, non-subordination.[99] Although it is consonant with both approaches, our anti-pornography statute emerges largely from an analysis of the problem under the second approach.

To define pornography as a practice of sex discrimination combines a mode of portrayal that has a legal history – the sexually explicit – with an active term that is central to the inequality of the sexes – subordination. Among other things, subordination means to be in a position of inferiority or loss of power, or to be demeaned or denigrated.[100] To be someone's subordinate is the opposite of being their equal. The definition does not include all sexually explicit depictions of the subordination of women. That is not what it says. It says, this which does that: the sexually explicit that subordinates women. To these active terms to capture what the pornography does, the definition adds a list of what it must also contain. This list, from our analysis, is an exhaustive description of what must be in the pornography for it to do what it does behaviourally. Each item in the definition is supported by experimental, testimonial, social, and clinical evidence. We made a legislative choice to be exhaustive and specific and concrete rather than conceptual and general, to minimise problems of chilling effect, making it hard to guess wrong, thus making self-censorship less likely, but encouraging (to use a phrase from discrimination law) voluntary compliance,

---

98 See eg Gloria Steinem, *Erotica v Pornography in Outrageous Acts and Everday Rebellions* (1983).

99 See Catharine A MacKinnon, *Sexual Harassment of Working Women* (1979), pp 101–41.

100 See Andrea Dworkin, 'Against the Male Flood: Censorship, Pornography and Equality' (1985) 8 *Harvard Women's Law Journal* 1.

knowing that if something turns up that is not on the list, the law will not be expansively interpreted.

The list in the definition, by itself, would be a content regulation. But together with the first part, the definition is not simply a content regulation. It is a medium-message combination that resembles many other such exceptions to First Amendment guarantees ...[101]

... This law aspires to guarantee women's rights consistent with the First Amendment by making visible a conflict of rights between the equality guaranteed to all women and what, in some legal sense, is now the freedom of the pornographers to make and sell, and their consumers to have access to, the materials this ordinance defines. Judicial resolution of this conflict, if the judges do for women what they have done for others, is likely to entail a balancing of the rights of women arguing that our lives and opportunities, including our freedom of speech and action, are constrained by, and in many cases flatly precluded by, in, and through, pornography, against those who argue that the pornography is harmless, or harmful only in part but not in the whole of the definition; or that it is more important to preserve the pornography than it is to prevent or remedy whatever harm it does ...[102]

... This ordinance enunciates a new form of the previously recognised governmental interest in sex equality. Many laws make sex equality a governmental interest. Our law is designed to further the equality of the sexes, to help make sex equality real. Pornography is a practice of discrimination on the basis of sex, on one level because of its role in creating and maintaining sex as a basis for discrimination. It harms many women one at a time and helps keep all women in an inferior status by defining our subordination as our sexuality and equating that with our gender. It is also sex discrimination because its victims, including men, are selected for victimisation on the basis of their gender. But for their sex, they would not be so treated.

The harm of pornography, broadly speaking, is the harm of the civil inequality of the sexes made invisible as harm because it has become accepted, as the sex difference. Consider this analogy with race: if you see black people as different, there is no harm to segregation; it is merely a recognition of difference. To neutral principles, separate but equal was equal. The injury of racial separation to blacks arises 'solely because [they] choose to put that construction upon it'.[103] Epistemologically translated is: how you see it is not the way it is. Similarly, if you see women as just different, even or especially if you don't know that you do, subordination will not look like subordination at all, much less like harm. It will merely look like an appropriate recognition of the sex difference.

Pornography does treat the sexes differently, so the case for sex differentiation can be made here. But men as a group do not tend to be (although some individuals may be) treated the way women are treated in pornography. As a social group, men are not hurt by pornography the way women as a social group are. Their social status is not defined as less by it. So the major argument does not turn on mistaken differentiation, particularly since the treatment of women according to pornography's dictates makes it all too often accurate. The salient quality of a distinction between the top and the bottom in a hierarchy is not

101 *Francis Biddle's Sister*, p 177.
102 *Francis Biddle's Sister*, p 178.
103 See *Plessey v Ferguson* 163 US 551.

difference, although top is certainly different from bottom; it is power. So the major argument is: subordinate but equal is not equal.[104]

ONLY WORDS[105]

Catharine MacKinnon

Preface[106]

On 17 August 1992, a small article in the *New York Times*, 'Police Seek People Who Cheered Killer On' reported this:

> A dozen people who chanted 'Kill her! Kill her!' as a woman was stabbed to death last Wednesday are being sought and could face charges of aiding and abetting a murder, the police say ... 'Usually, you hear of people who stand by and watch and do nothing,' said Sgt John McKenna of the Oakland Police Department. 'But this is the other end of things, where the people watched and participated.'

'Kill her! Kill her!' are only words, but the Oakland Police Department saw what they did: participation in a criminal act. Suppose, instead of a murder, the bystanders were watching a rape. Would chanting 'Rape her! Rape her!' not be participation? Suppose pictures were taken of the rape, and sold to people, some of whom chanted 'Rape her! Rape her!' as they watched.

The onlookers in Oakland just happened on a murder already in progress. Suppose they had paid to watch and chant during an arranged one? Imagine that a whole industry creates and sells pictures of women and children sexually violated and sometimes killed. Isn't this also participation? And those millions who create the market for those films, who watch them and chant 'Rape her! Rape her! and 'Kill her! Kill her'!' do they not also participate?

In the United States, this industry is not legally regarded as aiding and abetting violence against women. It is called protected speech. In this context, the chanters in Oakland could be considered to be expressing an idea; as could those in the extended examples. Will the United States continue to adhere to this view, which sounds so improbable in a British context? Canada has rejected its absolute priority on expression as a barrier to women's equality.[107] Will the rest of the world adopt it, in ever more absolute ways, along with the pornography with which it travels as a principled cover? This is an open question – but not for long.

This book attempts to move people to face the reality of harm done through what is called speech: what it does to women, children, the possibility of equality for oppressed groups and women's human rights, in particular. All reality of injury is entered through the experience of women used in pornography, as they have described it, over years of activism and research. Moving from this point, the discussion attempts to define and explore the legal and social terrain of inequality through expression, including through hate propaganda, racial harassment, sexual harassment and libel. It seeks to understand the role of speech in inequality and to expand the role of equality in speech. The point is to stop the harm and open a space for subordinated voices, those shut down and shut out through the expressive forms inequality takes.

---

104 *Francis Biddle's Sister*, p 179.
105 Harper Collins, 1995.
106 Footnotes edited.
107 *Butler v Regina* [1992] 2 WWR 577 (Can).

The claim that pornography 'is speech' is taken up with reluctance. This position conflates pornography with political, educational, artistic and literary expression, as if the two cannot be distinguished, so that if one is threatened, the other is threatened. The fact is, pornography, accurately defined, is readily distinguishable – on its face, in its making, in its use and in the effects of its use – from protected expression. To take the claim seriously enough even to rebut it, ie that this practice of sexual violation and inequality, this medium of slave traffic, is an opinion or a discussion is to collaborate, to some degree, in the legal and intellectual fraudulence of its position. It is to treat this position as what it pretends to be, one side in a *bona fide* discussion, rather than as what it is, a legitimising smokescreen for sexual exploitation. But, like pornography's lie that women want and choose to be used and hurt for sex, the lie that pornography 'is speech' has very real clout, in Anglo-American legal systems in particular.

Inequality based on sex and race is imposed through expressive means in England as well as in the United States. Accountability for it is almost equally rare. Both systems value freedom of speech, England without a written constitution, America with one. Both purport to hold equality as a legal and social norm, yet both are firmly hierarchical societies of inequality based on sex, race and class. British law permits restriction of hate speech (and libel) far more readily than does US law – showing less fetishism about speech and a greater sensitivity to its human consequences.[108]

In both nations, pornography is nominally criminal under obscenity law and is approached as a matter of morality. Both bodies of obscenity law have been equally useless in stemming the rising tide of pornography and equally blind to its material injuries. These failures are connected. Neither country has comprehended hate speech or pornography as matters of social inequality or legal equality, although scholarly dialogue in both countries, much of it drawing upon principles of international law, has more broadly speaking, neither country's law comprehends equality substantively.[109] Although there are exceptions, the legal definition of equality in both places tends to be a superficially mechanistic but deeply invidious abstraction that will never, and can never, produce social parity. One exception is sexual harassment, which both US and UK law recognise as sex discrimination, although it is pursued with greater vigour in the United States. So far, sexual harassment is not even arguably protected speech in either country. So while the case names differ, the social and legal issues are shared. And the failure to address the harm speech does to equality is virtually identical.

The fact that obscenity regulations in the United States parallels England is not surprising. American obscenity law (as much else legal) builds on English foundations. British obscenity law has centred its solicitude on the mind of the consumer, specifically on whether the materials have a tendency to 'deprave and

---

108 Public Order Act 1986. See also Geoffrey Bindman, 'Incitement to Racial Hatred in the UK: Have We Got the Law We Need?', S Coliver (ed), *Striking a Balance: Hate Speech, Freedom of Expression and Non-Discrimination* (London and Human Rights Centre, University of Essex, 1992), pp 258–62. See also RG Schneider, 'Hate Speech in the United States: Recent Legal Developments', in Coliver, *supra*, pp 269–83.

109 See Mari J Matsuda, Charles R Lawrence III, Richard Delgado and Kimberle Williams Crenshaw, *Words That Wound: Critical Race Theory, Assaultive Speech and the First Amendment* (Boulder and Oxford: Westview Press, 1993); Catherine Itzin (ed), *Pornography: Women, Violence and Civil Liberties* (Oxford University Press, 1993).

corrupt'[110] his morals. While one might well worry about what pornography does to those who use it, this test makes invisible those who are violated in making the materials, as well as those who are injured and subordinated by consumers acting on them. A substantive equality approach would make these harms visible.

Although activism and some scholarship in Britain has exposed pornography's harms, there has been little governmental response. The mainstream British policy debate has not yet integrated the empirical findings and conceptual advances of the last 15 years, and continues to rely largely upon the outdated *Williams Report*, which in 1979 found no clear consequential harms from exposure to pornography.[111] In the intervening period, more sophisticated, focused, reality-based, and less biased investigations, asking more of the right questions, have produced overwhelming scientific and experiential evidence of this connection. Parliament's attempt to update policy was frustrated by the biased Home Office report of December 1990, which ignored or misrepresented this newer research.[112]

The *Williams Report* did make clear that the widely reported drop in sex crimes in Denmark supposed to have attended the elimination of restrictions on pornography was an urban myth.[113] It also hypothesised harms of production, including 'the exploitation of children' and 'the infliction of physical harm'. Although it found no violated or exploited adults,[114] it concluded that both such acts and 'the material depicting them' should be prohibited when they occur.[115] Its legal approach did not keep the possibility of these harms in view, however, relying instead on the traditional, moralistic idea that 'the objective of law should be to prevent offence to the public at large and to protect young people from exposure to unsuitable material'. The profound lack of fit between harms of 'production and offensiveness to the community has gone mostly ummarked'[116] and wholly unaddressed by law.

Of course, the abandonment of those muted through expression is not limited to pornography or to the UK. As pornography has spread, at the same time and in the same places, racial and ethnic vilification have erupted. Following the break-up of the Soviet Union and Yugoslavia, hate speech, and organisations and activities which promote it have exploded into public view, escalating into genocide in Croatia, Bosnia-Herzegovina and Kosova. Just prior to the Serbian war of aggression in Bosnia and Herzegovina, pornography was everywhere; signs also appeared stating 'No Muslims or Croatians Allowed'. Both pornography and hate speech have been construed as expressions of freedom in formerly repressed and repressive states, but closer scrutiny shows them to be continuous expressions of social inequalities formerly carried out under

---

110 *R v Hicklin* (1868) LR 3 QB 371. See also *DPP v Whyte* [1972] 2 All ER 12 and *'Lady Chatterly's Lover'* [1961] *Crim LR* 177. This was the common law rule, embraced in the Obscene Publications Act 1959.

111 *Report of the Committee on Obscenity and Film Censorship* (London: HMSO, 1979).

112 Dennis Howitt and Guy Cumberbatch, *Pornography Impacts and Influence* (London: Home Office Research and Planning Unit, 1990). For discussion, see Itzin, pp 561–62.

113 *Williams, op cit*, para 81.

114 *Ibid*, para 91, see Itzin's commentary on this, pp 1–2.

115 *Williams op cit*, para 131.

116 Many authors in Itzin are exceptions.

centralised dominance in less visible ways. The 'gathering storm' of racial and ethnic incitement of which Edouard Shevardnaze warned Europe in 1990 has received some worried international attention. The escalating sexual hatred and incitement to sexual aggression against women and children, through pornography is denied, the flood of pornography itself celebrated as sign and substance of democracy and liberation.

The inter-connections between sexual issues on the one hand, and racial and ethnic issues on the other, have been little examined. Much pornography sexualises racial and ethnic hostility; it also desensitises the user to violence against powerless others by making aggression pleasurable. The Nazi propaganda machine sexualised hostility against Jews as preparation for their extermination. Under communism in what was Yugoslavia, visible pornography was a State monopoly. With the State's collapse just prior to the conflagration there, its pornography market, according to Yugoslav critic Bogdan Tirnanic, became 'the freest in the world'. In that war, pornography pervades the rape/death camps in which Serbian fascist forces have interned Muslim and Croatian women to rape and kill them. Women in those camps report that what they see done to women in pornography is also done to them.[117] They also report pornography being made of sexual atrocities committed against them. Ethnic epithets of sexual contempt, like 'ustasa whore', are routinely screamed at them as they are raped. Are the expressive tools of genocide also protected speech?

The sexuality of dominance and subordination that pornography engenders is also expressed in the often rabid hostility and irrationality of its public defenders. The materials create a visceral sexual attachment, a distinctive misogyny which impels and underlies its defence at any cost. Given that the commitment to pornography is through pleasure rather than through reason, it is worth asking: can any words be enough? Pornography is a problem that many people, including some with the power of the press and the law in their hands, do not want solved. This is also why no amount of evidence of the harm it does – of rape, battery, sexual abuse of children murder, sexual harassment, sex discrimination and denigration, necessary to its production and inevitable from its use, or its role in genocide – has been enough. In their way, its public defenders cheer the rapists and killers on. Pornography is not just the artefact, symbol, symptom its apologists say it is. This makes stopping it almost impossible – and, if freedom and equality are to be real, necessary.

PORNOGRAPHY AND THE TYRANNY OF THE MAJORITY[118]
Elizabeth Wolgast

The respect that atomism accords individuals justifies the maximum degree of freedom of expression, and that freedom protects pornography from public control. But many objectors to pornography, righteously indignant, also emphasise individual respect, particularly the respect due to women as sexual partners. Thus conflicting views, on both sides fervent and moralistic, draw their support from a single atomistic root. Where does this conflict lead us?

'If all mankind minus one were of one opinion', John Stuart Mill wrote, 'mankind would be no more justified in silencing that one person than he, if he had the

117 This is documented in CA MacKinnon, *Turning Rape into Pornography: Postmodern Genocide*, MS (July-August 1993).
118 *The Grammar of Justice* (Ithica: Cornell, 1987).

power, would be justified in silencing mankind'. No matter how great the majority, the very power to control opinion and expression is illegitimate, he argued. Worse, such power 'is robbing the human race' of the chance to hear different sides of a question whether right or wrong, and thus does injury to the whole community'.[119]

Society has no right to demand conformity to a set of beliefs, to 'maim by compression, like a Chinese lady's foot, every part of human nature which stands out prominently, and tends to make the person markedly dissimilar in outline to common place humanity'. A person needs opportunity to live as he chooses, to take up causes passionately, make mistakes, change his or her mind. Only in this way can anyone develop to the fullest potential. 'Human nature is not a machine to be built after a model, and set to do exactly the work prescribed for it, but a tree, which requires to grow and develop itself on all sides, according to the tendency of the inward forces which make it a living thing.'[120] Society will itself benefit when people have liberty to experiment in ideas and ways of living, Mill believed, for it is innovators, not conformists, who advance culture.

Truth also is advanced when people are allowed to express all opinions and to debate every question. And who is it argues against a popular view but a minority of dissenters? They are the ones, then, who need the most protection: 'On any of the great open questions ... if either of the two opinions has a better claim than the other, not merely to be tolerated but to be encouraged ... it is the one which happens at the particular time and place to be in a minority. That is the one which for the time being represents the neglected interests, the side of human wellbeing which is in danger of obtaining less than its share.'[121] Even in the gentler form of custom, majority tyranny is as much to be feared as political tyranny, Mill believes, and maybe more. His criterion for interference is that if only harm or injury to someone results should people be restrained from acting and living as they please. There is a presumption that in the absence of proof of injury, the individual should be left alone.

I quote extensively from Mill because his language is echoed in modern discussions of free speech, particularly those related to control of pornography. Control is seen as a simple case of the majority forcing others into conformity with their (puritanical) moral standard without argument. It appears a clear case of social compression, what Mill would call a 'Calvanistic' demand for 'Christian self-denial', aimed at at stifling the virtue of 'pagan self-assertion'. Similarly, Joel Feinberg refers to control as 'moralistic paternalism'. Other writers echo Mill's attitude.

For Americans this is a powerful and seductive argument against restrictions on any published material, including pornography. All the libertarian or the non-conformist minority asks of the majority is tolerance of its curious ways. What problem is there in that? Others don't have to look or buy; one person should be free to enjoy pornography even though others prefer not to, just as they are free to accept or reject escargots or dandelion wine. Passionate tastes are not a bad thing, Mill argued; they are the very 'raw material of human nature', capable of both more good and more evil than ordinary feelings. 'Strong impulses are but another name for energy. A person whose desires and impulses are his own – are

---

119 John Stuart Mill, *On Liberty*, p 76.
120 *Ibid*, p 135.
121 *Ibid*, p 123.

the expression of his own nature – is said to have a character.'[122] And society needs people of strong character: that is the romantic message.

To understand the role of Mill's argument, it is important to recognise that he wrote long after the Bill of Rights became law and that his view of freedom was not the one that prompted the First Amendment, or even one shared by the early Americans. The idea that truth depends on a 'marketplace of ideas', that freedom of expression advances the universal search for truth, that self-expression is an essential part of a person's self-development, that – most important – the only restriction rightly placed on a person's freedom is the injunction not to injure others – such ideas are those of Mill's time, not of Jefferson's. They originated with romantic philosophers of the 19th century, not with the political and moral thinkers of 17th century England and 18th century America, who stressed individual responsibility, restraint, and self-governance. Such virtues Mill would probably find much too straightlaced. It is therefore a wild anachronism to use Mill's *On Liberty* as a gloss on the First Amendment. But my argument does not turn on this point. I will argue that one kind of moral issue raised by pornography overshadows and requires us to reevaluate the free speech issue. Further, once the argument against protecting pornography is spelled out, I believe Mill can be rallied to its support instead of to the libertarian side.

Two points about 'harm' should be made. First, the language of injury and harm are no part of the First Amendment. The framers of that amendment did not suggest that if someone's practice of religion, for example, were to cause injury in some vague sense, the right of religious practice is restrictable. One might conclude from their terse statement that on the contrary, the right to practice religion should be very difficult to restrict. The 'injury' proviso, which may originate with utilitarians, is therefore a gauntlet I do not propose to pick up. Second, Mill's single proviso that a person's exercise of freedom should not harm others places a heavy burden of proof on anyone defending pornography's restriction and sets the presumption that freedom should prevail. How can injury be shown? How can it even be understood here? Who is injured when pornography is aimed at adult customers, free to decide whether they are interested in it?

To answer these questions we appear to need both a specific conception of harm and persuasive evidence of a causal connection, both of which various critics have shown to be problematic. I will argue, on the contrary, that to accept this burden of proof – that harm or injury to an individual has been caused – is an error of strategy. It is to accept a difficult or even impossible challenge when a more direct and powerful moral argument is available.

Freedom of speech and the press are commonly connected with democratic government and seen as essential to it. Tocqueville, for instance, wrote: 'In the countries in which the doctrine of the sovereignty of the people ostensibly prevails, the censorship of the press is not only dangerous, but it is absurd.' It was a connection not lost on the framers of the Constitution, who were on their guard against the danger that government might seek to impose its will on reluctant citizens. We don't need to doubt the connection here. The question is: does protection of free expression legitimately protect pornography?

A reasonable statement on this point is made by Ronald Dworkin, who argues that the right to have an equal voice in the political process is not denied when a person 'is forbidden to circulate photographs of genitals to the public at large, or

---

122 *Ibid*, pp 124–25.

denied his right to listen to argument when he is forbidden to consider these photographs at his leisure'.[123] Some other basis for protection is needed, according to him.

The Supreme Court argued along similar lines in *Roth v United States*.[124] What the amendment protects, it says, is the 'unfettered interchange of ideas for the bringing about of political and social changes desired by the people. And pornography is 'no essential part of any exposition of ideas'.

In my view the distinction set forth in *Roth* is important and should have been developed. But instead of developing it, the court went on to give another reason not to protect pornography, namely, that a 'social interest in order and morality' clearly 'outweighed' pornography's right to protection. Such a move was plainly hazardous: if other 'social interests' can 'outweigh' the right to free expression, then the protection of the First Amendment has been greatly diluted. The better argument would follow along the original lines, saying that pornography isn't in the category of 'expression' meant to be protected.

A knotty problem arises, however, when pornography is excluded from protection: the amendment speaks of freedom of the press. So from one angle it looks as if the amendment was meant to protect not citizens who want to read but publishers in the business of selling printed matter of whatever kind. And pornography certainly belongs in this large domain.

Were the framers trying to protect one kind of business while refusing to protect others? We are helped here by remembering that the First Amendment also dealt with freedom of worship and the right to congregate. The rights to worship and congregate in public rest on the respect of one's need to commune with God on the one hand and with one's fellow citizens on the other. The latter right has something to do with the role citizens in the whole process of government, their sense that the government is there to serve them and it is their job to monitor it. None of this suggests why publishers should protected by a fundamental constitutional right, rather than cobblers or hotel keepers. The more plausible connection is that between protecting the press and protecting citizens from oppression through censorship. The citizens have a need to know and hear printed opinions, just as they have a need to get together and talk, if they are to do their civic duty and live by their consciences. However, this ambiguity in the language of the First Amendment, this way of speaking of the press as if publishers *per se* are protected and not the free exchange of opinion, seems never to have been cogently dealt with by the courts, and it perennially causes problems, as it does in the present case.

The main point here is that if the amendment is understood to protect publishers as a special form of business protection, then it has no particular moral weight; business protections and trade restrictions may change with the times and do, and a business may seek protection for some political reason or other without invoking the First Amendment or any basic constitutional values.

Another problem with the *Roth* argument is that it invites the comparison of pornography with art, thereby suggesting that good art is more entitled to protection than bad. Good art presumably should survive lack of social value; bad art shouldn't. But what validity is there in this idea? It invites the comment

---

123 Ronald Dworkin, 'Do We Have a Right to Pornography?', in *A Matter of Choice* (Harvard University Press, 1985), p 336.

124 354 US 481.

that the degree of badness is relative, and may well be a matter of taste, that history has shown ... and so on. A more important point is that bad literature – bad essays on politics, appealing to weak and unworthy motives of a reader – are surely protected by the First Amendment. And bad political art too. Then why not the poor-quality stuff called pornography? The case made in *Roth* for restricting pornography is worse than unconvincing. It provides ground for a kind of moral repression that both the Constitution's framers and Mill would abhor. We still have to explain what is bad about pornography that is not bad about bad literature and bad art in general.

Joel Feinberg's use of pornography, he says, is 'purely descriptive'; he uses the term to refer to 'sexually explicit writing and pictures designed entirely and plausibly to induce sexual excitement in the reader or observer'.[125] According to this definition, pornography is a genre of materials of an erotic sort, some of which may be objectionable while the rest is not. Some Japanese prints or Indian murals could be described as pornographic and still appreciated as art by this characterisation, for 'pornography' is used in a morally neutral way. But since we are not concerned at the moment with erotic materials that are not offensive, I propose to use pornography as a pejorative term, which is to say in the way Feinberg would speak of offensive pornography. In response to the objection that the word is (most) commonly used in a descriptive and neutral way, I suggest that many ordinary people, including many feminists, commonly use it in a pejorative way and that in much ordinary speech to call something pornographic is to say that it is offensive. That is sufficient justification for using the term in this way.

It needs to be pointed out that to say that pornography is objectionable is not to demonstrate that it should be controlled. Many things that people do and say are acknowledged to be bad, including being unfaithful to one's spouse, misusing and deceiving friends, neglecting elderly parents, and lying. But we don't have laws against these things. As Feinberg says, in many respects 'the court has interpreted [the Constitution] to permit responsible adults to go to Hell morally in their own way provided only they don't drag others unwillingly along with them'. Such interpretations constitute a formidable defence against controls.

Though pornography may be objectionable in various dimensions (and I believe it is) I will focus on only one kind of objection that I claim to have moral weight. I will substantiate the claim that there is such an objection by citing expressions of it. Then I will defend the claim that this kind of objection should carry enough legal weight to justify the control of the objectionable materials. Last, I will argue that such control is quite compatible with the Constitution and the First Amendment and, finally, John Stuart Mill.

The objections I focus on are those expressed by women against certain representations of women in sexual situations: objections against representations of women 'being beaten or killed for sexual stimulation' and women enjoying brutal sexual treatment, usually at the hands of men. One pornography model demands censorship of 'all pornography which portrays torture, murder, and bondage for erotic stimulation and pleasure'.[126] What is objectionable is not just the representations but the lack of a context in which they are understood to be

125 J Feinberg, 'Pornography and the Criminal Law', in Copp and Wendell (eds), *Pornography and Censorship*, p 110.
126 Diana Russell with Laura Lederer, 'Questions We Get Asked Most Often', in L Lederer (ed), *Take Back the Night* (New York: Bantam, 1980), p 25.

reprehensible and condemnable. Without some such context. The representations carry the message that such treatment of women is all right. This is one kind of objection.

Another model protests against the circulation of any representation 'that reduces women to passive objects to be abused, degraded, and used in violence against women, because now every woman is for sale to the lowest bidder and to all men'.[127] She adds that a government that protects this kind of image making expresses 'an ideology of women as sexual objects and nothing else'. A related criticism was made by Gloria Steinem: '[Pornography's] message is violence, dominance, and conquest ... If we are to feel anything, we must identify with conqueror or victim.' It is a poor choice for women: 'We can only experience pleasure through the adoption of some degree of sadism or masochism ... We may feel diminished by the role of conqueror, or enraged, humiliated, and vengeful by sharing identity with the victim.'[128]

These quotations illustrate one general kind of objection made to pornography. That it is objectionable in these respects is an inference I make from the facts that (1) people do make vehement objections to it and (2) they see the offence as a moral one, concerning respect due any individual.

I emphasise that although I take it for granted that pornography deals with human sexuality, I am not defining it, although many writers consider a definition crucial for a coherent argument. There is a variety of erotic material that could be called pornographic, and whether we call something pornographic or not will depend in part on whether people find it seriously objectionable. But my argument isn't meant to fit all varieties of such material. I am testing only one dimension of objectionability against the First Amendment defence with the claim that it has moral weight.

My partial characterisation is this: some pornography is objectionable because it is perceived as seriously degrading and demeaning to women as a group. This characterisation draws on the fact that the materials are perceived by women as representing them as inferior or less-than-human beings to be used by others in sexual and sadistic ways.

Now, why should we take this complaint seriously, so seriously as to control a class of printed and pictorial materials? I hold that such complaints are the stuff of a serious moral issue.

Let us see how the reasoning works. Where is the moral problem? Who is to blame that the speaker was a pornography model? Presumably she chose to be one, and her choice – *volenti*, as Feinberg argues – applies to her as well as to the consumers. But this answer is not clearly adequate. The complaint is against the role in which women are portrayed, not against the working conditions, as it were.

The perception that one is being demeaned and that sanction is given to one's mistreatment as a means to sexual satisfaction here – is a complaint that touches an important moral nerve. It offends basic moral ideas, in particular the Kantian one that everyone should be treated with dignity and respect and not used as a means to another's end. The complaint or objection needs therefore to be taken seriously. That it is the first inference.

---

127 'Testimony against Pornography: Witness from Denmark', Diana Russell (ed), in *Take Back the Night*, Lederer (ed), pp 84–85.

128 'Erotica and Pornography', in *Take Back the Night*, *supra*.

But several questions leap to mind. First, what determines that this complaint justifies – or lays the foundation for justifying – control of the objectionable materials? Does just any group have the licence to insist that laws be changed to improve that group's image? How is the line to be drawn so as to prevent censuring of political caricatures, for instance?

The answer to this question is complicated but contains a general point. If respect for individuals is an important community value, then complaints by any group that their members are demeaned by some vehicle or other must have some weight. Such complaints must be addressed by the community seriously, for otherwise the value of respect is immediately and automatically undermined. The message conveyed that it doesn't matter if these people – members of this group – are demeaned suggests that some people are less important than others.

Therefore the answer to the question whose complaints count is that any complaint by any group that its members are not treated with respect deserves and needs to be treated seriously. To treat such complaints seriously isn't to concede automatically that the complainers are treated with disrespect or that the changes they want should be made. But at issue is not which is the right and which the wrong side of the question, justice doesn't have to be conceived in this way. The issue is the need to deal seriously with the complaint, the need to discuss it in a serious way and then either answer it or act upon it. Ignoring it, laughing at it, and dismissing it are self-incriminating responses that tend to undermine the trust that the emphasis on respect helps to guard.

An underlying theme here is that if respect is valued and presumed to prevail in the society, then the respect given one group cannot be casually evaluated by the perception of other groups. What respect for all others amounts to cannot be defined by a single authoritative group, say the group of the majority; the relation of this point to the pornography issue is explored below. Therefore if a number of members of some group perceive their treatment as demeaning, that is *prima facie* evidence that there is a problem. And given the seriousness of the matter, the rest of the community must take it seriously either by answering it or by making changes.

I conclude that although there may be different ways of responding to pornography and alternatives to control of such materials, this kind of complaint cannot be lightly dismissed. It needs to be handled in terms of the respect felt to be accorded the complainants by the rest of the community. One way the complaint against pornography by women is not addressed is by reference to the First Amendment and the possible 'slippery slope' to censorship.

Granted that there is a *prima facie* reason to think women are demeaned by pornographic materials, how does censorship become justified? Isn't some other means to deal with it available, and wouldn't that be preferable? The answer is that of course it's possible and other means may be preferable, for there certainly are dangers in permitting one group to control what others may read or see. It is not my thesis that censorship of pornography is the only answer to the moral complaint or that it should be invoked lightly. In fact, it might be invoked as a last resort when such moral protests are raised. But censorship is one answer, and my aim is to show that the justification for using it is not rebutted by an appeal to the First Amendment. Whatever answer is given, that answer needs to address the moral objection to the way treatment of women is represented. The establishment of guidelines for sexual representations might be a solution. Must we decide in general which kind of response is best? I propose rather that there is no theoretical and final answer but that an acceptable response will take serious account of the perceptions of the objecting group.

One has to ask, however, whether there isn't a danger in appealing to the moral standards of any one group when laws are formulated. As Mill suggests, shouldn't anyone have the right to live anyway he wishes? Isn't experimentation generally a good and not a bad thing?

One kind of answer to the libertarian would relate a society to a 'moral community', showing that morals and laws must be joined together. Harry Clor and Patrick Devlin each defend such views, the former defending a restrained use of censorship, the latter a freer use.[129] The problem with such views is that they are too broad. What is the 'moral community', and where is it to be found? Is it represented by the majority? If so, then surely moral constraints are worse than paternalistic: they are downright tyrannical, as Mill said.

Even though the complaint of women against pornography cannot be dismissed by appeals to freedom of the press, why shouldn't Mill's argument for freedom apply here? Why shouldn't the objection still hold that if women don't want to look at pornographic pictures or film, they shouldn't look? So long as there is 'reasonable avoidability' and people can avoid pornography if they want to, where, as Feinberg argues, is the offence? When the 'obscene' book sits on a shelf, who is there to be offended? If pornography lies between 'decorous covers', no one need look at it who doesn't want to. It is only when pornography produces an offence on a par with 'shame, or disgust, or noisome stenches' (however, they would translate in this case) that the law may justifiably interfere. That is to say, pornography should be restricted only when it becomes a nuisance difficult to avoid. To restrict it on other grounds would be to engage in moral paternalism. It would be to set standards for those who enjoy pornography in order to save them from themselves.

This protest, however, misses the point. The felt insult and indignity that women protest is not like a noise or bad odour, for these are group neutral and may offend anyone, while pornography is felt to single women out as objects of insulting attention. There is a clear division in the community here, unlike the division between people who mind an odour very much and others who can ignore it. The question of how the rest of the community should respond to the perceived debasement that women feel is not analogous to the way the community should treat people particularly sensitive to and offended by certain smells. There is a democracy with respect to smells, but with pornography there is felt hostile discrimination. One way to deal with objections to pornography has been to appeal to a typical member of the community, an 'average man' who can judge as a representative of the rest whether some material is sufficiently objectionable to warrant restrictions.

But there is an internal logical difficulty in this appeal. The 'average man' is understood not to be a woman, as is clear from the way the perceptions of the average man are viewed. *Roth*, for instance, speaks of the 'appeal to prurient interests', but such interests are surely interests predominantly of men, not of women. Feinberg, too, speaks to public nudity in terms of 'the conflict between these attracting and repressing forces, between allure and disgust', and again leaves the impression that he is speaking of general human reactions, while those he describes are characteristically male reactions. Other writers refer carelessly to the 'effects' of pornography – sexual arousal or even criminal behaviour – in such a way as to suggest that all people are included when in fact the effects referred to are specifically effects that pornography has on men.

---

129 H Clor, *Obscenity and Public Morality* (Chicago University Press, 1969); P Devlin, *The Enforcement of Morals* (Oxford University Press, 1965).

The premise is essential to my argument that pornographic materials may be seen differently by one group than by another. They may be felt as insulting by one group but inoffensive to another, as seriously demeaning by one and silly by another. An analogy can be drawn with the different perceptions of blacks and whites, or of Jews and Gentiles regarding certain materials: blacks may find demeaning an image that others think innocuous. It is crucial for my argument that such differences in perception be acknowledged as a social reality and that our understanding of what it is to treat everyone with respect allow for such differences in the perception of respect. It is important, in short, that we do not assume that there is one 'Everyman view', with the only question being which view that is. Only by respecting different perceptions about what is demeaning will we see that there may be a reason to limit materials that some group – even the largest – finds unobjectionable.

There is a further curious twist in the idea that there is an 'average man' who can judge whether some materials are offensive and obscene, a man such as the 'rational man' of English law or the 'man in the jury box', as Devlin calls him, someone who expresses 'the view' of the society. For presumably when such a person is called upon to judge the offending material, he is to judge it from his own character and conscience. And of course his character will influence what he finds: a man of very strong character may find pornography only mildly or not at all objectionable; a man of weaker character will find it has an influence on him but not in consequence call it objectionable; an 'average man' will fall somewhere in between. So sound judgment is difficult to come by.

But not only does a man's character influence his perception: the perception he expresses – his judgment as to the offensiveness of lewd materials – reflects back upon his character. Suppose he says that some materials are very provocative and could lead a viewer to do wicked things. He is testifying not only against the materials but also about his own susceptibility, and thus indirectly incriminating himself. We are told something about his own weakness if he sees pornography as dangerous. He is testifying about his character.

The result is that a bias is built into the testimony of the 'average man' and particularly of the 'right-minded man' regarding the offensiveness of pornography. A man – even a right-minded one – cannot judge that materials are 'corrupting' without revealing his own corruptibility. And so there is pressure both on men who are strong and on men who are not so strong to find pornography harmless. On the other side, a person who objects to it is likely to be characterised as 'often … emotionally disturbed', 'propelled by [his] own neurosis', or a 'Comstock'.

Given that there is a connection between a man's testimony about pornography and his character, should men who are weak and susceptible be consulted? That would be paradoxical: such people can hardly be counted on to give any reliable testimony. But a particularly upright and conscientious man (say a respected judge) is not qualified either, for he may be unable to see any problem. And the ordinarily upright but susceptible man may be reluctant to reveal his weakness. Then whose judgment should be given weight? Given the lack of any 'objective' or authoritative spokesman for the whole society, there's only one sensible answer.

If blacks are in a position to say what is demeaning to them, why shouldn't women's voices be heard on the pornography issue? Not because they are truly 'disinterested' parties and therefore qualified as authorities. On the contrary, I have been arguing that there are no disinterested authorities, no 'objective' representatives of the moral community. And if one group were acknowledged to be completely disinterested in regard to sex or disinterested in regard to heterosexuality, that would be no qualification but the contrary. The objectionability of pornography cannot be assessed in this way; there is no analogue here to the 'average consumer' who might represent the whole community in judging a retailing policy.

The reason that women should be viewed as particularly qualified is their charge that pornography is an offence against them. That charge puts them in a morally authoritative position, just as blacks are in such a position in regard to racial insults and Jews in regard to anti-semitic humiliations. Then we need only to add that a complaint of this kind demands to be addressed somehow. It does not follow what we should do.

What lies behind our invocation of an 'average man' in regard to such issues is a powerful tendency to treat pornography – and other ethically coloured issues – in androgynous terms. But common sense tells us that where sexuality is central, an androgynous point of view, even if there were one, would be irrelevant. Without sexuality and sexual difference, sexual attraction and sexual polarity, no pornography issue would ever arise. Therefore to treat the issue in terms of universal principles that hold objectively – atomistically – for all beings alike is to perpetrate a kind of legal comedy.

Feinberg questions Justice William Brennan's argument in *Roth* by asking, 'What is the alleged State interest that makes the unobtrusive and willing enjoyment of pornographic materials the State's business to control and prevent? What is the positive ground for interference?'

This demand is legitimate, and it needs to be answered in full. Even if a moral argument such as I have outlined can be made for control of pornography, how can the moral argument be translated into constitutional terms? If controls are justified, their justification should answer Feinberg's question. The need to protect respect may be clear, but the means for protecting it are not. Is there an analogy or a precedent to guide us?

I will argue at a common sense level, not meaning to interpret the notion of 'State interest' in its technical legal sense. Given that respect for persons is an important constitutional value, I propose to show a strategy that connects respect with controls on pornography, to show that the means, the logical path, is there already and has no need to be newly cut. The connection between respect and constitutional action has been made already.

What we need here is reasoning somewhat like that in *Brown v Board of Education*. There the court decided that educational facilities – equal 'with respect to buildings, curricula and other tangible factors' – might nevertheless be unequal in an important sense. And one of the reasons they might be counted unequal was (as one summary puts it) that 'to separate [children] from others ... solely because of their race generates a feeling of inferiority as to their status in the community that may affect their hearts and minds in a way unlikely ever to be undone'. Such an institution with the 'sanction of law' which thus produces the sense of inferiority of one race is unconstitutional. Respect is not to be measured in the specifics of equipment or curriculum but in the felt implication of inferiority.

In rejecting the justice of 'separate but equal' facilities, the court specifically rejected the protest that any 'badge of inferiority' supposed to be implied by segregation exist 'not by reason of anything found in the act, but solely because the coloured race chooses to put that construction upon it'.[130] The insult perceived by blacks has priority over protests of innocence by those charged with offending. It is not crucial that they see the offence in the same way. Thus the court answered by analogy two parallel arguments in the pornography issue, that women shouldn't be so sensitive about pornography, for since no one intends to demean them by it, there is nothing demeaning in it. The parallel answer is that whether there was intent to demean or not is irrelevant.

The argument in *Brown* exemplifies the general form of reasoning we need: an institution that perceptibly demeans some group and represents its members as inferior impugns the claim to equality of those members; in doing so it violates the Constitution's provisions; thus it shouldn't be protected by the federal government. There is no reference here to interpretations of other provisions of the Constitution. Of course the production of pornography isn't an institution, yet in so far as pornography is felt to demean women, its protection by the government under the First Amendment cannot be easily argued.

A *caveat* is needed here. This argument does not imply that if some group feels demeaned – say, by advertising or institutional arrangements – then censorship is automatically justified. Considerations other than the offence taken are often relevant, some of which may also be moral, and these considerations may overbalance the initial concern for respect. Nonetheless, if what is needed is a line of reasoning that can be used to support control of pornographic materials in the face of First Amendment protections, then such a line is clearly available.

In its general conception this approach accords with Ronald Dworkin's view that absolute principles are not what is needed in much legal reasoning. Instead, we often need to balance one kind of claim or principle against others. That's the case here. The First Amendment is terribly important to us as a democracy; there's no dispute about that. But it doesn't give the last word on the question 'What may a printer print, and what may a store sell?'. While this approach shows a way to defeat the absolutist claim of the First Amendment and open the possibility of censorship, I have no desire to insist that this course be taken. Other solutions may be preferable.

A number of features of the pornography issue are illuminated by its analogy with race discrimination. For one thing, it would be irrelevant to argue that the demeaning of blacks causes no 'injury' and therefore is harmless. What it causes is not the issue: the harm and the offence lie in the practices themselves and the felt implications for people's status, the light cast upon them as citizens, and the like. Second, just as it would be bizarre to appeal to a group of whites to determine whether racial inferiority is part of the message of segregation, it is curious to consult only men about the offence of pornography. Third, the protest that not all blacks were offended would be taken as specious. Even if many blacks denied that they felt offended, we might still acknowledge the vigorous complaints of others. The same holds for women; if some are not offended by pornography, it remains true that many are, and that they see the offence as one against women as a group.

But imagine that the Commission on Obscenity were to make the following argument: if we do nothing in the way of controls, we shall at least be doing nothing wrong. And in such a doubtful matter, with something as important as First Amendment protection at issue, it is better to do nothing. The answer to this argument contains a point often overlooked. When a powerful plea for respectful treatment is addressed by some group to the government, no 'neutral' or safe response is possible. Inaction is a kind of action; it signifies toleration of the practice and thus condones it, and in condoning endorses it. Thus to respond to discrimination by arguing that the rights of states and communities are sacred matters, and that one risks a slide down a 'slippery slope' if one interferes with them, would be hollow and disingenuous and recognised as such. Similarly, I propose that there is also no 'neutral' and safe response against pornography's demeaning of women. The issue demands to be addressed by a government that wants not to give sanction to the message carried by the images. A State that wants to ensure an atmosphere of respect for all persons has to face the issue in more decisive terms than protection of the First Amendment.

The Constitution does not lead us to believe that our first duty is to protect the First Amendment, as if its application needed no justification, as if it stood above other values, including that of respect for all persons. On the contrary, the rights of free speech, religion, and assembly are protected because of the respect due to citizens and their consequent need to be free of government control in certain ways. Freedom of speech is not a fundamental right of a certain kind of enterprise – namely, the press – but stems from a view of humans as morally autonomous.

Therefore it is curious that the court and libertarian writers show such dedication to freedom of the press as an abstraction, as a principle taken by itself. They deal with it, so it seems to me, as with an icon of a faith whose main tenets they have forgotten. In this respect theirs is less than a high moral stand. Remarking the irony of this liberal position, one writer comments that 'women may rightly ask why the Constitution must be read to value the pornographer's First Amendment claim to individual dignity and choice over women's equal rights claim to their own dignity and choice'. It is a curious way of thinking that asks citizens to lay down their claim to respect at the feet of this idol.

Mill warned us about the threat presented by people who think they have the 'right' moral perspective and therefore the only 'right' answers to serious questions. I agree; we need to beware of all sorts of tyranny, however righteous, well meaning, and scholarly. For on its side the protection of pornography also may represent a kind of tyranny of opinion, a libertarian tyranny that treats would-be censors as neurotic, misguided zealots and dismisses the moral complaint altogether.

Looked at from the perspective of women, the tolerance of pornography is hard to understand. Equally hard to understand is a point of view that sees the offence of pornography only in terms of its impact on and significance to men, as if the women of the society were irrelevant or invisible. And a more political point can be added. In the light of women's increasing protests against pornography and the proliferation of defences of it, the issue carries the hazard of generating conflict between two definable groups, roughly between libertarian men on the one hand and outraged women on the other. Given these dimensions, it seems imperative to straighten the arguments and the issue out.

I wish to say something more about the claim that a definition of pornography is needed for the present argument. My argument has followed the tactic of considering certain objections to pornography without a definition of pornography or a criterion as to what objections are valid. While it focuses on objections of a certain kind, those imputing a demeaning character to pornography, it doesn't specify what kinds of things are legitimately objected to or what is really objectionable.

Where could we get a definition of pornography suitable to the role I give it, the role of materials to which a certain vague kind of objection is made? Who should define it authoritatively? Common sense does not endorse the view that legal authority set standards for the rest of the community, should decide about the inherent rightness or wrongness of certain pictures, for example, for there might be no strong moral objection to pictures the community calls pornographic, and in the absence of such objection the pictures are not, on my view, pornographic at all. My argument says only that the law might justifiably restrict materials that are found insulting in a sexual way, as some materials are by women.

Because the argument is so vague, however, it arouses concern. How will pornographic pictures be distinguished from sexy art, and pornography distinguished from sexy literature – Lawrence's portrayal of Constance Chatterly, for instance? The answer is that the lack of a sharp line is precisely what I allow for, as I allow for changing attitudes. If a public work of art is found insulting by some part of the community that has to look at it, then that is a reason – though only one – for restricting it in some way. If no one objects then a definition that makes it objectionable would be superfluous and really besides the point.

The terms of the issue as I frame it require only the value of individual respect, which is part of our moral heritage, and the perceptions by members how they are respected. They therefore allow for changes in customs and tastes, allow that what is demeaning in one time may not be found so in another. When pornography is defined in terms of what is perceptibly demeaning, not what is permanently and abstractly so, there is no force to the protest that since 'Grandpa was excited even by bare ankles, dad by flesh above the knee, grandson only by flimsy bikinis', no standards can be set. As fashions change, their moral implications change too. So if what was found demeaning once is not found so any longer, any problem regarding it has vanished. It is better not to define pornography for all time, or to define it at all.

One important problem involving the First Amendment still needs to be considered. Suppose we are considering a work that asserts and argues that women are inferior to men, more animal than men, and that they enjoy brutal and sadistic treatment. Imagine such a work: it asserts that there is evidence to show that women enjoy a subservient, animal, victimised role and that this is a correct and proper way to treat women, particularly with regard to sex. Some evidence or other is cited, and it is argued that 'equality' is simply inappropriate for beings of this kind, belonging to an inferior level of sensibility or whatever. To be sure, these ideas run directly against the moral idea that an individual, *qua* individual, has worth. Nonetheless, we believe in free pursuit of all manner of debate, moral, scientific, and political, without government interference. So would such a work, purporting to be a scientific study, come under the protection of the First Amendment, or may it be treated like pornography and restricted on the same grounds? Does it differ from the case of hard pornographic pictures and films, and if so, how?

On this question I side with the libertarians, for the difference between pornographic pictures and such a report is a signal one for us and for the First Amendment. Mill also would recognise the difference, for he based the freedom of circulation of opinion on the possibility of refuting an opinion that is false and criticising one that is poorly founded. In his vision an opinion or argument is at continual risk of being refuted, and so it cannot endanger a community where reason and truth are valued. We can draw the distinction by saying that the materials that say nothing are beyond this risk of refutation and therefore, by protecting them, we give them an immunity to criticism that expressions of opinion do not enjoy. The argument of a work may be objectionable, but like all arguments, it is vulnerable to criticism, while pornography lacks such vulnerability.

This distinction is one I believe the framers of the Constitution would also have recognised. The need for opinions to be circulated freely is part of the respect for citizens which prompted the Bill of Rights. But protection of opinion could be distinguished then as well as now from protection of the press to print what it likes, including offensive pictures.

Defences of pornography have often turned on leaving this distinction obscure, arguing, for example, 'that pornography is intended not as a statement of fact, but as an opinion or fantasy about male and female sexuality'. Taken this way, it cannot be prohibited on the ground of being false. At the same time, however, one hears that 'correction of opinion depends ... on the competition of other ideas'. It is a Catch-22. Critics of pornography who are told that they should 'compete in the marketplace of ideas with their own views of sexuality' while pornography doesn't present ideas are placed in an impossible situation. The pictures don't argue for a demeaning attitude toward women in regard to sex or present a view of sexuality; at the same time they are demeaning. They don't argue that women enjoy being brutally handled; they show brutality and insinuate the victims' pleasure. While an author would be correct in saying that pornography carries an implied message that brutal treatment of women is acceptable, the fact that it is implied rather than explicit is important.

With this argument I believe Mill would concur, for he consistently maintained the need for respect of differences, including different points of view, and here the differences, including different points of view, is one relating to the two sex groups. Respect for persons in all their variety was at the heart of both his libertarianism and his ethical philosophy. However difficult they may be to understand in terms of one's own principles, people are worthy of respect: that was his repeated theme. 'Man is not a machine', he wrote, and he surely did not think women are machines for sex. To demean women in the way pornography does is to treat them as possessions or as servants. So in the end I think that Mill, who argued passionately for women's rights and equal worth and dignity, would find it intolerable to have his views invoked to protect pornography, as they have been.

Although the libertarian case against controls seemed clear-cut and irrefutable, appeal to atomistic ideas cannot solve such a powerfully felt moral issue. If respect for people really exists, it will appear in the way complaints of insult are handled and not only in the propositions used to rebut them. What is needed is not a vision of justice, a simple doctrinaire solution, but a carefully plotted middle way between broad and oppressive controls and reckless liberty. Such an approach will go beyond atomism and deal with injustice in a different and less theoretical way.

THE PROBLEM WITH PORNOGRAPHY: A CRITICAL SURVEY OF THE CURRENT DEBATE[131]

Emily Jackson[132]

There has, in recent years, been a proliferation of feminist debates around the issue of pornography. I do not wish to add to this massive literature by advocating either prohibition of, or free access to pornography. Instead I want to try to explain my agnosticism towards this stark dichotomous choice. There are

---

131 [1995] *Feminist Legal Studies* 49.

132 At the time of writing, Lecturer in Law, Birkbeck College, University of London.

compelling reasons for feminists to focus on pornography: discussion of pornography may focus on the impotence of rights; the superficiality of equality rhetoric; the construction of sexuality; the significance of representation and so on. It has proved to be a site where many of the most pressing issues facing women intersect. Moreover, few women fail to be moved and disgusted by descriptions of the abhorrent abuse that sometimes masquerades as 'adult' entertainment. So feminist responses to pornography consist in layers of theoretical arguments and emotional reactions. The picture is complicated still further by pornography's place within other non-feminist debates. Pornography has been a focus for a complex matrix of political, social and academic discourses not primarily motivated by the exploitation of women. Those concerned with freedom of the individual and those worried by the perceived moral degeneration of society have also fixed on pornography as a pivotal issue. Since the agendas of liberalism and the moralist right-wing both command weighty establishment support, feminists have frequently found themselves enmeshed in a series of arguments tangential to their central concerns.

At the root of this confusion is the unstated assumption that there are some basic shared understandings about what pornography is; what is wrong with it; and the role of law in its control. In this article I want to unpick these three overlapping questions. A precise definition of pornography is difficult, perhaps even impossible. Acknowledging this does not obviate the possibility of fruitful debate, but it does necessitate a closer look at the various ideological agendas which inform our preconceptions about pornography. I want to attempt to unravel the diversity behind the pornography debate, and examine the impact this diversity has had upon feminist responses. I then want to look closely at the feminist preoccupation with law reform in order to highlight some of the factors which serve to obstruct an indubitably well-intentioned crusade.

1. What is Pornography?

Much of the discourse appears to plunge into discussion about what should be done about pornography without first attempting to elucidate precisely what it is. Pornography is not a self-defining concept; indeed its connection with sexual arousal means that it is, probably, an inherently subjective notion. I am troubled by the possibility that pornography's meaning may be too fluid to serve as an adequate foundation for the layers of argument which rest upon some assumed definitional solidity. For example, does the intention of the consumer or the producer of the image have any impact upon what is categorised as pornography? Our instinct may be to deny emphatically any such suggestion, but there are difficulties with this. First, paedophiles are often attracted to images of children which might in other contexts be wholly innocent. If a paedophile ring traffics in 'holiday snaps' of children, do these images acquire illegitimacy through the purpose to which they are put? Can it become come an offence to sell pictures of naked children, when most parents have drawers full of such photos? Second, some feminists write about experiences of sexual abuse and exploitation in a way that might seem to mirror descriptions of such acts in pornographic magazines. For example, in Andrea Dworkin's novel *Mercy*, the heroine is repeatedly humiliated, sexually assaulted and tortured: is this then pornography? It might be argued that Dworkin's heroine does not appear to get pleasure from her abuse; but much hard-core pornography also shows women distressed by the sexual violence used against them. It might then be suggested that it should not be seen as pornography because we can be sure that was not what the author intended. Yet, if 'intention to exploit' becomes a necessary ingredient of the pornographic, we would have a readily manipulable defence which would effectively nullify attempts at regulation.

Furthermore, there are dangers in disallowing any expression which addresses sexual degradation. The paintings of René Magritte feature dehumanised images of women; in one picture, *Le Viol*,[133] a woman's face is replaced with a torso: her breasts become her eyes, and her pubic hair becomes a beard. Perhaps this shows women to be reducible to their sexual parts. But is it comment on a society that does this to women, or is it pornography?

It seems clear that any definition of pornography rests upon background assumptions about what, if anything, is wrong with it. If sexual explicitness is the central concern, lesbian erotica is undoubtedly pornography. If, on the other hand, the harm of pornography is perceived to be the exploitation of women, such imagery is relatively unproblematic. So the term 'pornography' would then seem easily manipulable. If its fluidity of meaning is directly related to its appropriation by those with divergent agendas, we should perhaps look more closely at the breadth of the pornography debate.

2. The Breadth of the Pornography Debate

Formulating a coherent strategy to deal with pornography depends, in part, on elucidating precise goals. The intersection of multiple political agendas must be acknowledged and understood. We could identify three broad types of perspective: right-wing moralist, liberal and feminist.

This split is plainly an over-simplification, within each category there will obviously be a plurality of different responses. Nevertheless it is clear that crisp analysis of the pornography issue is already seriously problematic. Does pornography threaten the moral fibre of society; or is a part of the individual's right to free expression; or does it exploit women? There will only be agreement on a definition of pornography when there is a coherent understanding about what it is that is problematic about particular types of imagery.

A. Moralists

For the moralist right, pornography synthesises all that is rotten in 20th century society. Its explicit representation of non-procreative sex is seized upon as a symbol of the corruption of modern morals. Mary McIntosh argues that this crusade is rooted in the 'paternalist form of patriarchal domination that had its heyday in the Victorian era'.[134] Immanent in the right-wing moralist criticism of pornography is the notion that sex and women should be protected by being kept within the family. The conservative agenda is to return to traditional religious values where sexuality, and in particular female sexuality is invisible. On this view increased openness about sexual desire is symptomatic of a modern moral decline. The moralist right perceive pornography to be part of a broader trend in which the privacy of procreative sex within the family unit is eroded. Pornography is then attacked in the same terms as the right wing assaults upon access to abortion or the growth in single parenthood.

The right-wing notion of a recent moral decline is in fundamental opposition to the feminist belief in pervasive and ongoing patriarchal values. The suppression of female desire through keeping women under the control of fathers and husbands is precisely what has been resisted by feminists. For example, for the moralist right-wing lobby sex education which does not simply explain reproductive functions is as much a target as conventional pornographic

---

133 Literally translated, *The Rape*.

134 M McIntosh, 'Liberalism and the Contradictions of Sexual Politics', in L Segal and M McIntosh (eds), *Sex Exposed: Sexuality and the Pornography Debate* (Virago, 1992), p 165.

imagery. In the UK AIDS groups which have produced explicit literature which 'presents an extensive, erotic series of non-penetrative sexual options' have been attacked by the right-wing lobby for promoting perverted practices. For feminists it is deeply troubling that current norms of sex education and information in teenage magazines convey disturbing messages for young girls. Sex, always assumed to be penetrative heterosexual intercourse, is explained in school as a source of pregnancy and disease, and magazines entreat them to 'hold out for love' and wait for 'Mr Right'. Lynne Segal argues that this 'sabotages sexual confidence, connecting girls' desire for love with the ignorance and guilt which will mean they leave the defining of sex up to boys and men'.[135] Young women need explicit sex education so that they do not feel impelled to tolerate unsatisfactory sexual relationships. Yet information which encourages young women to disengage themselves from traditional notions of female sexuality is precisely that which is routinely targeted and suppressed by the moralist lobby.

While concern about pornography has, for practical purposes, sometimes linked moralists with the feminist critique, it must be understood that their agendas are not simply different, but in fundamental opposition to each other. It is clear then that the same target of pornography can be approached from positions which are not simply disparate, but mutually contradictory.

B. Liberals

For liberals, freedom of expression is one of the fundamental tenets of individual autonomy. It is a basic principle of liberalism that the extreme views of minorities should be permitted in the interests of truth. The free flow of ideas, however unpalatable, is assumed to be conducive to rational argument and informed choice. This argument is regularly applied to pornography; Catharine MacKinnon suggests that putting the pornographers in the posture of the excluded underdog plays on the deep free speech tradition against laws that restrict criticising the government.[136]

Indeed some staunch liberals, such as Ronald Dworkin, have expressed concern that their principled objection to censorship is most often invoked not to protect political dissent, but to defend the free flow of pornography.[137] The tenacious liberal belief in the sanctity of free expression has exercised a considerable hold over the pornography debate and its suppositions need to be examined closely.

(i) The Constitutional Difference

The existence or not of a written constitution shapes the nature and impact of the discourse of rights. Giving constitutional guarantees of continued access to specific rights means that campaigners, of whatever political persuasion, will attempt to claim the language of rights in order to legitimate their stance, and confer the weight of constitutional machinery behind their crusade.

When the debate is about pornography, the First Amendment in the United States becomes an obvious pole on which to hang the pro-pornography flag. The link between the 'right' to free expression and the production, distribution, sale and use of pornography lends specious authority to the interests of an industry which is not, perhaps, self-evidently valuable. MacKinnon argues that this means that:

---

135 L Segal, 'Sweet Sorrows, Painful Pleasures', in Segal and McIntosh, *op cit*, p 88.

136 CA McKinnon, *Only Words* (Harvard University Press, 1993), p 39.

137 R Dworkin, *New York Review of Books*, October 1993.

> ... the operative definition of censorship accordingly shifts from government silencing what powerless people say, to powerful people violating powerless people into silence and hiding behind State power to do it.[138]

Flowing from this is an even more dangerous phenomenon. The staking out of a position of constitutional legitimacy to some extent forces the hand of groups or individuals who feel some disquiet about the prevalence of pornographic imagery. The terms of the debate have been set: access to pornography is a part of the freedom of expression upon which democratic society rests. In order to challenge this moral high ground, those concerned by pornography are manipulated into appearing to argue against freedom. There would seem to be no continuum here: speech is either free or not free. Those who want to argue that pornography is not an unqualified good are forced into arguing that it is an unqualified evil.

Nevertheless, all free speech clauses in rights-conferring documents allow for some restrictions: sensitive military information and incitement to racial hatred are examples. The difficulty is that any restrictions have to be proved necessary. Article 10 of the European Convention on Human Rights says that expression should be free save insofar as any restrictions are essential to the preservation of democracy. The assumption is, as Catharine MacKinnon has pointed out, that all speech, no matter how degrading or insulting, is a good thing. The burden of proof of harm is shifted to those seeking to restrict expression. The parameters are drawn narrowly and pornography must fit within the ill-defined rubric of obscenity.

If there is a written constitution, conflict between various fundamental rights is inevitable, and the resolution of such conflicts is a routine aspect of the judiciary's role. This makes pornography ordinances which rest on the protection of women's right to equal treatment, at least plausible. Feminists, it appears, have had to make a choice. Either they have to try to fit pornographic imagery within the recognised exception to free expression, ie obscenity. Or they have to mobilise another constitutionally protected right in an attempt to trump the First Amendment logic.

In countries without a written constitution, the debate is, to some extent, different, but it is crucially moulded by the assumptions which underlie the possible justifications for not having a bill of rights. In the UK there are vocal campaigns in favour of the creation of a written constitution. But they have not, as yet, succeeded. Why not? Many in the US regard a series of constitutionally guaranteed rights as self-evidently advantageous. How could another Western society resist the implementation of a solid buttress to their democracy? The answer may, I believe, lie in a peculiarly British phenomenon: that of placing great trust in those with power. In spite of evidence that suggests that power often slips into corruption, the British sometimes appear to believe that the benign exercise of authority is ultimately preferable to the creeping dangers inherent in a commitment to citizens' rights. In fact there would even be those within the UK who would argue that the British are more free as a result of the creativity of the common law tradition which allows incremental and possibly expansive development of autonomy, unhindered by rigid formulations of 'rights'.

In the UK there is no 'right' to produce, distribute, or consume pornography. Instead that which does not contravene the law against obscenity will, by default,

---

be permitted. The underlying assumption being that the law-makers and interpreters will leave a sufficiently wide lacuna such that individual autonomy is respected. It is crucial that those with power are entrusted with striking the correct balance. So the commitment to the pornographer's freedom is perhaps more insidious because it is unstated. It is an unseen assumption which undercuts any efforts to reform the law. While it is not constitutionally guaranteed, this means that it cannot be put into a balancing exercise with the 'rights' of women, as in the binary opposition posited by MacKinnon and Dworkin. Instead it rests as one of the fundamental background principles: free expression is unstated and hence unchallengeable.

Those worried by pornography then have their options limited. They cannot hope to challenge the free expression argument by pointing out its conflict with other 'rights'. Other rights, insofar as they exist, have already been weighed with free speech and, presumably, found to be of relative insignificance. The assumptions which underlie the common law are assumed to be so deeply embedded in that tradition that they cannot be questioned. So concern about pornography leaves only one option: that of strengthening existing obscenity law.

In spite of the constitutional difference it could be argued that Britain and America approach the free speech issue with essentially similar background assumptions. In the US the First Amendment protects expression by preventing its restriction, thus presupposing that the capacity for free speech exists. In the UK the absence of a constitution points even more clearly to an assumption that speech will be free provided the State does not intervene to curb it. This freedom need not be guaranteed because the legislature and the judiciary can be trusted to implement prohibitions on action in order to give maximum respect for individual liberty.

Equating the protection of pornography with the promotion of free speech has led to particular difficulties in Eastern Europe. Since pornography was suppressed by the communist regimes, the liberation of political expression has been accompanied by a celebration of the new ready availability of pornographic material.

In Hungary over 40 pornographic magazines have become available since the lifting of all restrictions on pornography in 1990. (Interestingly, *Playboy* is not considered to be pornographic). Laslo Voros, a self-styled 'King of Porn', claims that his seven sex magazines 'help people to overcome the legacy of communist sexual repression, teaching people about sex and helping those who cannot find partners'.[139] In Poland the law has not been changed, but pornography is now proliferating. Posters and calendars showing naked women are prevalent, and they are increasingly being used in advertisements. Corrin suggests that, in Poland, 'the general trend implies that freedom means, among other things, free access to women's bodies'.[140]

The Western linkage between pornography and freedom is partly to blame. Eastern European liberals have been convinced that access to pornography is a civil liberty and are resistant to any attempt to limit their new-found freedom.

---

139 'Superwoman and the Double Burden: Women's Experience of Change', in C Corrin (ed), *Central and Eastern Europe and the Former Soviet Union* (Scarlet Press, 1992).

140 *Ibid*, p 92.

(ii) The Congruence of Liberalism

For many feminists the ultimate goal is not the prohibition of pornography, but the marginalisation of the desire to consume it. New social taboos can be created: attitudes to drink-driving and smoking have shifted immeasurably in the last few years. But it must be acknowledged that, while the dissemination and consumption of pornography is legitimised by association, explicit or implied, with the first human freedom, attrition of the attitude that associates images of women in prone and subordinate positions with human (gender-neutral) freedom, will be problematic.

As I suggested above, in both the US and the UK, the assumption is that speech will naturally be free provided the State does not restrain it. This is a classic example of the liberal's preoccupation with negative liberty.[141] It is assumed that the important issue is the avoidance of restrictions on speech, rather than affirmative access to speech for those to whom it has been denied.[142] Pornography, with its tendency to strip women of credibility, may hinder, rather than promote free speech for women.

Joseph Raz has pointed out that liberty is meaningless without a range of valuable options.[143] True freedom entails the positive provision of resources, not just the protection of that which the subject already possesses. A real concern for freedom of expression then entails providing conditions in which women's speech will not be undermined by their status as objects for sexual consumption. MacKinnon argues that:

> censorship may occur not only through explicit State restriction, but also through the official and unofficial privileging of powerful groups and viewpoints.[144]

Censorship through relative powerlessness is invisible, it does not exist as a legal harm. Instead this is the marketplace of ideas, where those with the most power and confidence inevitably have access to the widest dissemination of their thoughts. The structural powerlessness of women which, according to some feminists is exacerbated by pornography, is a crucial determinant of the degree to which they have access to free expression.

Ronald Dworkin has argued that this argument means that feminists are demanding not just access to speech, but also a sympathetic reception for anything women say.[145] Yet I believe MacKinnon's point is chronologically prior: ending the silencing of women by encouraging any speech is content-neutral and does not imply any particular response to what women say.

So the libertarian slant of the American and British attitude to expression incorporates a very particular type of freedom. A freedom to retain the fruits of an already unequal distribution of power. While liberalism continues to confer legitimacy on negative freedom, the pornography debate will be stifled.

---

141 I Berlin, *Four Essays on Liberty* (Clarendon Press, 1969), pp 118–72; C Fried, *Right and Wrong* (Harvard University Press, 1978). For a lucid critique see C Taylor, *What's Wrong with Negative Liberty in Philosophy and the Human Sciences: Philosophical Papers 2* (Cambridge University Press, 1985), pp 211–29.

142 CA MacKinnon, *The Sexual Politics of the First Amendment* in *Feminism Unmodified* (Harvard University Press, 1987).

143 J Raz, *The Morality of Freedom* (Clarendon Press, 1986).

144 *Only Words, op cit*, p 77.

145 R Dworkin, *op cit.*

The rhetoric of equality is, in practical terms, undermined by the liberal tradition of neutrality. Catharine MacKinnon has argued that the legal commitment to impartiality leads to the 'stupid theory of equality'.[146] Where the legislature and the judiciary are avowedly neutral between groups of people whose positions may be deeply unequal, in treating the powerful in the same way as the powerless, the structural inequality persists and is legitimised by its association with the 'virtue' of neutrality. If equality and neutrality are not smoothly compatible, it may be necessary to clarify our priorities. Currently in the US and in the UK, neutrality effectively trumps the promotion of equality. But in Canada we can see how this could be reversed. The first goal of the Canadian courts is explicitly not neutrality, but equality. Their Constitution contains the familiar protection of free expression, but, crucially, laws which contravene a substantive part of the law can be justified under s 1 Charter of Rights and Freedoms if they *promote equality and are demonstrably justifiable* in a democratic State' (my emphasis). Restricting pornography is then constitutionally legitimate when it is established that its contents promote inequality. This step has been taken and Canada's Supreme Court has outlawed pornography not because of its lack of decency, but because it is incompatible with the promotion of women's equality. In *R v Butler*[147] the court held that if true equality between male and female persons is to be achieved, we cannot ignore the threat to equality resulting from exposure to audiences of certain types of violent and degrading material.

C. Feminism

Pornography is understandably of critical concern to feminists. No one who has heard the stories of abuse and desperation which lead women to be forced to perform for the pornographer's camera can fail to be moved and deeply troubled. Furthermore, many women feel instinctively that the message of pornography must have an impact upon its viewers attitudes towards women. Pornography has proved a fruitful area for debate for three reasons:

(a) The anti-pornography position taken by many feminists allows them, for a brief moment, to come closer to achieving their goals than ever before. They can command the weight of establishment support in the form of the moralist lobby. This may be, as I suggested earlier, a rather pernicious partnership. But for women who have lacked power, the clout of the unholy alliance may hold understandable appeal.

(b) I think pornography has also attracted debate because it is a sexy subject. Foucault has shown that the desire to translate sexual experience into discourse is an ahistorical human impulse.[148] Whatever one thinks about Camille Paglia's assertion that 'pornography and art are inseparable because there is voyeurism and voracity in all our sensations as seeing, feeling beings'[149] it is clear that sexuality inspires widespread fascination. Radical feminists, such as MacKinnon, have seized upon sexual norms as the defining moment in female subordination. Regardless of whether or not sexuality does constitute gender relations, it is clear that this assertion has been central to the degree of public and media interest in the radical feminist agenda.

(c) The substantive reason for focusing on pornography is then part of the feminist claim that the cultural construction of sexuality is of central

---

146 *Only Words, op cit*, p 98.

147 [1992] 2 WWR 577.

148 M Foucault, *The History of Sexuality*, Vol 1 (Penguin, 1979).

149 C Paglia, *Sexual Personae* (New York: Vintage Books, 1991), p 35.

importance. Feminists like Dworkin and MacKinnon have claimed that pornography damages all women by equating their sexuality with their abuse.

This last claim requires further investigation. Feminists often start from the supposition that women are harmed by pornography. There is a wealth of scientific evidence which suggests that exposure to pornography increases the likelihood that the average man will force sex on a woman. And there are interminable debates about whether this research documents a mere correlation, or a causal relationship between pornography and rape. Of course there are scientific reports which appear to show the opposite: that relaxation of censorship in Scandinavian countries is associated with a decrease in sexual violence. The latest piece of research in the UK found that it was not possible to prove that pornography caused sexual violence, but that neither was it proven that pornography had any beneficial effects in creating outlets for male aggression.[150]

I think it unhelpful to become entrenched in an unproductive series of claims and counterclaims. Deborah Cameron and Elizabeth Frazer[151] persuasively argue that causal explanations of human action are completely inappropriate. When a man sees a pornographic movie his response to it is not analogous to the behaviour of a heavy object dropped from a great height. Human behaviour is not susceptible to precise causal rules comparable to the laws of gravity. Reaction to pornography is not dictated by natural instinct, instead it consists in the interpretation of images. The meaning pornography has for its consumers is not self-constituting, it is one part of the cultural landscape, and its impact does not exist in isolation from broader experiences of sexuality.

Although we should clearly be concerned about evidence suggesting that men who are violent towards women often use pornography before or during that abuse, the problem with pornography should not be limited to the question of whether any single image is capable of creating an instant rapist.[152]

Indeed, Catharine MacKinnon, a staunch believer that 'porn is the theory, rape is the practice', does also suggest that pornography has an impact beyond that on its direct consumers and victims. In her view it does not simply present distorted images of sex to those who choose to consume it. Instead, it damages all women because it inescapably sets the ground rules for all sexual relations. She argues that pornography has made sex into an unequal encounter between a man who dominates and a woman who submits.[153] This image is reproduced so many times that it becomes inculcated into our consciousness as the way things are. MacKinnon argues that the resulting cultural hegemony is sustained by other media which affirm the values of pornography: the male is the possessor and the woman the possessed.

---

150 Documented in D Howitt and G Cumberbatch, *Pornography: Impacts and Influences. A Review of the Available Research Evidence on the Effects of Pornography* (London: Home Office Research and Planning Unit, 1990).

151 D Cameron and E Frazer, 'On the Question of Pornography and Sexual Violence: Moving Beyond Cause and Effect', in C Itzin (ed), *Pornography: Women, Violence and Civil Liberties* (Oxford University Press, 1993), pp 359–83.

152 L Segal, *Is the Future Female? Troubled Thoughts on Contemporary Feminism* (Virago, 1987), p 111.

153 CA MacKinnon, *Toward a Feminist Theory of the State* (Harvard University Press, 1989), p 69.

So pornography is one mechanism in the continuing process of gender definition. Pornography is one example, among many, from a cultural tradition that appears to devalue women. There is patently some connection between representations of sex and the sexual values of a community. But the relationship between the two is complicated. It is undeniable that pornography exists as one cultural medium in the ongoing social construction of reality. The gender hierarchy which dictates rigid and debilitating sexual identities is culturally constructed. Pornography presents particularly crude and polarised images of women and men, but it does not, on its own, create sexual inequality. Women can only think about their sexuality and articulate their desires though the filter of a deeply internalised set of patriarchal norms. It may then be true that feminine sexuality outside of its confining cultural representation has, historically, been profoundly silenced. We cannot easily articulate alternative sexual identities because our experience does not transcend our gendered culture. Feminism must struggle against the imposition of rigid sexual norms. This is, nevertheless, a vast project, and its success depends upon recognising the prevalence of pornography as but one link in the chain.

Indeed the fact that pornography is extreme may, according to some women, mean that it has less influence than other, more widely available material. In the UK Clare Short, a Labour MP, introduced a piece of draft legislation which, if implemented, would have prevented the most popular daily newspaper printing a provocative photograph of a topless model on its page three.[154] The inclusion or not of this sort of image under the rubric 'pornography' is controversial. But in being widely available, cheap, and published in the relatively privileged arena of the news media, it could be argued that these images have a profound effect on perceptions of women's sexuality. Not least because each morning *The Sun* will publish a new picture, and yesterday's copy is discarded. This disposability may amplify the objectification process.

Naomi Wolf has argued that images of women in 'legitimate' contexts such as women's magazines, Hollywood movies and pop videos have joined more traditional pornographic formats as means of disseminating dangerous images of women.[155] 'Beauty pornography' involves the use of perfected women's bodies in poses borrowed from soft and hard-core pornography to sell products to women. Women are told that the way to be sexy, desirable and to have self-respect is to be beautiful, skinny, and, increasingly, tied up and submissive. Movies portraying sexual exploitation and abuse have proliferated. Promotional pop videos have featured stylised images of women in danger. The mainstream cliché is thus one of stylish objectification and sado-masochism. Wolf is then not surprised that this has produced a generation that honestly believes that violence against women is sexual. The impact is not just on men, women's attitudes toward themselves are affected; Wolf finds it axiomatic that studies have found that 50% of women have submissive sexual fantasies. Wolf may then be close to MacKinnon in arguing that this has become the reality of sex.

It is irrefutable that current cultural representations of sexuality frequently articulate disempowering stereotype sex roles. Yet outlawing pornography, without altering its current definition would not even begin to deal with images that have become cloaked in respectability. Perhaps more fundamentally,

154 Indecent Displays (Newspapers) Bill, *Hansard*, 12 March 1986, 13 April 1988.
155 N Wolf, *The Beauty Myth* (Vintage, 1991), pp 131–78.

pornography just reinforces sexual identities which are simultaneously created and sustained in other ways.

If pornography is then simply one facet of an infinitely broader process, its legal proscription would not fatally undermine current sexual norms. Indeed, it could be argued that the pre-occupation with law reform may, in fact, be seriously obstructive.

3. The Problem with Law

Law's relationship with pornography is fraught with difficulty. Prohibiting or restraining certain forms of sexual expression is part of their appeal. Pornography is, in part, about the transgression of sexual norms. So to some extent the pornography industry is dependent upon the law to provide the rules which are then flouted in its images.

Within the existing ideological framework of current liberal legal systems, it is a fundamental principle that individuals' freedom should not be restricted unless such restraint is necessary to prevent harm to others.[156] Clearly the definition of harm is not static and is subject to renegotiation in order to encompass newly perceived injuries, recent prohibitions of racist speech are an example. Yet this 'harm principle' has proved peculiarly resistant to pornography.

Strengthening existing obscenity law is problematic. Obscenity means that which should not be publicly staged. Obscenity is a moral issue; its aim is to restrict the indecent. The crucial issue pornography raises for feminists is not its lack of decency, but its impact on female sexuality. The legal definition of obscenity in the US is based upon the 'prurient interest' test; in the UK, obscene publications must have 'a tendency to deprave and corrupt'. Neither test offers clear guidelines as to what will be considered obscene. Furthermore, the content of the law does not take pornography seriously since, in the UK and the US, the court must look at the work 'as a whole', thus allowing publishers to design their pornography so that crude visual images are legitimised by their juxtaposition with serious articles.

Indeed there have been times when it has been accepted that the generality of obscenity legislation is deficient and specific issue statutes have been passed. Detailed zoning restrictions on pornography have tended to be more effectively implemented than the outright proscription of obscenity. For example, in Hungary, feminist groups have organised campaigns to stem the proliferation of pornography, but their success has been limited to a 1991 ruling that pornography should not be displayed in certain newspaper kiosks. In the UK the Local Government (Miscellaneous Provisions) Act 1982 gave local authorities power to licence 'sex shops' and the Act offered a definition of the cinematic material to be controlled. It was that which portrays or is intended to stimulate 'sexual activity' or that which portrays 'genital organs or urinary or excretory functions'. These restrictions presuppose a very particular view of the problem with pornography. It might at first be thought that restricting the siting of pornography outlets is part of the 'moral corruption' view of pornography. But that would mean endorsing public interest litigation to enforce licensing restrictions or to sue for public nuisance. Nonetheless, in the UK it is clear that review of local authority licensing powers can only take place if the litigant has a 'sufficient interest', this would most easily be established if the applicant had a property right which was being harmed by the presence of a pornography

---

156 JS Mill, 'Essay on Liberty', in M Warnock (ed), *Utilitarianism* (Collins, 1962).

shop.[157] And, while it is clear from *Laws v Florinplace*[158] that a sex shop may be an actionable nuisance, one only has a right of action if one's right to peaceful enjoyment of one's own property is being interfered with. So perhaps the law is astute to protect property interests damaged by pornography, but other sorts of injuries are too diffuse, abstract and novel for public law or the tort system to recognise.

Feminists have tried to mobilise statistical data on the connection between pornography and rape, but, as I have explained, the evidence has remained inconclusive. Moreover, attempts by Catharine MacKinnon and Andrea Dworkin, with the support of the moralist lobby, to fit pornography within the guarantee of equal rights for all citizens do not necessarily provide a complete solution. Their ordinance would only work for women who were able to prove that a specific image interfered with a specific right of theirs. Such women do exist and may need this protection, but if the most wide-reaching effects of pornography consist in the transmission of cultural norms, the ordinance's efficacy is restricted. Before the ordinance could address the general impact of pornography, there would have to be an accompanying shift in the prevailing judicial framework. First, group actions would have to become possible. Second, the definition of harm would have to be amended so that it could include the diffuse effects of a cumulative impact on attitudes. Third, the doctrine of legal causation would need revision: partly because it is notoriously difficult to establish causation where the harm is mediated through the actions of a third party. Furthermore, extremely difficult speculative decisions are necessitated by the test which presently decrees that an act cannot be considered the legal cause of an event if, on the balance of probabilities, that event would have occurred anyway.

Moreover, the moralists have no complaint about other images of oppressive sex roles. They are concerned with the exposure of bodily functions, not exploitation. But for feminists it is the absence of dignity that is at issue. So any coalition between radical feminists and the moralist lobby represents a further obstacle to the potential efficacy of pornography ordinances: their aims are not co-extensive. And this divergence is a significant problem for a legal system which uses legislative purpose as an aid to statutory interpretation.

If feminists want to use the law to protect women, they must be specific about the object of their concern. There are clearly women who are directly harmed by pornography: in addition to the women whose abuse is motivated by pornography's consumption, the industry's workers may be particularly susceptible to exploitation. Some feminists have argued that pornography also harms all women by defining us in terms of our sexual availability. The cumulative interaction between pornography and the definition of male and female sexuality is important. Yet it is hard to see how one piece of statutory reform could intercept the diffuse and ongoing negotiation of sexual norms.

In the US Dworkin and MacKinnon have argued that devising an effective formulaic definition of pornography is relatively straightforward. They suggest that the images lack diversity and lend themselves particularly neatly to formulaic definition. Their ordinance would suppress 'pictures or words portraying the graphic, sexually explicit subordination of women (or men or children in women's place)'. I would suggest that the crucial word here is

---

157 K Schiemann, 'Locus Standi' [1990] *Public Law* 342.
158 [1981] 1 All ER 659.

'subordination', its dictionary definition is 'to treat or regard as of minor importance': what does this mean? How can we tell if an image treats women as 'of minor importance'? Representations which show women in positions of sexual dominance might, on a literal interpretation, fall outside of this definition. Yet clearly the sexual hierarchy is not dismantled when women are on top. There is the difficulty that an ordinance has to be interpreted and applied, and in that process of interpretation and application, its intent can be manipulated and its impact radically altered. Furthermore, I think that there would be the incipient danger that the ordinance, if enacted, would fall prey to the current practice whereby pornography is designed around obscenity law so that its sexual objectification of women is legalised as well as legitimised.

Simply stated, the problem seems to be that any legal definition will simultaneously be both under and over inclusive. There is a reflexive interaction between representations of sexuality and current sexual norms. Legal regulation of some of those representations cannot offer a complete renegotiation of sex roles. Legal discourse is a relatively autonomous system of communication. Pornography activists may strive to appropriate some of the power of the legal narrative, but in doing so they are forced to try to fit their agenda within the parameters of current legal methodology. Concentrating on prevention of harm has proved counter-productive. In legal discourse harm is narrowly understood and is subject to all the limitations of legal causation and an individualised system of justice.

Robin West has argued that 'women's injuries are often not recognised or compensated as injuries by the legal culture.'[159] And she maintains that translating women's injuries into the current legal framework is impossible because the norms of the legal system itself reflect male rather than female experience. The answer is not to manipulate the way we describe women's experiences in order to fit them into the legal tradition, since this will only perpetuate the silencing of women's real voices. Drucilla Cornell explains further that the adoption of traditional legal discourse, however well intentioned, may mean that 'the harm to women literally disappears because it cannot be represented as a harm within the law'.[160]

I think that the feminist preoccupation with law reform raises two compelling and contradictory arguments. First, feminist attempts to restrict or prohibit pornography are crucially motivated by taking seriously the invisible injury of gender hierarchy. Such efforts and the debate surrounding them have important symbolic significance, notwithstanding their somewhat patchy practical impact. Second, the campaigner's understandable desire to put such restrictions or prohibitions into practice has led to the pragmatic adoption of conventional legal methodology which carries with it inevitable debilitating constraints upon the breadth of the feminist argument.

To regard pornography as a problem is clearly one part of many feminist's agendas. The fact that it is already, albeit in a misguided and muddled way, recognised as such by the law makes expansion and rearticulation of legal restrictions appear both plausible and possible. My point is simply that any success will leave in place a gender hierarchy which will provide the background

159 R West, 'The Difference in Women's Hedonistic Lives: A Phenomenological Critique of Feminist Legal Theory', in M Fineman and N Thomadsen (eds), *At the Boundaries of Law* (Routledge, 1991), pp 115–34.
160 D Cornell, *Transformations* (Routledge, 1993), p 82.

legal framework and ideology informing the implementation of anti-pornography reform. This does not mean that such reforms may not have a valuable role in the gradual erosion of oppressive sexual identities. The danger lies in seeing this reform as a potential cure and glossing over or ignoring, for the sake of expediency, the fundamental obstacles immanent within conventional legal methodology.

4. Conclusion

Finally, I would like to conclude by asking why people produce pornography? I do not believe that most producers of pornography have, as their primary purpose, the inculcation of a value system which subordinates women. This may, or may not be the result of the pornography industry's proliferation and wider influence. The primary motive of pornographers is profit. The pornography industry has expanded and technological advances have not only made its mass production and wide dissemination cheaper, but have also introduced new media for the transmission of pornographic images. Worldwide, pornography is a multi-billion dollar industry, it generates more money than the legitimate film and music industries combined. Why is the pornography industry so profitable? Why is society attracted by images that portray powerlessness as sexy and desirable in women?

The supply of pornography is not the only factor maintaining its demand. Other institutions help sustain gender inequality. And it is this deeply ingrained gender imbalance that makes images of women's inequality sexy. Pornography is not the sole cause of women's sexual subordination, but neither is it simply a symptom. Representations of sexuality do have a reflexive interaction with sexual identities. Prohibiting one narrowly defined category of representations cannot overturn the complex process of construction of sexual desire. Moreover, there are compelling reasons to suppose that outright prohibition would be ineffective and even counter-productive. As I have suggested, the availability of pornography is not the only factor maintaining its appeal. If demand exists independently, preventing its supply will only succeed in pushing the sale of pornography underground. Having a flourishing black market is not necessarily preferable to the existence of a few 'adult' bookstores. It is even arguable that greater regulation is possible where a product is not prohibited absolutely. Anne McClintock argues that 'criminalising porn only drives the business underground, where it remains brutally managed by men'.[161] Clearly protection of women who work in the pornography industry is not best served by the obstinate refusal to believe that it would continue to exist if its production and sale were legally proscribed.

Pornography is a serious issue, but debate has been obfuscated by the repeated tendency to enmesh its discussion within suggested blueprints for legal reform. Perhaps the time has come to admit that the law cannot reverse a cultural obsession with sex by addressing one extreme means through which this obsession is expressed. Pornography will, I believe, continue to exist while the sexual *status quo* persists, but this should not lock us into inertia. Gender inequality and the desire for titillation are integral to current patterns of social interaction. This reality must be renegotiable and open debate about pornography is a valuable channel for the reassessment of our cultural values. Redefining the legitimate and helping to construct the socially unacceptable are

161 A McClintock, 'Gonad the Barbarian and the Venus Flagship', in Segal and McIntosh, *op cit*, p 130.

valuable roles for the law, and perhaps anti-pornography ordinances contain an important normative judgment about the acceptability of female exploitation. The surrounding debate has certainly raised awareness and facilitated discussion, and this in itself may have some transformative effect on attitudes towards pornography. It is, nonetheless, crucial that we should not pin all our hopes on the legal regulation of pornography as a panacea.

A preoccupation with law reform has led to factionalising and a tendency to oversimplify the exceptionally complex relationship between sexual representation and sexual experience. My point is simply that legal discourse sits uneasily with the agendas of those who are actively concerned about the ethos of current sexual imagery. Multiple points of tension make the arguments for reform appear fractured and incoherent. We should be talking about sex and its representation, but to force ourselves to do so in the language of a legal textbook impoverishes the debate.

CHAPTER 11

WOMEN AND MEDICINE

The treatment of women by the medical profession raises important issues for feminism. In the United States of America, for example, the battle has long raged – and continues to rage – over a women's right to abortion. The seminal decision of the Supreme Court of America in *Roe v Wade*[1] which confirmed that a women's right to abortion is a right to be guaranteed under the right to privacy under the American Constitution, has continued to be subjected to attack from those who advocate the right to life for a foetus, or, in their terms, an unborn child. The United Kingdom's more pragmatic attitude towards 'constitutional rights' whereby – subject to the jurisdiction of the European Court of Human Rights under the European Convention on Human Rights and Fundamental Freedoms to which the United Kingdom government is a signatory – citizens enjoy freedoms rather than constitutionally guaranteed rights. Results in the consequence that matters such as abortion rights are regulated – rather than enshrined – under an Act of Parliament which has the constitutional status and importance conferred on it by the prevailing political climate.[2] Accordingly, the Abortion Act 1967 conferred a limited right to abortion, subject to approval on medical grounds (which were loosely framed). Nevertheless, echoes of the American debate were heard in the late 1980s (if indeed they have ever been silent), when the time limit for abortion was reduced to 24 weeks.[3] As a result of the differing constitutional arrangements in the United Kingdom, however, the academic debate has not achieved the level of intensity which it has in the United States of America. While 'pro-life' campaigners fight for the greater protection of the rights of the foetus, thereby seeking to pit foetal rights against women's rights, in the United Kingdom the law has for long denied that a foetus has – prior to the point at which it is capable of being born alive[4] – any 'rights' in law. Nor will English law confer rights on any other person in relation to decisions as to a woman's choice to undergo an abortion.[5]

From a feminist perspective, the right of the individual to determine questions relating to her own body are of fundamental importance. To deny the right to take decisions is to treat the individual as unequal and inferior and to deny the rationality of the woman's decision-making process and her right to autonomy. Scientific and technological advances in reproduction raise a further set of complex questions.[6] In the United Kingdom, for example, the recent

---

1   93 SCt 705 (1973).

2   See Hilaire Barnett, *Constitutional and Administrative Law* (London: Cavendish Publishing 1995), Chapters II and XIV.

3   Abortion Act 1967, s 1(1)(a), as amended by the Human Fertilisation and Embryology Act 1990.

4   See the Infant Life Preservation Act 1929.

5   See *Paton v British Pregnancy Advisory Services* [1979] QB 276; [1978] 2 All ER 987; *Re F (In Utero)* [1988] 2 All ER 987; *C v S* [1987] 1 All ER 1230.

6   See the *Report of the Committee on Human Fertilisation and Reproduction (the Warnock Report)* (Cmnd 9314) (London: HMSO, 1984).

decision of the Court of Appeal that it could give no remedy to a woman wishing to use her deceased husband's sperm in order to conceive his child, on the basis that the husband had not given written consent, has raised the issue of women's rights once more to the fore.[7]

Implicit in issues relating to conception and childbirth are many traditional assumptions: the role of women in the 'private sphere'; women's 'unique' mothering abilities, which in effect keep women out of the public sphere[8] and the power relationships between women, their partners and the medical profession. The mythology surrounding motherhood is enduring. Has society moved on at all from the view expressed by anthropologist Bradislaw Malinowski in 1927?

> Maternity is a moral, religious and even artistic ideal of civilisation, a pregnant woman is protected by law and custom, and should be regarded as a sacred object, while she herself ought to feel proud and happy in her condition. That this is an ideal which can be realised is vouched for by historical and ethnographical data.[9]

Issues such as forced sterilisation, the right to abortion, the right of pregnant mothers to choose their own lifestyle, the treatment of women found guilty of infanticide and the legal regime surrounding assisted contraception and surrogacy agreements raise complex questions for women. In this chapter, issues raised by the law and practice relating to abortion, infanticide, sterilisation, and matters relating to the scientific relief of infertility are considered.

In the first extract, Elizabeth Kingdom considers feminist issues in relation to the sterilisation of women. As the author demonstrates in *Consent, Coercion and Consortium: the Sexual Politics of Sterilisation*[10] the traditional approach to issues of consent have been dealt with under English law as legal matters for the *ad hoc* determination of the courts. This 'rights-based' approach, the author argues, masks the need for the development of policies to regulate the complex questions raised by sterilisation. The author analyses the case-law and reveals the uncertainty surrounding the issue of legal consent to sterilisation. She then proceeds to analyse the differing approaches which may be taken in the formulation of policy.

In *Who is the Mother to Make the Judgment: the Construction of Women in English Abortion Law*,[11] Sally Sheldon examines the passage of the Bill leading to the Abortion Act 1967 through Parliament. The author argues convincingly that Members of Parliament (who are predominantly male), adopted very different constructions of the women subjects of abortion law, and the doctors who would be responsible for carrying out the operations. The woman is portrayed

---

7 *R v Human Fertilisation and Embryology Authority, ex p Blood* (1997) *Times LR*, 7 February 1997. The Court of Appeal remitted the case to the authority for reconsideration. See *The Times*, 26 February 1997.

8 See Shulamith Firestone, *The Dialectic of Sex* (1970).

9 B Malinowski, 'Sex and Repression', in CK Ogden (ed), *Savage Society* (London: Routledge and Kegan Paul, 1927).

10 From Elizabeth Kingdom, *What's Wrong with Rights?* (Edinburgh University Press 1991; 2nd edn 1996).

11 [1993] *Feminist Legal Studies* 3.

variously as 'immature; irresponsible; emotionally weak; marginal; deviant; a victim'. The doctors, by contrast, are constructed as 'mature; professional; sensitive; responsible.'

Katherine O'Donovan in *The Medicalisation of Infanticide*[12] traces the history of this sex-specific crime and analyses the manner in which women have been characterised by law: initially as criminals in need of punishment, through to psychologically damaged or insane, through to more recent perceptions about women's social and economic conditions. From her analysis the author identifies the difficulties in characterising infanticide in legal terms.

Rebecca Albury has analysed the implications for Australian women as that country sought to find the appropriate legal framework for the regulation of technological advances in the relief of female infertility. In *Law Reform and Human Reproduction: Implications for Women*[13] the author argues that the traditional 'public/private' dichotomy,[14] with all its implications for women in relation to assisted conception techniques and criticises the mechanisms of social control which are applied by the medical profession.

CONSENT, COERCION AND CONSORTIUM: THE SEXUAL POLITICS OF STERILISATION[15]

Elizabeth Kingdom

Introduction

Unlike abortion, sterilisation has not been a main target of feminist politics. There are several reasons, however, why it could become a major area of feminist struggle. Again, unlike abortion, sterilisation is not the subject of a specific act in statute law. Cases have been brought under a variety of legal headings, and the most frequently cited cases are characterised by a good deal of uncertainty, not to mention bizarre opinions. In the circumstances, it is perhaps not surprising that social commentators and members of the legal and medical professions should fall back on appeals to rights when debating these controversial cases. But there are good reasons why feminists should not follow that practice. Appeals to rights are notoriously vague and polemical. These qualities may be irresistible in the heat of an adversarial moment. Yet they inevitably frustrate the development of substantive and detailed policies. And in the particular case of sterilisation, uncertainty about which social, legal, and medical policies to adopt seems to invite the invocation of some uncomfortably atavistic rights which should be specially worrying to feminists.

Issues

In this section, I bring together a number of disparate issues relating to sterilisation, issues which are pertinent to the development of a sexual politics of sterilisation. As a preliminary, it will be useful to mention some standard terms which have been used to indicate the purpose of a sterilisation operation. As we shall see, the meaning and implications of these terms can become contentious.

---

12   [1984] *Criminal Law Review* 259.

13   *Australian Women and the Political System* (ed) Marian Simms (Melbourne Longman, 1984) Chapter 13.

14   On which see further Chapter 5.

15   *What's Wrong With Rights?* (Edinburgh University Press, 1991), p 63.

'Therapeutic' sterilisation is performed for medical reasons, for example where the removal of diseased tissue involves an operation which has the effect of making the patient sterile. 'Non-therapeutic' or 'eugenic' sterilisation is performed for social reasons. It may be because the patient is thought likely to produce children with certain undesired characteristics. It may be because the patient, typically a woman, is thought to be vulnerable to sexual attack and/or is thought to be incapable of managing any other form of contraception and/or is thought to be incapable of caring for any offspring. In the UK, the proposal to sterilise a person for eugenic reasons is made in the light of the person's individual characteristics and circumstances. In some other countries the proposal is made, initially at any rate, on the basis of the individual's membership of one or more specific categories of persons. These categories are defined in assorted medical, psychological, or social terms, such as epileptics, the feeble-minded, and the morally degenerate; the categories feature explicitly in legislation. Sterilisation for contraceptive purposes is sometimes called 'elective', sometimes sterilisation 'for convenience', and once, in *The Guardian*, 'recreational' sterilisation.

The Brock Report

In 1932, under the minute of the Chairman of the Board of Control and with the approval of the Minister of Health, a Committee was appointed under the Chairmanship of LG Brock:

> to examine and report on the information already available regarding the hereditary transmission and other causes of mental disorder and deficiency; to consider the value of sterilisation as a preventive measure having regard to its physical, psychological, and social effects and to the experience of legislation in other countries permitting it; and to suggest what further enquiries might usefully be undertaken in this connection.[16]

Appendix VIII summarises legislation on the subject of voluntary and compulsory legislation in 27 of the United States of America and nine other countries in which laws existed or in which bills were being drafted. In the UK, the Committee observed, 'the legal position in regard to sterilisation is not free from doubt'. The Committee drew a distinction between eugenic and therapeutic sterilisation, commenting that the legality of therapeutic sterilisation 'is not disputed in principle', but 'that there is general agreement that sterilisation of mental detectives on eugenic grounds is illegal'. It added that 'the legal position in regard to the eugenic sterilisation of persons of normal mentality is less certain, but most authorities take the view that it is illegal'.[17]

The Committee recommended the legalisation of voluntary sterilisation in the case of mental defectives or of people who had suffered from mental disorder, of people who suffered from or who were believed to be carriers of grave physical disabilities shown to be transmissible, and of people believed to be likely to transmit mental disorder or defect. Operations for sterilisation were to be performed only under the written authorisation of the Minister for Health, and in that respect a number of procedures were to be followed. These included the requirement of the patient's written consent or, if the patient were deemed incompetent to give a reasonable consent, the written consent of a parent, guardian or spouse.

---

16 *Report of the Departmental Committee on Sterilisation* (Cmd 4485), p 5.
17 *Ibid*, p 7.

Over 20 years later, Glanville Williams pointed out that the recommendations of the Brock Report were not implemented, although they were supported by a number of public bodies such as the Royal College of Physicians.[18] He might have added that, interestingly enough, they were also supported in a resolution passed by the Business Conference of Women's Sections at the 36th Annual Conference of the Labour Party.[19]

Re D (a minor) (wardship: sterilisation)[20]

As in 1934, the legality of therapeutic sterilisation is not in doubt today, but there is still uncertainty and disagreement about the legality of eugenic or non-therapeutic sterilisation. Robert Lee and Derek Morgan[21] have reviewed and analysed the tendency of recent cases of non-therapeutic sterilisation, but for purposes of this chapter I shall examine one of the most frequently cited cases. D was a girl with Sotos Syndrome. When D was a young girl her parents had decided that they should apply to have her sterilised when she was about 18 years of age to prevent her from having children who might be abnormal.[22] After discussion with a consultant paediatrician, however, arrangements were made to have D sterilised when she was ten. Among others, an educational psychologist challenged the social and behavioural reasons for sterilising D and applied to have her made a ward of court when the paediatrician refused to defer the operation. The case was heard in the Family Division. Heilbron J held that:

> ... the operation was one which involved the deprivation of a basic human right, ie the right of a woman to reproduce, and therefore, if performed on a woman for non-therapeutic reasons and without her consent, would be a violation of that right. Since D could not give an informed consent, but there was a strong likelihood would understand the implications of the operation when she reached the age of 18, the case was one in which the courts [sic] should exercise its protective powers. Her wardship would accordingly be continued ... A decision to carry out a sterilisation operation on a minor for non-therapeutic purposes was not solely within a doctor's clinical judgement. In the circumstances the operation was neither medically indicated nor necessary and it would not be in D's best interests for it to be performed.[23]

The leading article of *New Society*, written before the case was heard, commented that 'the plan to sterilise an 11-year-old Sheffield girl has quite rightly given rise to a sense of outrage about human rights'.[24]

What is the significance of this case? Feminists might be tempted to read it as a victory over paternalism in the matter of female reproductive capacities. But it is by no means obvious that it was D's sex that was the key issue. In *Re D* the court was preoccupied with, and the sense of outrage undoubtedly provoked by, the fact that D was a minor, mentally subnormal and incapable of giving informed consent to sterilisation proposed on non-therapeutic grounds.

---

18 G Williams, *The Sanctity of Life and the Criminal Law* (Faber and Faber, 1958).

19 J Weeks, *Sex, Politics and Society* (Longman, 1981), n 53.

20 [1976] 2 WLR 79.

21 R Lee and D Morgan (eds), *Birthrights: Law and Ethics at the Beginning of Life* (Routledge, 1989).

22 *Re D, op cit*, p 326.

23 *Ibid*, p 327.

24 *New Society* 1975, p 634.

This is not to say that there is no feminist interest in this case. Heilbron J's decision turned not only on the question of informed consent but also on the distinction between therapeutic and non-therapeutic sterilisation. For Heilbron J there seemed to be no difficulty in distinguishing the two types of sterilisation. Accordingly, and this is important to note, Heilbron J's stirring appeal to D's right to reproduce was predicated on the opinion that there were no medical reasons for sterilising her.

Fifteen years later, however, in a not dissimilar case, Lord Hailsham offered this critique of the distinction between therapeutic and non-therapeutic sterilisation:

> ... for purposes of the present appeal I find the distinction ... between 'therapeutic and non-therapeutic' purposes of this operation in relation to the facts of the present case above as totally meaningless ... To talk of the 'basic right' to reproduce of an individual who is not capable of knowing the causal connection between intercourse and childbirth, the nature of pregnancy, what is involved in delivery, unable to form maternal instincts or to care for a child appears to me wholly to part company with reality.[25]

Now feminists involved in the struggles leading up to the passing of the Abortion Act 1967 will recall that one of the toughest fights was over the inclusion of the so-called 'environment clause'. This made it permissible, if not mandatory, for registered medical practitioners to take account of the woman's actual or reasonably foreseeable environment in determining the risk to her health if she continued the pregnancy. Whilst this clause did not, as some feminists and some opponents of the new Act claimed, provide for independent social grounds for lawful termination, feminists and a good many doctors welcomed its provision in the Act. Doctors were relieved because it legitimated widespread medical practice. And, as we saw in the previous chapter, feminists took the clause to be critical in the struggle to weaken the ever-present tendency of legal and medical practitioners to treat women as legal subjects defined predominantly in terms of medical, specifically gynaecological, criteria rather than in terms of their economic and social status and situation.

In the context both of abortion and of sterilisation, then, the distinction between medical, or therapeutic, criteria and social, or non-therapeutic, criteria is contentious. Accordingly, to return to *Re D*, if that distinction is contentious, and if possession of the right to reproduce is dependent on a judgement about the presence or absence of medical or therapeutic grounds for sterilisation, then at the very least there is no clear basis for ascribing this right to an individual. This problem is intensified by a legal debate about the proper parties to reach a decision in these matters. In *Re D*, Heilbron J seemed to argue that the presence of medical grounds for sterilisation was one which came 'solely within a doctor's clinical judgement' and that it was the medical criterion and the medical professional that could override any claim to have a right to reproduce. In contrast, in *Re F*, Butler-Sloss LJ averred that the decision should not be left to the family and to the medical profession alone and that it should always be subject to the supervision of the courts.

These cases are instructive for feminists, because they signal that the right to reproduce is not something which in some sense exists, nor something which belongs to human beings by virtue of their membership of the species, *nem con*. Rather the ascription of the right to reproduce is just that – an ascription. As with all ascriptions, complex and competing criteria are deployed. It would, of course,

---

25 *Re F (Sterilisation: Mental Patient)* (1988) 138 NLJ 350.

be against the theme of this book to make these two cases carry a definitive argument about appeals to rights. In particular, it would be unwise to make generalisations on the basis of these two cases about the right to reproduce, since so much of what was at issue concerned the capacity to give an informed consent, but, as we shall see in the next section, the distinction between medical/therapeutic and social non-therapeutic criteria is also an issue where the capacity to give an informed consent is not in doubt.

Bravery v Bravery[26]

The problematic nature of consent, informed or not, and the slippery distinction between therapeutic and non-therapeutic sterilisation were also at issue in another controversial case. Mr and Mrs Bravery had married in 1934 and had their only child in 1936. Two years later, the husband had a vasectomy with the wife's knowledge. The couple continued to live together, sexual intercourse continued, but there were rows about, for example, the husband's dirty habits, his bad language, and his excessive interest in Indian philosophy. The wife left in 1951 and petitioned for divorce on grounds of cruelty, namely, his having had a vasectomy. It was held that:

> ... the wife had not made out a case of cruelty. As between husband and wife, for a husband to submit himself to an operation of sterilisation, without good medical reason, would, unless his wife were a consenting party, be a grave offence which could, without difficulty, be shown to be a cruel act, if it were found to have injured her health or to have caused reasonable apprehension of such injury. If a husband submitted to such an operation without the wife's consent, and if the latter desired to have children, the hurt might be progressive to the nerves and health of the wife.[27]

The case raises important questions. First, was Mrs Bravery a victim of gender stereotyping, explicit or covert, whereby a woman's capacity to control her sexuality is deemed less important than a man's? It is not clear how assiduous the surgeon was in eliciting Mrs Bravery's views on her husband's proposed vasectomy. In that respect, it is possible that she was the object of a particular form of discrimination which I discuss below. But as far as the court's deliberations were concerned, there was a strong suggestion that, had Mrs Bravery made it sufficiently clear, before the operation was performed, that she did not want Mr Bravery to be sterilised, the court would have expressed very different opinions, perhaps finding that she had made out a case of cruelty.

Now, on Mrs Bravery's own evidence, she knew that her husband was going to have the operation. What was at issue in cross-examination was whether she consented to it. As it happened, her husband worked at the hospital where the operation was performed, and she knew the surgeon and the nurse in question. She certainly did not give written consent, and it seems that at no time did she approach the persons concerned to say that she objected. What appears to have swayed Hodson LJ to the view that she did consent was, in the end, his finding it difficult to believe 'that any surgeon, a member of an honourable profession, would perform an operation of this kind on a young married man unless he was first satisfied that the wife consented'.

But, while there was doubt about whether the wife had consented to the operation, the court was in no doubt that the husband had given his consent.

---

26 [1954] 1 WLR 1169.
27 *Ibid*, p 1169.

Denning LJ did not dispute that; he dissented from the court's decision on altogether different grounds. He argued that an operation of sterilisation was, in the absence of some just cause or excuse, a criminal act in itself, an unlawful assault, to which consent gave no answer or defence. Denning LJ 's argument was based on the view that a person cannot effectively consent to mayhem (the act of maiming) against himself. Denning LJ was also concerned with a rather different form of assault when he concluded that 'if a husband undergoes an operation for sterilisation without just cause or excuse, he strikes at the very root of the marriage relationship'.[28]

Denning LJ's remark is clearly predicated on a view of the relation between marriage and the purpose of sexual intercourse which is at once familiar and horrifying to feminists. Since that view is discernible in all manner of legal proceedings and public debate, however, I shall not pursue the general feminist critique of it. But the possibility that non-therapeutic sterilisation might be a criminal act has given rise to conflicting legal opinions on the specific question of the legality of non-therapeutic sterilisation. In examining this legal controversy, I arrive at the consideration of a legal doctrine of serious concern to feminists, the doctrine of consortium.

The legality of non-therapeutic sterilisation

The reference to mayhem may seem bizarre in the context of sterilisation of a man, not least since mayhem has been defined as an injury to a man so that he is rendered less capable of defending himself.[29] But, whether they merited this attention or not[30] the grounds of Denning LJ's dissent continued to feature in discussions 'of the legality of sterilisation' for some years. AE Clark-Kennedy, for example, pointed out that all surgery is an assault on the body, irrespective of the patient's consent, and that it is justified only when a greater evil has been averted. Writing in 1969, he took the view that the sterilisation of a woman merely as a method of birth control and without any medical justification would probably be found to be illegal if the case were brought to court, and he thought the same might be true for sterilisation of a man.[31] It is interesting to note here that while the National Health Service (Family Planning) Act 1972 allowed local authorities to provide for sterilisation by vasectomy there was no mention of the various methods of female sterilisation. I shall return to this.

Similarly, Bernard Knight has pointed out that no Act of Parliament or judicial dictum has reversed the concept of law whereby sterilisation is a maiming operation. In contrast to Clark-Kennedy, however, he subscribes to the view held by the medical defence organisations that there has been a change in the climate of public opinion regarding sterilisation for purposes of birth control and that the courts would take a more liberal line than Denning LJ's about its legality.[32] J Leahy Taylor confirms this view when he says that a surgeon who performs a sterilisation operation on one of a married couple with the consent of both would not be putting himself at risk.[33]

---

28 *Ibid*, p 1171.

29 G Williams, *The Sanctity of Life and the Criminal Law, op cit*, pp 102–03.

30 *cf* B Dickens, 'Reproduction Law and Medical Consent' (1985) 35 *University of Toronto Law Journal* at 255–86.

31 AE Clark-Kennedy, *Man, Medicine and Morality* (US Distribution: Shoe String Press Inc), p 34.

32 B Knight, *Legal Aspects of Medical Practice* (Churchill Livingstone, 1987), pp 237–38.

33 J Leahy Taylor, *The Doctor and the Law* (Pitman Medical, 1970), p 81; *cf* JK Mason and A McCall Smith, *Law and Medical Ethics* (Butterworths, 1987) Chapter 4.

If, as seems likely, Knight and Taylor are right about the likely attitude of the courts to the legality of sterilisation for birth control purposes, then the question of consent will not be, as Denning LJ thought, an irrelevancy. On the contrary, it becomes one of the central issues.

Consent

In developing his argument about changing attitudes to non-therapeutic sterilisation, Knight cites the opinion of the representative body of the British Medical Association (BMA) in 1967 that 'if the doctor is satisfied that an operation for sterilisation is in the interests of the health of the patient and that the patient has given valid consent and understands the consequences of this operations there is no ethical reason why the operation should not be performed'.

The wording of the BMA's statement is noteworthy. It suggests that it is the valid consent of the patient alone that is required. In fact, both Knight and Taylor make a point of stressing the desirability – from the point of view of the surgeon's protection – of obtaining the consent of both husband and wife where the patient is married. Taylor suggests: 'Where sterilisation is being considered purely as an operation of convenience then, in all probability, no surgeon would be prepared to operate without the consent of both parties.'[34] Again, both Knight and Taylor take the view that a surgeon might proceed with an operation to sterilise a wife without the husband's consent if medical circumstances appeared to necessitate the operation, and Knight seems to countenance a similar possibility where the operation is on the husband.

On the other hand, the views of both Knight and Taylor are called into question on the issue of the spouse's consent by Appendix III of the Birth Control Trust's document *Sterilisation and the National Health Service*.[35] Written on information supplied by the Medical Defence Union, the Appendix states: 'only the patient can give consent. There is no legal requirement for the spouse's consent. However it is advisable in the interests of marital harmony to obtain the agreement of the spouse when the operation is done simply as a means of contraception.'[36]

The distinction between consent and agreement is not developed, however, and in the absence of precise clarification one imagines that surgeons might well want to cover themselves by getting the consent of the patient and the agreement of the spouse. In fact, the Liverpool Area Health Authority issues a form, to be used in cases of primary (that is, non-therapeutic) sterilisation if the patient is married and living with the spouse. There is provision on this form for the consent of the patient and the agreement of the spouse, and it urges that both parties should sign the form at the same time.

Discrimination and consent

Whatever the legalities of consent to non-therapeutic sterilisation, it would seem that surgeons' practices have not been uniform throughout the country. In 1976 it was reported that the NCCL was collecting evidence of cases where women were being denied intra-uterine devices and sterilisation for contraceptive purposes because they could not, or would not, get the written consent of their husband.

34 J Leahy Taylor, *The Doctor and the Law, op cit*, p 81.

35 Birth Control Trust 1978.

36 *Ibid*, p 104.

And, says the NCCI, the same doctors who demand a husband's consent will perform a vasectomy on a man without asking if she consents'.[37]

There can be no justification for this discrimination against women. One attempt to outlaw it might be made by bringing a test case under or proposing an amendment to the Sex Discrimination Act 1975, or through drafting a Bill dealing with this issue and others relating to sterilisation. In assessing the measures most likely to eliminate this form of discrimination, however, feminists will also need to investigate the various practices that have supported it. To help with that investigation, I put forward the following points.

Until recently at any rate, vasectomy has been a quicker and safer operation than the various methods of female sterilisation. It is possible, though not defensible, that the male patients and medical personnel have accordingly been inclined to see the decision to operate as unproblematic. On the other hand, as feminists involved in struggles to improve access to abortion facilities will testify, considerations of speed and safety do not appear to have been topmost in the mind of the majority of medical practitioners. It is the non-medical attitudes of those in a position to control access to wanted medical operations that have frequently been decisive.[38]

In the case of doctors' discriminatory practices over consent to non-therapeutic sterilisation, the inference must be that such doctors, consciously or not, attribute a legitimate interest in a spouse's potential fertility to husbands but not to wives. As it happens, that attitude could find support in law, at least until 1982, through the doctrine of consortium. Briefly, this is the ancient notion that a husband has a legitimate proprietary interest in his wife's services (servitium) or society (consortium). Very much in the spirit of this doctrine, it was possible, until 1982, for a husband to bring an action for loss of the services or society of his wife, but not vice-versa. The Administration of Justice Act 1982, however, rectified this anomaly in providing that no person shall be liable in tort to a husband for any such deprivation.

The precise nature of consortium has always been in doubt. In 1977, however, legal advice obtained by the NCCL contained a warning. A consortium probably would not be thought to include the right to a wife's potential fertility, there was still a risk that 'a husband could succeed in an action for damages against a doctor even though the wife had asked for and consented to the operation ... on the ground that the doctor has assisted in procuring damage to the husband's consortium'.[39]

The belated removal of the anachronistic doctrine of consortium in this context will rightly be a source of relief to feminists, but there is no reason to suppose that the atavistic rationale of the doctrine will be moribund forthwith. In this respect, it will be interesting to watch the progress of a recent claim for loss of consortium and distress brought by the wife of a haemophiliac who contracted HIV from infected blood. Her lawyer comments that 'interference with a sexual relationship is a recognised claim'.[40] So, the vestiges of the doctrine of consortium may have to be reckoned with for some time to come, if not through explicit reference to consortium then through ideologically related notions such as conjugal rights or the right to reproduce.

---

37   (1978) *New Society*, p 431; cf B Dickens *op cit*, p 277.

38   cf J Aitken-Swan, *Fertility Control and the Medical Profession* (Croom Helm, 1977).

39   *Re: Sterilisation* (National Council for Civil Liberties, 1977).

40   *The Independent*, 1990.

I would urge that feminists engaged in the development of a sexual politics of sterilisation should be extremely wary of formulating policies in terms of such rights – for fear of being drawn on to territory long dominated by ideologies and practices inimical to feminist objectives. There is a serious risk that the appeal to a woman's right to reproduce will be appropriated by those who would invoke a general right to reproduce or a human right to reproduce. Appealing to this more general right may in turn be a less than innocent practice, if the alleged general right is identified, covertly or not, with a man's, or worse, a husband's, right to reproduce. There are, furthermore, additional and independent reasons for not framing policies in terms of rights, and it is to this issue that the next section is addressed.

Policies

Two recurrent features of the literature on sterilisation provide the impetus for a review of the various policies which feminists might adopt. First, a good deal of research in the last decade or so has shown that there is increasing demand for sterilisation for contraceptive purposes. In 1972 it was found that hospitals which deliberately adopted a favourable attitude to sterilisation experienced a dramatic increase in spontaneous requests for sterilisation.[41] Two years later, a survey of 1,079 women in Coventry during their confinement produced the estimate that the potential demand for sterilisation was between 60 and 80 per 1000 confinements.[42] Two surveys by M Bone from the Social Survey Division of the Office of Population Censuses and Surveys on behalf of the Department of Health and Social Security showed a marked increase in favourable attitudes towards sterilisation for contraceptive purposes in the 1970s. Briefly, in 1973, of the total sample of women interviewed:

> only 20% said they would think about it if they had about the number of children they planned to have and most thought it only appropriate in more extreme circumstances, for example if further pregnancies would endanger their health or if they had had several more children than they wanted.[43]

The survey was admitted to give only a sketch of women's attitudes but it was surmised that the irrevocability of sterilisation made it 'very much a method of last resort for most women' (see *ibid*). In 1978, however, the picture had changed. The results of this survey suggested that:

> sterilisation was becoming less of a last resort for the desperate and more of a chosen method for couples who had just achieved the number of children they thought sufficient … Sterilisation was therefore not only spreading but increasingly impinging on young couples who had had few pregnancies and, it seems, quite soon after they had decided that their second or third baby was to be the last.[44]

Additional evidence for the demand for sterilisation for contraceptive purposes has been collected, and explanations for its increased popularity are available.[45]

The second recurrent feature of the literature on sterilisation has not been so thoroughly researched. It concerns a practice which is generally frowned on (or

41 AER Buckle and KC Young in (1972) *New Society*, 24 February, p 402.
42 LJ Opit and ME Brennan, in (1974) *New Society*, 18 July, p 157.
43 M Bone, *Family Planning Services in England and Wales* (Office of Population Censuses and Surveys, 1978).
44 *Ibid*, p 62.
45 *Birth Control Trust* (1978), Chapter 1.

at least seen as one which has to be justified) and about which it is extremely difficult to be precise. It is the practice which has come to be known as 'the package deal'. Briefly, a woman's request for an abortion is met on condition that she agrees to being sterilised at the same time. In 1974 the Lane Report on the working of the Abortion Act 1967 noted that, although the Committee had been unable to establish the facts in this matter, it was concerned by comments it had received about the large number of young unmarried women who had been sterilised as a condition of getting an abortion. The Report recommended that sterilisation should never be a condition for terminating an existing pregnancy nor be performed as a result of any other pressure.[46] In 1981 I Allen noted that fears were often expressed about women being pressurised into sterilisation when they had an abortion, although she was unable to find evidence to support those fears.[47] On the other hand, a 1971 survey of gynaecologists' attitudes showed:

> respondents to be evenly divided on the question, those in favour thinking that the abortion patient should accept sterilisation if there were medical or psychiatric indications, if the situation leading to abortion was unlikely to change, where there was multiparity, low IQ, 'irresponsibility', a previous abortion or other problems.[48]

In spite of the fact that evidence of the package deal is largely anecdotal, references to it persist, and it would appear that the practice continues.[49]

It is reasonable to suppose that, in responding to these trends, feminists will present their policies in terms of women's rights. Indeed, the package deal has been described in these terms. K Greenwood and L King connect it to the central demands of the Women's Liberation Movement for freely available contraception and abortion, observing that women have no right to abortion.[50] P Hewitt sees the package deal as a violation of a woman's right to choose, and she asserts that right on the basis of its relation to other rights, proposing that 'the freedom of a woman to control her own fertility is inextricably linked to fundamental principles of human rights'.[51] In this connection, too, it is worth recalling that in *Re D*, described above, it was held that the operation proposed was one which involved 'the deprivation of a basic human right, ie the right of a woman to reproduce'.

In the previous section, I drew attention to the risks of appealing to rights, such as the right to reproduce, when they are associated with ideologies and practices inimical to feminist objectives. In this section, I show that, even if feminists do present their policies in terms of rights, it is far from obvious that they will on that account be united in their policy preferences. On the contrary, I argue that appealing to women's rights can mask serious differences between feminists and can, in so doing, be an obstacle to the development of detailed policies and strategies in relation to sterilisation. To support this argument, I identify three

46 *Report of the Committee on the Working of the Abortion Act* (Cmd 5579) (1974).

47 I Allen, 'Family Planning, Sterilisation and Abortion Services' (1981) 595 *Policy Studies Institute* 65.

48 J Aitken-Swan, *op cit*, p 158.

49 Y Roberts (1988) *Independent*, 18 May.

50 K Greenwood, 'Contraception and Abortion', in *Cambridge Women's Studies Group* (1981), p 174.

51 P Hewitt, 'Women's Rights and Human Rights', in Birth Control Trust, *Abortion Ten Years On* (1987), p 29.

different ways in which feminists might take up the issue. For convenience, I label them as follows: Policy A: Deregulation; Policy B: Mandatory Provision; Policy C: Safeguards.

Policy A: Deregulation

Some feminists might respond to the trends outlined above by demanding the complete deregulation of sterilisation, meaning by this the abolition of all restrictions on it. Only in this way, it might be argued, can a woman enjoy genuine freedom to control her own fertility. That freedom cannot be enjoyed under present social conditions, since the existing legal and medical institutions and practices are necessarily geared to capitalist and patriarchal interests. It is therefore not merely futile or misguided to look to these institutions for recognition of a woman's absolute right to control her own body; it is to advocate reformist measures and, in so doing, to oppose the revolutionary demand for women's rights. The regulation of health care now is oppressive of women, and a socialist society will remove the need for that regulation. In the absence of socialism, but in order to advance towards it, women should concentrate their efforts on demystifying medicine and exploring alternative forms of health care by setting up self-help groups. In the specific matter of sterilisation, a woman's right to choose is both the expression of women's refusal to allow men in general, and doctors and lawyers in particular, to control women's fertility and the expression of their refusal to participate in social practices which support that control.

Clearly, this response has much in common with the way in which some feminists took up the issue of abortion in the USA and in this country, and I have already discussed some of these issues in the previous chapter, in relation to a woman's right to choose. As we have seen, the deregulation response has been forcefully pressed by Victoria Greenwood and Jock Young.[52] It was just as forcefully resisted by Paul Hirst.[53] Hirst's attack focuses on the absurdity of supposing that socialist states have or will have no need of regulation in the areas of health care, and he demonstrates the problematic politics of arguing for a woman's right to choose in the context of forming general social policy. He points out the dangers of demanding the demonopolisation of medical competence: 'Demonopolisation would mean that anyone was free to perform abortions; there would be no limit to personnel, methods or facilities. The possibility created by this laissez-faire is of a return to the era of the 'knitting needle', in the guise of alternative medicine and self-help.'[54] Hirst concludes that 'socialist states should take the control of medical competence and the determination of means of intervention more and not less seriously'.

Faced with this sort of criticism, proponents of deregulation might reply that nobody would seriously propose that personnel other than qualified surgeons should perform operations of sterilisation. It is worth noting, however, that there are continuing attempts to find a substitute for surgical sterilisation. One such attempt involves the relatively simple procedure of infusing a solution of quinacrine into the interior of the uterus.[55] Informal sources suggest that this sort of procedure could be performed very simply and that the kit could be

52   V Greenwood and J Young, *Abortion in Demand* (Pluto Press, 1976).
53   PQ Hirst, 'Law, Socialism and Rights', in eds P Carlen and M Collison, *Radical Issues in Criminology* (Martin Robertson, 1980).
54   *Ibid*, p 102.
55   Cf B Viel and J Walls, *The Demographic Explosion* (New York: Irvington, 1976), p 148.

marketed for a dollar. It would not be surprising if understandable apprehension at the implications of such a development led feminists to adopt an alternative to deregulation, namely mandatory provision.

Policy B: Mandatory provision

Resistance to the argument that law is necessarily oppressive of women, and alarm at the serious effects of deregulation in the sphere of health care in general, and sterilisation in particular, might make feminists adopt a different approach. This may invoke the rhetoric of a woman's right to choose, since it is a potent political slogan. But for these feminists it is not a knowingly unrealisable demand under capitalism and an unnecessary one under socialism. Instead, it is a convenient means of focusing attention on a particular area of health care the provision of which is currently disadvantageous to women, which on that account should not be tolerated now, and which certainly should not be tolerated under a socialist State committed to the removal of obstacles to women's full enjoyment of social benefits.

We have seen that there is a rising demand for female and male sterilisation as a form of birth control. One of the main sources of dissatisfaction with the present NHS sterilisation service, however, has been its uneven availability. In 1981, a survey of 30 area health authorities showed that in only six authorities was the average waiting time for female sterilisation three months or less, that in eight authorities it was two years or more, and that in one authority it could be four years. The average waiting time for vasectomies was just as uneven as between authorities, but generally it was shorter than for female sterilisation.

A major factor in this uneven availability was found to be the manner of its funding. Authorities and district management teams set aside money for item-of-service payments. The discretionary nature of this funding meant that doctors and health authorities were in a position to give priority to other operations and procedures in preference to sterilisation. It also allowed great scope for doctors and gynaecologists to exercise their personal as well as their professional judgements in relation to the moral aspects of sterilisation.

How can this situation be remedied? One obvious strategy would be for feminists to point to the cost-effectiveness of sterilisation in comparison with other forms of contraception, abortion, ante-natal maternity care and child care. WA Laing has estimated that, taking into account failure rates and the cost of unplanned conception, there is a break-even point of a little over a year for vasectomy.[56] Laing concludes that it seems illogical to restrict NHS sterilisations rather than reversible methods of contraception. It has also been shown that savings in in-patient costs are greatly reduced by the use of modern methods of female sterilisation, such as mini-laparotomy, and that the greatest savings would be effected by setting up special sterilisation units or clinics, perhaps in hospital wards closed as a result of financial cuts.

The argument for units specialising in sterilisation, contraception and abortion has been put forward by Wendy Savage. It is a powerful argument, since there is evidence that, for contraceptive and related matters, women would rather go to a specialised clinic than to their GP's surgery.[57] But that sort of provision would not by itself solve the problem of uneven availability, since the provision of such clinics would again be a matter of the political will of the relevant authorities to

56 WA Laing, 'Family Planning: the Benefits and Costs' (1982) 607 *Policy Studies* Institute 32.
57 Women's Health and Reproductive Rights Information Centre (1990).

fund them, and there is recent evidence of the reluctance of National Health Service regions to give priority to family planning services and Well-Woman Clinics.

To ensure even availability, it might be argued that it is necessary to effect a change in national legislation governing the provision of the health services. This would require close and expert scrutiny to identify the most effective legal reforms, and a difficulty here is the typical form of health service legislation. The National Health Service (Family Planning) Act 1972 allowed local health authorities to provide voluntary vasectomy services on the same basis as other contraceptive services. Interestingly, it made no reference to types of female sterilisation, provoking speculation about the role of that Act in the unevenness of sterilisation services as between women and men. But that Act is now repealed, and although it allows male and female sterilisation clinics to be held under the general provisions of family planning, the National Health Service Act 1977 makes no special mention of sterilisation. As in the National Health Service (Scotland) Act 1978 there is just the general requirement that the Secretary of State make such arrangements for contraceptive services as he considers necessary.

Feminists might want to look into how it would be possible to rectify this situation, with a view to making this sort of provision mandatory rather than discretionary, in the same way that they have argued for the mandatory provision of abortion facilities, and perhaps to have a minimal level of funding. Formidable obstacles to this sort of feminist intervention are apparent from commentaries on the passage of the National Health Service and Community Care Bill. The Women's Health and Reproductive Rights Information Centre (WHRRIC) has reported that:

> in the early days of the White Papers, five core services were mentioned ... Labour put forward an amendment listing the five core services: accident and emergency, geriatric, psychiatric, public health community-based services and services for the elderly and mentally ill. They also added maternity, gynaecology and family planning which had been left off the original list... the amendment was defeated, with the Conservatives arguing that market forces would ensure such services were provided![58]

Against this sort of political backdrop, the demand for mandatory provision begins to look Utopian. Also, it has to be said that even if mandatory provision could solve the problem of uneven geographical availability of sterilisation services, it would not necessarily deal with the problem of uneven availability as between women and men.

It is clear that the objective of a mandatory and non-discriminatory NHS sterilisation service requires close attention to the most effective means of changing existing legislation and medical practices, whether or not the objective is pursued in the name of a woman's right to choose. But this could hardly be more different from the use of that slogan to advocate deregulation of sterilisation services. A further contrast is that, even if the policy of mandatory provision is fought for in the name of a woman's right to choose, that right will have been converted, as it were, into a number of specific objectives. These objectives raise questions not of the rights of individual women but of general social policy in the sphere of health care, such as priorities in NHS spending. It is in this context that a third feminist response might be developed.

---

58   *Ibid*, p 18.

Policy C: Safeguards

Feminists might well be concerned that the setting up of special sterilisation clinics on the grounds of cost-effectiveness would not be in women's (or men's) interests. Local authorities would have strong incentives to ensure that such clinics were not under-used and, in consequence, they might be inclined to cut back their funding of existing contraceptive services, thereby reacting the scope of contraceptive choice. Further, the policy of mandatory provision of such clinics might not be implemented in full. Local authorities might be required to offer sterilisation services but not be required to do so through special sterilisation clinics. If, in addition, there were no change in the system of funding through items-of-service payments, there could be greater pressure than now on surgeons to make abortion conditional on sterilisation.

To prevent a resurgence or increase in the package deal, feminists might consider a policy which concentrates on strengthening safeguards in present and future provision. At least two such measures would be appropriate. Firstly, a case could be made for mandatory counselling before any decision to sterilise is made, given the mostly irreversible nature of sterilisation and the consequent social and moral questions peculiar to that form of contraception. While it would be difficult to enforce a policy of mandatory counselling, it would certainly be possible for the Department of Health and Social Security to toughen up its guidelines to local authorities on the provision of sterilisation. At present, the guidelines state only that full counselling is 'particularly important'. Allied to this, close attention should be given to the precise legal and practical meaning of 'consent' and of the distinction between 'consent' and 'agreement' as discussed above. Pressure could be brought on medical practitioners to ensure that consent is genuinely informed, in the sense of giving information both about what is known or believed to be the case regarding the possible effects of sterilisation but also about what is not known. For example, women should be advised about the uncertain state of knowledge concerning the effect of sterilisation on menstruation. Further, great care should be taken to define what counts as pressure or persuasion in the getting of a patient's consent and, where applicable, the agreement of the spouse. Secondly, feminists might consider the introduction of a compulsory period of time which must elapse – a breathing space – between a patient's having an abortion and her having an operation for sterilisation. This might be done by pressing for an amendment to the Abortion Act 1967 or by including the provision in a new Act concerned with sterilisation.

There are good reasons why feminists who supported these measures would think it inadvisable to campaign under the aegis of the slogan of a woman's right to choose. That slogan is clearly associated with pro-choice abortion campaigns. Insofar as abortion is thought not to be a desirable form of contraception, and because the breathing space is intended to dissociate abortion and sterilisation, it would be unfortunate if the two campaigns became identified with each other. Further, pro-choice campaigners have not been predominantly concerned that women would be pressured into having abortions, whereas the main burden of the safeguards under consideration here is to guard against women (and presumably men) being pressurised into operations of sterilisation by cost-conscious, disturbingly enthusiastic, or just plain busy medical practitioners. To that end, a much more appropriate slogan, if one were needed and if it had to be in terms of rights, would be a woman's right to refuse.

This outline of policy options open to feminists in the sphere of sterilisation provision and practice is obviously not exhaustive, although, under the present attack on the National Health Service and on such contraceptive services as exist at present, it may seem overly optimistic. Even so, the description of Policies A, B and C provides a basis for assessing different types of feminist response, especially where these policies are framed in terms of superficially similar appeals to women's rights.

'WHO IS THE MOTHER TO MAKE THE JUDGMENT?': CONSTRUCTIONS OF WOMAN IN ENGLISH ABORTION LAW[59]

Sally Sheldon[60]

1. Introduction

The title of this paper comes from the 'Parliamentary Debates on the Medical Termination of Pregnancy Bill (later to become the Abortion Act 1967). Kevin McNamara MP speaking with respect to the decision to abort a handicapped foetus, poses the question 'who is the mother to make the judgment?'.[61]

The continuing refusal of the law to recognise the decision of whether or not to terminate a pregnancy as one fundamentally belonging to the pregnant woman, forms the focus of this paper. I will argue that the reason why it is so unthinkable to give women self-determination (in the real sense of allowing them the final word in a decision to abort) is because of the constructions of woman upon which this law is predicated.

This paper conceptualises the legal subject as an internal construct of a given law, and as embodying certain characteristics. Law creates its own fiction of the subject that it seeks to regulate. Feminist texts have often discussed the construction of this subject as essentially male, existing either as a male universal legal subject, or as a construct of one particular law.[62] Abortion legislation, however, is one of the instances where law can be seen to posit a female legal subject.

This paper sets out to 'deconstruct' the Abortion Act 1967 to reveal the female legal subject created within it. It does not enter into the discussion of the morality of abortion, or the debate around the competing rights of foetus and woman. It will already be clear, no doubt, what my position within that debate would be. This paper also implicitly rejects the centrality normally granted to the foetus. It is often assumed that if we can accord the foetus one intrinsic ontological status (personhood or non-personhood) this in itself will provide a definitive solution to the problem of whether to allow abortion. Rather, I seek to recentre the notion of woman within discussions of abortion. She has been, in many accounts, the forgotten party.

---

59   [1993] 1 *Feminist Legal Studies* 3. (Footnotes edited.)

60   At the time of writing, University of Keele

61   McNamara, HC Debates Vol 730, Col 1129, 1966 (22 June).

62   N Naffine, *Law and the Sexes* (London: Unwin and Hymnan, 1990); K O'Donovan, 'Defences for Battered Women who Kill' (Summer 1991) *Journal of Law and Society* at 219–40. O'Donovan argues that the traditional defences to murder of provocation and self-defence have been constructed with regard to stereotypically male patterns of behaviour. R Holtmaat 'The Power of Legal Concepts: The Development of a Feminist Theory of Law' (1989) 17 *International Journal of the Sociology of Law* at 481–502. Holtman argues that the concept of employee supports the male model of paid labour, whilst excluding women who cannot or will not participate on the same footing as men.

This paper concentrates on the debates leading to the introduction of the 1967 Act, as played out in Parliament. It is beyond the scope of this paper to explore the exact relationship between the content of Parliamentary debates, and the final text of a debated statute. To say that the law is the product of debate within Parliament is obviously simplistic, not least because any new Bill is presented in draft form before ever coming under discussion (the text of the Abortion Act derives in large part from David Steel's original draft of the Medical Termination of Pregnancy Bill). Neither do I seek to deny the impact of extra-Parliamentary groups and in particular in this case, the medical profession on the formulation of statute. Rather, I content myself with a minimum assertion (that Parliamentary debates are in some way indicative of the predominant social discourses around the concept of woman which form the context within which the Abortion Act was conceived) and a more ambitious suspicion (that the statements made by MPs in this context provide particularly important and powerful 'telling instances' of this social and political discourse).[63]

This paper represents an attempt to draw out the way that the pregnant woman seeking abortion is constructed within these debates – to bring together dispersed comments of MPs to present a more unified account of the sort of general assumptions about the 'type' of woman whom the legislation must address (what kind of woman would seek to terminate a pregnancy?). I then very briefly outline the way that the figure of the doctor was constructed within the debates before examining how these constructions and the assumptions upon which they are predicated are reflected in the text of the Abortion Act itself.

Although the major thrust of this paper will be a criticism of the 1967 Act and the way that woman is constructed within it, I will at least begin to draw some more general conclusions about feminist strategies with regard to the law.

2. The Constructions of Woman Employed in Parliament

From my reading of the Parliamentary debates which preceded the passing of the Abortion Act 1967, two major constructions of the 'type' of woman who would want an abortion emerge. Both accounts reflect this woman as marginal and deviant, standing against a wider norm of women who do not need/desire abortion. These constructions reflect strategies used by the proponents and opponents of increasing access to abortion, and on a broader level, reflect images of women that were/are predominant in other social discourses. Both typifications are extreme – they are predicated partially on stereotypes, and partially on real and concrete examples which continually recur within the debates as *leitmotivs* to become generalised as representing the reality of the woman who seeks abortion.

The structure adopted within this section is to identify two major constructions of woman used within the debates which may be broadly (though not always consistently) identified with the reformer/opponent split. Thus, I would argue, whilst the reformers represent the woman who would seek to terminate a pregnancy as an emotionally weak, unstable (even suicidal) victim of her desperate social circumstances, the conservatives view her as a selfish, irrational

---

63   P Fitzpatrick, 'Racism and the Innocence of Law', in P Fitzpatrick and A Hunt (eds), *Critical Legal Studies* (Oxford: Blackwell, 1987), pp 11–132 esp, p 120.

child.[64] Such a schema is inevitably a simplification and imposes a unity and coherence which is doubtless lacking, but nonetheless it is useful in understanding and highlighting the kinds of constructions used in the debates.

(a) Woman as a Minor

This construction is typically adopted by opponents of abortion (although normally in their accounts the central place would be ceded to the foetus). It represents woman as a minor in terms of immaturity or under-development with regard to matters of responsibility, morality, and even to her very femininity or 'womanliness'. Her decision to abort is trivialised and denied rational grounding, being perceived as mere selfishness: she will abort 'according to her wishes or whims,'[65] for example, in order to avoid the inconvenience of having to postpone a holiday. She is immoral for being sexually active for reasons other than procreation; she is irresponsible for not having used contraception, and now for refusing to pay the price for her carelessness; she is unnatural and 'unwomanly' because she rejects the natural outcome of sexual intercourse for women: maternity. There is a hint that one day she will come to realise the error of her ways and want children, yet maybe will be unable to have them as a result of the abortion.[66]

Jill Knight plays heavily on the idea of the woman as selfish and irresponsible. She reveals an image of women seeking abortion as selfish, treating '[babies] like bad teeth to be jerked out just because they cause suffering ... simply because it may be inconvenient for a year or so to its mother'.[67] She later adds that '[a] mother might want an abortion so that a planned holiday is not postponed or other arrangements interfered with'.[68] The ability of the woman to make a serious decision regarding abortion is trivialised. It is not expected that the woman will make a careful decision considering all parties, but rather (like a child) she will make a snap decision for her own convenience.

The task of the law is thus perceived essentially as one of responsibilisation: if the woman seeks to evade the consequences of her carelessness, the law should stand as a barrier. It is often stated that allowing women to take the easy way out encourages them to be irresponsible:

> People must be helped to be responsible, not encouraged to be irresponsible ... Does anyone think that the problem of the 15-year-old mother can be solved by taking the easy way out? ... here is the case of a perfectly healthy baby being sacrificed for the mother's convenience ... For goodness sake, let us bring up our daughters with love and care enough not to get pregnant and

---

64   In view of Carol Smart's recent assertion that it is important to analyse how the female legal subject is constituted in classed and raced as well as gendered terms, it would perhaps be productive to view this distinction as one of class – ie the poor working-class woman fits the model of the unstable and desperate 'multi-child mother' who will have to resort to the back streets should legal relief be denied her; the rich, educated middle-class (working) woman is open to charge of selfishness for choosing to have a career rather than raise a child. See C Smart, 'Disruptive Bodies and Unruly Sex: The Regulation of Reproduction and Sexuality in the 19th Century', in C Smart (ed), *Regulating Womanhood: Historical Essays on Marriage, Motherhood and Sexuality* (London and New York: Routledge, 1992), pp 7–32.

65   Mahon, *HC Deb* Vol 750, Col 1356, 1967 (13 July).

66   See for example the comments of Knight, *HC Deb* Vol 749, Col 932, 1967 (29 June); Clover, *HC Deb* Vol 749, Col 971, 1967 (29 June).

67   Knight, *HC Deb* Vol 732, Col 1100, 1966 (22 July).

68   Knight, *HC Deb* Vol 749, Col 926, 1967 (29 June).

not let them degenerate into free-for-alls with the sleazy comfort of knowing, 'She can always go and have it out'.

By forcing her to continue with the pregnancy then, the law will seek to ensure that the pregnant woman will be more responsible in the future. As one MP comments with regard to whether abortion should be allowed to a 15-year-old girl: 'one needs to think twice before one removes all the consequences of folly from people'. The woman who seeks abortion is also seen as morally immature, and hence undeserving of help. Simon Mahon asks who is to be given priority in terms of treatment: is it the 'feckless girl who has an unwanted pregnancy from time to time' or the 'decent married woman' who is awaiting investigation or treatment for sterility? The use of this rhetorical trick of opposing the 'girl' to the 'decent married woman', serves to emphasise that the girl is not only feckless but is also decent and unworthy of respect.

The Parliamentary debates often reflect an implicit assumption that it is wrong for women to make a distinction between sex and procreation, they should not indulge in sex, if pregnancy is not desired. William Deedes makes these sentiments clear in expressing his concern that 'science and its little pill will enable so-called civilised countries to treat sex more and more as a sport and less and less as a sacrament in love', a divine instrument of procreation. Perhaps the single most telling quotation in this instance is that of David Steel himself, defending a clause which was included in the original wording of the Bill but dropped after debate in Parliament (for reasons that will be discussed later, see section 4(b) below). The clause sought to allow abortion to 'a pregnant woman being a defective or becoming pregnant while under the age of 16 or becoming pregnant as a result of rape'. He states:

> Most honourable members would agree that to have a woman continue with a pregnancy which she did not wish to conceive, or in respect of which she was incapable of expressing her wish to conceive, is a practice which we deplore, but the difficulty is to find an acceptable wording which will enable termination to be carried out following sexual offences of this kind but which does not allow an open gate for the pretence of sexual offences.

What is startling here is Steel's correlation of 'a pregnancy which she did not wish to conceive' with conception following rape. Steel fails to imagine that the vast majority of requests for abortion will be for pregnancies that the woman did not wish to conceive – thus in using this as an argument to justify abortion in cases of rape, he implicitly equates consensual intercourse with desired conception. Wanting sex equals wanting pregnancy and motherhood. The woman who rejects maternity is seen to reject the very essence of womanhood. Kevin McNamara provides a strong account of woman's maternal instinct: 'How can a woman's capacity to be a mother be measured before she has a child? Fecklessness, a bad background, being a bad manager, these are nothing to do with love, that unidentifiable bond, no matter how strange or difficult the circumstances, which links a mother to her child and makes her cherish it.'

This implicit assumption of woman as mother is further reflected in the consideration of her as having existing responsibilities to children and family, (and an apparent inability to see her outside of this role). Jill Knight informs us that: 'if it comes to a choice between the mother's life or the baby's, the mother is very much more important.' This is not, however, because the woman is more important in her own right, but rather because '[she] has ties and responsibilities to her husband and other children'.

(b) Woman as a Victim

The second construction strongly present in the Parliamentary debates is that of woman as victim. This construction is typically that of the reforming forces, where the woman and her social situation enjoy a far more central place. Advantage was taken of public sympathy for the situation of women at this time, given the highly restricted access to abortion. Newspapers and books had reported horror stories of back-street and self-induced abortions, and as David Steel noted in the debates, in the years preceding the introduction of the Abortion Act, an average of 30 women per year were dying at the hands of criminal abortionists.

The woman of this construction is not 'only on the fringe, but literally, physically inadequate'.[69] She is portrayed as distraught, out of her mind with the worry of pregnancy (possibly because she is young and unmarried, but normally because she already has too many children). She is desperate, and should the doctor not be able to help her, who knows what she will stop at (suicide is often discussed). Her husband is either absent or an alcoholic, her housing situation is intolerable. She is at the end of her tether simply trying to hold the whole situation together. As Madeleine Simms, of the Abortion Law Reform Association (ALRA), later wrote: 'It was chiefly for the worn out mother of many children with an ill or illiterate or feckless or brutal or drunken or otherwise inadequate husband that we were fighting.'

The following letter to Lord Silkin (referred to in the debates) provides a good example of the 'type' of woman envisaged by the reformist forces:

> Dear Lord Silkin
>
> I am married to a complete drunk who is out of work more than he is in. I have four children and now at 40 I am pregnant again. I was just beginning to get on my feet, and get some of the things we needed. I've been working for the last three years, and cannot bear the thought of that terrible struggle to make ends meet again. I've tried all other methods that I've been told about; without success, so as a last resort I appeal to you – please help me if you possibly can.

Lord Silkin himself comments, in presenting the Bill for its second reading that:

> the vast majority of women who are concerned with this are not, as I might have expected originally, single women, but married women, of an age approaching 40 or more, with a number of children, who have become pregnant again, very often unexpectedly, and who for one reason or another find themselves unable to cope with an additional child at that age ... [The kind of person that I really want to cater for is] the prospective mother who really is unable to cope with having a child, or another child, whether she has too many already or whether, for physical or other reasons she cannot cope.

The same kind of image is also drawn in the House of Commons, where one MP speaks of 'the mothers with large families and the burdens of large families very often with low incomes'. Another MP describes the illegal abortions he knows of:

> I have represented abortionists, both medical and lay. I have, therefore, met the 30 shilling abortion with Higginson's syringe and a soapy solution undertaken in a kitchen by a grey-faced woman on a *distracted multi-child mother, often the wife of a drunken husband*. I have also come across the more expensive back-bedroom abortion by the hasty medical man whose patient

---

69   V Greenwood and J Young, *Abortion in Demand* (London: Pluto, 1976), p 76.

returns to a distant town, *there to lie in terror and blood and without medical attention.*

Even Bernard Braine, a vocal opponent of the Bill accepts the image of the woman presented by the reformers: 'The hope of the sponsors of the Bill is to change the law that many abortions which take place at the moment illegally either in the back streets or, self-induced by some poor unfortunate woman, driven to desperation shall be brought into the framework of legality.'

The woman is portrayed as someone who is not completely in control of her actions, who will be driven to madness if relief is denied to her. David Owen states that: '[such] a woman is in total misery, and could be precipitated into a depression deep and lasting. What happens to that woman when she gets depressed? She is incapable of looking after those children so she retires into a shell of herself and loses all feeling, all her drive and affection.' A more extreme example is given by Lena Jeger, who speaks of the case of an 'honest young woman' with five children, recently deserted by her husband, who was refused an abortion because 'she did not seem quite depressed enough'. The woman was forced to continue the pregnancy, and her depression following the birth of her sixth baby was so extreme that she killed the baby by throwing it on the floor. The woman was now in Holloway prison and the children in care. Lord Strange notes that 'nearly every woman in this condition [of unwanted pregnancy] would be in a state bordering on suicide.

The woman's irrationality is sometimes conceptually linked to her pregnant condition, as David Owen states, for example: 'the reproductive cycle of women is intimately linked with her psyche.' This plays on notions of women as dominated by their biology, as existing through their ovaries. His image of the desperate woman is emphasised by contrasting it with the cool, impassive figure of the doctor (see section 3 below).

The idea that maternity is the female norm is exploited rather than challenged by the reformists. Madeleine Simms argued that it was precisely the woman with a fully developed 'maternal instinct' who might require an abortion, pointing out, however, that most women wished to have not more than two or three children, and they were appalled if they found they were having more children than they believed they could adequately care for. Should they accidentally become pregnant, she argued, they would then seek an abortion because of their feelings of responsibility to their husband and family, and because of their maternal instinct towards their existing children. In the House of Lords, Joan Vickers sums up sentiments which are often expressed or implicit in statements of other MPs when she notes that: 'I think that most women desire motherhood. It is natural for a woman to want to have a child ... It is only in extreme cases that a woman wants to terminate her pregnancy.'

In defending the need for a social clause (to allow abortion where the woman's social circumstances are deemed inadequate) within the Act, Roy Jenkins argued that without the presence of such a clause 'many women who are far from anxious to escape the responsibilities of motherhood, but rather wish to discharge their existing ones more effectively, would be denied relief. Edward Dunwoody argues, in similar vein, that in–

> many cases where we have over-large families the mother is so burdened down physically and emotionally with the continual bearing of children that it becomes quite impossible for her to fulfil her real function, her worthwhile function as a mother, of holding together the family unit, so that all too often the family breaks apart, and it is for this reason that we have all too many problem families in many parts of the country.

It is also argued that women should be allowed to abort handicapped foetuses, because the woman who is forced to give birth to a handicapped child will seldom allow herself to become pregnant again. This implicitly asserts that the role of the law must be to protect and entrench motherhood.

3. The Construction of the Doctor within the Debates

A very clear construction of the typical doctor also appears within the debates, in strong contrast to the figure of the woman. The doctor is a male figure, always referred to as 'he'. Doctors are referred to as 'medical men', 'professional medical gentlemen' and 'professional men'. William Deedes notes that 'the medical profession comprises a great diversity of men' and Jill Knight says that the GP is a skilled man. The doctor is perceived as the epitome of maturity, common sense, responsibility and professionalism. He is a 'highly skilled and dedicated', sensitive, sympathetic member of a 'high and proud profession', which acts 'with its own ethical and medical standard', displaying 'skill, judgment and knowledge'. Peter Mahon MP reminds us that 'it would be as well if we applauded the work of some of these men [gynaecologists] to keep our homes and families and country right'.

In presenting the Bill at its second reading, David Steel went so far to say that he felt that given more contact with her doctor and the ability to discuss her pregnancy with him, the woman would 'in some way be reassured and feel that she has been offered some guidance, and no abortion will take place at all'. David Owen echoes this sentiment later in the debates, noting that '[if] we allow abortion to become lawful under certain conditions, a woman will go to her doctor and discuss with him the problems which arise … he may well be able to offer that support which is necessary for her to continue to full term and successfully to have a child'.

4. The Construction of Woman and its Effect in Law

David Steel asserted that the Abortion Act (at the time, the Medical Termination of Pregnancy Bill) is what a 'reasonable man would regard as a reasonable statement of the law'. The Act is often depicted as a compromise between two competing sets of rights: the right to life of the foetus versus the right to choose (the right of the self-determination) of the woman. I would argue that this is a fictitious claim for if the law serves to protect and entrench any rights it is those of the doctor.[70] If the law has achieved any sort of compromise it is between the competing constructions of woman described above. In this section, I aim to show how law has incorporated the above constructions of woman in working with certain assumptions about (a) women's maternal role and (b) the essential irresponsibility and (c) sexual immorality of the sort of woman who would seek to terminate a pregnancy.

(a) An Assumption of Maternity as the Normal Role for Woman

The assumption of maternity as the female norm is reflected both in terms of the very structure of the law and in specific provisions which allow abortion in cases where the continuance of a pregnancy would involve injury to the health of any existing children of the woman's family, and (less obviously) in case of foetal handicap.

---

70 W Fyfe, 'Abortion Acts: 1803–1967', in Franklin, C Lury and J Stacey (eds), *Off-Centre: Feminism and Cultural Studies* (London: Harper Collins Academic, 1991), pp 160–74, esp at 165; M Berer, 'Whatever Happened to a Woman's Right to Choose?' (Spring 1988) *Feminist Review* at 24–37; L Clarke, 'Abortion: A Rights Issue', in R Lee and D Morgan (eds), *Birthrights: Law and Ethics at the Beginning of Life* (Routledge; 1990), pp 155–70.

The law regarding abortion functions in terms of a blanket ban (s 58 of the Offences Against the Person Act 1861) which renders abortion illegal. The Abortion (Amendment) Act 1967 offers a defence against this law where two doctors deem that the circumstances of the individual woman fall within certain general categories which are laid out within s 1 of the Act. The decision to abort is thus never seen as an intrinsically acceptable one, the possibility of which any woman could face at some time in her life. Rather, it is an option which may be justified only in certain cases by the individual circumstances (or inadequacies) of individual women, with the approval of two doctors. Conceptually then, abortion stands as the exception to the norm of maternity. No woman can reject motherhood: the only women who are allowed to terminate are those who can do so without rejecting maternity/familial norms *per se*, ie those who have reasons to reject this one particular pregnancy without rejecting motherhood as their destiny in general (they are carrying the wrong sort of foetus, they have obligations to meet to existing children, their living conditions are at present inadequate for a child, this particular pregnancy was thrust upon them through rape or incest, and could thus be psychologically damaging).

The woman's role as mother is again emphasised where s 1(1)(a) of the Abortion Act allows abortion where the continuance of a pregnancy 'would involve ... injury to the physical or mental health of ... any existing children of her family'. The woman is allowed to reject pregnancy in order to fulfil her existing responsibility as a mother more effectively. Here again, she is seen to reject one particular pregnancy rather than motherhood itself. Indeed, she may reject this particular pregnancy in order to be a better mother to those children already in her family.

Section 1(1)(b) of the Act provides that abortion can be allowed where 'there is a substantial risk that if the child were born it would suffer from such physical or mental abnormalities as to be seriously handicapped'. Whilst clearly displaying eugenicist considerations,[71] this clause can also be interpreted with regard to the status of the woman. It was justified in part on the grounds that to force a woman to carry an abnormal child to term will discourage her from future pregnancy and as Dr Winstanly points out that '[i]n every case the duty of the medical practitioners should be, wherever possible to encourage aid and support the mother towards term with the pregnancy'. Given that the handicapped baby or child is not seen as being as desirable as a 'normal' one (and does not feature in the romanticised family ideal), the woman can reject this pregnancy without rejecting the whole institution of motherhood itself.

(b) Female Irresponsibility

The assertion that many laws assume women to be irresponsible or irrational is a recurrent one within feminist writing. This construction of woman is clearly

---

71 Much of the debate in Parliament revolves around the number of healthy foetuses which must be sacrificed in order to pick out damaged ones. This appears to give official sanction to the notion that the lives of the handicapped are of less value than the able-bodied. For example, Peter Mahon, MP for Preston South: 'It is argued that if a mother has a particular disease in pregnancy ... there is a chance that her child will be deformed in some way. But the real tragedy would be that a large number of perfectly normal unmaimed human lives are to be sacrificed for the sake of one who would be born with some physical deformity. What kind of morality is that?' (see *HC Deb* Vol 750, Col 1358, 1967 (13 July)). See also Calperin: 'Surely it would be more reasonable to have the odd malformed child than to take the risk of killing a normal foetus.' *HC Deb* Vol 749, Col 1065, 1967 (29 June). For a strong criticism by a disabled feminist of the provision of abortion in case of handicap, see J Morris, 'Abortion: Whose Right to Choose?' (October 1991) *Spare Rib* at 16–18.

reflected in the text of the 1967 Act. The woman is seen as irresponsible in that she is deemed incapable of taking for herself this important decision of whether to terminate a pregnancy.

Section 1(1) of the Act provides that 'subject to the provisions of this section, a person shall not be guilty of an offence under the law relating to abortion when a pregnancy is terminated by a registered medical practitioner if two registered medical practitioners are of the opinion, formed in good faith' (the section goes on to lay out the necessary contra-indications).

The woman of the Abortion Act is clearly treated as someone who cannot take decisions for herself, rather responsibility is handed over to the reassuringly mature and responsible (male) figure of the doctor. The legislation assumes that the doctor is far better equipped to judge what is best for the woman, even though he may never have met her before, and have no real knowledge of, nor interest in, her concrete situation. This construction is perhaps an inevitable result of the constructions of woman used within the debates. If woman is distraught and irrational, then she is an unsuitable party to take such an important decision. Equally, if she is selfish and self-centred, intellectually and morally immature, portrayed as only considering her own needs, and giving no weight to other factors (such as the foetus) in her snap decisions, she is again incapable of taking such an important decision. She is thus in need of the normalising control of the doctor to impose either calm and rationality or morality and consideration of others.

The power of doctors in the field of abortion is very often justified by the argument that abortion is essentially a medical matter. However, the actual decision whether or not to abort is not normally one that requires expert medical advice. Further, the doctors' decision-making power is not contained within a narrow, limited medical field. In judging whether or not abortion could be detrimental to the mental or physical health of the pregnant woman or existing children of her family, 'account may be taken of the pregnant woman's actual or reasonably foreseeable environment', thus her whole lifestyle, home and relationships are opened up to his scrutiny, so that he may judge whether or not she is a deserving case for relief.

It is also worth mentioning the case of rape here, by way of explaining its absence in the English statute. Arguments for allowing abortion in the case of rape were dismissed for two main reasons. The first was that the woman would already be granted abortion under the law as it stood.[72] However a second reason which received much discussion, and stood as the final reason for not codifying the jurisprudential position within statute was that the woman cannot be trusted to tell the truth about whether she has been raped. One MP notes that: 'we also know that a great many charges of rape are made which are quite unfounded and which are made for quite different motives ...'. If verification by doctors had been possible, however, this would have provided grounds for rape to be included in the text of the Act: 'if there were a way in which doctors could decide whether or not a lady had been raped, I would be content to allow the provision on rape to go in.'

(c) Female Sexuality

The Abortion Act contains a strong moral element, distinguishing as it does between categories of deserving and undeserving 'victims' of unwanted

---

72 That is, under s 1(1)(a) of the Abortion Act. Continuance of the pregnancy would involve risk of injury to her mental health. Indeed, in practice, since *R v Bourne* [1938] 3 All ER 615 abortion had been permitted in cases of rape.

pregnancy. The former are allowed abortions, the latter denied them. This distinction works in part with regard to whether or not intercourse was wanted (hence the issue of rape), and whether the woman has a legitimate reason for changing her mind postconception – ie she did want to get pregnant, but now wants to reject this particular pregnancy (because of handicap).

Although, unlike most other European statutes, the English Abortion Act does not explicitly foresee abortion for cases of pregnancy resulting from rape (for the reasons noted above), there were lengthy discussions of this matter in Parliament which are informative with regard to constructions of woman's sexuality. There was practically unanimous agreement that women should be allowed abortion in case of rape, although the clause which allowed it within the statute was deleted for the reason that it is already enshrined in the Bill as amended.

I have argued that the provision with regard to handicap is strongly influenced both by eugenic considerations, and the construction of woman as mother. This clause also bears some relation to constructions of women's sexuality, as it serves to provide a 'get-out clause' for good women who want to become pregnant (and thus do not commit the sin of making the fatal distinction between sex and procreation), but through no fault of their own happen to be carrying a foetus 'of the wrong sort'.

5. Conclusion – Political Implications

I have argued that the law creates its own fiction of the woman it seeks to regulate through the partial legalisation of abortion in the 1967 Act. The statute is predicated upon certain assumptions of maternity as the female norm, female irresponsibility and emotional instability; it also carries implicit assumptions about appropriate female sexual morality.

What clues might this initially give us for how feminist strategies aimed at the law can be made more effective in the future? There are two points which I need initially to clarify. Firstly, legal reform need not be the inevitable focal point of every feminist campaign, indeed perhaps feminism has been too much seduced by what Smart has described as the 'siren call' of the law.[73] However, with regard to abortion, it is impossible to ignore the power exercised by and through the law or to bypass the necessity of engagement with law, even if this is just one focus of political activity amongst others. Secondly, I do not wish to dismiss or denigrate those political strategies which in 1966–67 succeeded in providing limited access to legal abortion. The partial legalisation of abortion has undoubtedly made a very real difference to the concrete possibilities open to many women. However, it is important also to realise the limitations of the 1967 Act, and to assess how it may best be challenged in the future.

I have argued that the law operates through constructing its own image of the legal subject which it seeks to regulate. The recognition that law operates in this way has certain implications for how we seek to address it. Notably, we have to take into account of this subject when constructing challenges to law. This has two implications. Firstly, it means that feminist challenges to law must be more aware of the way that they construct their subject. To take the example of the reformist strategies in 1966-67, to utilise the powerful image of the the 'worn out mother of many children with an ill or illiterate or feckless or brutal or drunken or other wise inadequate husband',[74] may have immediate political purchase at

---

73   C Smart, *Feminism and the Power of Law* (London: Routledge, 1989), p 160.
74   Simms, *supra*, p 81.

the expense of bringing its own, serious long-term limitations (reinforcement of the perceived need for normalising medical control over women in this situation). Secondly, it means that the most successful short-term strategies may be those which come closest to constructing the issue – and the legal subject – in the terms which are closest to the law's own, as this subject is most readily open to assimilation within the law.

Carol Smart has expressed this problem in the following terms:

> Law hears what we have to say about women as long as we are prepared to occupy the same epistemological and ontological space as law. In other words as long as we translate the vast and differentiated array of women into the more easily knowable woman we can gain a purchase. We may sometimes go even further and collude with the woman that legal discourse has constituted. But we do this at the expense of silencing and alienating many actual women for whom we do not speak.[75]

The tension between woman and women upon which Smart draws is one which has excited a great deal of attention in recent feminist writings. It starts from the recognition that feminism has often sought to create its own 'essential woman' – a unitary, generic woman[76] which seeks to offer one definitive account of women's experience of the world, but only at the expense of ignoring the voices of many real, concrete women. However, it is important to draw a distinction between the way that feminism seeks within itself to theorise issues of women's oppression, and the way that it seeks to develop concrete strategies aimed at achieving particular reforms. Feminist theory has been correctly criticised for falsely universalising from the experience of a relatively select group of women to present one generic woman. Feminist engagement with specific laws, however, may have no alternative but to do just this (albeit in a much more self-conscious way).

In my view, the tension between woman and women is always (and inevitably) present in feminist engagement with the law. This is not merely because the attraction of constructing a feminist truth of the essential woman in order to challenge law's powerful claim to reality is so tempting. Rather, if it is accepted that (criminal) law always works on the basis of constructing a legal subject (as I feel it does), then to mount any effective challenge to the law we have to construct a different subject: a feminist woman to challenge the legal woman. As Smart asserts, this will inevitably silence some women, but it will also give voice to others. The challenge for feminism is to work with an awareness of this tension in a pragmatic way.

The reform that was achieved in 1967 can thus be evaluated in terms of a trade-off between woman and women. In 1992, we are still in a position of having to make the same kind of trade off, but under somewhat different circumstances. With regard to abortion law, the aim must be to construct one feminist woman who can best serve the purposes of the array of concrete women who stand behind her. Given the circumstances, I would suggest the need to construct an image of the woman as rational, self-determining, responsible and mature, as the person best placed to consider the needs of herself and the foetus, and to make the correct decision with regard of whether or not to abort. This should form the

---

75   C Smart, 'Analysing Law: the Challenge of Feminism and Postmodernism', conference paper presented at Women's Studies in the European Community, European Culture Centre at the European University Institute, Florence, January 1991.

76   EV Spelman, *Inessential Woman* (Boston: Beacon Press, 1988).

basis for demanding a model of law which leaves the decision of whether or not to abort to the individual woman and therefore leaves the maximum amount of space for women's diversity. The feminist woman, then, will seek to leave maximum space to real and concrete women.

Some of the possible reforms which could ground themselves on this construction of woman were suggested in the 1990 Parliamentary debates on abortion, conducted within the ambit of the Human Fertilisation and Embryology Bill. The debates are interesting for the way that pro-choice advocates in the Commons combine traditional images of the woman seeking abortion (as described above) with much more positive images. Teresa Gorman, for example, argues that in 'supposedly a liberal society ... we should accord to the women ... the maturity and ability to make decisions about such matters for themselves'. Another MP asserts that the women of this country 'are perfectly capable of exercising their consciences over what they do with their bodies'.

Once the woman of abortion legislation is recognised as a creation (or artefact) of the law, then, she becomes the site of possible political struggle. The task facing feminism is to work within the tension between woman and women to construct a meaning in the interests of women, that is, a meaning which will serve as a basis for empowering, rather that disempowering women.

THE MEDICALISATION OF INFANTICIDE[77]
Katherine O'Donovan[78]

> The operation of the criminal law presupposes in the mind of the person who is acted upon a normal state of strength, reflective power, and so on, but a woman after childbirth is so upset, and in such a hysterical state altogether that it seems to me you cannot deal with her in the same manner as if she was in a regular and proper state of health.[79]

This statement, in its time, represented a new attitude to and a new language about the crime of infanticide. Fitzjames Stephen, the speaker, later wrote that:

> physical differences between the two sexes affect every part of the human body, from the hair of the head to the sole of the feet, from the size and density of the bones to the texture of the brain and the character of the nervous system ... Men are stronger than women in every shape. They have greater muscular and nervous force, greater intellectual force, greater vigour of character.[80]

Placing the two statements together poses the problem neatly. Does the acknowledgement of post-partum depression necessarily lead to statements about inequality of the sexes? Should the crime of infanticide be subsumed under the general law relating to diminished responsibility in homicide cases?

A brief history of the crime of infanticide

The first statute to create a crime of infanticide was passed in 1623.[81] It was a sex-specific crime committed by women and confined to bastard children as victims. The offence involved was concealment of death rather than death itself,

---

77 1984 *Criminal Law Review*, p 259.

78 Currently, Professor of Law, Queen Mary and Westfield College, University of London.

79 J Fitzjames Stephen (1866) 21 British Parliamentary Papers, pp 291–92.

80 J Fitzjames Stephen, Liberty, Equality, Fraternity (1873), p 212.

81 [1623] 321 Jac 1, c 27.

but the concealment operated as a presumption of guilt of murder. To rebut the presumption a witness had to be produced to give evidence that the child was born dead. Given the secrecy of the pregnancy and birth in most cases, this was difficult. By contrast, the suspected murder of children born in wedlock was treated as any other crime of homicide until 1922. The burden of proof was on the prosecution to show that the child had been born alive and had completely severed its connection with its mother's body.[82]

Aside from the jurisdiction of the King's courts over homicide the ecclesiastical court also dealt with infanticide. Parish priests were instructed to ask their parishioners in the confessional:

> Hast thou also by hyre I-Iyne,
>
> And so by-twene you they chylde I-slyne.[83]

Helmholz concludes, on the evidence from the Canterbury ecclesiastical courts, that 'medieval men did not regard infanticide with the horror we associate with pre-meditated homicide'.[84]

The statute of 1623 was considered harsh. Blackstone said it 'savours pretty strongly of severity'.[85] Public attitudes to infanticide by unmarried mothers were punitive, yet for single women in certain forms of employment there was considerable risk of pregnancy. It has been suggested that, in the 18th century half the unmarried women under the age of 26 were living-in servants, vulnerable to seduction and rape. Because their good 'character' was of economic and social value to them, pregnancy for these women was a catastrophe. Travelling and abandoning the child was not an available option, so concealment and infanticide were likely to follow pregnancy.[86] Even where the child was born dead, producing a witness to the court was probably difficult because of the secrecy of the affair. According to Blackstone the severity of the statute was mitigated in practice with the burden of proof shifting to the prosecution.[87]

Cases of child murder within wedlock were treated with less harshness. As Blackstone stated: 'to kill a child in its mother's womb is now no murder, but a great misprison'.[88] The reasons why married parents might not wish to accept a new child into the family could have been economic, or related to some physical problem the child had.

Langer argues that 'infanticide has from time immemorial been the accepted procedure for disposing not only of deformed or sickly infants but of all such new borns as might strain the resources of the individual family or the larger community'.[89] Opportunities for disposing of the child through overlaying, accident, sickness or infanticidal nursing were far greater than those available to single women. Writers on medieval coroner rolls suggest that the absence of

---

82   D Seaborne Davies, 'Child Killing in English Law' (1937) 1 *MLR* 203–23.

83   J Myre, *Instructions for Parish Priests 1359–68* (1902), p 42.

84   RH Helmholz, 'Infanticide in the Province of Canterbury during the 15th Century' (1975) 2 *History of Childhood Quarterly*, pp 379–90 esp, p 387.

85   W Blackstone, *Commentaries on the Laws of England* (1775) Vol IV, p 198.

86   RW Malcolmson, 'Infanticide in the 18th Century', in JS Cockburn (ed), *Crime in England 1550–1800* (1977), p 192.

87   *op cit*, n 7.

88   *Ibid* WL Langer, 'Infanticide: A Historical Survey' (1974) 1 *History of Childhood Quarterly* 353.

89   BA Kellum, 'Infanticide in England in the Later Middle Ages' (1974) 1 *History of Childhood Quarterly* 371; B Hanawalt, *Crime and Conflict in English Communities 1300–1348* (1979).

records on infanticide may be due to the public attitude, that such matters were insignificant.

In 1803 Lord Ellenborough's Act was passed, repealing the 1623 Act, and placing infanticide trials on the same footing as homicide trials. That change has been interpreted as meaning that infanticide could be committed with impunity: 'even the police seemed to think no more of finding a dead child than of finding a dead dog or cat.'[90] Throughout the 19th century there were scandals over burial clubs and baby-farming. The law was seen to be in disarray. There were numerous acquittals for lack of proof that the child had been born alive.[91] The 1803 Act contained a proviso whereby the jury could, in acquitting the defendant of murder, make a finding of concealment of birth which had a maximum two-year sentence. In his evidence to the Commission on Capital Punishment Byles J stated his belief that almost every case tried for concealment was a case of murder.[92] Trials for concealment increased threefold between the 1830s and the 1860s. There were 5,000 coroner's inquests a year on children under seven in the mid-19th century, yet only 39 convictions for child murder between 1849 and 1864. The victims in 34 of these cases were bastards. Recent evidence from the papers of the Thomas Coram Institute suggests that pregnancy for single female servants was still a social and economic disaster in Victorian times.[93]

In the 20th century a new legal approach to child murder was inaugurated by the Infanticide Act 1922. The Act reduced the offence from murder to manslaughter where a woman caused the death of her newly born child by any wilful act or omission 'but at the time of the act or omission she had not fully recovered from the effect of giving birth to such child, but by reason thereof the balance of her mind was then disturbed'.[94] It has been convincingly argued that the Act was the product, not of 19th century medical theory about the effects of childbirth, but of judicial effort to avoid passing death sentences which were not going to be executed.'[95] But medical theory provided a convenient reason for changing the law. Judicial evidence to the Commission on Capital Punishment was that juries would not convict for infanticide,[96] that the judiciary were concerned not to have to go through the 'solemn mockery' involved in a murder trial. Even where there was a conviction capital punishment was rarely carried out. Despite 39 convictions for child murder between 1849 and 1864, no woman was executed,[97] from 1905 to 1921, 60 women were sentenced to death, but in 59 of these cases the sentence was commuted.[98] It can be said however that in order to avoid 'solemn

---

90 Langer, *op cit*, n 11, p 360.

91 G Greaves, 'On the Laws referring to Child Murder,' *Transactions of the Manchester Stats Soc* (1863).

92 Commission on Capital Punishment (1866) Vol 21 *British Parliamentary Papers*, Seaborne Davies, *op cit*, n 4, p 218.

93 JR Gillis, 'Servants, Sexual Relations and the Risks of Illegitimacy in London 1801–1900' in ed JL Newton *et al*, *Sex and Class in Women's History* (1983).

94 Section 1(1) of the Infanticide Act 1922.

95 Seaborne Davies, *op cit*, n 4, Pt II, pp 269–87 esp, p 284.

96 Keating J in a memorandum to the Commission stated: 'It is in vain that judges lay down the law and point out the strength of the evidence, as they are bound to do; juries wholly disregard them, and eagerly adopt the wildest suggestions which the ingenuity of counsel can furnish ... Juries will not convict whilst infanticide is punished capitally.' (1866) Vol 21 *British Parliamentary Papers*, p 625.

97 Seaborne Davies, *op cit*, n 4, p 218.

98 Kenny's, *Outlines of Criminal Law by Turner* (19th edn, 1956), p 195.

mockery' the 1922 Act required a new pretence: that of endeavouring to fit what happened into medical theories about childbirth producing mental disorder.

The Infanticide Act 1938 reformed the 1922 Act in two directions. It altered the definition of the victims of infanticide from 'newly born' to 'under the age of 12 months' and it extended the medicalisation of the crime through the addition of language about 'the effect of lactation'. The cases which brought about the fixing of the age at 12 months illustrate the tension between the socio-economic model of the crime, which informed the statute of 1623, and the medical model which informed the 1922 and 1938 Acts. In *O'Donoghue*[99] the defendant who had killed her 35-day-old child was sentenced to death and duly reprieved. The admitted facts, on which her counsel based his argument on appeal, were that the mother 'was in great distress at the time of the birth for some weeks from poverty and malnutrition, and had only just obtained employment when she killed the child'. In an unsuccessful effort to persuade the court that the trial judge was wrong in holding that a 35-day-old child was not newly born, counsel also argued that 'there was between insanity and sanity a degree of mental derangement which the medical authorities called "puerperal"'.[100] Thus, a mixture of socio-economic causes and medical theory was used in argument. *Hale*[101] was a case in which the mother killed her second child when it was three weeks' old and inflicted injuries on herself. The medical evidence was that at the birth of her first child the mother had symptoms bordering on puerperal insanity. The trial judge, claiming himself bound by *O'Donoghue*, directed the jury to find the defendant 'guilty but insane'.

Medical or socio-economic model?

The Infanticide Act 1938 makes explicit the medicalisation of the crime. It provides for the reduction of the offence from murder to infanticide where the defendant is a woman who causes the death of her child under the age of 12 months by wilful act or omission:

> but at the time of the act or omission the balance of her mind was disturbed by reason of her not having fully recovered from the effect of giving birth to the child or by reasons of the effect of lactation consequent upon the birth of the child.[102]

As the wording makes clear, it is to the process of giving birth, the effect of this on the mother's body, and the hormonal and other processes that are involved in lactation that the statute refers. The idea behind this is that physical processes, whether they are called chemistry or hysteria, can influence behaviour in such a way as to reduce criminal responsibility. There is no apparent consistency to this theory, for if a woman who has given birth within 12 months kills adults or other children the Infanticide Act does not apply. This suggests statutory acknowledgement that social role change may produce psychosis. But other members of the household, such as fathers, who may also be affected by role change, cannot rely on the Act.

The medical model for the Act has come under attack in recent years. In 1975 the Butler Committee stated that the medical principles on which the Act is based

---

99 (1927) 20 Cr App R 132.

100 *Ibid*, p 133.

101 (1936) *The Times*, 22 July, p 13.

102 Section 1(1) of the Infanticide Act 1938.

are probably no longer relevant, and that 'puerperal psychoses are now regarded as no different from others, childbirth being only a precipitating factor'.[103] The Committee's view was that the purposes of an offence of infanticide 'are now sufficiently covered by the more recent provision for diminished responsibility'.[104]

The Criminal Law Revision Committee (CLRC) in its Fourteenth Report accepted that there is little or no evidence for an association between lactation and mental disorder, and that this reference should be removed from the Act. However, despite evidence from the Royal College of Psychiatrists that 'the medical basis for the present Infanticide Act is not proven',[105] the CLRC argued for the retention of an amended version of the present law. It is clear that both the Butler Committee and the CLRC were uneasy about the medical theory upon which the 1938 Act is based, yet neither found a satisfactory basis for their proposed reforms.

The Butler Committee recognised that 'the operative factors in child killing are often the stress of having to care for the infant, who may be unwanted or difficult, and personality problems'.[106] But if this is so, and if mental disorder is 'probably no longer a significant cause of infanticide' then diminished responsibility is not an appropriate defence plea. Even if the Butler Committee's other proposals for the abolition of the mandatory life sentence for murder and consequently of the necessity of a defence of diminished responsibility were to become law there would still be pressure in infanticide cases on psychiatrists 'to conform their medical opinion to the felt need for mercy',[107] by giving evidence of medical disorder so as to avoid a conviction for murder. The current 'stretching' of the law and medical principles because of sympathy for infanticidal mothers would continue, as would the myths that surround the crime.

The CLRC recognised that a medical model for infanticide as a crime is inadequate, and that mental disturbance may arise either from the effects of giving birth or from 'circumstances consequent upon the birth'. The recommended reform involved the inclusion of the latter phrase in the wording of the statute. From the report it is obvious that the Committee wished to extend the definition of the crime to cover 'environmental or other stresses,' including poverty, incapacity to cope with the child and failure of bonding. The social and economic nature of these factors was acknowledged in the report although the Committee was careful to link them to 'the fact of the birth and the hormonal and other bodily changes produced by it'.[108] Thus, to enable the court to take account of socio-economic factors, the medical model was retained. The CLRC was definite that cases 'where the social and emotional pressures on the mother consequent on the birth are so heavy that the balance of her mind is disturbed',[109] would not be covered by the defence of diminished responsibility.

---

103 *Report of the Committee on Mentally Abnormal Offenders* (Cmnd 6244, 1975), p 245.

104 *Ibid*, p 251.

105 Criminal Law Revision Committee, *Fourteenth Report, Offences Against the Person* (Cmnd 7844, 1980), para 103.

106 *op cit*, p 245, n 27.

107 AJ Ashworth, 'The Butler Committee and Criminal Responsibility' [1975] *Crim LR* 687 at 694.

108 *op cit*, n 29, para 105.

109 *Ibid*, para 102. The CLRC identified this type of case as 'battered baby syndrome'.

Conclusion

From its inception as a sex-specific crime in 1623 infanticide has been concerned with theories about women. The initial object of the law was to punish single women for becoming pregnant and for refusing to live with their sin. Thus the crime was created to affect moral and social behaviour. In the 19th century the discourse changed.[110] Symptoms of temporary madness were discerned including catatonia, hallucinations, delirium and depression. These were labelled lactational insanity, puerperal psychosis, or exhaustion psychosis. In the 20th century, in order to mitigate the severity of the crime this discourse was utilised by the law. It is only in the past 20 years that explanations for infanticide related to the mother's social and economic environment have been resurrected.

Proposals for reform have vacillated between the two models of the crime. It is not hard to understand why. To admit that social and economic circumstances, or motherhood, may cause crime is to open a hitherto tightly closed box. To deny recognition of infanticide as a separate, lesser crime is to invite juries to refuse to convict for murder. So the solution has been to fudge the issue by retaining discredited medical theory. Edwards has pointed out that 19th century discourse on puerperal psychosis was used to justify women's exclusion from participation in public life.[111] The danger is that continued emphasis on biological difference perpetuates that reasoning. Yet there is public sympathy for infanticidal mothers based on beliefs about childbirth. Perhaps this has something to do with the mystery of birth itself. F Tennyson Jesse's prison doctor expresses it thus: 'The dark consciousness of the womb was present with every man who had to do with the business, of the womb that was the holder of life, from which every living soul had issued in squalor and pain.[112]

LAW REFORM AND HUMAN REPRODUCTION: IMPLICATIONS FOR WOMEN[113]

Rebecca M Albury[114]

Biological reproduction, that most 'natural' of human activities, has been the subject of major technological change during the past 30 years. Although scientific understanding of the processes of reproduction is still under-developed, it is possible to intervene at several stages in the process, at least in the female body. The older technologies of contraception are well accepted if not understood by the majority of the population in industrial countries. They provide a model for some discussion about research on new techniques of abortion that will be separated from the physical termination of pregnancy just as the contraceptive pill and the IUD are separated from the physical activity of sexual intercourse. The new technologies of *in vitro* fertilisation (IVF) and embryo transfer (ET) are the subject of scientific, moral and legal interest. In combination with artificial insemination (AI) they open the possibility of technological reproduction for humans, a possibility that has provoked a growing debate in Australia and other countries where IVF teams are working.

---

110 N Walker, *Crime and Insanity in England* (1968), Chapter 7.

111 S Edwards, 'Medico-Legal Conundrums' paper given to the BSA Conference (1982).

112 F Tennyson Jesse, *A Pin to See the Peepshow* (1979), p 392.

113 Marian Simms (ed), *Australian Women and the Political System* (Melbourne: Longman, 1984), Chapter 13.

114 Susan Moller Okin (1979).

As the techniques have become more successful and better understood the debate has shifted to questions of how to reform the laws about paternity and custody to accommodate the new methods of conception, allowing less time for discussion of the social effects of the techniques themselves.

Law reform will certainly occur, the scientists, politicians, and law reform commissioners are all agreed that it must. They have not yet agreed on the nature of that reform and the discussions continue to formulate the questions the proposed legislation must answer. However, the general drift of the legislation can be predicted. A useful beginning for such a speculation is the course of debate and law-making about another contentious aspect of human reproduction – abortion. Many of the same issues are involved: the role of medical technology, the power of the medical profession, the needs of society, the desires of the woman, the place of her partner, the function of the law. In this paper I examine the similarities and differences in the formulation of the questions and the answers in the two points of intervention in the process of human reproduction. Throughout both debates run a set of related but unspoken assumptions about women in the family. By discussing those assumptions it is possible to point to the consequences of likely law reforms for women. Giving voice to the unspoken may also have the effect of shifting the terms of debate about the technologies of human reproduction by asking questions that previously did not have a place.

Women in the realm of private life

In common with other English-speaking countries, Australian political institutions are founded in liberal democratic theory. It is within the boundaries set by the definitions and categories of liberal democracy that the now familiar debates about human reproduction take place. At one level it is assumed that society is made up of individuals who share equally the responsibilities and benefits of their common life. This assumption is, however, a myth that denies the multitude of inequalities that are the consequence of another level of assumption: the profound separation of public and private (or personal) life. This division has served as a model for the division of many human experiences and institutionalised relations and thus has provided ways of viewing the world and of acting in it. Public life is the location of politics and the institutions of liberal democracy parties, parliaments, legal systems, trade unions and popular movements. The whole range of affective relations is located, by definition, outside of the public sphere in private life.

The separation of public and private life has been accompanied by the allocation of men and women into separate areas of action and concern. Women are commonly defined by their biological function as childbearers and assigned the social function as childrearers while men are defined by their capacity for rational thought and their transcendence of the purely biological.[115] This separation of public and private has contributed to the subordination of women by confining women to the private realm of the family, thus isolating them from the main arenas of political and social debate and by disguising the power relations between women and men. Liberal theorists seem to be discussing equal genderless individuals while it is clear that male heads of households are the actual theoretical individuals. The interests of all family members are assumed to be the same, though no argument has been produced for that position. At the same time, even the potential for women to take part in public life is denied on the grounds of their biological functions and the personal qualities that are said

115 A Rich, *Of Woman Born* (1976).

to come 'naturally' from those functions – emotional tenderness, empathy, nurturance, altruism – all qualities ill-suited to the harsh competitive public world, but assumed necessary for the survival of human beings.

Although feminist writers have long pointed to the conflict of interests in the power relations of family life their criticism of the contemporary social order has received little serious attention from social commentators with the exception of desperate defences of institutionalised sex roles and a gender-based division of human capacities and labour from both the left and right. The family is treated as a 'natural' and unproblematic feature of society and the contradictions that exist in any institution are ignored with the result that in any political debate a basic premise of liberalism remains unchallenged with women securely placed in male-headed families in the private sphere.

The assumed role of women in those families is central to the opposition to abortion and the justification of technological conception. In the family women gain their status from their relationship with men; they are daughters, wives, mothers. There are no words to describe autonomous women, all of the phrases used suggest the woman's deviance from the expected position of women as appendages of men – childless women, single mothers. Pregnancy and birth, or at least motherhood, are a part of the definition of women in our culture as in many others.[116] Motherhood is the foremost institutional structure in the lives of women; women who resist institutionalisation, even briefly, are regarded with suspicion and contempt – think of the abortion debate or the charge of selfishness levelled at women who remain child free by choice. It is no surprise, then, that infertile women in the *in vitro* fertilisation programme at Monash University/Queen Victoria Hospital speak of their childlessness in strong terms:

> I went through all those feelings about how unfair it was that women who don't really want kids can have them when I can't. I really felt I had a disability ... I don't see how being infertile is so different to being deaf or blind. You just aren't complete ... It was probably silly but I felt that Len might not love me as much if I couldn't have a baby. Perhaps he wouldn't consider me as feminine.

> Stephen is the child I have been attempting to conceive for the past 17 years. Stephen is why Toby and I are involved in the IVF programme: Stephen is waiting inside my mind. His spirit lives inside and waits for nature or my doctors to form his body – the body that will set him free to live ... Stephen's story started somewhere in my childhood when I began to realise I would have a child one day. Later on the seed began to take shape, and at the age of 14 I named him, and the seed started to grow roots ... Stephen and I are the survivors of a tragedy in which I lost my fertility and the body of my child. His deformed state is part of the quality of my life. What quality of life can I give him? ... The only way I can give quality to my child's life now is by giving him a body through which he can live. The only alternative is to destroy him. Who can help this mother practise euthanasia on her deformed child? How can you destroy a child with no body? How can you bury a child who hasn't known life, who is held back from any attempt at realising his life because of his mother's deformity?[117]

The desperation of these women who cannot meet the cultural definition of feminine womanhood by becoming mothers is accepted as unproblematic by

---

116 Walters and Singer (1982), pp 120–22.
117 (1982) *Sun-Herald*, 28 March.

medical researchers and law reformers. The Monash medical team says their work is the result of 'intense public demand',[118] but does not discuss the responsibility of the medical profession for establishing that demand. Both of the women quoted above lost their fallopian tubes as a result of misdiagnosed pelvic infections, of repeated complaints of pain that were ignored or dismissed as an excuse to get out of work.[119] Today women who were defined as malingering teenagers by medical professionals must rely on members of the same profession for a technical solution to the infertility created by that definition. Those women are not alone, but joined by thousands made sterile by contraceptives as well as misdiagnosis.[120] Further, the role of the medical profession in the definition of women's sexuality and life experiences is never raised, nor is the increasing literature analysing that role ever acknowledged, much less discussed. It would seem that medical technologists and their apologists are ignorant of a serious and systematic critique of their practices.

Mechanisms of control

Even if the assumptions about female sexuality and women's place in society are not formally articulated, they are present in the social practices surrounding the techniques of AI and IVF as they are in all other aspects of health-care delivery related to reproduction. Medical practitioners are acknowledged as experts about the functioning of female bodies and thus occupy a privileged place in defining the standards of normality and deviance.[121]

The laws of all states in Australia grant doctors the power to authorise abortion not women.[122] A woman must demonstrate her worthiness to become a part of a technological conception programme; she must fit the practitioners notion of a 'good mother'. First she must be married; the technical solution to the inability to give birth and fulfil the total definition of 'woman' is reserved for those who have indicated their willingness to accept the definition by the act of marriage. The Commission of Enquiry into IVF recommended that this become law in Victoria, but 'stable' *de facto* relationships will be included. In addition women must demonstrate the suitability of their skills and motives for parenting. Then a woman must be a 'good patient'. She must be willing to undergo a series of exhaustive and expensive tests to demonstrate her fertility before the relatively simple procedure of artificial insemination.[123] Couples must also submit to considerable counselling. Women in the IVF programme undergo considerably more testing and abdominal surgery but, at the Royal Women's Hospital, Melbourne, are not permitted open expression of their emotional reactions to the alternations of hope and disappointment. The Monash/Queen Victoria Hospital programme does not add this additional requirement.

The medical profession has added a new technique to its practice of social control of women; a control that remains unacknowledged either by the practitioners and their supporters or by the critics they recognise. For in the debate on *in vitro* fertilisation the feminist critiques of social attitudes and medical practices are dismissed as inappropriate to the questions at hand. One writer critical of

118 Walters and Singer (1982), pp 14, 121.
119 See now Artificial Conception Act 1984 (NSW); The Artificial Conception Act 1985 (WA); The Infertility Treatment Act 1995 (Vic); and see Gabrielle Woff (1966) 10 AJFL 71.
120 Seaman and Seaman (1978).
121 Ehrenreich and English (1979).
122 Finlay and Sihombing (1978); Treloar (1982).
123 Hanmer and Allen (1980).

technological conception, discussing the desire of an individual woman to have a baby says:

> An extreme feminist might take umbrage at such a feeling, and claim that the cure for it is not IVF but a change in the attitudes of society. I doubt if the woman in question would be much helped by this approach. Her need is real enough to her, and the object of it, surely is a good one: the having of a baby. I propose we accept that the desire of a childless couple to have a child of their own is a reasonable one.[124]

William Daniel SJ seems to be saying here that because some infertile women want babies then he need not think about the mechanisms of social control that made them feel 'that somehow you weren't a real woman unless you were fertile' (at p 73). He uses the word 'reasonable' in a way that suggests that any investigation into the social origin of the couple's desire is to call their rationality (sanity?) into question. It is also unlikely that anyone so unwilling to question the equation of woman with mother would notice the shift from a woman's 'need' to the couple's 'desire', much less examine the distribution of social power in a society in which that shift can be made.

While most writers are quick to dismiss feminist social criticism some are willing to use, out of context, Shulamith Firestone's vision of the technical eradication of childbirth as a means of ending women's oppression to appeal to sceptical women for support for research into the gestation of foetuses outside female bodies. They ignore the social structure of communal responsibility for children that Firestone postulates and the significant feminist literature that challenges her optimistic view of technology. Firestone's feminist critics emphasise the masculine control of science and the past, present and future potential of science to control and define women in the interests of a male-dominated vision of human life and social order.[125]

A brief examination of the rhetoric of the abortion debate raises a number of questions about the authenticity of the claim that medical services are delivered according to public demand and the desires of women. The laws in Australia give decision-making powers to doctors and the legal system not to women. The events in Queensland during March 1983 again demonstrated the willingness of the courts to grant every avenue to men who seek control of women. Women are exhorted to be responsible and unselfish, to use high technology contraception regardless of their personal evaluation of its dangers, to think of the moral fibre of the nation, and to support the hierarchy of authority in the family by submitting to the will of men or the inevitability of biology. The President of the National Right to Life Committee in the United States accused all of those who support the demand that women make the final decision about whether or not to terminate a pregnancy of doing 'violence to marriage by helping to remove the right of a husband to protect the life of the child he has fathered in his wife's womb'.[126] Fatherhood is reduced to an act of fertilisation and childhood is extended to before birth. The Right to Life has achieved a considerable success with this kind of polemic: the headlines of reports of the Queensland case asserted 'Father Fights For His Unborn Child!' even though the story made it clear that the man involved did not want to care for a living infant but proposed that the pregnant woman give birth then give the infant away for adoption.[127]

---

124 Walters and Singer (1982), p 73.

125 Rose and Hanmer (1976); Birke *et al* (1980); Roberts (1980).

126 Wilke as quoted in Petchesky (1981), p 221.

127 (1983) *The Telegraph*, 24 March.

What would happen to the terms of the abortion debate if it included the sympathy towards women's 'needs' that Daniel expresses when he opposes IVF? A paraphrase of his original argument reveals that his sympathy rests on the same assumptions of the social role for women as the practices of the doctors that he opposes. If the discussion is changed from a woman who wants a baby to one who wants to terminate an unwanted pregnancy his basic argument can be used to answer one of the many questions or statements of the Right to Life. Abortion is no solution to the social problems of women with unwanted pregnancies.

> An extreme anti-feminist might take umbrage at such a feeling, and claim that the cure for it is not abortion but a change in the attitudes of society. I doubt if the woman in question would be much helped by this approach. Her need is real enough to her, and the object of it surely, is a good one: the having of a baby when she wants one. I propose we accept that the desire of a woman [couple] to terminate an unwanted pregnancy is a reasonable one.

The assumption of the 'reasonableness' of the desire to terminate as well as the desire to achieve a pregnancy indeed changes the position of various parties to the abortion debate. Women seeking abortions are no longer distressed or misguided but fully rational decision-makers. Those with moral objection to abortion could continue to counsel women to avoid abortion but would find it more difficult to recommend laws that make abortion a criminal offence or that deny women their decision-making powers. Doctors might even begin to lobby through the AMA for the repeal of those laws that criminalise abortion just as they support efforts to clarify the law regarding technological conception. While such a course would be welcomed by many, including feminists (moderate or extreme), it is not very likely because it challenges the assumption that women are mothers and thus belong in families.

The law, like other liberal institutions, supports the assumption that women are not a part of public life. Its function as an enforcer of the dominant sexual politics can be seen in studies of judicial decisions of cases involving protective or exclusionary legislation (see Sachs and Wilson, 1978). Until the early 20th century judges ruled that women were not 'persons' under the law and could therefore be excluded from various professions, jury duty etc. Both United States and English courts ruled in similar ways leading scholars to point to an underlying shared double standard applied to women and men as an explanation for their consistency. The assumption that a woman's place is at home bearing and raising children and caring for men was/is central to judicial thinking, further supported by notions of women's physical weakness and moral inferiority to justify protective or discriminatory legislation.[128] In addition to continuing to serve men at home, women should not increase the competition for men at work.[129] Mary Eastwood suggests that many United States decisions were based on the relatively unsophisticated formulation: 'Men are in power; they have established their control, and it should stay that way.'[130] Australian law is based on the same assumptions and thus encodes the same social relations in both law-making and judicial decisions.[131] Similar beliefs inform the law reform process even though reformers recognise the injustice of some old laws.

---

128 Eastwood (1971).
129 Sachs (1978).
130 Page 285.
131 Ross (1982); NSW 1978.

Abortion law reform

During the 1960s and early 1970s one publicised type of law reform sought to relieve the unequal burden placed on different social groups by laws that were no longer suited to changing economic and social conditions. Changes in social services are an example of this type of law reform in its redistributive form, that is the reforms were an attempt to ease the effects of the unequal distribution of wealth. Abortion law reform has been claimed to be an example of the regulatory form of law reform, though with obvious redistributive aspects with regard to State responsibility for the cost of medical treatment for certain groups.[132] The social effect of illegal abortion was regarded as an individual problem of specific women not as a collective problem of an economic or ethnic group. Reformers sought to remove the stigma of criminal abortion from women who they regarded as marginal in a basically just social order. Such women were in need of abortion because of an individual problem: ignorance of contraception, irresponsibility in sexual activity, psychological disturbance, temporary or permanent social deprivation, extreme youth, or medical unfitness. In these special cases the decision-making was put into the hands of doctors and it was assumed that 'normal' women would not seek abortions.[133]

Abortion law reform was the focus of both feminist and anti-feminist organisation. In English-speaking countries abortion laws were changed to give more access to legal abortion during the years between 1967 and 1973. In Australia legal reform took place in some states in both judicial and legislative form. In other states the practice of law, enforcement has responded to political pressure in a variety of ways. The result of the formal and informal reforms has been to make medically safe abortions available at a greater or lesser cost for most women in Australia based on the right of a doctor to make decisions about medical treatment, not the right of a woman to control her fertility. Thus the reforms have also achieved the transfer of women from the control of individual men in families to the control of State sanctioned groups of specialist men. Located within the liberal tradition, the reforms to abortion laws have given 'women more rights without giving them a right to themselves'.[134]

The false assumption that only 'marginal' women demand abortions laid the groundwork for subsequent struggles. 'Normal' women also wanted abortions so demand was higher than anticipated. Most legislation introduced in English-speaking countries since 1973 has been to limit access to abortion either by increasing the obstacles to obtaining the operation or by denying medical benefits. These struggles have made clear the limitations of the reformist perspective as feminists argued for abortion on the demand of women and anti-feminist 'Right to Lifers' argued for an absolute prohibition on abortion. The reformist stance has been assumed to be a 'compromise' position which allows some abortions while maintaining a check on the 'frivolity' of women who might demand abortions for reasons the reformers think are specious. The reformist position can be located beside the anti-abortion position on the same side of a more basic contemporary political division than the abortion debate. Neither group is willing to acknowledge women as autonomous political and moral agents, though they differ on how to best enforce their views, the gender-based hierarchy that is sustained by the liberal democratic legal systems is supported

132 Randall (1982), p 171.
133 Greenwood and Young (1976).
134 Kickbusch (1981), p 153.

by both groups. The reformist approach to abortion law and, by extension, all aspects of human biological reproduction continues to regard regulatory reform as appropriate since they see redistributive reform as dealing with financial resources rather than access to social power (money being only a part of that power). Regulatory abortion laws establish the parameters of 'lawful' abortion – establishing who, what, where, when and why. A genuinely redistributive abortion law would reassign decision-making power over fertility to women and thus alter the social relations between women and men and challenge the function of the law as an enforcer of the sexual division of labour and power that places women in the politically subordinate domestic sphere under the authority of men.

Custody and technological conception

Law reform discussions in Australia about human reproduction have been largely technical examinations of how the accepted structure of law and legal practice can assimilate new technology, not about how the new technology reinforces the social relations already encoded in the law. This is no surprise since such discussions fall within the boundaries of liberal democratic categories that separate public and private life, that reinforce the male-headed family as the basic unit in a hierarchical society, that hold up a vision of a progressive and rational science. The Chairman of the Australian Law Reform Commission summarises the three elements of law reform as: assuming that a proposal will fit into the existing social order in a way that conserves what is good; it will involve some action as a recognition of the variety of social and technical changes that challenge the current legal system; and implementation of the proposals will mean a change for the better – though there are differences about what constitutes 'better'.[135]

Although the debate about *in vitro* fertilisation and artificial insemination includes a variety of legal and ethical questions, the law reformers see questions of property as their particular brief with the custody of the resulting child in cases of technological conception as an area of considerable concern. To what extent does the contribution of sperm to the biological process of reproduction entail legal and economic responsibilities? In the past the usual method of determining a man's legal relationship with a child was to enquire of his relationship with the child's mother – if he was married to her the child was deemed to be his and legitimate: the beneficiary of the man's rights and duties.[136]

Artificial insemination by donor (AID) raises a series of problems for this assumption because a child born within a marriage is demonstrably not the child of the husband. The problem for the law has been further compounded by the usual practice of such husbands, who declare themselves as the father when registering the birth of the child, though there is no provision for the legal recognition of a social rather than biological father except by adoption. Just as there has been little disapproval of the provision for *de facto* couples to register a child as legitimate there is likely to be little opposition to the legislation providing equal legal rights for children born as a result of AID, in spite of difficulties enacting uniform legislation throughout Australia. On the other hand, there is reluctance about allowing women without husbands to use artificial insemination; the opposition is usually couched in terms of the threat to marriage

---

135 Kirbyu (1983), p 10.
136 Mason (1982), p 349.

and the family posed by the practice.[137] Although the option of conception by means of sexual intercourse has no means of institutional regulation by the law or medical profession there is a desire to ensure that women using technological means of conception will be 'fit' to be mothers.[138] Both the law that does not recognise the concept of social fatherhood and the desire to restrict AID to married women rest on the assumption that a woman should be under control of a man in a family and that a man need only be responsible for a child to whom he has made a genetic contribution. The legal recognition of the child is dependent on the woman's legal relation to the man, that relationship is what legitimises the presence of his semen in her vagina.

International case law has not clearly determined whether the presence of semen alone is sufficient evidence of sexual intercourse making AID equivalent to adultery, or whether there must also be evidence of penetration of the woman's vagina by a penis.[139] (Remember that the presence of semen is often necessary to prove rape or sexual assault and that sexual assault has included attacks other than penetration of vagina by penis only during the last decade.) Laws regulating custody also establish the authority of men over the mothers of their children, an authority that continues after the marriage is dissolved.[140] Recent discussion of the rights of men over their biological children when they are not married to the woman who gave birth to and cares for them would further extend the control of women by men through the control of children.[141] The law reform literature seems to point to this as a possible outcome for custody law when it considers whether the sperm donor in AID could be made legally responsible for the child as its 'father'. Custody laws are to be reformed to preserve male authority in the family for any other change would not conserve the social order, might not allow the legal system to survive the challenge of social and technical change, certainly might not be a change for the 'better'.

In vitro fertilisation poses further legal problems of ownership. Who owns the components of the biological processes that are assisted by technology, the sperm, the ova, the embryo? The ownership of the embryo has profound implications beyond the often raised questions of frozen embryos in the laboratory. If the ownership of an embryo *in vitro* is legally established, what will the status of an embryo *in vivo*? Will a man be able to prevent an abortion because he is joint owner of the implanted embryo regardless of whether the woman consents to continuing the pregnancy? Could a man take out an injunction to enforce a particular diet, non-smoking, or regular exercise on a pregnant woman as an expression of his concern for the care of his property – his share of the foetus? Such speculations reduce women to little more than ambulatory incubators, but are not as far-fetched as they might seem, for men have already gone to court in attempts to deny women abortions in several countries. Again, the legal solution to the challenge of technical change could reinforce the social control of women by men.

While the custody of a child conceived *in vitro* using the sperm and ovum of the couple who will be her biological and social parents should pose no major legal difficulties, the custody of a child born of a 'surrogate mother' is highly

---

137 Walters and Singer (1982), p 78.

138 Scott (1981), pp 210–11.

139 Mason (1982), p 352; Scott (1981), p 206.

140 Delphy (1976); Brown (1981); Sutton and Friedman (1982).

141 Sutton and Friedman (1982), pp 124–25.

problematic. The hope (or is it fear?) of surrogate motherhood may be as a step in achieving the adherence of the equation of woman with mother for every woman. If a woman cannot sustain a pregnancy and adoptable babies are not available, then she and her husband could hire a woman to provide the life-support system for their genetic child – her body. A woman would need only some functioning ovarian tissue to become a mother and, of course, enough money to buy another woman's body. The naming of the hired woman as a surrogate 'mother' raises the primary question: what constitutes motherhood, a biological or social relation to the child? For the first nine months of its development both genetic parents would have the same relationship to the child – one similar to the man in conventional reproductive relationships – while the hired woman would experience the developing pregnancy with her body, in her life. When she gave birth she would give the baby to the employing couple as in a conventional adoption, severing the close relationship of the previous nine months.

Legal cases have so far involved women who were contracted to supply an ovum as well as a body for gestation. Judges have awarded custody to the birth-giving woman not the genetic 'father' and his wife when conflict has arisen, standard adoption laws apply when there is no conflict. The debate about the direction of legal regulation has focused on whether a contract between the couple and the woman would be binding and who would be the mother of the child for custody purposes (a concern similar to the issue of who is the father of the AID child, except that the surrogate would have already established a physical and social relationship with the child during the pregnancy).[142] The separation of pregnancy from childrearing has the potential to raise questions about the role of women in new ways, but only if the assumptions behind the use of the term 'mother' for both pregnant women and childrearing women are subjected to searching examination. In the absence of a critical examination technical developments and the legal responses to them may only serve to place further aspects of human reproduction under the control of specialist men and further deny the different experiences of women and men in the process of reproduction. There could also be increased pressure on women to conform to the definition of femininity that requires motherhood.

In addition to the custody questions there is the issue of the terms of a surrogacy contract; custody of the child is but one aspect of pregnancy with health insurance, smoking, diet and exercise among possible areas of regulation. This is an area with potential for many conflicts because, almost certainly if surrogacy becomes socially acceptable, poor women will be hired to have babies for wealthier couples. Class differences in attitudes toward pregnancy will become clear and with them the question of exactly what is paid for in the surrogacy agreement – must the surrogate live the life that the woman who will raise the child imagines she would live if she were pregnant? Law reformers also raise the question of who should be permitted to enter surrogacy contracts; some would exclude fertile women who want a genetic child without interruption to their careers. The only reference to the possibility of a man hiring a surrogate to provide an heir without the necessity of an emotional relationship with a woman dismisses Rorvik's[143] account on the grounds that the cloning aspect remains

---

142 Walters and Singer (1982), pp 97–109; Mason (1982), pp 354–56.
143 Rorvik (1978).

unproven,[144] rather than commenting on the possibility that wealthy men might buy a child like any other commodity. Is there a covert suggestion that surrogacy should be available only to women who will be 'good mothers' and stay at home with the child? All men who have children do so without interruption to their careers or alteration to their figures, nor do they stay at home by convention to do the daily tasks associated with child care. Certainly all discussions of surrogacy assume a conventional marriage with a couple who 'reasonably' desires a child to become a conventional family. As with AID, law reform proposals to meet the challenges of IVF and surrogacy contracts uphold those conventions.

Rights and needs in the family and society

Law reform proposals operate entirely within the constraints of liberal democratic thought and so support the separation of public and private life and the family structure implied by that division. The failure to examine the concept of the family in the debates about reproductive technology, regardless of whether the technology would prevent or allow conception or childbirth has led to a confusing repetition in the use of language. The same terms are used to support both sides in the debates about the use of the technologies. The proponents of the reform or repeal of laws that criminalise abortion demand the 'right to choose' for women while the opponents assert the 'right to life' for the foetus and point out the lack of 'choice' available to it. There was considerable debate in the Australian Parliament about whether the Human Rights Commission Bill should be extended to include foetuses within the definition of humans with rights to be protected. Proponents of the broad interpretation hoped to establish a basis for Commonwealth intervention into the provision of abortion services currently covered by State laws. They claimed that the Declaration of the Rights of the Child and the International Covenant on Civil and Political Rights are open to such an interpretation in spite of specific votes to the contrary in the drafting committees.[145] The covenant does contain a revealing statement about the family in Article 23:

> The family is the natural and fundamental unit of society and is entitled to protection by society and the State.

The family is assumed to be unitary rather than an association of individuals with unequal power and thus the possibility of conflicts of interest and conflicts of rights. This and similar formulations are used to reinforce the positioning of women in families by conservatives and liberals alike. The antecedent of contemporary thought is here revealed to be the legal fiction of the unity of the wife within the husband that served to exclude women from public life in the 19th century.[146]

One outcome of new technologies of human reproduction may be the provision of further dimensions to the definition of women as mothers by providing additional means of State intervention. Already commentators have asserted that the State has an obligation to provide IVF services because childless couples have a 'right' to bear children.[147] To use the term right here is to expand the conventional thinking about rights that requires the State not to stand in the way

144 Walters and Singer (1982), p 111.
145 UNESCO, 1977, 19.
146 Sachs and Wilson (1978), p 79.
147 (1982) *The Telegraph*, 12 May.

of the individual's exercise of her capacities so long as her activities do not cause harm. As a political right childbearing makes sense only in a State in which childbearing is an offence, not as a call for the establishment of services to reverse the effects of injury or disease. Childbearing, as a 'right' in a family perceived as a 'natural and fundamental unit of society', could become a compulsory symbol of adult good citizenship rather than an effect of heterosexual intercourse or a socially desirable option for couples. The State then would provide the means for achieving conception so good citizens could be distinguished from anti-social childless couples and individuals. The State provision of IVF or AID facilities offers the law opportunity for state-defined criteria of good motherhood which could be held up to all women. This is but a continuation of the forced choice of abortion or sterilisation by many poor women today because those services have State funding in combination with insufficient funding of childcare facilities, low welfare benefits and high unemployment.

Rights and needs are variously used to defend or attack uses of technology to intervene in the biological processes of reproduction. The demands of women for abortion are selfish or even anti-social according to some while the IVF programme is justified by the demands of women as a recognition of their 'need' to have children. Both arguments involve the definition of woman as mother: in one case to compel motherhood and in the other to provide a means to motherhood, a technological answer to the consequences of misdiagnosis and iatrogenic disease. Sterility is indeed a social problem for women, more so when childbearing is the only acceptable mode of acting a world divided into public and private realms. Human rights can be portrayed as excluding women's rights to abortion and perhaps even contraception while including the right to give birth, even if sterile, only from a political perspective in which rights depend on the division of society and the assumption that male-headed families constitute a 'fundamental unit'. In such a society, law reform to meet the challenge of medical technology is not discussed in the context of a critique of the social and political relations that the laws uphold; current power relations are taken as given. The demands of women for medical research into reliable woman-controlled contraception or relief from period pain cannot be heard much less met while medical research priorities are set according to the 'needs' of scientists to do exciting frontier research and their 'right' to be funded by bodies that accept those priorities.

Laws that criminalise abortion cannot be altered to acknowledge the control women have always sought to exercise over their fertility but only to hand control to a group of male-oriented specialists. The literature on law reform is singularly silent on the differing effects of the law on the lives of women and men. The literature on reproductive technology is silent about the social relations, whether familial or professional, which structure human reproduction. The consequences of the technological changes during the past 30 years will be better understood once those silences are broken and the network of power relations in which the changes are embedded are examined critically. Until such an examination is widespread the changes cannot be 'better' for women but only reinforce social relations as they exist.

CHAPTER 12

WOMEN AND INTERNATIONAL LAW

International law has been defined as:

> ... that body of law which is composed for its greater part of the principles and rules of conduct which states feel themselves bound to observe, and therefore, do commonly observe in their relations with each other, and which includes also:
>
> a   the rules of law relating to the functioning of international institutions or organisations, their relations with each other, and their relations with States and individuals; and
>
> b   certain rules of law relating to individuals and non-State entities so far as the right or duties of such individuals and non-State entities are the concern of the international community.[1]

In the last 50 years, the work of the permanent international organisations of international law such as the United Nations, World Health Organisation, International Labour Organisation has developed international law far beyond the traditionally adopted definition of being the law between nations alone. The commitment of the United Nations[2] and the Council of Europe[3] towards the definition, evolution and protection of human rights has created standards against which the law and practices of a State in relation to its subjects may be measured.[4] Conventions have been introduced for the advancement and protection of specific human rights.[5]

For feminist scholars the law and practice of international law in relation to the elimination of discrimination against women has proved a fertile source of study.[6] As the extracts which follow demonstrate, whilst great strides have been made in this direction, particularly in relation to State responsibility for

---

1   IA Shearer, *Starke's International Law* (Butterworths, 11th edn, 1994), p 3.

2   See the Universal Declaration of Human Rights adopted by the General Assembly of the United Nations in 1948; the Covenant on Economic, Social and Cultural Rights and the Covenant on Civil and Political Rights 1966.

3   See the European Convention for the Protection of Human Rights and Fundamental Freedoms November 1950.

4   See generally, P Alston (ed) *The United Nations and Human Rights* (1992).

5   See for example, the Convention for the Suppression of Traffic in Persons and of the Exploitation or the Prostitution of Others (1950); the Convention on the Status of Refugees (1951); the Supplementary Geneva Convention for Abolishing Slavery, the Slave Trade and Institutions and Practices Similar to Slavery (1956); Convention on the Suppression and Punishment of the Crime of Apartheid (1973); the Conventions of the International Labour Organisation: Freedom of Association and Protection of the Right to Organise (1948); Right to Organise and Collective Bargaining (1949); Equal Remuneration Convention (1951); Abolition of Forced Labour (1957); Discrimination (Employment and Occupation) (1958); International Convention of the Elimination of All Forms of Racial Discrimination (1965); Convention on the Elimination of All Forms of Discrimination against Women (1979); United Nations Declaration on the Elimination of All Forms of Intolerance and Discrimination Based on Religion or Belief (1981); Convention Against Torture and Other Cruel Inhuman or Degrading Treatment or Punishment (1984); International Convention on the Rights of the Child (1989).

6   Rebecca J Cook and Valerie L Oosterveld record that in 1995 the bibliography on the international right to non-discrimination on the basis of sex has now expanded to include over 400 entries: *A Select Bibliography of Women's Human Rights*.

women's rights, international law and practice has to date fallen far short of achieving adequate protection of all women's rights.

In the articles which follow, Hilary Charlesworth, Shelley Wright and Christine Chinkin examine the gendered nature of international law structures and question the application of international law norms – dominated by Western liberal perceptions and concepts – to Third World countries. It is the authors' submission that Western feminism, with its insistence on the extension of legal rights to ensure gender equality, misunderstands the feminist concerns of the Third World. The historical legacy of colonialism and post-colonialist nationalist raise special concerns. Western feminism needs, from this analysis, to expand its horizons and understandings to incorporate the women of the Third World. The internationally recognised rights to 'development' and 'self-determination' are examined by the authors and their potential for improving the status of women considered. Also analysed is the manner in which 'public/private' characterisations[7] exclude women from the protection of international law which focuses on groups of peoples in a gender-neutral manner.

The second extract is from the United Nations' Report, *The World's Women 1995: Trends and Statistics*. The Report highlights the need for women employees at the upper levels of the United Nations' organisations. The underrepresentation of women identified by the United Nations itself, is also considered by Charlesworth, Wright and Chinkin in their article.

Gender-based violence against women forms the focus of the next extract from the United Nations' Report. The Report catalogues domestic violence, rape and the sexual abuse of children throughout the world, together with forced prostitution and trafficking in women, the violence perpetrated against migrant domestic workers and the sexual abuse and rape of women during armed conflict.

It is violence against women on an international scale – its manifestations and settings – which forms the subject of Jane Connor's first article in this chapter. Jane Connors analyses the strategies which have been adopted by international law agencies to eliminate the multiple aspects of gender-based violence, and evaluates their successes and weaknesses. The 'public/private' split is also considered, and the pressing need for a deconstruction of the concepts discussed. The author concludes with an identification of the critical areas for action to further eradicate gender-based violence against women.

In Geraldine Van Bueren's extract, the role of international law in the protection of the rights of family members towards the close of the twentieth century are evaluated. The author analyses the potential for further protection against domestic violence by bringing it within the international law concepts of 'torture or cruel, inhuman or degrading treatment'. The author also analyses the problems posed in the elimination of cruel cultural practices against children such as female circumcision. The author analyses the traditional categorisations of rights under international law into civil and political on the one hand, and

7   Considered in Chapter 5.

economic, social and cultural rights on the other hand. It is her submission that whilst international law is experienced and well fitted for the protection of the former, there has been a traditional and well-documented unwillingness to extend the protection of law to economic, social and cultural rights – the very rights which have most relevance for women and children around the globe.

In *Women, Feminism and International Human Rights Law – Methodological Myopia, Fundamental Flaws or Meaningful Marginalisation?* Andrew Byrnes subjects the 'mainstream' of international human rights law to critical analysis from a feminist perspective. The author argues that the application of feminist legal methods to international law would bring about a greater awareness of and sensitivity to the issue of gender. International law, he argues, has traditionally failed to recognise the particular risks which women face. The failure to recognise the importance of gender, the reliance on the 'public/private' dichotomy and the implications of so doing are analysed. The author also examines the emergent and potentially fundamentally important concept of State responsibility for the acts of private individuals and its potential for women victims of private violence.

The final article by Jane Connors analyses recent developments in international law and its agencies in bringing the question of gender into the mainstream of international law. The language of human rights, she argues, has a particular moral authority, but the recognition of women's international human rights have been too long ignored. Nevertheless, as the author documents, there have been significant developments in 'mainstreaming' women's human rights. There remain many challenges for the future: the gender imbalance within the United Nations and its organisations; the difficulties in conceptualisation of rights into civil and political and economic and social and the need to broaden and modify the existing framework of international law agencies to fully recognise the special problems faced by women throughout the world.

FEMINIST APPROACHES TO INTERNATIONAL LAW[8]
Hilary Charlesworth, Christine Chinkin and Shelley Wright[9]

The authors commence the article with an overview of feminist jurisprudence, including a discussion of the 'sameness/difference' debate, considered in Chapter 6. Attention is then turned to the manner in which women's 'different voice' is apparently mirrored in the Third World. The differing historical and political backgrounds between First and Third World countries is also examined to reveal differing concerns of woman in differing societies but also the unifying situation of all women.

Feminist and Third World Challenges to International Law

Are women's voices and values already present in international law through the medium of the Third World? The divisions between developed and developing

8   (1991) 85 *American Journal of International Law* 613. The article has been abridged and footnotes edited.
9   At the time of writing, respectively, Senior Lecturer, University of Melbourne Law School; Senior Lecturer, University of Sydney Law School; and Lecturer, University of Sydney Law School.

nations (and between socialist and non-socialist states) have generated a lively debate over the universality of principles of international law. One consequence of decolonisation has been the great increase in the number of independent States, particularly in Africa and Asia. These States have challenged both substantive norms of international law and the traditional law-making processes as either disadvantageous to them or inadequate to their needs. The impact of this challenge to assumptions about the objective neutrality of norms by showing them to support Western values and interests has been substantial. Developing States have also emphasised decision-making through negotiation and consensus, and through the use of non-traditional methods of law-making such as the 'soft law' of General Assembly resolutions.[10] These techniques find some parallel in the types of dispute resolution sometimes associated with the 'different voice' of women. In his study of American diplomacy in the first half of this century, George Kennan implied that non-Western views of international relations and the feminine were linked:

> If ... instead of making ourselves slaves of the concepts of international law and morality, we would confine these concepts to the unobtrusive, almost feminine function of the gentle civiliser of national self-interest in which they find their true value – if we were able to do these things in our dealings with the peoples of the East, then, I think, posterity might look back upon our efforts with fewer and less troubled questions.[11]

This apparent similarity between the perspective culturally identified with women and that of developing nations has been studied in a different context. In *The Science Question in Feminism* Sandra Harding notes the 'curious coincidence of African and feminine "world views"' and examines them to determine whether they could be the basis of a 'successor', alternative view of science and epistemology.[12] Harding observes the association of the feminine with the second half of the set of conceptual dichotomies that provide the essential framework for traditional, enlightenment science and epistomology: 'Reason vs emotion and social value, mind vs body, culture vs nature, self vs others, objectivity vs subjectivity, knowing vs being'.[13] In the generation of scientific truth, the 'feminine' parts of these dichotomies are considered subordinate. Harding then notes the similarity of this pattern and the description of the 'African world view' identified by scholars in other disciplines. This world view is characterised by a 'conception of the self as intrinsically connected with, as part of, both the community and nature'.[14] The attribution to women and Africans of 'a concept of the self as dependent on others, as defined through relationships to others, as perceiving self-interest to lie in the welfare of the relational complex' permits the ascription to these groups of an ethic based on preservation of relationships and an epistomology uniting 'hand, brain and

---

10 See Chinkin, 'The Challenge of Soft Law: Development and Change in International Law' (1989) 38 *ICLQ* 850; Bedjaoue, 'Poverty of the International Legal Order', in *International Law: A Contemporary Perspective* pp 152, 157–58 (R Falk, F Kratochjwil and S Mendlovitz (eds) 1985).

11 G Kennan, *American Diplomacy 1900–1950*, pp 53–54 (1953); cf Jackquette, 'Power as Ideology: A Feminist Analysis', in J Stiehm (ed), *Women's Views of the Political World of Men* (1984), pp 9, 22.

12 S Harding, *The Science Question in Feminism* (1986), pp 173–74.

13 *Ibid*, p 170.

14 *Ibid*, pp 172–73; see also C MacKinnon, *Feminism Unmodified* (Harvard University Press, 1987), pp 39–40.

heart'. These perceptions contrast with the 'European' and male view of the self as autonomous, separate from nature and from others, and with its associated ethics of 'rule-governed adjudication of competing rights between self-interested, autonomous others' and its view of knowledge as an entity with a separate, 'objective' existence.[15]

There are problems in identifying these subordinate voices. For example: How far are these world views the product of colonial and patriarchal conceptual schemes? Are they in fact generally held by the groups they are ascribed to? How accurate are contrasting schemata in capturing reality? Harding argues that the linkage of the two discourse may nevertheless be useful as providing 'categories of challenge' – that is, naming 'what is absent in the thinking and social activities of men and Europeans' and stimulating analysis of how social orders based on gender and race can come into being.

More general analogies have been drawn between the position of Third World States and that of women. Both groups are said to encounter the paternalist attitude that they must be properly trained to fit into the world of developed countries and men, respectively.[16] Both feminists and developing nations have also resisted assimilation to prevailing standards and have argued for radical change, emphasising co-operation rather than individual self-advancement.[17] Both groups have identified unilinear structures that allow their systematic domination and the development of apparently generally applicable theories from very narrow perspectives.

Thus far, however, the 'different voice' of developing nations in international law has shown little concern for feminist perspectives. The power structures and decision-making processes in these societies are every bit as exclusive of women as in Western societies and the rhetoric of domination and subjugation has not encompassed women, who remain the poorest and least privileged.[18] Thus, at the United Nations Mid-Decade for Women Conference in Copenhagen in 1985, an Indian delegate could argue that since he had experienced colonialism, he knew that it could not be equated with sexism.[19] Although the developing nations' challenge to international law has been fundamental, it has focused on disparities in economic position and has not questioned the silence of half the world's population in the creation of international law or the unequal impact of rules of international law and many of its assumptions may have had an adverse effect on the development of a gender-based analysis of international law precisely because of the further level of confrontation it is assumed such an analysis would cause.

Feminism in the First and Third Worlds

An alternative, feminist analysis of international law must take account of the differing perspectives of First and Third World feminists. Third World feminists operate in particularly difficult contexts. Not only does the dominant European male discourse of law, politics and science exclude the kind of discourse characterised by the phrase 'a different voice', both female and non-European,

---

15 *Ibid*, p 171.

16 Brock Utne, 'Women and Third World Countries: What Do We Have in Common?' (1989) 12 *Women's Stud International F*, pp 495, 496–97.

17 *Ibid*, p 497.

18 K Jayawardena, *Feminism and Nationalism in the Third World* (1986); C Enloe, *Making Feminist Sense of International Politics: Bananas, Beaches and Bases* (1989), pp 42–64.

19 Quoted in C Bunch, *Passionate Politics* (1987), p 297.

but also feminist concerns in the Third World are largely ignored or misunderstood by Western feminists. Western feminism began as a demand for the right of women to be treated as men. Whether in campaigns for equal rights or for special rights such as the right to abortion, Western feminists have sought guarantees from the State that, as far as is physically possible, they will be placed in the same position as men. This quest does not always have the same attraction for non-Western women. For example, the Western feminist preoccupation with a woman's right to abortion is of less significance to many Third World women because population-control programmes often deny them the chance to have children. Moreover, 'non-positivist' cultures, such as those of Asia and Africa, are just as masculinist, or even more so, than the Western cultures in which the language of law and science developed. In the context of international law (and, indeed, domestic law), then, Third World feminists are obliged to communicate in the Western rationalist language of the law, in addition to challenging the intensely patriarchal 'different voice' discourse of traditional non-European societies. In this sense feminism in the Third World is doubly at odds with the dominant male discourse of its societies.

The legacy of colonial rule has been particularly problematic for many women in the Third World. Local women were seen as constituting a pool of cheap labour for industries, agriculture and domestic service, and local men were often recruited to work away from their families. Local women also provided sex to the colonisers, especially where there was a shortage of women from home. To local men, the position of their women was symbolic of and mirrored their own domination: while colonialism meant allowing the colonial power to abuse colonised women, resistance to colonialism encompassed reasserting the colonised males' power over their women.

Nationalist movements typically pursued wider objectives than merely to transfer power from white colonial rules to indigenous people: they were concerned with restructuring the hierarchies of power and control, reallocating wealth within society, and creating nothing less than a new society based on equality and non-exploitation. It was inevitable that feminist objectives, including the restructuring of society across gender lines, would cause tension when set beside nationalist objectives that sounded similar but so frequently discounted the feminist perspective.

Nevertheless, local women were needed in the fight against colonialism, which imposed numerous restrictions on them. The Sri Lankan feminist Kumari Jaywardena has shown that for many nationalists the objective of overthrowing colonial rule required both the creation of a national identity around which people could rally and the institution of internal reforms designed to present themselves as Western and 'civilised', and therefore worthy of self-rule. Thus, both the colonisers and the local men demanded that local women be modelled on Western women. On the one hand, 'ladylike' (Western) behaviour was regarded as a 'mainstay of imperialist behaviour', as 'feminine respectability' taught the colonised and colonists alike that 'foreign conquest was right and necessary'. On the other hand, many local males believed that 'women needed to be adequately Westernised and educated in order to enhance the modern and 'civilised' image of their country'. Of course, the model handed down by Western civilisation embraced all the restrictions imposed on Western women.

The need to rally around a national identity, however, required that local women, even while being groomed on the Western model, also take it upon themselves to be 'the guardians of national culture, indigenous religion and family traditions'. These institutions in many instances repressed women. Halliday points out that, despite the belief that the spread of nationalism and nationalist ideas is beneficial to women, 'nationalist movements subordinate women in a particular definition of their role and place in society, [and] enforce conformity to values that are often male-defined'.[20] Women could find themselves dominated by foreign rule, economic exploitation and aggression, as well as by local entrenched patriarchies, religious structures and traditional rulers.

These conflicting historical perspectives highlight a significant problem for many feminists in the developing world.[21] Feminist and women's movements have been active in numerous developing countries[22] since at least the late 19th and early 20th centuries, but too often women in nationalist movements have had to choose between pressing their own concerns and seeing those concerns crushed by the weight of the overall struggle against colonial rule.[23] Feminists in non-Western countries and, before independence, in the nationalist movements, were open to attack from their own people for accepting decadent Western capitalism, embracing the neo-colonialism of a foreign culture, and turning away from their own culture, ideology and religion. The explicit or implicit addition was that their acceptance of Western feminist values was diverting them from the revolutionary struggle against the colonial power. In other contexts, the emancipation of women has been regarded as a communist tactic to be resisted by resort to traditional values. Problems of loyalty and priorities arise in this context that do not exist for Western feminists. Many Third World feminist movements either were begun in co-operation with nationalistic, anti-colonial movements or operate in solidarity with the process of nation building. Overt political repression is a further problem for feminism in the Third World. In non-Western cultures there may be a much greater fear and hatred of the feminine, especially when it is not strictly confined to the domestic sphere, than is apparent or expressed in Western society.

Despite differences in history and culture, feminists from all worlds share a central concern: their domination by men. Birgit Brock-Utne writes:

> Though patriarchy is hierarchical and men of different classes, races or ethnic groups have different places in the patriarchy, they are united in their shared relationship of dominance over their women. And, despite their unequal resources, they are dependent on each other to maintain that domination.[24]

Issues raised by Third World feminists, however, require a re-orientation of feminism to deal with the problems of the most oppressed women, rather than those of the most privileged. Nevertheless, the constant theme in both Western and Third World feminism is the challenge to structures that permit male domination, although the form of the challenge and the male structures may differ from society to society. An international feminist perspective on international law will have as its goal the rethinking and revision of those structures and principles which exclude most women's voices ...[25]

---

20 Halliday, *Hidden from International Relations: Women and the International Arena* (1988) 17 Millenium 419, 424.

21 See C Chinkin, 'A Gendered Perspective to the International Use of Force' (1992) 12 *Australian Yearbook International* 1.

22 K Jayawardena, *op cit*; *cf* J Chafetz and A Dworkin, *Female Revolt: Women's Movements in the World and Historical Perspective* (1986), esp Chapter 4.

23 See R Morgan, *Going Too Far: The Personal Chronicle of a Feminist* (1977).

24 Brock-Utne, *op cit*, p 500.

25 *Feminist Approaches to International Law*, pp 616–21.

In the second part of the article the authors argue that in terms of the 'organisational and normative structures of international law', the 'international order is virtually impervious to the voices of women'. The authors conclude that in terms of decision-making, women have yet to exert an influence in international organisations:

> Women are excluded from all major decision-making by international institutions on global policies and guidelines, despite the often disparate impact of those decisions on women. Since 1985, there has been some improvement in the representation of women in the United Nations and its specialised agencies. It has been estimated, however, that 'at the present rate of change it will take almost four more decades (until 2021) to reach equality (ie 50% of professional jobs held by women)'. This situation was recently described as 'grotesque'.[26]

This critique is confirmed by the United Nations 1995 report, *The World's Women*, which records that:

> Women have always constituted a minority of United Nations professional staff. Many women joined the United Nations after the Second World War. Later, when the organisation expanded in the 1950s, mostly men were appointed, diminishing the proportion of women in professional positions. Not until the mid-1980s would the proportion of women again reach that of the earliest years ... Women have always been better represented at entry-level than at higher levels. Although the 1980s saw more women in entry and mid-level positions, women are still well below 20% at senior levels ... Beginning in 1985 the General Assembly set goals for increased women's representation. The first goal, to have 30% women in the Secretariat by 1990, was met in 1991. The current goal is 35% by 1995, with 25% at the higher management levels. At the end of 1993, the number of women in senior management had reached only 13% ... The first woman at the highest level of the United Nations below the Secretary-General was Helvi Sipila, appointed Assistant Secretary-General for Social Development and Humanitarian Affairs in 1972. From 1972 to 1979 there was always one woman serving at this level but never more than one for more than a few months. From 1979 to 1982 the number of women in the top echelon fluctuated between one and three, and from 1986 to 1991, between three and five. It rose to 12 in 1993–94.[27]

Charlesworth, Chinkin and Wright consider the significance of this under-representation of women in the United Nations:

> Why is it significant that all the major institutions of the international legal order are peopled by men? Long-term domination of all bodies wielding political power nationally and internationally means that issues traditionally of concern to men become seen as general human concerns, while 'women's concerns' are relegated to a special limited category. Because men generally are not the victims of sex discrimination, domestic violence, and sexual degradation and violence, for example, these matters can be consigned to a separate sphere and tend to be ignored. The orthodox face of international law and politics, would change dramatically if their institutions were truly human in composition: their horizons would widen to include issues previously regarded as domestic – in two senses of the word. Balanced representation in international organisations of nations of

26 *Ibid*, p 623.
27 United Nations Report, *The World's Women* 1995 (London: HMSO, 1995), p 154.

differing economic structures and power has been a prominent theme in the United Nations since the era of decolonisation in the 1960s. The importance of accommodating interests of developed, developing and socialist nations and of various regional and ideological groups is recognised in all aspects of the UN structure and work. This sensitivity should be extended much further to include the gender of chosen representatives.[28]

The Normative Structure of International Law

In this part of the article, the authors analyse the structure of international law, revealing that the traditional – male – conceptions of the 'public' and 'private' spheres of life which have so bedevilled the quest for true equality, have permeated the international order, the consequences of which are to delimit international law's concern with the plight of women. The authors then turn to analyse the potential for a feminist approach to international law.

Towards a Feminist Analysis of International Law

How can feminist accounts of law be applied in international law? Feminist legal theory can promote a variety of activities. The term signifies an interest (gender as an issue of primary importance); a focus of attention (women as individuals and as members of groups); a political agenda (real, social, political, economic and cultural equality regardless of gender); a critical stance (an analysis of 'masculinism' and male hierarchical power or 'patriarchy'); a means of reinterpreting and reformulating substantive law so that it more adequately reflects the experiences of all people; and an alternative method of practising, talking about and learning the law.[29] Feminist method must be concerned with examining the fundamentals of the legal persuasion: the language it uses; the organisation of legal materials in predetermined, watertight categories; the acceptance of abstract concepts as somehow valid or 'pure'; the reliance in practice on confrontational, adversarial techniques; and the commitment to male, hierarchical structures in all legal and political organisations.

Christine Littleton has said, 'Feminist method starts with the very radical act of taking women seriously, believing that what we say about ourselves and our experience is important and valid, even when (or perhaps especially when) it has little or no relationship to what has been or is being said about us'.[30] No single approach can deal with the complexity of international legal organisations, processes and rules, or with the diversity of women's experiences within and outside those structures. In this section we look at two interconnected themes developed in feminist accounts of the law that suggest new ways of analysing international law.

Critique of Rights

The feminist critique of rights questions whether the acquisition of legal rights advances women's equality.[31] Feminist scholars have argued that, although the

---

28 *Feminist Approaches to International Law*, p 625.

29 H Wishik, 'To Question Everything: The Enquiries of Feminist Jurisprudence' (1985) 1 *Berkeley Women's Law Journal* 64.

30 C Littleton, 'Feminist Jurisprudence: The Difference Method Makes' (1989) 41 *Stanford Law Review* pp 751, 764.

31 Some members of the critical legal studies movement have engaged in a parallel, but distinct, critique of rights See eg, Tushnet, 'An Essay on Rights' (1984) 62 *Texas Law Review* 1363; Hyde, 'The Concept of Legitimisation in the Sociology of Law' (1983) *Wisconsin Law Review* 379.

search for formal legal equality through the formulation of rights may have been politically appropriate in the early stages of the feminist movement, continuing to focus on the acquisition of rights may not be beneficial to women. Quite apart from problems such as the form in which rights are drafted, their interpretation by tribunals, and women's access to their enforcement, the rhetoric of rights, according to some feminist legal scholars, is exhausted.[32]

Rights discourse is taxed with reducing intricate power relations in a simplistic way. The formal acquisition of a right, such as the right to equal treatment, is often assumed to have solved an imbalance of power. In practice, however, the promise of rights is thwarted by the inequalities of power: the economic and social dependence of women on men may discourage the invocation of legal rights that are premised on an adversarial relationship between the rights holder and the infringer. More complex still are rights designed to apply to women only such as the rights to reproductive freedom and to choose abortion.[33]

In addition, although they respond to general societal imbalances, formulations of rights are generally cast in individual terms. The invocation of rights to sexual equality may therefore solve an occasional case of inequality for individual women but will leave the position of women generally unchanged. Moreover, international law accords priority to civil and political rights, rights that may have very little to offer women generally.[34] The major forms of oppression of women operate within the economic, social and cultural realms. Economic, social and cultural rights are traditionally regarded as a lesser form of international right and as much more difficult to implement.[35]

A second major criticism of the assumption that the granting of rights inevitably spells progress for women is that it ignores competing rights: the right of women and children not to be subjected to violence in the home may be balanced against the property rights of men in the home or their right to family life. Furthermore, certain rights may be appropriated by more powerful groups: Carol Smart relates that provisions in the European Convention on Human Rights on family life were used by fathers to assert their authority over ex nuptial children.[36] One solution may be to design rights to apply only to particular groups. However, apart from the serious political difficulties this tactic would raise, the formulation of rights that apply only to women, as we have seen in the international sphere, may result in marginalising these rights.

A third feminist concern about the 'rights' approach to achieve equality is that some rights can operate to the detriment of women. The right to freedom of religion, for example, can have differing impacts on women and men.[37] Freedom to exercise all aspects of religious belief does not always benefit women because many accepted religious practices entail reduced social positions and status for women. Yet attempts to set priorities and to discuss the issue have been met with

---

32 See C Smart, *Feminism and the Power of Law*, p 145; N Lacey, 'Legislation Against Sex Discrimination: Questions from a Feminist Perspective' (1987) 14 *Journal of Law and Society* 419.

33 For a discussion of the feminist ambivalence toward gendered laws such as statutory rape laws, see F Olsen, 'Statutory Rape: A Feminist Critique of Rights Analysis' (1984) 63 *Texas Law Review* 387.

34 European Convention on Human Rights and Fundamental Freedoms, Article 8.

35 See eg R Cranston, 'Are There Any Human Rights?', *Daedalus*, No 4, 1983, pp 1, 12.

36 C Smart, *Feminism and the Power of Law*, p 145.

37 Eg, International Covenant on Civil and Political Rights, Article 18.

hostility and blocking techniques. Thus, at its 1987 meeting the CEDAW[38] Committee adopted a decision requesting that the United Nations and the specialised agencies:

> promote or undertake studies on the status of women under Islamic laws and customs and in particular on the status and equality of women in the family on issues such as marriage, divorce, custody and property rights and their participation in public life of the society, taking into consideration the principle of El Ijtihad in Islam.[39]

The representatives of Islamic nations criticised this decision in ECOSOC and in the Third Committee of the General Assembly as a threat to their freedom of religion.[40] The CEDAW Committee's recommendation was ultimately rejected. The General Assembly passed a resolution in which it decided that 'no action shall be taken on decisions adopted by the Committee and request[ed that] the Committee ... review that decision, taking into account the views expressed by delegations at the first regular session of the Economic and Social Council of 1987 and in the Third Committee of the General Assembly'.[41] CEDAW later justified its action by stating that the study was necessary for it to carry out its duties under the Women's Convention and that no disrespect was intended to Islam.

Another example of internationally recognised rights that might affect women and men differently are those relating to the protection of the family. The major human rights instruments all have provisions applicable to the family. Thus, the Universal Declaration proclaims that the family is the 'natural and fundamental group unit of society and is entitled to protection by society and the State'.[42] These provisions ignore that to many women the family is a unit for abuse and violence; hence, protection of the family also preserves the power structure within the family, which can lead to subjugation and dominance by men over women and children.

The development of rights may be particularly problematic for women in the Third World, where women's rights to equality with men and traditional values may clash. An example of the ambivalence of Third World states toward women's concerns is the Banjul Charter, the human rights instrument of the organisation of African Unity.[43]

The Charter, unlike 'Western' instruments preoccupied with the rights of individuals, emphasises the need to recognise communities and peoples as

---

38 Convention on the Elimination of all forms of Discrimination Against Women.

39 UN Doc E/1987/SR 11 at 13, quoted in A Byrnes, Report on the Seventh Session of the Committee on the Elimination of Discrimination Against Women and the Fourth Meeting of States Parties to the Convention on the Elimination of All Forms of Discrimination Against Women (February-March 1988) at 13 *International Women's Rights Action Watch* 1988; *cf* An-Na'im, 'Rights of Women and International Law in the Muslim Context' (1987) 9 *Whittier Law Review* 491.

40 A Brynes, 13 International Women's Rights Action Watch 1988, p 6.

41 A Byrnes *supra*, pp 6–7.

42 Universal Declaration of Human Rights, GA Res 217A (III) Article 16(3) UN Doc A/810, at 71 (1948). *Cf* International Covenant on Economic, Social and Cultural Rights, 16 December, 1966, Article 10(1) 993 UNTS 3; International Covenant on Civil and Political Rights, Article 23.

43 African Charter on Human and Peoples' Rights, adopted 27 June 1981. OAU Doc CAB/LEG/67/3/Rev.5, reprinted in 21 *ILM* 59 (1982) (hereinafter 'Banjul Charter'). See Wright, 'Economic Rights and Social Justice: A Feminist Analysis of Some International Human Rights Conventions' (1992) 12 *Australian Yearbook International L.*

entities entitled to rights, and it provides that people within the group owe duties and obligations to the group. 'Peoples'' rights in the Banjul Charter include the right to self-determination, the right to exploit natural resources and wealth, the right to development, the right to international peace and security, and the right to a generally satisfactory environment.[44]

The creation of communal or 'peoples'' rights, however, does not take into account the often severe limitations on the rights of women within these groups, communities or 'peoples'. The Preamble to the Charter makes specific reference to the elimination of 'all forms of discrimination, particularly those based on race, ethnic group, colour, sex, language, religion or political opinion'. Article 2 enshrines the enjoyment of all rights contained within the Charter without discrimination of any kind. But after Article 2, the Charter refers exclusively to 'his' rights, the 'rights of man'. Articles 3–17 set out basic political, civil, economic and social rights similar to those contained in other instruments, in particular the International Covenants, the Universal Declaration of Human Rights (which is cited in the Preamble) and European instruments. Article 15 is significant in that it guarantees that the right to work includes the right to 'receive equal pay for equal work'. This right might be useful to women who are employed in jobs that men also do. The difficulty is that most African women, like women elsewhere, generally do not perform the same jobs as men.

Articles 17 and 18 and the list of duties contained in Articles 27–29 present obstacles to African women's enjoyment of rights set out elsewhere in the Charter. Article 17(3) states that '[t]he promotion and protection of morals and traditional values recognised by the community shall be the duty of the State'. Article 18 entrusts the family with custody of those morals and values, describing it as 'the natural unit and basis of society'. The same article requires that discrimination against women be eliminated, but the conjunction of the notion of equality with the protection of the family and 'traditional' values poses serious problems. It has been noted in relation to Zimbabwe and Mozambique that:

> [t]he official political rhetoric relating to women in these southern African societies may be rooted in a model derived from Engels, via the Soviet Union, but the actual situation they face today bears little resemblance to that of the USSR. In Zimbabwe particularly, policy-makers are caught between several ideological and material contradictions, which are especially pertinent to women-oriented policies. The dominant ideology has been shaped by two belief-systems, opposed in their conceptions of women. Marxism vies with a model deriving from precolonial society, in which women's capacity to reproduce the lineage, socially, economically and biologically, was crucial and in which lineage males controlled women's labour power.[45]

This contradiction between the emancipation of women and adherence to traditional values lies at the heart of and complicates discussion about human rights in relation to many Third World women. The rhetoric of human rights, on both the national and the international levels, regards as equal citizens, as 'individuals' subject to the same level of treatment and the same protection as

---

44 Banjul Charter *supra* Articles 20, 21, 22, 23, 24.

45 Jacobs and Tracy, 'Women in Zimbabwe: Stated Policies and State Action', in *Women, State Ideology: Studies From Africa and Asia* (11 Afshar ed 1988) pp 28, 29, 30.

men. But the discourse of 'traditional values' may prevent women from enjoying any human rights, however they may be described.[46]

Despite all these problems, the assertion of rights can exude great symbolic force for oppressed groups within a society and it constitutes an organising principle in the struggle against inequality. Patricia Williams has pointed out that for blacks in the United States, 'the prospect of attaining full rights under the law has always been a fiercely motivational, almost religious, source of hope'.[47] She writes:

> 'Rights' feels so new in the mouths of most black people. It is still so deliciously empowering to say. It is a sign for and a gift of self-hood that is very hard to contemplate restructuring ... at this point in history. It is the magic wand of visibility and invisibility, of inclusion and exclusion, of power and no power ...[48]

The discourse of rights may have greater significance at the international level than in many national systems. It provides an accepted means to challenge the traditional legal order and to develop alternative principles. While the acquisition of rights must not be identified with automatic and immediate advances for women, and the limitations of the rights model must be recognised, the notion of women's rights remains a source of potential power for women in international law. The challenge is to rethink that notion so that rights correspond to women's experiences and needs.

The Public/Private Distinction

The gender implications of the public/private distinction were outlined above. Here we show how the dichotomy between public and private worlds has undermined the operation of international law, giving two examples.

The Right to Development[49]

The right to development was formulated in legal terms only recently and its status in international law is still controversial. Its proponents present it as a collective or solidarity right that responds to the phenomenon of global interdependence, while its critics argue that it is an aspiration rather than a right.[50] The 1986 United Nations Declaration on the Right to Development describes the content of the right as the entitlement 'to participate in, contribute to, and enjoy economic, social, cultural and political development, in which all human rights and fundamental freedom can be fully realised'. Primary responsibility for the creation of conditions favourable to the right is placed on states:

> states have the right and the duty to formulate appropriate national development policies that aim at the constant improvement of the well-being of the entire population and of all individuals, on the basis of their active, free

---

46   See Amos and Parnar, 'Challenging Imperial Feminist' (1984) 17 *Feminist Rev* 3, 15.

47   Williams, 'Alchemical Notes: Reconstructing Ideals from Deconstructed Rights' (1987) 22 *Harvard CR-CL L Rev* 401, 417.

48   *Ibid* at 431. See also Schneider, 'The Dialectic of Rights and Politics: Perspectives From the Women's Movement' (1986) 61 *NYU Law Review* 589. Compare Hardwig, 'Should Women Think in Terms of Rights?' (1984) 94 *Ethics* 441.

49   For a fuller discussion see H Charlesworth, 'The Public/Private Distinction and the Right to Development in International Law' (1922) 12 *Australian Yearbook of International Law*.

50   Eg I Brownlie, 'The Rights of Peoples in Modern International Law', in J Crawford (ed), *The Rights of Peoples* (1988).

and meaningful participation in development and in the fair distribution of the benefits resulting therefrom.[51]

The right is apparently designed to apply to all individuals within a State and is assumed to benefit women and men equally: the Preamble to the Declaration twice refers to the Charter exhortation to promote and encourage respect for human rights for all without distinction of any kind such as of race or sex. Moreover, Article 8 of the Declaration obliges states to ensure equality of opportunity for all regarding access to basic resources and fair distribution of income. It provides that 'effective measures should be undertaken to ensure that women have an active role in the development process'.

Other provisions of the Declaration, however, indicate that discrimination against women is not seen as a major obstacle to development or to the fair distribution of its benefits. For example, one aspect of the right to development is the obligation of states to take 'resolute steps' to eliminate 'massive and flagrant violations of the human rights of peoples and human beings'. The examples given of such violations include apartheid and racial discrimination but not sex discrimination.[52]

Three theories about the causes of underdevelopment dominate its analysis: shortages of capital, technology, skilled labour and entrepreneurship; exploitation of the wealth of developing nations by richer nations; and economic dependence of developing nations on developed nations.[53] The subordination of women to men does not enter this traditional calculus. Moreover, 'development' as economic growth above all takes no notice of the lack of benefits or disadvantageous effects this growth may have on half of the society it purports to benefit.

One aspect of the international right to development is the provision of development assistance and aid. The UN General Assembly has called for international and national efforts to be aimed at eliminating 'economic deprivation, hunger and disease in all parts of the world without discrimination' and for international co-operation to be aimed, *inter alia*, at maintaining 'stable and sustained economic growth' increasing concessional assistance to developing countries, building world food security and resolving the debt burden.[54]

Women and children are more often the victims of poverty and malnutrition that men.[55] Women should therefore have much to gain from an international right to development. Yet the position of many women in developing countries has deteriorated over the last two decades: their access to economic resources has been reduced, their health and educational status has declined, and their work burdens have increased.[56] The generality and apparent universal applicability of

---

51 GA Res 41/128, Article 2(3) (4 December 1986).

52 *Ibid*, Article 5.

53 Thomas and Skeat, 'Gender in Third World Development Studies: An Overview of An Underview' (1990) 28 *Australian Geographical Stud* 5, 11; see also J Hanshall Momsen and J Townsend, *Geography of Gender in the Third World* 16 (1987).

54 GA Res, 41/133 (4 December 1986).

55 See M Waring, *Counting for Nothing* (1988).

56 See United Nations, *World Survey on the Role of Women in Development* 19–20 (1986); J Henshall and J Townsend, *op cit*; *Nairobi Review, Review and Appraisal of the Implementation of the Nairobi Forward-Looking Strategies for the Advancement of Women*, UN Doc e/CN.6/1990/5.

the right to development, as formulated in the UN Declaration, is undermined by the fundamentally androcentric nature of the international economic system and its reinforcement of the public/private distinction. Of course, the problematic nature of current development practice for Third World women cannot be attributed simply to the international legal formulation of the right to development. But the rhetoric of international law both reflects and reinforces a system that contributes to the subordination of women.

Over the last 20 years, considerable research has been done on women and Third World development.[57] This research has documented the crucial role of women in the economies of developing nations, particularly in agriculture. It has also pointed to the lack of impact, or the adverse impact, of 'development' on many Third World women's lives. The international legal order, like most development policies, has not take this research into account in formulating any aspect of the right to development.

The distinction between the public and private spheres operates to make the work and needs of women invisible. Economic visibility depends on working in the public sphere and unpaid work in the home or community is categorised as 'unproductive, unoccupied, and economically inactive'.[58] Marilyn Waring has recently argued that this division, which is institutionalised in developed nations, has been exported to the developing world, in part through the United Nations System of National Accounts (UNSNA).[59]

The UNSNA, developed largely by Sir Richard Stone in the 1950s, enables experts to monitor the financial position of States and trends in their national development and to compare one nation's economy with that of another. It will thus influence the categorisation of nations as developed or developing and the style and magnitude of the required international aid. The UNSNA measures the value of all goods and services that actually enter the market and of other non-market production such as government services provided free of charge. Some activities, however, are designated as outside the 'production boundary' and are not measured. Economic reality is constructed by the UNSNA's 'production boundaries' in such a way that reproduction, child care, domestic work and subsistence production are excluded from the measurement of economic productivity and growth.[60] This view of women's work as non-work was nicely summed up in 1985 in a report by the Secretary-General to the General Assembly: '*Overall socio-economic perspective of the world economy to the year 2000*'. It said: 'Women's productive and reproductive roles tend to be compatible in rural areas of low-income countries, since family agriculture and cottage industries keep women close to the home, permit flexibility in working conditions *and require low investment of the mother's time*'.[61] [Authors' emphasis.]

The assignment of the work of women and men to different spheres, and the consequent categorisation of women as 'non-producers,' are detrimental to women in developing countries in many ways and make their rights to

---

57 The first major study was E Boserup, *Woman's Role in Economic Development* (1970). See also Thomas and Skeat, *op cit*.

58 M Waring, *Counting for Nothing* (1988), p 13.

59 *Ibid*, p 27.

60 *Ibid*, pp 83, 27, 25.

61 UN Doc A/40/519, para 210, at 99 (1985).

development considerably less attainable than men's. For example, the operation of the public/private distinction in international economic measurement excludes women from many aid programmes because they are not considered to be workers or are regarded as less productive than men. If aid is provided to women, it is often to marginalise them: foreign aid may be available to women only in their role as mothers, although at least since 1967 it has been recognised that women are responsible for as much as 80% of the food production in developing countries.[62] The failure to acknowledge women's significant role in agriculture and the lack of concern about the impact of development on women mean that the potential of any right to development is jeopardised from the start.

Although the increased industrialisation of the Third World has brought greater employment opportunities for women, this seeming improvement has not increased their economic independence or social standing and has had little impact on women's equality. Women are found in the lowest-paid and lowest-status jobs, without career paths; their working conditions are often discriminatory and insecure.[63] Moreover, there is little difference in the position of women who live in developing nations with a socialist political order.[64] The dominant model of development assumes that any paid employment is better than none and fails to take into account the potential for increasing the inequality of women and lowering their economic position.

As we have seen, the international statement of the right to development draws no distinction between the economic position of men and of women. In using the neutral language of development and economics, it does not challenge the pervasive and detrimental assumption that women's work is of a different – and lesser – order than men's. It therefore cannot enhance the development of the group within developing nations that is most in need. More recent UN deliberations on development have paid greater attention to the situation of women. Their concerns, however, are presented as quite distinct, solvable by the application of special protective measures, rather than as crucial to development.

The Right to Self-Determination

The public/private dichotomy operates to reduce the effectiveness of the right to self-determination at international law. The notion of self-determination as meaning the right of 'all peoples' to 'freely determine their political status and freely pursue their economic, social and cultural development'[65] is flatly contradicted by the continued domination and marginalisation of one sector of the population of a nation-state by another. The treatment of women within groups claiming a right to self-determination should be relevant to those claims. But the international community's response to the claims to self-determination of the Afghan and Sahrawi people, for example, indicates little concern for the position of women within those groups.

The violation of the territorial integrity and political independence of Afghanistan by the Soviet Union when it invaded that country in 1979, and other strategic, economic, and geopolitical concerns, persuaded the United States of the

---

62 S Charlton, *Women in Third World Development* (1984), p 61.

63 See Molyneux, 'Women's Emancipation under Socialism: A Model for the Third World' (1982) 9 *World Dev* 1019.

64 See Thomas and Skeat *op cit*, p 11.

65 International Covenant on Civil and Political Rights, Article 1; International Covenant on Economic, Social and Cultural Rights, Article 1.

legality and morality of its support for the Afghan insurgents.[66] In deciding to support the rebels, the United States did not regard the policies of the mujahidin with respect to women as relevant.[67] The mujahidin are committed to an oppressive, rural, unambiguously patriarchal form of society quite different from that espoused by the socialist Soviet-backed regime. Indeed, Cynthia Enloe notes that '[o]ne of the policies the Soviet-backed government in Kabul pursued that so alienated male clan leaders was expanding economic and educational opportunities for Afghanistan's women'.[68] A consequence of the continued support for the insurgents was the creation of a vast refugee flow into Pakistan. Of these refugees, 30% were women and 40% were children under 13.[69] The *mullahs* imposed a strict fundamentalist regime in the refugee camps, which confined women to the premises, isolated them, and even deprived them of their traditional rural tasks. There is no indication that any different policy would be followed if the *mujahidin* were successful and able to form a government in Afghanistan. Indeed, this marginalisation and isolation of Afghan women is being projected into the future, as the educational services provided by the UN High Commissioner for Refugees are overwhelmingly for boys.[70] The vital impact of education on women and its effect in undermining male domination have been well documented.[71]

Morocco's claims to Western Sahara and the Polisario resistance to those claims have led to the establishment of Sahrawi refugee camps in Algeria that are mainly occupied by women and children. In these camps, however, women have been able to assert themselves: they have built hospitals and schools, achieved high rates of literacy, and supported 'the right of the woman and the mother' as well as the 'fight for independence'.[72] The international community, through the International Court of Justice and the General Assembly, has reiterated the right of the people of Western Sahara to self-determination.[73] Despite this legal support, the Sahrawis' only backing comes from Algeria, while Morocco is backed, *inter alia*, by France and the United States. The determination of these women to keep alive a 'democracy, based on proportional representation, with centralised and equal distribution, full employment [and] social and political parity between the sexes' in the adverse conditions of refugee camps has received little international support.

The international community recognises only the right of 'peoples' to self-determination, which in practice is most frequently linked to the notion of the independent state. Women have never been viewed as a 'people' for the purposes of the right to self-determination. In most instances, the pursuit of self-

---

66 See Reisman, 'The Resistance in Afghanistan is Engaged in a War of National Liberation' (1987) 81 *AJIUL* 906.

67 By contrast, the United States used the repression of women in Iran after the 1979 revolution as an additional justification for its hostility to the Khomaini regime.

68 C Enloe, *Making Feminist Sense of International Politics: Bananas, Beaches and Bases* (1989), P 587.

69 *New York Times*, 27 March 1988, p 16, col 1.

70 *Ibid*. The total enrolment in UN schools is 104,000 boys and 7,800 girls.

71 See eg, K Jayawardena, *op cit*, pp 17–19.

72 As demonstrated by the objectives of the Women's Union, founded in 1974. Cumming, 'Forgotten Struggle for the Western Sahara', *New Statesman*, 20 May 1988, p 14. ('Women are at the heart of the revolution; their own struggle for rights doesn't have to wait until the war is over, the two are indivisible.')

73 *Western Sahara Case*, 1975 ICJ Rep 12 (Advisory Opinion of 16 October).

determination as a political response to colonial rule has not resulted in terminating the oppression and domination of one section of society by another.

States often show complete indifference to the position of women when determining their response to claims to self-determination; the international invisibility of women persists. Thus, after the Soviet Union vetoed a Security Council resolution on the invasion of Afghanistan, the General Assembly reaffirmed 'the inalienable right of all peoples ... to choose their own form of government free from outside interference' and stated that the Afghan people should be able to 'choose their economic, political and social systems free from outside intervention, subversion, coercion or constraint of any kind whatsoever'.[74] The General Assembly's concern was with 'outside' intervention alone. Women arguably suffer more from 'internal' intervention: women are not free to choose their role in society without the constraints of masculine domination inside the State and are constantly subject to male coercion. The high-sounding ideals of non-interference do not apply to them, for their self-determination is subsumed by that of the group. The denial to women of the freedom to determine their own economic, social and cultural development should be taken into consideration by states in assessing the legitimacy of request for assistance in achieving self-determination and of claims regarding the use of force.

Conclusion

The feminist project, it has been said, has the 'twin aims of challenging the existing norms and of devising a new agenda for theory'. This paper emphasises the need for further study of traditional areas of international law from a perspective that regards gender as important. In a review of two Canadian legal textbooks on remedies, Christine Boyle points out that they simply do not address the concerns and interests of women.[75] She criticises this great silence and concludes: 'Men and Law' is tolerable as an area of intellectual activity, but not if it is masquerading as 'People and Law.'[76] International legal structures and principles masquerade as 'human' – universally applicable sets of standards. They are more accurately described as international men's law.

Modern international law is not only androcentric, but also Eurocentred in its origins, and has assimilated many assumptions about law and the place of law in society from Western legal thinking. These include essentially patriarchal legal institutions, the assumption that law is objective, gender neutral and universally applicable, and the societal division into public and private spheres, which relegates many matters of concern to women to the private area regarded as inappropriate for legal regulation. Research is needed to question the assumptions of neutrality and universal applicability of norms of international law and to expose the invisibility of women and their experiences in discussion about the law. A feminist perspective, with its concern for gender as a category of analysis and its commitment to genuine equality between the sexes, could illuminate many areas of international law; for example, State responsibility, refugee law, use of force and the humanitarian law of war, human rights, population control and international environmental law. Feminist research holds the promise of a fundamental restructuring of traditional international law

---

74 Thornton, 'Feminist Jurisprudence: Illusion or Reality?' (1986) 3 *Australian Journal of Law and Society* 5, 6–7.

75 C Boyle, 'Book Review' (1985) 63 *Can B Rev* 427.

76 *Ibid* at 430–31.

discourse and methodology to accommodate alternative world views. As Elizabeth Grosz points out, this restructuring will not amount to the replacement of one set of 'truths' with another: '[feminist theory] aims to render patriarchal systems, methods and presumptions unable to function, unable to retain their dominance and power. It aims to make clear how such a dominance has been possible; and to make it no longer viable.'[77]

The centrality of the State in international law means that many of the structures of international law reflect its patriarchal forms. Paradoxically, however, international law may be more open to feminist analysis than other areas of law. The distinction between law and politics, so central to the preservation of the neutrality and objectivity of law in the domestic sphere, does not have quite the same force in international law. So, too, the Western domestic model of legal process as ultimately coercive is not echoed in the international sphere: the process of international law is consensual and peaceful coexistence is its goal. Finally, the sustained Third World critique of international law and insistence on diversity may well have prepared the philosophical ground for feminist critiques.

A feminist transformation of international law would involve more than simply refining or reforming existing law. It could lead to the creation of international regimes that focus on structural abuse and the revision of our notions of State responsibility. It could also lead to a challenge to the centrality of the State in international law and to the traditional sources of international law.

The mechanisms for achieving some of these aims already exist. The Covenant on Economic, Social and Cultural Rights and the Women's Convention could be used as a basis for promoting structural economic and social reform to reduce some of the causes of sexual and other abuse of women. The notion of State responsibility, however, both under these Conventions and generally, will have to be expanded to incorporate responsibility for systemic abuse based on sexual discrimination (broadly defined) and imputability to the State will have to be extended to include acts committed by private individuals. An international mechanism to hear complaints of individuals or groups, such as a Protocol to the Women's Convention allowing for individual or representative petitions to the CEDAW Committee, could give women's voices a direct audience in the international community.

Is a reorientation of international law likely to have any real impact on women? Feminists have questioned the utility of attempts at legal reform in domestic law and warn against attributing too much power to law to alter basic political and economic inequalities based on sex.[78] Could this reservation be made *a fortiori* with respect to international law, whose enforcement and efficacy are in any event much more controversial? Would an altered, humanised international law have any capacity to achieve social change in a world where most forms of power continue to be controlled by men?

Like all legal systems, international law plays an important part in constructing reality. The areas it does not touch seem naturally to belong within the domestic jurisdiction of States. International law defines the boundaries of agreement by the international community on the matters that States are prepared to yield to supranational regulation and scrutiny. Its authority is derived from the claim of

---

77 E Grosz, p 197.

78 Eg, C Smart, *Feminism and the Power of Law, op cit*, pp 25, 81–82.

international acceptance. International legal concerns have a particular status; those concerns outside the ambit of international law do not seem susceptible to development and change in the same way. To redefine the traditional scope of international law so as to acknowledge the interests of women can open the way to re-imagining possibilities for change and may permit international law's promise of peaceful co-existence and respect for the dignity of all persons[79] to become a reality.[80]

INTERNATIONAL DATA ON VIOLENCE AGAINST WOMEN: THE UNITED NATIONS' REPORT: THE WORLD'S WOMEN 1995[81]

Gender-based violence against women crosses all cultural, religious and regional boundaries and is a major problem in every country in which it has been studied. It takes many forms, but studies and measurement techniques still little developed. Most data on violence against women are from small, *ad hoc* studies, but several countries have recently conducted national surveys on aspects of violence against women, particularly physical assault by an intimate partner. Data on sexual assault of women and girls are even more limited.

Domestic violence, rape and sexual abuse of children

The most pervasive form of gender-based violence against women is reported to be abuse by a husband or intimate partner. National studies in ten countries estimate that between 17% and 38% of women have been physically assaulted by an intimate partner. More limited studies in Africa, Latin America and Asia report even higher rates of physical abuse among the population studied – up to 60% or more of women. Women assaulted their partners too, but less frequently and seriously than man and usually in self-defence.[82]

Sexual assault is also common, but only a small fraction of rapes are reported to the police, making police-based crime statistics of limited use for evaluating the magnitude of the problem. In the United States more than 100,000 attempted and completed rapes of women and girls were reported to the police in 1990.[83] But a national survey found the rate was more than six times greater, even when considering only adult women and completed rapes.[84] In the Republic of Korea fewer than 2% of women rape victims ever contacted the police.[85]

In cities in six of 14 developing countries studied, sexual assault rates of 10% or more over five years were found – with the highest, 22%, in Kampala, Uganda. Rates less than 5% were found in cities of four other countries. Given their

79 UN Charter, Preamble.

80 *Feminist Approaches to International Law*, pp 634–45.

81 HMSO, 1995.

82 RP Dobash *et al*, 'The Myth of Sexual Symmetry in Marital Violence' (1992) 39 *Social Problems* 71–91; and *Violence Against Women in the Family* (United National Publication), pp 14–15.

83 United States Department of Justice, Federal Bureau of Investigation, Uniform Crime Reports (Washington DC, 1990).

84 DG Kilpatrick, CN Edmunds and AK Seymour, *Rape in America: A Report to the Nation* (Arlington VA: The National Victim Centre, 1992).

85 Young-Hee Shim, 'Sexual Violence Against Women in Korea'. Paper presented at the Conference on International Perspective: Crime, Justice and Public Order (St Petersburg, June 1992).

methodological limitations, these data can be considered only as very approximate estimates.

Most sexual crimes are committed by individuals known to the victims. Criminal justice statistics and data from rape crisis centres from six countries (Chile, Malaysia, Mexico, Panama, Peru and the United States) have been used to estimate that in more than 60% of all sexual cases the victim knows the perpetrator.[86]

The only data on forced sex that are roughly comparable across countries are from surveys among college-aged women which all used the same questionnaires. These studies report 8% to 15% of college-aged women have been raped. If attempted rapes are included, the rate of sexual assault jumps to between 20% and 27%.

Data from many countries indicate that sexual abuse is an all too common aspect of a girl's childhood. In national sample surveys in Barbados, Canada, the Netherlands, New Zealand, Norway and the United States, 27 to 34% of women interviewed reported sexual abuse during childhood or adolescence. Lower rates of abuse were reported in Great Britain (12%) and Germany (17%).

In a study of 450 school girls aged 13 and 14 in Kingston, Jamaica, 13% had experienced attempted rape, half before the age of 12. One-third had experienced unwanted physical contact and one-third had been harassed verbally. In India, close to 26% of 133 postgraduate, middle- and upper-class students reported having been sexually abused by the age of 12. From 40 to 60% of known sexual assaults have been found to be committed against girls [aged] 15 and younger, regardless of region or culture.

By far most child sexual abuse involves older men abusing young girls. In the United States 78% of substantiated child sexual abuse cases involved girls.[87] One South African study found that 92% of child victims were girls and all perpetrators but one were male – and two-thirds of them were family members.[88] In Costa Rica 94% of child sexual abuse victims are girls, and 96% of the perpetrators are male.

Gender-based violence against women and girls has been a focus of activism over the past decade. The majority of countries have more than one non-governmental organisation dedicated to the elimination of gender-based violence against women and girls. They provide services for survivors of abuse, work to change community attitudes and lobby for legal reform in North America, Europe, the Asia-Pacific region and Latin America and the Caribbean. There are fewer in Eastern Europe, Western Asia and Africa.

Activism in several countries has resulted in legal reform. In many countries, rape in marriage is now a crime. Domestic violence laws have been passed in Australia, the Bahamas, Barbados, New Zealand, Trinidad and Tobago, the United Kingdom and the United States. Generally, these acts clarify the definition of domestic violence and empower the courts to issue women 'orders

---

86   Lori Heise with Jacqueline Pitanguy and Adrienne Germain, 'Violence Against Women: The Hidden Health Burden', *World Bank Discussion Paper* No 255 (Washington DC, 1994), p 11.

87   Gail E Wyatt and GJ Powell, *Lasting Effects of Child Sexual Abuse* (California: Sage Publications, 1988).

88   Ismail E Hafejee, 'Sexual Abuse on Indian (Asian) Children in South Africa: First Report in a Community Undergoing Cultural Change, in Child Abuse and Neglect', Vol 15 (1991), pp 147–81.

of protection'. Some governments have funded services for victims and launched media campaigns against violence directed at women.

Other Violence Against Women

Forced Prostitution and Trafficking

Despite international legislation, including the 1949 Convention for the Suppression of the Traffic in Persons and of the Exploitation of the Prostitution of Others, trafficking in women for prostitution continues.

Little is known about the extent of this traffic, but several recent studies and international conferences show that countries all over the world are confronted with the problem:

The Commission on Human Rights Working Group on contemporary Forms of Slavery cites estimates of two million women in prostitution in India, roughly 400,000 of whom are under 18 years of age, and with 5,000 to 7,000 young girls from Nepal sold into brothels each year.[89]

Asia Watch and the Women's Rights Group report that at least 20,000 Burmese women and girls work in Thai brothels.[90]

A report to the 1991 Council of Europe Seminar on Action Against Traffic in women and Forced Prostitution describes the main international trafficking routes.[91]

A report by the Government of the Philippines to the International Organisation for Migration points to increases since 1982 in the numbers of Filipino women, usually between 16 and 23 years of age, migrating as entertainers. The report suggests that most of these women are the victims of traffic, being tricked into working as prostitutes or in sex-related businesses.

A 1992 report of the Netherlands Advisory Committee on Human Rights and Foreign Policy suggest traffic in thousands of women in the Netherlands alone for the purposes of prostitution.[92]

Papers presented at the 1994 Utrecht Conference on Traffic in Persons describe the growth in trafficking for sex work among Eastern European countries and from these countries to Western Europe.[93]

Victims of traffic are open to further abuses. The International Organisation for Migration reports in many cases that, once out of their countries, women are sold to brothel owners. Their documents are confiscated and to recover them, they are obliged to repay the costs of their transportation and subsistence. They are often imprisoned, and if they attempt to leave they are faced with physical assault or threats to their families. They are usually isolated and unable to speak the local

---

89 International Federation *Terre des Hommes*, as cited in United Nations, Commission on Human Right, Subcommission on Prevention of Discrimination and Protection of Minorities, Report of the Working Group on Contemporary Forms of Slavery on its Sixteenth Session (E/CN4/Sub2/1991/41), para 50.

90 *A Modern Form of Slavery: Trafficking of Burmese Women and Girls into Brothels in Thailand* (New York: Human Rights Watch, 1993), p 3.

91 Licia Brussa, 'Survey on Prostitution, Migration and Traffic in Women: History and Current Situation' (*EG/PROST* 92(2)).

92 Government of the Netherlands, Advisory Committee on Human Rights and Foreign Policy, Discussion Paper – the Traffic in Persons, Report of the Advisory Committee meeting held in the Hague, 27 April 1992.

93 Polish Feminist Association, 'Trafficking in Women – Report from Poland', and Lenke Feher, 'Forced Prostitution and Traffic in Persons' papers presented to the Conference on Traffic in Persons, Utrecht, Netherlands, November 1994.

language. Further their status as clandestine immigrants discourages them from coming forward to the authorities.[94]

Violence against migrant domestic workers

The demand for cheap domestic labour has led to the migration of women from poorer to richer countries in both developed and developing regions. The Asia and Pacific Development Centre has estimated one million to 1.7 million foreign women are currently working as domestic workers in the Asian countries studied. Some who migrate for promised jobs in domestic service, catering or entertainment find themselves tricked into prostitution. But it is not only in prostitution that women encounter maltreatment. Because these women are often illegal or undocumented immigrants and domestic work is unregulated, they are vulnerable to abuse. Migrant workers employed in domestic service often find their employers confiscate their passports and withhold their salaries, claiming outstanding debts.[95]

A recent report by Middle East Watch reports abuse, confinement and debt bondage of Asian maids working in Kuwait. It estimates that for the '12 months beginning in May 1991, 1,400 Filipino domestic servants and hundreds of Indian, Bangladeshi and Sri Lankan maids sought refuge in their home embassies. Others were picked up by the police after running away and either arrested or returned to their employers'.[96] A study of overseas domestic workers in Britain who had left their employers reported that most were not paid regularly, were subject to psychological abuse and had a work day that averaged over 17 hours with no time off. Two-thirds had their passports confiscated by their employer and one-third were physically abused.

Rape in war

Reports of mass rape of women in conflicts in the former Yugoslavia, the latest in a long history of sexual abuse of women during armed conflict, coincided with the growing consciousness of the gender basis of violence against women. The suffering of those women gained particular significance and helped focus attention on State responsibility for gender-based violence in wartime.

Quantifying wartime rape is even more difficult than quantifying sexual assault in other contexts. Estimates of the number of women raped in the former Yugoslavia vary widely. In its January 1993 report, the European Community investigative mission cited 20,000 rapes.[97] The United Nations Commission of Experts was able to identify 800 victims from Bosnia-Herzogovina by name.[98] Based on the number of pregnancies resulting from rape and a formula predicting a women's chance of becoming pregnant though one act of intercourse, a team of physicians estimated the number of rapes at 11,900.[99]

---

94 International Organisation for Migration, Trafficking in Migrants, *Quarterly Bulletin*, No 4 (Geneva, 1994).

95 Noeleen Heyser and Vivienne Wee, 'Domestic Workers in Transient Overseas Employment: Who Benefits, Who Profits', in *The Trade in Domestic Workers* (1992).

96 Middle East Watch, 'Punishing the Victim' (August 1992) cited in United Nations, Commission on Human Rights (E/CN4/1995/42), para 227–229.

97 European Community, *Report to European Community Foreign Ministers of the Investigative Mission into the Treatment of Muslim Women in the Former Yugoslavia*.

98 United Nations, *Final Report of the Commission of Experts Established Pursuant to Security Council Resolution* 780 (1992) (S/1994/674).

99 Shana Swiss and Joan Giller, 'Rape as a Crime of War: Medical Perspective', *Journal of the American Medical Association*, Vol 270, No 5, pp 612–15.

Reporting information suggesting over 254 rapes, the Human Rights Commission's Special Rapporteur on Myanmar pointed out that obtaining data on rape in armed conflict is particularly difficult because victims, if they are still alive, are ashamed, afraid or choose to obliterate the memory.[100] Further, the administrative chaos in armed conflict makes systematic collection of data almost impossible.

Sometimes evidence of sexual abuse in war emerges many years after the conflict. For example, the Japanese government recently acknowledged forcing tens of thousands of women from China, Indonesia, Korea and the Philippines into prostitution for the Imperial Army during the Second World War. These women, known as comfort women, now in their 70s, tell of being kidnapped or tricked into service.[101, 102]

VIOLENCE AGAINST WOMEN[103]

Jane Connors[104]

The Scope and Definition of Violence Against Women

(a) International definition

In December 1993, the United Nations General Assembly adopted the Declaration on the Elimination of Violence Against Women.[105] This Declaration categorises violence against women as both an issue of human rights generally and one of sex discrimination and inequality, in particular. It states, thus, that violence against women both violates and impairs or nullifies the enjoyment by women of human rights and fundamental freedoms and is a manifestation of the historically unequal power relations which have led to the domination over, and discrimination against, women by men and the prevention of their full advancement. It asserts, further, that violence against women is one of the crucial social mechanisms by which women are forced into a subordinate position to men.

Violence against women, for the purposes of the Declaration, is defined by both manifestation and site of violence. Thus, it includes physical, sexual and psychological violence or violence which results in, or is likely to result in, physical, sexual or psychological harm or suffering, whether this violence occurs in the family, the community or is perpetrated or condoned by the State.[106] The Declaration provides examples to elaborate this definition. They include battering, sexual abuse of female children in the household, female genital mutilation, marital rape, sexual abuse and sexual harassment and trafficking in women and forced prostitution. The Declaration makes clear, however, that whatever the manifestation or wherever the site of the violence, for the purposes of the instrument, violence against women goes beyond oppressive behaviour or

---

100 United Nations, Commission on Human Rights, Report on the Situation of Human Rights in Myanmar, prepared by Mr Yozo Yokota, Special Rapporteur of the Commission on Human Rights, in accordance with Commission resolution 1992/58 (E/CN4/1993/37).

101 United Nations, Commission on Human Rights (E/CN4/1995/42), para 286–92.

102 United Nations, *The World's Women 1995*, pp 158–68.

103 Background Paper, 'United Nations Fourth World Conference on Women' (1995). Previously unpublished.

104 At the time of writing, Senior Lecturer, School of Oriental and African Studies, University of London; currently Division for the Advancement of Women, United Nations, New York.

105 GA Res 48/104.

106 Articles 1 and 2.

discrimination generally and must constitute harm resulting from force or coercion.[107] Moreover, 'violence against women' is not random victimisation, but is gender-based.

The definition of violence against women elaborated in the Declaration is a distillation of many efforts to provide an appropriate definition of the issue. It is comprised of three elements: examples of various manifestations and sites or settings of female victimisation which have been identified by, in particular, women's activists and organisations; a narrow focus on violent conduct, rather than violation generally, and the element of gender, reflective of an analysis that violence, generally and certainly that against women, is gendered.

(b) Manifestations and sites of violence

Although women have been victims of violence in various forms and settings since the beginning of time, it has only been relatively recently that the scale and significance of such victimisation has been appreciated and, accordingly, that this victimisation has come to be regarded as a serious issue. It has only been relatively recently, further, that the myriad manifestations and settings of violence against women have been exposed and, to a certain extent, addressed.

Women's activists, predominantly drawn from Europe, North America and Australasia, drew attention to violence against wives in the family and rape as issues of concern related to female inequality and male control, on a sustained basis, only 30 years ago. Debates relating to women and development in the south led to the identification, frequently by grassroots women, of various manifestations of violence against women.[108]

Concentration by activists and scholars in both the north and south was initially on sexual violence by those outside the family, including sexual harassment in the workplace and elsewhere, forced prostitution and trafficking.[109] This was followed by attention to violence against women in the family, often described as domestic violence. Perhaps because violence in the family context challenges the universal image of the family as a supportive and loving haven, the natural and fundamental group unit of society[110] and because violence against women in the family represents the most fundamental example of the persistent inequality between women and men and, at the same time, serves to entrench that inequality in other spheres, violence against women in this context has remained the central focus of activism and scholarship within general issue of violence against women.

Attention to issues of sexual and domestic violence resulted in the revelation of further manifestations of violence against women. Very often these different manifestations occur within the family, but are tolerated or, indeed, condoned,

---

107 Article 1 states that 'the term "violence against women" means any act of gender-based violence'.

108 Margaret Schuler (ed), *Freedom From Violence: Women's Strategies From Around the World* (New York: UNIFEM United Nations, 1992); *Violence against Women in the Family* (New York: 1989 (Sales No E89.IV.5)).

109 Kathleen Barry, Charlotte Bunch and Shirley Castley (eds), *International Feminism: Networking Against Female Sexual Slavery* (New York: The International Women's Tribune Centre, Inc, 1984).

110 Article 16(3) of the Universal Declaration of Human Rights; Article 23(1) of the International Covenant on Civil and Political Rights; Article 18(1) of the African Charter on Human and People's Rights.

by the community and State. These include female foeticide,[111] and infanticide, the neglect, physical and sexual abuse of girl children, often by family members and marital rape. Forms of violence related to custom, culture or religion, some of which are a source of cultural pride, including the practice of sati – self-immolation – by widows;[112] female genital mutilation and other initiation practices, widowhood rites and violence related to the custom of dowry were also revealed as risks to women.

Economic, social and political developments, some postdating the adoption of the Forward-Looking Strategies,[113] led to the identification of other areas where women are at particular risk of violence. In some countries, structural adjustment policies have caused women to move from employment in the formal sector to that in the informal sector. There they are frequently subject to poor and unregulated working conditions and vulnerable to physical and sexual abuse.[114] The increasing participation of women, predominantly from the south and Eastern Europe, in international labour migration, the conditions of which are frequently unsatisfactory, has also provided a setting for physical and sexual abuse, with illegal immigrants most at risk. Poverty and lack of alternative employment has encouraged many women to turn to prostitution, both within their own countries and abroad. One of the results of HIV/AIDS has been increased sexual violence against girl children, who are not only the subject of victimisation by individuals, but also forced prostitution and national and international trafficking, as men seek younger and younger sexual partners so as to avoid infection.[115] Cheap and easy international tourism has brought with it the phenomenon of 'sex tourism' which has increased the risks of systematic and deliberate sexual exploitation and violence to women and girl children in the south.[116]

Ethnic, religious, communal and political conflicts have marked the end of the Cold War and these conflicts have proven to be the setting for much female victimisation. Female activists and often those whose campaigns concern women's issues, have been revealed as subject to physical and sexual violence, frequently by State agents, such as members of the military or the police.[117] Women who are detained have been abused, most often sexually, by prison

---

111 D D'Monte, 'Maharashtra Clamps Down on Prenatal Sex Tests', *People* (1988) 15(3) 26); A Pandya, 'Prenatal Attack on Women' (1988) *Christian Science Monitor*, 10 March p 23; V Patel, 'Sex Determination and Sex Preselection Tests: Abuse of Advanced Technologies', in (ed) Ghadially, R, *Women in Indian Society* (London: Sage, 1988), pp 178–85.

112 S Narasimhan, *Sati: A Study of Widow Burning in India* (New Delhi: Viking, 1988).

113 Nairobi Conference: Forward-Looking Strategies for the Advancement of Women (1985).

114 Middle East Watch/Women's Rights Project, 'Punishing the Victim: Rape and Mistreatment of Asian Maids in Kuwait', *Human Rights Watch*, Vol 4, Issue 8, August 1992.

115 Asia Watch/Women's Rights Project, 'A Modern Form of Slavery: Trafficking of Burmese Women and Girls into Brothels in Thailand' (New York: *Human Rights Watch*, 1993).

116 Douglas Hodgson, 'Sex Tourism and Child Prostitution in Asia: Legal Responses and Strategies' (1994) 19 *Melbourne University Law Review* 512 at 513–21.

117 Amnesty International, *Rape and Sexual Abuse: Torture and Ill-treatment of Women in Detention* (New York: Amnesty International Publications, 1991) (AI Index: ACT 77/11/91); Amnesty International, *Women in the Front Line* (New York: Amnesty International Publications, 1991) (AI Index: ACT 77/O1/91); Human Rights Watch and National Coalition for Haitian Refugees (1994). 'Rape in Haiti: A Weapon of Terror', *Human Rights Watch* Vol 6, No 8; Human Rights Watch and Women's Rights Project (1994); 'A Matter of Power: State Control of Women's Virginity in Turkey', *Human Rights Watch* Vol 6, No 7 pp 11–23.

officers, the police and the military. Women have been the victims of terrorism and specific targets for, particularly, rape and other sexual assault, during armed conflict. Clear evidence exists suggesting that sexual abuse by soldiers is widespread and that rape, sexual slavery and forced pregnancy are used systematically in some conflicts.[118] Most women who are subject to violence during wars take no active part in the conflict, but their abuse, which is very often sexual, is a deliberate tactic to intimidate or undermine the 'enemy' and often aims to inflict deep and lasting damage on entire communities. Frequently, like women in detention, women subjected to violence in conflict situations are abused because they happen to be the wives, mothers, daughters or sisters of the men the authorities cannot capture. These women become substitutes for the men in their families, with soldiers or government agents victimising them to shame their male relatives or to coerce them into surrendering. Many women who are abused during conflicts, moreover, are often from the most marginalised and vulnerable sectors of society, such as indigenous or peasant women or refugee or displaced women.

Conflicts and political and economic insecurity, as well as environmental degradation, have resulted in large refugee flows, with women forming the bulk of the refugee population. Refugee women and girls, particularly those with inadequate documentation or who are single and unaccompanied, are vulnerable to physical and sexual abuse during flight, on arrival in refugee camps and in the country of ultimate settlement.[119] Perpetrators of such violence include pirates, border guards, army and resistance units, as well as male refugees. Systematic sexual violence against women and girls, in the context of armed conflict and otherwise, as well as the sexual victimisation of individual women has also proved to be one of the major causes of internal displacement and the decision to seek asylum abroad.

In sum, thus, the focus on the issue of violence against women since the formulation of the Forward-Looking Strategies has shown that women are subjected to three main forms of violence: physical abuse, sexual abuse and psychological abuse. They are at risk of these abuses in all settings and contexts. The major site of violence against women is the family – where physical, sexual and psychological violence is a risk factor for girls and women throughout their

---

118 Although rape, as well as sexual slavery and forced pregnancy has been always been a feature of war, the conflicts in the former Yugoslavia have produced the most recent evidence women's vulnerability in conflict: see, Amnesty International (1993). 'Bosnia-Herzegovina: Rape and Sexual Abuse by Armed Forces' *AI Index* EUR 63/01/93; International Human Rights Law Group (1993). *No Justice, No Peace: Accountability for Rape and Gender-Based Violence in the Former Yugoslavia* (Washington DC: Amnesty International, 1994). Bosnia-Herzeqovina: '"You Have No Place Here": Abuses in Bosnian Serb-Controlled Areas' (*AI Index*: EUR 63/11/94, p 12); 'Rape and Abuse of Women in the Territory of Former Yugoslavia: Report of the Secretary-General' (UN Doc E/CN4/1994/5 (1993)). Evidence of sexual victimisation of women in the conflicts in the former Yugoslavia coincided with the revelation of systematic abduction of women, described as 'comfort women' who were subsequently forced into prostitution by the Japanese army during the Second World War: David E Sanger, 'Japan Admits It Ran Army Brothels During War' (1992) *New York Times*, 8 July.

119 S Wali, *Female Victims of Sexual Violence: Rape Trauma and its Impact on Resettlement* (World Health Organisation/UN High Commissioner for Refugees, 1990); UNHCR (1993). *The State of the World's Refugees: The Challenge of Protection* (London: Penguin Books), p 70; Executive Committee of the High Commissioner's Programme, *Note on Certain Aspects of Sexual Violence Against Refugee Women*, EC/1993/SCP/CRP.2, 29 April 1993; Africa Watch and Women's Rights Project, 'Seeking Refuge, Finding Terror: The Widespread Rape of Somali Women Refugees in North Eastern Kenya' (New York: *Human Rights Watch*, 1993).

lives and even from before birth. The community not only constitutes a site of violence against women, but also supports aspects of the family which make it the major site of victimisation for women. So also, the State constitutes a site of violence against women when, for example, it condones or tolerates the rape and torture of women in detention. Like the community, the State also provides the setting and justification for violence against women in the other sites of violence. The final site of violence against women is during international and civil war and general societal unrest. Again, this violence can take various forms and may or may not be related to the structure of a State.

(c) Violence as an issue of gender

Focus on the issue of violence against women has not only revealed the multifarious manifestations and settings of such violence, but has also suggested that although both women and men are at risk of personal victimisation, when women suffer such victimisation they usually are not random victims of violence, but that this violence frequently has a gender dimension. A number of aspects of violence suggest this analysis.

First, in general, although there are exceptions, irrespective of whether the victim is female or male, predominantly those who perpetrate violence are male. Second, the experience of violence for women and men is usually distinct, with women suffering different harms from men, these harms being determined by the sex of the victim. Women, for example, irrespective of setting or context, are at much greater risk of sexual violence than men. Third, those who perpetrate violent acts, particularly against others, are frequently motivated by factors concerned with gender, often the need to assert masculinity or enforce male power. Thus, for example, very often, but not exclusively, family violence is perpetrated by male members of the family who use humiliation, threats and/or force to maintain power and control over the female members of the household. Fourth, violence against women is very often associated with individual and societal conceptions of the distinct roles of women and men. Finally, the vulnerability of women to violence is integrally linked to the social, economic and political inequalities women experience as part of their daily lives, while, at the same time, violence and fear of violence have a symbolic impact and reinforces women's inequality of status in relation to men and deprives them of their ability to achieve ultimate equality.

Identification of the manifestations and sites of violence against women and the analysis of this violence as gendered provide a definitional context within which strategies to eliminate this problem can be formulated. The multifaceted nature of the problem clearly suggests that different strategies will be required for different forms and settings of violence against women. The gender analysis of the issue, however, indicates that efforts to address this violence must incorporate certain broad based strategic objectives concerned specifically with gender. These strategic objectives include de-legitimisation of male violence generally, confrontation of conceptions of gender roles and traditional values associated with such roles and transformation of the social, political and economic structures which entrench male privilege and maintain the subordination of women. These objectives must be considered and pursued in the context of overall efforts to achieve equality for women, which must, in turn, be pursued in the context of the achievement of universal human rights for all.

Until very recently, strategies at international, regional and national level employed in the context of the problem of violence against women have not incorporated such broad based strategic objectives, but have been narrow, concentrating on different aspects of violence against women.

In the following section the work of the United Nations concerning violence against women is described. It will be clear that until the beginning of this decade this work has concentrated on violence against women in the family, but in response to growing claims by women for equality in all spheres has broadened to address other forms of violence against women.

The United Nations and Violence Against Women

(a) The United Nations Decade for Women

The issue of violence against women did not feature as part of the agenda of the First United Nations Conference on Women at Mexico City in 1975. However, the result of the Conference, the World Plan of Action for the Implementation of the Objectives of the International Women's Year drew attention to the need for the family to ensure the dignity, equality and security of each of its members and to be provided with assistance in the solution of conflicts arising among its members.[120] Similarly, the Second United Nations Conference on Women at Copenhagen had few sessions focused on violence. Nevertheless, the Programme of Action stated that 'legislation should also be enacted and implemented in order to prevent domestic and sexual violence against women',[121] and in its Fifth Resolution, the Conference expressed the view that violence in the family was a serious social and inter-generational problem.

Following the Copenhagen Conference the issue of violence against women began to emerge as an international concern. The Sixth United Nations Congress on the Prevention of Crime and the Treatment of Offenders in 1980, in its Resolution 9, requested that at future Congresses and preparatory meetings for such congresses, as well as in the work of the Committee on Crime Prevention and Control, time should be allotted to the study of women as offenders and victims.[122] In 1982, on the recommendation of the Commission on the Status of Women at its 29th session, the Economic and Social Council adopted resolution 1982/22 in which it noted the concern expressed by the international community at the blatant and inhuman abuses of women and children, such as battery, violence in the family, rape and the resultant exploitation and violation of human dignity and indicated that the abuse of women and children constituted an intolerable offence to the dignity of the human being, requiring immediate and energetic action. Again in 1982, the seventh session of the Committee on Crime Prevention and Control identified violence as one of the most important issues in crime prevention and noted that consideration should be given to the victims of traditional crime, especially those involving violence in society at large and particularly within the family. It made clear that certain types of victimisation, particularly violence against female family members, were difficult to prevent or control, in view of cultural values, legal prescription and the response of criminal justice.[123]

---

120 Report of the World Conference of the International Women's Year, Mexico City, 19–22 July 1975 (*UN Sales* No E.76.IV.1) Chapter II, section A, paras 124 and 131.

121 Report of the World Conference of the United Nations 'Decade for Women: Equality, Development and Peace', Copenhagen, 14–30 July 1980 (*United Nations Sales* No E.80.IV.3) Chapter I, section A, para 141(f).

122 Sixth United Nations Congress on the 'Prevention of Crime and the Treatment of Offenders', Caracas, Venezuala, 25–25 September 1980: Report prepared by the Secretariat (*United Nations Sales* No E.81.IV.4) Chapter I, section B.

123 Report of the Committee on Crime Prevention and Control on its Seventh Session (E/CN5/1983/2) Chapter IV, section 8, paras 106 and 138.

It was at the 1985 Nairobi Conference, however, that violence against women truly emerged as a serious international concern and, many national, regional and international bodies began to take up the issue. The Nairobi Forward-Looking Strategies for the Advancement of Women[124] linked the promotion and maintenance of peace to the eradication of violence against women in both the public and private spheres. Chapter III of the Strategies, concerning peace, declared that violence against women existed in various forms in everyday life in all societies and was a major obstacle to the achievement of peace and the other objectives of the United Nations Decade for Women and that women victims of violence should be given particular attention and comprehensive assistance. Paragraph 258 went on to recommend the establishment of national machinery to deal with the question of violence against women within the family and society; the elaboration of preventive policies; and the adoption of legal measures to prevent violence and to assist women victims. Special attention was also paid in Chapter III to women in areas of armed conflict, with States being urged to apply the general framework of international humanitarian law for the specific benefit of women and children. The strategies identified a number of areas of special concern, including 'abused women', 'women victims of trafficking and involuntary prostitution' and 'women in detention and subject to penal law' where it was recommended that Member States should adopt specific measures. In order to counter abuse, governments were urged to affirm the dignity of women, intensify efforts to establish or strengthen forms of assistance to victims of violence through the provision of shelter, support, legal and other services, increase public awareness of violence against women as a societal problem, establish policies and legislative measures to ascertain the causes of violence and to prevent and eliminate its occurrence, in particular by suppressing degrading images and encourage the development of educational and re-educational measures for offenders.

Trafficking and forced prostitution were to be countered by the implementation of the United Nations 1949 Convention for the Suppression of the Traffic in Persons and the Exploitation of the Prostitution of Others, as well as by improved international strategies, including international co-ordination of police effort and measures to prevent prostitution by providing educational, employment and educational opportunities for women and children. Women deprived of freedom were acknowledged to be exposed to physical and sexual violence and moral harassments and States were directed to take into account the principles of the recommendations of the Sixth United Nations Congress on the Prevention of Crime and the Treatment of Offenders.[125]

(b) Post the Nairobi Forward-Looking Strategies

The Nairobi Forward-Looking Strategies had made clear that violence against women existed in various forms in all societies. However, the bulk of the text of the Strategies related to violence against women in the home. In consequence, predominantly, the work of the United Nations since the formulation of the Strategies has related to violence against women in the home.

The Seventh Congress on the Prevention of Crime and Treatment of Offenders held shortly after the Nairobi Conference identified violence against women in

124 Report of the World Conference to 'Review and Appraise the Achievements of the United Nations Decade for Women: Equality, Development and Peace', Nairobi, 15–26 July 1985 (*United Nations Sales* No E.85.IV.10).

125 *United Nations Sales* No E.81.IV.4

the domestic sphere as a major site of crime against women,[126] while United Nations General Assembly Resolution 40/36 of 29 November 1985 recognised the importance of violence in the home and advocated 'concerted and multidisciplinary action' both within and outside the United Nations system to deal with the problem, urging governments to adopt specific criminal legislation to obtain an equitable and human response from judicial systems to the victimisation of women. An Expert Group Meeting on Violence in the Family, with Special Emphasis on its Effects on Women,[127] convened in December 1986, made recommendations for concrete and immediate measures to confront violence against women in the home and long-term preventative measures aimed at improving the status of women and at ensuring a more accessible, sensitive, effective and fair response by civil and criminal justice systems to the victimisation of women in the family.

The Expert Group Meeting was followed by a special study on violence against women in the family, which revealed, alarmingly, that women irrespective of nationality, colour, class, religion or culture are at significant risk of physical, psychological and sexual violence in the home from male relatives, most frequently their husbands or partners.[128] Violence against women in the family was also part of the agenda of the Eighth United Nations Congress on the Prevention of Crime and the Treatment of Offenders held in Havana in 1990, as the result of which the General Assembly adopted resolution 45/114 in which it urged Member States to develop and implement policies, measures and strategies, within and outside the criminal justice system to respond to the problem of domestic violence. These policies were to include appropriate preventive measures, as well as treatment and effective assistance for victims of domestic violence. Resolution 45/114 also called for the preparation of a manual on domestic violence for practitioners, in response to which Strategies for Confronting Domestic Violence: A Resource Manual was published at the time of the World Conference on Human Rights in 1993. It is clear that the criminal justice organs of the United Nations will continue to pay close attention to the issue of domestic violence and other forms of violence against women. Resolution 3/1 of the Third Session of the Commission on Crime Prevention and Control condemns violence against women in all its forms, requests the Secretary-General to report at the third session of the Commission on the activities of United Nations bodies and institutions in this context and asks the Ninth United Nations Congress on the Prevention of Crime and Treatment of Offenders to be held in 1995 to further consider the issue.

Although the emphasis of the work of the United Nations in the field of violence against women has, thus, been with respect to violence in the domestic sphere, violence against women in other contexts has also been acknowledged. The Economic and Social Council has adopted, on the recommendation of the Commission on the Status of Women, several resolutions which relate to violence against detained women which is specific to their sex and has requested the Secretary-General to compile reports on this subject. The General Assembly has

---

126 Seventh United Nations Congress on the 'Prevention of Crime and the Treatment of Offenders', Milan, 25 August–6 September 1985: prepared by the Secretariat (*United Nations Sales* No E.86.IV.1) Chapter IV, section C, paras 230, 232 and 233.

127 Export Group Meeting on 'Violence in the Family with Special Emphasis on its Effect on Women', Vienna, 8–12 December 1986.

128 United Nations (1989) 'Violence Against Women in the Family' (*United Nations Sales* No E.89.IV.5).

adopted two resolutions concerning violence against women migrant workers, while the Commission[129] and Commission Working Group on Slavery, the Subcommission on Human Rights and the Working Group on Traditional Practices Affecting the Health of Women and Children[130] have all considered the issue of female genital mutilation. Forced prostitution and trafficking in women has been the concern of the Working Group on Contemporary Forms of Slavery, which in 1991 elaborated a Programme of Action for the Prevention of Traffic in Persons and the Exploitation of the Prostitution of Women, which has been endorsed by the Subcommission and the Commission on Human Rights.[131] So also, the Special Rapporteur on the Sale of Children, Child Prostitution and Child Pornography has devoted special attention, within his mandate, to the particular vulnerabilities of girl children.[132]

Specialised agencies of the United Nations, including the United Nations High Commission for Refugees (UNHCR) and United Nations UNIFEM, part of the United Nations Development Programme, have also addressed the question of violence against women. The UNHCR Executive Committee has agreed a number of resolutions concerning violence against refugee women[133] and in 1990 adopted a Policy on Refugee Women. General guidelines have been developed by UNHCR to help organisations working with refugees to ensure that women are protected against manipulation, exploitation and sexual and physical abuse and that they are able to benefit from protection and assistance programmes without discrimination,[134] while specific guidelines concerning the prevention of and response to sexual violence among refugees have just been completed. UNIFEM has linked the various forms of violence against women to development.[135]

Violence against women has, thus, attracted serious attention within the United Nations since the formulation of the Forward-Looking Strategies. However, up until the beginning of this decade, the approach taken has been, while acknowledging other aspects of the problem, to prioritise violence against women in the family as a matter of concern. During this decade, however, a combination of factors has changed this approach. Violence against women in

---

129 Resolution 1982/15 of 7 September 1982. The Subcommission appointed Mrs Halima Warzazi as the special rapporteur on traditional practices affecting the health of women and children. Her final report is to be found in UN Doc E/CN/4/Sub.2/1991/6 of 5 July 1991. In 1991, further, the Subcommission organised a seminar on traditional practices which called on States to draft legislation prohibiting female genital mutilation and create, in Member States, government bodies to implement official policy against the practice: UN Doc E/CN4/Sub.2/1991/48 at 29.

130 Report of the Working Group on 'Traditional Practices Affecting the Health of Women and Children', UN Doc E/CN4/1986/42 of 4 February 1986.

131 Report of the Working Group on 'Contemporary Forms of Slavery' on its Sixteenth Session, UN Doc E/CN4/Sub.2/1991/41 of 19 August 1991. See also Resolution 3/2 of the Commission on crime prevention and criminal justice which concerns international traffic in minors.

132 United Nations Special Rapporteur on the 'Sale of Children, Child Prostitution and Child Pornography, Preliminary Report on the Sale of Children', UN Doc E/CN 4/1991/51.

133 United Nations High Commissioner for Refugees, Executive Committee Conclusion, No 68 (XLIII) 1992; No 73 (XLIV) 1993.

134 'Guidelines on the Protection of Refugee Women' (Geneva: Office of the United Nations High Commissioner for Refugees, 1991).

135 Roxanna Carillo, *Battered Dreams: Violence Against Women as an Obstacle to Development* (New York: UNIFEM, 1992).

the family is now very clearly viewed as only one, albeit a large, part of the endemic problem of violence against women. The multifarious manifestations of this violence are subject to common analysis and attempts are being made to co-ordinate the work of the UN and its specialised agencies with respect to the problem.

(c) Widening the issue

The first factor contributing to this shift of approach was the emergence of violence against women as a priority for the Committee on the Elimination of Discrimination against Women, the treaty body established to monitor the implementation of the Convention on the Elimination of All Forms of Discrimination against Women.

The Convention on the Elimination of All Forms of Discrimination Against Women was elaborated by the Commission on the Status of Women prior to the Copenhagen Mid-decade Conference in 1980. The terms of treaty bind States Parties to condemn discrimination against women in all its forms and to take immediate and appropriate steps, in public and private life, to eliminate this discrimination. While the obligation to eliminate discrimination against women imposed by the treaty is broad, encompassing 'discrimination in all its forms', Part II of the Convention addresses particular areas of discrimination. At no point does the Convention specifically mention violence against women, although Article 6 obliges States Parties to take 'all appropriate measures, including legislation, to suppress all forms of traffic in women and exploitation of prostitution of women'.

The substantive work of the Committee on the Elimination of Discrimination against Women coincided with the revelation of the endemic nature of violence against women and the identification of this violence as related to the inequality of women with men. The absence of violence against women from the terms of the Convention encouraged States Parties to regard the issue, if they considered it at all, as outside their international treaty obligations. The Committee concerned, first, that States Parties frequently did not include information with respect to the problem in their treaty reports, thereby indicating that violence against women was not regarded as an issue of inequality and second, that States Parties might justify inaction because of the silence of the Convention on the matter, adopted, at its Eighth Session in 1989, General Recommendation 12. Recommendation 12 suggested that Articles 2, 5, 11, 12 and 16 required States Parties to act to protect women against violence of any kind in the family, the workplace or in any other area of social life and that States Parties report on legislative and other measures which have been taken to address violence against women, to protect the victims by providing support services and to compile statistics on incidence and victims. The following year, the Committee adopted General Recommendation 14 concerned with female circumcision and other traditional practices harmful to the health of women. This recommendation suggested various strategies, predominantly of an educational nature, that States Parties might take to eradicate, specifically, female circumcision.

General Recommendations 12 and 14 were tentative steps by the Committee to relate violence against women to discrimination and its elimination. In 1992, at its Eleventh Session, the Committee formulated the far more comprehensive General Recommendation 19 which specifically categorised gender-based violence, which it defined as violence that is directed against a women because she is a women or that affects women disproportionately, as a form of discrimination which supports other forms of discrimination and, accordingly, a breach of the general obligations of the Convention. Unlike General

Recommendations 12 and 14, General Recommendation 19 firmly places gender-based violence within the rubric of human rights and fundamental freedoms and makes clear that the Convention obliges States Parties to eliminate violence perpetrated by public authorities and by private persons, organisations or enterprises. The General Recommendation, further, elaborates programmatic measures States Parties should employ to address various manifestations of gender-based violence.

Prioritisation by the committee of the issue of gender-based violence, particularly in General Recommendation 19, was informed by the second factor which led to the broadening of the issue of violence against women within the United Nations: the categorisation of violence against women, because of its scale and gender dimension, as an issue of human rights. To concretise this categorisation and because international and regional human rights instruments and mechanisms, although implicitly concerned with gender-based violence, did not explicitly relate to the issue and had, in general terms, not been interpreted as concerned with it, the Commission on the Status of Women recommended the formulation of an international instrument on violence against women.[136]

The Declaration on the Elimination of Violence Against Women, the result of the Commission's recommendation, locates violence against women within the framework of violation of human rights obligations, inequality and discrimination[137] and sets out strategies that Member States and the organs and specialised agencies of the United Nations should employ to eliminate its occurrence. The Declaration's adoption was facilitated by the recognition by the World Conference on Human Rights, six months earlier, of the egregious nature of violence against women and the human rights dimensions of the problem[138] Further analysis the issue within this framework occurred in October 1993 at the United Nations Expert Group Meeting on measures to eradicate violence against women where recommendations were made with respect to human rights, law and justice, development, health and education and peace, peace-keeping, emergencies and conflict. The final step towards the broadening of the issue within the United Nations occurred in March 1994, when the United Nations Commission on Human Rights condemned all acts of gender-based violence against women and appointed a Special Rapporteur on violence against women to seek and receive information on violence against women, its causes and consequences; recommend measures at the national regional and international levels to eliminate violence against women; work with other mechanisms of the Commission on Human Rights and the Commission on the Status of Women and to report to the next session of the Commission on Human Rights.

---

136 ECOSOC Res 1991/18. See the report of the Expert Group Meeting on Violence Against Women, Vienna, 11–15 November 1991, EGM/VAW/1991/1.

137 Hilary Charlesworth disputes this, arguing that apart from a pre-ambular statement, the Declaration does not clearly present violence against women as a general human rights concern: it appears as a discrete and special issue rather than an abuse of, for example, the right to life or equality'. Hilary Charlesworth, 'What are Women's International Human Rights' in Rebecca Cook (ed), *The Human Rights of Women: National and International Perspectives* (Philadelphia: University of Pennsylvania Press, 1994), p 58 esp, p 73.

138 Article 18 of the Vienna Declaration; Article 38 of the Programme of Action. See also specific reference to violence against girl children in Article 21 of the Vienna Declaration and Articles 48 and 49 of the Programme of Action.

Existing strategies to confront violence against women

The previous section examined the development of policy within the United Nations with respect to violence against women, noting that the issue was initially viewed narrowly, with work concentrated on violence against women in the family. Coinciding with the identification of violence against women as gender-based, policy has broadened and the problem is considered as one of human rights and a dimension of discrimination between women and men.

The following section reviews strategies which have been introduced at international, regional and national level to address the issue. As will be seen, at all levels strategies fall into three broad categories: raising awareness of various forms of violence against women, advocating legal change and providing services for victims.

(a) International

As we have seen in the previous section, action at international level with respect to violence against women has incorporated the establishment of policy and the formulation of recommendations for Member States and United Nations activity with respect to the problem. Comprehensive recommendations relating to violence against women in the family, incorporating very specific suggestions for legal reform, with a concentration on a criminal justice approach to domestic violence, the role and training of the police, prosecutors and the health sector, social and resource support for victims and the compilation of research and data were made by the 1986 Expert Group on Violence in the Family, with Special Emphasis on its Effects on Women. Important recommendations were also made by the Group with regard to public awareness of violence against women, by education at all levels and in all forms and the elimination of images in education and the media entrenching the subordination and violation of women. Similar recommendations were made in the General Recommendations of the Committee on the Elimination of Discrimination against Women with regard to family violence. As has been noted, General Recommendation 19 was drawn more widely than the two earlier Recommendations on violence against women and thus incorporated suggestions relating to trafficking and sexual exploitation, sexual harassment, female circumcision and violence against rural women and domestic workers.

Strategies elaborated in the 1993 Declaration on the Elimination of Violence Against Women incorporated recommendations included in existing United Nations documents. Thus, recalling Paragraph 258 of the Forward-Looking Strategies, States are urged to consider the development of national plans of action to promote the protection of women against any form of violence and, if appropriate, co-operate with non-governmental organisations in this regard, entrench appropriate legal provisions, introduce training for relevant sectors, address issues of education and the portrayal of images of women, promote research and adopt measures directed to the elimination of violence against women who are especially vulnerable to violence. Unusually, however, the Declaration specifically addresses the organs and specialised agencies of the United Nations. They are requested to promote awareness of the issue and encourage co-ordination within the organisation with respect to efforts to eliminate gender-based violence.

It is the clear categorisation by the Declaration of Gender-Based Violence Against Women as both an issue of human rights and discrimination, however, which establishes the framework for the development of future strategies at international level. Within the Declaration itself, States are urged to condemn violence against women and refrain from invoking custom, tradition or religion to avoid this obligation, to ratify the Convention on the Elimination of All Forms of Discrimination Against Women without reservation or, if already State Party, remove any reservation to its terms as a means of eliminating violence against women. States are also urged to refrain from engaging in violence against women and exercise due diligence to prevent, investigate and punish acts of violence against women, whether perpetrated in the public or private sphere. This language not only sets strategic objectives for Member States, but encourages the interpretation of existing international standards and methods of implementation so as to address the issue of violence against women.

Action at international level has not been confined to the formulation of policy and recommendations, but has included the elaboration of international legislation. While much of this legislation is gender-neutral, applying equally to women and men, and does not relate specifically to violence against women, certain forms of gender-based violence are accorded special attention. Trafficking in women and the exploitation of prostitution are the subjects of a specialised treaty, the 1949 Convention for the Suppression of the Traffic in Persons and of the Exploitation of the Prostitution of Others[139] and are addressed by Article 6 of the Convention on the Elimination of All Forms of Discrimination against Women.

Most other forms of violence against women are addressed non-specifically and in gender neutral terms. For example, Articles 19 and 24(3) of the Convention on the Rights of the Child, although applying to both girl and boy children, create obligations on States Parties with respect to violence against girl children and traditional practices. Violence against women by State officials, both generally and where they are in detention, is prohibited by general international human rights norms including Articles 7 and 10 of the International Covenant on Civil and Political Rights 1966 and Articles 1 and 16 of the International Convention against Torture and Other Cruel, Inhuman and Degrading Treatment or Punishment 1984. Exploitation of and violence against female migrant workers is prohibited by several International Labour Organisation conventions, including the Migration for Employment Convention (Revised) of 1949 and the Migrant Workers (Supplementary Provisions) Convention 1975, as well as the United Nations Convention on the Protection of Migrant Workers and Their Families 1990, which has yet to enter into force.

Violence against women in situations of armed conflict[140] is addressed within the framework of international human rights and humanitarian law. Torture, cruel, inhuman or degrading punishment, slavery and servitude, wherever and whenever they occur, are prohibited by international human rights law.[141] In time of war, these obligations are reinforced by international humanitarian law standards, contained predominantly in the four Geneva Conventions 1949 and their two additional Protocols of 1977. Protection of women combatants and civilians is accorded within the general framework of humanitarian law,

---

139 GA Res 317 (IV) 2 December 1949, UN Doc A/1251 at 33–35 (1949).

140 Condemned in the Final Declaration of the International Conference of War Victims, held at Geneva from 30 August–1 September 1993, Chapter 1, paras 1 and 3.

141 Articles 7, 8 and 10 of the International Convention on Civil and Political Rights and Convention Against Torture and other Cruel, Inhuman or Degrading Punishment.

available on the basis of non-discrimination,[142] and by a number of provisions which are gender-specific.

Specific protections for female combatants were included in the 1929 Geneva Convention relating to the Treatment of Prisoners of War, with Article 3 of the Convention demanding that 'women shall be treated with all consideration due to their sex' and Article 4 allowing for differential treatment of women prisoners of war. The Third Geneva Convention of 1949 requires female supervision for and separate accommodation and sanitary conveniences from those of male prisoners to be provided for female prisoners of war,[143] while punishments in excess of those applicable to male prisoners of war may not be imposed on women prisoners.[144] Additional special protection is provided in Article 76(2) of Protocol I to prisoners of war who are pregnant or mothers of dependent infants whose cases are to be considered with 'utmost priority' with the object of early release and repatriation.

The Fourth Geneva Convention and the two Additional Protocols specifically prohibit any attack upon the 'honour' of non-combatant women, who are to be 'especially protected ... in particular against rape, enforced prostitution, or any form of indecent assault',[145] issues addressed in the 1974 Declaration on the Protection of Women and Children in Armed Conflict[146] which requires States to make all efforts to spare women from the ravages of war, including torture and degrading treatment and violence.[147]

Violations of international humanitarian law engage the international responsibility of the State. The Fourth Geneva Convention in Article 146 and 147 and its First Protocol in Articles 85 to 90 characterise certain violations in international, but not civil, war as 'grave breaches'. Characterisation of a violation as a grave breach not only imposes individual criminal liability on those who commit such a breach, but imposes responsibility on contracting parties to enact legislation to provide effective penal sanction for those ordering or committing grave breaches, as well as an obligation to search for such persons, irrespective of their nationality, and to bring them before the courts.

The definition of a grave breach, although encompassing wilful killing, torture or inhuman treatment, unlawful confinement, wilful causing of great suffering or serious injury to body or health, does not specifically incorporate gender-based violations. Thus, although it is highly likely that gender specific abuses, particularly sexual assault, during international conflicts, fall within the concept of grave breach, such a conclusion remains a matter of legal interpretation. It is unclear whether the United Nations considers that rape in international war amounts to a grave breach. Certainly, the United Nations Human Rights Commission has condemned, in the context of the former Yugoslavia the 'abhorrent practice of rape and abuse of women and children ... which, in the

---

142 The four Geneva Conventions and their Protocols all contain an identical prohibition on 'any adverse distinction founded on sex': Article 12, Geneva I; Article 12, Geneva II; Article 16, Geneva III, which also provides in Article 14 that women shall in all cases benefit by treatment as favourable as that granted to men; Article 27, Geneva IV; Article 75, Protocol I and Article 4, Protocol IV.

143 Articles 14(2), 29(2), 97 and 108 of Geneva III and Articles 75(5) and 5(2)(a), protocol I.

144 Geneva III, Article 88(3).

145 Article 27(2) Geneva IV; Articles 75 and 76 of Protocol I and Article 4, Protocol II.

146 GA Res 3318 (XXIX) 14 December 1974.

147 Paragraph 4.

circumstances constitutes a war crime'.[148] Similarly, the Vienna Programme of Action in paragraph 38 condemned systematic rape, sexual slavery and forced pregnancy in armed conflict and indicated that they required a 'particularly effective response'. In neither case, however, was a clear statement made that rape in war amounts to a grave breach. Whether rape in war amounts to 'torture' is also an issue of interpretation.

In 1992, the Special Rapporteur on Torture affirmed orally that rape of women in detention is a form of torture,[149] thus clearly suggesting that rape in war must also constitute torture. The International Committee of the Red Cross has, however, stated that rape and any other attack on a woman's dignity constitutes an act 'wilfully causing great suffering or serious injury to body or health' and accordingly falls squarely within the definition of grave breach within Article 147, a conclusion supported by *Cyprus v Turkey* where the European Commission concluded that rape of Cypriot civilian women by Turkish soldiers constituted inhuman treatment and thus contravened Article 3 of the European Convention on Human Rights and Fundamental Freedoms.

On a number of occasions the international community has established tribunals to determine whether parties to war have complied with their international human rights and humanitarian obligations. Following Second World War the International Military Tribunal was invested with jurisdiction to investigate and determine responsibility for 'crimes against peace', 'war crimes' and 'crimes against humanity'. Such crimes were, again, defined gender-neutrally, although, clearly, war crimes and crimes against humanity, which included enslavement and inhumane acts against the civilian population,[150] could be interpreted to include gender-specific abuses.

More recently, the UN Security Council has established an *ad hoc* international tribunal for former Yugoslavia[151] as an enforcement measure under Chapter VII of the UN Charter. This tribunal is mandated to prosecute for grave breaches defined by the Geneva Conventions and crimes against humanity. These latter are defined to include enslavement, imprisonment, torture and, in order to avoid any likely argument with regard to the matter, rape which is committed as part of a widespread or systematic attack against any civilian population on national, political, ethnic, racial or religious grounds. Although it is heartening that the tribunal has been specifically mandated to examine gender-based violations, the formulation in the statute concerning rape might serve to exclude rape which cannot be proven to be part of such a widespread or systematic attack. Currently, Member States of the United Nations are considering a draft statute to establish a permanent international criminal court which would have jurisdiction over war crimes, crimes against humanity and crimes against peace. No gender-specific crimes are incorporated within the present draft,[152] thus the issue of the jurisdiction of the proposed court of such crimes remains, as with the questions of grave breaches and torture, a matter for interpretation.

---

148 UN Commission on Human Rights, Rape and abuse of women in the territory of the former Yugoslavia, Report on 49th Session, 1 February–12 March 1993, ECOSOC Suppl No 3, E/CN4/1993/122.

149 UN Doc E/CN4/1992/SR.21, para 35.

150 Charter of the International Military Tribunal Annexed to the London Agreement, 8 August 1945, Article 6(b) and (c).

151 (1993) 32(4) ILM 1192–1194.

152 Article 20 of the draft statute of the International Law Commission.

To a large extent, international legal regulation governs the determination of those who meet the definition of refugee status and the protections which are available to such individuals.[153] Like most international regulation, international refugee law is gender neutral. Accordingly, although women are entitled to seek refugee status on the same basis as men and such status will confer on refugee women the same protections as on refugee men, the definition of such status and the protections afforded thereby do not incorporate any gender specific elements.

In order to qualify for refugee status in international law, a woman, like a man, must establish that she is a person who:

> ... owing to a well-founded fear of being persecuted for reasons of race, religion, nationality, membership of a particular social group or political opinion is outside the country of his nationality and is unable or, owing to such fear, is unwilling to avail himself of the protection of that country; or who not having a nationality and being outside the country of his former habitual residence (as a result of such events), is unable or, owing to such fear, is unwilling to return to it.[154]

Women seeking refugee status because of physical, sexual or psychological violence or because they fear such violence because, for example, they have contravened a society's cultural norms, are faced with two hurdles in meeting this definition. First, whether such violence amounts to 'persecution' and second, if this violence can be characterised as persecution, whether it can be linked to race, religion, nationality, membership of a particular social group or political opinion. Legal and policy directives within UNHCR suggest that, certainly, sexual violence and forced female genital mutilation can amount to persecution and thus provide the basis for a claim to refugee status.[155] The Executive Committee of the UNHCR has also adopted, in the light of a decision of the European Parliament in 1984, a conclusion to the effect that women asylum-seekers who face harsh or inhumane treatment due to their having transgressed the social mores of the society in which they live may be considered as a 'particular social group' within the meaning of the Convention definition. Despite the optional nature of the views of UNHCR on both these matters, governments of countries admitting refugees have increasingly, although not uniformly, recognised that sexual and other forms of violence against women can be used as an instrument of persecution, thereby providing valid grounds for refugee status. Some have also been prepared to conclude that women who have suffered or who have a well-founded fear of suffering sexual and other forms of violence form part of a particular social group and deserve the protection of

---

153 The 1969 OAU Convention Governing the Specific Aspects of Refugee Problems in Africa and the OAS Cartegena Declaration incorporate a definition of refugee which is less problematic for women. The former, which is similar in terms to that of the Cartegena Declaration extends the definition to encompass '... every person who, owing to external aggression, occupation, foreign domination or events seriously disturbing public order in either part or the whole of his country of origin or nationality, is compelled to leave his place of habitual residence in order to seek refuge in another place outside his country of origin or nationality.'

154 1951 Convention and 1967 Protocol Relating to the Status of Refugees; Statute of the UNHCR 1950.

155 Executive Committee of the High Commissioner's Programme, Subcommittee of the Whole on International Protection, 22nd Meeting, note on 'Certain Aspects of Sexual Violence Against Refugee Women', EC/1993/SCP/CRP.2, 29 April 1993, para 29. Forced female genital mutilation combined with absence of state protection is considered to be persecution owing to membership

asylum. Most notable in this respect is Canada, whose Immigration and Refugee Board issued guidelines relating to women refugee claimants fearing gender-related persecution on 9 March 1993. The Canadian guidelines provide that where a woman can establish a well-founded fear of persecution, gender can be included in the definition of social group. As refugee status is an individual remedy, however, a claimant seeking refugee status on gender-related grounds must show she has genuine fear of harm, that gender is the reason for the fear of such harm, the harm is sufficiently serious so as to amount to persecution, that there is a reasonable possibility for the feared persecution to occur if she returns to her country of origin and she has no reasonable expectation of adequate national protection.

No special regard is paid in international refugee law to the specific needs of refugee women, with women, again, being proferred protection in gender neutral terms. The issue of violence against refugee women has, however, as we have seen, been the concern of UNHCR which has issued policy directives and codes of practice for the treatment and protection of refugee women with the particular aim of adverting the risk of gender-based violence. These policy directives do not have the force of law and are, of course, not binding on States ...[156]

Problems with current strategies

The previous sections have canvassed current strategies that have been used to confront those forms of violence against women recognised by national governments. As has been noted, in most countries, forms of violence against women are addressed discretely, with few regarding these various manifestations as inter-related or inter-linked in any way. In most countries, further, responses have been law centred and have predominantly concerned law reform. The legal responses which have been applied to the various forms of violence against women are open to individual criticism. A general criticism of these legal responses is also pertinent: legal responses which are employed to confront violence against women and reforms that have been introduced are based on a model of gender-neutrality in a gender-specific area and do not take into account the reality of victimisation and the systemic inequalities in society. Very frequently, also, the laws which are applied are based on a perception that the law is neutral, but, in fact, perpetuate outdated sexual stereotypes and result in unfair and unequal treatment of women. Further, legal response has usually been piecemeal so that although useful legislative reform has been introduced, its effectiveness has been undermined by other laws or provisions which impact on the particular issue. For example, increased penalties for trafficking and better implementation of controls against trafficking are rarely accompanied by reforms which protect illegal immigrant women who have been the victims of trafficking. Where legal response has been concerned, also, there has been significant stress on criminalisation, which although of symbolic and rhetorical value, is that area of the law which is most informed by gender stereotypes and whose system is sympathetic in the context of crimes against women. Again, even where useful reform has been put in place, there has often been insufficient effort applied to harmonise law and practice, to implement the law and to monitor its implementation. Certainly, in many cases, key actors in the implementation of the law have received training, but this has been based on a misconception that training can change deep seated attitudes and beliefs about women.

---

156 *Violence Against Women*, pp 1–24.

The central difficulty with current strategies, however, is that, as yet, countries have been wary of allocating sufficient resources to create a harmonised and integrated response. It has been more convenient to concentrate on legal measures, where costs are few and rhetorical gains are high. Lack of resources, combined with competing values and beliefs about women, their place in the family, the community and society have been sufficient to dictate that the achievements so far, even in those countries where violence against women has been a priority concern for some time, are that individual women have been able to achieve individual resolution of their particular problems, but little substantial or substantive change has occurred. Countries must go beyond formalistic legal provisions and reach a deeper consensus and sustainable commitment to the eradication of violence against women. Violence must be made as costly to its perpetrators as it is to individuals, the community and to the State.

Strategic objectives

The ultimate goal of the international community and Member States must to be prevent violence against women in all its forms and in all contexts. This requires confronting the material reality of violence in women's lives, the particular conditions that facilitate its existence – family, economic dependency, lack of alternatives and, fundamentally, the way societies organise their beliefs and institutions to sustain gender violence.

As violence against women is ultimately linked to male privilege and public and institutional arrangements which serve to maintain that privilege, the central strategic objective must be to effect fundamental change in the social, political and economic structures that maintain the subordination of women, which must be considered and pursued in the context of overall efforts to promote equality for women and human rights for all. Relating abuse of women to their unequal status in society and societal beliefs, attitudes and values that condone violence against women leads, thus, to the inevitable conclusion that effective solutions to the problem must involve altering the status of women and traditional values that structure gender relations. Here notions of maleness and masculinity which incorporate the domination of women must be examined and revised. So also, the role of violence in dispute resolution generally, and in intimate relations in particular, must be addressed and reconstructed.

Critical areas for action

Different manifestations of violence against women, as well as the different contexts where such violence occurs call for discrete strategies. The section which follows, which draws on the recommendations of the United Nations Expert Group Meeting on Measures to Eradicate Violence against Women held in October 1993, outlines a number of these discrete strategies.

It is unlikely, however, that any strategy introduced to confront any manifestation of gender-based violence against women, in whatever context it occurs will be successful if violence against women is not confronted in an integrated and coherent way. Further, even in the context of an integrated approach, it is unlikely that any strategy – be it short, medium or long term – will succeed unless gender violence is made an issue of critical concern to everyone: women, men, the public, institutions and the state, as well as the individual community. Such an approach presents challenges at the individual level and creates a larger pool of people who are seeking solutions, as well as creating a base of political support that functions to pressure for change at the structural level both nationally and internationally.

A number of general challenges confront the construction of any integrated strategy to combat gender based violence against women. In the area of human rights, first, although the Vienna Declaration and Programme of Action explicitly mentioned women and gave recognition to violence against women and other types of abuses as violations of human rights, it and the UN Human Rights Conference did not effect significant expansion of the human rights framework so as to mandate the structural changes required for implementing its recommendations. The international community is thus faced with the challenge of determining how best to transform the current framework of human rights so as to take fully into account and address violence against women. Related to this is the fundamental challenge of the private, the domain in which women, in most societies exist and function. The private has served to insulate the most common, private forms of violence against women. The construction of the private has served to limit the effectiveness of human rights law as a strategy to confront violence against women and has States and their agents, including law-makers, judges and the police to ignore violence which occurs, particularly in the family context. Strategies must be developed, thus, to deconstruct the public/private dichotomy and make States accountable for violations of women's rights in all spheres. In this process, government responsibility for violations in the public must be remembered, so that States are held truly responsible for violence involving government agents and entrench effective measures to prevent public violence. Here the international community and Member States must face the challenge of specific risk groups: female political activists; refugees and women caught up in conflict and tension.

Two further general challenges face the international community and Member States. Firstly to move the definition and approaches to violence against women beyond a focus on violence against women in the family, while at the same time supporting the family as an egalitarian institution. Secondly, to see law reform as one aspect of the process of preventing violence against women, rather than the only aspect. States must be aware that although laws may establish a benchmark which formalises values of respect for women and intolerance of violence, no existing legislation deals adequately with the problem of violence. Indeed, in many cases laws that are currently in place are not only ineffective to stop violence, they perpetuate inequality and thus undermine any new strategies to address violent conduct. Laws, further, are only as effective as those who implement them, thus leaving States with the final challenge of the achievement of effective law enforcement.[157]

INTERNATIONAL PROTECTION OF FAMILY MEMBERS' RIGHTS[158]

Geraldine Van Bueren[159]

The extent of domestic violence against women was highlighted in a United Nations study on violence against women in the family.[160] The United Nations described this violence, which is regarded as universal, as follows: 'women have frequently been ... battered, sexually abused and psychologically injured by persons with whom they should enjoy the closest trust. This maltreatment has gone largely unpunished, unremarked and has even been tacitly ...

---

157 *Violence Against Women*, pp 54–56.

158 [1995] 17 *Human Rights Quarterly* 732.

159 Reader in Law, Queen Mary and Westfield College, University of London; Director of the Programme on International Rights of the Child.

160 See *Violence Against Women in the Family* (United Nations Division for the Advancement of Women, 1989).

condoned.'[161] In *Velasquez-Rodriguez v Honduras*[162] the Inter-American Court of Human Rights (Inter-American Court) specifically commented on State tolerance of human rights violations and stressed that '[what is decisive is whether a violation of rights recognised by the [American] Convention [on Human Rights] has occurred with the support or the acquiescence of the government, or whether the State has allowed the act to take place without measures to prevent it or to punish those responsible'. Thus, the court's task is to determine whether the violation is the result of a State's failure to fulfil its duty to respect and guarantee those rights, as required by Article 1(1) of the Convention. Importantly, the Inter-American Court determined that an illegal act which breaches human rights and is not directly imputable to the State (because it is an act of a private person or because the person responsible has not been identified) can lead to international State responsibility. This State responsibility does not derive from the act itself, but from the State's failure 'to prevent the violation or to respond to it as required by the [Inter-American] Convention'.[163] Furthermore, the Inter-American Court elaborated on the preventative obligation on states, explaining that this obligation included all means of a 'legal, political, administrative and cultural nature'. The Inter-American Court also concluded that where human rights violations by private parties are not seriously investigated, the parties are, in a sense, aided by the government making the State responsible under international law.

These parts of the *Velasquez-Rodriguez* decision were unanimous and reinforced the normative strength of a general recommendation of the Committee on the Elimination of Discrimination Against Women (CEDAW) that States Parties should take steps 'to overcome all forms of gender-based violence, whether by public or private act'.[164] However, before the *Velasquez-Rodriguez* principle of State accountability can be applied, the State must engage in some conduct that implies non-performance of an international duty. Therefore, domestic intra-familial violence must be analysed to consider whether it qualifies as a breach of international human rights.

Intra-familial violence includes battering, sexual abuse of children, dowry-related violence, marital rape, and female genital mutilation. In *Velasquez-Rodriguez*, the Inter-American Court was specifically concerned with the disappearance of Manfredo Velasquez and whether his disappearance could be linked to an official practice of disappearances in Honduras (either executed or tolerated by the Honduran government). The comments of the Inter-American Court are particularly apposite because violence within the family, whether of a sexual nature or otherwise, shares many of the characteristics of disappearances highlighted by the court, such as the suppression of information and the concealment of facts. The Inter-American Court specifically held that 'circumstantial or presumptive evidence is especially important in allegations of disappearances, because this type of repression is characterised by an attempt to suppress all information about the kidnapping or the whereabouts and fate of the victim'.[165] Additionally, the Inter-American Court criticised disappearances

---

161 *Ibid*, p 11.

162 Case 4, Inter-Am CHR OASC (1988).

163 *Ibid*, p 154.

164 UN GAOR Commission on the Elimination of Discrimination Against Women, 11th Session, Agenda Item 7, p 3, UN Doc CEDAW992.1. 15 (1992).

165 *Velasquez-Rodriguez supra* at 135.

because they were 'a means of creating a general state of anguish, insecurity and fear ...'.

Women and children victims of intra-familial violence testify that they experience similar feelings of insecurity, both physical and mental. Such feelings are contrary to the right to a sense of physical privacy as protected by international human rights law. Thus, States Parties to treaties that enshrine the protection of privacy have an emerging duty to prevent intra-familial violence where there is an established pattern of domestic violence that comes within the *Costello-Roberts* sufficiency test.[166] Furthermore, States Parties are obliged to investigate and punish those violations that do occur.

Whether domestic violence will amount to a breach of privacy; torture; or cruel, inhuman, or degrading treatment will depend upon the severity of the violence in each case. In *Soering v United Kingdom*, the European Court reiterated that the assessment of the minimum level of severity failing within the prohibited scope of torture, inhuman and degrading treatment, and punishment depends on all the circumstances of the case, including the gender and age of the victim.[167] However, taking the jurisprudence of both the Inter-American Court and the European Court together, there does appear to be a way forward in preventing and punishing domestic violence. Arguably, privacy in the sense of physical integrity offers greater latitude for countering forms of domestic violence less extreme than torture. This idea is again reinforced by dicta of the European Commission in *X and Y v Netherlands*. Although the European Commission did not consider it necessary to establish whether the particular mental suffering inflicted on Y was of such a nature and had reached such a degree of intensity as to bring it within the scope' of Article 3,[168] the Commission did observe that 'sexual abuse and inhuman or degrading treatment – even though they may overlap in individual cases – are by no means congruent concepts'.[169] This allows for two possibilities: first, in specific cases where the mental suffering might have passed the necessary threshold, such abuse (whether sexual or otherwise) will amount to inhuman or degrading treatment; and second, such abuse still might fall within the protection of an individual's private life, even if it does not amount to inhuman or degrading treatment. Hence, in States that do not investigate a persistent pattern of severe forms of domestic violence and that lack adequate civil remedies and criminal prosecutions, victims of such violence might have a cause of action under human rights treaties. These individuals might be able to petition international bodies to redress breaches of their right to be free from inhuman and degrading treatment and their right to privacy. Such an approach is consistent with the European Court's approach that the European Convention 'is a living instrument' that 'must be interpreted in the light of present day conditions,' because contemporary conditions have revealed the extent of domestic violence.

---

166 See G Van Bueren, 'Combating Child Sexual Abuse and Exploitation', in D Pearl and R Pickford (eds), *The Frontiers of Family Law* (1995).

167 See *Soering v United Kingdom* 161 Eur Ct HR (Ser A) (1989).

168 Report of the European Commission of Human Rights in the *X and Y v Netherlands* at 95 (5 July 1983).

169 *Tyrer v United Kingdom* 26 Eur Ct HR (Ser A) (1978), p 31.

The Children's Convention also reinforces State responsibility for intra-familial abuse. First, Article 19 of the Children's Convention clearly brings the concepts of 'child' and 'intra-familial' into the public sphere. Second, the Children's Convention extends the States' duties beyond prevention, investigation, and prosecution, to rehabilitation. Rehabilitation under the Children's Convention has a much broader application than is found in the 1984 Convention Against Torture and Other Cruel, Inhuman or Degrading Treatment or Punishment (Torture Convention), which only places a duty on State Parties to provide 'as full rehabilitation as possible' for acts that amount to torture; cruel, inhuman, and degrading treatment; and punishment as defined by the Torture Convention.[170] The duty incorporated in the Children's Convention is for any form of neglect, exploitation, or abuse. The Women's Convention has adopted an approach similar to that taken in the Children's Convention, specifically recommending that rehabilitation and support services be provided for women who have been victims of violence and abuse within the family.

The cumulative significance of this international legislation and jurisprudence, along with the recent adoption by the General Assembly of the Declaration on the Elimination of Violence against Women and the appointment of a Special Rapporteur on Violence Against Women, reinforces the duty upon States, as a matter of international law, to establish an effective legal system that does not tolerate assaults that threaten family members' physical integrity and life.

Such a reconceptualisation of intra-familial violence is already beginning to occur with regard to female circumcision. Within the framework of the Children's Convention, the abolition of traditional practices prejudicial to the health of the child implicates a prohibition on female circumcision. Such a prohibition is a specific facet of the right of the child to the highest attainable standard of health. The right to health traditionally has been classified by States as a social right, such that the States' only duty is to implement the right progressively. Hence, although States Parties are obliged to take 'all effective and appropriate measures' these measures are significantly weakened by the qualifier 'with a view to abolishing' such 'traditional practices'. A more effective approach would have States placed under an immediate duty to prohibit such practices. In an attempt to establish such a duty, female circumcision has been classified as genital mutilation and conceptualised as torture. Unfortunately, the definition of torture enshrined in the 1984 Convention on Torture and the Elimination of Cruel, Inhuman and Degrading Treatment or Punishment incorporates the notion of intentional infliction of severe mental or physical pain for specific purposes. Within such a restrictive and traditional definition, it is impossible to include every female circumcision (many of which are not inflicted with such an intent nor directly linked to the State), because they traditionally are performed by private individuals with the consent of the family (and sometimes with the consent of the girls).[171] Although it might be possible to invalidate the consent by adopting a psychoanalytic approach and arguing that the child has internalised her culture, this strategy has obvious dangers for those seeking to augment the autonomy of children. Because of these and other factors, female

---

170 Convention against Torture and Other Cruel, Inhuman or Degrading Treatment or Punishment, Article 14(1) adopted 10 December 1984, GA Res 396, UN GAOR Supp (No 51) at 197, UN Doc A/39/51 (1985) reprinted in (1985) 23 *ILM* 535.

171 However, State responsibility might arise if girls are circumcised in State hospitals or by State health officials.

circumcision is not classified as 'torture' by the Inter-African Committee on Traditional Practices Affecting Women and Children (who have set the goal of eradicating female circumcision by the year 2000), nor is it conceptualised as torture under the African Children's Charter.

Those who argue that female genital mutilation should be included within the definition of torture and cruel and inhuman treatment do so because the health consequences and the intensity of the pain and suffering are comparable to those experienced by torture victims. Therefore, the existing international protection machinery should be forced to confront the practice which the World Health Organisation estimates has affected 80–100 million women (of whom 15 million have been infibulated). In some States, such as Djibouti, Somalia, Eritrea, Ethiopia, Sierra Leone, and Sudan, more than 80% of girls have been circumcised'.[172] In addition, the issue of consent does not always arise because some girls suffer genital mutilation as early as the age of two.

Some female circumcisions, however, clearly come within the prohibition on torture. When girls are circumcised against their will, such circumcisions will clearly come within torture and other cruel, inhuman, and degrading treatment, and as such will be subject to immediate prohibition as a fundamental violation of a human right. Furthermore, when a girl flees her country because it is the only way to avoid circumcision, the *Conseil d'Etat* has accepted, as a matter of principle, that she will be entitled to refugee status on the grounds that she has a well-founded fear of being persecuted for reasons of membership in a particular social group. The same status would appear to be accorded to men who flee forced circumcisions and might be applicable to victims of other traditional practices.

The private sphere should not be eliminated completely in the field of international human rights law; however, States should no longer be permitted to claim non-interference as a defence to their failure to protect victims of intra-familial violence. The private/public distinction possibly bears some responsibility for the inequality in the societal power distribution, but the private/public distinction does not bear full responsibility for the failure of the international human rights legal system to protect women and children within the family. Rather, the failure to protect women and children results from the devaluation of the private sphere and the mistaken presumption of consent within the private realm. Women and children represent the majority of the world's population, but the international human rights legal system has failed to protect them; therefore, the boundaries of the private sphere must be reassessed. The historical origin of international human rights law should not predetermine its scope ...[173]

The Implementation of Family Members' Rights

The complexities inherent in protecting the rights and responsibilities of family members require sensitive decision-making and monitoring mechanisms. International obligations, which are difficult to supervise in any event, are even more difficult to monitor within the family. Although international substantive law is developing in order to protect more effectively family members' rights,

---

172 The World Health Organisation estimates that over 100 million girls and women have suffered female genital mutilation. It is common practice in 28 African states. Approximately 75% of the victims live in Nigeria, Ethiopia, Egypt, Sudan and Kenya.

173 *International Protection of Family Members' Rights*, pp 750–56.

such progress is being restrained artificially by the lack of accompanying developments in implementation procedures.

Although the family serves as the basic unit of society, international human rights law fails to enforce the rights of family members because its procedural focus is on the rights of individuals. Many of the obstacles to women's and children's equality within the family are structural. Civil and political rights, and economic, social, and cultural rights must be integrated, as a number of human rights instruments (including the Children's Convention, the Convention on the Elimination of All Forms of Discrimination Against Women, and the African Children's Charter) have done to better achieve equality for women and children. Clarence Dias correctly observes that civil and political rights have become justiciable and the focus of international human rights advocacy, while economic, social, and cultural rights remain mostly in the sphere of international development assistance. However, there is nothing inherent in these rights that necessitates this false dichotomy. A report on the implementation of economic, social, and cultural rights might reveal an underlying disparity of access that is based on gender or religious grounds, thus transforming an apparently economic, social, or cultural issue into a civil rights issue.

The real problem, as the prohibition on female circumcision demonstrates, is not the terminology, but rather the artificial distinctions in implementation. Prohibiting female circumcision through the drafting and adoption of national legislation requires minimal resources. Thus, it is difficult to defend the approach of international human rights law that States Parties have only a progressive (as opposed to an immediate) duty to prohibit female circumcision. The only resource demands would be for educational programmes that would accompany the implementation of such legislation. As long as protection from exploitation, be it sexual or economic, is classified as an economic or social right, the remedy for the victim is very indirect. In general, only violations of civil and political rights give rise to individual causes of action. Perhaps the reason for the division is fear: fear of opening perceived floodgates (if domestic violence, why not inadequate supplies of life support machinery?). However, the floodgates argument does not justify resisting reform. On the contrary, it justifies providing sufficient resources so that effective human rights machinery can function efficiently. Hence, the international human rights system should do more than simply 'mobilising shame', which is the objective of the reporting procedures. Even treaties that enshrine resource limitation clauses, such as 'to the maximum extent of their available resources, refer to resources that are unconstrained by concepts such as finances and economics. As James Himes notes, resources also include human resources, although this ought not justify placing a greater burden on the heads of households, frequently women.[174]

Although the international human rights legal system's reliance on the State nexus as the basis for responsibility has been criticised because it reflects men's subjugative experiences, the experiences of women and children are not necessarily excluded. The Committee on the Rights of the Child and the Commission on the Status of Women have attempted to integrate children's and women's rights into the mainstream. However, attention also should be focused on improving the implementation mechanisms for children's and women's rights.

---

174 The 'UN Convention on the Rights of the Child: More Than a New Utopia?' in James Himes (ed), *Three Essays on the Challenge of Implementation* (1993).

Neither the Children's Convention nor the Women's Convention incorporates a petition system, either Inter-State or individual. However, the Vienna Declaration and Programme of Action has mandated that the Commission on the Status of Women draft an optional protocol for complaints under the Women's Convention. In relation to children, the right to petition has already proven effective under the European Convention. During the drafting of the Children's Convention, the possibility of an individual petition system was raised informally by Amnesty International, but the idea was rejected. Many participants in the drafting process believed that an individual petition system would transform an implementation mechanism based on co-operation into one fraught with confrontation. This has not proven to be the case within the Council of Europe where States Parties generally abide by the judgments of the European Court.

Those critics who oppose incorporating an individual petition system into the Children's Convention argue that it is only appropriate for civil and political rights, and not suited to a treaty that also protects economic, social, and cultural rights. However, the incorporation of a right of individual petition into the African Children's Charter is evidence that it might be in the best interests of the child if such assumptions were challenged. Hence, it would be possible to have reporting, technical advice, and assistance, together with an optional petition system. For such a right to be included in the Children's Convention, either the Convention itself must be amended or an additional optional protocol must be attached. The latter is a more realistic option, although States Parties to the Children's Convention would not become automatic parties to the optional protocol. At present, a draft protocol has been drafted by the Committee on the Rights of the Child, but it focuses only on armed conflict. Extending the right of petition would be both egalitarian and evolutionary. However, under the existing regional and international petition mechanisms, it is only individual family members who may claim interferences with their family or family life. Although this does not prevent more than one family member from submitting a petition, as in *Johnston v Ireland*,[175] an individual family member may not petition on behalf of the entire family unit claiming that the State breached its obligations to protect the family as a group unit. Although class actions exist in a number of national jurisdictions, international law has not developed a similar procedure. The underlying purpose of a class action is to bind all parties represented and, in effect, implement rights that are of public concern. At first sight, the creation of an international legal class action appears to be unnecessary. A judgment from a regional human rights body, for example, occasionally prompts a State Party to amend its legislation, and thus, removes the necessity for future action. However, an international legal class action would have particular implications for the enforcement of a family's economic, social, and cultural rights.

Many of the concerns of children and women are in the economic, social, and cultural areas, and the lack of an international legal class action has had a significant negative impact on the protection of economic, social, and cultural rights. One of the reasons underlying the mistaken assumption that economic, social, and cultural rights are not justiciable is that they raise complex economic, social, and cultural questions that human rights fora have demonstrated a reluctance to consider within the confines of one case. As a result, the argument becomes circular. There is not a suitable implementation mechanism for

---

175 112 Eur Ct HR (Ser A) (1987).

economic, social, and cultural rights and, therefore, they are not justiciable. The creation of an international legal class action would assist states in reassessing the potential justiciability of these rights.

Conclusion

All reforms depend upon resources, which are not a matter of international law, but of international political will. Political will can be increased if the successes of human rights strategies are highlighted. This occurs too infrequently, and one cannot be surprised at the scepticism over the potential of international human rights law if international human rights lawyers themselves too often focus on failures rather than successes. International human rights law is standing at a crossroads. One route leads to the traditional private/public distinction; the other stretches over the horizon to effective protection for all family members. Although protecting family members was not the specific goal of the States that drafted the Children's Convention, Melton is correct when he notes that, if the Children's Convention were ever fully implemented, it 'would transform the social order, not only politically but even at the level of social relationships. The same is true of the Women's Convention. The challenge for international law in the 21st century will be to achieve this transformation.[176]

WOMEN, FEMINISM AND INTERNATIONAL HUMAN RIGHTS LAW – METHODOLOGICAL MYOPIA, FUNDAMENTAL FLAWS OR MEANINGFUL MARGINALISATION?[177]

Some Current Issues

Andrew Byrnes[178]

A. Introduction

Criticism of the 'Mainstream'

The last two decades have seen the emergence of a vast body of writing about women and the international system from a great variety of perspectives. Not surprisingly, this has included a proliferation of writing about women, women's rights and human rights in an international context. Much of that literature, fuelled by the energy that led to and was subsequently generated by the activities of the United Nations Decade for Women,[179] focused on the new norms, institutions and programmes established during this period which addressed in a focused way the concerns of women.

A number of writers also turned a critical eye on the response of the international system for the protection of human rights to the concerns of women and found it deficient in major respects. Two salient criticisms were made: issues of central concern to women found little place on the 'mainstream' agenda and the institutions and procedures concerned with 'women's issues' were the poor cousins of the 'real' human rights organs and procedures. These critics charged that the 'mainstream' 'human rights' community largely ignored or neglected blatant violations of women's human dignity, refusing to perceive them as gross violations of fundamental human rights. Such issues were left to be taken up, if

---

176 *International Protection of Family Members' Rights*, pp 762–65.

177 (1992) 12 *Australian Yearbook of International Law* 205. (Article abridged and footnotes edited.)

178 University of Hong Kong.

179 See generally, A Fraser, *The UN Decade for Women: Documents and Dialogue* (1987); H Pietila and J Vickers, *Making Women Matter: The Role of the United Nations* (1990).

at all, as social and humanitarian issues in marginalised, procedurally weak fora dealing with women's issues.[180] These perceptions gave rise to demands not only that the women's institutions be strengthened but also that greater attention be given to issues affecting women in the mainstream organs.

Implicit in these critiques was the assumption that it is both possible and desirable to deal with many of these violations of women's human dignity within the established human rights framework, in particular the civil and political rights framework. However, apart from some fairly general explanations of the reasons for the alleged exclusion of women's experiences from the dominant practice, these critiques did not explore the conceptual, doctrinal and institutional hurdles which need to be overcome if this goal is to be achieved.

B. A Resurgence of Interest

The concern to ensure a greater prominence for violations of 'women's rights' in the human rights 'mainstream' appears to have gathered momentum in the last couple of years (particularly in North America, but elsewhere as well).[181] The slogan 'women's rights are human rights' has been invoked frequently and there have been a number of conferences and seminars exploring the relationship between 'women's rights' and 'human rights'. This interest has come not only from women's groups; increasingly feminists or those sensitive to feminist issues in 'mainstream' organisations or who are working within a more traditional framework have begun to address the issue in earnest. Under pressure from such groups governmental bodies have also begun to address the issue.

Despite this interest, there has so far been relatively little exploration of the implications from an international human rights law perspective of attempting to give greater prominence to gender in the mainstream discourse. Much still needs to be done to define the terms used in the discussion, to document in detail the inclusion or exclusion of violations of women's human rights within the dominant discourse, to ascertain the reasons for this, and to develop strategies to ensure that greater account is taken of these issues in the mainstream. This paper is intended to contribute to that process. Much of it is tentative, suggesting areas for further research and action, rather than stating definitive conclusions. ...

Looking at the 'Mainstream': Definition and Justification

This paper focuses on the so-called 'mainstream' of international human rights practice and seeks to place issues of the violation of women's human rights in that context. The concept of 'the mainstream' requires definition and the decision to focus on it justification.

The 'mainstream' has institutional, substantive and geographical dimensions. I use the term 'mainstream' to refer to those institutions entrusted with responsibility for 'general' human rights matters – within the United Nations system, primarily the Geneva-based political and expert bodies; within the regional systems, the organs charged with responsibility for the administration and enforcement of human rights such as the Strasbourg organs and the Inter-American Commission of Human Rights and the Inter-American Court. They

---

180 See eg L Reanda, 'Human Rights and Women's Rights: The United Nations Approach' (1981) 3 *Human Rights Quarterly* 11; Fran Hosken, 'Introduction', *ibid* 1; M Galey, 'International Enforcement of Women's Rights' (1984) 6 *Human Rights Quarterly* 463.

181 For a recent restatement and development of a number of the criticisms, see C Bunch, 'Women's Rights as Human Rights: Toward a Re-vision of Human Rights' (1990) 12 *Human Rights Quarterly* 486.

may be contrasted with those bodies which have a 'specialist' jurisdiction in relation to 'women's issues', such as the Commission on the Status of Women and the Inter-American Commission of Women.

Substantively, the term is used to refer to human rights guarantees contained in the 'general' human rights instruments, in particular the two International Covenants and the European Convention (as well as the American Convention and the African Charter).

However, it is also clear that within the human rights 'mainstream' as defined above traditional civil and political rights have enjoyed and continue to enjoy a particularly privileged position – much of the attention, resources and activities of those involved in the mainstream is devoted to these issues. They accordingly receive prominence (as always) in this paper.

Focusing on the 'mainstream' in contrast to the 'women's rights' bodies has its problems. For instance, talking about the mainstream and recognising its dominant role reinforces its conception of itself as the centre and the marginalisation of those that it defines as on the margins. Nonetheless, the practice relating to the major civil and political rights catalogues is in many respects a privileged and powerful discourse, reinforced by a considerable allocation of institutional resources and the reality is that these institutions have the prestige, resources and perhaps the power to bring about change.

The existence of a privileged dominant practice and a 'specialised' marginal one presents a strategic dilemma in this area, as in many areas where the goal is to bring about the advancement of women: how does one ensure that feminist perspectives are incorporated within the dominant discourse while maintaining the separate focus which is apparently necessary to ensure that these issues are not submerged or overwhelmed. In strategic terms any attempt to increase the attention given by the 'mainstream' to gender issues in human rights must therefore also be accompanied by steps to strengthen the existing 'women's rights' rights institutions and to lessen their marginalisation.

The Importance of Method

A feminist approach or method? 'Asking the Woman Question'[182]

A characteristic feature of feminist enquiry has been the insistence that women's experiences be the starting point for analysis:

> One of the methodological devices feminists have introduced into the study of human societies and of political and social theory has been to keep at the forefront questions such as: What about the women? What are women's lives like in such a society? How is their work assessed and valued? What are the prevailing attitudes about women? What notions are there of 'women's nature'?[183]

> One distinctive feature of feminist research is that it generates its problems from the perspective of women's experiences. It also uses these experiences as a significant indicator of the 'reality' against which hypotheses are tested.[184]

---

182 For a description of the 'woman question' and its origins, see K Bartlett, 'Feminist Legal Methods' (1990) 103 *Harvard Law Review* 829, 837. (Extracted in Chapter 4.)

183 See eg E Spelman, *Inessential Woman* (1989), p 47; H Wishik, 'To Question Everything: the Enquiries of Feminist Jurisprudence' (1985) 1 *Berkeley Women's Law Journal* 64; E Minnich Karmarch, *Transforming Knowledge* (1990).

184 S Harding, 'Introduction: Is There a Feminist Method?' in S Harding (ed), *Feminism and Methodology* (1987), pp 1, 7.

This method of enquiry – asking where women are in the dominant account of the way things are and whether dominant standards and models reflect the reality of women's perspectives – has had a major impact on many disciplines, in some cases transforming basic concepts and undermining established truths. In a number of areas feminist scholarship has moved 'from simply adding women into existing schemes of knowledge into more fundamental reconstructions of the concepts, methods and theories of the disciplines'.

The Importance of Method in Relation to Women and Human Rights Violations

A failure to be aware of the relevance of gender can result in a distorted picture of patterns of human rights abuses, and can lead to an androcentric definition of substantive norms. Furthermore, an awareness of the role that gender may play in a given context may alert one to the need to adopt a particular response tailored to that context.

A failure to realise that women may have suffered violations whose form has been influenced by the fact that they are women and to enquire specifically about such violations may mean that certain types of human rights violations which have a gender-specific cause or form are not detected. For example, in the area of refugee law,[185] women refugees are frequently subjected to various forms of sexual abuse which may form part of the persecution from which they have fled or which they may have experienced while travelling or while living in refugee camps. The failure to be aware of the possibility of such violations and the fact that women will often be reluctant to talk about them, particularly to the interviewers, can mean that not only may a woman's claim to refugee status never be uncovered but the need for appropriately formulated medical or other programmes to address the results of gender-specific violations may not be perceived.

Similarly, if women prisoners or detainees are being subjected to regular sexual abuse in special women's prisons, this is more likely to be uncovered if issues of gender are specifically considered by those enquiring into the existence of torture in a country rather than as the result of general enquiries about the maltreatment of detainees in prisons.[186]

Another important aspect of sensitivity to gender is that it can have an impact on the content of substantive norms by leading to their reinterpretation in a way which reflects women's perspectives. The question here might be, for example, whether particular forms of conduct amount to degrading treatment and violate various guarantees. It is well accepted that some of the answers to that question may vary according to the cultural context; they may also vary according to sex within that cultural context. Similarly, with refugees, an awareness of the particular forms of persecution from which women are fleeing may lead to the reinterpretation of the grounds of persecution to include those forms of persecution.[187]

---

185 See generally A Johnson, 'The International Protection of Women Refugees: A Summary of Principal Problems and Issues' (1989) 1 *International Journal of Refugee Law* 221.

186 A Bynes, 'The Committee Against Torture', in P Alston (ed), *The Human Rights Organs of the United Nations* (1992).

187 See generally J Greatbatch, 'The Gender Difference: Feminist Critiques of Refugee Discourse' (1989) 1 *Int J of Refugee Law* 518; DE Neal, 'Women as a Social Group: Recognising Sex-Based Persecution as Grounds for Asylum' (1988) 20 *Columbia Human Rights LR* 203.

Thus, by being aware of gender issues, one is more likely to uncover the full range of violations in a particular context, as a result of which one may need to reinterpret previously accepted substantive interpretations of rights guarantees in order to reflect adequately the experiences of women, as well as to devise different strategies for addressing problems.

Quite simply, if you are not looking for something (or at least aware that it might exist), then your chances of finding it are significantly reduced. The importance of being aware that sex and gender may be significant, asking what the position of women is and whether that is reflected in universal norms and taken into account in designing responses to social problems has been demonstrated time and time again. However, in the area of human rights abuses it appears that too often this dimension of a situation may not be explored thoroughly, and such examination as there may be is limited to the relatively formalistic invocation of androcentric standards of non-discrimination.

The Accusations of Neglect and the Extent of the Inclusion of Women's Human Rights Issues in the Mainstream

1 Nature of the critique

The major human rights instruments all grandly proclaim that women are entitled to enjoy the rights guaranteed on a basis of equality with men. The charges laid at the door of the mainstream human rights community by feminist critics vary in the extent of their denunciation of the system for its failure to promote the realisation of this entitlement. The more sweeping ones argue that these guarantees of equal enjoyment of rights are little more than empty rhetoric and that women are neglected entirely within the mainstream practice, while more moderate critics argue that there is a low level of awareness of these issues and that the attention paid to them is insufficient.

Some of the important criticisms that have been voiced are allegations that:

- even those violations suffered by women that appear indistinguishable from those suffered by men are not adequately taken cognisance of within the 'mainstream';

- the failure to be aware that sex and gender are important determinants of human rights violations means that gender-specific variants of violations may be missed or not adequately responded to;

- standard interpretations of particular rights and of the entitlement to equal enjoyment of those are androcentrically biased;

- the public/private distinction that underpins the traditional civil and political rights framework has the effect of rendering gross violations of women's rights at the hands of private individuals largely invisible;

- the prevailing preoccupation with civil and political rights at the expense of economic and social rights diverts resources away from areas in which they could more effectively be used to promote the advancement of women;

- gender is also largely neglected in the interpretation of economic, social and cultural rights, despite the fact that considerable effort is now being devoted to exploring the detailed substantive content of those rights.

These charges appear to have a large measure of truth in them. Many issues of importance to women have been consigned to marginalised and less powerful institutions within the United Nations human rights system. The violations suffered by women are a relatively minor concern of the mainstream human rights community, unless they happen to fall into a small number of narrowly defined categories. Otherwise, there is considerable evidence of sex/gender blindness or myopia within that system.

Nevertheless, both the terms of the charges themselves and their accuracy need to be examined in greater detail if the indictment is to be made to stick and a convincing case made for change. In general terms the following are the questions which need to be addressed:

a.   To what extent have women's experiences been included within the purview of mainstream human rights practice at the international level and why have the particular violations that have been addressed been taken up in preference to others?

b.   What are the reasons for the limited extent to which women's experiences have been included within that discourse?

c.   Is it possible for that neglect to be remedied within the established conceptual framework? What changes would be needed and what limits are there?

2 'Violations' of 'women's rights' or 'women's human rights'

In order to assess the accuracy of the charges of neglect and bias made against the 'mainstream' it is necessary to examine in more detail the terms of the debate. Reference is made to 'violations' of 'women's rights', 'women's human rights', 'gender-specific human rights violations', and 'human rights violations against women'. It is important initially to define some of these terms and to delineate the nature of the experiences and perspectives which, it is argued, are not adequately taken into account in the dominant institutions.

The term 'violation(s)' (of 'women's rights' or of 'women's human rights') is not used by the critics in a merely technical international law sense, but refers to serious infringements of human dignity suffered by women, whether or not they would constitute a violation of human rights guarantees under accepted interpretations. These 'violations' include violations that fall within the classical categories of civil and political rights violations (such as torture and maltreatment in detention) with or without a gender-specific element; violations suffered at the hands of the State or its officials, or at the hands of private individuals acting in a private capacity; denials of access to social and economic benefits on a discriminatory basis; and a disproportionate denial of access to social benefits and opportunities because of the use of models or definitions derived from the experience and life patterns.

Women suffer violations of their human dignity for many different reasons and in many different ways.[188] In some cases the reason for the violation and the form it takes may appear indistinguishable from those leading to violations against men in similar circumstances. In other cases their sex or gender may be the occasion for or determine the form which the violation takes. In many other cases there may be a complex interaction between sex, gender, race, class, political activities or some other factor in explaining the origin and form of human rights violations from which women suffer.

The types of violations which have been frequently referred to as of particular significance to women or which are determined to a significant extent by gender include:[189]

---

188 See J Neuwirth, 'Towards a Gender-Based Approach to Human Rights Violations' (1987) 9 *Whittier LR* 399 and F Gaer, 'Introduction in International League for Human Rights, Human Rights Abuses Against Women' (1990).

189 See generally Amnesty International, *Women in the Front Line: Human Rights Violations Against Women* (1991) and F Gaer, *supra.*

- rape by State officials or by private individuals
- dowry deaths
- family and domestic violence
- forced prostitution and trafficking in women
- denial of equal rights to participate in political life (including denial of the right to vote)
- harassment of politically active women
- denial of inheritance and property rights
- sexual surgery/female circumcision
- denial of reproductive rights
- discriminatory provisions in nationality law both as to the acquisition and transmission of nationality
- unequal access to health care and unequal enjoyment of the right to life and right to adequate food
- discrimination against women refugees
- persecution of women because of their family relationships
- denial of access to land and economic opportunities.

The terms 'violations of *women's rights*' and 'violations of *women's human rights*' frequently appear in the discussion. However, there is some lack of clarity as to the scope of each of those terms. The first term is apparently intended to refer to 'gender-specific' violations, that is, violations which may be suffered only or predominantly by women or which appear to be based on sex or gender (for example, rape, female circumcision, forced prostitution, trafficking in women, discrimination in nationality laws). The second term is broader in its coverage, encompassing human rights violations where women 'just happen to be the victims', that is, the violations are not gender-specific and men are or could equally well be victims of essentially similar violations (for example, persecution of politically active women, discrimination against members of an ethnic minority, forced evictions).

It is easy to see that it may be difficult to assign particular violations unambiguously to one of these categories, a fact which reflects the inter-play of sex, race, class and other factors in the form a human rights violation may take. Even in cases in which the reason for the persecution of a woman is her political activities, the form the violation takes may be influenced by her sex and gender.

However, the institutional allocation of responsibility for 'human rights issues' and 'women's issues' within a system such as the UN human rights system may make it important to ask whether every human rights violation suffered by a woman is 'violation of women's rights' or whether the fact that race, class or political opinion are the determinative factors in many human rights violations against women, perhaps to the exclusion of sex and gender, means that women 'just happen to be the victims' of them and gender plays no significant role and, if so, which ones they are.

Criticism of the 'mainstream' practice is that it fails to take adequate account of 'human rights violations against women', as well as 'violations of women's rights'. More prominence has been given to the latter in the debate, but both categories require investigation. The point is that in both cases there is a danger that the gender dimension of a human rights abuse may not be perceived if one is not looking for it – the failing is one of method, but one which affects questions of substance.

An evaluation of the criticisms made of the 'mainstream' thus requires an examination of how human rights violations against women in all their forms are dealt with, not just clear cases of gender-related violations but also cases of violations in which 'women just happen to be the victims'.

Silences/Omissions/Myopia: Is Gender on the Agenda?

It is not difficult to point to instances in which gender appears to have been neglected when its inclusion is of considerable importance. The practice of the Human Rights Committee, widely regarded as the leading human rights treaty body within the UN system, provides a number of examples. The Committee, in addition to its function of considering individual complaints under the First Optional Protocol to the International Covenant on Civil and Political Rights (ICCPR), has adopted the practice of issuing general comments dealing with the articles of the Covenant. These are intended to be an authoritative exegesis of the content of the rights guaranteed by the ICCPR and they identify what the Committee considers to be the most important dimensions of those rights.

In these interpretative comments there is virtually no recognition that sex or gender can be a significant dimension in defining the substantive content of individual rights or that it can affect the choice of methods that must be adopted by states to ensure that all individuals within their jurisdiction enjoy those rights equally.

In its general comment on the right to privacy, for example, there is not even a passing reference to the importance that this right has assumed in the struggle of women in many countries for control over their reproductive lives; traditional concepts such as the inviolability of the home and restrictions on the use of sensitive personal information by governments and others are the major preoccupations of the Committee. Similarly, the Committee's view of the scope of the right of a person to fair and non-discriminatory treatment by the legal system is expounded without any suggestion that the relationship of women to the criminal justice system as victims of crime and as defendants raises important issues of fairness that differ in many ways from those that arise in relation to men.

Similarly, the Committee's general comments on the right to bodily integrity and the right to life give not the faintest intimation that women face major, different threats to their enjoyment of these rights than do men or that this fact may have important implications for the obligations assumed by governments under the Covenant to ensure equality in the enjoyment of these rights. In many parts of the world women are at a considerably higher risk of death from avoidable causes than are men.[190] The reasons for this include horrifyingly high levels of maternal mortality, preferential treatment of men and boys in providing access to food and health care, and the perpetuation of traditional practices such as genital mutilation of young girls. The differences in the nature and level of threats to the enjoyment of their rights to life and to bodily integrity that women and men face justify the conclusion that women and men do not enjoy these rights on an equal basis, which is the promise held out to women by the major human rights instruments.

---

190 R Cook, 'Human Rights and Infant Survival: A Case for Priorities' (1986–87) 18 *Columbia Hum Rts LR* 22–24; R Cook, 'Reducing Maternal Mortality' in S McLean (ed), *Legal Issues in Human Reproduction* (1989), p 185; A Sen, 'More than 100 Million Women are Missing', *New York Review of Books*, 10 December 1990, p 61.

The Human Rights Committee is not atypical in the lack of importance it gives to gender as a component of the definition of human rights; this pattern appears regularly in the work of publicists, activists and other bodies concerned with the implementation of the major civil and political rights catalogues. For example, a collection of essays which is the major work on the ICCPR in English and which is authored exclusively by males ignores the relevance of gender in its elaboration of the normative content of the Covenant, except in cases where the subject of women is forced upon it by the specific language of the Covenant.[191]

Similarly, a recent major treatise on torture and international law runs to several hundred pages without any discussion of the way in which sexual violence against women is a major component of the practice of torture. Nor does it even address the question of the inadequacies of the international law definition of torture which, by restricting its scope to acts committed by or at the instigation of State officials, excludes from the purview of international law major areas in which women suffer similar treatment at the hands of non-State officials. United Nations Rapporteurs preparing studies of particular human rights, thematic reports on human rights violations or reports on individual countries where one would expect some discussion of well-known violations of the rights of women, often compile reports which make no reference to the fact that women suffer not only many of the same violations as men but different ones as well. And many traditional NGOs are simply not interested in exploring the gender dimensions of human rights violations, although there have been some encouraging developments in recent years.

Nature of the Inclusion

Yet the more extravagant critiques of the 'mainstream', that women are completely ignored, go too far. Firstly, despite the apparently pervasive disregard of gender, a number of gender-specific issues are addressed within the mainstream. Secondly, it is clear that attention is given to women who are victims of classical human rights violations (where the victims 'just happen to be women'). For example, issues of discrimination on the basis of sex, torture or arbitrary imprisonment of women, and practices of particular importance for women (such as trafficking in women, forced prostitution and female genital mutilation) have a place on the agenda of 'mainstream' bodies. There have been some indications in recent years that some of the human rights bodies are becoming more aware of the issue of gender and are attempting to respond to it, though how wide-ranging these responses will be remains to be seen. For example, the Committee on Economic, Social and Cultural Rights in its General Comment No 4 (1991) on the right to adequate housing contained in Article 11(1) of the International Covenant on Economic, Social and Cultural Rights noted:[192]

> 6.   The right to adequate housing applies to everyone. While the reference to 'himself and his family' reflects assumptions as to gender roles and economic activity patterns commonly accepted in 1966 when the Covenant was adopted, the phrase cannot be read today as implying any limitations upon the applicability of the right to individuals or to female-headed households or other such groups. Thus, the concept of 'family' must be understood in a wide sense. Further, individuals, as well as families, are entitled to adequate housing regardless of age,

---

191 See L Henkin (ed), *The International Bill of Rights: The Covenant on Civil and Political Rights* (Columbia University Press, 1981).

192 UN Doc E/C.12/1991/4, Annex III, para 6.

> economic status, group or other affiliation or status and other such factors. In particular, enjoyment of this right must, in accordance with Article 2(2) of the Covenant, not be subject to any form of discrimination.

Apart from this passage, the Committee does not develop its analysis of right to housing with explicit reference to gender dimensions of the right. Nonetheless, it does incorporate within its discussion issues which may be of particular importance to women rather than men in a number of societies (for example, the availability of potable water, energy for cooking, sanitation and washing facilities and food storage).

Despite this sort of example, one may perhaps be justifiably sceptical about the significance accorded to these issues within the 'mainstream' and the effectiveness of the monitoring and enforcement procedures or the manner in which those issues are handled. One might also ask about the cases of 'classical' violations against women which are not being noticed because of the use of flawed methods which do not explicitly take gender into account.

However, the question then becomes not whether violations of women's human rights are dealt with but the terms of the inclusion (and the exclusion). How much is included and what is left out? What are the terms and extent of the inclusion (are only those violations that conform to an androcentric model taken cognisance of)? Are the issues that are dealt with important issues, or relatively minor issues, thus distracting attention from more fundamental issues? How are these matters disposed of – are effective responses devised (and are they in accordance with the women whose interests are affected?)? What level of resources and institutional support is given to this work? Is there a real commitment (as evidenced by effective procedures and enforcement mechanisms) to addressing these problems?

To date many of these questions have only been examined briefly – much of the discussion has been fairly descriptive – and provide fertile ground for further research. They are important questions to address because, whenever one raises the question of what the 'mainstream' is doing to address violations of the human rights of women, in particular gender-specific violations, one is referred to the work of bodies which have these issues on their agenda. The task then becomes one of evaluating the extent to which issues of real importance to women are covered and the effectiveness of the substantive work and the monitoring procedures which are in place – and then upon close examination these may turn out to be less impressive than portrayed.

For example, 'mainstreamers' frequently point to the body of international case law which has dealt with issues of particular importance for women (including sex discrimination and reproductive rights issues) and cases in which women have been successful in vindicating their rights as evidence of the contribution being made by the mainstream to the promotion of women's human rights.

While these cases are significant, it is also important to be aware of their conceptual limitations. Furthermore, it is instructive to see exactly what claims of women have been addressed and to ask why others have not been raised in these fora.

The international cases in which women figure as authors of complaints (or in which issues of sex discrimination otherwise arise) fall into a number of broad categories:

1.   Those in which women suffer violations which are basically identical to those suffered by men.

2. Those involving claims of non-discrimination in which women are claiming an entitlement to the same treatment, rights or privileges as men.

3. Those involving claims by women of an entitlement to have control over their reproductive capacity or claims by others to attempt to limit that control.

The first category of cases in practice involves no particular recognition that sex or gender can be an important factor in the definition, cause, or form of violations of bodily or psychic integrity. The second and third categories do involve some recognition that sex and gender can play a role in the definition of what constitutes a human rights violation, particularly in cases which do not turn on a simple discrimination point because there is no male comparator.

Both the first and second categories embody essentially androcentric models of women's entitlements: if men are entitled to a particular benefit and women claim an identical benefit or if they put forward a claim sufficiently analogous to those of men, then the mainstream may take cognisance of it.[193]

The third category has been far more problematic from women's point of view with rather mixed outcomes if one is concerned to have an international endorsement of women's control over their own reproductive capacity.

Nearly all the leading international cases involving issues of sex discrimination in which a claim has been successful have been relatively 'easy' ones in analytical terms. While the outcome of a number of cases may have had important political and economic consequences and required the rejection of traditional or stereotyped ideas, giving to women the identical privileges (in most cases at a formal legal level) as are enjoyed by men does not involve a major theoretical reorientation. While important in what they do achieve, one should not overestimate their significance – they do not undertake the rethinking that is necessary if one approaches the area with a feminist perspective of even moderately radical ilk.

In summary, while there is still much detailed work to be done to determine the extent to which human rights violations against women and violations of women's rights are dealt with by the 'mainstream', one gains a firm initial impression that by and large there is relatively little acknowledgment that gender is an important dimension in defining the substantive content of rights, in particular those rights that do not refer specifically to women or that embody a guarantee of non-discrimination, and that equal enjoyment of rights is defined in terms of a male-centred model. The corollary of this is that there is also little recognition that a State's obligation to ensure equal enjoyment of a right by women may entail the taking of measures quite different from those which may be necessary to ensure that men enjoy that right.

Reasons for the Limited Recognition of the Role of Gender in Defining and Responding to Human Rights Violations

Thus, while there remains much work to be done in further documentation of the extent to which human rights violations against women are dealt with in the 'mainstream', there are certainly strong indications that the relevance of gender to the definition of human rights violations and responses to them is much neglected within that 'mainstream', rendering invisible many violations of women's human dignity.

---

193 *Cf* CA MacKinnon, *Toward a Feminist Theory of the State* (1989), pp 215–34.

Why is this so? A number of reasons for this neglect have been suggested.[194] They include overwhelmingly the membership of the bodies charged with the implementation and interpretation of these instruments, the apparent reluctance historically of human rights groups and women's human rights groups to insist that these issues be addressed in the mainstream, the institutional separation between the bodies concerned with 'human rights' and those concerned with 'women's issues', and the conceptual framework of traditional civil and political rights analysis.

Despite the rhetoric about the inter-dependence and indivisibility of human rights, traditional civil and political rights have received the lion's share of the attention of the international human rights community. Many of the violations suffered by women are bound up with the disadvantages they suffer in the economic and social field, and the lack of attention devoted to these economic, social and cultural rights has accordingly involved a neglect of areas important for the facilitation of the advancement of women. Furthermore, violations of 'women's human rights' are often regarded neither as pressing nor as important as the other violations of human rights being perpetrated in many parts of the world or as too sensitive to deal with in light of possible accusations of cultural imperialism.

There is a certain reluctance within the civil and political rights world to address social and economic inequalities of a structural nature which effectively negate the possibility of the exercise of guaranteed civil and political rights. Much of current human rights practice has concerned itself, quite understandably, with symptoms rather than the underlying causes of human rights violations. To respond to clear cases of gross violations of human rights where victims are suffering in a direct and visible way and where one can point to the perpetrator of the violation and demand that the perpetrator desist from its conduct is in some ways easier than attempting to respond to violations of human rights arising from social and economic arrangements which can only be addressed by fundamental changes in those relations (such as starvation of a large proportion of a country's population unnecessarily). However, even those institutions which have attempted to focus on the conditions giving rise to gross violations of human rights do not see gender or violations against women as an identifiable area requiring urgent study. Nor do some clear cases of gross violations against women attract the same attention as some which are seen not to raise 'sensitive' issues of culture and tradition which so often spell 'hands off' in relation to violations of women's rights. Two prominent examples are the practice of female circumcision or female genital mutilations and the position of women in various religions (in particular under some interpretations of Islam).[195]

One other reason why mainstream bodies may not be paying adequate attention to gender-related issues may be the nature of their information-gathering techniques. Many of the United Nations human rights bodies, for example, obtain a great deal of their independent information about human rights violations from the many non-governmental organisations which form part of

---

194 See eg F Gaer, 'Human Rights at the United Nations: Women's Rights are Human Rights', in *Brief No 24*, November 1989 (International League for Human Rights).

195 See D Sullivan, 'Advancing Freedom of Religion or Belief through the UN Declaration on the Elimination of Religious Intolerance and Discrimination' (1988) 82 *AJIL* 487; D Arzt, 'The Application of International Human Rights Law in Islamic States' (1990) 12 *Hum Rts Q* 202; A Rahman, 'A Religious Rights Versus Women's Rights in India' (1990) 28 *Columbia J Trans L* 473.

the Geneva or US-based human rights community. While there are certainly women's organisations which are part of that community, many of them have traditional human rights concerns or agendas or are not particularly interested in pursuing women's issues in 'mainstream' human rights terms. The many networks of women's organisations which are working in the area of gender-specific violations know little about or have limited access to these international fora and do not appear to be sought out by those responsible for gathering information. A further factor is the location in Vienna of the UN bodies with primary responsibility for 'women's issues', the Commission on the Status of Women and the Committee on the Elimination of Discrimination Against Women, while the other human rights bodies are based in Geneva. This means that the Geneva-based NGOs are often not aware of what is happening in Vienna.

Another feature of the 'mainstream's' treatment of gender issues has been the rather limited notion of the concept of equality and non-discrimination in the enjoyment of rights. To date, the main model used has been a largely androcentric one – if men are entitled to something, then women should be entitled to the same thing; whereas true equality may involve the reworking of the core concept of the right to ensure that women enjoy that right fully.

But perhaps the most important reason has been the conceptual framework of the 'mainstream' with its public/private split, which has obscured many of the violations of human dignity suffered by women at the hands of private individuals. In the next section some of the ramifications of this public/private distinction are explored and in the following one the conceptual structure of the 'mainstream' civil and political rights framework is examined in the context of violence against women.

The Public/Private Distinction: State Responsibility Arising out of the Acts of Private Individuals

The theoretical framework of traditional human rights analysis has been a major contributor to the neglect of violations of particular concern to women; it also poses a number of serious obstacles which need to be overcome if women's legitimate claims in relation to the right to life and the right to bodily integrity are to be addressed within that framework. These problems arise from a focus on direct State violations of individual rights, an acceptance of a division between public and private spheres of social life, and a reluctance to address the existence of economic and social conditions which affect the ability to exercise the basic civil and political rights guaranteed.

The primary orientation of civil and political rights analysis has been direct violations of the rights of individuals by the State. These violations have generally taken one of two forms: the adoption of legislation or practices which discriminate against particular groups or unjustifiably limit the exercise of rights, or the actions of State officials directed against individuals which violate their rights – classic cases being torture, wrongful imprisonment and summary or arbitrary executions.

Women do, of course, suffer serious violations of their rights directly at the hands of the State and, as indicated above, sex and gender may play a role in the instigation of such violations and the particular form they take. However, women also suffer major violations of their physical integrity at the hands of private individuals. The extent of State involvement and complicity in these violations is its responsibility for the maintenance of a legal and social system in which these violations occur and may legitimate such violations or allow them to pass unpunished. However, the liability of the State for such 'complicity' under international human rights law is far from self-evident.

Further, the conceptual framework of civil and political rights is built on a separation of public and private realms. The cordoning off of particular activities from direct State intervention by adopting the notion of a sphere of private life (the very area in which women suffer many infractions of their rights at the hands of men) renders the vindication of these rights difficult within that framework.

State Responsibility Arising out of the Acts of Private Individuals

Despite the achievements of the international human rights movement in bringing about a situation in which it can be said that States owe duties to their own citizens, our present system of international law is still fundamentally a State-centred one of reciprocal rights and obligations enjoyed and borne by States among themselves. International law has had difficulty in dealing with the question of the liability of States in relation to the acts of private individuals which cause damage to other individuals and States. It is a still a relatively undeveloped subject in the area of international human rights.

The major exploration of the issue in general international law has been in relation to the liability of governments for harm caused by individuals within their territory to nationals of another country or to their property. Diplomats and other foreigners within the jurisdiction of a State who suffer physical or material damage at the hands of private individuals have been the two basic categories with which international law traditionally concerned itself. In such cases, depending on the circumstances and the status of the individual who suffers damage, the position has been that a failure to take reasonable steps to prevent harm to aliens or, at the very least, the failure to provide a legal system within which claims for redress can be pursued by private individuals or are pursued by public authorities can amount to a violation of international law by the authorities of the host State. This is so even though the State was not directly responsible for the original actions of the private individuals who caused the damage.

Thus, even where private individuals have violated others' rights in the first instance, the host State has been held liable for a failure to take reasonable steps to prevent these violations or for the failure to have an appropriate system of laws and institutions to punish or remedy such transgressions. Under some circumstances, then, international law requires a State not to just stand idly by while private individuals infringe the rights of other individuals; they must take positive steps to stop those violations or to offer redress for them.

The Obligation of the State to Prevent or Provide a Remedy for Infringements of Rights by Private Individuals

While the traditional liberal conception of human rights guarantees was protection against the direct exercise of State power against a private individual, it has become increasingly accepted at the international level that the interests protected by human rights guarantees may in many cases be encroached on by private individuals as well as government, and that this has implications for the responsibility of the State under international law.

As a result, there has been an expansion of the traditional content of States' obligations in the area of protection of human rights, with parallels being drawn from the more traditional doctrines of the law of State responsibility. Under the general human rights treaties (as well as other treaties), the State is considered to be under an obligation not only to refrain from taking direct action which infringes individual rights but also to take positive steps to ensure that individuals actually enjoy those rights. This latter aspect of the obligation includes in certain circumstances a duty to take appropriate measures to protect individuals against violation of those rights by private persons. This approach has been adopted under the ICCPR, the European Convention and the American Convention on Human Rights.

The textual basis for these positive obligations has been the obligations assumed by the State under the treaties to take appropriate measures to ensure that individuals actually enjoy the rights guaranteed to them. For example, the obligations of the State under the ICCPR extend to ensuring in some circumstances that the rights of individuals are not infringed by other private persons or that adequate remedies are provided or appropriate punishment imposed if such rights are infringed.

As one commentator puts it:[196]

> The obligation 'to ensure' these rights encompasses the duty 'to respect' them, but is substantially broader ... the provision implies an affirmative obligation by the State to take whatever measures are necessary to enable individuals to enjoy or exercise the rights guaranteed in the Covenant, including the removal of governmental and possibly also some private obstacles to the enjoyment of those rights ... as regards some rights in some circumstances, it may perhaps require the State to adopt laws and other measures against private interference with enjoyment of rights, for example against interference with the exercise of the right to vote and other political rights.

This approach to the general obligation to respect and ensure the enumerated rights against infringement by private persons has also been taken by the Inter-American Court of Human Rights when interpreting the similar language of the American Convention on Human Rights.

In *Velasquez Rodriguez v Honduras*,[197] a case involving 'disappearances' in Honduras, the court accepted that the Honduran government could be liable internationally if it failed to take appropriate steps to prevent or punish private individuals who caused others to 'disappear'. The court discussed the extent of the obligation in Article I of the American Convention 'to respect' and 'to ensure' the full and free exercise of the rights guaranteed in the Convention. It concluded that, while the obligation clearly extended to violations of rights carried out by the act of a public authority or by persons who use their position of authority:[198]

> 172 ... [This] does not define all the circumstances in which a State is obligated to prevent, investigate and punish human rights violations, nor all the cases in which the State might be found responsible for an infringement of those rights. An illegal act which violates human rights and which is initially not imputable to a State (for example, because it is the act of a private person or because the person responsible has not been identified) can lead to international responsibility of the State, not because of the act itself, but because of the lack of due diligence to prevent the violation or to respond to it as required by the Convention ...

---

196 T Buergenthal, 'To Respect and to Ensure: State Obligations and Permissible Derogations', in L Henkin, *op cit*.

197 Inter-American Court of Human Rights, Ser C No 4, Judgment of 29 July 1988 (1989) 28 ILM 291.

198 *Ibid*, paras 172, 174–5; 28 ILM 291, 325.

174. The State has a legal duty to take reasonable steps to prevent human rights violations and to use the means at its disposal to carry out a serious investigation of violations committed within its jurisdiction, to identify those responsible, to impose the appropriate punishment and to ensure the victim adequate compensation.

175. This duty to prevent includes all those means of a legal, political, administrative and cultural nature that promote the protection of human rights and ensure that any violations are considered and treated as illegal acts, which, as such, may lead to the punishment of those responsible and the obligation to indemnify the victims for damages.

The general obligation 'to respect' and 'to ensure', the obligation to prevent, remedy or punish violations by private individuals has been examined in the context of a number of specific rights under the general human rights treaties.

For example, at the time the ICCPR was drafted, it was contemplated that the State had the obligation not merely to refrain from taking life under circumstances not consistent with the Covenant, but that the obligation to ensure enjoyment of that right included a duty to protect life against the actions of private persons. The Human Rights Committee has expressed a similar view. The European Commission of Human Rights has also recognised that the guarantee of the right to life under the European Convention requires the State in certain circumstances to take positive measures to protect the right to life against violations by private individuals.[199]

Both the European Court of Human Rights and the European Commission of Human Rights have recognised in a number of cases that effective guarantees of the enjoyment of individual rights require that the State protect individuals against the actions of other individuals infringing on those rights. One example is a case brought against the United Kingdom in which the court held that the right of freedom of association includes the right not to he a member of a trade union. The court also held that the failure of United Kingdom legislation to prevent an employer from discriminating against an employee on the ground of a refusal to join a union was a failure on the part of the United Kingdom to fulfil the obligation it had assumed under the Convention to 'secure to everyone within its jurisdiction ... the rights and freedoms' defined in the Convention.[200]

The general position under that Convention has been expressed by the Commission in the following terms:[201]

It is true that the Convention fundamentally guarantees traditional freedoms in relation to the State as the holder of public power. This does not, however, imply that the State may not be obliged to protect individuals through appropriate measures taken against some forms of interference by other individuals, groups or organisations. While they themselves, under the Convention, may not be held responsible for any such acts which are in breach of the Convention, the State may, under certain circumstances, be responsible for them.

199 *W v UK*, Application No 9360/81, European Commission of Human Rights, decision on admissibility of 28 February 1983, 32 D & R 211, 213; *X v Ireland* Application No 6040/73, 44 CE 121, 122.

202 *Young, James and Webster v UK*, judgment of 26 June 1981, Ser A, No 44, para 49, 62 ILR 359, 4 EHRR 38.

201 *National Union of Belgian Police* case, Report of the Commission, Ser B, No 17, para 59 (1976).

In *Plattform Ärzte für das Leben v Austria*, a case involving the disruption of anti-abortion demonstratiqns in Austria by those who supported the wider availability of abortion, the court also recognised that the State may be under a duty to take steps to ensure that the rights of freedom of assembly of some groups can he exercised without excessive interference from opposition groups.[202] The Human Rights Committee has also recognised that the classical civil and political rights impose some positive obligations on states to prevent infringements by private individuals, as has the Inter-American Court of Human Rights in the context of freedom of expression.

Thus, the State is required in certain circumstances to take positive action to ensure the enjoyment of those rights against interference by other private individuals. This action will generally include the enactment of laws and the fashioning of administrative and other arrangements so that individuals can actually enjoy the rights guaranteed by the relevant treaties. The various human rights bodies have recognised that positive obligations are implied in many of the classical civil and political rights and have begun to explore the extent of those rights. What is surprising is that the issue has barely been formulated in terms which raised issues of particular concern to women, either by complaints lodged by individuals or by the interpretative bodies themselves on their own initiative.

'Private' Violence

The widespread problem of violence against women which is not directly attributable to the State is more problematic for the human rights 'mainstream'. A recent United Nations study on violence against women in the family context described its dimensions:

> Research indicates that violence against women is not confined to violence perpetrated by strangers. Indeed, it has become clear that women are more often at risk from those with whom they live and many of them live constantly with the threat of 'domestic violence', whether battery, rape, incest or emotional abuse.

> In all countries and cultures, women have frequently been battered, sexually abused and psychologically injured by persons with whom they should enjoy the closest trust. This maltreatment has gone largely unpunished, unremarked and has even been tacitly, if not explicitly, condoned.[203]

The issue of violence against women has been at the forefront of the critique of the 'mainstream's' failure to recognise violations of women's human dignity. The assertion frequently made by feminists (admittedly in some cases as an attempt to change perceptions rather than as a statement of the existing legal position) that 'rape is a human rights violation' is met with the response from traditional human rights groups and the 'mainstream' that this is only the case if it is carried out by officials of the State (for example, the rape of women prisoners by prison guards).

This example highlights the conceptual difficulties that the established framework of international human rights law has in recognising that pervasive patterns of private violence against women may involve a failure by the State to respect the human rights of women.

---

202 Judgment of 21 June 1988, Ser A, No 139, para 32, 13 EHRR 204.

203 United Nations: *Violence Against Women in the Family*.

Yet the gulf between the two positions is by no means completely unbridgeable. While international law is traditionally reluctant to recognise the acts of private individuals as acts of the State, the discussion above has made clear that States are under an obligation in certain circumstances to take preventive or punitive measures against violations of the rights of individuals by private parties.[204]

To date, little has been done to explore the implications for violence against women of the recent developments in the area of State responsibility arising out of the acts of private individuals, despite the fact that considerable attention has been paid to that latter issue in other contexts. It is an important area well deserving of further work.

The Committee on the Elimination of Discrimination Against Women recently addressed the issue of violence against women in a general recommendation adopted at its 1992 Session. In its General Recommendation No 19 the primary aim of the Committee was to clarify the extent to which different forms of violence against women were in its view covered by the Women's Convention (in which the term 'violence' does not appear). Another, related goal of the General Recommendation was to emphasise the overlap between the obligations which States Parties to the Women's Convention had assumed in relation to violence against women and the obligations which States Parties to other human rights treaties had assumed in relation to such violence.

In its discussion the Committee characterised violence against women as a form of 'discrimination against women' as defined in Article 1 of the Convention and noted that the Convention obliged States Parties to eliminate all forms of discrimination, whether perpetrated by public officials or private individuals:

> 7. This definition of discrimination [in Article 1 of the Convention] includes gender-based violence – that is violence which is directed against a woman because she is a woman or which affects women disproportionately. It includes acts which inflict physical, mental or sexual harm or suffering, threats of such acts, coercion and other deprivations of liberty. Gender-based violence may breach specific provisions of the Convention, regardless of whether those provisions expressly mention violence.

Gender-Based Violence Violates Human Rights

> 8. Gender-based violence which impairs or nullifies the enjoyment by women of human rights and fundamental freedoms under general international law or under specific human rights conventions is discrimination within the meaning of Article 1 of the Convention. These rights and freedoms include, *inter alia*:
>
> – the right to life,
>
> – the right not to be subject to torture or to cruel, inhuman or degrading treatment or punishment,
>
> – the right to the equal protection of humanitarian norms in time of international or internal armed conflict,
>
> – the right to liberty and security of person,
>
> – the right to the equal protection of the law,
>
> – the right to equality in the family,

---

204 See eg the change in attitude adopted in the US State Department's 1990 Country Reports on Human Rights which reflects the stance that government tolerance of systematic violence and abuse directed at women engages the responsibility of the State.

- the right to the highest standard attainable of physical and mental health, and
- the right to just and favourable conditions of work.

The Convention covers public and private acts

9. The Convention applies to violence perpetrated by public authorities. Such acts of violence may also breach that State's obligations under general international human rights law, and under other Conventions, in addition to being a breach of this Convention.

10. It should be emphasised, however, that discrimination under the Convention is not restricted to actions by or on behalf of governments (see Articles 2.e, 2.f and 5). For example, under Article 2.e the Convention calls on States to take all appropriate measures to eliminate discrimination against women by any person, organisation or enterprise. Under general international law and specific human rights covenants, States may also be responsible for private acts if they fail to act with due diligence to prevent violations of rights, or to investigate and punish acts of violence, and to provide compensation.

11. States Parties should take appropriate and effective measures to overcome all forms of gender based violence, whether by public or private act.

Absence of Complaints in International Fora

There appear to have been virtually no cases at the international level in which violence against women has been explicitly raised by complainants. The closest instance seems to be *X and Y v Netherlands*,[205] a case under the European Convention in which a challenge was made to Netherlands law under which for various technical reasons a criminal prosecution could not be brought against a person who had sexually abused a mentally handicapped woman.

In that case, the European Court and Commission held that the failure of Netherlands law to provide for the possibility of criminal proceedings for this type of sexual violation while providing such remedies for others was a failure to fulfil its obligation to ensure that persons in the victim's position could enjoy the right to respect for their private life guaranteed by the Convention. In so holding, the court stated its view that, while the object of the guarantee of the right to privacy was 'essentially that of protecting the individual against arbitrary interference by public authorities', it did not stop there; it may impose positive obligations on the State which 'may involve the adoption of measures designed to ensure respect for private life even in the sphere of the relations of individuals between themselves'.

In view of this approach to positive obligations, one must ask why it is that there have there been no international cases in which women have alleged violations against States whose legal systems fail to make marital rape a crime or which provide inadequate administrative and legal preventive and remedial measures for rape and acts of violence committed against women. A number of possible explanations suggest themselves. One is that many of the groups active in combatting violence against women may know little about the international procedures that are available to them. A second reason may be that these international procedures are largely ineffectual in terms of producing practical results which benefit those whose rights are being violated or, at least, that there

205 European Court of Human Rights, Judgment of 26 March 1985, Ser A, No 91, 8 EHRR 235, 81 ILR 103.

are more productive ways in which human, financial and material resources can be utilised than in pursuing international complaint procedures. It may also be that the track record of these institutions to date in cases involving issues other than fairly straightforward discrimination is not so promising that one could presume that the outcome of any such case would serve women's interests.

If such cases were brought, what sort of positive steps could be required of a State internationally to ensure that it carries out its obligation to ensure women's rights to freedom from violation of their bodily integrity? Plainly they would include the requirement that a State have in place criminal legislation or some appropriate substitute to punish serious violations of women's physical integrity. They would presumably also include an obligation on State officials to take active steps to protect women against such violence where that is reasonably feasible, as well as punishing those who commit such crimes. Thus far, we are in well-charted territory internationally.

There appears to be no reason why the obligation could not be extended further to impose on the State an obligation to undertake major education and training programmes for women and men in relation to domestic violence or even to do something about some of the social structures which promote violence against women (assuming one can reach agreement on what the causes of the violence are). These requirements would involve an extension beyond the range of measures which is normally suggested as appropriate in cases involving infringements of the right to physical integrity. Nonetheless, they have parallels in obligations imposed by the Racial Discrimination Convention and the Women's Discrimination Convention and the types of measures which States undertake to adopt in the area of economic and social rights.

There are, of course, other problems which need to be addressed in this context, among them the ambiguity of the role of the State from a feminist perspective and the dangers of imposing duties on a State where the performance of those duties may encroach upon the enjoyment of other rights which are valuable for women. Nonetheless, the issues need to be further explored.

Conclusion

This paper has attempted to survey some of the current issues of concern to those who are seeking to ensure that major violations of women's human dignity are recognised by the international human rights community as violations of human rights in the technical sense and that the institutions concerned with the promotion of human rights give greater attention to these issues in their work.

There are many issues which still need further detailed examination as part of this effort. They include more concerted efforts to identify the role of sex and gender in constituting all human rights violations of which women are the victims, further in-depth examination of the extent to which human rights violations against women are dealt with within the 'mainstream' (and what is excluded and why), and further consideration of the reasons for the apparent lack of receptivity to these issues in order to develop strategic responses. In particular, more attention needs to be given to the development in the law of State responsibility arising out of the acts of private individuals and to explore how those developments may be turned to advantage in furthering the promotion of the human rights of women internationally.

One suspects that the permeability of the 'mainstream' to these issues may be limited; this makes it all the more important not just to infiltrate or utilise the 'mainstream', but also to strengthen those existing institutions which address the problems facing women – and to increase the awareness, in both directions – of the work being done in the 'mainstream' and 'on the margins'.

MAINSTREAMING GENDER WITHIN THE INTERNATIONAL FRAMEWORK[206]

Jane Connors[207]

1. Introduction

During this decade, the approach of international advocacy for the advancement of women has shifted significantly. Whereas during the period of the United Nations Decade for Women and throughout the first five years after the agreement of the Nairobi Forward-Looking Strategies for the Advancement of Women, advocacy for women's equality with men was situated squarely within the context of advocacy for development, increasingly, since 1990, advocacy for women's advancement has taken the form of claims for the 'human rights of women'.

A number of reasons underlie this shift in approach. First, the framework of human rights offers direct practical advantages for women. Unlike the framework of development, the framework of human rights law provides a forum for asserting individual claims of human rights violation and thus allows individuals, and sometimes groups, to seek relief and remedies through international, regional or, where such exist, national human rights mechanisms.

Second, and more importantly,[208] the framework of human rights has an important political meaning. The language of international human rights allows the legitimate claims of women to be articulated with a moral authority, seriousness and importance that other approaches do not. It is a language that is recognised by the powerful and a discourse which stimulates popular response.

Human rights speak in broad terms about the fundamental entitlement of all human beings to live in dignity and in conditions of social justice. The approach of human rights provides a foundation from which to mount a set of demands premised on the intrinsic worth of women. Claims based on human rights require no justification, with claimants entitled to human rights as of right. Unlike other approaches, entitlement is not predicated on the achievement of some other end, such as sustainable development or effective population or environment policies. Again, the human rights approach resists a tendency to defend values on a cost effective basis. Rather, realisation of the entitlements of human rights is, in the words of the Programme of Action of the International Conference on Population and Development, a highly important end in itself'.[209]

The human rights approach offers other advantages. Unlike other approaches to women's claims, an approach based on human rights promises the engagement of the responsibility of the State in a way that is internationally recognised and acknowledged. Where claims fulfil the definition of internationally guaranteed

---

206 1995 Conference Paper, previously unpublished.

207 At the time of writing, School of Oriental and African Studies, University of London; now United Nations, Division for the Advancement of Women.

208 As Andrew Byrnes points out in 'Towards More Effective Enforcement of Women's Human Rights Through the Use of International Human Rights Law and Procedures' in Rebecca J Cook (ed), *Human Rights of Women: National and International Perspectives* (University of Pennsylvania Press, 1994), pp 189–227 esp, p 192: 'recourse to international procedures is likely to have a very limited direct impact in redressing violations of human rights. [It] follows ... that any use of international procedures must form part of a broader political strategy.'

209 International Conference on Population and Development, Programme of Action, Chapter IV, 4.1.

human rights, their denial or violation immediately raises the question, both at national and international level, of the legal responsibility of the State. Women's claims, thus, when conceived of as human rights, are elevated from the realms of State and international promises premised on good faith and moral obligation, to a level of binding legal obligation, requiring immediate national and international recognition and implementation and, in the case of violation, urgent response. Women's claims, when conceived of as human rights, become fundamental and immutable obligations.

Advocacy for women's advancement rooted in the framework of human rights – an approach often described as the 'human rights of women' – although recent – has been repaid by impressive gains. Over the past three years, the international community has shown greater awareness of the gender implications of human rights, acknowledged some of the specific concerns of women to be issues of human rights and facilitated the introduction of new measures to protect and advance those rights.

Nevertheless, significant gaps remain. Primary among these is that although gender is now clearly part of the agenda in mainstream international human rights thinking, it is not completely within the mainstream of that thinking. Second, advances in human rights thinking relating to the concerns of women have so far been narrowly confined and have focused predominantly on the issue of gender-based violence against women and, to a lesser extent, reproductive health. Third, while there has been some progress in bringing consideration of the human rights of women into the mainstream of the international framework, which I have chosen to define as the United Nations system, this progress so far has been limited, in the main, to the United Nations Human Rights Programme, which, in essence, is comprised of the Centre for Human Rights and the various human rights bodies and mechanisms serviced by that Centre. Within the United Nations Human Rights Programme itself progress has been mixed, with some bodies and mechanisms showing greater understanding of the meaning of bringing the human rights of women into mainstream human rights work.

The mainstreaming of the human rights of women within the international framework, therefore, poses two challenges:

–   how best to move the human rights of women from the agenda of the United Nations Human Rights Programme into the mainstream of the work of that Programme; and

–   how best to ensure that the human rights of women are part of the approach to women's concerns throughout the entire UN system.

What follows seeks to provide a context for addressing these challenges. Divided into three sections, it begins with a definition of the 'human rights of women' as currently understood. It then moves on to assess the progress that has been made in mainstreaming of the human rights of women within the international framework so far. Finally, it points to obstacles to further mainstreaming.

2. The human rights of women

In 1993, the Vienna Declaration and Programme of Action, the final document of the Second World Conference on Human Rights, declared the human rights of women and the girl-child as an 'inalienable, integral and indivisible part of human rights'.[210] By virtue of the Vienna Document the international

---

210 Paragraph 18 of the Vienna Declaration.

community made clear that the human rights of women and the girl child are part of human rights, but did not go further to define the human rights of women and the girl child.

Although there are a handful of international instruments which elaborate human rights which are particular to women,[211] there are no separate human rights for women and men. Rather, human rights instruments prescribe that the rights they define are available to all, irrespective of 'race, colour, sex, language, religion, political or other opinion, national or social origin, property, birth or other status'.[212] The general norm of non-discrimination on the basis of sex, guaranteeing women equal rights with men, is found in United Nations human rights treaties,[213] conventions concluded by the International Labour Organisation (ILO)[214] and in the Convention Against Discrimination in Education 1960 elaborated by the United Nations Economic, Social and Cultural Organisation (UNESCO).

Detailed explanation of the specific meaning of discrimination against women is to be found in the Convention on the Elimination of All Forms of Discrimination Against Women. This Convention is the definitive legal instrument requiring respect for and the observance of the human rights of women. It is universal in reach and comprehensive in scope, binding States Parties, of which there are now 151, with the legal duty of eliminating all forms of discrimination against women in civil, political, economic, social and cultural fields.

While all human rights apply equally to women and men, with the full and equal participation of women in political, civil, economic, social and cultural life at the national, regional and international levels and the eradication of all forms of discrimination on the grounds of sex constituting priority objectives of the international community, the *de facto* situation of women predicates that some human rights are of particular importance for them.

The Vienna Declaration and Programme of Action made clear that women are subject to violations of their human rights in all spheres, but it highlighted certain violations as gender specific. Gender-based violence, sexual harassment, exploitation and trafficking in women and forms of violence specifically directed against women in situations of armed conflict[215] were described as human rights violations particular to women. Certain human rights – to health, education, equality in access and participation in decision-making[216] – were also isolated as having singular importance for women.

---

211 For example, the 1902 Hague Conventions concerning conflicts of national laws concerning marriage, divorce and the Guardianship of Minors; the International Agreement for the Suppression of the White Slave Traffic 1904, The International Convention for the Suppression of the White Slave Traffic 1910, the International Convention to Combat the Traffic in Women and Children, 1910, the International Convention for the Suppression of Traffic in Women of Full Age 1933; ILO Conventions No 3, relating to the Employment of Women Before and After Childbirth and No 45 relating to the employment of women in underground work in mines of all kinds; the Convention on the Political Rights of Women 1952; the Convention on the Nationality of Married Women 1957.

212 Article 2(1) of the Universal Declaration of Human Rights.

213 Article 3 of the International Covenants on Civil and Political Rights and Economic, Social and Cultural Rights; Article 2(1) of the Convention on the Rights of the Child.

214 ILO Conventions No 100, 111 and 156.

215 Paragraph 18 of the Declaration; para 38 of the Programme of Action.

216 Paragraphs 41 and 43 of the Programme of Action.

The human rights implications of gender-based violence against women were further clarified by the Declaration on the Elimination of Violence Against Women, which categorises such violence as an issue of human rights generally and one of sex discrimination and inequality in particular.[217] The importance of the right to health and reproductive choice for women was underscored by the Programme of Action of the International Conference on Population and Development.[218] Most recently, the Beijing Declaration and Programme for Action confirmed women's rights as human rights and the human rights of women and the girl child as an inalienable, integral and indivisible part of all human rights and fundamental freedoms.[219] The Programme for Action underlined the human rights implications of gender-based violence against women, particularly in armed conflict.[220] It also focused on violations of the human rights of women resulting in refugee flows and the vulnerability of refugee women to further violations of their human rights.[221]

In light of the conclusions of the Second World Conference on Human Rights and international consensus since that time, including the conclusions of the Fourth World Conference on Women, 'the human rights of women' must be taken to encompass those defined universal human rights to which women are entitled by virtue of their equal access with men, but as mediated by gender. 'The human rights of women', thus, predicates an understanding that women are denied enshrined human rights in many different ways. They are denied economic, social, cultural, civil and political rights in the same way that men are denied those rights. As victims of discrimination on the basis of sex, women are denied these rights on a basis of equality with men. They are also denied human rights in ways that are particular to them because of their gender. This denial takes two forms. Women are disproportionately victims of gender-specific abuses, the most obvious and egregious examples being the myriad forms of gender-based violence. Further, women are denied enjoyment of enshrined rights by social and economic factors that affect them more than men. Their reproductive role and their almost total responsibility for young children and the elderly impacts on their enjoyment of many enshrined rights in ways that do not affect men. The right to life for women requires greater attention to reproductive health; the right to work for women includes greater attention to facilities for child care. Their economic inequality, similarly, impacts on their enjoyment of enshrined rights in many ways that do not affect men.

3. Mainstreaming the human rights of women

Mainstreaming means bringing about desired change by influencing decisions at the highest levels. Mainstreaming of the human rights of women within the international framework aims to introduce a qualitative change in the approach of that framework to women.[222] It aims to ensure that the concerns of women feature as priority concerns within all parts of the framework. Moreover, it aims to ensure that the concerns of women are defined as issues of human rights so that the claims of women are construed as valid human rights claims.

---

217 GA Res 48/104.

218 See, in particular Principle 3, Chapter IV and paras 8.19–8.27.

219 Platform for Action, paras 213–216.

220 Platform for Action, paras 133–136.

221 *Ibid*, para 226.

222 'Technical Assistance and Women: From Mainstreaming Towards Institutional Accountability', E/CN6/1995/6, para 9.

Mainstreaming of the human rights women within the international framework involves two levels of action. First, guaranteeing that the United Nations Human Rights Programme brings the human rights of women into the mainstream of human rights work and second, guaranteeing throughout the rest of the UN system, women's concerns are viewed as issues of human rights and, accordingly, priorities for action.

The following section outlines progress in mainstreaming the human rights of women within the United Nations system. It reviews, first, the Human Rights Programme, where there has been some progress in mainstreaming. Mainstreaming of the human rights of women in the balance of the system, where progress has been less marked is then considered.

(i) Mainstreaming within the United Nations Human Rights Programme

Effective mainstreaming of the human rights of women requires the Human Rights Programme to take account of gender-specific abuses and treat these as violations of human rights and, also, to understand the gender dimensions of human rights generally. Impressive progress has been made within the Programme with respect to the first requirement,[223] but progress with respect to the second requirement has been slower. With respect to progress with regard to the first requirement, further, the shift in terms of policy has been greater than in terms of application.[224]

Reference has already been made to the conclusions of the United Nations World Conference on Human Rights which significantly expanded the international human rights agenda to include gender-specific violations and identified particular examples of gender-specific examples as human rights abuses. The Conference also called for the equal status of women and the human rights of women to be integrated into the mainstream of United Nations system-wide activity.[225] One of the specific mandates of the Conference was that the human rights of women should form an integral part of United Nations human rights activities. To this end, it urged treaty-monitoring bodies to include the status of women and the human rights of women in their deliberations and findings, making use of gender-specific data and welcomed resolution 1993/46, adopted by the 49th Session of the Commission on Human Rights, which had encouraged human rights rapporteurs and working groups to take account of gender in their work. The theme of integration of gender into the mainstream human rights programme has been further underlined in a series of resolutions of the Commission on Human Rights[226] the Commission on the Status of Women[227] and the General Assembly.[228]

Concrete progress in mainstreaming the human rights of women into the United Nations Human Rights Programme was made in March 1994 by the United

---

223 The extent to which gender concerns have been included in the activities of the United Nations human rights mechanisms, Report by the Secretary-General, A/Conf.177/9, 21 August 1995.

224 Similar conclusions have been made with respect to mainstreaming women in technical assistance: see E/CN6/1995/6 and mainstreaming gender throughout the United Nations: see E/CN6/1885/Add.10.

225 The Vienna Declaration and Programme of Action, UN Doc A/Conf.157/23 (1993); para 18 of the Declaration; paras 36–44 of the Programme of Action.

226 1994/45; 1994/53; 1995/86.

227 37/4; 38/2; 39/5.

228 GA Res 49.161.

Nations Commission on Human Rights when it agreed to appoint a Special Rapporteur on Violence against women, including its causes and consequences.[229] Until the appointment of the Special Rapporteur on Violence against women, the Human Rights Programme, which clearly took the view that the parallel 'women's rights programme', comprised of the Commission on the Status of Women and the Committee on the Elimination of Discrimination Against Women, had institutional responsibility for the human rights of women, had devoted little attention to the human rights of women. Women who suffered violations of enshrined human rights in the same ways as men and women whose enjoyment of enshrined rights was unequal with that of men because of discrimination on the basis of sex had received some attention within the human rights programme.[230] In addition, the Human Rights Committee in its General Comment 18(7) had sought to give guidance on the meaning of discrimination on the basis of sex in the enjoyment of civil and political rights.

Some sustained attention to the human rights of women within the Human Rights Programme had been paid by the Subcommission on the Prevention of Discrimination and the Protection of Minorities, which initially appointed a working group and then a special rapporteur on traditional practices affecting the health of women and children and has adopted a plan of action directed at eradication of these practices[231] Further progress within the Programme can be seen by the decision of the Subcommission to consider the human rights of woman and the girl child under every relevant item of its agenda and in all relevant studies and by its appointment of a special rapporteur on 'systematic rape, sexual slavery and slavery-like practices during wartime, including internal conflict'.

Progress can also be seen in the approach of some of the treaty bodies. In 1990 the Economic, Social and Cultural Rights Committee revised its reporting guidelines to require minimal specific coverage of the position of women in their enjoyment of rights guaranteed by the Covenant and a number of its general comments on the content of rights, particularly more recently, have shown an awareness of the gender dimension of those rights.[232]

At its October/November 1994 Session, the Human Rights Committee decided to consider the possibility of updating its General Comment relating to the equal rights of men and women and it agreed that the lists of issues to be taken up in the consideration of States Parties reports should include more concrete and detailed information on the equal status and the human rights of women. During its session in March/April 1995, it amended it guidelines for the preparation of

---

229 Res 1994/45.

230 Andrew Byrnes, 'Women, Feminism and International Human Rights Law: Methodological Myopia, Fundamental Flaws or Meaningful Marginalisation? Some Current Issues', 12 *Australian Yearbook of International Law* 205 (extracted, *supra*). For examples of how the human rights of women have been considered by the mainstream programme see the various decisions of the Human Rights Committee under the First Optional Protocol which concern discrimination against women, for example *Aumeeruddy-Cziffra v Mauritius* Communication No 35/1978; *Broeks v Netherlands* Communication No 172/1984; *Ato del Alvellanal v Peru* Communication No 202/1986.

231 E/CN4/Sub.2/1994/10/Add 1.

232 General comment 4(1991) on the right to adequate housing; General comment 5 (1994) concerning persons with disabilities; see also, draft general comment on the economic, social and cultural rights of the elderly (E.C.12/1994/WP.16).

initial and periodic reports so as to request States Parties to provide gender-specific information.

The youngest treaty body, the Committee on the Rights of the Child has, since its first meeting in 1991, incorporated issues of gender into its analysis. This has been facilitated by the fact that its Convention, the Convention on the Rights of the Child, is the only treaty which avoids gender-inclusive language, by employing both the female and male pronoun, and by the fact that although the rights enshrined in the Convention are available to female and male children equally, some articles have greater relevance for the girl child. The Committee's reporting guidelines require States Parties to include in their reports gender disaggregated information and statistical data and indicators with respect to the enjoyment of rights established by the Convention. During the consideration of reports, the Committee has raised issues of early marriage, maternal health care, early pregnancy, family planning education and services, adverse health practices, the denial of educational opportunities for girls, as well as sexual and other abuses. These concerns, as well as suggestions for measures of prevention and rehabilitation, are reflected in the concluding observations adopted by the Committee. Moreover, in its regular discussion days, the Committee on the Rights of the Child has examined the particular problems of the girl child. Early in 1995, for example, in preparation for the Fourth World Conference on Women, the Committee comprehensively discussed the girl child.

Since August 1984, the Secretary-General of the United Nations has periodically convened a meeting of persons chairing the various treaty bodies. At their fifth meeting in 1994, the chairpersons emphasised the necessity of adequate meeting and time and resourcing for the Committee on the Elimination of Discrimination against Women, suggesting that it should, like all the other human rights treaty bodies, be based at the Human Rights Centre and thereby be integrated into the mainstream of other United Nations Human Rights activities. Reiterating that all human rights contained in international instruments apply fully to women, they urged treaty bodies to closely monitor the enjoyment by women of those rights and suggested the development of a common strategy by the treaty bodies to achieve this objective, which would include the amendment of reporting guidelines to include incorporate information on women, including gender-disaggregated statistical data.[233] Their sixth meeting in September 1995 was devoted to the exploration of ways of more effectively monitoring the human rights of women within the treaty supervision system.

Some evidence of mainstreaming of the human rights of women can also be seen in the work of the non-treaty mechanisms. In 1993, the report of the special rapporteur on the situation of human rights in the former Yugoslavia reported systematic rapes of women and requested a team of medical experts to investigate allegations of rape and make detailed recommendations for action.[234] In his analysis of patterns of torture, the special rapporteur on the situation of human rights in occupied Kuwait examined the use of gender specific methods of torture, identifying women as a category among torture victims and recognising 'sexual torture' as a method of torture.[235]

---

233 Note by the Secretary-General, *Effective Implementation of International Instruments on Human Rights, Including Reporting Obligations under International Instruments on Human Rights*, A/49/537 (19 October 1994), paras 19, 20, 49, 50.

234 1993 Report, para 552 and UN Doc E/CN4/1993/50 Annex II.

235 UN Doc E/CN4/1992/26, paras 105, 111, 181, 182.

Since the 1993 resolution of the Commission on Human Rights directing special rapporteurs and working groups of the Commission and the Subcommission to regularly and systematically to include in their reports available information on human rights violations affecting women[236] 'more progress has been made'.[237] Statistics relating to women detained were included in the report of the Working Group on Enforced or Involuntary Disappearances[238] and the Working Group on Arbitrary detention now provides a gender-disaggregated breakdown of the cases it has dealt with.[239] Similarly, the most recent report of the Special Rapporteur on Torture in response to resolution 1994/37 of the Commission on Human Rights, inviting him to examine questions concerning torture directed disproportionately or primarily against women, conditions conducive to such torture and to make appropriate recommendations, examines methods of torture involving sexual abuse, which he describes as a common means of torture in some countries and which he describes as 'essentially gender-based'.[240] Again, the special rapporteur on extra-judicial, summary or arbitrary executions has specifically reported on female victims.[241]

The increased gender-awareness and growing appreciation of the human rights of women by the treaty bodies and other human rights mechanisms marks a significant step towards mainstreaming the human rights of women within the United Nations Human Rights Programme. However, it is important to note that not all treaty bodies and mechanisms have to date addressed the human rights of women. Although the Committee on the Elimination of Racial Discrimination has decided one communication from a woman under its optional communication procedure concerning discrimination on the basis of race,[242] there is, as yet, no evidence of gender analysis apparent in its questions during the reporting process or in its general recommendations. Similarly, the Committee on Torture has exhibited little awareness of the gender dimensions of its Convention. Specific mention has been made above of the other human rights mechanisms that have addressed gender in their work. Suffice to say, these are the minority of the working groups and thematic and country rapporteurs of the Commission and Subcommission. Moreover, there is some evidence of resistance to the mainstreaming of the human rights of women by these mechanisms.[243]

Progress in the mainstreaming of the human rights of women within the Human Rights Programme is determined not only by whether the human rights of

---

236 1993/46.

237 CHR Res 1994/53 calling for thematic special rapporteurs and working groups to include in their reports gender-disaggregated data and to address the characteristics and practices of human rights violations under the mandates that are specifically or primarily directed at women, or to which women are particularly vulnerable, has also affected the approach of these mechanisms.

238 UN Doc E/CN4/1994/260.

239 UN Doc E/CN4/1994/27, Annexes V and VI and UN Doc/ECN4/1995/31/Annex II.

240 E/CN4/1995/34, paras 15–24 and 333–338.

241 UN Doc C/CN4/1994/7, paras 715–716; UN Doc E/CN4/1995/34.

242 *Yilmaz Dogan v The Netherlands Communication* No 1/1984.

243 'Integration of the Human Rights of Women into the activities of the human rights bodies and mechanisms' HR/GENEVA/1995/EGP/BP.1, p 15: 'There is a lack of understanding on (sic) the issues of integration of women's rights into the mainstream of United Nations system-wide human rights activities. This was reflected at a recent meeting of the special rapporteurs, representatives, experts and chairmen (sic) of working groups.'

women are addressed or acknowledged within the mainstream human rights mechanisms, but also by the nature of the inclusion within the mainstream.

There are two comments which can be made about the nature of the inclusion of the human rights of women within the mainstream of the human rights programme. First, and not surprisingly because of the lobbying surrounding the elaboration of the Declaration on the Elimination of Violence Against Women and the establishment of the Special Rapporteur on Violence, mainstream mechanisms have shown themselves to be amenable to the view that gender-based violence is an issue of the human rights of women and, accordingly, have been willing to address forms of violence against women and girl-children as questions of human rights. So far, however, these mechanisms have not begun to employ gendered analysis of human rights norms in a pro-active manner to promote pro-woman policies and practices.

Second, inclusion of the human rights of women by these mechanisms has not had an apparent analytical basis, but has, rather, taken the form of considering whether women are an affected group – an approach which can be described as 'just add women'. There has been little analysis of why women do or do not feature in the work of the relevant mechanism and no real examination of the economic and social characteristics which might explain the presence or absence of women. A notable exception in this context is the Special Rapporteur on Extrajudicial, Summary or Arbitrary Executions who has twice reflected on why the victims he deals with during the course of his work are disproportionately male. As he points out women continue to play a small role in the political and economic life of many countries. The under-representation of women in positions of influence, for example in political parties or trade unions, or in professions such as law or journalism, means that they are also less exposed to acts of violence at the hands of governments that may perceive them as a threat. On the other hand, in areas where women are actively participating in public life, they do not seem to be in a different position from their male counterparts.[244] This reflection is interesting in that it represents a high level of gender awareness in a mainstream mechanism, thereby testifying to success in attempts to mainstream the human rights of women. It is also interesting in that it reveals the limits of these attempts at mainstreaming, indicating that the vulnerability of women to 'execution', which is extrajudicial, summary or arbitrary outside the traditional public sphere has not been encompassed within the mandate of the rapporteur, either at an official level or by the rapporteur personally.

Efforts to mainstream the human rights of women within the United Nations Programme of Human Rights have not been confined to human rights mechanisms, but have extended into the secretariat of the Human Rights Centre and into its work. In 1994, a focal point on women's issues was established in the office of the Secretary-General for Human Rights to deal with matters relating to the human rights of women within the Centre for Human Rights as well as system-wide. The focal point also advises the Assistant Secretary-General for Human Rights and the High Commissioner for Human Rights on measures to be taken to integrate gender concerns within human rights activities. The Centre has amended its Plan of Activities for the Implementation of the Vienna Declaration and Programme of Action to incorporate activities related to the human rights of women and in 1995, prepared, with the Division for the Advancement of

---

244 UN Doc E/CN4/1997/7, para 716; UN Doc E/CN4/1995/61, para 415.

Women, a joint workplan relating to the human rights of women.[245] In 1995, the Centre, in collaboration with the United Nations Development Fund for Women (UNIFEM), organised an expert-group meeting to develop guidelines to incorporate gender perspectives into the work of the United Nations human rights system.

There is some evidence of the introduction of gender within the Centre for Human Rights programme of advisory services and technical assistance in the field of human rights,[246] which takes the form of advisory services of experts, human rights seminars, training courses and workshops and fellowships and scholarships. Women have been recruited to implement human rights technical assistance projects in some countries and a roster of women experts in the field of human rights is being developed. Some attempt has also been made to integrate gender in the Centre's public information activities. Number 22 in the Human Rights Fact Sheet series, which are translated into the six official languages of the United Nations and distributed worldwide free of charge, published in 1995, concerned the Convention on the Elimination of All Forms of Discrimination Against Women. There is a commitment to incorporate a gender-perspective in other publications, although to date the practical results of this commitment are difficult to discern.[247] Many of these efforts coincided with preparations for the Fourth World Conference for Women, during which the Human Rights Centre participated in a number of special activities, including a panel discussion on the human rights of women and a panel discussion on violence against women. Representative of the importance of the human rights for women for the Centre was the presence of the High Commissioner for Human Rights, Mr Jose Ayala-Lasso and the Assistant Secretary-General for Human Rights, Mr Ibrahima Fallh.

Conclusion

The above review indicates solid evidence of attempts by the United Nations Human Rights framework to mainstream the human rights of women. However, it is clear that the aim of mainstreaming requires further and significant efforts. At this point, certainly, the human rights mechanisms and the Centre that services them are clearly aware that gender is an important dimension of human rights. Nonetheless, the real implications of gender for the work of these mechanisms and for the Centre has not yet been understood. Mainstreaming of the human rights of women has been confined to the formulation of the human rights agenda and has had little impact on the shaping of the agenda or the work within the agenda. With isolated exceptions, the approach has been to add women to the existing framework, not to modify the existing framework to take account of the gender dimensions of human rights.

---

245 E/CN6/1995/13.

246 It is interesting to note that the first resolution concerning technical assistance in the field of human rights adopted by the General Assembly (res 729 (VIII, 23 October 1953)) approved a decision by the Economic and Social Council to render, at the request of Member States, services which did not fall within the scope of current technical assistance programmes, in order to assist those States in promoting and safeguarding the rights of women. More recent activities are described in the integration of the human rights of women into the activities of the human rights bodies and mechanisms, HR /Geneva/1995/EGP/BP. 1, pp 6–8.

247 The various volumes in the *ad hoc* publications series and the human rights study series pay little regard to the gender-dimension of their subjects. It is disappointing also to observe that the Centre for Human Rights Professional Training Series, which was initiated after the Vienna Conference, does not routinely address the human rights of women. No mention is made in the human rights and pretrial detention monograph, for example, of the particular threats to women in detention.

The conclusion that can be drawn is that while the gender dimensions of human rights are perceived as important, there is no real understanding of these dimensions and the implication of the dimensions for the work of the mechanisms or the Centre. To date, understanding appears to be confined to the issue of gender-based violence against women, with concentration being squarely upon violations of rights by such violence. The question of mediation of rights by issues other than gender-based violence, both insofar as violation and opportunity for enjoyment are concerned, has not been a subject within the human rights mainstream. Moreover, a gendered reading of existing human rights so as to promote pro-active, pro-woman policies and programmes has not, so far, occurred within the Programme ...[248]

4. Challenges to mainstreaming

Future efforts to mainstream the human rights of women throughout the international framework face a number of challenges. Perhaps the fundamental challenge is that of attitude. Both within the human rights programme of the United Nations and system-wide there is a continuing need to convince people of the importance of mainstreaming the human rights of women. Insofar as the system outside the human rights programme is concerned, the challenge of convincing people of the importance of mainstreaming the human rights of women is combined with the challenge of convincing people of the importance of the human rights approach to issues generally.

Another important challenge which faces the mainstreaming process flows from the gender of those charged with the mainstreaming mission. Many commentators have drawn attention to the fact that experts nominated to the United Nations system are overwhelmingly male. With the exception of the Committee on the Elimination of Discrimination Against Women which, since its inception, with one exception, has been composed entirely of women, most experts who have served on treaty bodies have been men. Few human rights special rapporteurs and members of working groups have been women.

Despite Article 8 of the United Nations Charter which provides that no restrictions shall be placed on the eligibility of men and women to participate in any capacity and under conditions of equality in its principal and subsidiary organs and a succession of policy statements and affirmative action guidelines, male dominance in these bodies is mirrored by male dominance at the decision-making level in the bureaucracy of the United Nations.[249]

Gender imbalance is even greater with older agencies, for example the ILO, being particularly affected in this way.[250] While there is no conclusive evidence indicating that a gender-balanced bureaucracy would lead inevitably to more gender-conscious policy-making in the United Nations system, there are reasons to believe that this may be the case. Certainly, as Hilary Charlesworth has pointed out, the current imbalance makes it difficult for the realities of women's lives to contribute in any significant way to the shaping of the organisation's

---

248 *Mainstreaming Gender Within the International Framework*, pp 1–10.

249 Brian Urquhart and Erskine Childers describe the situation as 'appalling' and 'grotesque' in 'A World in Need of Leadership: Tomorrow's United Nations' (1990), pp 30, 60.

250 *Technical Assistance for Women: From Mainstreaming Towards Institutional Accountability*, Note by the Secretary General E/CN6/1995/6, 19 December 1994, paras 25-31; Hilary Charlesworth, 'Transforming the United Men's Club: Feminist Futures for the United Nations' (1994) 4 *Transnational Law and Contemporary Problems* at 422–54.

policy.[251] Gender imbalance has also facilitated the construction of a category of 'women's concerns' within the system and the establishment of special women's institutions, such as CSW and CEDAW, to promote these concerns. These institutions have been crucial for women, but at the same time have confined women's views within their narrow mandates, creating yet another obstacle to mainstreaming.

While it is likely that a gender-balanced staff would facilitate the mainstreaming of gender within the system, this does not mean that it would bring about the mainstreaming of the human rights of women. Mainstreaming of the human rights of women requires mainstreaming a gender and human rights approach. Outside the Human Rights Programme and the ILO there is a dearth of expertise in human rights, let alone the human rights of women, again creating an obstacle to system-wide mainstreaming. Mainstreaming of the human rights of women is likely, further, to be more difficult in those agencies dominated by staff who have been educated in disciplines which blind them to relevance of gender.

The effect of male domination at decision-making levels system-wide and lack of expertise in human rights can be addressed by training in gender sensitivity and analysis and human rights and specific training and guidelines relating to the human rights of women to some extent, but training and guidelines can never fully replicate the effect that a gender-balanced and human rights-aware staff can have on mainstreaming. There is a danger also that current efforts at mainstreaming women in development – incorporating the establishment of a centralised WID focal point, generally short of staff and resources and working in relative isolation[252] – might be replicated in this context. This has proven to be insufficient in the absence of institutional commitment and education, accompanied by post-training follow-up and support.

The continuing institutional and geographical separation between the Human Rights Programme and the Commission on the Status of Women and the Committee on the Elimination of Discrimination against Women, system-wide regarded as the bodies concerned with 'women' s issues' and, accordingly, the Women' s Rights Programme, remains a powerful obstacle to mainstreaming of the human rights of women within the work of that Programme. Failure to mainstream within that Programme has further implications for mainstreaming system-wide, with other programmes and agencies prepared to remain unconvinced of the importance of the human rights of women if the Human Rights Programme is not prepared to accept their importance. The establishment of focal points for women and the development of workplans and co-operation guidelines can go some way to create greater integration, but the institutional and geographical separation of CEDAW, in particular, from the mainstream human rights programme will inevitably slow further progress. Mainstreaming of the human rights of women within the human rights programme will be facilitated with institutional and geographical integration of CEDAW, but at the same time, raises the further challenge of ensuring that this mainstreaming does not overwhelm or obscure the perspective of the human rights of women.

---

251 Hilary Charlesworth, *op cit*, p 444. UNICEF, Gender Equality and Empowerment of Women and Girls, E/ICEF/1994/L.5 para 20 points out that mainstreaming women's concerns in UNICEF programmes has been influenced in some instances by the varying levels of commitment to gender equality and women's empowerment among UNICEF staff.

252 'Technical Assistance and Women', *op cit*, E/CN6/1995/5 para 12.

The traditional priority given to civil and political rights at the expense of economic, social and cultural rights, similarly presents an obstacle to the mainstreaming of the human rights of women. Human rights discourse subscribes to the indivisibility and inter-dependence of rights and emphasises that the promotion of certain fundamental freedoms cannot justify the denial of other fundamental rights and freedoms, but more attention is devoted to civil and political rights at the expense of economic, social and cultural rights. This has meant that denial of the human rights of women in the context of these rights – such as the impact of structural adjustment, denial of cultural difference – issues of pressing concern to most women in their everyday lives and rights of importance to the work of many UN agencies have been marginalised. Until proper attention is paid to these rights and the gendered dimensions of the enjoyment is elaborated, the mainstreaming of the human rights of women is likely to be confined to acknowledgement of gender-based violence as an issue of human rights. Further, until the gender dimensions of economic, social and cultural rights are elaborated those bodies of the United Nations concerned with economics and development are likely to remain resistant, certainly at the level of operations, if not at the level of policy, to the idea of system-wide mainstreaming of the human rights of women.

Challenges posed by attitude, gender-imbalance in the international framework, location of bodies concerned with the human rights of women and the prioritisation of agreed 'indivisible and inter-dependent' human rights while real, are nonetheless capable of realisation. Deeper obstacles, related to the doctrinal framework of international law – of which human rights law is a branch – also stand in the way of effective mainstreaming of the human rights of women.

One of the reasons why the concerns of women have so far failed to be integrated into the discourse of human rights law or into its jurisprudence is the historic focus of international law on violations committed directly by the State. Within this conceptualisation of the law as a constraint on the power of the State many abuses against women have not been acknowledged as human rights violations because they are committed by private persons very often husbands, lovers, family or community members rather than agents of the State. The focus of human rights law on the direct actions of the State serves to marginalise the concerns of women at two levels: at the level of definition of human rights and at the level of the responsibility of the State.

It has already been noted that there are no special human rights for women, but that they, like men, are entitled to universal human rights. Human rights as currently defined, are not only usually limited to State actions and obligations, but envisage a human condition unmediated by issues of gender. Moreover, as currently framed non-discrimination in enjoyment of rights is measured against male standard. The challenge is thus to broaden the normative framework of human rights to include abuses suffered by women and to take account of the realities of women's lives – in other words, issues of gender. Without a gendered-approach to human rights, efforts in mainstreaming will outweigh the value in its achievement.

The effects of the focus of international law on the direct actions of the State are not only seen in the definition of human rights, but are apparent in the international principle of State responsibility which divides public actions for which the State is accountable from those private ones for which it does not have to answer internationally. In general, the State is answerable internationally for abuses for which it has direct or indirect responsibility, with other abuses being within its domestic jurisdiction. Inevitably, until the notion of State responsibility is broadened, everyday abuses that women suffer will not involve the State internationally.

The challenges to a notion of women's human rights and accordingly its further integration into the mainstream have so far been discussed within the context of gender-based violence against women and some progress has been made. This progress has come at a price, however, as the discussions of the relevance of gender in human rights appear to include only gender-based violence against women. It is essential that the current view of the relevance of gender in the context of human rights moves beyond a narrow focus of violence to a gendered reading all rights.

Conclusion

Enormous progress has been made within the international framework towards mainstreaming gender in the guise of the notion of the human rights of women. Much more remains to be done and a number of challenges remain. Strategies are currently being formulated and within those strategies perhaps the most effective will be to 'mainstream' the Convention on the Elimination of All Forms of Discrimination Against Women. Now ratified by 151 nations – over two-thirds of the members of the United Nations – the Convention remains little known within the Human Rights Programme and in other areas of the UN system. It is crucially important that the Convention constitutes a force internationally. Here, again, obstacles exist. These include the various well-known weaknesses of the Convention, including the absence of a method to resolve the large number of substantive reservations that States have entered to its terms and the fact that it lacks investigatory and enforcement powers and has no capacity to resolve interstate or individual complaints. Yet, weaknesses aside, were the Convention to be the focus of sustained attention, particularly in view of current plans to provide for an optional complaints and enquiry mechanism the capacity for progress in gender mainstreaming in the international framework would be significant.

INDEX